Biblical Eschatology

Biblical Eschatology

Second Edition

Jonathan Menn

Forewords by Dr. Robert Yarbrough
and His Grace, The Most Reverend, Stanley Ntagali

RESOURCE *Publications* · Eugene, Oregon

BIBLICAL ESCHATOLOGY
Second Edition

Resource Publications
An Imprint of Wipf and Stock Publishers
199 W. 8th Ave., Suite 3
Eugene, OR 97401
www.wipfandstock.com

PAPERBACK ISBN: 978-1-5326-4317-0
HARDCOVER ISBN: 978-1-5326-4318-7
EBOOK ISBN: 978-1-5326-4319-4

Manufactured in the U.S.A.   02/28/18

To my wife Nancy—the love of my life, my best friend,
and my partner in the journey through this life with Jesus.

Contents

Permissions

Unless otherwise indicated, all Scripture quotations are taken from the New American Standard Bible`, Copyright © 1960, 1962, 1963, 1968, 1971, 1972, 1973, 1975, 1977, 1995 by The Lockman Foundation. Used by permission. (www.Lockman.org)

Scripture quotations marked RSV are from the Revised Standard Version of the Bible, copyright 1952 [2nd edition, 1971] by the Division of Christian Education of the National Council of the Churches of Christ in the United States of America. Used by permission. All rights reserved.

Scripture quotations marked ESV are from the ESV The Holy Bible, English Standard Version® (ESV®), copyright © 2001 by Crossway, a publishing ministry of Good News Publishers. All rights reserved.

Scripture quotations marked NKJV are taken from the New King James Version®. Copyright © 1982 by Thomas Nelson, Inc. Used by permission. All rights reserved.

Scripture quotations marked NIV are taken from the THE HOLY BIBLE, NEW INTERNATIONAL VERSION®, NIV® Copyright © 1973, 1978, 1984, 2011 by Biblica, Inc.™ Used by permission. All rights reserved worldwide.

Quotations taken from *Triumph of the Lamb* by Dennis Johnson, ISBN 978–0–87552–200–5 are used with permission of P&R Publishing Co P.O. Box 817, Phillipsburg N.J. 08865.

Quotations taken from *Daniel* by Iain Duguid, ISBN 978–1–59638–068–4 are used with permission of P&R Publishing Co P.O. Box 817, Phillipsburg N.J. 08865.

Quotations taken from *The Israel of God* by O. Palmer Robertson, ISBN 978–0–87552–398–9 are used with permission of P&R Publishing Co P.O. Box 817, Phillipsburg N.J. 08865.

Quotations taken from "Old Testament Prophecy and the Future of Israel: A Study of the Teaching of Jesus" by R. T. France, *Tyndale Bulletin* 26 (1975) 53–78 are used with permission of Tyndale House.

Quotations taken from the Lausanne Covenant© are used with permission of the Lausanne Movement.

Quotations taken from *New American Commentary Zechariah* by George Klein © 2008 B&H Publishing Group, are used with permission.

Quotations taken from the article "The Purpose of Symbolism in the Book of Revelation" by G. K. Beale, *Calvin Theological Journal* 41 (2006) 53–66 are used with the permission of the Calvin Theological Journal.

Quotations taken from *Daniel: An Introductory Commentary* (TOTC), by Joyce Baldwin © 1978 InterVarsity Press, are used with permission.

Quotations taken from *Daniel* (AOTC 20), by Ernest Lucas © 2002 Apollos, are used with permission.

Quotations taken from *The Millennial Maze* by Stanley J. Grenz © 1992 by Stanley J. Grenz, are used by permission of InterVarsity Press, PO Box 1400, Downers Grove, IL 60515. www.ivpress.com.

Quotations taken from *Collected Works,* by John Murray © 1977, published at Edinburgh by Banner of Truth, are used with permission.

Quotations taken from *The Abomination of Desolation in Biblical Eschatology,* by Desmond Ford © 1979 University Press of America, are used with permission.

Foreword

by Dr. Robert Yarbrough

It is a joy to commend this book, first of all, because of who the author is. Jonathan Menn spent much of his adult life as an attorney. But in his 50s he applied his trained mind to theological studies at Trinity Evangelical Divinity School, graduating with a Master of Divinity degree in 2007. I was privileged to have him in class at the time. I recall a term paper he wrote on 1 Corinthians 15:20–28. It argued for an amillennial understanding of New Testament eschatology, a view I have not been persuaded to adopt. Yet the quality of the essay was undeniable. Here was an author who, already at the student level, was serious and knowledgeable about Scripture, investigating it with intelligence and zeal, and capable of articulating his ideas with logical order and rhetorical force.

Since that time Jonathan's commitment to interpreting Scripture aright and spreading knowledge of its message has only grown. He is currently East Africa Director of Equipping Pastors International. In the first eleven months of 2012 alone, he conducted training seminars in Burundi, Rwanda, Uganda, Kenya, and Tanzania. Nearly 900 leaders were impacted by these seminars. Many times that number have been impacted through those whom Jonathan trained and equipped to take better knowledge of God's Word back to their people in villages and other locations across numerous African nations. Nor is knowledge Jonathan's only emphasis: action in keeping with the Bible's teaching receives equal attention.

Jesus said that by their fruits we will know much about people. The fruit of Jonathan's labor is this: To understand Scripture and then with eagerness and a self-sacrificial outlook to travel long distances and work hard hours to help others know and teach God's Word better worldwide. This kind of pastoral and missionary commitment (and experience) is not strictly necessary for writing about a subject like biblical eschatology. But it may point to a writer who knows his Bible and is growing into the pastoral and missiological heartbeat of its authors. I believe in this case it does. Jonathan Menn's take on biblical eschatology is worth pondering because he has credibility as a recognized student and international teacher of Scripture, especially in its end-times implications.

A second reason for commending this book is the contribution it makes. While there are many books on eschatology, this one has features that set it apart: (1) It is wide-ranging yet not superficial. Menn considers most major issues (e.g., the Antichrist, the Millennium, the rapture), all the major positions, and every major biblical passage directly relevant to eschatology in the course of his investigation. This includes detailed analyses of the Olivet Discourse and book of Revelation, plus overviews of Daniel 9, Ezekiel 40–48,

Zechariah 14, and Romans 11. (2) The book includes a selective history of eschatological thought, from the first century to the present time, with an emphasis on the views of the apostolic and post-apostolic fathers (quotations from whom also recur throughout the book). (3) Menn also grounds eschatology in the overall biblical structure and storyline, which renders eschatology clearer than when it is treated merely as a separate topic of systematic theology. (4) The last chapter discusses the importance of eschatology practically—i.e., the question of "What difference does it make?" Menn's research indicates that one's views on eschatology are important not only theologically but also in terms of evangelism and social action.

These are all the more reasons for me to commend the book, and for readers to pay attention to it. True, no publication can say everything about this subject. Moreover, until the day when this world's future is fully known because the Age to Come has arrived, none of us can say for sure just how some elements of the Bible's end-time projections will play out. Also, there are specialized scholarly monographs covering most topics and passages that Menn treats in less detail in this book. But informative and provocative "big picture" reconstructions are no less important than micro-level technical analyses.

Despite limitations inherent in any synthesis of the eschatology found in the Bible—and therefore present in this book too—readers will find themselves challenged, informed, and most likely even energized by careful interaction with the exposition and argumentation found in the pages ahead. Revelation 1:1 pronounces a blessing on all who read, hear, and heed the "prophecy" that makes up the New Testament's last book. I have no doubt that many a similar blessing will accrue to readers who wrestle with the presentation set before us in Jonathan Menn's thorough, carefully reasoned, and at times passionate presentation.

Dr. Robert W. Yarbrough
Professor of New Testament
Covenant Theological Seminary, St. Louis, Missouri
January 2013

FOREWORD

by His Grace, The Most Reverend, Stanley Ntagali

I FIRST MET JONATHAN Menn in 2006 when he and his teaching team from Equipping Pastors International came to the Masindi-Katara Diocese, Church of Uganda (Anglican) of which I was Bishop. One of my concerns as Bishop was to provide sound biblical instruction and training for the pastors of my diocese. In the years he worked with the diocese, teaching such subjects as biblical counseling and through books such as 1 Corinthians, Jonathan's teaching proved to be biblically sound, theologically deep, while at the same time being clear, practical, and challenging.

Since my election as Archbishop of The Church of the Province of Uganda, my concern over the theological education of both clergy and laity has increased. Perhaps the area where sound teaching is most needed is in the area of eschatology. It is a mystery to many, and is exploited and sensationalized by some. I was therefore excited to learn of this book, and to have been asked to write this foreword. Although many books on eschatology exist, Biblical Eschatology does several things that I have never before seen in one volume.

First, this book is comprehensive, but not superficial. It deals with every major position, issue, and passage of Scripture pertaining to eschatology: the millennium; the rapture; the Antichrist; and contains excellent analyses of the Olivet Discourse and the book of Revelation, as well as good overviews of Ezekiel 40–48, Daniel 9, Zechariah 14, and Romans 11. The scholars are allowed to speak for themselves. And, as an African, I am pleased to note that, in addition to drawing on the best of Western Evangelical and Reformed scholarship, Jonathan has also quoted from more than one African scholar.

Second, this book has the rare virtue of being not only biblically sound and theologically deep, but also being clear, logical, and readable. One important aspect of the clarity of which I speak is the chapter on how to interpret prophecy and apocalyptic. This helped me to understand the nature of prophecy much better and removed the veil that shrouds the subject for so many people. Many of today's so-called "prophecy experts" would do well to read it.

Third, this book does something I very much applaud: it has a chapter on the history of eschatological thought, with particular attention to the apostolic and post-apostolic fathers. They also reappear throughout the book. We often tend to forget our spiritual forefathers and fail to see how our views are in continuity with, or depart from, theirs. My Anglican heritage attunes me to this, but my Pentecostal and Evangelical brothers and sisters who come from newer Christian traditions would, I think, appreciate this facet of the book.

Fourth, this book does something I do not see in most other works on eschatology: it firmly grounds eschatology in the larger biblical story and structure. This, to me, serves to make eschatology much more understandable than when (as is usually the case) it is treated apart from the rest of biblical theology. Since most Christians are interested in the "end-times," seeing how eschatology fits into the Bible's overall structure serves as a corrective to the speculative sensationalism that is rampant today.

Finally, this book is unique in that it talks about why eschatology matters. Most people think that one's eschatological views have no real effect on their lives. Not only does the last chapter of the book dispel that notion, but the chapter on the book of Revelation demonstrates how that book is designed to affect our lives by again and again confronting us with the ultimate question of who is our real Lord.

In short, this book is like Jonathan's teaching at my diocese years ago: biblically sound and theologically deep, yet clear, practical, and challenging. It is a book for clergy and laity alike. It is not slanted toward any particular denomination, but is for the whole church. I highly recommend it.

His Grace, The Most Reverend, Stanley Ntagali
The Archbishop of the Church of the Province of Uganda.

Preface

Every book represents the completion of a journey—indeed, sometimes of an odyssey. That is certainly true of this book.

In the mid-1980s, my wife and I began attending an evangelical church that took eschatology seriously. The pastor preached on the subject frequently. That, in itself, is quite rare. Although the pastor prided himself on "teaching through the entire Bible, verse by verse," the more I listened to his sermons the more I realized that, regardless of what his text was, he always seemed to find a way to bring the "pretribulational rapture" into the picture. Something was amiss; but the realization that something was amiss was one of the factors that motivated me to begin studying eschatology on my own.

In 1988 Edgar Whisenant came out with his book *88 Reasons Why The Rapture Will Be In 1988*. It created quite a stir in some circles, including among several people in the church we were attending. By then I knew enough to realize that Whisenant was wrong on several counts, so I told the pastor and others, "I will bet you any sum of money that the rapture will not happen this year." I had no takers of my wager, particularly after I added, "Honesty compels me to tell you that this is a bet I cannot lose: when the rapture doesn't happen, I will have your money; if it were to happen, we would all be in a place where there is no money."

Ideas have consequences. I led home Bible studies for several years while attending that church. Although the specific eschatological view of the pastor was not listed as part of the church's statement of faith, it nevertheless proved to be the litmus test of orthodoxy. I found that out while teaching through the book of Mark. When we got to the Olivet Discourse in Mark 13, I presented an alternative view of things, in line with the views of historic Christianity (and in line with the discussion of the Olivet Discourse in chapter 8 of this book). The historic exegesis of the Olivet Discourse was not, however, the view of the church I was attending, and such alternative views were not welcome. As a result, my family found that we "would be happier in another church."

That proved to be a great blessing. We began attending a large church where I was able to teach through several books of the Bible in adult education Bible studies on Sunday mornings, and my wife and I have since joined an excellent small church where I have the opportunity to preach during the months I am at home.

After I had been practicing law for approximately 25 years, although my practice was successful, I desired to leave the practice of law and do something more directly to help advance Christ's kingdom. I am grateful my wife, Nancy, had the good sense to say, "If you don't want to practice law anymore then quit. Go to seminary, and do what you want." Fortunately, Trinity Evangelical Divinity School has an extension campus in Milwaukee, WI, only about one hundred miles from our home in Appleton. Therefore, in the fall of 2003 I began pursuing an MDiv at night while continuing to practice law during the day. Dr. Steven Roy was my professor for a number of classes, including a NT Theology class that included eschatology. His presentation was not the propaganda of one narrow view but the presentation of the strengths and weaknesses of different views. His example is one of the important influences behind this book.

In Dr. Roy's class I also did a lengthy paper that was the genesis of what, in this book, is Appendix 2—The Millennium: An Amillennial Synthesis of the Biblical Data. Even though I advocated the amillennial position while he has an historic premillennial view, Dr. Roy encouraged me, both by requesting to keep a copy of the paper for his files and by commenting that "this is one of the best arguments for the amil position I've read," and "it gives me much to think about." However, he also challenged me to pay greater attention to the NT's revelation of the overlap of the "two ages" and "the impact of the reality of the overlap of the ages for a possible millennium." Consequently, I have revised, expanded, and deepened that paper several times since it originally was prepared in December 2004 and have tried to meet Dr. Roy's challenge, particularly in chapters 3–5 as well as in Appendix 2.

My time at Trinity proved crucial in other ways, both for my career and for this book. As a result of taking an introductory course on world missions, I began thinking seriously about teaching in the non-Western world. Through God's providence, I got connected with Equipping Pastors International in early 2005, made my first trip to East Africa in May of that year, and realized that I had found my calling to teach and equip pastors and church leaders in East Africa. I have been doing that full time since I received my degree in May 2007. While studying under Dr. Robert Yarbrough at Trinity's main campus (I had quit the practice of law completely at the end of 2005), I wrote a lengthy paper on 1 Cor 15:20–28, a small portion of which is incorporated in this book.

It truly has been said, "If you want to learn, teach." That has been the case with respect to this book. The essential outline of this book was generated when I first taught biblical eschatology at the Mbarara Bible College, Mbarara, Uganda, in 2008. Appendix 6–Zechariah 14 (its relation to Christ's two advents) was added as a result of a discussion I had with one of the pastors I work closely with in Kenya.

While every book represents the completion of a journey, no such journey is undertaken alone. In addition to Dr. Roy and Dr. Yarbrough, I also wish to acknowledge Dr. Eckhard Schnabel who was my professor for a number of classes at Trinity. His handout comparing the "signs" Jesus listed in the Olivet Discourse and the "seals" in Revelation was important. I highly respect Dr. Schnabel, and interact with him, particularly in chapter 7 (although I disagree with him on one important issue).

I would also like to acknowledge and thank the following people for their assistance in bringing this book to fruition. My friend Rev. John McFadden (author with his wife, Dr. Susan McFadden, of *Aging Together: Dementia, Friendship, and Flourishing Communities*) got me connected with Wipf & Stock. The helpful staff at Rolfing Library of Trinity International University, where I did much of my research, was invaluable. Mike Stratton assisted with some formatting issues. The proofing and suggestions of Chris Moran and Shari Klika have made this a better book. It is my hope that this book will contribute to the ongoing discussion of eschatology, to the end that our theology, our eschatology, and our praxis will all cohere to the glory of God and the advancement of Christ's kingdom here on earth until he returns in glory.

Preface to the Second Edition

It has been over four years since *Biblical Eschatology* was originally published. I am happy that the book generally was well-received[1] and am grateful that Wipf & Stock Publishers have agreed to publish this second edition. The format and objectives of this edition remain the same as the original. It analyzes all of the major eschatological passages, issues, and positions in a fair, clear, but not superficial way. It tries to make understanding eschatology easier by including a history of eschatological thought and by showing how eschatology fits into the overall biblical storyline and structure. And it shows the importance of eschatology theologically and the relevance of eschatology for practical life. Nevertheless, I have endeavored to do four things in this edition:

- Correct some typographical and other errors and correct links in the bibliography to sources that are available online.

- Flesh out the discussion of a few areas; this augmented discussion is found particularly in chapters 4 and 5 and appendix 2.

- Delete appendix 3 (regarding the "rapture"), since I believe that issue is adequately covered in chapter 9, and add a new appendix 7 on 1 Cor 15:20–57 (regarding the resurrection, the *parousia*, and the millennium), since that passage is Paul's longest discussion of the resurrection, and the passage has generated a fair amount of scholarly debate. It is therefore worthy of special attention.

- Interact more with different eschatological views, particularly with preterism (which I believe was unduly slighted in the first edition) and with J. Webb Mealy's "new creation millennialism" form of premillennialism. I also interact somewhat more with postmillennialsm and the pre-wrath rapture position.

Part of the impetus for this was J. Webb Mealy's contacting me, forwarding to me his written work, requesting my critique, and giving me his critique of portions of this book. While he has not persuaded me of the correctness of his position (nor have I persuaded him of the correctness of mine), our interchanges were in the highest tradition of scholarly give-and-take. Further, he forced me to consider some issues I had not previously thought much about and to "go deeper" with respect to some other issues. The result, I hope, is that this second edition has been improved and strengthened.

Finally, I would like to thank all those who pointed out to me various typographical errors or areas that could have been more clearly stated in the first edition. I also want to specifically thank Kim Riddlebarger and especially R. Fowler White and Sam Storms who

---

1. It was listed as the "book of the year" for 2013 by Michael Newnham (http://michaelnewnham.com/?s=biblical+eschatology), who also lists it among the top 10 books he recommends that every Christian should read (http://michaelnewnham.com/?p=20063). The book also was listed as the number 6 best book of 2014 by Sam Storms (http://www.crossmap.com/blogs/the-best-books-in-2014-part-two-5782).

were kind enough to respond to my unsolicited email, answer a number of questions that I had, and (in the case of Drs. White and Storms) even send me some material to review. Their consideration was both very kind and helpful.

I hope that this second edition will prove to be helpful to all those who are interested in developing a coherent position with respect to an important area of the Bible that, unfortunately, has often either been ignored or abused. I continue to believe what I said at the conclusion of the main text of the first edition (and this one): "By understanding eschatology, we can have a well-integrated theology that enables us to live authentic Christian lives with confidence and hope. Such lives will demonstrate the present reality of the kingdom while we look forward to the final consummation in all its glory."

List of Abbreviations

AB	Anchor Bible
ABD	Anchor Bible Dictionary
ANF	*Ante-Nicene Fathers,* 10 vols. Edited by Alexander Roberts and James Donaldson Peabody, MA: Hendrickson, 1994
Ant.	Josephus, *The Antiquities of the Jews*
ANTC	Abingdon New Testament Commentary
AOTC	Apollos Old Testament Commentary
AUSS	*Andrews University Seminary Studies*
Barn.	*Epistle of Barnabas*
BDAG	Walter Bauer, Frederick W. Danker, W. F. Arndt, and F. W. Gingrich. *Greek-English Lexicon of the New Testament and Other Early Christian Literature,* 3rd ed. Chicago: University of Chicago Press, 2000
BECNT	Baker Evangelical Commentary on the New Testament
BJRL	*Bulletin of the John Rylands Library*
BNTC	Black's New Testament Commentary
BSac	*Bibliotheca Sacra*
CBQ	*Catholic Biblical Quarterly*
Civ.	Augustine, *The City of God*
Comm. Dan.	Hippolytus, *Commentary on Daniel*
CTJ	*Calvin Theological Journal*
CTR	*Criswell Theological Review*
Dial.	Justin Martyr, *Dialogue with Trypho*
ESV	English Standard Version
EvQ	*Evangelical Quarterly*
Haer.	Irenaeus, *Against Heresies*
HALOT	*The Hebrew and Aramaic Lexicon of the Old Testament,* study edition. 2 vols. Edited by Ludwig Koehler and Walter Baumgartner. Revised by Walter Baumgartner and Johann

	Jakob Stamm. Translated and edited under the supervision of M. E. J. Richardson. Leiden: Brill, 2001
Hist. eccl.	Eusebius, *Ecclesiastical History*
HLD	*Harpers' Latin Dictionary*
HNTC	*Harper New Testament Commentary*
ICC	International Critical Commentary
Int	*Interpretation*
Int	Interpretation: A Bible Commentary for Teaching and Preaching
IVPNTC	InterVarsity Press New Testament Commentary
JATS	*Journal of the Adventist Theological Society*
JBL	*Journal of Biblical Literature*
JETS	*Journal of the Evangelical Theological Society*
JSNT	*Journal for the Study of the New Testament*
JSOTSup	*Journal for the Study of the Old Testament,* Supplement series
JTS	*Journal of Theological Studies*
J.W.	Josephus, *The Wars of the Jews*
MNTC	Moffatt New Testament Commentary
MSJ	*The Master's Seminary Journal*
NAC	New American Commentary
NASB	New American Standard Bible
NCBC	New Cambridge Bible Commentary
NIBC	New International Biblical Commentary
NICNT	New International Commentary on the New Testament
NIDNTTE	*New International Dictionary of New Testament Theology and Exegesis, 2nd ed.* Edited by Moisés Silva. 5 vols. Grand Rapids: Zondervan, 2014
NIDOTTE	*New International Dictionary of Old Testament Theology and Exegesis.* Edited by Willem VanGemeren. 5 vols. Grand Rapids: Zondervan, 1997
NIGTC	New International Greek Testament Commentary
NIV	New International Version
NIVAC	NIV Application Commentary
NKJV	New King James Version

NovT	*Novum Testamentum*
NSBT	New Studies in Biblical Theology
NT	New Testament
NTC	New Testament Commentary
NTS	*New Testament Studies*
NTSup	New Testament Supplement
OT	Old Testament
PC	Proclamation Commentaries
PNTC	Pillar New Testament Commentary
REC	Reformed Expository Commentary
Res.	Tertullian, *on the Resurrection of the Flesh*
RevExp	*Review and Expositor*
RSV	Revised Standard Version
RTR	*Reformed Theological Review*
SBJT	*Southern Baptist Journal of Theology*
SC	Sources Chrétiennes
SP	Sacra Pagina
TDNT	*Theological Dictionary of the New Testament.* 10 vols. Edited by Gerhard Kittel and Gerhard Friedrich. Translated by Geoffrey W. Bromiley. Grand Rapids: Eerdmans, 1964–76
TNTC	Tyndale New Testament Commentary
TOTC	Tyndale Old Testament Commentary
TynBul	*Tyndale Bulletin*
UBS4	*The Greek New Testament,* 4th rev. ed. Edited by Barbara Aland, Kurt Aland, Johannes Karavidopoulos, Carlo M. Martini, and Bruce Metzger. New York: United Bible Societies, 1993
USR	*Union Seminary Review*
WBC	Word Biblical Commentary
WTJ	*Westminster Theological Journal*
ZNW	*Zeitschrift für die Neutestamentliche Wissenschaft*

ESCHATOLOGY—THE STUDY OF THE "last things" or "end-times"—is important. It is important because approximately 27 percent of the Bible contains prophetic or predictive elements.[2] Although not all prophecy relates to the end of history, lengthy and important passages in both the OT and NT concern the last things. Major OT prophets such as Isaiah, Ezekiel, Daniel, and Zechariah wrote about eschatology. Jesus spoke at length concerning eschatology in the Olivet Discourse, and the apostles Peter, Paul, and John all wrote in some detail regarding eschatology. Consequently, not to have a good grasp of eschatology means that much of the Bible will remain closed, or be a mystery, to us.

However, eschatology can be contentious. Several different schools of eschatological thought have arisen during the course of Christian history. Indeed, different schools of eschatological thought were present even in the first two centuries of the church. Eschatological views have proven to be the basis of major divisions among denominations and Christian traditions.

Eschatology also is a great fascination for most people. Much has been written, and continues to be written, on the subject. Most books on eschatology, however, tend to address only a particular aspect of the topic (e.g., the "millennium"), or they present only one viewpoint, or they treat eschatology as if it were a subject that stands on its own apart from the rest of biblical theology.

This book takes a different approach. What I endeavor to do is to study biblical eschatology comprehensively. While I, of course, have and clearly state my own views (see especially Appendix 2–The Millennium: An Amillennial Synthesis of the Biblical Data), I discuss and critique all of the major eschatological positions (see especially chapters 1–Eschatology: Introduction, 7–The Millennium, and 12–The Importance of Eschatology; the introductory portions of chapters 8–The Olivet Discourse: the Tribulation and the Second Coming and 11–The Book of Revelation; and Appendices 1–The Four Basic Millennial Views, 4–Dan 9:24–27 [the "seventy weeks"], 6–Rom 11:25–26 ["and so all Israel will be saved"], and 7–1 Cor 15:20–57: The Resurrection, the *Parousia*, and the Millennium). The book also deals with all of the major eschatological issues. These include the Antichrist (see especially chapter 10–The "Antichrist"); the second coming of Christ (see especially chapter 5–The Eschatological Significance of Christ's Second Coming and much of chapters 8–The Olivet Discourse: the Tribulation and the Second Coming and 11–The Book of Revelation); the rapture (see especially chapter 9–The "Rapture": Pretribulational or Part of the Second Coming?); and the millennium (see especially chapter 7–The Millennium and Appendices 2–The Millennium: An Amillennial Synthesis of the Biblical Data and 7–1 Cor 15:20–57: The Resurrection, the *Parousia*, and the Millennium).

---

2. Payne, *Encyclopedia*, 12–13.

In addition to being comprehensive, this book attempts to make eschatology understandable and clear. It does this in several ways. First, as an evangelical who has a high view of the Bible, I regard exegesis of Scripture as fundamental. Therefore, chapters 8 and 11 provide detailed analyses of the two primary eschatological texts—the Olivet Discourse and the book of Revelation. Other major eschatological texts are analyzed in connection with the discussions of particular issues, such as Christ's *parousia*, the rapture, the millennium, or the Antichrist, or in appendices 3–Ezekiel 40–48 (Ezekiel's vision of a new temple), 4–Dan 9:24–27 (the "seventy weeks"), 5–Zechariah 14 (its relation to Christ's two advents), 6–Rom 11:25–26 ("and so all Israel will be saved"), and 7–1 Cor 15:20–57: The Resurrection, the *Parousia*, and the Millennium). Sound exegesis, however, can only take place within the domain of good hermeneutics. Consequently, chapter 2–Interpreting Prophecy and Apocalyptic and the beginning part of chapter 11–The Book of Revelation provide the hermeneutical tools to enable us to understand the genre of prophecy and apocalyptic and interpret such texts well.

Second, context is essential for sound interpretation of any text, particularly prophetic, apocalyptic, and other texts dealing with eschatology. Most other works concerning biblical eschatology treat it on its own as a subject of systematic theology. I believe that is a mistake. In fact, one reason eschatology is considered by many people to be so difficult to understand is that it usually is divorced from the broader context of biblical theology—both the broad biblical storyline and the Bible's overall eschatological structure. I have endeavored to rectify that situation by including three chapters that discuss the biblical storyline and structure and show how eschatology coherently fits into that storyline and structure: chapters 3–Old Testament Eschatological Expectations and the Significance of Christ's First Coming, 4–Interpreting Biblical Eschatology in Light of its Overall Structure, and 5–The Eschatological Significance of Christ's Second Coming. When considered in light of the Bible's overall storyline and eschatological structure, I think that eschatology actually is relatively easy to understand and fits coherently into the rest of the Bible.

Third, just as understanding eschatology is made easier by approaching it within the context of biblical theology, so understanding is augmented by considering historical theology. Although most books on eschatology treat it almost as if we were "reinventing the wheel," the fact is that the apostolic and post-apostolic fathers of the church wrote a considerable amount on eschatology (as have theologians throughout the last two millennia). Understanding their views helps us critique our own views. C. S. Lewis pointed out that every age tends to have its own outlook and make its own mistakes and that "all contemporary writers share to some extent the contemporary outlook."[3] Consequently, each new book of theology "has to be tested against the great body of Christian thought down the ages."[4] I have therefore included chapter 6–Historical Overview of Eschatological Thought to help us put our eschatology in the context of historical theology. In that chapter, I pay particular attention to the apostolic and post-apostolic writers who also make their appearance from time to time throughout the book.

Finally, many people seem to be of the opinion that one's eschatological views have no practical importance. They are "pan-millennialists" who think that "everything will

---

3. Lewis, "Introduction," 5.

4. Ibid., 4.

pan-out in the end." After all, we will not be able to absolutely confirm which view is correct until Christ comes again, and then, so the thinking goes, it won't matter. That type of thinking, although probably not consciously articulated, may be behind the fact that most books on eschatology do not deal with the practical implications of one's eschatological views. Such thinking, however, is contrary to the very nature of prophecy and apocalyptic prophecy such as the book of Revelation. All prophecy has an underlying moral or ethical purpose and is designed to confront and change people's attitudes and behavior. That is seen again and again, particularly in the book of Revelation. I have therefore included chapter 12–The Importance of Eschatology to deal specifically with the issue of what difference our eschatological views make with respect to how we live. As that chapter makes clear, eschatology is important both theologically and practically. Indeed, historically, eschatological views have played a very important role—both for good and for bad—in people's engagement with or withdrawal from the world.

In sum, the Bible tells a coherent story from beginning to end. It shows us that history is meaningful, and it points us to a bright consummation. Eschatology is the last act of the biblical drama and informs everything else that takes place throughout the Bible. To have a good understanding of the Bible as a whole, we need a good understanding of eschatology. When we do, the entire Bible becomes much more meaningful since we now can understand how it all fits together. Further, our general theology, our eschatology, and how we live our lives should all be coherent. Our beliefs—including the hope and perspective that sound eschatology imparts—should motivate us to live lives worthy of Jesus Christ our Lord. It is my hope that this book, by conveying a sound understanding of the many facets of eschatology, will assist that process to the glory of God and the furtherance of his kingdom.

1

Eschatology: Introduction

THE WORD "ESCHATOLOGY" COMES from two Greek words, *eschatos* ("farthest" or "last") and *logos* ("word," "instruction," "teaching").[1] Eschatology, therefore, has been defined as: "the word concerning, or the study of, what is ultimate or last, that is, what is final in the program of God";[2] or "teaching about the end," i.e., "any theology of history based upon a divinely revealed message about the last events";[3] or "the doctrine of the last things."[4]

Eschatology in the context of the overall biblical story

The overall biblical story

The basic biblical story may be summarized as follows: God created a beautiful world and human beings to live joyful, fulfilled lives in fellowship with him. Through our sin we lost that fellowship and brought evil and death into the world. However, God did not leave us in our sin and death. By means of a grand plan which involved calling Abraham and the nation of Israel, he prepared the way for his own coming to earth in the person of Jesus Christ to bring forgiveness of sin and to restore fellowship with him. He is coming again to utterly destroy sin and death without destroying us. He will consummate our restoration and our relationship with him. And he will renew the earth to be even more glorious than when it was first created. His goal is to live in a perfect, holy, loving, familial relationship with humanity, in a perfect environment, in which all relationships have been restored to perfection. God himself is both the author of the story and its primary character.[5]

Stanley Grenz summarizes the role of eschatology vis-à-vis the overall biblical storyline: "Within the context of Christian doctrine the topic of eschatology provides an

1. BDAG, *"eschatos,"* 397; *"logos,"* 598–99.
2. Grenz, *Millennial Maze,* 16.
3. McGinn, *Anti-Christ,* 2.
4. Vos, *Pauline Eschatology,* 1.
5. Stephen Sykes puts it this way, "In Christian narrative, God's world is the *setting,* the *theme* is the rescue of the fallen world and of humankind; the *plots* are the biblical narratives, from creation, election, to incarnation, crucifixion, resurrection and ascension; the *resolution* is the last judgement, heaven and hell." Sykes, *Atonement,* 14.

overarching vision of the faith. It seeks to set forth what is the ultimate goal toward which God's work in the world is directed, how that work will be consummated and in what manner that goal is already in the process of being realized. . . . The Bible presents history as meaningful, in that it is directed toward a goal—namely, the reign of God or the presence of the will of God throughout the earth. . . . John's vision [in Revelation] forms the climax to a long history of prophetic promise that stretches back to the Garden of Eden."[6]

Individual versus corporate eschatology

There are two main types or foci of eschatology: "individual eschatology" (i.e., what happens to individuals after death), and "corporate eschatology" (i.e., God's overall plan for human beings and creation as a whole and how that plan is consummated). This book deals primarily with corporate eschatology rather than individual eschatology, although there is some overlap between them.

Major hermeneutical issues

The basic questions that people have to wrestle with as they try to understand what the Bible says about eschatology include: Do the second coming of Christ, the resurrection and judgment of all humanity, and the inauguration of the eternal kingdom, occur as aspects of one great event, or are they separated by a temporary messianic kingdom that lasts a thousand years? Are we able to predict when any of the the "end-time" events will occur by paying attention to the events transpiring in the Middle East or other geopolitical occurrences? What is the role of the church in all of this?

The major positions regarding eschatology differ over two main issues:

(1) *The nature of the "thousand years" (Rev 20:2–7)*: Is the "thousand years" a discrete period of time distinct from the rest of history, or not? and What does it look like? (i.e., Is it a "golden age" on earth that can be experienced in the flesh, or can it be apprehended only by faith?); and

(2) *The timing of the "thousand years"*: Is the "thousand years" a past, present, or future period of time? and Does it occur before or after Christ comes again?

The different answers to the main eschatological issues tend to be based on different answers to three hermeneutical issues: (1) The role of the NT in interpreting the OT; (2) How to interpret the Bible's symbolic language; and (3) The relationship between Israel and the church.

Brief definitions of major eschatological terms

"On the simplest level . . . there are two basic schemes of prophecy: Premillennialism Versus Non-Premillennialism."[7] In other words, the primary issue is whether Christ's second

---

6. Grenz, *Millennial Maze*, 16, 27, 28; see also Vos, *Pauline Eschatology*, 1.
7. Waldron, "Structural Considerations," n.p.

coming (*parousia*) precedes (premillennialism) or follows (non-premillennialism) the "thousand years" of Rev 20:2–7. Two main camps hold that the *parousia* will precede the "thousand years": historic premillennialism and dispensational premillennialism. Three main camps hold that Christ's second coming will come after the "thousand years": postmillennialism, amillennialism, and preterism.

- *Millennium.* The term is from the Latin for "thousand years."[8] The term "thousand years" occurs only in Rev 20:2–7. All standard Bible translations of Revelation 20 use the term "thousand years." However, many writers who discuss eschatology in general and Revelation 20 specifically employ the term "millennium." One problem with doing that is that the term "millennium" is loaded with connotations of a "golden age," which *may not at all be* what the term "thousand years" as used in Revelation 20 suggests. Don Garlington therefore observes, "It would be preferable not to speak of a 'millennium' at all in this sense, given the context-specific coloring of John's 'thousand years.'"[9] Since the term is so popular, however, there is little chance that Garlington's prudence will be followed.

- *Premillennialism.* Premillennialism is any belief that Christ will come *before* the "thousand years." Premillennialists believe that at his coming Christ will institute a thousand-year reign ("golden age") on the earth, after which he will institute the eternal state. In older writings, "premillennialism" is often called "chiliasm" from the Greek *"chilioi"* which means "thousand." Premillennialists are divided into two main camps: historic premillennialists and dispensational premillennialists.

    (1) *Historic Premillennialism.* Historic premillennialists believe that any doctrine of the millennium must be based on the NT and be consistent with Christ's present reign. They believe that there will be two bodily resurrections separated by the "thousand years": the resurrection of the righteous when Christ comes again and then the resurrection of the unrighteous after the thousand years. After that, the eternal state will be instituted.[10]

    (2) *Dispensational Premillennialism.* Dispensational premillennialists hold that there is a radical distinction between Israel and the church and that all prophecies must be interpreted "literally": prophetic promises to OT Israel must literally be fulfilled in the physical nation of Israel, not in the church. They view the millennium as the climax of God's dealings with Israel. They hold that Christ will actually have two "second comings": the first one, which they call the "pretribulational rapture," is only "for" his church (i.e., the church will leave the earth and meet Christ in the air and then go back with him to heaven). Later, after the "great tribulation," Christ will physically come with his church to the earth and set up a thousand-year kingdom in which Israel is dominant.[11] They also believe that there will be three resurrections: the first for the righteous dead

---

8. *Mille* = "thousand"; *annus* = "year." See Schnabel, *40 Questions*, 267.

9. Garlington, "Reigning," n.p.

10. Ladd, "Historic Premillennialism," 17–40. A recently-developed variant of premillennialism called "new creation millennialism" will be discussed in chapter 7–The Millennium.

11. Boyd, "Dispensational Premillennial Analysis," 4–13; Hoyt, "Dispensational Premillennialism," 63–92.

at the rapture; the second at the end of the tribulation for those saints who have died during the tribulation; and the third at the end of the millennium for the unbelievers.[12] After that there will be a great rebellion which Christ will overcome. He will then institute the eternal state.

- *Postmillennialism.* Technically, any belief that Christ will come *after* the "thousand years" is postmillennial. As popularly used, however, postmillennialism is the belief that the "millennium" is a future, discrete period of unprecedented Christian influence in the world (a "golden age"), based on the work of the church and the Holy Spirit in the world, that gradually emerges before Christ's return. Christ will then come again, receive the kingdom, and initiate the eternal state.[13]

- *Amillennialism.* Amillennialists believe that the "thousand years" is a symbolic reference to the entire period between Christ's resurrection until shortly before his return. That period will be characterized by the spread of the gospel but also by the spread of sin, i.e., there will be no "golden age" before Christ returns. Christ's return will result in the general resurrection and judgment, and will usher in the eternal state.[14]

- *Preterism.* The term comes from the Latin *"praeter"* which means "past" or "beyond."[15] Preterism is divided into two main camps: "full preterism" and "partial preterism." Full preterism holds that all significant events of prophecy, including the "millennium" and Christ's second coming (which preterists see as a spiritual coming), took place in AD 70 when the Jewish temple was destroyed by the Romans. Partial preterism holds that most of the major eschatological events were fulfilled by AD 70 but that Christ will physically come again in the future and set up the eternal state.[16]

- *Tribulation and Great Tribulation.* "Tribulation" refers to the persecution of believers. Based on their interpretation of Dan 9:24–27, dispensationalists and some others think that there will be a seven-year tribulation, primarily directed against the nation of Israel, just before the *parousia.* The "great tribulation" is thought to be a time of even more intense persecution in the last half of the tribulation. Most historic premillennialists, amillennialists, and postmillennialists disagree with dispensationalists concerning the interpretation of Dan 9:24–27. They see tribulation as one of the things that characterizes the entire period between Christ's first and second comings, although the intensity of persecution may increase shortly before Christ returns. Preterists hold that the tribulation was a past event related to the siege and overthrow of Jerusalem in AD 70.

- *Pretribulationism, Midtribulationism, and Posttribulationism.* "Pretribulationism" is a distinctively dispensationalist idea. Pretribulationists believe that *before* the

12. Erickson, *Christian Theology,* 1225.

13. Boettner, "Postmillennialism," 117–41. Postmillennialist Greg Bahnsen states that "it is more common today for postmillennialists to refer to the whole period, from the first advent to the second, as the millennium," but they contend that "Christianity will become the dominant principle rather than the exception to the rule." Bahnsen, *Victory,* 34, 92; see also Kik, *Eschatology,* 17.

14. Hoekema, "Amillennialism," 155–87.

15. See *HLD, "praeter,"* 1433–34; Gentry, *Dominion,* 159; Gentry, "Foundation," 13.

16. Sproul, *Last Days,* 24–25.

"tribulation" Christ will come part-way from heaven to earth to "rapture" ("take away" to heaven) the church. A variant of this is "midtribulationism" which believes that Christ will rapture the church in the middle of a seven-year tribulation (i.e., just before the "great tribulation").[17] Both pre- and mid-tribulationists believe that *after* the tribulation Christ will come *again,* this time all the way to earth, to set up a thousand-year kingdom. After that he will establish the eternal state. On the other hand, "posttribulationism" holds that Christ will return only *after* the church goes through tribulation. Posttribulationists believe that the rapture of living believers will take place along with the resurrection of the dead when Christ returns.

Pretribulationism must not be confused with premillennialism. All pretribulationists and midtribulationists are also premillennialists. However, not all premillennialists are pretribulationists. Most historic premillennialists are posttribulationists. By definition, all amillennialists, postmillennialists, and preterists also are posttribulationists.

Resources to compare different eschatological systems

One good way to see the strengths and weaknesses of different eschatological systems is by reading books in which a proponent of one view makes his case and then is critiqued by advocates of other views. Such books include: Robert Clouse, ed., *The Meaning of the Millennium: Four Views* (Downers Grove, IL: InterVarsity, 1977); Darrell Bock, Craig Blaising, Kenneth Gentry, and Robert Strimple, *Three Views on the Millennium and Beyond* (Grand Rapids: Zondervan, 1999); Gleason Archer, Paul Feinberg, Douglas Moo, and Richard Reiter, *The Rapture: Pre-, Mid-, or Post-Tribulational?* (Grand Rapids: Academie, 1984); Craig Blaising, Alan Hultberg, and Douglas Moo, *Three Views on the Rapture: Pretribulation, Prewrath, or Posttribulation,* 2nd ed. (Grand Rapids: Zondervan, 2010); Thomas Ice and Kenneth Gentry, *The Great Tribulation: Past or Future? Two Evangelicals Debate the Question* (Grand Rapids: Kregel, 1999); and C. Marvin Pate, Kenneth Gentry, Sam Hamstra, and Robert Thomas, *Four Views on the Book of Revelation* (Grand Rapids: Zondervan, 1998).

Books in which one author does a fair job of describing the different eschatological positions include: Millard Erickson, *Contemporary Options in Eschatology: A Study of the Millennium* (Grand Rapids: Baker, 1977); Stanley Grenz, *The Millennial Maze* (Downers Grove, IL: InterVarsity, 1992); C. Marvin Pate, *Reading Revelation: A Comparison of Four Interpretive Translations of the Apocalypse* (Grand Rapids: Kregel, 2009); and Steve Gregg, ed., *Revelation: Four Views: A Parallel Commentary* (Nashville: Thomas Nelson, 1997).

---

17. A variant of *this* is the "pre-wrath" rapture position which contends that the rapture will take place during the "great tribulation" but before the "wrath of God" is poured out. See Marvin Rosenthal, *Pre-Wrath, passim.* Subsequent discussions of pre-tribulationism (see particularly chapter 9–The "Rapture": Pretribulational or Part of the second coming?) include the midtribulation and pre-wrath views even if they are not mentioned explicitly, since all are based on dispensationalist premises and the basic principles that pertain to pretribulationism pertain to its variants as well.

2

Interpreting Prophecy and Apocalyptic

PROPHECY CAN BE ONE of the most challenging areas of biblical interpretation. Three main reasons for that are: (1) failure to apply the basic principles of biblical interpretation; (2) misunderstanding the genre of prophecy; and (3) failing to understand basic biblical theology.[1]

The nature of biblical prophets and prophecy

God gave Israel his revelation and established his covenant. In this context, God instituted the prophets through Moses. The prophet was to be a man of God, a witness for God, a servant of God, and committed to God. He was to speak the voice of God, in contrast to listening to the voice of the people. Likewise, he served as a critic of the culture from a godly perspective.[2]

God's prophets applied God's word during crises in the covenant relation between God and his people. The main activity of OT prophets was *not* predicting the future. Rather, OT biblical prophecy was as interested in the present as in the future. The prophets all had essentially a two-fold message and ministry: (1) They warned God's people of the consequences of disobedience to the Lord's ways by *oracles of judgment*; and (2)

---

1. There are many good books on biblical interpretation and biblical theology. These include:

Biblical Interpretation: Kay Arthur, *How to Study Your Bible* (Eugene, OR: Harvest House, 1994); Gordon Fee and Douglas Stuart, *How to Read the Bible for All Its Worth* (Grand Rapids: Academie, 1982); Grant Osborne, *The Hermeneutical Spiral* (Downers Grove, IL: InterVarsity, 1991); William Webb, *Slaves, Women & Homosexuals: Exploring the Hermeneutics of Cultural Analysis* (Downers Grove, IL: IVP Academic, 2001); Bennie Wolvaardt, *How to Interpret the Bible: A Do-It-Yourself Manual.* (London: Veritas College, 2005); Jonathan Menn, *Biblical Interpretation* (2017), online: http://www.eclea.net/courses.html#interpretation.

Biblical Theology: T. Desmond Alexander, *From Eden to the New Jerusalem: Exploring God's Plan for Life on Earth* (Nottingham, England: Inter-Varsity, 2008); G. K. Beale, *A New Testament Biblical Theology: The Unfolding of the Old Testament in the New* (Grand Rapids: Baker Academic, 2011); Graeme Goldsworthy, *According to Plan: The Unfolding Revelation of God in the Bible* (Downers Grove, IL: Grove, IL: InterVarsity, 1991); Jonathan Menn, *Biblical Theology* (2016), online: http://www.eclea.net/courses.html#theology.

2. VanGemeren, *Interpreting*, 41–69.

They called God's people back to faithfulness by *oracles of salvation*.[3] In other words, all OT prophets were concerned with changing people's behavior.[4] Their message was, "if you do this, judgment will come; if you follow the Lord, blessings will come." As such, much of OT prophecy was "conditional" on people's repentance and behavior, even when a prophecy appeared to be unconditional (e.g., Jonah 3).

The prophets primarily were oral communicators; the prophetic writings were secondary. Prophetic books often contain many collections of spoken oracles that are not always presented in chronological order. The metaphorical language they often use is grounded in imagery meaningful to their own culture.

General considerations for interpreting prophecy

Emphasis on God, not on specific events

Prophetic messages are more the "*forth*-telling" of God's word, than the *fore*telling of specific, inevitable, future events. The *fulfillment* of prophecy lies in a *person* (God), and he may fulfill his word *however* and *whenever* he chooses. For example, the prophets spoke of David returning or his descendant coming to Israel (e.g., Isa 11:1; Jer 30:9; Ezek 37:24); God actually came in the flesh in the person of Jesus Christ, and the kingdom of God became manifested through Jesus in ways the OT prophets could not conceive (see Mark 1:15; Luke 17:21; Matt 16:19 [compare Isa 22:22]). Stephen Travis notes, "It was the literalists of Jesus's day who found it hard to recognise in him the fulfillment of their expectations. Those who looked for a military and political Messiah, the natural counterpart to David, failed to see that Jesus had more, not less, to offer. Those who accused him at his trial could not get beyond a literal understanding of his prediction that within three days he would rebuild the ruined Temple (Matthew 26:61; cf. John 2:18–22)."[5] In light of this, "If we acknowledge that ancient prophecies may be fulfilled in ways we do not expect, it follows that we cannot employ prophecies as detailed blueprints of the future. We may see general parallels between the prophet's situation and our own; however, we must leave room for unforeseen variations."[6]

Emphasis on patterns and themes

Because of their two-fold message (judgment and salvation), even though the prophets spoke about specific crises, their underlying messages of judgment and salvation are relevant for many generations. Further, "Old Testament end-time predictions commonly are connected by themes and key words rather than by a strict chronological order (for example, see Dan 7:8–27; 8:9–26; Rev 16–19)."[7] Similar themes run throughout the prophets. Those themes include: God's covenant with his people; the presence of God; God as king;

---

3. Ibid., 78–79.

4. See Schnabel, *40 Questions*, 13.

5. Travis, *I Believe*, 139.

6. Green, *How to Read Prophecy*, 105.

7. Oropeza, *99 Reasons*, 195n.10.

God's Messiah; the Day of the Lord; the kingdom of God; and the Spirit of the Lord. The NT writers saw the OT prophetic writings primarily as *patterns* that were fulfilled in the NT. Thus, just as Rachel wept when going into exile (the context of Jer 31:15), so Rachel weeps again when Herod killed the children (the context of Matt 2:18 in which Matthew quotes Jeremiah's prophecy). We need to look for those themes and patterns. In them we begin to see the mind of God.

Contingency in prophecy

As oracles of judgment and salvation, prophecy has an underlying moral purpose. Prophecy is designed to change people's behavior; it is not designed as something that is to be regarded with an attitude of fatalistic resignation. Desmond Ford observes that modern Western readers who have a "fatalistic or predestinarian outlook often take as absolute, Semitic pronouncements which in their own day would have been considered as less than absolute. . . . The biblical view of prophecy is that a forecast is not necessarily a prediction to be fulfilled at all hazards. Rather a prediction of disaster is a hint in order that proper steps might be taken to avert the evil. Similarly a prediction of blessing is an encouragement, that there might be perseverance in the right course."[8]

God is not a static, impersonal force. Rather, to use anthropomorphic language, God reacts to the choices made by people in response to his decrees which have been articulated by his prophets. We see this, for example, in God's "changing his mind" in response to Moses' intercession on behalf of Israel after God had threatened to destroy Israel (Exod 32:9–14) and in his not destroying Nineveh after it repented (Jonah 3:1–10). J. Barton Payne summarizes, "Prophecy in particular has been designed by God for moral ends so as to motivate men into conformity with divine holiness. Should men, therefore, seek to take advantage of its holy assurances . . . change becomes then not only possible but inevitable."[9]

God announced this principle of contingency in Jer 18:6–11; 26:12–13; 36:1–3; Ezek 18:1–32; 33:10–20. Sometimes the conditional nature of a prophecy is explicitly stated.[10] Sometimes a prophecy is unconditional on its face, but the character of God and the responses of people provide unstated conditionality to the prophecy.[11] Actions taken in response to a prophecy might either postpone or hasten its fulfillment.[12] In 1 Sam 23:10–14, David avoided entirely the consequences that God had revealed to him by taking prudent action. In Acts 21:10–14, "Paul's Christian friends did not regard the prophecy [of Agabus] as of inevitable fulfillment. Instead they treated it as a kindly warning whereby the disaster might be averted."[13]

---

8. Ford, *Abomination of Desolation*, 75, 99n.72.

9. Payne, *Encyclopedia*, 62; see also Schnabel, *40 Questions*, 11. A good recent analysis of the contingent and hortatory nature of prophecy is Chisholm, "When Prophecy Appears to Fail," 561–77.

10. E.g., Jer 38:17–18; 42:7–17; Acts 27:21–44; Rom 11:17–24.

11. E.g., Exod 32:9–14; 1 Kgs 20:26–42; 21:17–29; Isa 38:1–5; Jonah 3:1—4:2; Matt 19:27–28. In Matt 19:27–28 the promise by Jesus to the Twelve that they would judge the twelve tribes of Israel included *Judas*.

12. See 2 Kgs 22:14–20; Hab 2:2–3; 2 Pet 3:8–12.

13. Ford, *Abomination of Desolation*, 99n.72.

Prophets build on earlier prophecies

God's covenants grow and develop through the prophets who develop and transform them through their proclamations of judgment and salvation. The following are two examples of prophetic development within the OT itself:

- *The promise of the land in the Abrahamic Covenant (Gen 12:1–3).* The "land" promised to Abraham initially was undefined (Gen 12:1). It was first defined as what Abram could see (Gen 13:14–15), then was geographically described (Gen 15:18–21; 17:8), and finally was included in the comprehensive statement that "your seed shall possess the gates of their [lit., 'his'] enemies" (Gen 22:17). The OT indicates that the promise of land was physically fulfilled at least twice: in the days of Joshua (Josh 21:43–45), and during the reign of Solomon (1 Kgs 4:20–21). However, because of disobedience Israel was dispossessed from the land, so the promise was never ultimately fulfilled during the OT. The land was still longed for, and restoration was promised during the exile (see Ezek 20:1–44). The promise was again partially fulfilled physically after the exile.

- *The Davidic Covenant (2 Sam 7:12–16).* Jeremiah recalled Nathan's promises to David concerning a Davidic king and Levitical priesthood in order to assure the exiles that God would restore them to their land (Jer 33:19–22). Jeremiah also built on Isaiah's prophecy that a righteous branch would come from David's line and added that the Levitical priests would never lack a man to offer sacrifices before the Lord (Jer 33:14–18; cf. Isa 11:1).

Prophetic idiom

The OT prophets spoke within the framework, and used terms, they were familiar with and that made sense to their hearers. The OT prophets spoke of Messiah's eternal kingdom using the language and limited frame of reference of their own physical, Israelite context. E. F. Kevan correctly observes that "in all of their statements about the kingdom of God, even when uttering the most spiritual and glorious truths regarding it, the vocabulary which the prophets employ is always that of the kingdom of God in the forms in which they knew it in their own day."[14] Thus, the OT prophets used the imagery of the temple and Zion, and they spoke of the kingdom in terms of a literal king from the line of David sitting on a throne in a palace in Jerusalem. This is known as "prophetic idiom."[15]

Even in the NT, when God revealed the fulfillment of OT prophecy and when the NT writers point forward to the consummation of God's plan, they use the language that their contemporaries would understand. As Steve Lehrer describes it, "when God used the prophets to explain the spiritual fulfillment of God's plan in the New Covenant era, God decided to use the language of types and shadows. He was describing the New

---

14. Kevan, "Covenants," 24; see also Lehrer, *New Covenant Theology*, 85 ("In the Old Covenant era we see spiritual truths being related in picture form"); Lewis, *Dark Side*, 37 ("Isaiah often saw the future reign of the Lord in limited and metaphoric terms").

15. Irons, "Prophetic Idiom." Chisholm refers to this as "contextualization." Chisholm, "When Prophecy Appears to Fail," 572–74.

Covenant in the language of the Old Covenant. He pointed toward the spiritual goal of God's plan in the brightest and clearest way that the physical types and shadows would allow."[16] Examples of this include: Jesus describes his body as the "temple" (John 2:18–22); the church as a whole is called the "temple" or the "tabernacle" in 1 Cor 3:9, 16–17; 2 Cor 6:16—7:1; Eph 2:21; 1 Pet 2:5; Rev 3:12; Rev 13:6; Paul uses OT language of burnt offerings to describe money given to assist his ministry (Phil 4:18; see Exod 29:18); in Revelation the leaders of end-time nations are referred to as "kings" (e.g., Rev 16:14; 19:18); and the bringers of catastrophe are compared to horses whose riders are equipped with ancient armor and weapons (e.g., Rev 6:2, 4, 5, 8; 9:7, 9, 17).

Non-literal fulfillment

Because God's purposes develop in interaction with human choices and events, prophecies are not always fulfilled "literally." Stephen Travis gives examples of this:

> Jeremiah and Isaiah predicted that Babylon would fall to the Medes (Jeremiah [51]:11, 28; Isaiah 13:17), and Isaiah described graphically the total destruction of Babylon and the merciless killing of its people (Isaiah 13:14–22). But in fact Babylon fell to the Persians who had gained control of the Medes before capturing Babylon. And Babylon surrendered without a struggle. The city was not destroyed, and continued to be inhabited. So, the prophecy of Babylon's fall was fulfilled substantially, but not literally. Similarly, Isaiah 10:28–34 prophesied the Assyrian invasion, vividly describing how the Assyrian army would come from north to south, city by city along the hills through Ai [Aiath], Geba, Gibeah, Anathoth and Nob to Mount Zion itself. In fact, when Sennacherib came with his invading force he followed the sea coast and approached Jerusalem from the west.[17]

Changed circumstances and the manner of fulfillment

Prophecies were based on specific historical situations; therefore, changed circumstances affect the way in which the prophecies are fulfilled. There have been momentous geopolitical changes that have altered the social landscape since the OT prophecies were given. More importantly, the coming of Jesus Christ altered the "theological landscape" in profound ways.[18] This means that, although similar themes and principles run throughout the prophets, and God's character remains the same, we cannot expect apparently unfulfilled OT prophecies to be fulfilled exactly as the people (or even the prophets themselves) may have envisioned. Travis explains:

> Because prophecy is tied to a particular historical situation, it uses terms appropriate to those times. Abraham is promised land. Exiles from a ruined Jerusalem are promised a new Temple (Ezekiel 40–48). . . . And it is because the prophecies

16. Lehrer, *New Covenant Theology*, 85.

17. Travis, *I Believe*, 137–38.

18. The effect of Jesus' first coming, and the consequent change from the Old Covenant to the New Covenant era, is discussed in the next two chapters of this book.

address one particular situation that, once they are fulfilled (for example, in the return from exile), we cannot apply them in detail to another, later historical situation (for example, the Middle East today). At most we can draw general parallels, as the New Testament does, between the situation addressed by the prophet and the situation of today's 'Israel', the church. . . . Because the form of a prophecy reflects the conditions of the time when it is uttered, we should not be surprised to find it being fulfilled substantially but not literally. A moment's reflection will confirm how inappropriate it is to envisage a literal fulfillment of some prophecies. For instance, there is Isaiah's prophecy of a time when Assyria, Egypt and Israel will live in harmony and be a blessing to the world (Isaiah 19:19–25). Today Assyria does not exist as a nation, and most of the inhabitants of Egypt are racially quite different from the Egyptians of Isaiah's day. Such a prophecy can hardly be fulfilled literally, though it could be a picture of the peace between Jew and Gentile made possible by Christ (cf. Ephesians 2:11–22), or the ideal relations between people of all nations in God's ultimate kingdom.[19]

The profound effect of the NT on OT prophecy

The full meaning of any particular passage or prophecy may not be clear unless the whole Bible and the stage of redemptive history are taken into consideration. Dennis Johnson makes this point clearly: "To read the Bible contextually *as the Word of God* must include the completed canon as the ultimate context of any particular passage."[20] The NT profoundly affects OT prophecy. In fact, one may say that the NT transforms OT prophecy and is the best interpreter of OT prophecy. Prophecy is an important area in which "the New [Testament] is in the Old [Testament] *concealed,* and the Old is in the New *revealed*."[21]

Progressive revelation

Graeme Goldsworthy states an important hermeneutical point: "It is impossible from the Old Testament alone to understand the full measure of God's acts and promises that it records."[22] The reason why the OT alone does not convey its full underlying meaning is the doctrine of progressive revelation. "Progressive revelation means that God's revelation was not given all at once in the beginning, but was revealed by stages until the full light of truth was revealed in Jesus Christ."[23] Thus, the OT is the preparation of the gospel; the Gospels are the manifestation of the gospel; Acts is the expansion of the gospel; the Epistles are the explanation of the gospel; and Revelation is the consummation of the

---

19. Travis, *I Believe*, 136, 138.

20. Johnson, *Him We Proclaim*, 156, emphasis in original.

21. This quotation is credited to Augustine (354–430) and is adapted from his *Quaestiones in Heptateuchum* 2.73, which Paul Wendland translates as follows, "This passage [Exod 20:19] signifies a great and lasting truth: that fear pertains to the Old Testament just as love does to the New—even though the New lies hidden in the Old Testament, and the Old Testament is opened up in the New." Wendland, "Another Latin LXX quote," n.p. The same idea had been expressed earlier by Lactantius in his *Divine Institutes* 4.20.

22. Goldsworthy, *According to Plan*, 54; see also Schnabel, *40 Questions*, 11.

23. Goldsworthy, *According to Plan*, 64.

gospel. Jesus and the NT authors understood this. They saw the entire OT as in some way a book about Jesus. He is its central person and integrating theme[24] and is "the final and the fullest revelation of what the promises are really about."[25]

Typology and the transformative effect of Christ's first coming

Because the Bible ultimately is the story about Jesus Christ who is explicitly revealed only in the NT, the NT writers generally look at the OT in a "typological" way.[26] The NT reveals that OT Israel as a nation, and all of its laws, ceremonies, and institutions, and the OT prophecies concerning it, were "types," "symbols," "shadows," "copies," or "examples" of NT realities that were fulfilled and superseded in Christ and his church.[27] Edward Young points out that, in approaching OT prophecies, "since the revelation granted to the prophets was less clear than that given to Moses; indeed, since it contained elements of obscurity, we must take these facts into consideration when interpreting prophecy. We must therefore abandon once and for all the erroneous and non-Scriptural rule of 'literal if possible.' The prophetic language belonged to the Mosaic economy and hence, was typical. Only in the light of the New Testament fulfillment can it properly be interpreted."[28] Willem VanGemeren adds, "The coming of our Lord radically altered the understanding of the Old Testament. The apostles understood the canon in the light of Jesus' ministry, message, and exaltation. The traditional understanding of Moses' words and the Prophets had to undergo a radical transformation in view of the coming of our Lord."[29] Consequently, we must "always read the Old Covenant Scriptures through the lens of the New Covenant Scriptures."[30]

The form of prophetic fulfillment

How the NT fulfills the OT "types" and promises is not self-evident. Goldsworthy points out, "It was not self-evident that Jesus fulfilled the Old Testament promises. Those Jews who looked for a literal fulfillment of the Old Testament promises failed to recognize Jesus as the fulfillment."[31] Because of the transformative nature of the coming of Christ and the inauguration of the New Covenant, the *form* in which OT prophecies are fulfilled in the future are likely to be different from the Old Covenant *form* in which the prophecies themselves were originally given. In the New Covenant we should not expect OT prophe-

---

24. Luke 24:25–27, 44–45; John 5:39–40, 46; Acts 3:18, 24; 10:43; 26:22–23; 2 Cor 1:20; 1 Pet 1:10–12; Heb 1:1–3. See Gaebelein, "Unity of the Bible," 392–95.

25. Goldsworthy, *According to Plan*, 65.

26. Ramm, *Interpretation*, 260–69; Goldsworthy, *According to Plan*, 67–69.

27. See Matt 5:17; 1 Cor 10:1–6; 2 Cor 3:12–16; Gal 3:23—4:7, 21–31; Col 2:16–17; Heb 1:1–2; 8:1—10:22.

28. Young, *My Servants*, 54, 215n.21.

29. VanGemeren, *Interpreting*, 83.

30. Lehrer, *New Covenant Theology*, 177. As P. W. L. Walker states, it is "illegitimate to approach the Old Testament text as though the New Testament had not been written." Walker, *Jesus*, 313.

31. Goldsworthy, *According to Plan*, 65–66.

cies to be fulfilled in an Old Covenant way. The NT builds upon OT concepts, often in surprising ways. This has an important corollary or effect with respect to the form and content of the fulfillment of OT prophecy. David Holwerda explains, "When fulfillment happens, the institutions that were types or symbols of that reality are no longer necessary. They are displaced by the reality they symbolize."[32] Goldsworthy adds, "This means that the form and the content of the fulfillment exceeds by far the form and content of the promises themselves. . . . *Literalism* involves the very serious error of not listening to what the New Testament says about fulfillment. It assumes that the fulfillment must correspond exactly to the form of the promise."[33] Although the original OT audience may have understood a prophecy in one way, where the NT either explicitly or implicitly interprets the OT prophecy, it is not proper "to attempt a mediating position whereby the New Testament critique of [the OT prophecy] is acknowledged, but the Old Testament understanding of the [prophecy] is somehow allowed to stand, unaltered and unscathed."[34]

NT reinterpretation of OT prophecy

The NT demonstrates that the ultimate meaning and fulfillment of OT prophecies go far beyond the "physical" aspects of ancient Israel. In fact, as George Eldon Ladd states, "the Old Testament did not clearly foresee how its own prophecies were to be fulfilled. They were fulfilled in ways quite unforeseen by the Old Testament itself and unexpected by the Jews."[35] E. F. Kevan observes, "Examples of the transmutation of the prophecies may be seen in the Davidic Kingship, the Servant, the Chosen People, the Hill of Zion, the institution of worship through Priest and Sacrifice, and the Messianic hope. . . . Our Lord himself transmuted many of the Old Covenant conceptions, such as the Sabbath, Ceremonial Defilement, the Temple, and the Davidic Kingship. It was because of His transmutation of the last that the Jews drove Him to His death."[36] While some might say the NT "spiritualizes" much of OT prophecy, it is probably more accurate to say that the NT *reinterprets* or *reapplies* OT prophecy[37] or reveals the true, ultimate meaning of the OT prophecies that God intended from the beginning.

In the NT, prophetic fulfillment is played out in the physical realm but in a new, spiritual key. The "land" promise in the Abrahamic Covenant and the prophecies of a king and Levitical priesthood in the Davidic Covenant, discussed earlier, show how the NT radically reinterprets OT prophecies:

32. Holwerda, *Eschatology*, 74–75.

33. Goldsworthy, *According to Plan*, 65, 67; see also Ramm, *Interpretation*, 260.

34. Walker, *Jesus*, 313.

35. Ladd, "Historic Premillennialism," 27.

36. Kevan, "Covenants," 27. The transmutation and fulfillment of these prophecies is discussed in greater detail in chapter 3.

37. We will see this when we consider the Olivet Discourse and "Antichrist." This phenomenon occurs throughout the NT, culminating in Revelation. With respect to Revelation, Richard Bauckham observes, "John is very conscious of writing in a long tradition of prophetic oracles and so is constantly echoing and reapplying the oracles of his predecessors." Bauckham, "Economic Critique," 53; see Appendix 5: Zechariah 14 (its relation to Christ's two advents) for examples of how Revelation takes every OT image and limited frame of reference in Zechariah 14 and expands or transforms it.

- *The promise of the land in the Abrahamic Covenant (Gen 12:1–3).* The NT reinterprets the OT physical Canaan as a figure of the true "land": the earth in its entirety (Rom 4:13); and the heavenly city, the New Jerusalem (Heb 11:8–16; Revelation 21–22).[38] Thus, Deut 30:12–14 dealt with obeying the Law of Moses and God's promise to return repentant Israel to the land. In Rom 10:1–10 Paul quotes that passage but reinterprets those OT promises as promises that faith in Christ will result in salvation. Further, the heart of the land promise was Israel's "rest" from all of its enemies and full provision for all of its needs.[39] That has been transformed into the believers' salvation or spiritual rest (Heb 3:7—4:11).[40]

- *The Davidic Covenant (2 Sam 7:12–16).* Jeremiah's prophecies concerning the king and Levitical priesthood in the Davidic Covenant (Jer 33:19–22) are fulfilled in Jesus Christ. Unlike the form of Jeremiah's prophecies, Christ's reign is from heaven as Lord not from an earthly throne as a political/military king.[41] Further, a "literal"

38. "The land was a concrete expression of God's promise. As such, it was only a pointer to 'the city with foundations, whose architect and builder is God' (Hebrews 11:10). . . . Prosperity in the land was to be an index of Israel's faithfulness (Deuteronomy 28:1–14). Exile and loss of the land would result from continued disobedience (Deuteronomy 28:15—29:28). These arrangements prefigured the inheritance of the new heaven and new earth, which we receive now on the basis of Christ's obedience, not our own (1 Peter 1:4)." Poythress, *Shadow of Christ,* 106, 72.

39. See Deut 12:9–11; 25:19; Josh 1:2–8; Ps 95:10–11.

40. With respect to the promise of the land, Heb 3:7–11, 15, 4:3, 5, 7 quote from Ps 95:7–11 and allude to Num 14:23 and Deut 1:34–35, where "entering God's rest" is equated with entering the promised land of Canaan. However, Heb 3:11; 4:3, 5 also quote that part of Ps 95:11 which says, *"they shall not enter my rest."* Heb 4:9–11 concludes by saying that there is a rest that we should be diligent to enter. Hebrews is reinterpreting the meaning of "rest" and "land," compared to how those words were used in the OT. The Israelites in the wilderness did not "enter God's rest" in the sense that they were not allowed to enter the Promised Land. Hebrews 3 interprets that to mean that they did not obtain salvation. Joshua, of course, *did* lead Israel into the Promised Land, and they *were* given rest from their physical enemies! "But the author of Hebrews is pointing past a physical fulfillment concerning physical land and rest from war into a spiritual rest. The promise of Canaan as an everlasting possession is finally and ultimately fulfilled with the everlasting possession of our eternal salvation." Lehrer, *New Covenant Theology,* 36

The NT's reinterpretation of "rest" entails a redefinition of the "Sabbath." In the OT there were two rationales for the Sabbath: God's resting from his work of creation (Exod 20:11), and the exodus from Egypt (Deut 5:15). Heb 4:4, 8 apply both rationales to the New Covenant "Sabbath rest." Although the *consummation* of our rest remains future (Heb 4:11), Heb 4:3, 10 state that those who believe in Christ *"enter that rest"* or *"have entered His rest."* In other words: "God's rest is entered by believing (4:3). Therefore the New Covenant people of God discharge their duty of Sabbath observance, according to the writer, by exercising faith. . . . Thus the true Sabbath, which has come with Christ, is not a literal, physical rest but is seen as consisting in the salvation that God has provided. . . . Christ brings the spiritual reality; His work fulfills the intent of the Sabbath, and with Christ comes that for which the Sabbath existed. The reality of salvation rest supersedes the sign." Lincoln, "Sabbath, Rest, and Eschatology," 213, 215.

41. Before Jesus was born the angel Gabriel promised Mary that God would give Jesus *"the throne of his father David; and he will reign over the house of Jacob forever, and his kingdom will have no end"* (Luke 1:32–33). After his resurrection, Jesus told his disciples, *"All authority has been given to me in heaven and on earth"* (Matt 28:18). It was at his ascension, however, that the final aspect of the Davidic Covenant was fulfilled—the true "seed" of David, the Son of God, sat down on the "throne of David" where he is reigning now with all power (see Mark 16:19; Luke 22:69; Eph 1:20–23; Col 3:1; Heb 1:3; 1 Pet 3:21–22; Rev 1:5; 3:21). On the Day of Pentecost, Peter demonstrated how Jesus, through his resurrection and ascension, fulfilled the Davidic Covenant (Acts 2:22–36). Darrell Bock summarizes that Peter, by quotation and allusion, connected 2 Samuel 7 and Psalms 16:8–11, 110:1, and 132:11, to the effect that, *"Being seated on David's throne is linked to being seated at God's right hand. In other words,*

interpretation of Jeremiah's prophecy of a permanent Levitical priesthood cannot be reconciled with NT reality: the Levitical priesthood was only a "type" or "shadow"; the NT makes clear that Christ and the church now constitute the everlasting priesthood under the New Covenant.[42] Thus, Lehrer concludes, "When Jeremiah speaks of a restoration of the nation of Israel and the city of Jerusalem, an eternal dynasty sitting on the throne of David ruling Israel and keeping them safe, and an eternal and exceedingly numerous Levitical priesthood continuously making sacrifices, he is using the language of the picture to describe God's New Covenant fulfillment; one that is far better than the Old Covenant pictures."[43]

Specific considerations for interpreting prophetic language

"Literal," "metaphorical," "physical," and "spiritual"

We must be careful in our use of language: do not confuse "literal" with "physical." The "literal" meaning of a text is that which is "natural," "proper," "obvious," and "normal."[44] The "literal" manner of interpretation "takes as the primary range of designation the customary, the usual, the socially-acknowledged designations. Thus the literal meaning of a word is its designation in the common stock of the language."[45] This means that the genre of the text one is interpreting is of crucial importance. In other words, the "literal" way to interpret poetry is "poetically"; the "literal" way to interpret symbols is "symbolically"; the "literal" way to interpret metaphor is "metaphorically."[46]

Many contemporary "prophecy interpreters" do not understand how the NT applies OT prophecies because they look at OT prophecies as if they stand alone and must be fulfilled in a literal, physical way in the modern nation of Israel. Their view is something like that of the Pharisees who failed to recognize Jesus as the Messiah because he did not conform to their limited, "physical" ideas of what Messiah would be (i.e., a military and political ruler of Israel). They miss the theological truth that the OT forms were *"a mere shadow of what is to come; but the substance belongs to Christ"* (Col 2:17).

The problem for such interpreters is that they wrongly think that "literal" means the same as "physical" and that the opposite of "literal" is "spiritual." Although many think

---

Jesus' resurrection-ascension to God's right hand is put forward by Peter as a fulfillment of the Davidic covenant." Bock, "The Reign," 49, emphasis in original; see also Ladd, "Historic Premillennialism," 31. How Christ fulfilled the Davidic Covenant is discussed in detail in Menn, *Biblical Theology,* 34–37.

42. Heb 4:14–15; 7:11—8:2; 1 Pet 2:5, 9; Rev 1:6; 5:10. In connection with Heb 7:11–12, T. Desmond Alexander notes, "The reference here to 'a change in the law' indicates that the regulations associated with the Levitical priesthood were no longer in force once the church became the new temple of God." Alexander, *From Eden,* 150.

43. Lehrer, *New Covenant Theology,* 91. The same is true with respect to the New Covenant as originally given to Jeremiah (Jer 31:31–34). Although in its *form* the New Covenant was with *"with the house of Israel and with the house of Judah,"* the NT affirms that the New Covenant actually is fulfilled in Christ and the church, not with the physical nation(s) of Israel and Judah. See 2 Corinthians 3; Hebrews 8–10; see also Grenz, *Millennial Maze,* 109.

44. Ramm, *Protestant,* 119–23.

45. Ibid., 120.

46. See Garlington, "Reigning," n.p.n.27; Poythress, "Genre and Hermeneutics," 48–52.

that what is "literal" can only be physical, and what is non-literal must be non-physical, the author of Heb 8:1—10:1 "gives precisely the opposite definition: the literal sanctuary is the heavenly one and the figurative sanctuary is the earthly."[47] In fact, the opposite of "literal" is "metaphorical," not "spiritual"; "spiritual" is the opposite of "physical." The senses of the words are as follows:

- *Physical*: tangible, made of matter.

- *Spiritual*: non-physical objects or concepts, or the spiritual domain.

- *Literal*: the normal, straightforward sense of the text, something that describes true reality.

- *Metaphorical*: the characters, events, and objects that are not intended to be taken "literally" as true reality in and of themselves but represent something else and point to another meaning.

Visions and symbolic language

Much biblical prophecy, and most of the book of Revelation, was given in visions and is couched in symbolic language. Visions and symbolic language are *not like* the didactic prose of the Epistles or the narrative stories of the Pentateuch, the historical books of the OT, the Gospels, or Acts. The OT prophets typically prophesied in the form of *visions, parables, and "dark sayings."*[48] The broad context of Revelation, beginning with Rev 1:1's use of *sēmainō* ("communicate by symbols") and *deichnumi* ("show"), together with the repeated formula "I saw" (or similar expressions) that introduces symbolic visions throughout the book,[49] denote "the general symbolic nature of the communication," as opposed to the simple conveyance of facts and historical information.[50]

The meaning of visionary terms is not self-evident. Visions and symbols are more like pictures or editorial cartoons. Elisabeth Schüssler Fiorenza puts it this way, "Apocalyptic language functions not as predictive-descriptive language but rather as mythological-imaginative language. . . . It does not appeal to our logical faculties but to our imagination and emotions."[51] The visionary and symbolic language used in much of prophecy requires that we distinguish four levels of communication: (1) *the linguistic level* (i.e., the textual record itself); (2) *the visionary level* (i.e., what the prophet actually saw; his "visual experience"); (3) *the referential level* (i.e., the historical reference of the various particulars in the description); and (4) *the symbolic level* (i.e., the interpretation of what the symbolic imagery actually connotes about its historical referent).[52]

This is hermeneutically and exegetically significant. The idea that one should interpret "literally" except where one is forced to interpret symbolically by clear contextual indications "should be turned on its head" in connection with the interpretation of

47. Beale, *Temple*, 295.
48. Ps 78:2; Ezek 17:2; 20:49; 24:3; Hos 12:10; Matt 13:35.
49. Rev 4:1; 12:1–3; 13:1–3; 14:1; 17:1–3.
50. Beale, *Revelation*, 973.
51. Schüssler Fiorenza, *Revelation*, 25.
52. Poythress, "Genre and Hermeneutics," 41–42.

Revelation and other prophecy (especially the apocalyptic form of prophecy) since, although some parts are not symbolic, "the essence of the book is figurative."[53] An example of this is seen in Rev 20:1–6. In that passage, John:

> employs the words "one thousand years," "resurrection," and "life" because he saw, at the *visionary* level, people who were resurrected and given life for one thousand years. Because the objects he sees and what he hears are seen and heard in a vision, they are not *first* to be understood literally but viewed as symbolically portrayed and communicated, which is the *symbolic* level of the vision. That this vision is shot through with symbols is apparent merely from the obvious symbolic nature of such words as "chain," "abyss," "dragon," "serpent," "locked," "sealed," and "beast." Therefore, the words "resurrection" and "life," for example, do not by themselves give a clue about whether the visionary, symbolic portrayal has a one-to-one (literal) correspondence to its historical referent together with a figurative meaning or only an indirect figurative relation. Thorough exegesis must decide in each case.[54]

The same could be said for the phrase "thousand years" in that passage. To hold to a "literal" thousand years requires, to be consistent, that the "key" and "chain" held by the angel in Rev 20:1 are a physical key and chain, and that the "abyss" of Rev 20:3 is an actual pit in the earth which has a physical lock and physical "seal."[55] However, the abyss is not spatial, but "represents a spiritual dimension existing alongside and in the midst of the earthly, not above or below it . . . The abyss is one of the various metaphors representing the spiritual sphere in which the devil and his accomplices operate."[56] Further, numbers in apocalyptic literature typically are symbolic of ideas.[57] Kenneth Gentry observes, "In Revelation perfectly rounded thousands all appear to be symbolic."[58] Premillennialist Grant Osborne similarly states, "Multiples of tens were commonly used in Jewish writings symbolically, and it is likely that this refers to an indefinite but perfect period of time."[59] Thus, most commentators, including premillennialists Ladd[60] and Osborne,[61] agree that the "thousand years" is a symbolic or figurative term.

Final guidelines for interpreting prophecy

Given the significance of the change from the Old Covenant to the New Covenant, our focus should be on the general spiritual principle or idea of the prophecy rather than

---

53. Beale, *Revelation*, 52.

54. Ibid., 973–74.

55. Waltke, "Kingdom Promises," 273; Jackson, "Examining," n.p.

56. Beale, *Revelation*, 987.

57. Summers, "Revelation 20," 180.

58. Gentry, "A Preterist View," 56.

59. Osborne, *Revelation*, 701.

60. Ladd, *Commentary*, 262.

61. Osborne, *Revelation*, 701.

on some supposed "predictive event." The following are suggestions for interpreting prophetic symbolism:[62]

- *Approach symbolism with humility.* A spirit of humility is important since much prophetic language is both ambiguous and figurative. Even Daniel found his vision beyond his own understanding (Dan 8:27). It therefore should not surprise us that biblical prophecy may be difficult to understand.

- *Recognize the primacy of imagination over reason.* Prophecy is not straightforward didactic teaching like that in the epistles. The nature of prophetic language allowed prophecies to be applied to different time periods, circumstances, and manners of fulfillment which were not apparent when the prophecies were originally uttered. Logical analysis does not unlock fantastic symbolism. Instead, we must "train ourselves to think in pictures."[63]

- *Find the meaning in context.* Imagery in the book of Revelation can be found in the OT. That establishes a context, but we must then ask how did *John* use the symbol.

- *Look for the prophet's pastoral concern.* For example, in Rev 2:10; 13:9–10; and 14:12 John calls his readers to steadfastness and perseverance.

- *Look for the main point.* Details serve to reinforce the main point the prophet is making.

- *Avoid sensational prophetic materials.* Those who claim to have discovered some "hidden" truth about the end times, or who have deciphered a biblical "code," usually are proven false.

- *Realize that many OT and some NT prophecies have already been fulfilled.* Fee and Stuart highlight a perhaps little-known fact regarding OT prophecy: "Less than 2 percent of Old Testament prophecy is messianic. Less than 5 percent specifically describes the New Covenant age. Less than 1 percent concerns events yet to come. The prophets *did* indeed announce the future but it was usually the immediate future of Israel, Judah, and other nations surrounding that they announced, rather than *our* future."[64]

Apocalyptic

During and after Judah's exile in Babylon, a subgenre of prophecy arose called "apocalyptic."[65] This genre flourished from about 250 BC until AD 200 in Jewish and then in some Christian literature. It is found in several extra-biblical writings. Apocalyptic writing in the Bible is primarily represented in the books of Daniel and Revelation (Isa-

---

62. See Green, *How to Read,* 74–79; Oropeza, *99 Reasons,* 181–83.

63. Green, *How to Read,* 75; see also Schüssler Fiorenza, *Revelation,* 25.

64. Fee and Stuart, *How to Read the Bible,* 150.

65. The word "apocalyptic" is used both as an adjective and as a noun. Some researchers suggest that "apocalyptic" describes a certain kind of eschatology and "apocalypse" denotes a particular literary genre. See Carson and Moo, *Introduction,* 714. Most writers, however, use "apocalyptic" to signify both a literary genre and a type of eschatology. The term will be used in its broader sense here.

iah, Ezekiel and Zechariah also contain apocalyptic elements). Common themes include history and the end of history, cosmic cataclysm, the battle between cosmic powers, the righting of wrongs, and the consummation of God's plan and kingdom.

Apocalyptic and prophecy

Apocalyptic is a form of prophecy that "contains a heightening and more intense clustering of literary and thematic traits found in prophecy."[66] Thus, all of the considerations for understanding and interpreting prophecy apply to the apocalyptic form of prophecy. As Joel Green summarizes, the essential differences between the apocalyptic versus the non-apocalyptic forms of prophecy concern apocalyptic's dependence on symbolism and imagery and its concentration on the end or consummation of history:

> In distinguishing apocalyptic from prophecy, the most obvious difference concerns the means by which the message is communicated. The prophetic "word of the Lord" gives way to revelation through a vision or dream. Symbolism, imagery, numbers—seen already in prophetic texts—come to the fore with greater elaboration in apocalyptic. Apocalyptic texts sometimes reinterpret earlier prophecies; for example, Daniel refers to Jeremiah's "seventy years" in Daniel 9:2. Most important, though, is the difference in focus of the message. The prophets proclaimed God's working in and through the course of history. The apocalyptists anticipated a radical intervention by God at the end, beyond history.[67]

Apocalyptic and history

Although apocalyptists focused on the end of history, contemporary historical events were significant. Apocalyptists viewed God as sovereignly in control of history. He is moving history to his ordained end. In the consummation, God's faithful will be delivered and rewarded. This is particularly true in a Christian apocalypse such as Revelation. Håkan Ulfgard points out, "A significant fact separating it [Revelation] from Jewish apocalypses and of the greatest importance for all exegesis is its affirmation that the turning-point in history has already taken place. After God's decisive act of salvation in Christ, the destiny of the world is in the hands of God and the Lamb."[68] Thus, although much apocalyptic writing features great conflict and what, to our eyes, may seem like bizarre imagery, apocalyptists remained people of hope.

---

66. Beale, *Revelation*, 37.

67. Green, *How to Read*, 62; see also Carson and Moo, *Introduction*, 714.

68. Ulfgard, *Feast and Future*, 11; see also Carson and Moo, *Introduction*, 715.

3

Old Testament Eschatological Expectations and the Significance of Christ's First Coming

Old Testament eschatological expectations

OT eschatological terminology

SEVERAL OT PASSAGES USE the phrase "last days," "latter days," "latter years," "days to come," or "end time" in an eschatological sense. In the OT, the phrase *"acherith hayamim"* has generally been translated as "last days," "latter days," "latter years," "days to come," or "end time." Geerhardus Vos points out that, in the OT, *acherith hayamim* "belongs strictly to the field of eschatology. . . . This should, however, not be confounded with the idea of chronological fixity. It is peculiar to the Old Testament that it makes this 'acherith' a sort of movable complex, capable of being pushed forward along the line of prophetic vision."[1] The idea of the *acherith hayamim* is "elastic as to its extent, no less than movable as to its position. It covers . . . unfavorable and favorable happenings occurring in the farthest visible plane to which the prophetic vision extends, and there is not clear marking of the sequence of these in time. . . . Sometimes *points* are mentioned as falling within the 'acherith,' sometimes a *condensation of events* occupying apparently a certain stretch of time."[2] Thus, some of the uses of *acherith hayamim* (or similar phrases) appear in the context of Israel's situation following its exile in Babylon, whereas other such uses appear to be related to events of the absolute end of history.

According to the OT, in the *acherith hayamim* (or similar concepts):[3]

- "Shiloh" will come from Judah (Gen 49:1, 10).

- A star and scepter shall come from Israel (Num 24:14, 17).

- Israel will return to the Lord and listen to his voice (Deut 4:30).

---

1. Vos, *Pauline Eschatology*, 5.
2. Ibid., 5–6; see also Venema, *Promise,* 22–23.
3. See Vos, *Pauline Eschatology,* 1–5.

- Israel will act corruptly, provoke the Lord, and evil will befall it (Deut 31:29).

- The mountain of the house of the Lord will be established and the nations will stream to it (Isa 2:2).

- The anger of the Lord will not turn back (Jer 23:20).

- The fierce anger of the Lord will not turn back until he has accomplished his intent (Jer 30:24).

- God will restore the fortunes of Moab (Jer 48:47).

- God will restore the fortunes of Elam (Jer 49:39).

- Gog will come against Israel (Ezek 38:1–16).

- Four kingdoms will arise and then God will set up his kingdom (Dan 2:28–45; 8:17–25).

- Out of the Greek empire different kings will arise, fight, and control Israel (Dan 11:35–45).

- Many will be purged and refined but the wicked will act wickedly (Dan 12:4–10).

- Israel will return and seek the Lord (Hos 3:5).

- The mountain of the house of the Lord will be established and the peoples will stream to it (Mic 4:1).

OT eschatological themes[4]

Before the exile of Israel to Babylon, the prophets tended to stress Israel's rebelliousness. After the exile, the prophetic emphasis shifted toward the responsibility of God's people to prepare for the full establishing of God's kingdom.[5] Those prophetic themes included:

- *A new exodus.* God's people will be rescued from captivity.[6] They will be rescued from their false shepherds (Ezekiel 34).

- *A new people.* Sometimes this is depicted as God's faithful remnant.[7] God's failed, captive, and divided people will be remade, reanimated, and reunited.[8] God also will bless the nations.[9] Eckhard Schnabel synthesizes the data from Isaiah 56–58 to show that Isaiah appears to redefine the "people of God" contrary to the limitations of the Mosaic Covenant (see Deut 23:1–8):

  > Isaiah announces that in the last days, when God will reveal his righteousness, biological descent or bodily mutilation [i.e., eunuchs] will no longer determine membership in his people. Foreigners will "join themselves to the Lord, to min-

---

4. For a summary of OT prophetic motifs see VanGemeren, *Interpreting*, 212–44.

5. VanGemeren, *Interpreting*, 57–58, 68, 213–14.

6. Isa 43:1–7, 15–21; 48:20–21; 49:24–26; 51:9–11; 52:1–12; Jer 23:7–8; 30:4–11.

7. Isa 10:20–23; 11:11–12; 14:1–4; 46:3–4; 51:11; 61:4–7; Jer 23:1–8; 29:10–14; 30:10–11; 31:7–9; Mic 2:12.

8. Isa 11:11–16; Jer 30:18–22; Ezek 36:22–24; 37:1–28; Amos 9:11–15; Mic 4:6–13; Zeph 3:14–20.

9. Isa 2:2–4; 19:18–25; 49:5–6; 56:1–8; Mic 4:1–4; Zeph 3:9; Zech 8:20–23.

ister to him, to love the name of the Lord, and to be his servants" (56:6). . . . The criterion for being a part of YHWH's future restoration and establishment of his kingdom is not ethnic descent but a contrite spirit and a contrite heart [57:15] and a righteous response to God's will on the part of those individuals who belong to the remnant for whom God has compassion (58:7–14)—those who "take refuge" in YHWH "shall possess the land and inherit my holy mountain" [57:13], both "the far and the near" [57:19]. This means that in the Isaianic prophecies the criteria for membership in the eschatological people of God have changed in a fundamental way: when YHWH restores the earth, both repentant Jews and repentant Gentiles will constitute the covenant people.[10]

- *A new agent to fulfill God's purposes.* God's agent is his anointed servant (Isa 42:1–9; 61:1–3). He appears as a suffering servant.[11] He appears as a mysterious "son of man" (Dan 7:13–14). He is a new David.[12] Elijah also will appear (Mal 4:5–6).

- *A new land.* There will be a new Zion.[13] It will be a land of peace, plenty, and prosperity.[14] There will even be a new heaven and earth (Isa 42:14–17; 65–66).

- *A New Covenant.* The OT promise of a "New Covenant" is explicitly made only in Jer 31:31–34 but is implicit elsewhere in Jeremiah and Ezekiel.[15] The New Covenant would not be like the Old, Mosaic Covenant which Israel broke. The New Covenant "internalizes" and "personalizes" God's relationship with his people in ways that none of the other covenants ever attempted.

- *A new rule of God.* There will be a new presence of God and a new temple.[16] God will pour out his Spirit on his people.[17] Sometimes God himself is described as returning to Zion.[18] His relationship with his people will be restored and renewed (Hos 2:16, 19–20; 3:5).

- *The "day of the Lord."* The concept of "the day of the Lord" emerges out of the above prophecies. Sometimes it is described as a day coming in the near future;[19] in such cases it often appears to be talking about God's destroying OT Israel's enemies.[20] Sometimes the time is not specified. The day of the Lord is frequently described as a fearsome day of wrath and judgment.[21] Other passages speak of salvation for the

---

10. Schnabel, "Israel, the People," 41.

11. Isa 42:1–9; 49:1–6; 50:4–9; 52:13—53:12.

12. Isa 9:2–7; 11:1–5; 16:5; Jer 23:1–6; Ezek 34:23–24; 37:24–25; Amos 9:11.

13. Isa 1:27; 2:1–3; 11:6–9; 35:1–10; 54:1–17; 61:3—62:12; Ezek 34:11–16, 25–31; 36:35–38.

14. Hos 2:14–18; Joel 3:18; Amos 9:13–15; Mic 4:3–4.

15. Jer 32:38–40; 50:4–5; Ezek 11:16–20; 36:24–32; 37:15–28.

16. Isa 12:6; Ezek 37:27–28; 40–48; Joel 3:16–17; Zeph 3:14–17.

17. Joel 2:28–32; Isa 32:9–20; 44:3–5; Ezek 36:25–28; 37:14.

18. Isa 4:1–6; 26:21; 52:7–9; 66:15; Ezek 43:2–7; Zech 2:10; 8:3; 14:3–5; Mal 3:1.

19. Isa 13:6; Ezek 30:1–3; Joel 1:15; 2:1; 3:14; Obad 15; Zeph 1:7, 14.

20. Joel 3:4; Obad 18–21; Zeph 1:7–11; 2:4–15.

21. Isa 2:12–21; 10:3 (*"day of punishment"*); 13:6–13; 26:21; 34:8; 63:1–4a (*"day of vengeance"*), 6; Jer 46:10 (*"day of vengeance"*); Ezek 7:19; 13:1–5; 30:1–3; Hos 1:11 (*"day of Jezreel"*); Joel 1:15; 2:1, 11; 3:14; Amos 5:18–20; Obad 15–16; Zeph 1:7—2:3; Zech 14:1–7; Mal 4:5.

Lord's people on that day.[22] These latter senses depict the *"day of the Lord"* as a final, eschatological day of God's visitation in grace and judgment.

No OT synthesis

The above prophetic themes were not systematized into a coherent whole. The OT prophetic themes created hope and expectation that God would visit his people in grace and his enemies in judgment. The prophetic themes outlined above found partial fulfillment with the return of Israel from exile, the rebuilding of the temple, and the re-establishment of the priesthood and sacrificial system. But such fulfillment fell short of the eschatological language the prophets had used and the expectations they had raised. Nevertheless, these provisional fulfillments within history sustained hope that the final eschatological kingdom itself would appear in all its fullness.[23]

Christ's first coming and the fulfillment of the OT eschatological prophecies concerning Israel

The NT reveals that the synthesis and fulfillment of the OT promises are found in Christ, of whom Paul says, *"For as many as are the promises of God, in Him they are yes"* (2 Cor 1:20). The OT prophets mingled items connected with the first coming of Christ and items connected with his second coming. Anthony Hoekema reminds us that "not until the New Testament times would it be revealed that what was thought of in Old Testament days as one coming of the Messiah would be fulfilled in two stages: a first and second coming."[24]

Christ and his church fulfill the OT prophecies in ways that were not anticipated by the OT prophets themselves.[25] That fact has tremendous eschatological significance: since Christ and the church fulfill the OT prophecies concerning Israel, including the prophecies concerning the restoration of Israel, it is *not legitimate* hermeneutically to contend that those same OT prophecies also must have a future "literal" fulfillment in the physical nation of Israel. To contend that is to miss the *entire storyline of the Bible,* which finds its culmination in Christ and his people, the church. Some of the ways in which Christ and the church fulfill the OT prophecies regarding Israel are the following:

---

22. Isa 35:4; 40:9–11; 63:4b–5; Joel 2:30–32; Obad 17; Zech 2:10–13.

23. See Bauckham, *Theology,* 154; Venema, *Promise,* 23.

24. Hoekema, *Bible and Future,* 12.

25. Because the church is "in Christ," the church also fulfills the OT promises regarding Israel, as will be discussed. Because of limitations of space, this book can only show a few of the ways in which Christ and the church fulfill OT prophecy regarding Israel. For more, see Menn, *Biblical Theology,* 26–93.

Jesus is the new, true Israel, the true "seed" of Abraham, the fulfiller of the Abrahamic Covenant

God's mercy and his covenant with Abraham, referred to in Jer 33:26, are cited by Mary in Luke 1:54–55 as pertaining to the coming of Jesus. Zacharias likewise viewed the coming of Jesus and his forerunner John as fulfilling the covenant with Abraham (Luke 1:67–79). Jesus himself stressed that the Abrahamic Covenant ultimately was spiritual and that he fulfilled it (John 8:31–58). Gal 3:16 points out that the promise was made to Abraham *"and to his seed."* Paul emphasizes that the word for "seed" is *singular* and refers to Christ. Holwerda discusses the significance of this: "If Jesus is the one through whom the [Abrahamic] promise is being fulfilled, then he can lay claim to being Abraham's true descendant, the one who is what a descendant of Abraham is supposed to be. Jesus, then, is true Israel, the one who does everything that Israel was supposed to do and who is everything that Israel was supposed to be."[26]

Jesus fulfills the prophecies regarding the new exodus and the rescue of Israel from false shepherds

In connection with the exile, the prophets frequently speak of God "gathering" again the remnant of Israel.[27] Jesus said, *"I am the good shepherd"* (John 10:11–15) and claimed to "gather" Israel.[28] Eckhard Schnabel points out, "When Jesus speaks of himself as the shepherd who has a flock (John 10:11), he alludes to a rich biblical tradition that describes Israel as YHWH's flock, with either YHWH (Ps 23) or Israel's leaders (Ezek 34) as shepherds."[29] R. T. France adds, "When he announced that his mission was to seek and save the lost (Luke 19:10) he was, surely consciously, echoing Ezekiel's description of God as the shepherd who will rescue his scattered flock (Ezekiel 34, esp. verses 16, 22)."[30]

Jesus fulfills the prophecies of the anointed servant and new messianic agent

As described by Isaiah, the Servant:

- has the Spirit of God upon him (42:1);
- will bring salvation to Israel and the Gentiles and is a *"light of the nations"* (42:6; 49:6);

26. Holwerda, *Jesus and Israel,* 33. The argument of Galatians 3–4 as a whole is that Christ and the church are the true fulfillment of the Abrahamic Covenant. Essentially, what Paul presents in this passage is a Christocentric and Christological reinterpretation of the Abrahamic covenant. . . . In short, Paul is reinterpreting the Abrahamic covenant, where the priority is to belong to Christ, and *all* who are in him, Jew and Gentile alike, also qualify as the seed of Abraham." Burke, *Adopted,* 112, 114n.33. Thus, in Gal 3:29 Paul specifies, *"if you belong to Christ, you are Abraham's descendants, heirs according to promise."* That occurs *not* by physical descent but through *faith* (Gal 3:7–9, 14).

27. Ps 147:2; Isa 11:12; 27:12; 49:5; 56:8; Jer 6:9; 31:10; Ezek 11:17; 28:25; 34:13; 37:21; 38:8; 39:28; Hos 1:11; Mic 2:12; 4:6; Zeph 3:18–20; Zech 10:8, 10.

28. Matt 3:12; 12:30; 13:30, 47–48; 18:20; 22:10; 23:37; 24:31; Mark 13:27; Luke 3:17; 11:23; 13:34.

29. Schnabel, "Israel, the People," 44.

30. France, "Old Testament Prophecy," 57.

- is beaten and afflicted (50:6; 52:14, 53:4–5, 7, 10);

- is despised and forsaken (53:3);

- despite persecution, he does not open his mouth (42:2; 53:7);

- dies as an offering, bearing the sins of many (53:4–6, 8–12).

Jesus both lived like a Servant and described himself as a Servant.[31] Jesus quoted Isa 61:1–2 and applied it to himself: *"The Spirit of the Lord is upon Me, because He has anointed Me"* (Luke 4:18). The NT writers describe Jesus as the "Servant."[32] Further, the NT specifically quotes and applies the Servant passages to Jesus as the fulfillment of prophecy.[33]

Jesus fulfills and inaugurated the New Covenant

At the Last Supper Jesus explicitly stated that he was inaugurating the New Covenant in his blood.[34] Jesus himself drew connections between what he was about to do on the cross and the OT prophetic expectations. Paul Williamson states, "The allusions to both the forgiveness anticipated by Jeremiah (Matt. 26:28; Jer. 31:34) and the blood associated with the establishment of the original Mosaic covenant (Luke 22:20; Exod. 24:7) further underline that Jesus understood his death as the inauguration of the new covenant."[35]

This is made clear in the book of Hebrews. David Peterson states, "In so many of his [the writer of Hebrews] references to the 'new' or 'better' covenant, it is the blood of Jesus that is stressed by our writer (10:29, 12:24, 13:20). He interprets the oracle of Jeremiah in priestly and sacrificial terms because he views the Old Covenant in those terms and sees the work of Christ as *the reality towards which the cult and the prophecy were both pointing.*"[36] The covenant was confirmed and finalized on the cross (Heb 9:12–17). It was ratified when Jesus rose from the dead, then ascended to heaven and sat down on the throne with the Father (Heb 10:11–18). Although in its form as originally given by Jeremiah the New Covenant was *"with the house of Israel and with the house of Judah,"*

---

31. Matt 20:28; Mark 10:45; Luke 22:27; John 13:5–16.

32. Acts 3:13, 26; 4:27, 30; Phil 2:7.

33. The Spirit of God is upon him (Isa 42:1): see Matt 3:16; Mark 1:10; Luke 3:22; 4:18, 21; John 1:32.

He brings salvation to Israel and the Gentiles and is a *"light of the nations"* (Isa 42:6; 49:6): see Luke 2:32; John 8:12; 9:5; 12:46.

He is beaten and afflicted (Isa 50:6; 52:14, 53:4–5, 7, 10): see Matt 27:26–31; Mark 10:33–34; 15:15–20; Luke 22:63–65; 23:11; John 18:22; 19:1–3.

He is despised and forsaken (Isa 53:3): see Matt 26:38, 56, 69–75; Mark 14:50, 66–72; Luke 22:54–61; John 18:15–18, 25–27.

Despite persecution he does not open his mouth (Isa 42:2; 53:7): see Matt 26:62–63; 27:12–14; Mark 14:60–61; 15:3–5; Luke 23:9; John 19:9; Acts 8:26–35.

He dies as an offering, bearing the sins of many (Isa 53:4–6, 8–12): see John 1:29; 1 Cor 15:3; 2 Cor 5:21; Heb 9:28; 1 Peter 2:21–24.

34. Luke 22:20; 1 Cor 11:25; see also Matt 26:27–29; Mark 14:23–25.

35. Williamson, *Sealed with an Oath*, 184.

36. Peterson, "Prophecy of the New Covenant," 77, emphasis in original.

the NT repeatedly affirms that the New Covenant actually is fulfilled in Christ and the church, not with the physical nation(s) of Israel and Judah.[37]

Jesus fulfills the prophecies regarding the new people and rule of God

Jesus forced his contemporaries to make a choice: "What does loyalty to Israel's god mean for a Palestinian Jew faced with the announcement that the long-awaited kingdom is now at last appearing? Jesus' zealous contemporaries would have said: Torah provides the litmus test of loyalty to Israel's god and to his covenant. Jesus said: what counts is following me."[38] Unlike the political nation of OT Israel, Jesus now governs his people internally, by giving them new hearts and pouring out his Spirit on them.[39] "Whereas in the Old Testament God was perceived as dwelling *among* his people, in the New Testament he is viewed as dwelling *within* his people."[40] In fact, Jesus saw "loyalty to himself and his kingdom-movement as creating an alternative family."[41]

Jesus fulfills the prophecies regarding the restoration of Israel

The prophets (e.g., Isaiah 60–62; Jeremiah 30–33; Ezekiel 34–37) had prophesied the restoration of Israel under the leadership of God's anointed king who would reign from Jerusalem or Mount Zion. This was still hoped for by the people in Jesus' day.[42] In Jesus, those prophecies are fulfilled (Luke 1:68) but in an unexpected way: the new Zion, the restored Israel, is not identified with a place or a nation but with the person of Christ and his people. Before Pentecost, even Jesus' disciples did not understand how Jesus had redefined what the "restoration of the kingdom of Israel" was all about. They thought that Messiah would politically restore only a small nation, not spiritually redeem the entire world. However, in Acts 1:6–8 Jesus' answer to their question about *"restoring the kingdom to Israel"* reorients them to a very different idea of what that really means.

---

37. 2 Cor 3:2–18; 4:3–6; Hebrews 8–10.

38. Wright, *Victory*, 381.

39. See John 14:16–17; Acts 2:14–18; Rom 8:9, 14; 1 Cor 3:16; 6:19; 2 Cor 3:2–3. The New Covenant represents a radically new way by which God's people are governed. In Gal 3:22—4:11 Paul contrasts governance under the Law and the Spirit. He argues that the Law was a *"pedagogue"* (3:24–25), a *"guardian and manager"* (Gal 4:2), which had custody over *"minor children"* (Gal 4:1–3). Linda Belleville notes, "The Law orders the daily affairs of its wards until sonship is realized. It was established as a temporary but necessary expedient given the operative principle of sin and functions as a 'bridle' for a people that are prone to sin, bringing to light the defined will of God as a basis for covenant obligation. With the coming of faith in Christ, the Law's function as guardian and custodian ceases and the Spirit becomes the internal guiding principle." Belleville, "Under Law," 70.

40. Alexander, *From Eden*, 69.

41. Wright, *Victory*, 401. See Matt 8:21–22; 10:34–39; 12:46–50; 19:29; Mark 3:21, 31–35; 10:29–30; Luke 8:19–21; 9:59–60; 11:27–28; 12:51–53; 14:25–27; 18:29.

42. See Luke 2:25, 38; 19:11; 24:21; Acts 1:6.

A new definition of "restoration of the kingdom"

P. W. L. Walker compares what Jesus told the two disciples on the road to Emmaus in Luke 24 and what he tells his disciples in answer to their question about restoring the kingdom to Israel in Acts 1:

> The background in Luke 24 suggests that Jesus is criticizing their very concept of 'restoration'. He reaffirms the expectation, but alters the interpretation. His emphasis is on the 'kingdom of God' (v. 3), not Israel's political kingdom; the Spirit will be given (vv. 4–5), not for the 'restoration of the kingdom to Israel', but to enable them to witness far beyond the borders of Israel. . . . In Luke 24 the disciples were invited to see Jesus' work of redemption by looking *back* to his crucifixion, now they are invited to look *forwards* to their mission 'to the ends of the earth' (Acts 1:8). The 'redemption of Israel' is a two-fold entity—inaugurated through Jesus' death and resurrection, but implemented through the disciples' mission. . . . Israel was being restored through the resurrection of its Messiah and the forthcoming gift of the Spirit. The way in which Israel would then exert its hegemony over the world would not be through its own political independence, but rather through the rule and authority of Israel's Messiah. The chosen method of this Messiah's rule was through the apostles' proclamation of his gospel throughout the world bringing people into the 'obedience of faith' (*cf.* Rom. 1:5). Jesus' concern, now as before, was not for a political 'kingdom of Israel', but rather for the 'kingdom of God' (Acts 1:3).[43]

Although the first part of Jesus' answer in Acts 1:7–8 could be viewed simply as correcting the disciples' "time-table" (i.e., "this restoration will take place, but not now"), the second part of his answer (beginning in Acts 1:8) indicates that Jesus really is talking about a different concept of "restoration of the kingdom" altogether. In other words, "the kingdom is indeed being restored, but it will come to Jew and gentile alike through the preaching of the gospel."[44]

Jesus' definition of "restoration of the kingdom" signifies a redefinition of the true "Israel"

The early church quickly came to understand that in Christ not only had the true "Israel" been restored, but it had been redefined.[45] At the Council of Jerusalem in Acts 15:15–18, James quotes from Amos 9:11–12 (which concerns rebuilding *"the fallen tabernacle of David"*) and concludes that the Gentiles coming into the church *is* the rebuilding of the

43. Walker, *Jesus*, 96, 292; see also Peterson, *Acts*, 109–10. The background in Luke 24 may be more significant than is usually appreciated. The two disciples on the road to Emmaus had noted that *"it is the third day since these things happened"* (Luke 24:21). In Luke 24:46 Jesus mentions that his resurrection on *"the third day"* had been "written" about in the OT. Walker states, "Yet to what verses is he referring? Whilst it is possible that there is an allusion to the story of Jonah, the far more likely reference is Hosea 6:2 ('after two days he will revive us; on the third day he will restore us'). If so, Jesus has taken a verse which originally referred to the restoration or revival of Israel and applied it instead to himself as Israel's Messiah. . . . As Dodd rightly concluded: 'the resurrection of Christ *is* the resurrection of Israel of which the prophets spoke.'" Walker, *Jesus*, 285.

44. Goldsworthy, *Whole Bible*, 238.

45. In other words, Jesus "was *affirming* Israel's election even as he *redefined* it." Wright, *Victory*, 390.

"tabernacle of David" (i.e., the restoration of Israel). In fact, the coming to faith by the Gentiles shows that the "tabernacle of David" *already had been rebuilt* since, as Walker observes, "the text suggests there must indeed be a 'restoration' before the Gentiles can come in ('I will restore it, *so that . . .* the Gentiles'). James' using it to affirm the validity of Gentile mission must indicate acceptance that Israel had *already* been restored."[46]

Hoekema discusses how the Septuagint[47] clearly reveals that the OT terminology for Israel is reapplied by the apostles to now apply to the church: "The Hebrew term *qāhāl,* commonly rendered *ekklēsia* in the Septuagint is applied to Israel in the Old Testament. To give just a few examples, we find the word *qāhāl* used of the assembly or congregation of Israel in Exodus 12:6, Numbers 14:5, Deuteronomy 5:22, Joshua 8:35, Ezra 2:64, and Joel 2:16. Since the Septuagint was the Bible of the Apostles, their use of the Greek word *ekklēsia,* the Septuagint equivalent of *qāhāl,* for the New Testament church clearly indicates continuity between the church and Old Testament Israel."[48]

However, that continuity is not complete identity. In the Bible the crucial distinction is within Israel itself, between the faithful remnant and the mass of Israelites who were apostate.[49] The NT clarifies that the church *is* "remnant Israel" and, indeed, represents a great worldwide expansion of remnant Israel, "encompassing both elect Jews and Gentiles who, together, make up 'the Israel of God' (Gal. 6:16)."[50] Consequently, as William Everett Bell says, "The New Testament actually speaks not so much of the Old Testament saints being admitted to the church, but of the Gentile believers of the New Testament age being admitted to Israel."[51]

The fact that the church is the new, true Israel is indicated by the NT's applying to the church the same descriptions that the OT applied to Israel, including:

- *A chosen race, a royal priesthood, a holy nation, a people for God's own possession* (Eph 1:4–5; Col 3:12; Titus 2:14; 1 Pet 2:5, 9; compare Exod 19:5–6; Deut 4:20; 7:6–7; 14:2; Isa 43:20–21).

- *The people of God* (Rom 9:22–26; 1 Pet 2:10; compare Hos 1:10; 2:23).[52]

- *The called* (Rom 1:6–7; 1 Cor 1:2; compare Isa 41:9; 43:5–7; 48:12).

- *The sons or children of God* (Rom 8:14, 16; 9:26; Gal 3:26; 1 John 3:1–2; compare Exod 4:22; Deut 14:1).

- *The seed (descendants) of Abraham* (Rom 4:13–16; Gal 3:29; compare Ps 105:6–7).

46. Walker, *Jesus,* 97.

47. The Greek translation of the Hebrew Bible, also known as the LXX. It dates to the third century before Christ.

48. Hoekema, *Bible and Future,* 215.

49. See, e.g., 1 Kgs 19:10, 18; John 8:44; Rom 9:6–8; 11:2–5. See also Gay, "Remnant Theology," n.p.; Grenz, *Millennial Maze,* 125; Lehrer, *New Covenant Theology,* 65–84.

50. Williamson, *Sealed with an Oath,* 191. See Matt 13:31–32, 47–48; 16:18; Rom 9:27; 11:1–7; Heb 11:40; Rev 5:9; 7:9.

51. Bell, "Critical Evaluation," 102. This is particularly seen in Paul's figure of the "olive tree" in Rom 11:17–24 in which, through faith in Christ, Gentiles are grafted into the olive tree of remnant Israel. See Gay, "Remnant Theology," n.p.

52. In Rom 9:24–26 Paul not only quotes Hosea but specifically says that Hosea (who was talking about Israel) applies to "us" (i.e., the church).

- *The wife of God* (Eph 5:25–32; Rev 21:9–14; compare Isa 54:4–7).

- *The household of God* (Eph 2:19; 1 Tim 3:15; compare Num 12:7).

- *The flock of God* (John 10:15–16; 1 Pet 5:2–3; compare Ezek 34:12–16).

- *God's field* (1 Cor 3:9; compare Jer 12:10).

- *The olive tree* (Rom 11:17–24; compare Jer 11:16; Hos 14:6).

- *The (true) circumcision* (Rom 2:28–29; Phil 3:3; Col 2:11; compare Gen 17:9–15; Deut 30:6; Acts 7:51; Eph 2:11; Phil 3:2).

- *"I will be their God, and they shall be My people"* (2 Cor 6:16; Heb 8:10; Rev 21:3; compare Gen 17:8; Exod 6:7; 29:45; Lev 26:12; Jer 7:23; 11:4; 24:7; 30:22; 31:1, 33; 32:38; Ezek 11:19–20; 14:10–11; 36:28; 37:23, 27; Hos 2:23; Zech 8:8; 13:9.).

- *"The Israel of God"* (Gal 6:16).[53]

Jesus fulfills the prophecies regarding Mount Zion

At the end of his answer to the disciples concerning restoring the kingdom to Israel (Acts 1:8), Jesus told them to go *"to the ends of the earth."* That recalls the Great Commission (Matt 28:18–20) where he gave his disciples a similar charge and assured them, *"I am with you always."* Jesus' charge also echoes Ps 2:8 which says that the *"ends of the earth"* have been given to the messianic king as his possession. Schnabel comments how, again, Jesus takes OT concepts and reformulates them to demonstrate his redefinition of the kingdom: "In Jesus' charge to the disciples to go to all the nations 'until the ends of the earth,' the prophetic vision of the nations coming to Jerusalem (Isa 2:2–5, Mic 4:1–5; Zech 8:20–23) is replaced by the reality of Jewish missionaries going to the nations. The anticipated movement from the periphery to the center is redirected in terms of a mission from the center (Jerusalem, where Jesus had died and was raised from the dead) towards the periphery (the ends of the earth)."[54] In other words, the new kingdom, the new Mount Zion, is where the king is. It is no longer a specific geographical location but is spiritual. It is everywhere Christ's people are (see John 4:21–24; Heb 12:22–24). Christ has replaced Zion as the center of God's dealings with his people, and in Christ all of the hopes associated with Zion have been fulfilled.

The NT writers understood that Jesus had completely reoriented OT prophecy. The OT picture of the *"mountain of God"* (e.g., Isa 56:7) was a "shadow" or "copy," using picture or physical language, to denote the greater living and spiritual reality of Christ himself (Col 2:16–17; Heb 8:1—10:22). Thus, while the Old Covenant was still in effect,

---

53. This phrase occurs only here in the NT, and who it is specifically referring to is disputed: the church as a whole; certain Jewish Christians; the "all Israel" who will be saved (referred to in Rom 11:26 [itself a disputed term]); or possibly Jews as Jews. Given the argument of Paul and the context of Galatians as a whole, the idea that Paul is giving a blessing to non-believing Jews is not plausible. Therefore, this phrase probably refers to the church as a whole. At minimum, it would apply to Jews who had become believers in Jesus. See LaRondelle, *Israel of God*, 108–14; McKnight, *Galatians*, 302–4; Longenecker, *Galatians*, 297–99; Sizer, *Zion's Christian Soldiers*, 48–50.

54. Schnabel, "Israel, the People," 47.

even during Jesus' earthly ministry, Jerusalem was called the "holy city."[55] However, Simon Kistemaker points us to the significant fact that "after that period, the term 'holy city' no longer occurs, for God took up residence not in Jerusalem but in the church; and at Pentecost the Holy Spirit filled not the temple or Jerusalem but the apostles and all those who repented and were baptized (Acts 2:1–4, 38–39)."[56] Heb 12:18, 22 therefore concludes by saying that in Christ we have *not come to a mountain that can be touched . . . but you have come to Mount Zion and to the city of the living God, the heavenly Jerusalem"* (see also Gal 4:21–31).

The kingdom of God[57]

In one sense the kingdom of God is eternal

God always has been, is now, and always will be sovereign and reigning over everything.[58] The primary meaning for both the OT Hebrew and NT Greek words translated as God's "kingdom" is "His reign, His rule, His sovereignty . . . not a realm or a people."[59]

In another sense the kingdom of God is a spiritual reality that is present and may be entered now

Some passages speak of God's kingdom as a realm into which we may now enter to experience the blessings of his reign.[60] In Rev 1:9 John says that the kingdom is a present reality and describes himself as *"your brother and fellow partaker in the tribulation and kingdom."* The very nature of the kingdom is different from the expectations of the Jews and even of Jesus' own disciples (at first). Jesus began his public ministry by announcing the presence of the kingdom (Mark 1:15). He specified that the kingdom of God is spiritual (John 3:5–8) and can only be entered by means of the new birth (John 3:3). Instead of renewing

---

55. Isa 48:2; Dan 9:24; Neh 11:1, 18; Matt 4:4; 27:53.

56. Kistemaker, "Temple," 437. Paul made the same point in Gal 4:21–31, where he said that the physical Mount Sinai and physical Jerusalem were actually in slavery, but *"the Jerusalem above"* is free, and *"she is our mother."* Significantly, "Paul not only applied to the *heavenly* Jerusalem an Old Testament text (Isa. 54:1 in Gal. 4:27) which had originally applied to the *earthly* Jerusalem; he also denied that the latter was in any way connected to the 'Jerusalem above.'" Walker, *Jesus*, 131.

57. The NT uses the phrases *"kingdom of heaven"* and *"kingdom of God"* synonymously. "Mark, Luke, and John always speak of the Kingdom of God, Matthew alone has the Kingdom of Heaven; and in 12:28; 19:24; 21:31, 43, Matthew has the Kingdom of God. The difference between the two phrases is to be explained on linguistic grounds. The Kingdom of Heaven is the Semitic form and the Kingdom of God is the Greek form of the same phrase." Ladd, *Gospel of the Kingdom*, 32. Jesus uses both phrases together in Matt 19:23–24 and "makes it quite clear that the two phrases are interchangeable and that no difference of meaning is to be sought between them." Ibid.

58. See, e.g., Gen 1:1; Job 12:9–10; Ps 103:19; Isa 44:24–28; 66:1–2; Dan 4:34–37; 6:26–27; Matt 5:34–35; Acts 4:27–28; 7:49–50; Eph 1:11.

59. Ladd, *Gospel of the Kingdom*, 19–21; see Ps 103:19; 145:11, 13; Matt 6:33; Mark 10:15; Luke 19:11–12.

60. Matt 21:31; 23:13; Mark 10:14–15; Luke 11:52; 16:16.

Israel's earthly status and power, Jesus ordained his church as the visible representation of the kingdom on earth (Matt 16:18–19).

Proclaiming the kingdom was the primary focus of Jesus' teaching[61] and parables.[62] He commissioned his disciples to proclaim the kingdom of God (Luke 9:1–6; 10:1–12). Both before and after Christ's death, "the kingdom of God" was equated with *"preaching the gospel"* (Luke 9:2, 6) and *"the gospel of the grace of God"* (Acts 20:24–25). Acts 28:23–31 equates the *"kingdom of God"* with the *"salvation of God."* When Jesus cast out demons he told the Pharisees, *"The kingdom of God is not coming with signs to be observed; nor will they say, 'Look, here it is!' or, 'There it is!' For behold, the kingdom of God is in your midst"* (Luke 17:20–21; see also Matt 12:28). He told Pilate, *"My kingdom is not of this world"* (John 18:36). In Rom 14:17 Paul says, *"The kingdom of God is not eating and drinking, but righteousness and peace and joy in the Holy Spirit."*[63] In answering his disciples' question about restoring the kingdom to Israel (Acts 1:6–8), Jesus in effect responded: "The kingdom is being restored now. . . . It comes through the preaching of the gospel under the influence of the Holy Spirit."[64]

In another sense the kingdom of God is eschatological

Some passages speak of God's kingdom as a future realm which will come only with the return of Christ.[65] In other words, the kingdom of God is the eschatological goal of all history, when all of God's enemies are defeated, all evil vanquished, and God reigns with his people in perfect righteousness, happiness, and goodness.[66] In this sense, the kingdom of God is future. It is "an inheritance which God will bestow upon His people when Christ comes in glory."[67]

Christ's first coming and the "already, but not yet" nature of the kingdom of God

Even though the eschatological kingdom of God is future and awaits Christ's coming again in glory, Christ's first coming *inaugurated* that same eschatological kingdom. "Not clearly foreseen, apparently, by either Old Testament prophets or the earliest New Testament disciples, was the already-not yet complexion of the messianic age,"[68] i.e., the kingdom of God and reign of Christ have been inaugurated, realized in principle, and are present now (the "already" of the kingdom); however, they have not yet been fully mani-

---

61. Matt 4:17, 23; 9:35; Luke 4:43.

62. Matt 13:1–50; 21:28—22:14; 25:1–13.

63. See also 1 Cor 4:20; Col 1:13; 4:11.

64. Goldsworthy, *According to Plan*, 212. In what he told his disciples, "Jesus thus gives the definitive interpretation of the Old Testament prophecies concerning the day of salvation." Ibid.

65. Matt 7:21; Mark 9:47; 10:23; 14:25; Luke 22:15–16; 2 Thess 1:5; 2 Tim 4:18; 2 Pet 1:11.

66. Dan 2:44; Zech 14:9; Matt 6:9–10; 1 Cor 15:20–28; Rev 21:1—22:5.

67. Ladd, *Gospel of the Kingdom*, 17. See Matt 25:34; 1 Cor 6:9–10; 15:50; Gal 5:21; Eph 1:14, 18; 5:5; Col 3:24.

68. Yarbrough, "Biblical Theology," 65.

fested but await a future consummation in all their glory (the "not yet" of the kingdom).[69] Currently, good and evil co-exist, but there will come a time of harvest and of separation of good from evil.[70] Believers already have come to the heavenly Jerusalem (Heb 12:22); yet the full, glorious presence of the New Jerusalem is future (Rev 21:10–11).

The "already, but not yet" schema has been discussed by many commentators.[71] Geerhardus Vos shows this in a helpful diagram:[72]

The world to come,
realized in principle

[in heaven]

Resurrection of Christ

Parousia

Future age and world fully realized in solid existence

[on earth]

This age or world

George Eldon Ladd discusses the central concept of NT theology that Vos's diagram depicts:

> This diagram is intended to suggest that all of the redemptive blessings already enjoyed in Christ are, to use Vos's words, "semi-eschatological" realities. *This is to the present writer the unifying centre of New Testament theology.* The Kingdom of God, which is the central theme of Jesus' preaching, belongs essentially to the age to come. God's rule will never be fully realized in this age. The Gospels, like Jewish apocalyptic, recognize the role of evil spirits in this age. Satan and his angels must be destroyed (Matt. 25:41) before God's Kingdom is consummated. However, this does not mean, as in Jewish apocalyptic, that God has abandoned his world and human history. In fact, *history has become the scene of the conflict between the Kingdom of God and the powers of evil.* "But if it is by the Spirit of God that I cast out demons, then the kingdom of God has come upon you" (Matt. 12:28). The Kingdom of God belongs to the age to come, but in the person and mission of Jesus, that Kingdom has invaded history to bring to men living in the old age the blessings of the age to come.[73]

69. The "already, but not yet" nature of the kingdom is reflected in Christ's beatitudes in Matt 5:2–10. T. Desmond Alexander notes, "Whereas the rewards of verses 2 and 10, which frame the Beatitudes, are in the present ('for theirs is the kingdom of heaven'), all of the other rewards are future oriented: they shall. . . . This distinction is significant, for it underscores that although the kingdom of God (the reign of Christ) is a present reality, the consummated kingdom awaits his return in glory." Alexander, *From Eden*, 95.

70. This is reflected in Jesus' parable of the wheat and the tares (Matt 13:24–30, 36–43) and parable of the dragnet (Matt 13:47–50). See Alexander, *From Eden*, 95.

71. See Ladd, *Gospel of the Kingdom*, 13–23; Hoekema, *Bible and Future*, 13–22; Venema, *Promise*, 12–32.

72. Vos, *Pauline Eschatology*, 38.

73. Ladd, "Apocalyptic," 293–94, emphasis in original.

The present reality of the eschatological kingdom

The present reality of the eschatological kingdom of God (the "already" of the kingdom) is seen in many ways.

- Jesus Christ is on the throne and is reigning now. Eph 1:20–22 tells us that even now Christ is *"far above all rule and authority and power and dominion,"* and that the Father has *"put all things in subjection under his feet."* Heb 2:8 likewise says that God has put *"all things in subjection under his [Jesus'] feet,"* and *"He left nothing that is not subject to him."* Since the reign of Christ has already begun, the eschatological kingdom in a certain sense has begun (Rev 1:5–6).

- We have a new citizenship and have been transferred into the kingdom. In Christ we are *"new creatures"* (2 Cor 5:17). God already has *"raised us up with Him in the heavenly places in Christ Jesus"* (Eph 2:6; see also Eph 1:3; 2:19; Col 3:1–4). God has *"rescued us from the domain of darkness, and transferred us to the kingdom of his beloved Son"* (Col 1:13). We *"have come to Mount Zion and to the city of the living God, the heavenly Jerusalem"* (Heb 12:22). Therefore, even though we live on the earth, *"our citizenship is in heaven"* (Phil 3:20).

- The presence of the king implies the presence of the kingdom (Matt 21:5; 28:18–20).

- The preaching of the kingdom implies the presence of the kingdom (Luke 10:8–11; 16:16).

- The power of the king implies the presence of the kingdom.[74]

- Forgiveness of sins implies the presence of the kingdom. Hoekema states, "In the Old Testament prophets, the forgiveness of sins had been predicted as one of the blessings of the coming Messianic age (see Isa. 33:24; Jer 31:34; Mic. 7:18–20; Zech. 13:1). When Jesus came, he not only preached about the forgiveness of sins but actually bestowed it [Matt 1:21; Mark 2:10; John 1:29]."[75] Thus, Jesus' ability to bestow forgiveness of sin fulfills the prophets and indicates that the kingdom is present.

- The kingdom of God is equated with "eternal life."[76] Since the eternal life of the kingdom is present now (John 3:36; 17:3; 1 John 1:2–3; 5:13), the kingdom itself in a certain sense also is present now.

---

74. See Matt 10:5–8; 12:22–28; 21:21–22; Mark 11:23–24; 16:15–18; Luke 10:17–20; John 14:11–14; Acts 1:8; 10:38; Rom 15:18–19; 1 Cor 4:20; 5:4; 2 Tim 1:7; Heb 2:1–4; 6:5. That power included power over nature, supernatural healings, and other manifestations. Dan McCartney states, "Jesus casts demons out by the Spirit of God, and this is a sign that 'the kingdom of God has come upon you' (Matt 12:28; Luke 11:20). This is one of the clearest statements by Jesus that the kingdom has already arrived." McCartney, *"Ecce Homo,"* 9; see Longman and Reid, *Warrior,* 107. Healing also is associated with the reign of God. See Luke 9:1–6; Matt 9:35; 10:1, 9–11; Mark 6:6–12. John Gray points out that Jesus' miraculous healings indicated "the breaking of the power of evil spirits, which disrupted God's order. Healing thus implied the victory of the Divine King in the cosmic conflict and Creation as an aspect of the imposition of His government." Gray, *Biblical Doctrine,* 1n.1.

75. Hoekema, *Bible and Future,* 47.

76. Matt 19:16, 23–24, 28–29; 25:34, 46; Mark 10:17, 23–25, 29–30; Luke 18:18, 24–25, 29–30.

- The kingdom brings with it resurrection.[77] Christ is the first fruits of the resurrection (1 Cor 15:23). Even now we have been raised with Christ and seated in heavenly places.[78] Thus, in a certain sense the kingdom already has begun.

Summary of the "already, but not yet" nature of the kingdom of God

"The blessings of the present age are the pledge and guarantee of greater blessings to come."[79] Ladd summarizes this:

> At the Second Coming of Christ, His Kingdom will appear in power and glory. But this glorious Kingdom of God, which will be manifested at Christ's return has already entered into history, but without the outward glory. The future has invaded the present. . . . The power of God's Kingdom which in The Age to Come will sweep away both evil and all its influence has come among men in the present evil Age to deliver them from the power of sin, from servitude to Satan, and from the bondage and fear of death. The life of God's Kingdom which will be realized in its fullness when Christ comes, when our very bodies shall be redeemed—that life of the future Kingdom has entered into the present so that men may now be born again and enter into God's Kingdom—the sphere of His reign, the realm of His blessings. The Holy Spirit who one day will completely transform us so that we become like the Lord Jesus Christ in his glorified body has come to us before the arrival of the New Age to dwell within our hearts, to give us the life of the Kingdom here and now that we may enjoy fellowship with God. Tomorrow is here today. The future has already begun. We have tasted the life, the powers, the blessings of The Age to Come.[80]

Consequently, "What Christ gives to his people then will not be compensation for what they lack now, so much as the full experience of what they now know in part."[81]

The fact that the kingdom is already present (the "already" of the kingdom) but has not yet been consummated (the "not yet" of the kingdom) creates a tension while we live on this earth

Even though in this age Christ has been given all authority *"in heaven and on earth,"*[82] we still suffer and face persecution, hatred, tribulation, and death.[83] God has put *"all things in subjection under his feet,"*[84] although *"now we do not yet see all things subjected to him"* (Heb 2:8). Jesus is reigning now but still faces enemies (1 Cor 15:25–27). Already *"our citi-*

---

77. Matt 24:29–31; Mark 13:24–27; Luke 17:22–37; John 5:25–29; 1 Cor 15:22–23, 50; 1 Thess 4:13–17.

78. Rom 6:4–11; 7:4; 8:10–11; Eph 2:5–6; Col 2:12–13.

79. Hoekema, *Bible and Future*, 22.

80. Ladd, *Gospel of the Kingdom*, 95.

81. Travis, *I Believe*, 96.

82. Matt 28:18; see also Matt 11:27; Eph 1:20–22; Col 2:10; Heb 1:3–4; 1 Pet 3:22.

83. See Matt 23:34; 24:9; Mark 10:29–30; John 15:20; 16:33.

84. 1 Cor 15:27; Eph 1:22; Heb 2:8.

zenship is in heaven" (Phil 3:20), but we still eagerly wait for Christ who *"will transform"* us into his glory *"by the exercise of the power that he has even to subject all things to himself"* (Phil 3:20–21). This causes a tension as we live in this world.

Because of the tension between the reality of the "already" of the kingdom and the hope of the "not yet," the NT constantly exhorts us to *"walk in a manner worthy of the God who calls you into His own kingdom and glory."*[85] The NT frequently explains this situation through the metaphor of light and darkness. Both Jesus and the NT writers contrast the "darkness" of this age and those who are not following the Lord, with the "light" of Christ and those who are believers. The light has invaded the darkness. Therefore, Christians are to live as "sons of light."[86] We can do so with confidence and hope. Oscar Cullmann explains why:

> *The decisive battle in a war may already have occurred in a relatively early stage of the war, and yet the war continues.* Although the decisive effect of that battle is perhaps not recognized by all, it nevertheless already means victory. But the war must still be carried on for an indefinite time, until "Victory Day." Precisely this is the situation of which the New Testament is conscious, as a result of the recognition of the new division of time; the revelation consists precisely in the fact of the proclamation that *that event on the cross, together with the resurrection which followed, was the already concluded decisive battle.*[87]

85. 1 Thess 2:12; see also Eph 4:1; 2 Thess 1:5; see Hoekema, *Bible and Future,* 68–75; Green, *How to Read,* 114–16; Travis, *I Believe,* 216–26.

86. See Matt 4:16; Luke 1:79; 16:8; John 1:5; 3:19; 8:12; 12:35–36, 46; Acts 26:18; Rom 13:12; 2 Cor 6:14; Eph 5:8–9; 1 Thess 5:5–6; 1 Pet 2:9; 1 John 1:5–7; 2:8–11.

87. Cullmann, *Christ and Time,* 84, emphasis in original.

4

Interpreting Biblical Eschatology in Light of its Overall Structure

THE BOOK OF REVELATION, and much other prophecy (especially apocalyptic), is largely visionary and highly symbolic. Therefore, it should be interpreted in light of clear didactic prose, illustrations, and parables elsewhere in Scripture that deal with eschatology.[1] In interpreting prophecy, we need to look for clear passages on the same subject in the broader context of the rest of the book, testament, and Bible as a whole. We should try to harmonize isolated and unclear passages with clear and frequent passages. Clear passages may at least tell us what the obscure passages do *not* mean.

The OT had various prophetic and eschatological themes and expectations but never synthesized them into a coherent whole. The OT did not have an overall interpretive structure which could clearly account for the fact that Messiah would come twice. The NT has changed that. We now have *"the whole counsel of God"* (Acts 20:27). What was unclear to the OT prophets has been made clear to us. Most OT prophecy was fulfilled in the first coming of Christ. The interpretation of what remains (i.e., the "not yet" of the kingdom) is made easier because the NT now gives us a clear, consistent, and comprehensive eschatological interpretive structure. That structure is the "two ages" (Greek = *aiōn* ["age"]): *"this age,"* and the *"age to come."*[2]

---

1. Riddlebarger, *Amillennialism*, 36–38, 197–200; Beale, *Revelation*, 973–74.

2. The *New American Standard Bible* (NASB) has been used in this book unless otherwise stated. However, because the Greek term *aiōn* ("age") sometimes is translated as "world," I have compared the NASB with the Greek NT. Whenever the Greek NT uses *aiōn* I have rendered it "age," even though the NASB may have translated it as "world."

It should be noted that the "two-age" structure was implicit, if not fully developed, in the OT. For example, VanGemeren states, "The phrase 'the age to come' relates to the prophetic designation 'in that day,' 'in the last days,' or 'in those days' (Isa. 2:2; Jer. 33:16; Joel 2:29)." VanGemeren, *Interpreting*, 92. However, in the OT this idea appears to have been primarily related to a new beginning for the nation of Israel after the exile. VanGemeren therefore notes that the prophets "comforted the godly remnant with the eschatological hope that after the Exile, the Lord will open up a new era of forgiveness, covenant renewal, and restoration." Ibid. As was discussed in chapter 3, and as will be discussed in this and the next chapter, the coming of Christ and the completion of the NT demonstrate that the OT prophecies in fact find their ultimate fulfillment not in the restoration of Israel after the exile, but in the restoration of the cosmos and people of all nations through Christ.

The "two-age" model

The terminology of the two ages is the key concept for understanding biblical eschatology. A proper understanding of how this age and the age to come fit together renders biblical eschatology both understandable and coherent. Samuel Waldron mentions that the importance of the two ages derives from the fact that that terminology "pervades the New Testament, is homogeneous and provides us with a truly structural concept for biblical eschatology. It means the same thing—assumes the same, basic structure—wherever it is used."[3] M. C. de Boer adds that "the scope of the two ages is cosmic: they both involve all people and all times."[4]

"This age," "the age to come," and variants of those terms are used to describe the two ages

Multiple places in the NT describe the two ages by using the terms *"this age"*[5] and *"the age to come."*[6] Sometimes a variant or distinctive part of those terms is used. *"This age"* sometimes is called *"the age"*[7] or *"this present age."*[8] The *"age to come"* sometimes is called *"that age"* (Luke 20:35) or *"the one to come."*[9] In several passages only *"this age"* or *"this present age"* appears, but "the other member of the contrast is nevertheless present by implication."[10]

The Bible also uses related terminology to describe the two ages

- In Mark 10:30 and Luke 18:30 Jesus contrasts *"this time"* with *"the age to come."*

- Rom 8:18 contrasts *"this present time"* with *"the glory that is to be revealed."*

- Rom 13:12–13 contrasts *"The night [which] is almost gone"* with *"the day [which] is near,"* i.e., "The 'night' is the present evil age (Gal. 1:4); 'the day' is the day of the Lord. Paul's assertion that 'the day is almost here' (Rom.13:12 NIV) means that the day

---

3. Waldron, "Structural Considerations," n.p.n.3. The material quoted herein from Waldron has been incorporated in his book *The End Times Made Simple: How Could Everybody Be So Wrong about Biblical Prophecy* (Amityville, NY: Calvary, 2007). See also Ladd, "Revelation of Christ's Glory," 13 ("Underlying biblical theology is the structure of the two ages: This Age and the Age to Come"); Ladd, *Gospel of the Kingdom*, 26–34; Vos, *Pauline Eschatology*, 12–38; Hoekema, *Bible and Future*, 13–22.

4. de Boer, "Paul and Apocalyptic Eschatology," 349.

5. Matt 12:32; Luke 16:8; 20:34; Rom 12:2; 1 Cor 1:20; 2:6, 8; 3:18; 2 Cor 4:4; Eph 1:21; 1 Tim 6:17. In the Bible, "this age" refers to the time after the fall of Adam and Eve into sin and the concomitant entry of sin and death into the world. It does not refer to the period of time from creation until the fall.

6. Mark 10:30; Luke 18:30; Eph 1:21; Heb 6:5.

7. Matt 13:22, 39–40, 49; 24:3; 28:20; Mark 4:19.

8. Gal 1:4; 1 Tim 6:17; 2 Tim 4:10; Titus 2:12.

9. Matt 12:32; Eph 1:21; 1 Tim 6:19 (the same Greek word as in Matt 12:32 and Eph 1:21, the present active participle of *mellō* ["coming"], is translated "future" in 1 Tim 6:19).

10. Vos, *Pauline Eschatology*, 12. See Rom 12:2; 1 Cor 1:20; 2:6, 8; 3:18; 2 Cor 4:4; Gal 1:4; Eph 2:2; 1 Tim 6:17; 2 Tim 4:10; Titus 2:12.

when God will bring to an end human history as we know it is fast approaching."[11] Consequently, we are to *"lay aside the deeds of darkness and put on the armor of light. Let us behave properly as in the day."*

- First Cor 13:9–10 contrasts *"the partial"* with *"the perfect."*

- First Cor 13:12 contrasts *"now"* with *"then,"* i.e., "Now, in This Age, we see in a mirror, imperfectly; 'but then face to face.' In The Age to Come, we shall no longer see a reflected likeness, we shall see face to face."[12] Similarly, 1 John 3:2 contrasts *"now"* with *"what we will be."*

- In 1 Cor 3:19 *"this world"* (ho kosmos houtos) is a synonym for *"this age"* (see also 1 Cor 5:10; 7:31; Eph 2:2). This is seen in the parallelism in 1 Cor 3:18–19: *"If any man among you thinks that he is wise in this age, he must become foolish, so that he may become wise. For the wisdom of this world is foolishness before God."*

- Second Cor 4:17–18 contrasts our *"momentary, light affliction"* which is producing for us *"an eternal [aiōnion, adjective from the noun aiōn ('age')] weight of glory"* and also contrasts *"the things which are seen"* with *"the things which are not seen; for the things which are seen are temporal, but the things which are not seen are eternal [aiōnia, adjective from the noun aiōn ('age')]."*

- In Eph 2:1–2 Paul says that the Ephesians had been dead in their trespasses and sins in which they had formerly walked according to *"the age of this world"* (synonymous with *"this age"*). Similarly, in Luke 16:8 Jesus contrasts *"the sons of this age"* with *"the sons of light."*

- First Tim 4:8 contrasts *"the present life"* with *"the life to come."*

- Heb 1:6 and 2:5 contrast *"the world"* (tēn oikoumenēn) with *"the world to come"* (tēn oikoumenēn tēn mellousan).

- Heb 13:14 contrasts *"here we do not have a lasting city"* with *"the city which is to come."*

- In several places, instead of using *"the age to come"* or *"eternal life"* (zōēn aiōnion, lit. "life of the age [to come]"), Jesus and Paul use the phrase "kingdom of God," just as we "more easily speak of 'heaven' or 'eternity' than of 'the future age.'"[13]

- In Matt 19:28 Jesus called the age to come *"the regeneration"* (Greek = paliggenesia).[14]

11. Schnabel, *40 Questions,* 22.

12. Ladd, *Gospel of the Kingdom,* 74.

13. Vos, *Pauline Eschatology,* 12. See 1 Cor 6:9–10; 15:50; Gal 5:21; Eph 5:5; 1 Thess 2:12; 2 Thess 1:5; 2 Tim 4:18.

14. Tim Keller points out that Stoic philosophy held that history was an endless cycle. "Every so often the universe would wind down and burn up in a great conflagration called a *palengenesia,* after which history, having been purified, started over. But in Matthew 19:28 Jesus spoke of his return to earth as *the* palingenesis. 'I tell you the truth, at the renewal of all things (Greek *palingenesis*), the Son of Man will sit on his glorious throne.' This was a radically new concept. Jesus insisted that his return will be with such power that the very material world and universe will be purged of all decay and brokenness. All will be healed and all might-have-beens will *be.*" Keller, *Reason for God,* 32–33.

There is a qualitative difference between "this age" and the "age to come"

Ladd states an important hermeneutical fact:

> The New Testament sets The Age to Come in direct opposition to This Age.... When we ask what Scripture teaches about the character of these two ages, we find a sharp contrast. This Age is dominated by evil, wickedness, and rebellion against the will of God, while the Age to Come is the age of the Kingdom of God.... In This Age there is death; in the Kingdom of God, eternal life. In This Age, the righteous and the wicked are mixed together; in the Kingdom of God, all wickedness and sin will be destroyed. For the present, Satan is viewed as the 'god of this age;' but in The Age to Come, God's Kingdom, God's rule will have destroyed Satan, and righteousness will displace all evil.[15]

The qualitative difference between the two ages is seen in the following scriptural comparison:

Characteristics of "this age"	*Characteristics of the "age to come"*
Direct comparisons and contrasts	*Direct comparisons and contrasts*
(1) It will end (Matt 13:39–40, 49; 24:3–30), and signs will mark the end of this age (Matt 24:3, 29–30; Mark 13:4, 24–26; Luke 21:7, 25–27)	(1) It will last forever (Luke 1:33; 2 Pet 1:11; Rev 11:15)
(2) It is the age of things that do not last (1 Cor 15:50; Heb 13:14)	(2) It will be the age of things that last forever (1 Cor 15:50)
(3) It is "of the world" (Rev 11:15)	(3) It is heavenly and "of the Lord" (2 Tim 4:18; Rev 11:15)
(4) Satan is the god of this age (2 Cor 4:4)	(4) God will be "all in all," and Satan will be tormented forever (1 Cor 15:28; Rev 20:10)
(5) Wicked and righteous people co-exist (Matt 13:24–30, 36–43)	(5) The wicked and the righteous will be separated and will not co-exist (Matt 13:40–43)
(6) It is the age of worry, persecution, and suffering (Matt 13:22; Mark 10:30; Rom 8:18)	(6) There will be no mourning, crying, or pain (Rev 21:4)
(7) It is the age of death (Luke 20:29–36; 2 Cor 4:3–4)	(7) It will be the age of eternal life; there will be no death (Mark 10:30; Luke 18:30; Luke 20:36; Rev 21:4)
(8) People marry and are given in marriage (Luke 20:34)	(8) There will be no marriages or giving in marriage (Luke 20:35)
(9) Now we see dimly, know only in part, and have been blinded (1 Cor 13:12; 2 Cor 4:4); the rulers of this age do not understand God's wisdom (1 Cor 2:6–9)	(9) Then we will see clearly and will know fully (1 Cor 13:12)

15. Ladd, *Gospel of the Kingdom*, 31, 28, 34; see also Riddlebarger, *Amillennialism*, 241 ("The contrast between this age and the age to come is a contrast between things eternal and things temporal"); Bahnsen, *Victory*, 169 ("This age" denotes "an *ethical* sphere more than a temporal dispensation," an ethical sphere which is antagonistic to God). Very early in church history, the distinction between the two ages was recognized and was used as the basis for leading a godly life now. The *Epistle of Barnabas* 4:1 states, "Let us, therefore, avoid absolutely all the works of lawlessness lest the works of lawlessness overpower us, and let us hate the deception of the present age, so that we may be loved in the age to come." See also *Shepherd of Hermas, Vision* 4.3.2–5.

(10) This present age and its ways are evil (Gal 1:4); people walk in trespasses and sins (Eph 2:1–2)	(10) Evildoers and immoral, impure, covetous people and idolaters will not inherit the kingdom, but only the worthy will inherit the kingdom (1 Cor 6:9–10; Gal 5:21; Eph 5:5; 1 Thess 2:12; 2 Thess 1:5)
(11) Now it has not appeared what we will be like (1 John 3:2)	(11) We will be like Jesus (1 John 3:2) and will be "like angels" (Luke 20:36)
(12) Christ is reigning and is above all names in this age and will be with us until the end of the age (Matt 28:20; Eph 1:21)	(12) Christ will reign and be above all names in the age to come (Eph 1:21)
(13) Blasphemy against the Holy Spirit will not be forgiven in this age (Matt 12:32)	(13) Blasphemy against the Holy Spirit will not be forgiven in the age to come (Matt 12:32)

Characteristics of "this age"	*Characteristics of the "age to come"*
Other comparisons and contrasts	*Other comparisons and contrasts*
(14) It is the age of material homes, fields, families, and material rewards (Mark 10:30; Luke 18:30)	(14) It will be an age of revealed glory (Rom 8:18)
(15) Love of "this present age" causes people to stop being faithful (2 Tim 4:10)	(15) Flesh and blood will not inherit the kingdom (1 Cor 15:50)
(16) The sons of this age are more shrewd in relation to their own kind than are the sons of light (Luke 16:8)	(16) We will see Jesus just as he is (1 John 3:2)
(17) We are not to be conformed to the pattern of this age but are to live Godly lives in "this present age" (Rom 12:2; Titus 2:12)	(17) God will show the "surpassing riches" of his grace to us (Eph 2:7)
(18) The wisdom of this age is foolishness to God (1 Cor 1:20; 2:6–8; 3:18)	(18) The age to come has life which is truly life (1 Tim 6:19)
(19) Those who are rich in this age are not to fix their hope on their wealth but can store up "the treasure of a good foundation" for the age to come now by generosity (1 Tim 6:17–19)	(19) The age to come will be as different from this age as the day is from the night (Rom 13:12–13)
(20) Some people in this age have tasted "the powers of the age to come" (Heb 6:5)	(20) It will be the age of perfection (1 Cor 13:9–10)

There is a quantitative difference between "this age" and the "age to come"

The term *aiōn* (the noun for "age") may refer to a long, but finite, period of time or to an everlasting or eternal period of time depending on the context. For example, "this age" is temporal, finite, and will come to an end (Matt 13:39, 40, 49; 24:3; 28:20; Heb 9:26). However, the "age to come" will last infinitely, without end (Luke 1:33; 2 Pet 1:11; Rev 11:15). The everlasting nature of the age to come is implied from the above qualitative differences with this age: e.g., *"the perfect"* (1 Cor 13:9–10) cannot be subject to termination or be succeeded by anything better; clearness of sight and fullness of knowledge (1 Cor 13:12) can never be surpassed; imperishability (1 Cor 15:50) by definition cannot end.[16] The unending nature of the age to come is particularly seen when the adjective *aiōnios* (which is based on *aiōn* and pertains to the "age") is used in conjunction with the attributes of God and the promises, blessings, and curses that find their fulfillment in the age to come.[17] As such, *aiōnios* is typically translated "eternal" or "everlasting":

- *Tou aiōniou Theo* ("the eternal God," Rom 16:26).

- *Pneumatos aiōniou* ("the eternal Spirit," Heb 9:14).

- *Kratos aiōnion* (Christ's "eternal dominion," 1 Tim 6:16).

- *Zōēn aiōnion* ("eternal life," e.g., Matt 19:16, 29; 25:46; Mark 10:30; Luke 10:25; 18:18, 30; John 3:15, 36; 4:14, 36; 5:24, 39; 6:27, 40, 47, 68; 10:28; 12:25, 50; 17:2, 3). In Matt 25:46 the judgment of the "goats" ("eternal punishment," *kolasin aiōnion*) is specifically contrasted with the reward of the righteous "sheep" ("eternal life," *zōēn aiōnion*). That indicates that, in both cases, *aiōnion* is everlasting.[18]

- *Aiōniou kriseōs* ("eternal judgment," Mark 3:29). Mark 3:29 states that whoever blasphemes against the Holy Spirit does not have forgiveness *eis ton aiōna* ("unto the age," i.e., forever) but is subject to *aiōniou kriseōs* ("eternal judgment"); the coupling of "age" with "eternal judgment" shows that the lack of forgiveness is everlasting as is the judgment. That is made explicit in the parallel passage of Matt 12:31–32 where Jesus contrasts any other sins and blasphemies with the blasphemy against the Holy Spirit; the former will be forgiven, but whoever blasphemes against the Holy Spirit the Holy Spirit shall not be forgiven "either in this age, or in the age to come." See also Heb 6:2 (*krimatos aiōniou*, "eternal judgment"), 2 Thess 1:9 (*olethron aiōnion*, "eternal destruction").[19]

- *Tas aiōnious skēnas* ("the eternal dwellings," Luke 16:9). The contrast in this verse is the "wealth of unrighteousness" which will "fail" compared to the "eternal dwellings" into which the person who has used his wealth wisely will be received.

---

16. Robert Peterson puts it like this, "The state of affairs after the resurrection of the dead is characterized by the life of God himself; the age to come lasts as long as he does—forever." Peterson, *Hell on Trial*, 35.

17. In fact, it appears that every time the adjective *aiōnios* is used in the NT "endlessness" is meant. See BDAG, *"anōnios,"* 33; Zodhiates, *Complete Word Study, "anōnios,"* 107–08. Even the few instances where something in the past is referred to (Rom 16:25; 2 Tim 1:9; Titus 1:2), the use of *anōnios* renders the sense as "time eternal," "before time was," or "from eternity." Zodhiates, *Complete Word Study, "anōnios,"* 107; see also Walvoord, "The Literal View," 24–25.

18. See Augustine, *Civ.*, 21.23; Carson, "Matthew," 8:522. Spiros Zodhiates also points out that *zōe aiōnios* "is to be understood as referring not only to duration, but more so to quality. That is, it is not merely a life that is eternal in duration, but is primarily something different from the natural life of man, i.e., the life of God. Since it is His life God gives to the believer through Christ, and He is endless, His life imparted must be endless, although the life He gives to the believer has a beginning." Zodhiates, *Complete Word Study, "anōnios,"* 107.

19. Zodhiates notes, "All of these designations of punishment stand in contrast to eternal life as the inherent punishment for those who reject Christ's salvation in that they will be separated from the life of God which they rejected. As to the duration of what is designated as *anōnios* when it comes to punishment, it is only proper to assign it the same duration or endlessness as to the life which is given by God." Zodhiates, *Complete Word Study, "anōnios,"* 108.

- *Aiōnion en tois ouranois* ("eternal in the heavens," 2 Cor 5:1). The contrast in this verse is between our "earthly tent" (body) which will be "torn down" and our "building from God, a house not made with hands, eternal in the heavens." To this same effect is 2 Cor 4:18 which contrasts the temporary nature of the "things which are seen" with the everlasting (*aiōnia*) nature of the "things which are not seen"; the contrast is not primarily between visibility and invisibility but the impermanence of the things of this age and the permanence of the age to come.

- *Doxēs aiōniou* ("eternal glory," 2 Tim 2:10).

- *Sōtērias aiōniou* ("eternal salvation," Heb 5:9).

- *Aiōnian lutrōsin* ("eternal redemption," Heb 9:12).

- *Tēs aiōniou klēronomias* ("the eternal inheritance," Heb 9:15).

- *Diathēkēs aiōniou* ("eternal covenant," Heb 13:20).

- *Euggelion aiōnion* ("eternal gospel," Rev 14:6).

On a number of occasions, biblical writers use the plural "ages." They do this in connection with the past and current age, e.g., 1 Cor 10:11 (*"upon whom the ends of the ages have come"*); Heb 9:26 (*"now once at the consummation of the ages he has been manifested to put away sin"*); in connection with the future age to come, e.g., Dan 7:18 LXX (lit. the saints will possess the kingdom "to the age of the ages"); Dan 12:3 LXX (lit. those who lead many to righteousness will be like the stars "to the ages and still [further]"); Rom 16:27 (lit. to the wise God . . . "be glory to the ages"); Eph 2:7 (*"in the ages to come"* he will show the surpassing riches of his grace); Heb 13:8 (lit. Jesus Christ is the same yesterday, today, "and to the ages"); Jude 25 (lit. to God be . . . authority "before all of the age and now to all the ages"). On multiple occasions the phrase *eis tous aiōnas tōn aiōnon* (lit. "into the ages of the ages") is used.[20] The phrase is an intensive form and is correctly translated "forever and ever" or "forevermore" since every use shows something exhibiting an eternal or everlasting duration.

The use of the plural appears to be largely stylistic. For example, Geerhardus Vos comments that the phrase *"ages to come"* in Eph 2:7 "is a plural of immensity; it expresses itself in terms of time, whereas eternity marks the pleroma [fullness] of time."[21] The same could be said for the other uses of "ages" instead of "age." Stephen Smalley notes that the literal phrase "to the ages of the ages" in Rev 22:5 "is liturgical in character; see 1:6; et al."[22] *TDNT* states, "In order to bring out more fully the stricter concept of eternity, religious usage generally prefers the plural. . . . This plural us is simply designed to emphasise [sic] the idea of eternity which is contained in but often blurred in the singular *aiōn*."[23]

The following examples show the equivalence of the use of the singular and the plural:

---

20. Gal 1:5; Phil 4:20; 1 Tim 1:17; 2 Tim 4:18; Heb 13:21; 1 Pet 4:11; Rev 1:6, 18; 4:9, 10; 5:13; 7:12; 10:6; 11:15; 15:7; 19:3; 20:10; 22:5.

21. Vos, *Pauline Eschatology*, 316n.20.

22. Smalley, *Revelation*, 566.

23. Sasse, *"aiōn,"* 1:199.

- Dan 7:18 LXX talked about the saints possessing the kingdom *"for ever and ever"* (lit. "to the age of the ages," *eōs aiōnios tōn aiōvōv*), i.e., plural. However, immediately before that, in Dan 7:14 LXX, God's dominion is described as *"an everlasting dominion"* (*exousia aiōnios*), i.e., singular; immediately after, in Dan 7:27 LXX, God's kingdom is likewise described as an *"everlasting kingdom"* (*Basileia aiōnios*), i.e., singular.

- In Matt 18:8 and 25:41 Jesus speaks of the *"eternal fire"* (*pur to aiōnion*), i.e., singular. He says it *"has been prepared for the devil and his angels"* (Matt 25:41). Rev 20:10 then describes the torment of the fire in the plural, i.e., the devil is thrown into *"the lake of fire . . . and will be tormented forever and ever"* (*eis tous aiōnas tōn aiōnon*).[24]

- In Luke 1:33 Christ's everlasting kingdom is described both in the plural, *"He will reign over the house of Jacob forever"* (lit. "to the ages," *eis tous aiōnas*) and in the singular, *"and His kingdom will have no end"* (*telos*, "end" is singular). In 2 Pet 1:11 the singular "age" likewise is used to describe Christ's eternal kingdom (*tēn aiōnion Basileian*)

- Heb 7:24 describes Jesus' everlasting existence and priesthood in the singular, *eis ton aiōna* (lit. "into the age," i.e., forever); Heb 7:28 similarly uses the singular to say that Jesus has been made perfect "forever" (*eis ton aiōna*). On the other hand, Heb 13:8 uses the plural, *eis tous aiōnas* ("into the ages," i.e., forever) to describe how Jesus *"is the same yesterday and today and forever."*

- Heb 9:26 speaks in the plural about the *"consummation of the ages"* (*sunteleia tōn aiōnōn*) which appears to be synonymous with Jesus' statement in the singular that he is with us to *"the end of the age"* (*sunteleias tou aiōnos*) (Matt 28:20).

- 1 Pet 5:10 speaks of *"His eternal glory"* (*tēn aiōnion autou doxan*) in the singular; 1 Pet 5:11 then speaks of that same glory (and might or dominion) in the plural (*autō hē doxa kai to kratos eis tous aiōnas tōn aiōvōv*) as does 1 Pet 4:11 (*hē doxa kai to kratos eis tous aiōnas tōn aiōvōv*).

The above table and examples reveal that, although there may be different aspects of "this age" (for example, the period before Christ came and the period after his coming), the whole of this age is of the same essential nature. Likewise, although we do not have detailed information about everything that will characterize the "age to come" after Christ returns, the information we do have indicates that the whole of the age to come (i.e., the "ages of the ages") will be of the same essential nature for all of eternity.

The two ages comprehend all of time, and the age to come immediately succeeds this age

Eph 1:21 says that Christ is *"far above all rule and authority and power and dominion, and every name that is named, not only in this age but also in the one to come."* Additionally, in Matt 12:32 (see also Mark 3:29) Jesus states that whoever speaks against the Holy Spirit

---

24. Robert Peterson points out that "as a comparison of Matthew 25:41 with Revelation 20:10 makes clear . . . [t]he Devil's being cast into eternal fire means that he will be perpetually tormented. When Jesus, therefore, says that wicked human beings will share the Devil's fate, he means that they too will suffer eternal torment." Peterson, *Hell on Trial,* 46.

shall not be forgiven, *"either in this age, or in the age to come."* Those passages indicate that there is no intervening or temporary time period between *"this age"* and the *"age to come."*[25] The reason why this necessarily is true is pointed out by Vos: "The very name 'coming aion' is not merely expressive of futurity, but also carries within itself the element of direct successiveness. Were this otherwise, then the entire closely-knit scheme intended to comprehend all happenings in the universe from beginning to end would fall to pieces, because of the lacking link in the middle. To say that a sin will not be forgiven either in this age or in the age to come could never have served as a formula for absolute unforgivableness ad infinitum, Matt. xii. 32, if there were conceivable a gap between the two aions."[26]

Transformation by resurrection is required in order to enter the age to come/ kingdom of God

The necessity of resurrection as a condition to enter the age to come or consummate kingdom of God is stressed by Ladd: "The Kingdom of God, like The Age to Come, will follow the resurrection. In I Corinthians 15:50, Paul says that 'flesh and blood cannot inherit the kingdom of God.' Paul here is speaking about the resurrection. *Flesh* and *blood* cannot inherit the Kingdom of God. Our bodies must undergo a transformation so that they no longer consist of flesh and blood but are incorruptible, glorious, powerful, 'spiritual' bodies (vv. 42–44). Only in these transformed bodies will we enter the Kingdom of God."[27]

Christ's first coming brought with it an overlapping of the "two ages"

The breaking in of the *"age to come"* into *"this age"* is parallel to the "already, but not yet" nature of the kingdom. Thus, the age to come is the reign of Christ; the reign of Christ has already begun (Acts 2:29–36; Eph. 1:21). The age to come is the age of resurrection (Luke 20:34–36); the resurrection has already begun (1 Cor 15:23). The age to come is the age of eternal life (Mark 10:30); eternal life has already begun (John 3:36; 17:3; 1 John 1:2–3;

---

25. This same thing is indicated in 2 Pet 3:3–13. In that passage, Peter does not use the terms "this age" or "the age to come." Instead, he speaks of the "heavens and earth" God had created and "the world" (*kosmos*) that was destroyed by the Flood (2 Pet 3:5–6). He then says that *"the present heavens and earth are being reserved for fire, kept for the day of judgment"* (2 Pet 3:7; see also vv. 10–12). On the heels of that he concludes that we are *"looking for and hastening the coming of the day of God"* because *"according to his promise we are looking for new heavens and a new earth, in which righteousness dwells"* (2 Pet 3:12–13). Two observations are important: First, as mentioned above, there are different aspects to "this age" (here, the pre-Flood and post-Flood worlds), although the entirety of this age has the same essential character. Second, the "new heavens and new earth" immediately succeed the destruction of "the present heavens and earth"—there is no interregnum allowed for or hinted at, and such a temporary, non-final period would be contrary to Peter's argument. Further, since *"righteousness dwells"* in the "new heavens and new earth," that new order of existence (i.e., "the age to come") will, by its very nature, be permanent and everlasting.

26. Vos, *Pauline Eschatology*, 25–26.

27. Ladd, *Gospel of the Kingdom*, 34. First John 3:2 indicates the same thing.

5:13). The age to come is the age of the new creation (Rom 8:18–22; Rev 21:1–4); in a sense the new creation already has begun (2 Cor 5:17; Gal 6:15).[28]

The early church understood the essentially eschatological nature of Christ's first coming and our life in the kingdom now. Gordon Fee states:

> The absolutely essential framework of the self-understanding of primitive Christianity . . . is an eschatological one. Christians had come to believe that, in the event of Christ, the New (Coming) Age had dawned, and that, especially through Christ's death and resurrection and the subsequent gift of the Spirit, God had set the future in motion, to be consummated by yet another coming (Parousia) of Christ. Theirs was therefore an essentially eschatological existence. They lived "between the times" of the beginning and the consummation of the End. Already God had secured their eschatological salvation; already they were the people of the future, living the life of the future in the present age—and enjoying its benefits. But they still awaited the glorious consummation of this salvation. Thus they lived in an essential tension between the "already" and the "not-yet."[29]

The overlapping of the two ages and the "breaking in" of the age to come into this age explains why the Bible constantly assumes a "two-stage" character of salvation. Justification (Rom 5:1; Matt 12:37), adoption (Rom 8:14–16, 23; Gal 4:4–6), redemption (Eph 1:7; 4:30), and other biblical realities associated with salvation are spoken of both as past realities and future blessings. The overlapping of the two ages does not change the character either of "this age" (which still remains temporal and evil) or of the "age to come" (which is the age of life, righteousness, and God's kingdom). There will be an end of *this age* and a consummation of the kingdom, which will be manifested in all its glory. Until then, Christians are to be "in the world, but not of the world" (John 17:13–18). While we are on earth we are to remember that *our citizenship is in heaven* (Phil 3:20) and live accordingly.

Christ's first coming and the "last days"

The NT makes clear that Christ's first coming (or, more specifically, the complex of his death, resurrection, ascension, and pouring out of the Spirit at Pentecost) is of great eschatological significance.[30] Some people think that the "last days" is a period of time in the future which will occur just before Jesus comes again. That is not true. Oscar Cullmann, building on his metaphor of Christ's first coming as the decisive battle of war (e.g., D-Day in World War II), states that our "post-Easter present stands in a different relation

---

28. See Ladd, "Revelation 20," 173; Wright, *Resurrection,* 332; Waldron, "Structural Considerations, n.p.

29. Fee, *1 and 2 Timothy,* 19.

30. Allison summarizes the understanding of the NT writers and the early Christians as follows: "When [Jesus] suffered and died and subsequently appeared alive to his followers, they concluded that the eschatological drama had opened, that the final tribulation had begun with the suffering and death of the Messiah, that the general resurrection had begun with his resurrection. In brief, the eschatological expectations of the pre-Easter period were drawn upon in the attempt to understand the crucifixion and Jesus' conquest of death." Allison, *End of the Ages,* 170.

to the end from all the preceding epochs since the creation of the world; it is *the final time before the end* (I John 2:18), because, no matter what its still undetermined duration may be (Acts 1:7), the mid-point [the first coming of the Messiah] has been passed."[31] Thus, Christ's first coming: (A) marked the beginning of the "last days" which will continue until his return; and (B) fulfilled the OT prophecies concerning the "latter days" or "last days."[32]

The first announcement of the "last days" in the NT

The first announcement of the "last days" in the NT was Peter's speech on the Day of Pentecost in Acts 2. Anthony Hoekema notes the significance of the wording Peter uses when he quotes the prophet Joel in his speech:

> New Testament writers are conscious that they are already living in the last days. This is specifically stated by Peter in his great sermon on the day of Pentecost, when he quotes from Joel's prophecy as follows: "For these men are not drunk, as you suppose, since it is only the third hour of the day, but this is what was spoken by the prophet Joel: 'And in the last days it shall be, God declares, that I will pour out my Spirit upon all flesh . . .'" (Acts 2:16–17). The words "in the last days" (*en tais eschatais hēmerais*) are a translation of the Hebrew words *'acharey khēn*, literally *afterwards*. When Peter quotes these words and applies them to the event which has just occurred, he is saying in effect: "We are in the last days now."[33]

Every other use of the phrase "last days" in the NT presupposes that we are in the "last days" now

The following are the other uses of "last days" in the NT. In each case the passage explicitly or implicitly applies to the present time (i.e., the period between Chrst's first and second comings):

- 2 Tim 3:1–5: *"But realize this, that in the last days difficult times will come. For men will be lovers of self, lovers of money . . . Avoid such men as these."*

- Heb 1:1–2: *"God, after He spoke long ago to the fathers in the prophets in many portions and in many ways, in these last days has spoken to us in His Son."*

- Jas 5:1–3: *"Come now, you rich, weep and howl for your miseries which are coming upon you. . . . Your gold and your silver have rusted; and their rust will be a witness*

---

31. Cullmann, *Christ and Time*, 145, emphasis in original.

32. The preterist view is that the "last days" refers to "the period from the Advent of Christ until the destruction of Jerusalem in A.D. 70, the 'last days' of Israel during the transition period from the Old Covenant to the New Covenant (Heb. 1:1–2; 8:13; 1 Pet. 2:20; 1 John 2:18)." Chilton, *Vengeance*, 16n.35. All believers hold that the "last days" herald the *parousia*, but for preterists the *parousia* is a past event: "The definitive Parousia occurred at the Ascension, resulting in Christ's Parousia against Jerusalem in A. D. 70." Ibid., 434–35.

33. Hoekema, *Bible and Future*, 16.

against you and will consume your flesh like fire. It is *in the last days* that you have
stored up your treasure!"

- 2 Pet 3:1–4:"*I am writing you . . . that you should remember the words spoken of be-
forehand by the holy prophets and the commandment of the Lord and Savior spoken by
your apostles. Know this first of all, that* *in the last days* *mockers will come . . . saying
'Where is the promise of his coming?'"*

The NT writers use other phrases to show that we are now in the "last days"

In the following passages the NT writers use equivalent phrases to the "last days," but they
have the same meaning as the "last days." Again, the context indicates that the present
time (between Christ's first and second comings) is indicated.

- 1 Cor 10:11: "*Now these things happened to them as an example, and they were written for our instruction, upon whom* *the ends of the ages* *have come.*"

- Gal 4:4: "*But* *when the fullness of time came,* *God sent forth His Son, born of a woman,
born under the Law.*"

- Eph 1:9–10: "*He made known to us the mystery of His will . . . with a view to an administration suitable to* *the fullness of the times,* *that is, the summing up of all things in
Christ.*"

- 1 Tim 4:1–6: "*But the Spirit explicitly says that* *in later times* *some will fall away from
the faith . . . men who forbid marriage and advocate abstaining from foods which God
has created to be gratefully shared in . . . In pointing out these things to the brethren,
you will be a good servant of Christ Jesus.*"

- Heb 9:26: "*But now once* *at the end of the ages* *He has been manifested to put away sin
by the sacrifice of Himself.*"

- 1 Pet 1:3–5: "*Blessed be the God and Father of our Lord Jesus Christ, who . . . has
caused us to be born again . . . [and we] are protected by the power of God through faith
for a salvation to be revealed* *in the last time.*"

- 1 Pet 1:20: "*He was foreknown before the foundation of the world, but has appeared* *in
these last times* *for the sake of you.*"

- 1 John 2:18: "*Children,* *it is the last hour;* *and just as you heard that antichrist is coming, even now many antichrists have appeared; from this we know that it is the last
hour.*"

- Jude 17–19: "*But you, beloved, ought to remember the words that were spoken before-
hand by the apostles of our Lord Jesus Christ, that they were saying to you, 'In the last
time there will be mockers, following after their own ungodly lusts.' These are the ones
who cause division, worldly-minded, devoid of the Spirit.*"

Even though we are in the "last days" now, there will be a "last day" when this age ends and the eschatological fullness of the age to come begins

The distinction between the "last days" and "the last day"

There is a distinction between the "last days" and "the last day." On the day of Pentecost, Peter said that pouring out of the Holy Spirit was proof that the "last days" are here now. In other words, the "last days" are not a brief period of time shortly before Christ comes again; rather, the complex of Jesus' death, resurrection, ascension, and the pouring out of the Holy Spirit inaugurated the "last days." The last days have lasted approximately two thousand years so far. However, there will be a "last day" when the "last days" of this present age end. That "last day" will be the day of Christ's return, the *parousia*.[34] Hoekema explains how the grammar of the NT makes this clear: "When the expression is found in the singular, however ('the last day'), it never refers to the present age but always to the age to come, usually the Day of Judgment or the day of resurrection. . . . New Testament eschatology, therefore, looks back to the coming of Christ which had been predicted by the Old Testament prophets, and affirms: we are in the last days now. But New Testament eschatology also looks forward to a final consummation yet to come, and hence it also says: the last day is still coming; the final age has not yet arrived."[35] Thus, in John 6:39, 40, 44, 54 Jesus does not speak about the *"last days"* (plural), but in each of those verses says that he will raise up the faithful on *"the last day"* (singular). In John 11:24 Martha says that she knows her brother Lazarus *"will rise again in the resurrection on the last day"* (singular). In John 12:48 Jesus says, *"The word I spoke is what will judge him at the last day"* (singular).

The "end of the ages" versus the "end of the age"

The distinction between the "last days" and "the last day" is also found when the Greek noun *synteleia* ("end" or "consummation") is used with either the plural or singular of the word "age" (i.e., "the end of the ages" versus "the end of the age"). Hoekema explains that this NT grammar reveals that there will be a specific end of this age:

> In the one instance where this word [*synteleia*] is used with the plural of *aiōn* (age), it means the present era: "Now once at the end of the ages (*epi synteleia tōn aiōnōn*) hath he [Christ] been manifested to put away sin" (Heb. 9:26, ASV). But when this word is used with the singular of *aiōn*, it always refers to the final consummation which is still future: "Lo, I am with you always, to the close [end] of the age (*tēs synteleias tou aiōnos*)" (Matt. 28:20). When Jesus is explaining the meaning of the Parable of the Tares, he says, "the harvest is the close [end] of the age (*synteleia aiōnos*)" (Matt. 13:39; cf. vv. 40, 49); and when the disciples ask Jesus about the future, they say, "Tell us, when will this be, and what will be the sign of your coming and the close [end] of the age?" (Matt. 24:3).[36]

---

34. See Schnabel, *40 Questions*, 22–24.

35. Hoekema, *Bible and Future*, 19–20.

36. Ibid., 19.

Consequently, the biblical pattern reveals a clear and consistent eschatological structure. There are two ages: "this age" and the "age to come." Christ's first coming—particularly in the complex of his death, resurrection, and ascension—entailed the in-breaking of the "age to come" into "this age." His first coming means that this age is in its "last days." Christ's first coming, however, did not mean the total *replacement* of this age with the age to come. Rather, since his first coming, the two ages are overlapping. Nevertheless, there will be a "last day" in which "this age" will end and will be replaced by the "age to come" in all its fullness. To that we now turn.

5

The Eschatological Significance of Christ's Second Coming

THE SPECIFIC TIME WHEN "this age" will end and the "age to come" will be consummated in all its glory is the second coming of Christ. "The Scriptures explicitly tell us that the line of demarcation between these two ages is our Lord's second advent."[1] The "last day" is equivalent to "the end of the age." In other words, "the last day of *this age* is the day of Christ's second coming and it is the first day of *the age to come*."[2] Titus 2:12–13 clearly implies that the second coming (the "appearing") of Christ Jesus is the *"blessed hope"* for which we look, which brings to a close *"the present age"* and inspires believers *"to live sensibly, righteously and godly in the present age."* Heb 9:28 says the same thing: *"So Christ also, having been offered once to bear the sins of many, will appear a second time for salvation without reference to sin, to those who eagerly await Him."*

The second coming is a definite event

Acts 3:19–21; Heb 9:28; Jas 5:8; 2 Pet 3:10; and Rev 22:20 all speak about the second coming of Christ as a definite event that will occur in the future and not simply as a spiritual event that is ongoing now or a definite event that occurred sometime in the past. Christ's return will be personal (John 14:3; 1 Thess 4:16); physical (Acts 1:11); visible (Matt 24:26–27, 30); audible (1 Thess 4:16); triumphant and glorious (Matt 24:30; Mark 13:26; Luke 21:27; Rev 19:11–16).

---

1. Riddlebarger, *Amillennialism*, 85; see also Venema, *Promise*, 90–95 ("the return of Christ marks the close of the present age"); Ladd, *Gospel of the Kingdom*, 27 ("these two ages are separated by the Second Coming of Christ and the resurrection from the dead"); Charles, *Eschatology*, 448 ("the parusia [sic], accompanied by the final judgment and the resurrection, marks the end of the present age and the beginning of the new").

2. Waldron, "Structural Considerations," n.p.

The Bible uses specific terms to describe Christ's second coming

The "coming" (parousia; erchomai; analuō; panerchomai; hupostrephō; hēkō)

"This word [*parousia*] means 'presence' or 'arrival'. It was used in the Greek world to describe the visit of a ruler to a city, with all the festive atmosphere which surrounded such a visit. Often a party of civic dignitaries, or even the whole population, would go out to meet the ruler as he approached the city. It was a day of festival."[3] Every time the word *parousia* is used in the NT with reference to Christ it is used in the singular with the definite article (i.e., "*the parousia*"). Thus, in the NT *parousia* essentially is a technical term for the eschatological coming of Christ in glory.[4]

- *The following verses use the Greek noun parousia ("coming") to describe Jesus' second coming*: Matt 24:3, 27, 37, 39; 25:19; 1 Cor 15:23; 1 Thess 2:19; 3:13; 4:15; 5:23; 2 Thess 2:1, 8; Jas 5:7, 8; 2 Pet 1:16; 3:4, 12; 1 John 2:28.

- *The following verses describe the second coming with the Greek verb erchomai ("come") instead of the noun parousia*: Matt 16:27; 23:39; 24:30; 24:42–44, 46; 25:19; 26:64; Mark 8:38; 13:26; 14:62; Luke 9:26; 12:36–40, 43, 45; 18:8; 19:13; 21:27; John 14:3; 21:22–23; Acts 1:11; 1 Cor 4:5; 11:26; 2 Thess 1:10; Heb 10:37; Jude 14; Rev 1:4, 7–8; 2:5, 16; 3:11; 16:15; 22:7, 12, 20.

- *The following verses describe the second coming with the Greek verbs analuō, hupostrephō, and epanerchomai ("return"; "come again")*: Luke 12:36; 19:12, 15.

- *The following verses describe the second coming with the Greek verb hēkō ("come")*: Matt 24:50; Luke 12:46; Heb 10:37; Rev 2:25; 3:3.

The "revelation" (apokalupsis; apokaluptō) and the "appearance" (epiphaneia; phaneroō; horaō)

Travis discusses the essential equivalence of the "revelation" (*apokalupsis*) and the "appearing" (*epiphaneia*) of Jesus Christ: "Paul speaks of Christ's coming as his 'being revealed' or 'appearing' (Greek *apokalypsis* [2 Thess 1:7]). This description, like the equivalent word for 'appearing' (*epiphaneia*) in [2 Thess 2:8], repeats a theme which we have already noticed in Jesus's teaching. One of the purposes of Christ's coming will be to reveal what is now hidden, to make clear-cut what is now open to doubt, to demonstrate the glory of Christ in contrast to the 'incognito' element in his first coming."[5]

- *The following verses use the Greek noun apokalupsis to describe Jesus' second coming*: 1 Cor 1:7; 2 Thess 1:7; 1 Pet 1:7, 13; 4:13.

- *In the following verses the verb form (apokaluptō) is used to describe the second coming instead of the noun form*: Luke 17:30; Rom 2:5; 8:18–19; 1 Pet 5:1.

---

3. Travis, *I Believe*, 84.

4. Oepke, "*parousia*," 5:865–66.

5. Travis, *I Believe*, 86.

- *The following verses describe the second coming with the Greek noun epiphaneia*: 2 Thess 2:8; 1 Tim 6:14; 2 Tim 4:1, 8; Titus 2:13.

- *The following verses describe the second coming with the Greek verb phaneroō ("appear"), which is related to epiphaneia*: Col 3:4; 1 Pet 5:4; 1 John 2:28; 3:2.

- *The following verse describes the second coming with the Greek verb horaō ("appear")*: Heb 9:28.

"The day of the Lord (or of Christ)"

Just as the OT prophets spoke of the *"day of the Lord,"* so does the NT. However, in the NT that phrase no longer refers to temporal judgments on Israel's enemies. Instead, it refers to the great eschatological climax of this age: the day of condemnation of the ungodly but salvation and vindication for those who are Christ's. The OT examples are instructive, however, because the *"day of the Lord"* typically meant judgment involving the concurrent destruction of the wicked and salvation of the righteous (see Isa 13:1—14:23; Joel 1:13—3:21; Amos 5:18—9:15; Obad 15–17; Zeph 1:7—3:20). That pattern indicates that the eschatological *"day of the Lord"* likewise will be a general judgment involving all people, both the wicked and the righteous.

The *"day of the Lord"* is sometimes called the *"day of the Lord Jesus Christ"* or, more simply, *"the day"* or *"that day."* In the NT, as John Murray tells us, *"that day"* is "a well-defined eschatological denotation to designate the day of the Lord, the last day (cf. Matt. 7:22; Luke 10:12; 21:34; 2 Thess. 1:10; 2 Tim. 1:12, 18; 4:8). So much is this the case, that the expression 'the day' has taken on a distinctly technical meaning (cf. Rom. 13:12; 1 Cor. 3:13; 1 Thess. 5:4; Heb. 10:23; 2 Pet. 1:19)."[6] It is equated with *"the last day."* It is sometimes called the *"day of judgment"* (Matt 10:15; 11:22, 24; 12:36; 2 Pet 2:9; 3:7; 1 John 4:7). It will come unexpectedly, so Christians should be living alert and sober lives in order not to be "overtaken" by it (1 Thess 5:2–6; 2 Thess 2:2–4; 2 Pet 3:10).[7]

- *The following verses express the above idea with the phrases "the day (of the Lord or of Christ)," or "his day," or "that day"*: Matt 24:36; Mark 13:32; Luke 17:24, 31; 21:34; Acts 2:20; Rom 13:12; 1 Cor 1:7–8; 3:13; 5:5; 2 Cor 1:14; Phil 1:6, 10; 2:16; 1 Thess 5:2, 4; 2 Thess 1:10; 2:1–2; 2 Tim 1:12, 18; 4:8; Heb 10:25; 2 Pet 3:10.

6. Murray, "Interadventual Period," 394–95; see also Ewert, "1–2 Thessalonians," 1082.

7. The one possible exception to this is Acts 2:20, in which Peter quotes Joel 2:28–32 as having been fulfilled in the outpouring of the Holy Spirit on the day of Pentecost. That passage includes the sentence, *"The sun will be turned into darkness and the moon into blood, before the great and terrible day of the Lord shall come."* Hoekema comments: "Unless one interprets these signs in a nonliteral way (in which case the turning of the sun to darkness could be understood as fulfilled in the three hours of darkness while Jesus was on the cross), it would appear that Joel in his prophecy sees as coming together in a single vision events actually separated from each other by thousands of years." Hoekema, *Bible and Future*, 9; see also Schnabel, *40 Questions*, 20–21. Or, Peter is seeing the culmination of Jesus' first coming as a single, multifactorial event (death, resurrection, ascension, outpouring of the Holy Spirit) which inaugurates God's judgment on Satan and the world that rejects Christ (see. e.g., Luke 10:18; John 3:18–19; 12:31; Rev 12:9). Preterists contend that the "day of the Lord" refers to the destruction of Jerusalem in AD 70: "This is why the Bible speaks of the outpouring of the Holy Spirit upon the Church and the destruction of Israel as being *the same event*, for they were intimately connected theologically." Chilton, *Paradise*, 100.

- *The following verses express the same idea but are phrased slightly differently:* Acts 17:31 (*"a day in which He will judge the world in righteousness"*); Rom 2:5 (*"the day of wrath and revelation of the righteous judgment of God"*); Eph 4:30 (*"the day of redemption"*); 1 Pet 2:12 (*"the day of visitation"*); Rev 6:17 (*the great day of their [God's and the Lamb's] wrath"*); 16:14 (*"the great day of God"*); Jude 6 (*"the judgment of the great day"*).

Christ's second coming does not stand alone but entails both resurrection and judgment

The second coming ushers in and entails a complex of events. From the standpoint of corporate eschatology, the *parousia* entails resurrection and judgment. The resurrection and judgment applies to human beings (both Christians and non-Christians) and to creation itself (i.e., the purging of evil from the universe and the renewal of creation by the institution of the "new heaven and new earth" [Rev 21:1]). Vos points out, "The two overtowering final events in the drama of eschatology are the Resurrection and the Judgment. . . . The Judgment is, of course, the inevitable summing up of a world-process that has fallen subject to the moral abnormality of sin; the Resurrection, after a parallel manner, serves for restoring what has become the prey of decadence and death."[8]

"Corporate eschatology" has profound implications for "individual eschatology." Vos explains, "The eschatological process is intended not only to put man back at the point he stood before the invasion of sin and death, but to carry him to a higher plane of life, not attained before the probation, nor, so far as we can see, attainable without it."[9] Johannes Schneider discusses the significance of the *parousia* for our transformation: "Divine sonship is not the highest stage in the being and nature of the Christian. Fulfillment is reached only when Christians are like Christ. This likeness will be achieved when Christ is manifested. The *parousia* of Christ thus brings perfection to Christians. Then the transfiguration of Christians will enable them to see the transfigured Christ as He is."[10] Thus, 1 John 3:2 states, *"Beloved, now we are children of God, and it has not appeared as yet what we will be. We know that when He appears, we will be like Him, because we will see Him just as He is."*

Christ's second coming brings with it the resurrection of the just and the unjust alike (including the transformation of believers who are living at the time of the parousia [the "rapture"])

- *The following passages speak of Christ's second coming as entailing the resurrection of the just and unjust alike:* Dan 12:2; Matt 13:30, 39–42, 48–50; 25:31–32; Luke 17:22–37; John 5:25–29; Acts 24:14–15; Rev 20:11–15.

---

8. Vos, *Pauline Eschatology*, 72.

9. Ibid.

10. Schneider, *"homoios,"* 5:188.

- *The following passages correlate the resurrection with the second coming but only explicitly talk about the resurrection of believers, not the resurrection of unbelievers*: Matt 24:29–31; Mark 13:24–27; Luke 14:12–14; John 6:39, 40, 44, 54 (in each of these passages in John 6 Jesus repeatedly and unambiguously says that he will raise up his people *"on the last day"*); 11:24; 1 Cor 15:20–26, 35–57; 1 Thess 4:13–17.

The context of those passages makes it clear why only believers are referred to. Jesus was giving assurance to believers based on the unity of believers with Christ (John 6:35–58), was giving assurance to believers and warning them to remain faithful (Matt 24:4–44; Mark 13:5–37), or was giving an incentive to believers that their acts of kindness to those who could not repay them in this world would be rewarded in the judgment that accompanies the resurrection (Luke 14:12–14).

The Pauline passages are similar. In 1 Corinthians 15 Paul expresses his surprise that some people in the church did not believe that there would be a bodily resurrection (15:12). In 15:12–19 he explains how deadly that idea is to the faith. In 15:20–28 he then articulates the heart of his argument that believers are united with Christ and will be bodily raised at his coming. He concludes his argument in 15:35–58 by discussing how the resurrection will occur and why such transformation is necessary to enter into the fullness of the kingdom. The issue of the fate of unbelievers simply is not relevant to that passage.[11] Similarly, the purpose of 1 Thess 4:13–17 is to provide hope and comfort to living believers concerning the resurrection of those believers who had already died.[12]

Christ's second coming brings with it the judgment of all people: rewards for the righteous and punishment for the unrighteous

- *The following passages speak of the second coming of Christ as entailing the judgment of all people, believers and unbelievers alike*: Matt 7:21–23; 10:32–33 (Mark 8:38); Matt 13:24–30, 36–51; 16:27; 24:42–51; 25:10–13, 14–30, 31–46; Luke 12:35–48; 17:22–37; 19:12–27; 21:26–28; John 5:25–29; Acts 17:31; Rom 2:5–16; 14:10–12; 1 Cor 4:5; 2 Cor 5:10; 2 Thess 1:6–10; 2 Tim 4:1; Heb 6:2; Jas 5:7–9; 2 Pet 3:7–13; Rev 11:18; 14:14–20; 19:11–21; 20:11–15; 22:12.

- *The following passages speak of the second coming of Christ as entailing the judgment (vindication) of believers*: Luke 18:17–18; Rom 8:18; 1 Cor 1:7–8; 3:12–15; 1 Thess 3:13; 5:23; 2 Tim 4:8; Heb 9:28; 1 Pet 1:7, 13; 4:13; 5:1, 4; 1 John 2:28; 4:17.

- *The following passages speak of the second coming of Christ as entailing the judgment of unbelievers*: 2 Thess 2:8; 2 Pet 3:3–12; Jude 14–15.[13]

11. This passage is discussed in detail at Appendix 7: 1 Cor 15:20–57: The Resurrection, the *Parousia*, and the Millennium.

12. Additionally, in all of the above passages the term "resurrection" may not have been used for unbelievers because they will not be resurrected to eternal life, but will be resurrected only to be judged and cast into the lake of fire (i.e., the "second death"). See Kline, "First Resurrection," 371; Mealy, *After the Thousand Years*, 230n.5.

13. Jude 14–15 quotes from the ancient (c.300BC?) book of *1 Enoch* 1:9 and says that the Lord is coming *"to execute judgment upon all."* Steven Kraftchick states, "The context of *1 Enoch* 1:9 suggests that God's judgment will be passed on 'all flesh' i.e., all the inhabitants of earth, righteous and ungodly (*1*

The Bible teaches that there is one general resurrection, and one general judgment, of both believers and unbelievers

The day of judgment is always spoken of in the singular, e.g., *"day of judgment"* (Matt 10: 15; 11:22–24; 12:36); *"that day"* (Matt 7:22; Luke 10:12); *"the judgment"* (Luke 10:14; 11:31); *"a day in which he will judge the world"* (Acts 17:31); *"a day of wrath"* (Rom 2:5); *"a day of judgment"* (2 Pet 3:7); *"the day of judgment"* (1 John 4:17); *"the great day of their [God's and the Lamb's] wrath"* (Rev 6:17); *"the time for the dead to be judged"* (Rev 11:18); *"the great day of God"* (Rev 16:14). That day—which involves both resurrection and judgment—takes place on "the last day," the "end of the age."[14]

Both believers and unbelievers will participate in the one great judgment. The universality of the judgment is specified in the following passages: Acts 17:31 says, *"He has fixed a day in which He will judge the world in righteousness through a Man whom He has appointed, having furnished proof to all men by raising Him from the dead."* Jesus says in Rev 22:12, *"I am coming quickly, and my reward is with me, to render to every man according to what he has done."* Acts 10:42; 2 Tim 4:1; 1 Pet 4:5 all speak of Christ who will judge *"the living and the dead."*[15] The phrase is an expression of universality, "all" people. J. Ramsay Michaels observes that Peter's "whole argument extending from [1 Pet] 3:13 to 4:5 is . . . God will vindicate those who suffer and hold their oppressors accountable at the day of judgment."[16]

The presence of believers and unbelievers being present together is made clear in the following passages which speak of those who are vindicated and those who are condemned at the same judgment: In Matt 12:35–37 Jesus says, *"35 The good man brings out of his good treasure what is good; and the evil man brings out of his evil treasure what is evil. 36 But I tell you that every careless word that people speak, they shall give an accounting for it in the day of judgment. 37 For by your words you will be justified, and by your words you will be condemned."* Rom 2:5–8 speaks of *"the day of wrath and revelation of the righteous judgment of God, 6 who will render to each person according to his deeds: 7 to those who by perseverance in doing good seek for glory and honor and immortality, eternal life; 8 but to those who are selfishly ambitious and do not obey the truth, but obey unrighteousness, wrath and indignation."* Rev 11:18 says, *"The time came for the dead to be judged, and the time to reward Your bond-servants the prophets and the saints and those who fear Your name, the small and the great, and to destroy those who destroy the earth."*

Enoch 1:7). But 'all' for Jude refers only to all those who commit ungodly deeds. He thereby underscores the adverse judgment that will be passed on the 'ungodly.'" Kraftchick, *Jude*, 55; see also Harvey and Towner, *2 Peter*, 216; Schreiner, *1, 2 Peter*, 472.

14. Matt 13:30, 39–42, 48–50; John 6:39, 40, 44, 54; 11:24; 12:48.

15. While the context appears to speak of the universality of the judgment—those alive when Christ comes and those who previously have died—some have found in the phrase *"the living and the dead"* a reference to "the elect, who live by grace, and the reprobate, who are spiritually dead." Haydock, *Catholic,* Acts 10:42; "It is more correct to understand the *living* of those who enjoy spiritual life, and the *dead* of those who remain spiritually dead; which makes the distinction a more important one, and renders the phrase parallel to all those passages which treat of the judgment of the good and the bad." Olshausen, *Commentary,* 4:497. Whichever way one construes these verses, the conclusion is the same: the righteous and the unrighteous are both present and judged at the same judgment.

16. Michaels, *1 Peter,* 235.

In Matt 12:39–42 (Luke 11:29–32) Jesus says that the men of Nineveh *"will stand up with this generation at the judgment, and will condemn it because they repented,"* and *"the Queen of the South will rise up with this generation at the judgment, and will condemn it, because she came from the ends of the earth to hear the wisdom of Solomon."* *"Stand up"* is the future middle indicative of the verb *anistēmi*, from which the noun *anastasis* (resurrection) is derived. *"Rise up"* is the future passive indicative of the verb *egeirō* (lit., "will be raised up"), which is essentially synonymous with *anistēmi*.[17] These are the primary words signifying resurrection in the NT. Davies and Allison point out that *"at the judgment"* and *"this generation"* "both have eschatological content. In addition, the scene painted presupposes a universal judgement, for it involves the Ninevites and the Israel of Jesus' time, as well as the queen of the South."[18] Thus, we see the redeemed and the unredeemed from different times and places being resurrected together (i.e., *"with this generation"*) at the time of the judgment, with the redeemed playing a part in the judgment of the unredeemed.[19] Further, "the judgment" is a noun, and includes the definite article, which specifies that there is only one judgment (as opposed to an indefinite "will rise up *in judgment*").[20]

Two other factors indicate that at the judgment believers and unbelievers are resurrected alike. First, while J. Webb Mealy acknowledges that Luke 20:34–36 and Matt 25:31–46 describe a general judgment of all humanity, he contends that only a *"partial, selective resurrection* for those judged 'worthy'" (i.e., the believers) takes place; the unbelievers are being judged in their unresurrected state to determine whether they will be deemed "worthy" to achieve resurrection and take part in resurrection life in the age to come.[21] However, the believers are standing before the judgment seat, the glorious throne of God (Matt 25:31; Rom 14:10–12; 2 Cor 5:10; Rev 20:11–13), in their resurrected state and evidently have to be in their resurrected state to be there; unbelievers are together with the believers at the same place and time. It is therefore incredible to believe that the unbelievers will not of necessity also be in their resurrected state. Thus, in Matt 25:31–46

17. "Both verbs can mean 'will rise up', but in the present context the passive form of the second invites the sense 'will be raised up [by God].'" Nolland, *Matthew,* 512; see also France, *Matthew,* 487n.2, 492n.17.

18. Davies and Allison, *St. Matthew,* 2:358.

19. In addition to denoting resurrection, to "stand up" (*anistēmi*) and "rise up" (*egeirō*) can also mean to appear as a witness in court. See Mealy, *The End,* 150–52 for biblical examples of this. Here the words are being used in both senses.

20. Holleman comments, "The idea here is that the unrighteous generation of Jesus' time will be convicted by the righteous generations of former times, since the latter repented and believed while Jesus' generation did not. In order to judge, the people of Nineveh will rise [*anastēsontai*], i.e., they will share in the eschatological resurrection. The relationship assumed here between resurrection and judgement is traditional: it is often said that people will be raised to be judged." Holleman, *Resurrection and Parousia,* 81–82. That is corroborated in Rev 20:11–15 which speaks of the judgment: "We know that these people who come before God are resurrected because John writes of the sea, death, and hades giving up the dead (v. 13). Since it makes no sense to speak of the sea containing souls, John must mean that God will raise the bodies of all who died at sea. In addition, God will raise all who were buried ('hades') here means the grave). Indeed, God will raise *all* the dead, since the term 'death' covers all those not includeed in the categories of those who are buried or those who died at sea." Peterson, *Hell on Trial,* 90.

21. Mealy, "Revelation is One," 137–39. Mealy acknowledges that Hades is "the abode of the spirits of those who have died or have been killed. Human beings who are in Hades await resurrection and final judgment (see Lk. 16:19–31)." Mealy, *The End,* 53n.61.

it is "sheep" and "goats" who stand before the throne, not "sheep" and "spirits of goats."[22] Mealy's proposal would mean that the unbelievers are raised from Hades to the judgment throne in spirit form only to be thrown back into Hades for a thousand years.[23] Nothing in the context of any passage concerning the judgment suggests that unbelievers are in some sort of incorporeal state fundamentally different from the state of believers who are subjects of the same judgment or that unbelievers are the subjects of multiple judgments.

Second, human beings are body-soul unities. The Bible repeatedly says that we will be judged "according to our deeds."[24] Our bodies are integral components of who we are and are integral participants in our sins. Consequently, resurrection of the whole person, body and soul, believers as well as unbelievers, is both necessary and implied whenever the judgment is spoken about in the Bible. This is indicated in the images used of the judgment in a number of passages: Pss 9:8; 96:10; 98:9 say that God will judge *the peoples,* not just their spirits;[25] Ps 73:20, in discussing the judgment of the wicked, says that God *will despise their form*; Jesus warned to *fear Him who is able to destroy both soul and body in hell*" (Matt 10:28); Rom 9:22–23 speaks of *vessels of wrath prepared for destruction* in the same way that it speaks of *vessels of mercy . . . for glory*"; 2 Cor 5:10 specifies that *we must all appear before the judgment seat of Christ, so that each one may be recompensed for his deeds in the body, according to what he has done, whether good or bad*"; Phil 2:10–11 speaks of how *every knee will bow* and *every tongue will confess*"; Jas 5:1–3 speaks of how the witness of the "rust" of people's gold and silver *will consume your flesh like fire*"; 2 Pet 3:7 speaks of *the day of judgment and destruction of ungodly men.*" All these images indicate that the whole person is subject to the judgment, just as the whole person committed deeds worthy of reward or condemnation. Unbelievers will indeed be resurrected along with the believers, but the former are resurrected to judgment and destruction whereas the latter are resurrected to life. All of the above passages uniformly contradict the idea of multiple partial or selective resurrections or judgments.

---

22. Mealy speaks of "the shades of the dead [who] stand before the throne to be judged as to whether they are worthy of a part in resurrection and the new age of Christ's kingdom." Mealy, *After the Thousand Years,* 180. Contrary to that, Heb 6:2 speaks of the foundational or elementary teachings of the faith, concluding its list with *"the resurrection of the dead and eternal judgment."* Thus, judgment is closely associated with resurrection. Although it is not absolutely clear that the resurrection referred to pertains only to the just or to the just and unjust alike, the immediate association of the phrase *"eternal judgment"* and the reference in vv. 4–6 of those who have fallen away indicates that the general resurrection and judgment of all people—the just and unjust alike—is being referred to. O'Brien, *Hebrews,* 215n.27; Allen, *Hebrews,* 343; Hughes, *Hebrews,* 205.

23. See Mealy, *The End,* 47–56 (he contends the unbelievers will be resurrected for their final judgment after spending the "thousand years" of Revelation 20 in Hades).

24. E.g., Matt 16:27; 25:14–30; Luke 12:47–48; John 5:28–29; Rom 2:1–6; 12:19; 1 Cor 3:8, 11–15; 2 Cor 5:10; 11:15; Gal 6:7–8; Eph 6:8; Col 3:25; 2 Tim 4:14; Heb 10:26–27; 1 Pet 1:17; 2 Pet 2:20–22; Jude 14–15; Rev 2:23; 14:13; 20:11–13; 22:12.

25. "The psalms are referring to a future occasion that was naturally identified subsequently as the last judgment." Marshall, "Acts," 595.

Christ's second coming brings with it the destruction or cleansing of the present world and the restoration of creation

Acts 3:19–21; Rom 8:17–25; Heb 1:10–12, and 2 Pet 3:3–13 all speak of the destruction or cleansing of the present world and the restoration of creation.[26] The destruction and renewal of the earth can be seen as a special aspect of the judgment and resurrection that Christ's coming entails.[27] Both the creation as a whole and we ourselves are described as "groaning" until we receive *"the redemption of our body"* (Rom 8:22–23; see also 2 Cor 5:1–4). Nevertheless, the creation itself is said to be *"waiting eagerly"* in *"anxious longing"* to be *"set free from its slavery to corruption"* (Rom 8:19, 21). That restoration of creation at the *parousia* is described in Ps 96:11–13a which says, *"[11] Let the heavens be glad, and let the earth rejoice; Let the sea roar, and all it contains; [12] Let the field exult, and all that is in it. Then all the trees of the forest will sing for joy [13] Before the Lord, for He is coming, For He is coming to judge the earth."* The sin of human beings and the groaning of the earth are related; indeed, the "curse" of the earth is part of God's judgment on mankind's initial sin (Gen 3:14–19). That is reflected in Rev 11:17–18 and Rev 20:11–15 which depict the final judgment and refer to the earth as part of that judgment (see also Ps 96:13). Thus, resurrection and judgment of people do not stand alone but are part of the restoration of all of creation.[28]

26. The end of 2 Pet 3:10 says that *"the earth and its works will be burned up."* A footnote to the NASB notes, "Two early mss read *discovered*"; *UBS4*, 806n.2 refers to multiple manuscripts that have this reading. N. T. Wright points out that the use of "discovered" or "being found out" is used in Jewish texts and elsewhere in the NT in connection with the eschatological judgment. If that is the proper reading, then what is being implied is not the abolition of creation but that "the only way to the fulfillment of the creator's longing for a justice and goodness which will replace the present evil is for a process of fire, not simply to consume, but also to purge." Wright, *Resurrection*, 463. In commenting on 2 Pet 3:7, Douglas Harink similarly says, "If creation is finally to be fully liberated and made new by the Word and the Spirit, the divine parousia must consume everything that now holds creation and history in bondage to unrighteousness, death, and decay. The coming fiery purification and glorious transfiguration of creation are not two events in a sequence; they are the double effect of the final divine parousia of the Spirit and the Word of God." Harink, *1 & 2 Peter*, 178.

27. See Riddlebarger, *Amillennialism*, 138 (the *parousia* entails resurrection, judgment, and re-creation of all things); Shepherd, "Resurrections," 37–43 (the "resurrection of all things at the end of the age" is cosmic in scope and involves individual resurrection, judgment, the restoration of creation, and the reconciliation of all things to Christ); Mealy, *After the Thousand Years*, 89, 192 (the *parousia* entails "the righting of all wrongs, and the giving of all rewards, both positive and negative," the "dissolution of the existing heaven and earth," and the "re-creation of the world").

28. Tim Keller observes, "Outside of the Bible, no other major religious faith holds out any hope or even interest in the restoration of perfect *shalom* [absolute wholeness; peace; full, harmonious, joyful, flourishing life], justice, and wholeness in this material world. Vinoth Ramachandra, a Sri Lankan Christian writer, can see this very clearly. All other religions, he says, offer as salvation some form of liberation from ordinary humanness. Salvation is seen as escape from the shackles of individuality and physical embodiment into some kind of transcendent spiritual existence." Keller, *Reason for God*, 223–24. Christianity alone holds out hope for the salvation of the *world*: human beings who have glorious new bodies living in a renewed earth, with God directly in their midst.

The NT identifies Christ's second coming as being "the last day," "the end of the age," "the day of the Lord," the day of the resurrection, and the day of judgment

The events which will take place on "the last day" or "the end of the age" or "the day of the Lord"—the resurrection of both believers and unbelievers, judgment of both believers and unbelievers, and the renewal of the earth—all take place (or are initiated) when Christ comes again. The NT ties together all of those events, although some passages emphasize only some of them while other passages emphasize others of them. When we see the overlap of multiple passages, we clearly see that the second coming of Christ is equivalent to "the last day," "the end of the age," and "the day of the Lord," and it entails resurrection, judgment, and renewal of the earth. In other words, if A includes B; and B includes C; then A also includes C. Or, to put it another way, if in one place A is said to include B; and elsewhere A is said to include C; then we may conclude that A includes both B and C.

- *"The end of the age," the resurrection, and the judgment of believers and unbelievers alike are all correlated.* Matt 13:24–30, 36–43 (parable of the wheat and the tares) brings together in one passage resurrection (13:28–30, 39–41), *"the end of the age"* (13:39–40), and the judgment of believers and unbelievers alike (13:30, 40–43). Matt 13:47–50 (parable of the dragnet) similarly brings together in one passage *"the end of the age"* (13:49), resurrection (13:49), and the judgment of both believers and unbelievers (13:48–50).

- *"The revelation of the Lord Jesus Christ," "the end [of the age]" and "the day of the Lord" are correlated* in 1 Cor 1:7–8; 2 Cor 1:13–14 connects *"the end"* with *"the day of the Lord."*

- *"The last day" and the resurrection are correlated* in John 6:39, 40, 44, 54; 11:24.

- *"The last day" and the judgment are correlated* in John 12:48.

- *The second coming, "the day of the Lord," the resurrection, and the judgment are all correlated.* Second Thess 1:6—2:8 brings together in one passage the "revelation" (*apokalupsis*, 1:7), the "coming" (*erchomai*, 1:10), the *parousia* (2:1, 8), the resurrection and rapture (2:1), *"the day of the Lord"* (2:2), and the vindication of believers and judgment of unbelievers (1:6–10; 2:8).

- *The second coming, "the day of the Lord," and the judgment are all correlated.* Matt 24:36–51 brings together in one passage *"that day"* (24:36), the "coming" (both *parousia* [24:37, 39] and *erchomai* [24:42–44, 46]), and the separation and judgment of both believers and unbelievers (24:37–41, 45–51). Rom 2:1–16 brings together in one passage the "revelation" (*apokalupsis*, 2:5), *"the day"* (2:5; 16), and the judgment of God on both believers and unbelievers (2:1–16). Second Tim 4:8 brings together in one passage *"that day,"* the "appearing" (*epiphaneia*), and the judgment (reward) of believers. Second Pet 3:3–12 brings together in one passage the "coming" (*parousia*, 3:4), the *"day of judgment"* (3:7), the *"day of the Lord"* (3:10), the judgment of unbelievers and the destruction of the earth (3:3–12).

- *"His day," "the day the Son of man is revealed [apkaluptetai]," "that day,"* and the Judgment are all correlated in Luke 17:24–37.

- *The second coming and the resurrection are correlated.* See above section regarding "Christ's second coming brings with it the resurrection of the just and the unjust alike (including the transformation of believers who are living at the time of the *parousia* [the 'rapture'])."

- *The second coming and the judgment are correlated.* See above section regarding "Christ's second coming brings with it the judgment of all people: rewards for the righteous and punishment for the unrighteous."

- *The resurrection and the judgment are correlated.* Dan 12:2; John 5:28–29; Rom 14:10–12 (resurrection is implied from the phrase *"stand before the judgment seat of God"*); 2 Cor 5:10 (resurrection is implied from the phrase *"appear before the judgment seat of Christ"*); Heb 6:2 bring together in one passage the resurrection and the judgment of both the good and the evil.[29]

- *The second coming, "the day of the Lord," and "that day" are all correlated.* Just as *"the day of the Lord"* will come *"like a thief"* (1 Thess 5:2, 4; 2 Pet 3:10), so Christ says, *"I will come like a thief"* (Rev 3:3; 16:15; see also Matt 24:42–44; Luke 12:39–40). *"That day"* is used for the second coming (Luke 17:30–31; 2 Thess 1:6–10). Similarly, *"the day of the Lord"* is used for the second coming (1 Cor 1:7–8; 2 Thess 2:1–2; 2 Pet 3:3–4, 9–10). See also Luke 17:24 [*"His day"*]); 2 Pet 3:12 (*"the day of God"*).

- *"The day of the Lord" and the judgment are correlated.* The same phrase, *"the day of the Lord"* (or *"of Christ"*), is used for the final day of judgment of believers (1 Cor

---

29. Dan 12:2 says, *"Many of those who sleep in the dust of the ground will awake, these to everlasting life, but the others to disgrace and everlasting contempt."* "This is the first and only unambiguous reference to resurrection from the dead in the OT, although the concept is not entirely foreign to Hebrew thought, given the statement by Isaiah that 'your dead will live' (Isa 26:19; [other OT hints of resurrection include Job 14:14; 19:25–27; Ps 16:10; 49:15; Isa 25:8; Hos 13:14])." Hill, "Daniel," 205. "The word 'many' (Heb. *rabbim*) may have the force of 'all.'" Ibid., 206. In light of the progressive revelation of the doctrine of the resurrection in the NT, that is probably the meaning. That is indicated by Christ Himself: "When our Lord Jesus quotes this verse, as He without a doubt does in John 5:28, 29 (the points of coincidence between Daniel's and the Savior's statements are too many to be an accidental similarity) He substitutes 'all' for 'many.' This substitution is evidently interpretive." Leupold, *Exposition*, 529. The parallels between the two passages are exact and demonstrate the simultaneousness of the resurrection and the judgment of both the righteous and the unrighteous:

Dan 12:2	*John 5:28–29*
Many of those who sleep in the dust of the ground	An hour is coming, in which all who are in the tombs
will awake,	will hear His voice, and will come forth;
these to everlasting life,	those who did good deeds to a resurrection of life,
but the others to disgrace and everlasting contempt	those who committed evil deeds to a resurrection of judgment

Regarding John 5:28–29, see also Appendix 2: The Millennium: An Amillennial Synthesis of the Biblical Data, the section "Parallels of other NT and OT passages with Rev 20:4–6 indicate that the 'first resurrection' is spiritual and takes place before the final, general, physical resurrection at the *parousia*."

1:8; 2 Cor 1:13–14; Phil 1:6, 10; 2:14–16; 1 Thess 5:2–9); unbelievers (1 Cor 5:5); and unbelievers, believers, and the earth itself (2 Pet 3:3–13).

- *"The day" and the judgment are correlated.* The same phrase, *"the day,"* speaks about the judgment of believers (Rom 13:12; 1 Cor 3:11–15); and speaks about or implies the joint judgment of believers and unbelievers (Rom 2:16; Heb 10:23–27).

- *"That day" and the judgment are correlated.* The same phrase, *"that day,"* speaks about, or implies the vindication of or rewards to believers (2 Tim 1:12, 18; 4:8); the judgment of unbelievers (2 Thess 1:6–10); and speaks explicitly about the judgment of unbelievers and implicitly of the vindication of believers (Matt 7:22–23).

- *"The day of judgment"* is used for the final day of judgment of believers (1 John 4:17); unbelievers (Matt 10:15; Matt 11:22, 24; Luke 10:14; 2 Pet 2:9; 3:7); the earth (2 Pet 3:7, 12); and angels (Jude 6).

- *Other passages and phrases correlate the parousia with the day of judgment.* The *parousia* and the general judgment of all, including the earth, are brought together in Acts 17:31 (*"a day in which he will judge the world"*); Rom 2:5–6 (*"the day of wrath and revelation of the righteous judgment of God"*); 2 Pet 3:12 (*"the day of God"*); Rev 11:17–18 (*"the time came for the dead to be judged . . . to reward your bond-servants . . . and to destroy those who destroy the earth"*); Rev 14:14–20 (*"the hour to reap"*); Rev 20:11–15 (*"a great white throne"* and *"the dead, the great and the small, standing before the throne . . . and the dead were judged"*). The *parousia* and the judgment of unbelievers are brought together in Rev 6:16–17 (*"the great day of their wrath"*); Rev 16:14 (*"the great day of God, the Almighty"*). The *parousia* and the judgment of believers are brought together in 1 Pet 2:12 (*"the day of visitation"*).

6

Historical Overview of Eschatological Thought

William Everett Bell reminds us of the importance of historical study for sound hermeneutics and interpretation: "The importance of a study of the history of a doctrine as a preliminary step in arriving at a proper interpretation is a generally-accepted hermeneutical principal. As Ramm points out, it is the better part of wisdom not to ignore the exegetical labors of past generations. An interpretation that is quite apart from foregoing interpretations is not necessarily wrong, but it is at least suspect. It might be said that the burden of proof falls on the innovator."[1] The same view was held by the post-apostolic fathers.[2] For example, Tertullian (c. 160–220) stated, "That which was first delivered is of the Lord and is true, whilst that is strange and false which was afterwards introduced. . . . For their very doctrine, after comparison with that of the apostles, will declare, by its own diversity and contrariety, that it had for its author neither an apostle nor an apostolic man."[3] Clement of Alexandria (c. 150–215) similarly said, "It is evident, from the high antiquity and perfect truth of the Church, that these later heresies, and those yet subsequent to them in time, were new inventions falsified [from the truth]."[4]

---

1. Bell, "Critical Evaluation," 25–26.

2. There are several compilations of the writings of the apostolic and post-apostolic fathers, including: Michael Holmes, ed. *The Apostolic Fathers*, 2nd ed. Trans. J. B. Lightfoot and J. R. Harmer (Grand Rapids: Baker, 1989); Alexander Roberts and James Donaldson, ed. *Ante-Nicene Fathers*, 10 Volumes (Peabody, MA: Hendrickson, 1994). Philip Schaff, ed., *Nicene and Post-Nicene Fathers*, first series, 14 Volumes (Peabody, MA: Hendrickson, 1994) (Augustine and John Chrysostom); Philip Schaff and Henry Wace, ed., *Nicene and Post-Nicene Fathers*, second series, 14 Volumes (Peabody, MA: Hendrickson, 1994) (Eusebius and other post-apostolic fathers from the Council of Nicea in AD 325 and later). Those works (or similar editions) are available online at: http://www.ccel.org.

3. Tertullian, *Prescription Against Heretics* 31–32.

4. Clement of Alexandria, *Stromata* 7.17.

The seeds of what are now called "amillennialism" and "historic premillennialism" were both present in the writings of the early church fathers

The apostolic and post-apostolic fathers

The term "apostolic fathers" applies to the writings of the late first and early second centuries. They include: the *Didache* (c. 70–110); the *Epistle of Barnabas* (c. 70–131), Clement of Rome, author of *1 Clement* (c. 95–96); *2 Clement* (an early Christian sermon, c. 98–100); Ignatius (c. 35–117), bishop of Antioch; Papias (c. 60–135), bishop of Hierapolis; Polycarp (c. 69–155), bishop of Smyrna; and the *Shepherd of Hermas* (c. 95–154). The term "post-apostolic fathers" is the name given to the writers who established Christian doctrine before the eighth century. They include: Justin Martyr (c. 100–165); Irenaeus (c. 130–200); Clement of Alexandria (c. 150–215); Tertullian (c. 160–220); Origen (c. 185–254); Eusebius (c. 263–339), Athanasius (c. 296–373), and Augustine (354–430).

The early Christian writings

There exists a fairly sizable amount of writing of the early church fathers concerning eschatology. Those that have come down to us tend to be fragmentary. Such patristic writings generally were not prepared as systematic theologies. Rather, the prospect of martyrdom, political factors, geographical influences, the inheritance of Jewish eschatology, and responses to Gnosticism all were influences on the early fathers' eschatological writings.[5] Ken Klassen also notes that "the primary concern of the Apostolic Fathers was pastoral, rather than interpretive."[6] Despite differences among the early Christian writers, they nevertheless hold much in common.

Proto-amillennialism and proto-historic premillennialism

The seeds of both amillennialism and historic premillennialism were present early on. Some people maintain that some form of premillennialism "was probably the dominant millennial view during the early period of the church."[7] However, that is not correct. Justin Martyr (c. 100–165), himself a premillennialist, wrote concerning premillennialism that "many who belong to the pure and pious faith, and are true Christians, think otherwise."[8] D. H. Kromminga states, "The evidence is uniformly to the effect, that throughout the years from the beginning of the second century till the beginning of the fifth chiliasm [i.e., premillennialism] . . . was extensively found within the Christian Church, but that it never was dominant, far less universal; that it was not without opponents, and that its representatives were conscious of being able to speak only for a party in

---

5. Klassen, "Reexamination of the Nature," 9–23; see also Boyd, "Dispensational Premillennial Analysis," 18–19.

6. Klassen, "Reexamination of the Nature," 25.

7. Erickson, *Christian Theology*, 1215.

8. Justin Martyr, *Dial.* 80.

the Church. It may be added, that chiliasm never found creedal expression or approbation in the ancient Church."[9]

In his detailed study of the millennial thought of early Christianity, Charles Hill found among many writers "the existence of an early non-chiliastic interpretation of Rev. 20," and concludes, "A solidly entrenched and conservative, non-chiliastic eschatology was present in the Church to rival chiliasm from beginning to end."[10] In fact, Alan Patrick Boyd's comprehensive survey of the eschatological writings of the apostolic and post-apostolic fathers until the death of Justin Martyr in AD 165 demonstrates that "perhaps seminal amillennialism . . . ought to be seen in the eschatology of the period."[11]

Leading premillennialists and amillennialists of the apostolic and early post-apostolic era, and the basis of their thought

Premillennialists

Only fragments of the writings of Papias (c. 60–135) still exist. Irenaeus called Papias "the hearer of John [the apostle],"[12] but based on a writing by Papias, Eusebius contends that the "John" Papias learned from was not the apostle but a presbyter in the church.[13] In any event, Eusebius reports that Papias taught that there would be a thousand-year kingdom of Christ on the earth, following the resurrection, which would precede the final state.[14] The supposed connection of Papias with John has led some to posit that John was the source of the premillennial view;[15] there is no direct evidence of that, and the actual data concerning the nature of any such millennium and what Papias' millennial beliefs actually were is quite meager. Justin Martyr (c. 100–165), Irenaeus (c. 130–200), and Tertullian (c. 160–220) also were premillennialists. Much of this early millennialism, which was drawn largely from Jewish eschatological ideas, had a physical, sense-oriented quality in which the blessings of the millennium were amplified versions of contemporary, earthly life.[16]

9. Kromminga, *Millennium*, 51.

10. Hill, *Regnum Caelorum*, 260, 253. Hill quotes from, among others, 2 *Clement*, Melito of Sardis, Claudius Apollinarius of Hierapolis, Irenaeus, Hippolytus, Origen, Clement of Alexandria, Dionysius of Alexandria, and Cyprian to this effect. Ibid., 260–68. The purpose of Ken Klassen's master's thesis was "to analyze the eschatology of the Ante-Nicene Fathers on the nature of the *first resurrection* of Revelation 20:4–6." Klassen, "Reexamination of the Nature," 4. He found three streams of thought in the early church: non-millennial (i.e., the "first resurrection" was viewed as the intermediate state in heaven when the soul is separated from the body at death); "millennial" (i.e., a literal, physical resurrection for a thousand years); and anti-millennial (i.e., the "first resurrection" was viewed spiritually [that was the dominant view in Alexandria]). Klassen, "Reexamination of the Nature," 4–5.

11. Boyd, "Dispensational Premillennial Analysis," 91. Boyd's conclusion is credible since, when he wrote his thesis, he was a dispensational premillennialist who "undertook the thesis to bolster the system [dispensationalism] by patristic research, but the evidence of the original sources simply disallowed this." Ibid., 91n.2. See also Klassen, "Reexamination of the Nature," 25 ("there is no ground for the assertion that *millennialism* was prevalent in the subapostolic period ending with the year 150 A.D.").

12. Irenaeus, *Haer.* 5.33.4.

13. Eusebius, *Hist. eccl.* 3.39.

14. Ibid.

15. Crutchfield, "The Apostle John" 411–27.

16. Erickson, *Contemporary Options*, 95.

For example, Irenaeus quoted Papias, who himself had quoted from the late first/early second-century Jewish *Apocalypse of Baruch* (*2 Baruch*), that in the millennium "the days will come, in which vines shall grow, each having ten thousand branches, and in each branch ten thousand twigs, and in each true twig ten thousand shoots, and in each one of the shoots ten thousand clusters, and on every one of the clusters ten thousand grapes, and every grape when pressed will give five and twenty metretes [each metretes = 39.4 liters] of wine."[17]

Justin, Irenaeus, and others such as Hippolytus (c. 170–236) and Lactantius (c. 240–320), believed that the earth would exist for six thousand years, corresponding to the six days of creation.[18] Millard Erickson summarizes that these early church fathers believed that "Christ's first coming had taken place within the sixth thousand-year period and that His second coming would take place at its close. The seventh thousand-year period, the millennium, would then correspond to the day of rest. This meant that the second coming could not be more than one thousand years away. This led to attempts to calculate the date of the second coming."[19]

Irenaeus also developed a two-fold theological rationale for the thousand-year millennium: it accustoms the saints "gradually to partake of the divine nature," and it serves as a recompense for the suffering they endured in this life.[20] The Montanists (late second–early third centuries), an ascetic (and in some respects heretical) reform movement that emphasized the charismatic gifts and the nearness of the end of the world, also were premillennial.[21]

Amillennialists

The *Didache* (c. 70–110) (an early Christian manual of instruction) discusses the last days in some detail; it refers to the resurrection of the righteous and the Lord's coming with his saints but contains no hint of premillennialism.[22] Boyd's study of the early church fathers until the death of Justin Martyr revealed that "Clement of Rome [late first century], Barnabas [c. 70–131], Hermas [c. 95–154], Ignatius [c. 35–117], Polycarp [c. 69–155], and Hegesippus [c. 110–180] cannot be claimed as premillennialists."[23] In his

---

17. Irenaeus, *Haer.* 5.33.3, quoting *2 Baruch* [Syriac Apocalypse], 29:1–8.

18. That idea is based on the statement in 2 Pet 3:8, *"with the Lord one day is like a thousand years, and a thousand years is like one day."* Even today, some people try to make eschatological predictions using the "day = 1000 years" idea. That entire approach is false. Peter's statement was not designed to prove that a day equals a thousand years, or that a thousand years equals a day. Peter's meaning simply is that God is not limited by our notions of time. "The verse contrasts man's transience with God's everlastingness, the limited perspective of man whose expectations tend to be bounded by his own brief lifetime with the perspective of the eternal God who surveys the whole of history." Bauckham, "Delay of the Parousia," 26.

19. Erickson, *Contemporary Options*, 95.

20. Irenaeus, *Haer.* 5.32.1.

21. Berkhof, *Christian Doctrines*, 54, 262.

22. *Didache* 16:6–7.

23. Boyd, "Dispensational Premillennial Analysis," 92n.1; see also Gentry, *Dominion*, 58 (Hermas, Polycarp, Clement of Rome, and Ignatius "seem best to fit in with the amillennial viewpoint").

recent comprehensive study of orthodox non-premillennialism (i.e., amillennialism) up to the mid-third century, Charles Hill concluded:

> The express statements of the grandsons of Jude as reported by Hegesippus, of Hermas, the author of 2 *Clement,* the *Epistula Apostolorum,* and the *Apocalypse of Peter,* as well as of Hippolytus, Clement of Alexandria, Origen, Dionysius of Alexandria, and Cyprian, concerning general eschatology enable us to say with little or no hesitation that all held amillennial expectations of the return of Christ. All of these also held to some form of a heavenly intermediate state, and this fact further verifies that we have in early Christianity competing patterns or 'complexes' of eschatological teaching. This verification has a reflexive impact on our interpretation of several other authors. It makes possible the inference that Clement of Rome, Ignatius, Polycarp, Athenagoras, Melito of Sardis, the martyrs of Scilli in 180 and those of Carthage in 203, the authors of the *Ascension of Isaiah,* 5 *Ezra,* the *Odes of Solomon,* the *Epistle to Diognetus,* the *Martyrdom of Polycarp,* the *Epistle of Vienne and Lyons,* and the *Acts of Thomas* would not have been at home within the chiliast [premillennialist] camp, for, though we have found only half the bones of their eschatological "skeleton," the skeleton to which these bones belong is of the non-chiliast species.[24]

The *Epistle of Barnabas* (c. 70–131) represents "a very early amillennial type of eschatology, as early as any chiliasm can be shown to have appeared in the ancient Church."[25] In *Barnabas* the OT promises to Israel are applied to the church. Like the early premillennialists, *Barnabas* uses the six thousand year age of the earth, based on the days of creation methodology. When he expounds this and the meaning of the Sabbath, *Barnabas* holds that on the "seventh day" (i.e., the second coming) Christ "shall abolish the time of the Lawless One, and shall judge the ungodly, and shall change the sun and the moon and the stars, then He shall truly rest on the seventh day."[26] He then equates the "seventh day" with the "eighth day" (the eternal rest of the saints).[27] In other words, "The day of rest that is coming is one and the same day, viewed from two different aspects. From the viewpoint of continuity the great world-sabbath is the seventh day; but from the viewpoint of discontinuity it is the eighth, beyond and outside the present world-week. The future state is the last, reckoning from creation; it is new, because of sin and redemption. This is the simplest meaning which I can discover in Barnabas' words; but this is plain and pure Amillennialism."[28]

Opposition to premillennialism arose early in church history, especially in the East. Erickson tells us why: "The excesses of Montanism [late second–early third centuries], helped to discredit it and to stamp it as Jewish in origin and character rather than Christian. This rejection was due, at least in part, to the chiliasts' ideas of the millennium being so realistic (materialistic) and crass. This certainly helped to repulse the more intellectually inclined Christians like the Alexandrian school—Clement [c. 150–215], Origen [c.

---

24. Hill, *Regnum Caelorum,* 249.

25. Kromminga, *Millennium,* 40; see also Boyd, "Dispensational Premillennial Analysis," 101–06.

26. *Barn.* 15:5.

27. Ibid., 15:8.

28. Kromminga, *Millennium,* 36.

185–254], and Dionysius [c.?–265]—which led the opposition to chiliasm."[29] Caius of Rome (early 3rd century), in commenting on Rev 20:2–3, propounded the amillennial position that Satan had been bound at Christ's first coming, citing Matt 12:29; in this he was opposed by Hippolytus.[30]

Although some have considered Hippolytus (c. 170–236) a premillennialist, the authentic corpus of his writings is "very much under dispute"; moreover, Hippolytus himself wrote of Christ's loosing people from the bonds of death, binding him who was strong against us (i.e., Satan), and setting humanity free.[31] His *Commentary on Daniel* includes a "non-chiliastic exegesis of Rev. 20:4–6, wherein John's 'first resurrection' is viewed as taking place when the martyred soul rises to join Christ the judge in his heavenly dominion."[32] Further, Cyprian (c.?–258), bishop of Carthage, was both "an amillennialist and a proponent of a 'heavenly' intermediate state."[33] Cyprian's writings, which include an exposition of Rev 20:4–6, "establish beyond a reasonable doubt that he has in mind the enjoyment of the millennium of Rev. 20:4–6 in heaven by the faithful during the interadvent period."[34] Probably the most influential figure in the demise of premillennialism was Augustine (354–430), bishop of Hippo. Augustine had drawn on the work of Tyconius (c.?–390).[35] In his influential book *The City of God,* Augustine interpreted the "thousand years" as the present age, "from the first coming of Christ to the end of the world."[36]

Summary of the eschatology of the apostolic and early post-apostolic fathers

Most of the apostolic fathers and early post-apostolic fathers were generally in accord with the principles stated by the *Epistle of Barnabas*. The major features of the eschatology of the apostolic and early post-apostolic fathers are as follows:

- *The "last days" are present and would unfold with the occurrence of various events, which would bring about Christ's second coming in the relatively near future: 1 Clement 23:1–5; 42:3; 2 Clement 11:1—12:1; 14:2; Ignatius, To the Ephesians 11:1 ("These are the last times"); To the Magnesians 6:1 (Christ "was with the Father and appeared at the end of time"); To Polycarp 3:2; Epistle of Barnabas 4:3–6, 9; Didache 10:6; 16:1–8; Shepherd of Hermas, Vision 2.2.5; 3.8.9; Parable 9.12.3;[37] Justin Martyr, Dialogue with Trypho 32; 49;[38] Tertullian, The Shows 30* ("But what a spectacle is that fast-approaching advent of our Lord").

29. Erickson, *Contemporary Options,* 96.

30. See Dionysius Syrus, *Rev 20:2, 3.*

31. Hill, *Regnum Caelorum,* 262, quoting Hippolytus's *Comm. Dan.,* 4.33.4.

32. Ibid., 160, 169, citing *Comm. Dan.* 2.37.4; cf. 3.31.3 (from *Hippolyte Commentaire sur Daniel*).

33. Ibid., 192.

34. Ibid., 198.

35. Erickson, *Christian Theology,* 1213; Grenz, *Millennial Maze,* 42–43.

36. Augustine, *Civ.,* 20.8.

37. Hermas later allows for a delay to allow for repentance (*Parable* 9.14.2).

38. The delay in the *parousia* is to allow people time to repent and to complete the number of the just (*First Apology* 28, 45).

- *The destruction of Jerusalem in AD 70 was the result of Israel's rejection of Christ and fulfilled prophecy*: Justin Martyr (*First Apology* 47), Tertullian (*An Answer to the Jews* 13; *Against Marcion* 3.23; *Apology* 26), and Irenaeus (*Against Heresies* 4.4.1–3) all saw the destruction of Jerusalem as the result of Israel's rejection of Christ in fulfillment of OT prophecy. Origen (*Against Celsus* 2.13), and Eusebius (*Ecclesiastical History* 3.5–7), appear to be the first to explicitly set forth the view that the destruction of Jerusalem in AD 70 was the fulfillment of Christ's prophecy in the Olivet Discourse.

- *Although the church was in the "last days" and the events of history were eschatologically relevant, the second coming would not be immediate, but the Roman Empire first would be broken, Antichrist would arise, and the church would have to pass through tribulation which would serve to purify it*: Epistle of Barnabas 4:3–5; Shepherd of Hermas, Vision 2.2.6–8, 4.1.1—4.3.6; Didache 16:1–8; Justin Martyr, Dialogue with Trypho 110; Irenaeus, Against Heresies 5.25.1—26.1, 28.4, 30.4, 35.1; Tertullian, On the Resurrection of the Flesh 22, 24–25, 27, 41.

- *The second coming will be visible*: 2 Clement 17:4–5; Didache 16:8; Justin Martyr, Dialogue with Trypho 32; 64.

- *The second coming entails resurrection of the dead and the rapture of the living saints*: 1 Clement 50:3–4; 2 Clement 9:1–6; 12:1; 17:4–5; Didache 16:6–7; Epistle of Barnabas 21:1–3; Polycarp, To the Philippians 2:1–2; 5:2 (Polycarp clearly implies that the second coming entails resurrection: "If we please him in this present world, we will receive the world to come as well, inasmuch as he promised to raise us from the dead"); Justin Martyr, First Apology 52; Dialogue with Trypho 52; Tertullian, On the Resurrection of the Flesh 24–25, 41.

- *The second coming brings with it the judgment of believers and unbelievers alike*: 1 Clement 34:3; 2 Clement 16:3; 17:4–7; 18:2; Epistle of Barnabas 4:12; 5:7 ("after he has brought about the resurrection he will execute judgment"); 15:5; Polycarp, To the Philippians 2:1–2; Shepherd of Hermas, Vision 3.8.9; 3.9.5 (the second coming is implied since judgment comes when "the tower"—the church [Parable 9.12.1—13.2]—is completed); Parable 4.1–8 (the second coming is implied since judgment occurs in the age to come, which is "summer to the righteous, but winter to the sinners," when the fruit of "all people will be revealed"); Justin Martyr, First Apology 52; Dialogue with Trypho 32; 35; 45; 49; 117; 121; Tertullian, On the Resurrection of the Flesh 24.[39]

---

39. Justin indicated that the second coming would inaugurate the eternal kingdom (*Dial.* 34; 36; 39; 113), and that the second coming entails the general resurrection of all men and the judgment of both the righteous and the wicked (*First Apology* 52). However, in *Dial.* 80–81 he alludes to Rev 20:4–5 and says that the general resurrection and judgment would take place after the "thousand years." He makes no attempt to reconcile the two positions. Little stress is made on the millennium, and it appears almost to merge into the eternal state. Similarly, Tertullian in *Against Marcion* 3.24 indicated that the *parousia* would result in bodily resurrection for a thousand years, after which the world would be destroyed and believers changed "into the substance of angels" and removed to heaven. However, in *Res.* 25 he indicates that the "first resurrection" of Rev 20:4–6 is "a spiritual resurrection at the commencement of a life of faith" which comes to "full completion" by the "final and universal [bodily] resurrection "at the very conclusion of all the periods" (i.e., "at the end of the world"). Again, he does not attempt to reconcile those two positions.

- *The second coming will bring about the destruction or renewing and transformation of the earth*: 2 Clement 16:3; *Epistle of Barnabas* 15.5; Papias, *Fragment* 14; Justin Martyr, *Dialogue with Trypho* 81; Irenaeus, *Against Heresies* 5.33.3–4.

- *The second coming ushers in the kingdom of God, which is a time of the worldwide rule of Christ, and rest, rule, and holiness of believers on or over the earth*: 2 Clement 6:7; 11:7—12:1; 17:5; *Epistle of Barnabas* 6:17–19; 10:11; Polycarp, *To the Philippians* 2:1–2; 5:2 (Polycarp clearly implies that the second coming ushers in the kingdom: "If we please him in this present world, we will receive the world to come as well, inasmuch as he promised to raise us from the dead . . . [and] we will reign with him"); Justin Martyr, *Dialogue with Trypho* 34; 36; 39; 113.

- *The promises given to OT Israel are not taken "literally" as applying to the physical nation of Israel, but are applied to the church which has taken the place of Israel*: 1 Clement 32:1–4; *Epistle of Barnabas* 2:4–10; 4:6–8; 6:1–19; 9:8; 10:1–12; 13:1–6; 14:4–5; 16:1–10;[40] *Didache* 14:1–3; *Shepherd of Hermas, Parable* 9.16.1–7; 9.17.1–2; Justin Martyr, *Dialogue with Trypho* 34; 44; 113; 119–20; 121; 123–25; 130–31; 135; 140; Irenaeus, *Against Heresies* 5.32.1–2; Tertullian, *Against Marcion* 3.24; *On the Resurrection of the Flesh* 26.

Distinctions between ancient and modern premillennialists

An important hermeneutical distinction between ancient and modern premillennialism

The ancient premillennialists were adherents of a "continuous-historical" approach to interpreting Scripture, i.e., the entire book of Revelation was relevant and understandable and was related in some way to ongoing history. They believed that "the events revealed in the pictures of the Apocalypse were in the making, [and] had begun to come about in their own days. . . . [T]hey expected the events to come to pass in a relatively short time."[41] In contrast, most modern premillennialists (especially dispensationsalists), even those who think the second coming will occur soon, have divorced eschatology from history. They relate eschatology solely to a period of time shortly before Christ comes again. For them, most of the book of Revelation (at least from chapter 4 onward) is unrelated to anything that has happened in the last two thousand years and will continue to be unrelated to anything in the future until some specific event triggers the "running of the eschatological clock." Kromminga points out that the modern premillennialist position concerning the stopping and restarting of the "eschatological clock" amounts to an "implicit denial of the continuity of historical developments, the extraction of the eschatological quality from the course of Christian history so far, and its concentration into a final period of history," all of which make both Revelation and history "quite unintelligible for us who are not yet

---

40. "The purpose of the Epistle of Barnabas is to demonstrate that the Church is the heir of the covenant which YHWH made with the nation of Israel at Sinai." Boyd, "Dispensational Premillennial Analysis," 101–02.

41. Kromminga, *Millennium*, 314.

living it."[42] In its hermeneutics, therefore, ancient premillennialism is closer to modern amillennialism, postmillennialism, and preterism than it is to modern premillennialism.

None of the distinctive beliefs of dispensational premillennialism were present in the apostolic and post-apostolic era

Boyd's study of the eschatology of the early apostolic and post-apostolic fathers demonstrates that the profound eschatological differences between the apostolic and post-apostolic fathers (including those who were premillennialists) and modern dispensationalists "disqualify any claim that pretribulational, dispensationalism existed *in any form* in the period. First of all, a consistently applied literal interpretation and a distinction between Israel and the Church are missing, and these are the foundation stones of the modern [dispensational] system. Secondly, there is no concept of dispensations or dispensationalism at all. Thirdly, there was only the concept of a visible Second Advent, immediately preceding the establishment of the kingdom. Fourthly, although they believed in the kingdom, it certainly was not the climax of God's program for Israel [as dispensationalists claim]."[43] Further, there is no hint of an "any moment" coming of Christ for the church [the dispensationalist doctrine of "imminency"] or a "pre-tribulational rapture" of the church.[44] Instead, all of the apostolic and post-apostolic fathers who discussed the issue stated that the church would pass through the "tribulation."[45]

Amillennialism was the dominant eschatological position from Augustine until the Reformation

Amillennial eschatology: virtually universal

Augustine's essentially amillennial eschatology was predominant throughout the Middle Ages.[46] The Middle Ages also became dominated by a "static" view of history. Consequently, relatively little attention was paid to eschatology since "eschatology was not really concerned with history" and "there was no sense of a dynamic movement in history."[47] The kingdom of God generally was seen as being "embedded in the permanent and unchangeable structure of the church."[48]

---

42. Ibid.

43. Boyd, "Dispensational Premillennial Analysis," 49–50, emphasis in original.

44. Ibid., 62, 72–73, 86, 89. See also Bell, "Critical Evaluation," 55–56.

45. Ladd, *Blessed Hope,* 19–31 ("Every church father who deals with the subject expects the Church to suffer at the hands of Antichrist"); Bauckham, "Great Tribulation," 27–40 ("The central and positive role given to the sufferings of the Church is the distinctive shift of emphasis which characterizes early Christian apocalyptic and which Hermas faithfully represents"); Bell, "Critical Evaluation," 27–56; Klassen, "Reexamination of the Nature," 6; and Boyd, "Dispensational Premillennial Analysis," 107–112 (regarding *Shepherd of Hermas* and the tribulation).

46. Grenz, *Millennial Maze,* 44; Erickson, *Christian Theology,* 1213.

47. Holwerda, "Eschatology and History," 312.

48. Ibid.

Premillennial eschatology: still alive

Some mystical sects and reform-minded orders within the Roman Catholic Church revived or kept premillennial ideas alive. Perhaps the most important medieval eschatological writer was the founder of a monastic order, Joachim of Fiore (c. 1132–1202). He rejuvenated the literal hermeneutic of Irenaeus and Hippolytus, against Jerome, Augustine, and Pope Gregory the Great (540–604). He historicized the book of Revelation, finding its symbols to refer to historical events implicating the whole history of the Church: past, present, and future. He also taught a literal one thousand year golden age to come after the defeat of the Antichrist.[49] Finally, Joachim implied that an evil pope would play the role of Antichrist, an idea that grew in the late Middle Ages and Reformation era, although such an idea had been voiced even in the late tenth century.[50]

Postmillennial eschatology: incipient

Some Medieval ideas have certain commonalities with later postmillennialism.[51] The progress of the church would be gradual, but it would be sure. In fact, Erickson states, "It is likely that postmillennialism and amillennialism simply were not differentiated for much of the first nineteen centuries of the church."[52]

Amillennialism has continued to be the dominant eschatological position since the Reformation, but the Reformation era unleashed new ideas that led to the rise of other eschatological views

During the Reformation the "magisterial reformers" (Lutherans and Reformed groups) generally followed Augustine with respect to eschatology. The "radical reformers" (Anabaptists) emphasized the expectation of Christ's earthly reign.[53] As a result of extremist actions by some Anabaptists, both Catholics and Protestants rejected millenarianism as heretical.[54] Even the Second Helvetic [Zwinglian, Swiss Reformed] Confession of 1566, which "occupies the first rank among the Reformed Confessions" and has been described as "scriptural and catholic, wise and judicious, full and elaborate, yet simple and clear,"[55] rejects "the Jewish dream of a millennium, or golden age on earth, before the last judgment."[56] However, the Reformation set in motion events that would profoundly affect eschatological views in ironic ways long after the Reformation era itself was over.

---

49. McGinn, *Anti-Christ*, 137.

50. Ibid., 7, 100, 142–72.

51. Grenz, *Millennial Maze*, 46.

52. Erickson, *Christian Theology,* 1219; see also at 1213–14.

53. Erickson, *Contemporary Options,* 97.

54. Grenz, *Millennial Maze*, 51.

55. Schaff, *Creeds of Christendom,* 1:394–95.

56. "Second Helvetic" 1990: 404.

Luther's eschatology

Although he maintained an amillennial position, in two ways Martin Luther's (1483–1546) eschatology substantially advanced matters beyond the medieval consensus. First, although John Wycliffe (c. 1320–1384) had first identified the papacy itself (as opposed to an evil individual pope) as Antichrist, the mainspring for the ascendancy of the "papacy as antichrist" position proved to be Martin Luther.[57] This view became a standard part of Protestant belief.[58] It is based on Roman Catholic canon law concerning the pope, which holds, "By virtue of his office he possesses supreme, full, immediate, and universal ordinary power in the Church, which he is always able to exercise freely,"[59] and "No appeal or recourse is permitted against a sentence or decree of the Roman Pontiff."[60] The pope's own chief theologian, Sylvester Prierias, had written, "A *Pontifex indubitatus*[61] cannot lawfully be deposed or judged either by council or by the whole world, even if he is so scandalous as to lead people with him by crowds into the possession of hell."[62] Luther responded, "Be astonished, O heaven; shudder, O earth! Behold, O Christians, what Rome is!" and "It must, therefore, have been the chief devil himself who said what is written in the canon law, that if the pope were so scandalously bad as to lead crowds of souls to the devil, still he could not be deposed."[63]

Second, "In keeping with his antipapal polemic, Luther altered his interpretation of Revelation, as he came to see in it a prophecy of the history of the church. Consequently, he sought to match the various symbols in the book with events of church history. . . . He did not anticipate a future era of peace and righteousness on the earth, but rather saw the biblical vision of the golden age as being fulfilled, beginning in the patristic era and concluding with the triumph of the papacy."[64] That historicist view of Revelation remained the standard Protestant view for at least the next two hundred years.[65]

Roman Catholic eschatological responses to Luther

In trying to refute Luther's identification of the papacy with Antichrist, Roman Catholic theologians (primarily Jesuits), including Robert Bellarmine (1542–1621), Francis

---

57. The papacy-as-antichrist idea "became a central tenet of the Lollard movement" (mid-fourteenth-century English religious and social movement inspired by Wycliffe) and "among the radical Hussites [Czech followers of John Hus (c. 1369–1415)] . . . became a part of a revolutionary ideology that encouraged overthrowing the social and religious order." McGinn, *Anti-Christ*, 182, 187. Since Wycliffe and Hus were betrayed and killed, and the Lollards and Hussites were largely suppressed, once he accepted this view Martin Luther advanced it with fierce conviction. Ibid., 201–02.

58. McGinn, *Anti-Christ*, 202; Grenz, *Millennial Maze*, 50. Although that view has lost much of its appeal, a contemporary variant—the Roman Catholic Church is the "whore of Babylon" (Rev 17:1–18)—is advocated by Dave Hunt in *A Woman Rides the Beast* (Eugene, OR: Harvest House, 1994).

59. Canon 331.

60. Canon 333 §3.

61. I.e., a pope not accused of heresy or schism.

62. Luther 1970: 18n.28.

63. Ibid., 18, 18n.28.

64. Grenz, *Millennial Maze*, 50–51.

65. Ibid., 51.

Suarez (1548–1617), and Francis Ribera (1537–1591), reintroduced the medieval *futurist* rendering of Antichrist. They contended that Antichrist was an individual who would conclude history.[66] Other Catholic apologists took the opposite approach. Although certain partial-preterist ideas are implicit in the NT, the first systematic preterist exposition of prophecy was written by the Spanish Jesuit Luis De Alcasar (1554–1613) during the Counter-Reformation. Alcasar "contended that the Apocalypse describes the twofold war of the church in the early centuries—one with the Jewish synagogue, and the other with paganism—resulting in victory over both adversaries."[67] He viewed the New Jerusalem as the Roman Catholic Church. Thus, Ribera thrust Antichrist into the future, whereas Alcasar pushed Antichrist back into the early centuries of Christianity. Both moves served to insulate the papacy from being identified with the Antichrist, which the Protestants had done.

The rise and decline of postmillennialism

Even in the ancient church, some had views which contained "the germs for later full-fledged Postmillennialism."[68] Kenneth Gentry sees incipient postmillennialism in some of the writings of Origen (c. 185–254), Eusebius (c. 263–339), Athanasius (296–372), and Augustine (354–430).[69] In later centuries, the Roman Catholic Joachim of Fiore (c. 1132–1202) and others in the thirteenth and fourteenth centuries held proto-postmillennial views.[70] Following the Reformation, John Calvin (1509–1564) held seemingly postmillennial views.[71]

Postmillennialism was developed in the seventeenth century by Lutheran and Reformed theologians who advocated a more spiritual conception of the millennium.[72] However, postmillennialism's "most important systematizer" was English Puritan Thomas Brightman (1562–1607); its most important popularizer was Anglican Daniel Whitby (1638–1726).[73] Although neither the Augsburg nor the Westminster Confessions (the

---

66. McGinn, *Anti-Christ*, 226–28; Grenz, *Millennial Maze*, 51.

67. Froom, *Prophetic Faith*, 2:507; see also McGinn, *Anti-Christ*, 228.

68. Kromminga, *Millennium*, 76. For an historical overview of eschatological thought similar to this one, see Mathison, *Postmillennialism*, 23–53. As a postmillennialist, Mathison discusses important postmillennialists in somewhat greater detail than is done here.

69. Gentry, *Dominion*, 80–87.

70. Ibid., 87–88.

71. Ibid., 88–89 see also Mathison, *Postmillennialsim*, 38–40; Bahnsen, *Victory*, 93–100. Calvin has never been particularly noted for his eschatology. The one NT book notable by its absence from his commentaries is Revelation. W. Gary Crampton says, "Calvin is claimed by advocates of both postmillennialism and amillennialism. . . . Some postmillennialists have called Calvin's millennial view 'incipient postmillennialism.' Others refer to him as an 'optimistic' amillennialist." Crampton, *What Calvin Says*, 102. David Holwerda, in his analysis of Calvin's eschatology, arrives at this conclusion: "Calvin's view of history is hopeful rather than optimistic, because he believed that the power of the kingdom of God would continually defeat the power of evil. But until that final return of Christ when God will be all in all, there will always be constant turmoil, conflict, and suffering." Holwerda, "Eschatology and History," 336.

72. Berkhof, *Christian Doctrines*, 263–64.

73. Gentry, *Dominion*, 77–78, 89–91. Interestingly, Brightman was strongly Calvinistic and Whitby was strongly Arminian.

basic creedal statements of the Lutheran and Reformed churches) includes an explicit statement concerning millennialism, the Savoy Declaration of 1658, which modified the Westminister Confession in accord with Congregational practice, does include an explicitly postmillennial provision.[74]

The close link of Ribera's and other Catholic apologists' *futurism* "led English Puritans in the seventeenth century to reject the futurist hermeneutic *en masse.*"[75] Among the Puritans and post-Puritans in England and America from the seventeenth–nineteenth centuries, the dominant eschatological position was postmillennialism. Postmillennialism "steeled confidence in progress, and specifically it reinforced the secular version of progress inherited from the Enlightenment."[76] James Turner found that "Evangelicals expected that progress toward the millennial day would come through the same technical and scientific advances on which secular reformers pinned their hopes."[77] It is not surprising that postmillennialism therefore developed in a new, more secular, form—a new, just, social order—among liberals in the nineteenth century.[78]

Postmillennialism's influence waned considerably, especially after the world wars and tragedies of the twentieth century showed that society, even in supposedly "Christian" countries, was in many respects not getting better.[79] However, in recent years postmillennialism has experienceed a renaissance and has largely been coupled with partial preterism in the writings of such scholars as J. Marcellus Kik, David Chilton, Kenneth Gentry, Keith Mathison, and Greg Bahnsen.

The rise and decline of dispensational premillennialism

The rise of dispensational premillennialism

Historic, futuristic premillennialism began to gain increasing numbers of advocates and adherents beginning in the late 1700s.[80] A completely new and different system of futurism—dispensationalism—began in the 1830s. Dispensationalism usually traces its origins to the Plymouth Brethren movement in England. The Brethren were a separatist group, highly critical of the organized church.[81] Dispensationalism embraced futurist

---

74. *Savoy Declaration,* ch. 26, sec. 5.

75. Grenz, *Millennial Maze,* 52.

76. Turner, *Without God,* 87.

77. Ibid., 88.

78. Berkhof, *Christian Doctrines,* 264; Bloch, *Visionary Republic,* 131; Turner, *Without God,* 88–89.

79. Donald Dayton makes an interesting observation about the different millennial schools' views of the world: "Those conditioned to think that Evangelical theological discussions are resolved exclusively by scriptural exegesis would be astonished to discover the extent to which resolution of these eschatological issues depended upon matters of taste and perceptions of the direction in which the world was moving. Much of the appeal in the argumentation was to empirical evidence. The postmillennialists pointed to the progress of foreign missions and the spread of literacy to prove that the world was in fact getting better and better. Premillennialists, on the other hand, cited the rise of crime and social problems, often primarily in the cities, as evidence that the world was growing more evil." Dayton, *Evangelical Heritage,* 126–27.

80. Bloch, *Visionary Republic,* 130–39; Turner, *Without God,* 87.

81. Grenz, *Millennial Maze,* 60; Rowden, "The Brethren," 526.

premillennialism, a focus on Israel, and the "pretribulational rapture" of the church, as the hallmarks of its eschatology. Dispensationalism grew rapidly in popularity, especially among American fundamentalist churches. It is "very popular today in the more conservative Baptist movements and is almost universally accepted among independent, fundamental [and Pentecostal] churches."[82] The birth of the modern state of Israel in 1948 was instrumental in the acceptance of dispensationalism.[83]

The decline of dispensational premillennialism

Beginning in the 1980s, even dispensationalists have recognized that various aspects of traditional dispensationalism are biblically indefensible. This has led to the rise of what is known as "progressive dispensationalism," led by such men as Craig Blaising, Darrell Bock, and Robert Saucy. Progressive dispensationalists have endeavored to bring dispensationalism closer to historical Christianity while, at the same time, not abandoning such dispensational *sine qua non* as the sharp Israel-church distinction and the pretribulational rapture. Others have seen that effort as an attempt to "square the circle" and have left dispensationalism entirely. Grenz observes that "the dominance of this viewpoint—at least in its classical expression—may be on the wane, just as the fate of other eschatological systems in previous eras."[84]

Part of the reason for the decline of dispensational premillennialism may lie in dispensationalists' "remarkable ingenuity in adapting their message to current historical fears, especially since the 1960s."[85] The Nazi-Soviet pact of 1939, the Soviet Union after World War II, the founding of modern Israel in 1948, the rise of the European Common Market and European Community, the disintegration of the Soviet Union and the rise of radical Islam, Saddam Hussein and Babylon, "Y2K," and other political and economic actors and events, all have been seen by dispensationalists as the fulfillment of biblical prophecy and the malevolent harbingers of the "end times."[86]

However, typically when one such candidate of prophetic fulfillment passes from the scene and a new one takes its place, dispensationalists never admit (or even mention) their error in having found prophetic significance in the no-longer viable candidate. In discussing dispensationalist pronouncements concerning the actors and events surrounding World War II, for example, Timothy Weber notes that "premillennialists had shown more enthusiasm than accuracy in their interpretations of the roles of Italy, Germany, and Russia before and during the war. Their leaders were confident *that* biblical prophecy was being fulfilled, but events kept forcing them to reevaluate their interpretations of *how* it was being fulfilled. One is struck by how forgiving and forgetful the premillennialist rank and file must have been during this period. They stuck by their leaders even when

---

82. Erickson, *Contemporary Options*, 97.

83. See Grenz, *Millennial Maze*, 62; McGinn, *Anti-Christ*, 255–56; Boyer, *When Time*, 187–95.

84. Grenz, *Millennial Maze*, 63; see also Weber, *Living in the Shadow*, 241–42; Gentry, *Dominion*, 38–41.

85. McGinn, *Anti-Christ*, 257; see also Oropeza, *99 Reasons*, 87–89 for examples of how dispensationalist date-setters are "flexible" in their calculations.

86. See McGinn, *Anti-Christ*, 257–60; Gentry, *Dominion*, 39–41; Wilson, *Armageddon Now*, 216; Oropeza, *99 Reasons*, 72–112, 148–66.

they misread the signs of the times. The leaders themselves seemed little deterred by their mistakes."[87]

Stephen Sizer observes that the same thing continues to occur today:

> Hal Lindsey insisted that Russia's place in history was predicted in the Bible. . . . As Russia declined, Lindsey switched his emphasis to Islamic fundamentalism. While *The Late Great Planet Earth* (1970) suggested that we were threatened by 'The Russian force', in the *Oracle Commentaries* (2006), that had morphed into a 'Russian-Syrian-Iranian Axis'. . . . Charles Dyer's *The Rise of Babylon: Sign of the End Times* indeed suggested that Babylon would be rebuilt before the final battle of Armageddon, and he showed how Saddam Hussein was apparently rebuilding it. The cover shows Saddam in uniform, in front of a statue of Nebuchadnezzar. With Saddam's untimely demise, events in Iraq do not appear to be heading in the predicted direction. In 2004, Dyer's sequel presents a toppled Saddam alongside an image of the new enemy—Osama Bin Laden. The actors may change, but the same confident assurance of "Bible prophecy coming true" remains.[88]

The issue goes beyond the credibility of the specific predictions and interpretations of current events, to the credibility of the underlying theology and methodology. "When Hal Lindsey, for example, claims that the 1980s are the 'terminal decade' in human history and that 'all these things' must come to pass within a generation of the founding of the state of Israel, he is placing [dispensational] premillennialism's credibility on the line."[89] In his study of the premillenarian response to Russia and Israel since 1917, Dwight Wilson similarly concludes, "The premillenarians' credibility is at a low ebb because they succumbed to the temptation to exploit every conceivably possible prophetic fulfillment. . . . It is not likely that the situation will change greatly."[90] One can only "cry wolf" so many times before people start questioning not only one's conclusions but also one's underlying theological presuppositions and methodology.

The contemporary situation

The amillennial position has continued to be the major eschatological position among Anglicans, Presbyterians, Lutherans, Methodists, Roman Catholics, and Eastern Orthodox since the post-Reformation era. Premillennialism, divided into its dispensational and historic varieties, remains the dominant eschatological view among Baptists, Pentecostals, and other Evangelicals, although Evangelicals are now looking much more favorably on amillennialism than in the past.[91] Postmillennialism is held primarily in the Reformed camp. Full preterism received its first systematic expression by J. Stewart Russell in his

87. Weber, *Living in the Shadow*, 201–02.

88. Sizer, *Zion's Christian Soldiers*, 31–32. See also Pate and Haines, *Doomsday Delusions*, 133–38; Oropeza, *99 Reasons*, 86–112 (reasons why no one knows the date of the end based on current world affairs).

89. Weber, *Living in the Shadow*, 242; see also Gentry, *Dominion*, 39–41. This is particularly true since Lindsey is "the most widely read writer on prophetic themes in history." Weber, *Living in the Shadow*, 211.

90. Wilson, *Armageddon Now*, 218.

91. See Grenz, *Millennial Maze*, 150.

book *The Parousia,* first published in 1878. It is believed by a relatively small number but is being actively promoted by several authors including Don Preston, Max King, John Noe, Ed Stevens, and Gene Fadeley. Partial-preterism has been systematized by several scholars (see above regarding the coupling of partial preterism and postmillennialism), and finds acceptance among many amillennialists and postmillennialists. The major views concerning the "millennium" will, therefore, be considered next.

7

The Millennium

Overview of major millennial positions[1]

THERE ARE SIGNIFICANT DIFFERENCES between historic and dispensational premillennialism, particularly over the *nature* of the "millennium." However, both historic and dispensational premillennialism have certain beliefs in common.[2] Likewise, there are significant differences between postmillennialism and amillennialism over both the timing and nature of the "millennium." However, both of these positions also have certain beliefs in common.

Essential beliefs of both premillennialist positions	*Essential beliefs of both non-premillennialist positions*
1. The "1000 years" is a discrete period of time in the future, which follows Christ's second coming. It may not be exactly 1000 years, but it is a discrete and special period of time.	1. Christ's second coming follows the "1000 years" of Rev 20:2–7.
2. There will be two bodily resurrections and two judgments: the resurrection and judgment of believers at the time of the second coming; and the resurrection and judgment of "the rest of the dead" at the end of the 1000 years.	2. There will be one general resurrection and judgment of all people, both believers and unbelievers, at the time of the second coming.

---

1. Historic premillennialism, dispensational premillennialism, postmillennialism, and amillennialism also are summarized in a comparative table in Appendix 1: The Four Basic Millennial Views.

2. Although his is a premillennial position, J. Webb Mealy's "new creation millennialism" (discussed later in this chapter) accepts the amillennial position with respect to point 8 in the table comparing premillennialist and non-premillennialist positions and significantly differs from both the historic and dispensational premillennial positions with respect to points 4–7.

Essential beliefs of both premillennialist positions	Essential beliefs of both non-premillennialist positions
3. Revelation is essentially chronological. Specifically, the events of Revelation 20 chronologically follow those of Revelation 19.	3. There is chronological movement within Revelation, but the visions of that book are largely parallel accounts of similar events with different emphases. Specifically, Revelation 20 recapitulates, rather than follows, the major events of Revelation 19.
4. Non-resurrected people in their natural bodies and resurrected people in their glorified bodies will co-exist after the second coming during the "millennium."	4. Non-resurrected people in their natural bodies and resurrected people in their glorified bodies will not co-exist after the second coming.
5. Both human sin and physical death will continue to exist for 1000 years after Christ's second coming.	5. Both human sin and physical death will not continue to exist after Christ's second coming.
6. Unbelievers will still have the opportunity to come to faith in Christ for 1000 years after his return.	6. Unbelievers will not have the opportunity to come to faith in Christ after his return.
7. The natural creation will continue for 1000 years after Christ's second coming and will be subjected to the curse imposed by the fall of man, although it will be modified.	7. The natural creation and the curse imposed by the fall of man will not continue after Christ's second coming. Instead, Christ's second coming will bring with it the renewal of creation and the removal of the curse.
8. The new heavens and new earth will not be introduced until 1000 years after the return of Christ.	8. The new heavens and new earth will be introduced at the return of Christ.

Historic premillennialism

Essential beliefs of historic premillennialism

Historic premillennialists look for two clusters of end-times events: (1) The second coming follows a great worsening of persecution of Christians (the "tribulation"); it results in the binding of Satan and initiates Christ's millennial reign on the earth. During the millennium, glorified saints and unredeemed, natural people (survivors of the "battle of Armageddon" and of Christ's *parousia*) will co-exist. (2) After the millennium, Satan is freed, which results in a great rebellion against Christ. Christ then destroys all his enemies, carries out the final judgment, and initiates the eternal state (the new heavens and new earth).[3] Historic premillennialists view the millennium as part of the way in which Christ puts all his enemies under his feet, as manifesting publicly his reign (that now is visible only to the eye of faith), and/or as revealing the sinfulness in the hearts of people and thereby vindicating God's justice at the final judgment.[4]

---

3. Ladd, "Historic Premillennialism," 17–18.
4. Ibid., 39–40; see also Schnabel, *40 Questions*, 276–77.

Biblical bases of historic premillennialism

Rev 20:1–6

Leading historic premillennialist spoksman George Eldon Ladd holds that any doctrine of the millennium must be based on the NT and be consistent with Christ's present reign.[5] Only Rev 20:2–7 mentions the "thousand years" (millennium). Thus, Ladd's view is based almost entirely on his exegesis of Rev 20:4–6, which deals with the reign of the saints and the "two resurrections." Particularly important is the Greek verb *ezēsan* ("they lived" or "they came to life"), found in Rev 20:4–5. He concludes that, since the same word applies both to those of the *"first resurrection"* and to *"the rest of the dead who did not come to life until the thousand years were completed,"* it must mean the same thing in each case, namely, bodily resurrections separated by an intervening thousand years.[6] Historic premillennialists see the events depicted in Revelation 19–20 as being chronologically sequential.

Other OT and NT passages

Some historic premillennialists look to certain OT passages (e.g., Ps 72:8–14; Isa 11:6–11; 65:17–25; Zech 14:5–17) which, if taken literally, seem to suggest a future stage in the history of redemption that is greater than the present age but still does not see the removal of all sin and death from the earth. A NT passage along the same lines is Rev 2:26–27. Some cite 1 Cor 15:22–24 as implying a three-fold series of resurrections: (1) Christ the first fruits; (2) then those who belong to him; (3) then "the end" (which they interpret as "everybody else").[7]

Critique of historic premillennialism

The "binding of Satan"

On the surface, the premillennialist exegesis of Rev 19:11—20:6 appears to have the advantage of seemingly being the more natural reading regarding chronological sequence, the "binding of Satan" as implying a greater restriction on his activities than is apparent to us now, and the nature of the "two resurrections." On the other hand, premillennialist exegesis does not take into account the pattern of recapitulation throughout the book of Revelation or the many indications that Rev 19:11—20:6 are not chronologically sequential but are parallel and recapitulative. Premillennialist exegesis of Rev 20:4–6 also has not dealt with the verbal indicator (the use of "first" with "resurrection") that signifies *contrast* of dissimilar things, not sequence of similar things.[8]

---

5. Ladd, "Historic Premillennialism," 29–32.

6. Ibid., 32–38.

7. See, e.g., Zaspel, "The Kingdom," n.p.

8. For a detailed discussion of these points see Appendix 2: The Millennium: An Amillennial Synthesis of the Biblical Data.

The "two ages"

Premillennialism faces the serious challenge of being contrary to the overall biblical eschatological structure of the "two ages." Waldron asks, "Where in the two-age structure can the millennium be placed? Shall it be put in *this age* or in *the age to come*? The fact is that it fits into neither age. Why does it not fit in *this age*? Because the millennium occurs after Christ's second coming. Why does it not fit in *the age to come*? Because no wicked men in an unresurrected condition remain in that age. When we remember that there is no intermediate period between the two ages and no other period beside the two ages, no place for premillennialism remains."[9] This is, of course, indicated by the language the Bible uses to describe the time in which we live since Christ's first coming: these are the "last days," which indicates that there are no days *in history* to follow—"no millennium that will introduce another grand redemptive era in man's history. . . . The idea of the appearance of Christ as the 'Last Adam' (1 Cor. 15:45) is indicative that there is no different historical age to follow."[10]

The second coming

Premillennialism's view of the *parousia* is seriously inadequate. It turns the second coming, which is the climax of this age and of history, into an anti-climax. The *parousia* brings with it the resurrection and judgment of all people, the destruction or cleansing of the world and the restoration of creation, the end of "this age," the beginning of the "age to come," and the inauguration of God's perfect and eternal kingdom.[11] Premillennialism qualifies, downplays, minimizes, or denies every one of those fundamental aspects of the *parousia*.

For example, according to Paul, Christ's final enemy is death. This last enemy is destroyed at the *parousia* of Christ (1 Cor 15:25–26, 50–55).[12] The destruction of death at the *parousia* is consistent with the clear NT teaching that "Christ is coming back in the fullness of his glory to usher in, not an interim period of qualified peace and blessing, but the final state of unqualified perfection."[13] Premillennialism contradicts the essential nature of the *parousia* because it teaches that death is not destroyed until the end of the millennial reign of Christ, a full thousand years after the *parousia*.[14]

---

9. Waldron, "Structural Considerations," n.p.

10. Gentry, *Dominion*, 327.

11. See above, chapter 5–The Eschatological Significance of Christ's Second Coming.

12. Lincoln, *Paradise Now*, 66; Venema, *Promise*, 250. Additionally, 1 Cor 1:7–8 "brings together the revelation (*apokalypsis*) of our Lord Jesus Christ, the end [*to telos*], and the day of our Lord Jesus Christ." Strimple, "Amillennialism," 110. "The point is that the 'end' does not come, say, a thousand years after the second coming; for Paul, the second coming *is* the end." Davis, *Christ's Victorious Kingdom*, 57. In Matt 24:14, Christ himself equated "the end" [*to telos*] with the *parousia*. For these and other reasons, the idea that 1 Cor 15:22–24 implies a three-fold series of resurrections ending a thousand years after the *parousia* is incorrect. This is discussed in more detail in Appendix 7: 1 Cor 15:20–57: The Resurrection, the *Parousia*, and the Millennium.

13. Hoekema, *Bible and Future*, 185.

14. See Grenz, *Millennial Maze*, 143–44. This contradiction between the Bible and premillennialism goes to the heart of premillennialism, because the *sine qua non* of premillennialism is its view of

The inhabitants of the millennial kingdom

Premillennialism entails the belief that people in natural bodies and resurrected people will co-exist. However, that idea contradicts the very nature of Christ's second coming which begins the *"age to come,"* in which the temporal has passed away and which is the age of resurrection where there are no marriages or sexual relationships because people in that age are no longer mortal but are *"like angels, and are . . . sons of the resurrection"* (Luke 20:34–36). None of the passages that discuss the "two ages" hint at the possibility of glorified and natural people co-existing, and all such passages appear to contradict that idea.

Additionally, 1 Cor 15:50 tells us that *"flesh and blood cannot inherit the kingdom of God."* Jesus' kingdom parables tell us that all nonbelievers will be gathered out of the kingdom at the end of this age (Matt 13:41–43; 25:31–46). All believers will be raptured or resurrected and given glorified bodies at the second coming. According to Rev 19:21, *"everybody else was killed"* when Christ comes again. As Mealy clearly sees, "The sense of these words is as plain as it is consistent with the pattern leading up to them: no one on earth survives the confrontation with the returning Christ."[15] To the same effect is Rev 6:12–17 which is "the first of many scenes in Revelation depicting the coming in judgment of God and the Lamb. . . . The key point, in regard to Rev. 6:12–17, is that it depicts no room for earthly survivors in the great crisis of God's and Christ's intervention to judge humanity on the earth."[16] Consequently, no unglorified human beings remain to enter an earthly millennial kingdom.[17]

The nature of the millennial kingdom

Premillennialism asserts that after Christ returns in all his glory at the *parousia* he will have to rule his enemies with a "rod of iron" and will have to crush a final rebellion at the end of the millennium. This is a fatal problem for all forms of premillennialism. Kim Riddlebarger discusses this:

> The most serious problem to be faced by all premillenarians is the presence of evil in the millennial age. . . . The last day has already come, and our Lord has raised his own and sent those who are not his into the fires of eternal judgment. There simply cannot be people in unresurrected bodies on the earth after our Lord's return, for the wheat has already been separated from the weeds (Matt. 13:37–43), the sheep have already been separated from the goats (Matt. 25:31–46), and the elect have already been gathered from the four corners of the earth by the angelic host (Matt. 24:30–31).[18]

---

the "thousand-year" (as opposed to everlasting) earthly reign of Christ following the *parousia*. See Bell, "Critical Evaluation," 85, 136; Grenz, *Millennial Maze*, 141–42.

15. Mealy, *After the Thousand Years*, 91; see also Schnabel, *40 Questions*, 237.

16. Mealy, *New Creation*, 51.

17. With respect to premillennialist attempts to solve this problem by claiming that the nations of Rev 20:3 are survivors of the battle of Rev 19:19–21, or that only armies were killed and the survivors are those who supported, but were not actual members of, the armies, see Appendix 2: The Millennium: An Amillennial Synthesis of the Biblical Data.

18. Riddlebarger, *Amillennialism*, 86–87.

How extensive is this problem? Premillennialists conceive of the millennium as a "golden age" of peace and "political, social, and economic righteousness" under the rule of Christ.[19] However, such a state is, at best, only superficial. Death and crime will continue to exist, and people who are "openly rebellious will be put to death."[20] The church "will be the enforcers of righteousness. . . . There will be an ironclad rule of righteousness over the world. People who have survived the Great Tribulation and enter into the Kingdom Age will not be allowed to live in greed or sin. They will be ruled over with a rod of iron."[21]

The problem, inherent in premillennialism, is that it does not recognize the epoch-changing significance of the *parousia* and the change from "this age" to the "age to come." It does not appreciate that the fundamental transformation of the ages (corporate eschatology) entails a fundamental transformation of people (individual eschatology). Instead, all forms of premillennialism insist that, following the second coming and all it entails, people and their fundamentally sinful nature will remain as they are now. The power of indwelling sin, which so corrupts humanity today,[22] will continue to indwell and corrupt people in this supposedly new, Christ-centered "golden age."

Premillennialist Ladd admits that "even in such a society the hearts of men remain rebellious and respond to the devil when he is released."[23] John Phillips explains:

> Children born during this age will be born with sinful natures, needing to be saved, just as today. Children of believing parents today sometimes become gospel-hardened; so, during the Millennium many will become glory-hardened. They will submit to Christ's rule and to the stern laws of the kingdom because to rebel will mean instant punishment. During the Millennium, many will render only feigned obedience. . . . Thus, many will abide by the laws of the kingdom only because they have to. Sin will reign in secret in their hearts, and they will long for the time when the strict rules will be relaxed. The devil will find fertile soil in their souls.[24]

As a result, even during this supposed "golden age," "a special, millennial missionary effort" will be required.[25] Premillennialist G. R. Beasley-Murray agrees and contends that the reference in Rev 20:6 to Christians acting as "priests" in the millennium "hints that there is a ministry for them to perform in that age amongst earth's inhabitants, perhaps with especial reference to evangelism."[26] Nevertheless, when Satan is released, he is able

---

19. Ladd, *Last Things*, 110; see also Phillips, *Exploring Revelation*, 236–38.

20. Walvoord, *Millennial Kingdom*, 302, 316, 318–19; Smith, *What the World*, 184–85.

21. Smith, *What the World*, 185; see also Hoyt, *Dispensational Premillennialism*, 82, 92.

22. See, e.g., Gen 3:6–19; Ps 51:5; Rom 3:9–18; 5:12–21; 6:6; 7:14–25; Eph 4:22. The most thorough treatment of the power of indwelling sin is John Owen, *Indwelling Sin in Believers* (Grand Rapids: Baker, 1979).

23. Ladd, *Last Things*, 110.

24. Phillips, *Exploring Revelation*, 240; see also Pache, *Return*, 431; Walvoord, *Millennial Kingdom*, 302. Chuck Smith puts it this way, "Many people wouldn't have had a chance to make a real choice for Jesus Christ, because they were *forced to serve* Christ during the Millennium." Smith, *What the World*, 185, emphasis added.

25. Payne, *Encyclopedia*, 319.

26. Beasley-Murray, "The Revelation," 1306.

to gather together unsaved rebels against Christ, the number of whom *"is like the sand of the seashore"* (Rev 20:8)!

That entire scenario is completely contrary to the Bible's description of the nature of existence following Christ's second coming. The renewal of creation (e.g., *"the wolf will dwell with the lamb, and the leopard will lie down with the young goat,"* Isa 11:6–9) at the second coming is contrary to premillennialism because it means that the curse is removed. Rom 8:21 says that *"the creation itself also will be set free from its slavery to corruption."* That indicates a complete, not partial, removal of the curse and renewal of the earth. If the curse of the ground is removed then sin itself has been removed since the curse of nature was because of human sin (Gen 3:14–19; Rom 8:20–21). It also means that death has been removed because death was the result of human sin (Gen 2:17; Rom 5:12–14, 21). Thus, premillennialism divorces what God joined together by inconsistently maintaining that human beings in the millennium will still sin, rebel against God, and die, even though creation itself has been renewed and the curse removed.

Further, as Arthur Lewis points out, the idea inherent in premillennialism that the preaching of the gospel in the whole world as a testimony to all the nations (Matt 24:14) will not be completed by the end of this age or before the return of Christ "is patently contrary to the admonitions of Christ for all men to heed and believe now, before the judgment, when it will be too late (Matt. 13:37–39; 22:8–14; John 12:48). This view also denies the Lord's clearly stated intention that the age to come will be for the rewarding of the saints, not for an extension of evangelism to the lost (Matt. 25:31ff.)."[27] On the other hand, "When the 'thousand years' is understood to be coterminous with this day and age, the pieces all fall in place. Unbelief, sin, war, and death belong to the present and will intensify at the time of the 'great tribulation' just before the return of Christ. Therefore, the dark side of the millennium strongly suggests that it is not future but actual."[28]

Jesus and Paul

Since the millennium is so important, one would have expected Jesus and Paul to discuss it, or even mention it—but they never do. The Olivet Discourse[29] is Jesus' longest and most comprehensive discourse on eschatology; yet he never said anything about a millennium or millennial kingdom. First Cor 15:20–57 is Paul's longest and most comprehensive discourse on eschatology; yet he never said anything about a millennium or millennial kingdom. It is incredible to claim that a millennial kingdom will occur, when it is not mentioned where one would expect it to be mentioned if it existed. Indeed, the *entire corpus* of Paul's eschatological writing "contains no reference to a Messianic Kingdom."[30] Premillennialists maintain that the reference to the "thousand years" in Rev 20:2–7 is sufficient to establish the existence of a millennial kingdom. That would be true if Rev 20:2–7 could *only* be understood as teaching a temporary millennial kingdom after the *parousia*. However, that passage can reasonably be interpreted *not* to teach the existence of a future

27. Lewis, *Dark Side*, 17.

28. Ibid., 19.

29. Matthew 24–25; Mark 13; Luke 21:5–36; see also Luke 17:22–37.

30. Davies, *Paul and Rabbinic Judaism*, 297.

temporary millennial kingdom.[31] Therefore, better hermeneutics would interpret the passage consistent with the thrust of the rest of the NT.

Dispensational premillennialism

Differences between historic and dispensational premillennialism

Historic premillennialism and dispensational premillennialism are different eschatological systems.[32] Historic premillennialists dispute the radical distinction between Israel and the church, the hermeneutical principles that underlie dispensationalism, and much of dispensationalist exegesis. Dispensationalist Charles Ryrie admits, "All other views bring the Church into Israel's fulfilled prophecies except dispensationalism."[33] Historic premillennialist Ladd disputes dispensationalist "literalism": "It is difficult to understand the thousand years for which [Satan] was bound in strict literalness in view of the obvious symbolic use of numbers in Revelation."[34] He also disagrees with the dispensationalist understanding that the binding of Satan is "absolute": "This is obviously symbolic language describing a radical curbing of Satan's power and activities. . . . His incarceration in the abyss does not mean that all of his activities and powers are nullified, only that he may no longer deceive the nations as he has done through human history and lead them into active aggression against the saints during the thousand years."[35]

Essential beliefs of dispensational premillennialism

Dispensationalists look for three clusters of end-times events: (1) Christ will come for his church (the "pretribulational rapture") before the tribulation. (2) The second coming will follow the tribulation; it results in the binding of Satan and initiates Christ's millennial reign on the earth. (3) After the millennium, Satan is freed, which results in a great rebellion against Christ. Christ destroys all his enemies, carries out the final judgment, and initiates the eternal state (the new heavens and new earth).[36]

---

31. Recall "the existence of an early non-chiliastic interpretation of Rev. 20" and the fact that "a solidly entrenched and conservative, non-chiliastic eschatology was present in the Church to rival chiliasm from beginning to end." Hill, *Regnum Caelorum,* 260, 253. See Appendix 2: The Millennium: An Amillennial Synthesis of the Biblical Data.

32. Bell, "Critical Evaluation," 43–45; Boyd, "Dispensational Premillennial Analysis," 88–91; Riddlebarger, *Amillennialism,* 28.

33. Ryrie, *Dispensationalism Today,* 159.

34. Ladd, *Commentary,* 262.

35. Ibid. Amillennialists agree with Ladd on those points. E.g., Venema, *Promise,* 315–27.

36. Probably the most comprehensive and standard text of classical dispensational premillennialist eschatology is J. Dwight Pentecost, *Things to Come: A Study in Biblical Eschatology* (Grand Rapids: Zondervan, 1958).

Israel and the church

Dispensationalism holds that the Church and Israel are radically disconnected.[37] Stanley Grenz discusses this key distinction of all varieties of dispensationalism, "Traditionally dispensationalists have asserted that Israel is God's national people, whereas the church of Jesus Christ constitutes God's spiritual or heavenly people. . . . Dispensationalists of all varieties adamantly reject the contention that the church is the New Israel."[38] They believe that God's *primary* dealings are with the nation of Israel; the church is something like an after-thought or interruption in God's program concerning Israel. In fact, dispensationalist Harry Ironside even published a book in which he called the church the "Great Parenthesis" in God's eschatological plan.[39] Progressive dispensationalists have tried to soften these positions, speaking of a "united people of God" within which lie important differences and seeing the church and Israel as inaugurating the kingdom in two stages.[40] All dispensationalists believe that the unfulfilled OT national promises made to Israel are to be fulfilled "literally."[41]

The tribulation

Dispensationalists believe that neither the tribulation nor the millennium properly concerns the church. Rather, "the tribulation concerns Israel, not the church."[42] Dispensationalists believe that God will resume his involvement with Israel at the time of the rise of Antichrist. They foresee a seven-year tribulation primarily directed against Israel and hold that the church cannot be present on the earth during the tribulation. That leads to the dispensationalist idea of the "pretribulational rapture": the belief that Christ will come again part way to the earth exclusively for the church and "rapture" it away to heaven for seven years (or three and a half years for midtribulationalists). At the end of the tribulation, Christ will come again, this time all the way to the earth, and set up his millennial kingdom.

The millennium

The millennial kingdom is seen as the fulfillment of the OT promises to Israel. Thus, a dispensationalist millennium has a decidedly Jewish flavor in which the nation of Israel is dominant.[43] After the millennium, Satan will be freed, which results in a great rebellion against Christ. Christ will destroy all his enemies, carry out the final judgment, and initi-

37. Ryrie, *Dispensationalism Today,* 44–45, 137–40, 154–55.

38. Grenz, *Millennial Maze,* 95–96; see Pentecost, *Things to Come,* 201–02; MacDonald, *Believer's,* 2351.

39. Ironside, *Great Parenthesis,* 13.

40. Grenz, *Millennial Maze,* 102.

41. Ryrie, *Dispensationalism Today,* 96–98; see also Grudem, *Systematic Theology,* 1113–14.

42. Walvoord, *Rapture Question,* 62; see also Pentecost, *Things to Come,* 193, 197–98; Smith, *What the World,* 70; Higgins, *Manasseh Effect,* 51.

43. Hoyt, "*Dispensational Premillennialism,*" 63–92.

ate the eternal state.[44] Thus, dispensationalism not only necessitates "two second comings of Christ, but it sees a proliferation of resurrections and judgments as well—those for Israel and those for the church."[45]

Biblical bases of dispensational premillennialism

Revelation 19–20

Dispensationalists essentially agree with historic premillennialists' interpretation of Revelation 19–20 and those passages that historic premillennialists view as indicating that the millennium is a "hybrid age" that fits into neither this age nor the age to come.

A literal interpretation of the OT

Dispensationalists admit, "Premillennialism is founded principally on interpretation of the Old Testament."[46] Herman Hoyt concurs, "Little is said in the New Testament about the vast changes that will occur in this realm [i.e., in the millennial kingdom]. These must be found in Old Testament prophecy."[47] Dispensationalists think that all the promises given to OT Israel regarding the kingdom that were not fulfilled "literally" (i.e., physically) await fulfillment in the millennium. Those promises include: the primacy of Jerusalem and vicinity;[48] a real king will sit on a material throne (Isa 33:17); the curse will be lifted in part;[49] there will be a temple and temple sacrifices (Ezekiel 40–48); Israel will rule over the Gentile nations;[50] yearly pilgrimages to Jerusalem will be required and Jewish feast days reinstituted;[51] retribution against anyone violating the law will be swift and harsh.[52]

Dan 9:24–27

This is a foundational passage for dispensationalism. Christian interpreters generally have taken Daniel's "seventy weeks" to refer to seventy periods of seven years, or a total of 490 years, dealing with God's plan for Israel which culminated in the first coming of the Messiah (Jesus Christ). The traditional, conservative Christian view of the passage holds that

---

44. Boyd, "Dispensational Premillennial Analysis," 4–13.

45. Bell, "Critical Evaluation," 4.

46. Walvoord, *Millennial Kingdom*, 114. A historic premillennialist like George Ladd disagrees with John Walvoord's statement. See Ladd, "Historic Premillennialism," 29–32. Walvoord apparently was equating premillennialism with *dispensational* premillennialism.

47. Hoyt, *"Dispensational Premillennialism,"* 92.

48. Isa 2:3; 24:23; Obad 12–21.

49. Isa 32:15–16; 35:1–2, 7; 65:20–23.

50. Deut 28:1, 13; Isa 41:8–16; 60:1–3, 12.

51. Zech 8:18–23; 14:16–19.

52. Isa 11:3–4; Mal 3:1–5. Hoyt says, "It will be necessary to exercise a stern and inflexible rule of righteousness to control sin and perpetuate the virtues of this kingdom." Hoyt, *"Dispensational Premillennialism,"* 92.

Daniel's "seventy weeks" are an unbroken group. The sixty-ninth week ends with Christ's baptism. He then ratifies the New Covenant and is "cut off" (crucified) in the middle of the seventieth week.

The dispensationalist interpretation is fundamentally different from the historic Christian view, as Grenz describes: "When Israel rejected Jesus, 'God's prophetic clock' was stopped . . . and consequently the church program, which was unknown in the Old Testament, was inaugurated. One future day the church phase of God's program will be completed, and the church will be raptured. That great event will commence the restarting of God's prophetic clock to tick off the seventieth week of Daniel's prophecy, which is the seven-year tribulation period."[53]

Critique of dispensational premillennialism

The critique of historic premillennialism also applies to dispensational premillennialism. Further, dispensationalism is subject to several additional criticisms.[54]

The nature of the millennium

Dispensationalism's idea of the nature of the millennium is without basis. Dispensationalists think that the purpose of the earthly millennium is to fulfill OT promises to Israel. Thus, the dispensationalist version of the millennium restores Israel to its land and, in fact, exalts the nation of Israel above all other nations. Jesus will rule from an earthly throne in Jerusalem, akin to king David, as an all-powerful earthly potentate. Hoekema astutely notes the vast amount of eschatological data concocted by dispensationalists from the key passage that deals with the "millennial reign," Rev 20:4–6:

> If this is to be the purpose of the millennium, is it not passing strange that Revelation 20:4–6 says not a word about the Jews, the nation of Israel, the land of Palestine, or Jerusalem? This would not be so serious if the idea of the restoration of Israel were only an incidental aspect of the millennium. But, according to dispensational teaching, the restoration of Israel is the *central purpose* of the millennium! It is therefore all the more significant that nothing of this alleged central purpose is mentioned in the only biblical passage which deals directly with Christ's millennial reign, Revelation 20:4–6. We conclude that dispensational premillennialism must be rejected as a system of biblical interpretation which is not in harmony with Scripture.[55]

53. Grenz, *Millennial Maze*, 104; see Ice, "Old Testament," 84–87. For a detailed discussion of the major views concerning Dan 9:24–27, see Appendix 5: Dan 9:24–27 (the "seventy weeks").

54. A critique of dispensationalism's doctrine of the pretribulational rapture is in chapter 10–The "Rapture": Pretribulational or Part of the Second Coming?

55. Hoekema, *Bible and Future*, 221–22.

The Israel-church dichotomy

Dispensationalism's rigid distinction between Israel and the church and the primacy it gives to Israel are unbiblical. Dispensationalism misses the truly significant biblical distinction concerning Israel: the distinction between the unbelieving nation and the faithful remnant. Erickson comments on the highly selective nature of dispensationalist passage-selection used to bolster their system, "Dispensationalists have carefully selected passages that favor (or at least can accommodate) their interpretation. Other passages, however, are not so easily disposed of. In Romans 9 and Galatians 3, for example, it is difficult to escape the conclusion that Paul regarded the church, Jew and Gentile alike, as the true heir to the promises originally made to national Israel."[56] In Eph 2:11–22 Gentiles are described as having been *"excluded from the commonwealth"* and *"strangers to the covenants"* (2:12). However, 2:19 says that "in Christ" the Gentiles *"are no longer strangers and aliens, but are fellow citizens with the [Jewish] saints."* The passage is clear that, as Bell remarks, "Believing Gentiles, members of the church, have been admitted as citizens to the commonwealth of Israel, from which they had been aliens previously, and thus share in the covenants made by God with Israel in Old Testament times. There is no doubt that this commonwealth has undergone a transformation, but the continuity remains."[57]

To hold that the church is a "parenthesis" of history is utterly false. Indeed, just the opposite is true. OT Israel, its laws, ceremonies, and institutions, were "types," "symbols," "shadows," "copies," or "examples" of NT realities that were fulfilled in Christ and his church.[58] Stanley Grenz concludes that "the New Testament clearly teaches that the church is neither a secondary nor a preliminary program, but the crowning product of all God's activity in history. . . . The New Testament presents the coming of Jesus to die for the sins of the world as the central, eternal plan of God. Christ's death—and consequently the founding of the church to proclaim the gospel of forgiveness through Christ—is not some second-order program subservient to God's working with Israel."[59] Thus, dispensationalism in general, and dispensationalist eschatology in particular, have the entire storyline of the Bible essentially backwards.

Progressive dispensationalists try to paper over the problem. However, the problem of the nature of the church vis-à-vis Israel is inherent in all forms of dispensationalism. The distinction made by progressive dispensationalists who "speak of Israel and the church as 'distinguishable covenant participants' who 'comprise differing peoples' . . . only serves to continue the dispensationalist denial that the church is the climax of the divine program inaugurated in the Old Testament."[60]

---

56. Erickson, *Contemporary Options*, 123.

57. Bell, "Critical Evaluation," 105; see also above, chapter 3, the section "Jesus' definition of 'restoration of the kingdom' signifies a redefinition of the true 'Israel.'"

58. Matt 5:17; 1 Cor 10:1–6; 2 Cor 3:12–16; Gal 3:23—4:7, 21–31; Col 2:16–17; Heb 1:1–2; 8:1—10:22; see above, chapter 3, particularly the section "Christ's first coming and the fulfillment of the OT eschatological prophecies concerning Israel."

59. Grenz, *Millennial Maze*, 123, 117; see also Baldwin, *Daniel*, 177.

60. Grenz, *Millennial Maze*, 117–18.

Progressive revelation

Dispensationalism fails to take progressive revelation seriously. The OT does not stand on its own. The NT provides us with *"the whole counsel of God"* (Acts 20:27). The NT is, in fact, the best commentary on the true meaning of the OT. Thus, it is "illegitimate to approach the Old Testament text as though the New Testament had not been written."[61] Just as dispensationalism sees the nation of Israel as the primary vehicle in God's redemptive plan and the church as a "parenthesis" rather than the culmination of that plan, so it sees the OT as primary and the NT as secondary in biblical interpretation, especially the interpretation of prophecy. Thus, dispensationalism essentially rejects the foundational hermeneutical principles of "progressive revelation" and the primacy of the NT in interpreting the OT.

The problem of dispensationalism is fundamentally a hermeneutical one. Ladd observes that dispensationalism's fundamentally different hermeneutical presuppositions distinguish it from all other forms of Christianity: "Here is a basic watershed between a dispensational and a nondispensational theology. Dispensationalism forms its eschatology by a literal interpretation of the Old Testament and then fits the New Testament into it. A nondispensational eschatology forms its theology from the explicit teaching of the New Testament."[62] Ironically, therefore, despite having a serious and "high view" of the Bible, dispensationalism does not take the whole of biblical revelation seriously enough. William Everett Bell summarizes:

> The final test for the meaning of an Old Testament passage is not necessarily its literal meaning, but the meaning given to it by the inspired New Testament writers, whether that meaning be literal or typical. . . . The dispensationalist practice of deciding the meaning of a concept at its first embryonic appearance in the Old Testament, together with the refusal to expand, restrict or otherwise modify the concept in the light of additional and fuller subsequent revelation, must be rejected as an unacceptable hermeneutical method, because it must frequently distort New Testament revelation in order not to disturb a premature "literal" Old Testament interpretation, and thus it simply does not account satisfactorily for the totality of the Biblical data.[63]

Arbitrariness and inconsistency

Dispensationalism's supposedly "literal" hermeneutic is inherently arbitrary and inconsistent. Dispensationalists depart from "literalism" whenever necessary to save their system. For example, The OT made at least ten promises to Abraham and his descendants in OT Israel which were to last "forever":

61. Walker, *Jesus*, 313.

62. Ladd, "Historic Premillennialism," 27.

63. Bell, "Critical Evaluation," 131, 133. Graeme Goldsworthy similarly concludes: "Dispensationalism, along with some other forms of premillennialism, is a system of biblical theology that is flawed because it does not draw its interpretive presuppositions from the Bible. For example, it stresses that all prophecy is fulfilled in a literal sense. That is not according to the evidence of the New Testament, which interprets prophecy in the light of Christ." Goldsworthy, *Whole Bible*, 75–76.

- possession of the land of Canaan (Gen 13:15);

- circumcision (Gen 17:13);

- the feast of Passover (Exod 12:14);

- the feast of Unleavened Bread (Exod 12:17);

- the lampstand in the tabernacle (Exod 27:21);

- the Sabbath day (Exod 31:16–17);

- the Day of Atonement (Lev 16:29–30);

- the throne of David (2 Sam 7:13);

- the city of Jerusalem (1 Chron 23:25);

- Christ's personal rule in Jerusalem (Mic 4:7).

A consistent "literal" interpretation of those passages would require an unending Jewish national existence in the literal land of Canaan.

According to dispensationalism, however, the "literal" earthly promises made to Israel are not to be fulfilled by Abraham, or OT Israel, or believing Jews who have become a part of the Christian church, but are to be fulfilled only by the one generation of Israelites living at the time of the second coming, and then only for a thousand years (i.e., in the millennium). Bell concludes, "Whatever else may be said of this interpretation, which seems to be that of the leading contemporary dispensationalists, it is not literal. One thousand years is not forever and the New Jerusalem is not literal Canaan. Once again, it is seen that dispensationalists . . . modify their literalism in interpreting Old Testament prophecies in order not to contradict openly the plain teaching of the New Testament. . . . By such an admission, however, it would seem that dispensationalists have actually surrendered their case."[64]

---

64. Bell, "Critical Evaluation," 85, 136. Other examples of dispensationalism's abandoning its "literal" hermeneutic whenever necessary to save its system could be multiplied at length. One notable example is its interpretation of Ezekiel's vision of a new temple in Ezekiel 40–48. Dispensationalists believe that this is a "picture of the millennial Temple" that will be literally built. Scofield, *New Scofield*, 884n.1. The problem for dispensationalism is that Ezek 43:19–27 speaks specifically of animal sacrifices of young bulls, goats, and rams *"for a sin offering."* Despite the clear language of Ezekiel, *The New Scofield Reference Bible* claims that these animal sacrifices either will be "memorial in character [and] have no expiatory value," or "the reference to sacrifices is not to be taken literally, in view of the putting away of such offerings [by Christ's sacrifice on the cross], but is rather to be regarded as a presentation of the worship of redeemed Israel, in her own land and in the millennial Temple, using the terms with which the Jews were familiar in Ezekiel's day." Ibid., 888n.1. That admission, however, is fatal to dispensationalism and to its entire "literal" hermeneutical method of reading prophecy. Cornelis Venema comments, "The same reason that leads the dispensationalist to read the language about sacrifices in this passage in a non-literal way—because it would lead to conflict with other portions of Scripture—could equally well apply to other aspects of this prophecy." Venema, *Promise*, 285–86. Further, the text does not call for "memorial" sacrifices but for "sin offerings." As Stephen Sizer points out, "It is impossible to confuse or equate the sacrifice of a young bullock with a memorial offering, which consisted of grain and oil (Lev. 2:2, 9, 16)." Sizer, "The Temple," 254; see also Sizer, *Zion's Christian Soldiers,* 119.

New Creation Millennialism

A recent variant of premillennialism is that proposed by J. Webb Mealy and adopted by Eckhard J. Schnabel which Mealy calls "new creation millennialism."[65] This view is the most detailed and sophisticated premillennial position.

Nature and biblical bases of new creation millennialism

Mealy's agenda underlying his articulation of new creation millennialism was "to discover a passage in Revelation that pictures the ultimate fate of the unrepentant as annihilation rather than endless torment."[66] New creation millennialism is based on a detailed exegesis not only of Rev 19:11–21:8[67] but also on a detailed analysis of biblical passages dealing with fire and being consumed.[68] It sees several correspondences between its view of how eschatology unfolds and that set forth in the "Isaiah's apocalypse" of Isaiah 24–27.[69]

Mealy recognizes that the key premillennial tenets of natural people surviving Christ's *parousia* and the earth's not being completely restored at the *parousia* are not biblically sustainable. Consequently, new creation millennialism affirms the biblical (and amillennialist) positions that no one survives the *parousia* (Rev 19:11–21) except the saints (who are given resurrection);[70] the new earth of Revelation 21–22 appears at the time of the *parousia* (not a thousand years later).[71] Rev 20:4–6 depicts the resurrected saints reigning on the new earth, beginning at the *parousia,* for a thousand years. The unbelieving dead are imprisoned with Satan in Hades for a thousand years. They are then resurrected to life and given a "final chance" to turn to Christ but reject the offer, continue in their rebellion, and are judged.[72] Rev 20:7–10 depicts the release and judgment of Satan and the resurrection and judgment of unbelievers at the end of the thousand years. Rev 20:11–15 presents a composite of two separate judgments: 20:11–12 is the judgment at the *parousia* on the basis of one's conduct in this life (corresponding to 20:4–6); 20:13–15 presents the resurrection and judgment at the end of the 1000 years of those who been granted the "final chance" and is based on their conduct in their resurrection life (corresponding to 20:7–10).[73] The judgment of those who were granted the "final chance" but continued in their rebellion is annihilation.[74]

---

65. Mealy, *After the Thousand Years, The End of the Unrepentant,* "Revelation is One," *New Creation Millennialism*; see also Schnabel, *40 Questions,* 227–28, 268–69, 275–78, 288–91.

66. Mealy, "Revelation is One," 135.

67. Mealy, *After the Thousand Years,* 59–233.

68. Mealy, *The End, passim.*

69. Mealy, *The End,* 106–18; Mealy, *New Creation,* 107–11.

70. Mealy, *After the Thousand Years,* 91; see also Schnabel, *40 Questions,* 237.

71. Mealy, *After the Thousand Years,* 223–27; see also Schnabel, *40 Questions,* 277.

72. Mealy, *After the Thousand Years,* 59–235; see also Schnabel, *40 Questions,* 276–77, 288–90.

73. Mealy, *After the Thousand Years,* 173, 177–89; see also Mealy, *The End,* 173 ("In Rev. 20:12–13, John simply sees the two phases of the judgment of the unrepentant juxtaposed: judgment in a state of death, based on the evidence in books that record their actions in mortal life, followed by resurrection and judgment, based on each person's actions in a resurrected state").

74. Mealy *The End,* 91–93; Mealy, "Revelation is One," 135–36. Mealy gives a succinct summary of

Critique of new creation millennialism

As noted above, Mealy and Schnabel recognize the fatal problem inherent in the other forms of premillennialism which claim that unresurrected sinners and resurrected saints will co-exist in the post-*parousia* millennium. New creation millennialism endeavors to escape this problem by positing that all the unredeemed die and are cast into Hades at the *parousia,* only to be resurrected at the end of the thousand years. However, that attempted solution to the problem renders Satan's binding in Rev 20:1–3 unnecessary. Sam Storms points out, "What need is there for Satan to be bound at all? According to Revelation 20:3, the purpose of Satan's incarceration is to prevent him from deceiving the nations. But if the nations no longer exist on the earth . . . who could possibly constitute those who are the potential objects of his deceptive lies?"[75] Additionally, Rev 20:8 speaks of Satan being released from the abyss *"to deceive the nations which are in the four corners of the earth."* Yet new creation millennialism contends that "the nations" are not living living human beings "in the four corners of the earth" at all, but are *the dead* who have been incarcerated in the abyss with Satan for a thousand years and now are coming out of the abyss with Satan![76] Not only does such an idea seem bizarre, but it amounts to equating Hades and the abyss with the earth, the dead with the living, and Satan's accomplices with his victims.

New creation millennialism also founders on its conception of the judgment. Mealy and Schnabel rightly see Rev 20:7–10 and 20:11–15 as dual depictions of the judgment, one as a battle and one as a courtroom proceeding.[77] However, they err in that they do not see one general judgment of all humanity. Instead, they see believers as undergoing one judgment at the *parousia* but unbelievers undergoing two judgments: one at the *parousia* and a second judgment a thousand years later, which they refer to as a "retrial."[78] Such multiple judgments are never hinted at in the Bible, which always speaks of the eschatological judgment in the singular, often preceded by the definite article, i.e., "*the* judgment."[79] The basis of the judgment always is the deeds done in this life, not something done after death (e.g., Matt 24:45–51; 25:31–46; 2 Thess 1:6–10). The rewards or punishments always are said to be everlasting, as opposed to being a temporary "sentence to prison" only to be released.[80]

---

his entire eschatological scheme in *The End,* 195–97.

75. Storms, *Kingdom Come,* 447.

76. Mealy, *After the Thousand Years,* 129–30; Schnabel, *40 Questions,* 227–28, 276.

77. Mealy, *After the Thousand Years,* 180; Schnabel, *40 Questions,* 290.

78. Mealy, *After the Thousand Years,* 185; Schnabel, *40 Questions,* 290.

79. E.g., Matt 12:41–42; Luke 10:14; 11:31–32; Acts 24:25; Rom 2:3; 14:10; 2 Cor 5:10; Jude 6. See above, chapter 5, the section "The Bible teaches that there is one general resurrection, and one general judgment, of both believers and unbelievers."

80. E.g., Matt 24:45–51; 25:31–46; Mark 9:41–48; Rom 2:1–8; compare Mealy, *After the Thousand Years,* 124, 130; Schnabel, *40 Questions,* 227, 268, 276. It is beyond the scope of this critique (or this book) to analyze Mealy's case for the ultimate annihilation of the unrepentant. Suffice it to say the following: (1) Although annihilationism and other views of the ultimate fate of the unrepentant have been proposed (see, e.g., Crockett, ed., *Four Views on Hell*), no other proponents of annihilationism have found it necessary to come up with a new, comprehensive scheme of eschatology to justify such a belief. That, of itself, does not make Mealy's view wrong, but it does suggest that it is unecessary. (2) If the traditional and majority view of hell as eternal punishment for the unrepentant is valid, then of necessity

Further, Mealy's position takes Rev 20:11–15, which clearly is a unity, and divides it into two pieces, separated by a thousand years. Mealy correctly sees Rev 20:11–12 as describing the judgment at the *parousia*.[81] However, he sees Rev 20:13–15 as a description of the judgment of resurrected unbelievers after the millennium.[82] On the other hand, Schnabel first says that Rev 20:11 takes place at the *parousia* but then inconsistently indicates that *all* of Rev 20:11–15 takes place a thousand years after the *parousia*.[83] Schnabel himself recognizes that Rev 20:11–15 "poses a problem for the timing of the final judgment if Revelation 19:11–21 is interpreted as the day of judgment taking place on the day of Jesus' second coming, as expected by Jesus and Paul."[84] He also acknowledges, "The problem disappears if the millennium is not seen as a thousand-year period between Jesus' second coming and the final judgment, but as referring to the church period. If there is no millennium, then the judgment of Revelation 19:11–21 can be seen as being recapitulated in Revelation 20:11–15."[85]

Although new creation millennialism purports to have a high view of the *parousia* and all it entails, there is an incompleteness about it that even Mealy recognizes.[86] For example, Mealy concedes that "according to the world view of most readers (ancient or modern!), there would not be much joy in picturing oneself on a renewed earth built over an underworld populated by hostile and unrepentant nations. Such a picture might have the unsavoury effect as imagining oneself living in a beautiful palace above a basement full of corpses, or of hungry crocodiles."[87] Further, new creation millennialism does not eliminate the problem of sin and death existing after the *parousia*. Unbelievers are said to reside in Hades for a thousand years while the redeemed live over them on the re-created earth; after the thousand years the unredeemed ascend to the earth, attack the saints, and are destroyed a second time.[88] Thus, even according to new creation millennialism, after the thousand years unredeemed (albeit resurrected) people, together with sin, evil, and death, will co-exist with redeemed, glorified people on the new earth. Whether during or after the thousand years, the presence of the unredeemed, sin, evil, and death following the *parousia* is contrary to the perfect peace, holiness, and harmony of the New Jerusalem. Rev 21:8 makes clear that no unredeemed person *ever* can enter the new earth, because *"their part will be in the lake that burns with fire and brimstone, which is the second death"* (it does not say, "they will be sentenced to prison for a thousand years, then may enter the new earth as enemies and *then* will be cast into the lake of fire").

Mealy's scheme fails. For a good defense of the traditional view see Peterson, *Hell on Trial*.

81. Mealy, *After the Thousand Years*, 180.

82. Ibid., 180, 185.

83. Schnabel, *40 Questions*, 277, 290–91.

84. Ibid., 289.

85. Ibid., 289n.5. It is somewhat unclear how many resurrections the unrepentant undergo according to new creation millennialism. Storms plausibly observes that, after their resurrection in Rev 20:8–9, the unrepentant apparently are killed in Rev 20:10 and *again* are cast into Hades only to be resurrected yet again to be judged at the Great White Throne, since Rev 20:13 says, *"Death and Hades gave up the dead which were in them; and they were judged."* See Storms, *Kingdom Come*, 449.

86. Mealy, *After the Thousand Years*, 212, 227.

87. Ibid., 212.

88. Ibid., 127–30, 136–39; see also Schnabel, *40 Questions*, 227, 269, 275, 278, 280.

Another fundamental problem with new creation millennialism is that it is contrary to the Bible's clear eschatological structure of the "two ages." Based on the fact that the Bible sometimes uses the plural ("the ages of the ages") to describe the age to come, Mealy holds that the "age to come" refers only to a finite period of "the thousand years" (i.e., a post-*parousia* "millennium"); he contends that the age to come is followed by a never-ending sequence of additional ages.[89] This amounts to an underinterpretation of the phrase "age to come" and an overinterpretation of the phrase "the ages of the ages" and draws a distinction where none exists. It does not take into account the equivalence of the two phrases and thereby would limit many of the descriptions of God, Christ, and the promises made to believers as finite, applicable only for the "thousand years." Finally, this view does not appreciate that, although the Bible is not explicit about all that will be occurring throughout the eternity to come following the *parousia*, the essential character and nature of that time is the same throughout, and it excludes the very presence of sin, evil, and death which new creation millennialism, like other forms of premillennialism, posits will be present during or after the "millennium."[90]

Postmillennialism

Essential beliefs of postmillennialism

Postmillennialists look to a future distinct period of unprecedented Christian influence in the world before Christ's return. For postmillennialists, the millennial "golden age" will occur *in history.*[91] Christ's second coming will occur after the millennium and will result in the resurrection and rapture, the final judgment, and the initiation of the eternal state. The basic postmillennial concept of the "millennium" is that it arrives, not by the ending of this age and this world at the *parousia*, but gradually through the working of the Holy Spirit through the church *in* history, *in* this world. As Grenz puts it, "The changes that will emerge in the future age will be differences of *extent*, not *content.*"[92]

89. Mealy, *New Creation,* 20n.46, 96–99; see also, *The End,* 53–55. For a detailed discussion of the two ages, including a discussion of the use of the singular and the plural in describing them, see above, chapter 4.

90. For a lengthy, general review of Mealy's position, see Beale, "Review Article," 229–49.

91. While some postmillennialists have referred to the "golden age" that will be brought about by the working of the Holy Spirit through the church before the second coming of Christ as the "millennium" (e.g., Boettner, "Postmillennialism," 117), postmillennialist Greg Bahnsen states that "it is more common today for postmillennialists to refer to the whole period, from the first advent to the second, as the millennium." Bahnsen, *Victory,* 34; see also Kik, *Eschatology,* 17. Thus, postmillennialists agree with amillennialists regarding the *timing* of the "millemnnium"; what distinguishes postmillennialism from amillennialism (and from premillennialism) is "the optimistic confidence that the world nations will become disciples of Christ, that the church will grow to fill the earth, and that Christianity will become the dominant principle rather than the exception to the rule." Bahnsen, *Victory,* 92.

92. Grenz, *Millennial Maze,* 70–71.

Biblical bases of postmillennialism

The "Great Commission"

Postmillenialists hold that, because Christ gave the church the "Great Commission" (Matt 28:18–20) and empowered the church with the Holy Spirit, the church will successfully complete the Great Commission to all people groups. The Great Commission is more than just evangelism; it includes teaching, discipling, and living out Christ's commands. Because God is sovereign, Christ has *all authority*, and the Holy Spirit is more powerful than anything or anyone else, the church ultimately will overcome its enemies and bring about a time of unprecedented blessings in history.[93]

The triumph of God's people in history

Postmillennialists look to passages like the following, which indicate the spread and influence of God's people over all of the earth in history: Gen 1:28; Ps 2:8–9; 22:27–28; 86:9–10; 110:1; Isa 2:1–4; 9:6–7; Dan 2:34–35; Matt 13:31–35; 16:18; Rev 7:9; 21:16, 24.[94] Consequently, postmillennialists generally see Revelation 21–22 as depicting the victorious church in history, not the consummate, eternal state.[95]

Revelation 19–20

Postmillennialists see Rev 19:11–21 not as a description of the eschatological second coming, but as the victory of Christ through the church's successful completion of the "Great Commission" in this age.[96] Regarding the "two resurrections" of Rev 20:4–6, postmillennialists are united with amillennialists in finding it impossible that two physical resurrections are being described, the first of the righteous and the second of the unrighteous. That contradicts the clear teaching of Scripture that the second coming marks the resurrection of all people for the general judgment. Consequently, most postmillennialists interpret Rev 20:4–6 as referring to spiritual resurrection before the millennium and the physical resurrection following the millennium.[97]

---

93. Gentry, *Greatness*, 98–108; Mathison, *Postmillennialism*, 115–16, 191–94.

94. See, e.g., Kik, *Eschatology*, 16–29; Bahnsen, *Victory*, 54–64, 78–80.

95. Kik, *Eschatology*, 20–21; Mathison, *Postmillennialism*, 157–58.

96. Boettner, "Postmillennial Response," 200–02. On the other hand, Mathison sees the passage as Christ's fulfilling Psalm 110 by triumphing over his enemies in connection with his ascension. Mathison, *Postmillennialism*, 154.

97. Kik, *Eschatology*, 42–44, 209–13 (contrary to most amillennialists, Kik believes the "thrones" signify the reign of the saints *on earth*, not in heaven during the "intermediate period"); Mathison, *Postmillennialism*, 156; see also Grenz, *Millennial Maze*, 73–74.

Critique of postmillennialism

"This age" versus the "age to come"

Postmillennialism's teaching of a Christianized "golden age" of righteousness and peace that occurs in "this age" is not consistent with the clear biblical teaching that "this age" is and always will be an evil age. The NT has many passages that describe this age as evil, warn Christians of persecution, and exhort Christians not to be conformed to the pattern of this age.[98] If postmillennialism's golden age were to occur, it would have significant implications for those passages and others like them. Waldron points out that such passages "would no longer be accurate descriptions of this age or the experience of Christians in this age. This, however, would be a dangerous viewpoint because it would directly undermine the authority of the New Testament for the believer."[99]

The triumph of God's people in history

Although Christ commissioned Christians to go into all the world, and the church will grow like a mustard tree and spread like leaven, none of those passages state or imply the extent to which the kingdom will grow. The NT has texts such as the parable of the wheat and the tares (Matt 13:24–30, 36–42) that indicate both the spread of the church and the increase of evil at the same time. Jesus also said, *"The gate is small and the way is narrow that leads to life, and there are few who find it"* (Matt 7:14). Wayne Grudem comments, "Rather than teaching that a majority of the world will become Christians, Jesus seems here to be saying that those who are saved will be 'few' in contrast to the 'many' who travel toward eternal destruction." [100] Similarly, in Luke 18:8 Jesus asks, *"When the Son of man comes, will He find faith on earth?"* That question suggests that the earth will not be filled with believers, but by those who do not have faith, when Christ returns.

Amillennialism

Essential beliefs of amillennialism

Amillennialists look for one cluster of end-time events: the second coming entails a complex of events involving the resurrection of the righteous and the unrighteous, the judgment of the righteous and the unrighteous, the renewal of the earth and the cosmos, and the inauguration of the eternal state. There will be no thousand year interregnum of Christ between the second coming and the eternal state. The basic amillennial view of the "first resurrection" (Rev 20:6) is that it is a symbolic term for the believers' regeneration and new life on earth (i.e., their spiritual resurrection in Christ) or the death of the

---

98. See Mark 10:30; Luke 16:8; 18:30; Rom 12:2; 2 Cor 4:4; Gal 1:4; Eph 2:2; 2 Tim 3:12–13; 4:3–4.

99. Waldron, "Structural Considerations," n.p.

100. Grudem, *Systematic Theology,* 1124.

believer which translates him to the intermediate state to "live and reign with Christ" (Rev 20:4).[101]

Revelation 20 depicts three scenes: Satan bound (Rev 20:1–3); the reigning saints (Rev 20:4–6); and the nations in revolt (Rev 20:7–10). "All of these scenes fit the present conditions of the earth below and the glorified saints above."[102] Amillennialists thus hold that the "thousand years" is a symbolic reference to the entire period (which we are now in) between Christ's resurrection until shortly before his return. This age will be characterized by the spread of the gospel but also by the spread of sin, i.e., there will be no "golden age" before Christ returns. Satan is now bound in the sense that he can no longer absolutely prevent the spread of the gospel to the nations or unite the world to destroy the church. Shortly before the second coming, he will be loosed and persecution will increase. That will be ended by Christ's return in victory. "The biblical millennium, therefore, is not the glorious age to come, but this present era for giving the message of salvation to the nations."[103]

Biblical bases of amillennialism

Revelation 19-20

Amillennialists typically adopt the "progressive parallelism" view of Revelation whereby major sections of the book tend to repeat the history of the entire church age from different points of view. Thus, events of Revelation 20 do not chronologically follow the events of Revelation 19 (as premillennialists believe) but recapitulate those events. Revelation is consistent with every other reference in the Bible that the final judgment (Rev 20:7–15) is associated with the *parousia*. Therefore, the thousand-year reign of Rev 20:4–6 must occur before, not after, the second coming.[104] The "thrones" and "souls" in that passage are in heaven.[105] Rev 20:3 says that the "binding of Satan" is limited for a specific purpose: *"that he would not deceive the nations any longer."* That occurred at the first coming of Christ (Matt 12:28–29; Luke 10:18) and, following Pentecost, as the gospel was proclaimed to all the nations (Matt 24:14; 28:18–20; Acts 2:1–11; Col 1:23).

Rev 20:4–6 does not refer to two bodily resurrections as premillennialists believe. The joining of "first" with "resurrection" only occurs here in the entire Bible. In Revelation 21 and elsewhere when "first" is used, it is *not* used as the first in a series of things that are of the same kind but as something that stands in *contrast* to what is described as the "new" or the "second." Thus, in Rev 20:4–6 the *"first resurrection"* does not stand for the first of two bodily resurrections but is *antithetically contrasted* with the *"second death."*

---

101. See, e.g., Augustine, *Civ.,* 20.6–10; White, "Death and the First Resurrection," 22; Kline, "First Resurrection," 371.

102. Lewis, *Dark Side,* 65.

103. Ibid.

104. Hoekema, "Amillennialism," 160.

105. Ibid., 165–67.

The second coming, resurrection, and judgment

Multiple passages point to only one cluster of events (not two or three) as including the second coming, the general resurrection, and the general judgment. Heb 9:28 says that Christ will come *"a second time,"* not a "second and third time." Amillennialists look to the structure of biblical eschatology as a whole as supporting their position, including texts which link the final judgment of both the righteous and the wicked with second coming[106] and texts which link the general resurrection with the second coming.[107]

1 Cor 15:20–57

Christ's reign does not begin sometime in a future millennium, but he is reigning now (Acts 2:29–36). First Cor 15:20–57 does not establish three sequential orders of resurrection (Christ; those who are his; and "the end") but two: Christ; and those who are his (unbelievers are not specifically referred to in the passage). Death, which is *"the last enemy that will be abolished"* (15:26), is clearly abolished at the *parousia* (15:23–26, 52–54). The passage contradicts the premillennial idea that after the *parousia* death still exists.[108]

Critique of amillennialism

The chronology of Revelation 19–20 and the two resurrections

Premillennialists contend, in contrast to amillennialists, that Revelation 20 follows chronologically in history from where Revelation 19 left off rather than recapitulating Revelation 19. Further, they see the "two resurrections" of Rev 20:4–6 as two sequential, physical resurrections of the same kind, separated by one thousand years, rather than two different types of "resurrection." In this latter regard, the words or Henry Alford are often quoted: "If, in a passage where *two resurrections* are mentioned, where certain *psuchai ezēsan* at the first, and the rest of the *nekroi ezēsan* only at the end of a specified period after that first,—if in such a passage the first resurrection may be understood to mean *spiritual* rising with Christ, while the second means *literal* rising from the grave;—then there is an end of all significance in language, and Scripture is wiped out as a definitive testimony to anything."[109] Those are the two major objections to amillennialism.[110]

---

106. Matt 13:24–30, 36–43, 47–50; 16:27; 25:31–46; Luke 17:22–37; John 5:25–29; 2 Thess 1:6–10; 2 Tim 4:1 (implicitly); Jas 5:7–9; Rev 19:11–21; 20:11–15; 22:12.

107. Matt 13:30, 40–41, 48–49; 24:29–31; 25:31–32; Mark 13:24–27; Luke 17:22–37; John 5:25–29; 1 Cor 15:20–26, 35–57; Phil 3:20–21; 1 Thess 4:13–17.

108. See Appendix 7: 1 Cor 15:20–57: The Resurrection, the *Parousia*, and the Millennium.

109. Alford, *Greek Testament*, 4:732; quoted in Ladd, *Commentary*, 267.

110. Amillennial responses to this critique are set forth in Appendix 2: The Millennium: An Amillennial Synthesis of the Biblical Data.

The binding of Satan

The other main objection to amillennialism is that the "binding of Satan" in Rev 20:1–3 implies "a far greater restriction of his activity than anything we know in this present age."[111] Wayne Grudem articulates this objection:

> The imagery of throwing Satan into a pit and shutting it and sealing it over him gives a picture of total removal from influence on the earth. To say that Satan is now in a bottomless pit that is shut and sealed over simply does not fit the present world situation during the church age, in which Satan's activity is still very strong, in which he "prowls around like a roaring lion, seeking someone to devour" (1 Peter 5:8), in which he can fill someone's heart "to lie to the Holy Spirit" (Acts 5:3), and in which "what pagans sacrifice they offer to demons and not to God" (1 Cor. 10:20).[112]

Travis responds to that critique by remarking:

> The source of the language about 'binding Satan' (Revelation 20:2) is naturally found in Jesus's image of the binding of the strong man in Mark 3:27. By general agreement, Jesus is there referring to the overcoming of Satan which he began in his ministry and demonstrated in his exorcisms. Thus John's statement that Satan is bound 'So that he could not deceive the nations any more until the thousand years were over' (Revelation 20:3) would be another way of saying that Jesus's first coming involved decisive victory over Satan's power (cf. Luke 10:17f.; John 12:31; Colossians 2:15) and heralded the preaching of the Gospel to Gentile nations who had previously been deceived by Satan (cf. Matthew 28:18–20). Some may argue that Satan at present seems to enjoy fairly unrestricted power, and that amillennialism therefore fails to do justice to Revelation's assertion that Satan is bound and put out of action. But they must argue their case not only with amillennialists but also with Jesus and Paul and their insistence that in a real sense Satan has been defeated, even though that defeat will not be finalized until Jesus's second coming.[113]

Additionally, that criticism fails to take into account the "epic idiom" John uses to describe the binding of Satan.[114]

Preterism

Essential beliefs of preterism

There are different varieties of preterism.

---

111. Grudem, *Systematic Theology*, 1130.

112. Ibid., 1117–18.

113. Travis, *I Believe*, 145. Even some premillennialists essentially agree. Ladd states that the language of "binding" is obviously symbolic and "does not mean that all of his activities and powers are nullified, only that he may no longer deceive the nations as he has done through human history and lead them into active aggression against the saints during the thousand years." Ladd, *Commentary*, 262.

114. See White, "On the Hermeneutics," *passim*; see also below, chapter 11, the discussion of the binding of Satan.

Full preterism

Full preterist advocate Don Preston calls full preterism "covenant eschatology" because "it defines Biblical eschatology as the end of the Old Covenant age of Israel—i.e. AD 70—and not 'historical eschatology' i.e. the end of time and human history."[115] Hence, "The true [full] preterist view is that the second coming of Christ was to finally judge and remove the last vestiges of the Old Covenant system and fully establish the kingdom and the New Covenant system by 70 A.D."[116] Full preterists see "the second advent (including the 'rapture,' resurrection, and judgment) as occurring in A.D. 70."[117] The "resurrection of the dead and transmutation of the living take place in the realm of the spiritual, into which earthly spectators and reporters do not enter, and could see nothing if they did."[118] In short, full preterism holds that "every facet of New Testament eschatology is applicable exclusively to the final period of the Old Testament aeon."[119] Consequently, full preterism denies the future second coming of Christ.[120]

Partial preterism

Partial preterism, on the other hand, holds that Christ's ascension and enthronement in heaven represents his *parousia*, which led to his coming (*parousia*) in judgment against Israel in A.D. 70.[121] Partial preterists likewise view the bulk of Bible prophecy, including the "Great Tribulation," as being related to and fulfilled in the events surrounding the destruction of Jerusalem and the temple in A.D. 70.[122] Nevertheless, partial preterists agree that the "second advent" of Christ will occur at the end of history, accompanied by resurrection, judgment, and the institution of the final state.[123]

Biblical bases of preterism

OT prophecy

Preterism correctly sees OT Israel as a "type" or "shadow" that pointed to and finds its fulfillment in New Covenant realities.[124] It seeks the OT background of NT texts and synthesizes multiple lines of OT prophecy into a coherent whole. Thus, preterists cite such

115. Preston, *AD 70*, 3n.6.

116. Scott, "But What Will They Do," n.p.; see also Preston, *Like Father*, 17–18, 58, 206–07.

117. Gentry, *Dominion*, 271; see also Preston, *Like Father*, 200; Sproul, *Last Days*, 157.

118. Russell, *Parousia*, 210; see also Preston, *Like Father*, 288–89.

119. King, *The Cross*, xi; see also Preston, *Like Father*, 306, 313n.32 ("We hold that eschatologically Jesus did not see beyond AD 70"); Preston, *AD 70, passim*.

120. Don Preston states, "Jesus never predicted a physical visble return to end human history." Preston, *Like Father*, 57.

121. Chilton, *Vengeance*, 434–35; DeMar, *Last Days*, 157–69.

122. Sproul, *Last Days*, 157; Kik, *Eschatology*, 112–57; Gentry, "Exposition," 16–66.

123. Sproul, *Last Days*, 157; Gentry, *Dominion*, 276–77; Chilton, *Vengeance*, 494, 589; Kik, *Eschatology*, 158.

124. See Preston, *Like Father*, 114, 203–204, 300–301; Preston, *AD 70*, 10–12.

passages as Isaiah 24–27 (the destruction of God's enemies and resurrection), Isaiah 62 (the messianic marriage), Isaiah 65–66 (the messianic banquest and the new creation), along with multiple other OT passages, as finding their fulfillment in AD 70 since Luke said of that time, *"These are days of vengeance, so that all things which are written will be fulfilled"* (Luke 21:22).[125]

The Olivet Discourse

Christ's Olivet Discourse was his major discourse concerning eschatology. The context of the Olivet Discourse was Jesus' condemnation of the scribes and Pharisees (Matt 23:1–36), his lament over Jerusalem (Matt 23:37–39), and his prophecy of the destruction of the temple (Matt 24:1–3). There are multiple time indicators (*"this generation,"* Matt 23:36; 24:34); personal references ("you," "your," Matt 23:34–36; 24:2, 6, 9, 15, 20, 23, 25, 26, 32–34); obvious references to Jewish circumstances (Matt 24:15–20); and the facts of history (Luke 21:20). Those all clearly relate the context to the events surrounding the destruction of the temple and Jerusalem in AD 70.

The book of Revelation

The book of Revelation is both a prophecy and an epistle (the prescript in Rev 1:4 establishes that it is an epistle). All epistles were expected to be understood by the people to whom they were addressed. The book was addressed to then-existing churches. Apocalyptic descriptions (e.g., beasts and Babylon the great) could easily be taken as coded descriptions of Rome and Jerusalem. Rev 1:1, 3; 2:16; 3:10, 11; 22:6, 7, 10, 12, 20 all contain time indicators (e.g., *"the time is near,"* *"I am coming quickly"*) that suggest first-century fulfillment.

Critique of preterism

Time indicators

Preterism is strongest in dealing with the time indicators and the references to the "abomination of desolation" and "great tribulation" in the Olivet Discourse as relating to the destruction of Jerusalem in AD 70. As R. C. Sproul states, "Whatever else may be said of preterism, it has achieved at least two things: (1) It has focused attention on the time-frame references of New Testament eschatology, and (2) it has highlighted the significance of Jerusalem's destruction in redemptive history."[126]

---

125. See Preston, *AD 70*, 49–58.

126. Sproul, *Last Days*, 25; see Otto, "Jesus the Preterist," n.p.; see also below, chapter 8, regarding the "signs of the times" that all occurred in principle before AD 70.

Typology and prophetic language

Preterism also is strong in recognizing that the entire Old Covenant system, including Israel itself, represented physical, earthly "types" or "shadows" which pointed to future, New Covenant, spiritual realities.[127] As Leonhard Goppelt says, "there is no typology that by-passes Christ; he is the antitype of the entire OT."[128] Preterists are also sensitive to the fact that prophetic language often was figurative.[129]

The second coming, resurrection, and judgment

Preterism is weakest in dealing with the passages that deal with the second coming, the resurrection, and the judgment. Full preterism falsely holds that the second coming, the resurrection, the judgment, the new earth, etc., all have occurred. Partial preterist commentators have made strong arguments pertaining to Christ's ascension and his coming in judgment as being a *parousia*.[130]

The idea that the events of AD 70 constituted an eschatological *"parousia"* of Christ is problematic in at least two ways: (1) Such a view teaches multiple *"parousias"* of Jesus, when the NT is clear that there will be only one; and (2) Christ's "coming" in AD 70 was a local judgment on Jerusalem and his *"parousia"* was invisible,[131] whereas the NT makes clear that the second coming will be visible (Matt 24:27, 29; Rev 1:7) and will involve judgment of the entire earth.[132] J. C. Ryle discusses the preterist view of the second coming of Christ described in Matt 24:29–31 as follows:

> In this part of our Lord's prophecy He describes His own second coming to judge the world. This, at all events, seems the natural meaning of the passage: to take any lower view appears to be a violent straining of Scripture language. If the solemn words here used mean nothing more than the coming of the Roman armies to Jerusalem, we may explain away anything in the Bible. The event here described is one of far greater moment than the march of any earthly army; it is nothing less than the closing act of the present dispensation,—the second personal advent of Jesus Christ.[133]

Ryle's comment highlights the underlying theological problem of preterism: it essentially is not Cristocentric. It was not just the coming of the kingdom that was the focus

127. See Gal 4:21–31; Col 2:16–17; Heb 8:5; 9:15–10:22; 12:18–24.

128. Goppelt, *Typos*, 116.

129. See below, chapter 8, the section "The signs in the sky and on the earth (Matt 24:29; Mark 13:24–25; Luke 21:25–26)."

130. See Chilton, *Vengeance*, 64–67; DeMar, *Last Days*, 159–69; France, *Matthew*, 919–28; Storms, *Kingdom Come*, 259–73.

131. Don Preston maintains that, just as God had come in judgment in the past and "was *perceived* but not *visible*," so in AD 70 "Jesus was coming on the clouds of heaven in judgment of those who pierced him." Preston, *Like Father*, 230.

132. See Matt 13:24–30, 36–51; 16:27; 24:42–51; 25:14–30, 31–46; Luke 12:35–48; 17:22–37; 19:12–27; John 5:25–29; Acts 3:19–21; 17:31; Rom 8:17–25; 1 Cor 4:5; 2 Thess 1:6–10; 2 Tim 4:1; Jas 5:7–9; 2 Pet 3:3–15; Rev 11:18; 19:11–21; 22:12.

133. Ryle, *Expository Thoughts*, 321.

of those who were looking for the Messiah, but they were looking for the *personal* Coming One (see, e.g., Luke 2:25–38; 7:19). J. E. Fison observes, "We are apt to-day to recognize the practical identity of the coming of Jesus in the past with the coming of the kingdom of God, but we [at least preterists] are loath to commit ourselves to a similar identity in the future. Yet there is no getting away from the latter if we accept the former."[134] A. L. Moore picks up on this insight and says:

> If we recognize this, we shall be careful to see that the concept of the Son of Man coming in clouds with great glory and the concept of the Kingdom of God come with power have a strictly Christocentric interpretation. . . . To be sure, the fall of Jerusalem is rightly understood as a signal manifestation of God's sovereignty in Christ, exercised in judgment upon recalcitrant Israel, but it is not *specifically* Christocentric. . . . [Mark 9:1; 14:62] speak of a *visible manifestation* of the Kingdom of God and of the Son of Man, and this in both instances is contrasted with the hiddenness of the Kingdom and of the Son of Man in the ministry of Jesus. It is this manifestation of the sovereignty of God in the triumphant revelation of the Son of Man in glory and power which alone can fulfil [sic] the expectation of the New Testament. The resurrection appearances were witnessed, to be sure, by the disciples: yet the resurrection was no open, universal manifestation and must therefore be distinguished sharply from the Parousia.[135]

Preterism also cannot account for the fact that the apostolic and post-apostolic fathers, some of whom lived through the momentous events of AD 70, did not view the destruction of Jerusalem as a secret, spiritual *"parousia"* of Jesus but instead looked to a future second coming.[136] Randall Otto correctly asks, "If the eschatological scenario and parousia Jesus predicted in the Olivet discourse was fulfilled in AD 70, where did the apostles get the notion of another, yet future, parousia?"[137] Further, all the early ecumenical creeds "declared the *future* coming of Christ, the resurrection of all men, and the general judgment to be fundamental, non-negotiable articles of the Christian faith."[138] Keith Mathison comments on the significance of the ecumenical creeds: "If creedal orthodoxy is not maintained as a boundary, biblical interpretation necessarily sinks into the sea of subjectivity and thereby loses any claim to absolute authority. . . . If we do not believe that God providentially guided the church to establish a basic rule of faith (the creed), then there is no such thing as Christian orthodoxy."[139]

The full preterist view that the resurrection has already occurred is similarly problematic. Kenneth Gentry points out:

> Christ's resurrection is expressly declared to be the paradigm of our own (1 Cor. 15:20ff). Yet we know that his was a physical, tangible resurrection (Lk. 24:39), whereas ours is (supposedly) spiritual. What happens to the Biblically defined analogy between Christ's resurrection and ours in the hyper-preterist

134. Fison, *Christian Hope*, 138.

135. Moore, *The Parousia*, 104–05.

136. See *1 Clement* 50:3–4; *2 Clement* 12:1; 17:4–5; *Didache* 10:5; 16:3–8; *Barn.* 7:2.

137. Otto, "Jesus the Preterist," n.p.

138. Chilton, *Paradise*, 138–39; see Apostles' Creed (c. 2nd cent.); Nicene-Constantinople Creed (325/381); Athanasian Creed (c. late 5th-early 6th cent.).

139. Mathison, *Postmillennialism*, 239.

system? . . . There are numerous other theological and exegetical problems with a spiritual-only resurrection. For one thing, the hyper-preterist view tends to diminish the significance of the somatic implications of sin: Adam's sin had physical effects, as well as judicial and spiritual effects; where are these taken care of in the hyper-preterist system? Death's implications are not just judicial and spiritual, but also physical (Gen. 3:14, 19; Rom. 6:23). If Christians now are fulfilling the resurrection expectation of Scripture, then the gnostics of the early Christian centuries were correct! . . . We must wonder why Paul was mocked by the Greeks in Acts 17 for believing in the resurrection, if it were not a physical reality. We must wonder why Paul aligned himself with the Pharisees on the issue of the resurrection (Ac. 23:6–9; 24:15, 21). We must wonder why we Christians still marry and are given in marriage, since Christ said in the resurrection we will not marry (Lk. 20:35). We must wonder why we "resurrected" Christians must yet die; why should we not leave this world like Enoch and Elijah?[140]

"The end of the age"

Preterism holds that "the end of the age" in Matt 24:3 "entails the emergence of the church as the distinctive people of God at the end of the Jewish age in the day of the Lord's coming in judgment to destroy the temple."[141] However, that view is subject to two formidable objections. First, it undermines the significance of what Christ accomplished on the *cross.* The cross (which entails the resurrection, ascension, and the pouring out of the Holy Spirit), not the events of AD 70, ended the Old Covenant and instituted the New Covenant (Luke 22:20; John 19:30). The cross ended the efficacy and significance of the temple (Matt 27:51; Mark 15:38; Luke 23:45; John 2:19–22). Jesus' ascended to the "true tabernacle" and established a new relationship between God and humanity (Heb 8:1—10:22). The cross inaugurated the "last days" (Acts 2:16–17).

Second, turning "the end of the age" into "the end of the *Jewish* age" is contrary to the clear NT meaning of *"this age"* versus *"the age to come,"* which find their line of demarcation not in the events of AD 70 but in the yet future second coming of Christ and the consummation of his everlasting kingdom. Riddlebarger discusses this:

> Perhaps the most serious problem associated with all varieties of preterism is the failure to acknowledge that the end of the age and the dawn of the age to come are not mere shifts in redemptive history. There is no doubt that the events of A.D. 70 do, in part, fulfill our Lord's words to his apostles of immanent judgment on Israel. The destruction of Jerusalem and its temple does not mark the end of the age; the final consummation does (Matt. 13:40). The events of A.D. 70 do not mark the dawn of the age to come; the final consummation does (Luke 20:35). This indicates that the events of A.D. 70, while vital to the course of redemptive history, do not constitute our Lord's Parousia or the judgment. The contrast between this age and the age to come is a contrast between things eternal and things temporal. This contrast presents a major problem for preterist interpreters, who seek to limit this shift to the destruction of Jerusalem. The two ages are not merely two periods in redemptive-history time but are two distinct

140. Gentry, "A Brief Theological," n.p.

141. Otto, "Jesus the Preterist," n.p.; see also Preston, *Like Father,* 52–53, 218; Preston, *AD 70,* 68–77.

eschatological epochs, with the age to come not being fully realized until our Lord's second advent.[142]

As we saw earlier, individual eschatological passages need to be interpreted in light of the clear, overall "two-age" eschatological structure of the Bible. That, of course, has implications for all eschatological systems. The following two points, discussed by Wayne Jackson, show specific implications of preterism's erroneous understanding of the "end of the age" when viewed in light of the Bible's overall two-age structure:

> 1. The responsibilities of the Great Commission—to teach and immerse lost souls—was commensurate with that era preceding the "end of the world [age]" (Matthew 28:18–20). If the "end of the world [age]" occurred in A.D. 70, then the Lord's Commission is valid no longer. This conclusion, of course, is absurd.
> 2. In the parable of the tares, Jesus taught that at "the end of the world [age]" the "tares" (i.e., evil ones) would be removed from his kingdom and burned (Matthew 13:39–40). Did that transpire with the destruction of Judaism? It did not. The notion that the "end of the world [age]" is past already is false.[143]

Another problematic implication of preterism's redefinition of the "two ages" is that, just as "this age" is redefined to be the Old Covenant Jewish age so the "age to come" is redefined to be the New Covenant age in which we are now living.[144] According to full preterism, the age in which we are now living will last forever.[145] That means that sin and death also will continue to exist forever.[146] Gentry observes, "There is no final conclusion to the matter of man's rebellion; there is no final reckoning with sin. Christ tells us that the judgment will be against rebels in their bodies, not 'spiritual' bodies (Mt. 10:28). The hyper-preterist system does not reach back far enough (to the Fall and the curse on the physical world) to be able to understand the significance of redemption as it moves to a final, conclusive consummation, ridding the cursed world of sin. The full failure of the First Adam must be overcome by the full success of the Second Adam."[147]

With that background of the major systematic theological approaches to eschatology, we now turn to Christ's most detailed discussion of eschatology: the Olivet Discourse.

---

142. Riddlebarger, *Amillennialism*, 241–42.

143. Jackson, "Preterism," n.p.

144. Preston, *Like Father*, 52–57; Preston, *AD 70*, 159.

145. Preston, *Like Father*, 54–55, 95; Preston, *AD 70*, 21.

146. Preston, *Like Father*, 262–63, 266; Preston, *AD 70*, 22.

147. Gentry, "A Brief Theological," n.p.

8

The Olivet Discourse: the Tribulation and the Second Coming

THE OLIVET DISCOURSE[1] IS Jesus' longest, most important and detailed discussion of eschatology. In it he deals with the destruction of Jerusalem and the temple which occurred in AD 70, discusses his second coming, exhorts his followers in light of these eschatological events, and concludes (in the Matthew account) by discussing, both in parables and direct discourse, the final judgment that will occur when he returns. D. A. Carson points out that the Olivet Discourse "is undoubtedly a source for the Thessalonian Epistles and Revelation. If so, then we may say that Jesus himself sets the pattern for the church's eschatology."[2]

Interpretive approaches to the Olivet Discourse

The Olivet Discourse is Jesus' response to his disciples' two-fold question: *"Tell us, when will these things happen, and what will be the sign of your coming and of the end of the age?"* (Matt 24:3) Using the Matthew 24 account as the guide, there are three general approaches to interpreting the Discourse:

The preterist interpretation

Full preterists view the entire discourse as referring to the events surrounding the destruction of Jerusalem in AD 70. Most partial preterists see the destruction of Jerusalem as the subject of Matt 24:1–35 and the future second coming beginning with Matt 24:36.[3]

---

1. Matt 24:1—25:46; Mark 13:1–37; Luke 21:5–36; see also Luke 17:20–37 for a similar discourse.

2. Carson, "Matthew," 8:489, citations omitted; see also Charles, *St. John,* I:158.

3. A variant partial preterist position holds that in the Olivet Discourse speaks primarily of Christ's own impending death and resurrection, rather than of the events of AD 70 or the *parousia*. Bolt, "Mark 13," 10–32.

All preterists see Matt 24:29–31 as relating to the destruction of Jerusalem in AD 70, i.e., Jesus "comes" in judgment *on Jerusalem*.[4]

These approaches have the following strengths

(1) They take seriously the context of Matt 23:34—24:2.

(2) They answer the first and central question of the disciples regarding the timing of the destruction of the temple, *"Tell us, when will these things happen?"* (Matt 24:2–3). The partial preterist view answers both that question and the disciples' second question, *"What will be the sign of your coming and of the end of the age?"* (Matt 24:3).[5]

(3) They are sensitive to the figurative use of prophetic language (Matt 24:29; Mark 13:24–25; Luke 21:25–26).

(4) They correctly note that the reference in Matt 24:30; Mark 13:26; Luke 21:27 to *"the Son of Man coming on the clouds"* is drawn from Dan 7:13. N. T. Wright states that the Danielic background of Jesus' reference "would not advance the cause of those who read [Matt 24:30; Mark 13:26; Luke 21:27] as predicting a downward cloud-borne movement for the 'son of man', since Daniel 7 conceives the scene from the perspective of heaven, not earth. The 'son of man' figure 'comes' to the Ancient of Days. He comes *from* earth *to* heaven, vindicated after suffering."[6]

(5) They take *"this generation"* (Matt 24:34) in its normal sense as referring to the generation then alive when Jesus was speaking.

(6) They have the virtue of simplicity. The full preterist view sees the discourse as Jesus' way of synthesizing almost all OT prophecy regarding the *parousia* of Christ and the change from the Old Covenant to the New Covenant as occurring at one time. Similarly, the partial preterist view "has the advantage of being neat. There is a clear division [at Matt 24:36; Mark 13:24] between the two parts of the discourse, and it eliminates flipping back and forth or appealing to 'prophetic foreshortening' or the like."[7]

These approaches have important weaknesses

(1) They do not take into account the time reference *"immediately after the tribulation of those days"* in Matt 24:29. If Matt 24:15–21 refers to the destruction of the temple and Jerusalem in AD 70, but Christ's "coming" *is* his "coming in judgment" against Jerusalem, then *"immediately after the tribulation of those days"* has no meaning because both 24:15–21 and 24:29 would be talking about the same event.

---

4. Mathison, *Postmillennialism,* 114; Preston, *Like Father,* 219.

5. As will be discussed below in the section "The content and structure of the Olivet Discourse," the *disciples* evidently believed that the destruction of the temple, Jesus' coming, and the end of the age were a single complex of events. Full preterism continues that outlook.

6. Wright, *Victory,* 361; see also Kik, *Eschatology,* 142.

7. Carson, "Matthew," 9:553.

(2) They do not account well for the Son of Man's *"coming in the clouds"* (Matt 24:30). Elsewhere in the NT *"coming in the clouds"* refers to the second coming.[8] No NT writer uses *"coming in the clouds"* to refer to the destruction of Jerusalem.

(3) They do not account well for the apparently visible, audible, and public *"coming of the Son of Man"* (Matt 24:27, 30–31). D. A. Carson notes that multiple other passages are involved with respect to the *parousia*.[9] Those other passages are not descriptive of the events of AD 70. "Here are references to the Son of Man's coming, angels gathering the elect, trumpet call, clouds, glory, tribes of the earth mourning, celestial disturbances—all unambiguously related to the Second Advent. It seems very doubtful, to say the least, that the natural way to understand vv.29–35 is a reference to the Fall of Jerusalem."[10] The "angels," "trumpet," "gathering," etc. all appear to be global, public, visible, and audible events, but preterism makes them unseen, unheard, and local events. To those who would apply such verses metaphorically, Desmond Ford asks, "Just how could Christ have made the point of His return, if words as clear as these are capable of another meaning? We would also enquire whether the New Testament teaching on the resurrection and the Age to come is not evaporated by such exegesis."[11]

(4) They do not properly take account of the meaning of *parousia* (Matt 24:3, 27, 37, 39). Preterism inconsistently interprets the key term *parousia* to make it conform to preterism's own pre-existing theological presuppositions. Stanley Toussaint discusses this:

> The problem with this interpretation is the meaning of *parousia* before verse 36 and after. Since the coming of the Son of Man in verses 37 and 39 is the Second Advent, one would expect the identical words ("the coming [*parousia*] of the Son of Man") in verse 27 to refer to the same event. The word would also have the same meaning in verse 3. In each case the Second Advent must be in view. Furthermore the word *parousia* in the New Testament is always used of an actual presence. In 1 Corinthians 16:17; 2 Corinthians 7:6–7; 10:10; Philippians 1:26; 2:12; and 2 Thessalonians 2:9 *parousia* refers to a person's bodily presence. In all the other cases *parousia* is used of the Lord's presence at his second coming (1 Cor. 15:23; 1 Thess. 2:19; 3:13; 4:15; 5:23; 2 Thess. 2:1, 8; James 5:7–8; 2 Pet. 1:16; 3:4, 12; 1 John 2:28). Since the only occurrences of *parousia* in the Gospels are in Matthew 24, it would seem that they too refer to a yet-future coming of Christ.[12]

(5) Full preterists do not appreciate factors and time indicators described by Jesus that differentiate the events of AD 70 that are "near" and which "you [will] see" from

---

8. Matt 26:64; Acts 1:9–11; 1 Thess 4:16–17; Rev 1:7.

9. Carson cites Matt 13:40–41; 16:27; 25:31; 1 Cor 11:26; 15:52; 16:22; 1 Thess 4:14–17; 2 Thess 1:7; 2:1–8; 2 Pet 3:10–12; Rev 1:7. Carson "Matthew," 8:493.

10. Ibid.

11. Ford, *Abomination of Desolation*, 65.

12. Toussaint, "A Critique," 475–76; see also above, chapter 5, regarding the nature of the second coming and what it entails.

the events surrounding his second coming that will not occur for "a long time" and which "you do not know."[13]

The dispensationalist/futurist interpretation

This interpretation views the entire discourse (at least the Matthew and Mark accounts) as pertaining to future events surrounding Christ's *parousia*.

This approach has the following strengths

(1) It answers the second question of the disciples, *"What will be the sign of your coming, and of the end of the age?"* (Matt 24:3).

(2) It takes the time reference *"immediately after the tribulation of those days"* (Matt 24:29) in a straightforward manner.

This approach has important weaknesses

(1) It is completely divorced from the context of Matt 23:34—24:2. The disciples were discussing the then-existing temple building. In Matt 23:34–38; 24:2; Mark 13:2; and Luke 21:20–24, Jesus is obviously referring to the destruction of that temple. Nothing in the context supports the idea that Jesus is talking about another temple to be rebuilt centuries later, only to again be destroyed.[14]

(2) It divorces Matthew's and Mark's version of the discourse from Luke's. Dispensationalist Thomas Ice agrees that Matthew, Mark, and Luke all "record the Olivet discourse as given by Jesus [but] Matthew and Mark focus exclusively upon the future events of the Tribulation, while Luke's version includes past and future elements."[15] That *in effect* amounts to saying that Jesus gave two separate discourses. In fact, Matthew's, Mark's, and Luke's accounts of the discourse are consistent with each other, supplement and complement each other, and mutually interpret each other. All three versions arise from the context of Jesus' rejection of Israel and deal both with the events of the first century (the fall of Jerusalem) and the second coming. Even dispensationalist David Turner admits, "It must be concluded that the futurist view, held by traditional dispensationalists, is unconvincing. It does not satisfactorily handle the contextual emphasis on the fall of Jerusalem."[16]

(3) It ignores the first and central question of the disciples regarding the timing of the destruction of the temple, *"Tell us, when will these things happen?"* (Matt 24:2–3).

---

13. These are discussed in the sections of this chapter entitled "The parable of the fig tree: "all these things" and "this generation" versus "that day and hour" (Matt 24:32–36; Mark 13:28–32; Luke 21:28–36)" and "The second coming of Christ is totally unpredictable."

14. See Blomberg, "Matthew," 86.

15. Ice, "New Testament," 96.

16. Turner, "Structure and Sequence," 10.

D. A. Carson observes that the dispensationalist/futurist interpretation has serious implications for Jesus' own credibility because, according to the dispensationalist interpretation:

> Jesus' answer must have not only been opaque to his auditors but almost deceptive. Their first question concerns Jerusalem's judgment. But since a substantial part of Jesus' answer is couched in terms dealing with Jerusalem's destruction, how could the disciples think Jesus was *not* answering their question but describing a *second* destruction of the city, unless Jesus explicitly disavowed their understanding? But he does nothing of the kind. So perhaps it is not surprising that the dispensational identification of vv.15–28 *exclusively* with the great tribulation after the rapture of the church, whether revealed or unrevealed, finds no exponent till the nineteenth century. The dispensational approach to the Olivet Discourse must be judged historically implausible in reference to both the history of Jesus and the history of interpretation.[17]

(4) It ignores the AD 70 context of the references to *"the abomination of desolation,"* fleeing from Judea, and the *"great tribulation"* in Matt 24:15–21. Futurism supposes that the references in this portion of the discourse pertain to events that will occur after a future Antichrist comes and there is great tribulation just before the second coming. However, as Carson discusses, "the details in vv.16–21 are too limited geographically and culturally to justify that view. . . . The instructions Jesus gives his disciples about what to do in view of v.15 are so specific that they must be related to the Jewish War [of AD 66–70]. . . . Jesus clearly expects these events to take place while the strict Sabbath law is in effect."[18]

(5) It has to reinterpret *"this generation"* (Matt 24:34) in an unnatural way to mean "the nation of Israel," "the Jewish race," or to mean "that generation" (i.e., believers [or Jews] alive at the time of the second coming).[19]

The combined interpretation

This interpretation views the discourse as applying to the entire period between Christ's first coming and his second coming. Some portions of the discourse deal with the fall of Jerusalem in AD 70, and some portions deal with Christ's second coming at the end of the age. This view has always been the approach taken by the vast majority of conservative Christian scholars, although there are differences among them concerning exactly how the different parts of the discourse fit together. This is the approach that will be presented here.

17. Carson, "Matthew," 9:556.

18. Carson, "Matthew," 8:499, 501.

19. This is discussed below in this chapter in the section "The parable of the fig tree: 'all these things' and 'this generation' versus 'that day and hour' (Matt 24:32–36; Mark 13:28–32; Luke 21:28–36)."

The context of the Olivet Discourse

> "Most agree that the Olivet Discourse relates to (a) Israel's rejection of Christ, (b) Christ's rejection of Israel, and (c) the disciples' questions in Matthew 24:3."[20]

The broader context: judgment

Following his triumphal entry into Jerusalem, Jesus rejected Israel, condemned the Jewish leaders, and foreshadowed the destruction of Jerusalem and the temple. The theme of Jesus' judgment, condemnation, and rejection of the nation of Israel as his people is clear and pervasive, as Desmond Ford lists:

> Christ's pronouncement of divine visitation at the time of His triumphal entry [Matt 21:1–11; Mark 11:1–10; Luke 19:29–40], the cleansing of the temple [Matt 21:12–17; Mark 11:15–18; Luke 19:45–48], the cursing of the fig-tree [Matt 21:18–19; Mark 11:12–14], the utterance of judgment parables—vineyard and rejected stone [Matt 21:33–46; Mark 12:1–12; Luke 20:9–18], the marriage of the king's son [Matt 22:1–14], the woes on the Pharisees [Matt 23:1–39]; all take place as a series of thunderclaps of Judgment.[21]

Craig Blomberg adds that, in context, the parables of the two sons (Matt 21:28–33), the vineyard (Matt 21:33–46; Mark 12:1–12; Luke 20:9–18), and the marriage feast (Matt 22:1–14) function as "three parables that sequentially depict Israel's indictment (21:28–32), sentence (21:33–46), and execution (22:1–14)."[22]

The rejection of Jesus

The judgment upon Israel was based primarily on Israel's rejection of Jesus. In his triumphal entry into Jerusalem, Jesus was fulfilling the OT expectations that "YHWH is returning to Zion. He will do again what he did at the exodus, coming to dwell in the midst of his people."[23] However, Israel did not recognize that the OT was being fulfilled, the king had come, and God was visiting his people. Consequently, as N. T. Wright describes the scene, Jesus:

> bursts into tears and solemnly announces judgment on the city for failing to recognize 'its time of visitation' [Luke 19:41–44]. YHWH is visiting his people, and they do not realize it; they are therefore in imminent danger of judgment, which will take the form of military conquest and devastation. This is not a denial of the imminence of the kingdom. It is a warning about what the imminent kingdom will entail. . . . It was a warning that, when YHWH returned to Zion, he would come as judge for those in Israel who had not been faithful to his

---

20. Toussaint, "A Critique," 474.

21. Ford, *Abomination of Desolation*, 36.

22. Blomberg, "Matthew," 74; see also Longman and Reid, *Warrior*, 121–24.

23. Wright, *Victory*, 616. See Isa 4:2–6; 24:23; 25:9–10; 35:3–6, 10; 40:3–5, 9–11; 52:7–10; 59:15–20; 60:1–3; 62:10–11; 63:1–9; 64:1; 66:12–19; Ezek 43:1–7; Hag 2:7–10; Zech 2:4–5, 10–12; 8:2–3; Mal 3:1–4.

commission. . . . 'Why do you desire the day of YHWH? It is a day of darkness, not of light' [Amos 5:18]. Israel's hopes of national victory would be set aside; the only people vindicated when their god returned, to act in fulfillment of his promise, would be those who responded to the divine summons now being issued in Jesus' kingdom-announcement.[24]

The basis of judgment in his parables of the vineyard and rejected stone (Matt 21:33–46; Mark 12:1–12; Luke 20:9–18) and the marriage of the king's son (Matt 22:1–14) was the Jewish leaders' rejection of him. In his lengthy discourse against the scribes and Pharisees (Matt 23:1–39), Jesus made the same connection. He said he was sending prophets, wise men, and scribes whom they would kill and persecute, *"so that upon you may fall the guilt of all the righteous blood shed on earth, from the blood of righteous Abel to the blood of Zechariah. . . . Truly I say to you, all these things will come upon this generation"* (23: 34–36). Jesus concluded by connecting himself with Jerusalem's fate: *"Jerusalem, Jerusalem, who kills the prophets and stones those who are sent to her! How often I have wanted to gather your children together, the way a hen gathers her chicks under her wings, and you were not willing. Behold, your house is being left to you desolate! For I say to you, from now on you will not see Me until you say, 'Blessed is He who comes in the name of the Lord!'"* (23:37–39).[25]

Jesus even reiterated the connection between rejection of himself and the judgment that would soon fall on Jerusalem and the temple as he was being led to his crucifixion (Luke 23:28–31). Wright states, "The judgment of which Jesus was warning the women of Jerusalem was the devastation which would result from the city's rejection of him as the true king, and his message as the true way of peace. His own death at the hands of Rome was the clearest sign of the fate in store for the nation that had rejected him."[26] To put it another way, "(1) If the Romans treat Me, whom they admit to be innocent, in this manner, how will they treat those who are rebellious and guilty? (2) If the Jews deal thus with One who has come to save them, what treatment shall they receive themselves for destroying Him?"[27] One commentator summarizes, "As far as the New Testament is concerned, the events at the close of the Old Testament era, the death of Christ and the fall of Jerusalem, were the beginning of the End. They were the first act in the drama of the end time, and the last act would be the Parousia."[28]

The immediate context: the temple

When Jesus left the temple for the Mount of Olives, his disciples mentioned how beautiful and wonderful the temple buildings were. Jesus responded by telling them, *"Do you not see all these things? Truly I say to you, not one stone here will be left upon another, which will*

---

24. Wright, *Victory,* 636–37.

25. "There is no consensus on the exegesis of this passage, whether the acclamation of Jesus as king implies the conversion of at least some Jews, or whether it is a reluctant admission of his sovereignty when he comes as Judge." France, "Old Testament Prophecy," 76n.41.

26. Wright, *Victory,* 569.

27. Plummer, *St. Luke,* 529.

28. Ford, *Abomination of Desolation,* 31.

not be torn down." (Matt 24:2; see also Mark 13:2; Luke 21:6). That statement regarding the temple prompted the disciples' questions, *"Tell us, when will these things happen, and what will be the sign of Your coming and of the end of the age?"* (Matt 24:3; see also Mark 13:4; Luke 21:7). The Olivet Discourse is Jesus' answer to those questions.

The parallel with the Babylonian destruction of Jerusalem

The Olivet Discourse is parallel to Jeremiah's and Ezekiel's prophecies of the destruction of the temple that occurred when the Babylonians took Jerusalem in 586/587 BC:

In Jer 12:7; 22:5 God said that he was abandoning his "house," which would become "desolate."	In Matt 23:38 Jesus said *"Your house is being left to you desolate."* At his death, when *"the veil of the temple was torn in two from top to bottom"* (Matt 27:51), the temple was exposed as desolate of God's presence or even the physical indicators of God's presence (e.g., the ark of the covenant and the mercy seat).
In Ezek 10:1–19 God's glory left the temple.	In Matt 24:1; Mark 13:1 Jesus left the temple.
In Ezek 11:6–7 God commanded a man clothed in linen to scatter coals of fire over the city. "The vision was prophetic of the fires that actually destroyed Jerusalem in 587 BC (2 Ki. 25:9); but more significant than the prediction is the revelation of the identity of the Destroyer, God Himself."*	In Matt 24:2; Mark 13:2; Luke 21:6 Jesus said, *"not one stone will be left upon another."*
In Ezek 11:22–23, before departing the city, the glory of God was last seen when it *"stood over the mountain which is east of the city"* (i.e., the Mount of Olives).	The Mount of Olives is where Jesus prophesied the destruction of the temple and Jerusalem (Matt 24:3; Mark 13:3).

*Beasley-Murray, *Ezekiel,* 671

Both Luke 19:42–44 (in which Jesus also predicts the destruction of Jerusalem) and Luke's account of the Olivet Discourse are "composed *entirely* from the language of the Old Testament. . . . So far as any historical event has coloured the picture, it is not Titus's capture of Jerusalem in A.D. 70, but Nebuchadrezzar's capture in 586 B.C. There is no single trait of the forecast which cannot be documented directly out of the Old Testament."[29] The OT description of the destruction wrought by the Babylonians (Ezek 5:9; 7:5–6; Dan 9:12) and Jesus' description of the destruction to be wrought by the Romans (Matt 24:21), are virtually identical. Additionally, both the Babylonians in 586 BC and the Romans in AD 70 invaded Jerusalem, destroyed the temple, destroyed much of Jerusalem, and took most of the people who were not killed into captivity.[30]

Despite these parallels, the judgment and rejection of Israel by Jesus is unlike even the earlier destruction by the Babylonians in 586 BC. That event, profound as it was, was not a final, theological, rejection of the nation. Israel had been permitted to return after the exile. They rebuilt the temple. However, as we have seen, the temple, indeed the nation

29. Dodd, *More,* 79.
30. Blomberg, "Matthew," 69.

itself, existed as a "type" or "shadow" to point to something greater than itself—namely, Jesus Christ. Now, Jesus had come—and was rejected. N. T. Wright notes, "As a prophet, after the manner of Elijah, Jeremiah or Ezekiel, he had solemnly announced that Israel—Jerusalem—the Temple—were under judgment. The prophets had come and gone, and been ignored. He came as the last in the line, and they were planning to kill him."[31] Therefore, as R. T. France points out, after Jesus entered Jerusalem that last time—in his actions, parables, and direct statements of the coming judgment on Israel—there is "an inescapable note of finality. The blood of all the prophets from the beginning will be required of this generation: it is the final reckoning. The Lucan version of the prediction of the fall of Jerusalem contains the solemn words, 'These are the days of vengeance, to fulfil all that is written' (Luke 21:22). The note of climax we have seen in Jesus' declaration that in him all the hopes of the Old Testament were finding fulfilment [Mark 1:15; Luke 4:21; 24:27, 44–47] is paralleled by this idea of the coming disaster as the culmination of all Israel's rebellion."[32]

The theological significance of the destruction of the temple in AD 70

Although the destruction of Jerusalem and the temple in AD 70 was not the "end of this age" as preterists claim, it nevertheless was theologically significant.

Superseding the Old Covenant

The destruction of Jerusalem and the temple fulfilled Christ's prophecies and demonstrated God's rejection of the nation of Israel as his chosen people and as the vehicle for spreading his truth. Jesus' death on the cross ended the Old Covenant and instituted the New. At that time *"the veil of the temple was torn in two from top to bottom"* (Matt 27:51), symbolizing the destruction of the temple and, more importantly, the Old Covenant temple system. The destruction of Jerusalem and the temple in AD 70 was the outward, visible sign that confirmed the truth of the supreme theological event that had occurred forty years before: that the Old Covenant system was no longer effective and had been abrogated by the death, resurrection, and ascension of Jesus Christ. The destruction of the temple rendered the keeping of the Torah impossible, thus confirming that the Old Covenant had been superseded. J. C. Ryle remarks on the significance of the destruction of the temple:

> Jerusalem and the temple were the heart of the old Jewish dispensation: when they were destroyed, the old Mosaic system came to an end. The daily sacrifice, the yearly feasts, the altar, the holy of holies, the priesthood, all were essential to the revealed religion, till Christ came,—but no longer. When He died upon the cross, their work was done: they were dead, and it only remained that they

31. Wright, *Victory,* 594.

32. France, "Old Testament Prophecy," 62. The rejection of the *nation* of Israel of necessity is final because Jesus had redefined "Israel" to now be all who are united with and loyal to Jesus himself (see chapter 3 above, particularly the section "Christ's first coming and the fulfillment of the OT eschatological prophecies concerning Israel").

should be buried.—But it was not fitting that this thing should be done quietly. The ending of a dispensation given with so much solemnity at mount Sinai, might well be expected to be marked with peculiar solemnity; the destruction of the holy temple, where so many old saints had seen "shadows of good things to come," might well be expected to form a subject of prophecy: and so it was.[33]

Vindication of the church

The destruction of Jerusalem and the temple also vindicated the church as God's chosen people and as the vehicle for spreading his truth.[34] Many of the early church fathers recognized this:

- *Epistle of Barnabas* (c. 70–131):

  I will also speak to you about the temple, and how those wretched men went astray and set their hope on their building, as though it were God's house, and not on their God who created them. . . . But let us inquire whether there is in fact a temple of God. There is—where he himself says he is building and completing it! . . . Before we believed in God, our heart's dwelling-place was corrupt and weak, truly a temple built by human hands, because it was full of idolatry and was the home of demons, for we did whatever was contrary to God. . . . By receiving the forgiveness of sins and setting our hope on the Name, we become new, created again from the beginning. Consequently, God truly dwells in our dwelling-place—that is, in us. . . . This is the spiritual temple that is being built for the Lord.[35]

- *Tertullian* (c. 160–220): "Judea . . . would never have been beneath your [Rome's] sceptre but for that last and crowning offence against God, in rejecting and crucifying Christ."[36] "Let us show that Christ is already come, (as foretold) through the prophets, and has suffered, and is already received back in the heavens, and thence is to come accordingly as the predictions prophesied. For, after His advent, we read, according to Daniel, that the city itself had to be exterminated; and we recognise that so it has befallen."[37]

- *Hippolytus* (c. 170–236): "But why, O prophet, tell us, and for what reason, was the temple made desolate? Was it on account of that ancient fabrication of the calf? Was it on account of the idolatry of the people? Was it for the blood of the prophets? Was it for the adultery and fornication of Israel? By no means, he says; for in all these transgressions they always found pardon open to them, and benignity; but it was because they killed the Son of their Benefactor, for He is coeternal with the Father. Whence He saith, 'Father, let their temple be made desolate [Matt 23:38].'"[38]

33. Ryle, *Expository Thoughts*, 317.
34. See Gentry, "A Preterist View," 80.
35. *Barn.* 16:1–10.
36. Tertullian, *An Answer to the Jews* 13.
37. Tertullian, *Apology* 26.
38. Hippolytus, *Expository Treatise Against the Jews* 7.

- *Cyprian* (c. 208–258): "Did not the Jews perish for this reason, that they chose rather to envy Christ than to believe Him?"[39]

- *Lactantius* (c. 240–320): "Why hath God done these evils to this land and to this house? . . . Because they forsook the Lord their God, and persecuted their King most beloved by God, and crucified him with great degradation, therefore hath God brought upon them these evils [1 Kgs 9:6–9]."[40]

Separation of Judaism and Christianity

The destruction of Jerusalem and the temple led to the formal separation of Judaism and Christianity. Jews were exempt from having to worship the Roman emperor. "Up until the era of the mid-A.D. 60s (but not after A.D. 70) the Romans were prone to identify Christianity as a sect of Judaism, intimately and necessarily bound up with it."[41] That is because, as Beale tells us, "According to Roman law, religions were considered illegal outside their country of origin, though this was not enforced unless there was overt social misbehavior associated with the practice of a religion. The only exception to this law was Judaism, the practice of which was allowed throughout the Empire."[42]

However, Christians did not support the Jewish revolt and escaped from Jerusalem before its destruction by the Romans. The Christians' failure to support the revolt and their escape from Jerusalem were regarded by their Jewish fellow-countrymen as apostasy. As a result, after AD 70 the Jewish leaders attacked Jewish Christians, their presence in the synagogues, and their status as Jews. J. G. Davies says, "Seeking to establish a new uniformity in religion as a necessary basis for a new unity, the rabbis introduced into the synagogue service a formula which the Jewish Christians could not pronounce [known as the *'minim'* (lit., 'heretics')] to the effect that 'for the Nazarenes [followers of Jesus] there may be [or 'let there be'] no hope'. They followed this by sending letters to all Jewish congregations in the Diaspora denouncing the practice and faith of Christianity."[43]

This had several consequences, one of which was immediate and ultimately proved costly to many Christians. After the formal separation from Judaism, "Jewish Christians were no longer perceived by the Roman government as under the umbrella of Judaism

---

39. Cyprian, *Treatise on Jealousy and Envy* 5.

40. Lactantius, *Divine Institutes* 4.18.

41. Gentry, *Before Jerusalem Fell,* 227.

42. Beale, *Revelation,* 30–31.

43. Davies, *Early Christian Church,* 46; see also Barrett, *New Testament Background,* 210–11; Gentry, *Before Jerusalem Fell,* 226–30. This was the twelfth of the "Eighteen Benedictions" that were part of the synagogue service. Barrett quotes the twelfth benediction as follows: "For the renegades let there be no hope, and may the arrogant kingdom soon be rooted out in our days, and the Nazarenes and the *minim* perish as in a moment and be blotted out from the book of life and with the righteous may they not be inscribed. Blessed art thou, O Lord, who humblest the arrogant." Barrett, *New Testament Background,* 211. Barrett notes that the benediction has taken various forms, and that "and the Nazarenes" may not have been part of the original text, although the wording just quoted "is probably very close to the original wording." Ibid.

and, therefore, faced the cruel dilemma of either forsaking Christ (if they were to be read-mitted into the synagogues) or worshiping Caesar."[44]

The content and structure of the Olivet Discourse

The disciples asked a two-fold question: "When?" and "What?" (Matt 24:3; see also Mark 13:4; Luke 21:7). The "when" concerns the destruction of the temple; the "what" concerns the coming of Christ and the end of the age. The disciples' questions to Jesus indicate that they viewed the destruction of the temple, Jesus' coming, and the end of the age as a single complex of events.[45] Although the form of the question varies from gospel to gospel, D.A. Carson points out that "if we make the reasonable assumption that in the disciples' mind their question as to the temple's destruction and the signs that will presage it are linked to the end of the age and Jesus' return (cf. 16:27–28; 23:39; Luke 19:11–27), there is little problem. Matthew makes explicit what was implicit and what Jesus recognized as implicit in their question."[46] Jesus' answer to the disciples' questions is nuanced and distinguishes the events that the disciples had conflated.[47]

The structure of the discourse may be outlined as follows:

Topic	Matthew 24	Mark 13	Luke 21
1. Occasion of the address	24:1–3	13:1–4	21:5–7
2. Signs of the times between Jesus' 1st & 2nd Comings	24:4–28	13:5–23	21:8–24
A. General description of the "birth pains"	24:4–14	13:5–13	21:8–19
B. A "sharp pain": The Fall of Jerusalem	24:15–21	13:14–19	21:20–24
C. Special dangers: False Christs & deception	24:22–28	13:20–23	21:8
3. The coming of the Son of Man	24:29–31	13:24–27	21:25–28
4. The significance of the signs of the times	24:32–35	13:28–31	21:29–33
5. Warnings against presumption & unpreparedness	24:36–51	13:32–37	21:34–36

The signs of the times (Matt 24:4–28; Mark 13:5–23; Luke 21:8–24)

"Literary and structural arguments suggest that [Matt 24:4–28; Mark 13:5–23; Luke 21:8–24] must be taken as one time period [culminating in the second coming] with [the destruction of the temple and Jerusalem—Matt 24:15–21; Mark 13:14–19; Luke 21:20–24] a critical part of it."[48] Structurally, this is especially seen in Mark's account, since Mark "brackets" the entire section with the Greek word *blepete* ("watch out"; "take heed"; "see") at the beginning (Mark 13:5) and at the end (Mark 13:23).[49]

44. Pate, "Progressive Dispensationalist View," 140; see also Schüssler Fiorenza, *Revelation,* 55; Stylianopoulos, "I Know," 22n.19.

45. See Toussaint, "A Critique," 474.

46. Carson, "Matthew," 9:558.

47. See Blomberg, "Matthew," 86.

48. Carson, "Matthew," 8:502.

49. For a comparative table of the "signs of the times" listed in Matthew's, Mark's, and Luke's accounts

Matt 24:4–14; Mark 13:5–13; Luke 21:8–19

In this part of the discourse, "Jesus deals with certain outstanding features of the inter-adventual period. We are reminded at [Matt 24:6] that the end is not immediately, that the activity of deceivers, and reports of wars and rumours of wars, are not to be regarded as portents of an imminent consummation (cf. Luke 19:11); and at [Matt 24:7–8] that wars, famines, and earthquakes are but the beginning of sorrows."[50] John Murray observes that Christ's reference to the disciples' being *"hated by all the nations"* (Matt 24:9; Mark 13:13; Luke 21:17) and the preaching of the gospel *"in the whole world . . . to all the nations"* (Matt 24:14; Mark 13:10) are reminders "of the extended period that the events of interadventual history require for their fulfillment. However, this section of the discourse brings us to what is surely of the same purport as 'the consummation of the age' in the question of the disciples [Matt 24:3], namely, 'the end'—'then shall the end come'. So we are compelled to construe [Matt 24:4–14; Mark 13:5–13; Luke 21:8–19] as, in brief outline, a forecast of interadventual history."[51] That is how *Didache* 16 (c. 70–110) applied this portion of the discourse.

Matt 24:15–28; Mark 13:14–23; Luke 21:20–24

This section begins with the fall of Jerusalem in AD 70 and then recapitulates the entire inter-advent period. Murray notes that it "cannot be a continuation, because [Matt 24:14; Mark 13:10] brought us up to the end. It must be, to some extent, recapitulation. Our Lord forecasts to the disciples certain additional features of the period that had been delineated in [Matt 24:4–14; Mark 13:5–13; Luke 21:8–19] and gives the warnings and exhortations appropriate to the events involved. Here we have a principle that must be applied in the interpretation of prophecy. Delineation of the eschatological drama is not always continuously progressive; it is often recapitulatory."[52]

Luke's parallel account is more focused on Jerusalem. Nevertheless, Luke 21:24b (*"and Jerusalem will be trampled under foot by the Gentiles until the times of the Gentiles are fulfilled"*) also covers the entire inter-advent period until the *parousia*. This is seen in light of Zech 14:2 which, if taken literally, speaks about the future subjugation of Jerusalem just before the second coming. Kenneth Barker discusses the theological significance of Zechariah vis-à-vis the "times of the Gentiles":

> This eschatological verse alone—with its statement that "the city will be captured"—is sufficient to refute the notion popular in certain circles that "the times of the Gentiles" (Lk 21:24) were fulfilled at the rebirth of the modern state of Israel in 1948. According to Lukan theology, after "the times of the Gentiles are fulfilled," Jerusalem will be trampled on no more. Since Zechariah 14:2 clearly indicates that Jerusalem will be "trampled on" again in the future, the "times of the Gentiles" would seem to extend to the Messiah's second advent, when those

---

of the Olivet Discourse, see Schnabel, *40 Questions*, 32–33.

50. Murray, "Interadventual Period," 388.

51. Ibid.

52. Ibid.

"times" will be replaced by the final, universal, everlasting, messianic kingdom of Daniel 2:35, 44–45.[53]

The same result obtains if one looks at Jerusalem spiritually. In its rejection of Jesus, Jerusalem lost its claim to be called the holy city. Its true character is seen as Sodom and Egypt (Rev 11:8). Simon Kistemaker points out, "God took up residence not in Jerusalem but in the church; and at Pentecost the Holy Spirit filled not the temple or Jerusalem but the apostles and all those who repented and were baptized (Acts 2:1–4, 38–39). [Thus, in Revelation] John describes the new Jerusalem as the holy city (21:2, 10; 22:19). He explains that this is 'the camp of the saints and the beloved city' (20:9) which Jesus calls 'the city of my God' (3:12). The holy city is the spiritual Jerusalem of the saints."[54] Consequently, in the most important (spiritual) sense, *physical* Jerusalem will continue to be *"trampled under foot by the Gentiles"* until Christ returns.

Before AD 70 all of the "signs of the times" that Jesus predicted occurred in principle

Before Jerusalem fell in AD 70 all of the predicted "signs of the times" had begun to occur. Acts 5:36–37; 8:9–10; 13:6; 1 John 4:1 record different "false prophets" who had arisen, and 1 John 2:18 reports that *"many antichrists have appeared."* Josephus reported the same thing.[55] Following the death of Nero in AD 68, "wars and rumors of war" erupted throughout the Roman Empire.[56] The war against the Jews lasted from AD 66–70. Regarding "famines and earthquakes," Acts 7:59–60; 11:19, 28; 12:1–2, Josephus,[57] and Eusebius[58] report great famines. Both Acts 16:26 and Josephus[59] report earthquakes. The references in Mark 13:9 to the "courts" (or Sanhedrin) and "synagogues" indicate first-century Jewish persecution of Christians. Acts 4:3; 5:17–41; 6:11—8:3; 12:1–5; 14:1–6, 19; 16:19–24; 17:5–8, 13; 18:12–17; 20:3; 21:27—28:20; 2 Cor 11:24–33; Heb 10:32–34 all report the same thing. First Tim 1:19–20; 6:10; 2 Tim 1:15; 4:10; Heb 2:1–4; 6:1–6; 10:26–31 record betrayals and falling away from the faith by professed believers. "Lawlessness" was characteristic of the time during the Jewish War.[60] Mark 13:9–11 links the preaching of the gospel to *"all the nations"* with the first-century Jewish persecution of believers. Acts 2:5–11; Rom 1:8; 16:25–26; Col 1:6, 23 also record that the gospel was *"preached in the whole world."*[61] With the fall of Jerusalem, *"all these things"* that Jesus had prophesied in the

---

53. Barker, "Zechariah," 824–25; see also Walker, *Jesus*, 100–101; Schnabel, *40 Questions*, 132–33.

54. Kistemaker, "Temple," 437.

55. Josephus, *Ant.* 20.5.1; 20.8.6; *J.W.* 2.13.4; 6.5.2.

56. Josephus, *J.W.* 4.9.2–3.

57. Josephus, *Ant.* 20.2.5; *J.W.* 6.3.3.

58. Eusebius, *Hist. eccl.* 2.8–26.

59. Josephus, *Ant.* 15.5.2; *J.W.* 4.4.5; 5.10.3.

60. Josephus, *J.W.* 4.6.3; 5.10.2–3; 7.8.1. The excerpts from Josephus's writings pertaining to the fall of Jerusalem are helpfully collected, organized, and given subheads and explanatory footnotes as Appendix B in Chilton, *Paradise*, 237–90.

61. See also Schnabel, *40 Questions*, 132.

Olivet Discourse had been initiated and had taken place *in principle*.[62] Consequently, after Jerusalem and the temple were destroyed in AD 70, Jesus could return in any generation, suddenly and unexpectedly.[63]

The occurrence of the "signs" before AD 70 and the "delay" of the parousia

While the form of the disciples' question indicates that they viewed the first century and "end times" as a single complex of events, Jesus' answer separates the two. The difficulty is finding the precise point of separation in the answer because all the events in different ways appear to be linked.[64] Here is where the "contingent" element of prophecy may be at work. Desmond Ford suggests that Christ may have "believed that if the early church proved faithful to its missionary commission, and if the chastened Jewish nation repented, the end would transpire in that same Age. It is this linkage of the gospel proclamation to the world with the end of the Age that provides the hint of the contingent element. Such proclamation would be dependent upon the whole-hearted dedication of the church. An uncertain human element is involved."[65] Similarly, G. B. Caird writes, "Jesus clearly indicated that in its final manifestation the Day was known only to God, not because God had fixed a date which he guarded as a close secret, but because the coming of the Day was contingent upon the full realization of the purposes of God."[66] Inasmuch as the end did not occur in the first century, the "signs of the times" have continued since AD 70 and will continue to occur until Christ returns. When he returns is known only by God.[67]

The "abomination of desolation" (Matt 24:15; Mark 13:14)

Prophetic use of "abomination of desolation"

The *"abomination of desolation"* (or *"abomination that causes desolation"*—NIV; or *"desolating sacrilege"*—RSV) was referred to in Dan 8:13; 9:27; 11:31; 12:11. This prophecy not only was known by the Jews of the second temple era but was applied by them to the events of their own time. In 167 BC Antiochus Epiphanes, the Seleucid king, had

---

62. See Matt 24:33–34; Mark 13:29–30; Luke 21:31–32. Partial preterists, of course, cite this in support of their contention that *"all these things"* had occurred in full by AD 70. Mathison, *Postmillennialism*, 111–15. Full preterists contend that not only were these signs completely fulfilled, but all prophecies were fulfilled by AD 70 which therefore marked the *consummation* of all prophecy. Preston, *AD 70*, 43–58; Preston, *Like Father*, 301–08.

63. Schnabel, *40 Questions*, 157. The events surrounding Christ's own death have similar eschatological import: Judas is called *"the son of perdition"* (John 17:12), the same phrase used to describe the *"man of lawlessness"* in 2 Thess 2:3 who must come before *"the day of the Lord."* At Christ's death there were signs in the sky (Matt 27:45; Mark 15:33; Luke 23:44–45); an earthquake and resurrection of saints occurred (Matt 27:51–53). Thus, both the fall of Jerusalem and Christ's own death "were eschatological in import—the signs of the times had already begun." Pate and Haines, *Doomsday Delusions*, 47.

64. Ford, *Abomination of Desolation*, 68.

65. Ibid., 76.

66. Caird, *Apostolic Age*, 189.

67. Matt 24:36; Mark 13:32; see also below, the section "The second coming of Christ is totally unpredictable."

sacrificed a swine on the altar and had made the practice of Judaism illegal. That prompted the Maccabean revolt of 167–164 BC.[68] In 1 Macc 1:54, the *"abomination of desolation"* was applied to the desecration of the altar of the temple by Antiochus.[69] Nevertheless, in the first century many in Israel believed that Antiochus had not completely fulfilled Daniel's visions of the *"abomination of desolation."* Desmond Ford relates that Daniel "had promised the advent of the kingdom of God after the profanation of the sanctuary by the willful king. But certainly the kingdom had not come with the rededicated sanctuary in 165 B.C. Therefore, they reasoned, the woes under Antiochus must have been prefigurative of worse woes to come."[70]

In the Olivet Discourse, Jesus likewise views the times of Antiochus as prefigurative of what lay ahead. He takes the same prophetic language and reapplies it—or, rather, is saying that the true fulfillment related to the nation's rejection of *him*.[71] The temple would again be desecrated and, indeed, destroyed.[72] That happened in AD 70 when the Romans again desecrated the building by virtually razing it to the ground.[73]

After the fact, that is how first-century Jewish historian Josephus took it, although he did not understand that the reason for the fulfillment of the prophecy was because of Israel's sin and rebellion in rejecting Jesus, Israel's Messiah. Josephus wrote, "And indeed it so came to pass, that our nation suffered these things under Antiochus Epiphanes, according to Daniel's vision, and that he wrote many years before they came to pass. In the very same manner Daniel also wrote concerning the Roman government, and that our country should be made desolate by them."[74] Clement of Alexandria (c. 150–215),[75] Tertullian (c. 160–220),[76] and early church historian Eusebius (c. 263–339)[77] also took Daniel's vision that way.

Identity of the "abomination of desolation"

The specific identification of the *"abomination of desolation"* is unclear but is related to the events of AD 66–70 in Jerusalem and the temple. The *"abomination of desolation"* has been identified with: the Zealots who defiled the temple, killed the priests, and deposed the

---

68. Bartlett, "Maccabees," 476; Metzger, *Introduction*, 132.

69. See also Josephus, *Ant.* 12.7.6; Schnabel, *40 Questions*, 154.

70. Ford, *Abomination of Desolation*, 157.

71. Compare Dan 7:13 and Mark 13:26; Dan 8:13 and Luke 21:24; Dan 9:27 and Mark 13:14; Dan 11:31 and Mark 13:14; Dan 12:1 and Mark 13:19; and possibly Dan 11:45 and Matt 24:15 (*"in the holy place"*).

72. "Jesus' appeal to Daniel's 'abomination of desolation' should be understood in a typological sense. That is, the crisis of long ago, which threatened to bring Judaism and Israel's national life to an end, will once again threaten Israel and Jesus' followers." Evans, *Mark 8:27—16:20*, 319; see also Schnabel, *40 Questions*, 38–39.

73. "Titus' savagery surpassed that of Antiochus with the city and temple almost completely destroyed and the temple cult eradicated." Such, *Abomination*, 98.

74. Josephus, *Ant.* 10.11.7.

75. Clement of Alexandria, *Stromata* 1.21.

76. Tertullian, *An Answer to the Jews* 8.

77. Eusebius, *Hist. eccl.* 3.5.4.

high priest;[78] the invading Roman armies;[79] the Roman eagle military standards which had religious significance and which the Roman army brought into the temple where they offered sacrifices to them;[80] Titus's standing in the temple;[81] and other things.[82]

The actions of the Zealots and the Romans may be linked as the *"abomination of desolation."* Peter Gentry describes this linkage:

> The "abominations" refer to the sacrilege which resulted from the struggle between [Zealots] John, Simon, and Eleazar ("people of the coming ruler" [Dan 9:26]) for control of Jerusalem, and the "war" [Dan 9:26] refers to the destruction of Jerusalem and Temple by Vespasian/Titus (the "one causing desolation" [Dan 9:27]). The "one causing desolation" (Titus) comes "on the wing of," [Dan 9:27] i.e., in connection with, those causing "abominations" (Jews), the one (i.e., people) being desolated. Jesus' mention of the "abomination of desolation" in the Olivet Discourse supports this understanding since he is probably speaking of the sacrilege of John of Gischala [Zealot leader] as the "abomination" which forewarns of the impending "desolation" of Jerusalem and the Temple by the Romans.[83]

Luke 21:20 (*"When you see Jerusalem surrounded by armies, then recognize that her desolation is near"*) picks up on Jesus' statement in Matt 23:38 that *"your house is being left to you desolate."* That the surrounding armies signal *"desolation is near,"* indicates that the desolation itself is the destruction of the temple and the city.[84] In light of all of the above, Rikk Watts wisely cautions, "Perhaps the attempt at an overly precise identification [of the *"abomination of desolation"*] is misguided. Mark 13, although clearly referring to a historical event, does so using prophetic topoi [rhetorical conventions or motifs]. As with all such prophetic language, the concern is the significance of the event, not an exact description."[85]

"Abomination of desolation": AD 70 versus end-time Antichrist

Both the historical and the literary contexts of the reference to the *"abomination of desolation"* indicate an historical event surrounding the AD 70 destruction of Jerusalem, not an "end-time" Antichrist.[86] Christ's admonition to his disciples, *"when you see"* the abomi-

---

78. Gentry, "Exposition," 47; Schnabel, *40 Questions*, 156; Carson, "Matthew," 8:501. See Josephus, *J.W.* 4.6.3; see also ibid., 4.3.4—4.7.2; 5.1.1—5.3.1; 5.6.1; 5.13.1–7.

79. Ford, *Abomination of Desolation*, 163–66.

80. Josephus, *J.W.* 6.6.1; Gentry, "Exposition," 48; Carson, "Matthew," 8:501.

81. Such, *Abomination*, 96–98.

82. Watts, "Mark," 224; Ford, *Abomination of Desolation*, 158–62.

83. Gentry, "New Exodus," 39. Concerning John of Gischala, see Josephus, *J.W.* 2.21.1–8; 4.3.1–2, 13–14; 4.4.1; 4.7.1; 7.8.1.

84. See Pao and Schnabel, "Luke," 376.

85. Watts, "Mark," 224.

86. Nevertheless, R. Fowler White observes that the biblical prophetic repetition of similar themes and language regarding the *"abomination of desolation"* recurs in the book of Revelation: "By the time of creation's destruction in [Rev] 16:18, 20, the dragon, the sea beast, and the land beast-false prophet will have defiled the entire earth through 'unclean spirits' (16:13), thus turning the world into an

nation of desolation or Jerusalem surrounded by armies (Matt 24:15; Mark 13:14; Luke 21:20) suggests the events of AD 70, since Jesus was talking to his disciples, "you" is in the second person plural, and the events of AD 70 were in the lifetime of the disciples. Kenneth Gentry articulates what should otherwise be self-evident: "Surely Jesus does not denounce the first-century temple in which He is standing (24:1) by declaring it 'desolate' (23:38), prophesying its total destruction (24:2), then answering the question 'when shall these things be?' (v.3), and warning about the temple's 'abomination of desolation' (v.15) only to speak about the destruction of a totally different temple some two thousand years (or more) later!"[87]

Further, both the references in Dan 9:27 and 11:31, which suggest a human instigator of the abomination, and the Maccabean historical background "indicate a historical, not a supra-historical individual" as the abomination.[88] "In fact, a supra-historical Antichrist figure in [Mark 13:14a] would leave no room for the subsequent 'false christs' in [Matt 24:24; Mark 13:22]."[89] Finally, because Israel as a nation and its temple were "types," "symbols," "shadows," "copies," or "examples" of NT realities, the temple and its sacrifices have been fulfilled and superseded in Christ.[90] Therefore, even if a temple is rebuilt in Jerusalem it would be an idol temple, with no more theological significance than a Hindu temple or an Islamic mosque. Nothing that might occur in a rebuilt temple could be an *abomination of desolation.*

The exhortation to flee from Judea (Matt 24:16–20; Mark 13:14–18; Luke 21:21)

The case is overwhelming for interpreting Matt 24:16–20; Mark 13:14–18; Luke 21:21 as local and historical, i.e., related to the war of AD 66–70, not to an "end-time" event. Desmond Ford remarks: "V. G. Simkhovitch long ago lunged at the heart of the matter when he asked 'If it refers to the end of the world, what difference does it make whether that end is to come in the winter or in the summer?' And C. H. Dodd in similar vein affirmed that the description in these verses fits precisely a condition of besiegement. Unless these verses have reference to the destruction of Jerusalem and the temple, Christ has not truly replied to the enquiry from His disciples which provoked the discourse."[91] Fourth-century church historian Eusebius recognized that Matt 24:19–21 (pertaining to flight) concerned the events of the AD 66–70 war.[92]

In Luke 21:20 the exhortation to flee is triggered *"when you see Jerusalem surrounded by armies."* In Matt 24:15 and Mark 13:14 the triggering event is seeing the *"abomination*

---

abomination of desolation. Also, by the time of her destruction in 16:19, Babylon will have been filled with 'uncleanness' (cf. 17:4; 18:2), having become 'the mother of the abominations of the earth.'" White, "On the Hermeneutics," 60n.30.

87. Gentry, "Exposition," 24.

88. Such, *Abomination,* 95.

89. Ibid., 96.

90. Matt 5:17; Mark 14:58; John 2:18–22; 1 Cor 10:1–6; 2 Cor 3:12–16; Gal 3:23—4:7, 21–31; Col 2:16–17; Heb 1:1–2; 4:14–5:10; 7:1—10:22.

91. Ford, *Abomination of Desolation,* 65–66.

92. Eusebius, *Hist. eccl.* 3.7.1–2.

of desolation . . . standing in the holy place" (or *"where it should not be"*). Jerusalem was, in fact, encircled by the Romans several times (in AD 66, 68, and 70) before it was finally destroyed.[93] Eusebius reports that the church at Jerusalem had been commanded by a divine revelation given before the war [evidently the Olivet Discourse] and therefore left the city and dwelt in the town of Pella beyond the Jordan.[94] That may have occurred in AD 68.[95]

One objection to identifying Titus's standing in the temple or the Roman army worshiping their standards in the temple area as the *"abomination of desolation"* is that by the time that occurred it was too late to flee from Jerusalem. If that is the case, then the exhortation to *"those who are in Judea"* (Matt 24:16; Mark 13:14; Luke 21:21) is actually a *post-war* measure (since the entry of the Romans into the temple marked the end of the war). The exhortation is not directed to those in Jerusalem itself, from which flight was by that time impossible. However, even after Jerusalem was destroyed, W. A. Such tells us there was still "reason to believe that Judean Christians, vulnerable in places like Lydda, might suffer from the continuing activity of the Romans in Judea. . . . Such continuing after-shocks from Jerusalem's fall [e.g., various massacres and other acts by the Romans against Jews] would have unsettled Judean Jews rebuilding their synagogues and Jewish Christians trying to return to their homes and would have raised the possibility of worse to come. In this context Mark's injunction for Judeans to flee makes sense in light of events from Jerusalem's fall."[96]

The "great tribulation" (Matt 24:21; Mark 13:19; Luke 21:22–23)

Both Matt 24:21 and Mark 13:19 state that the events of AD 70 *"will be a great tribulation, such as has not occurred since the beginning of the world until now, nor ever will."* There have been greater numbers of deaths, including Jewish deaths, in wars since that time (e.g., World Wars I and II, and the holocaust of approximately six million Jews in WWII). Therefore, many people do not see how the *"great tribulation"* can refer to the events of AD 70. There are at least four reasons why the *"great tribulation"* refers to the events of AD 70, not to some "end-time" event shortly before the second coming.

The context of the Olivet Discourse

The context of the Olivet Discourse establishes the AD 70 context for the *"great tribulation"* to which Christ refers. Both Christ's statement in Matt 23:38 that *"your house is being left to you desolate"* and the occasion of the Olivet Discourse itself (Matt 24:1–3; Mark 13:1–4; Luke 21:5–7) primarily concern the destruction of the temple and Jerusalem. Likewise, the *immediate* context of Christ's reference to the *"great tribulation"* concerned the events of AD 70.

---

93. Gentry, "Exposition," 48–50.

94. Eusebius, *Hist. eccl.* 3.5.3. Many Jews fled the city after the first attempt to take Jerusalem in AD 66 failed. Such, *Abomination,* 118–19.

95. Carson, "Matthew," 8:501.

96. Such, *Abomination,* 129–30.

Grammatically, both Matt 24:21 and Mark 13:19 tie the *"great tribulation"* to the immediately preceding AD 70 context (i.e., fleeing from Judea) since both verses begin with the word "for" (Greek = *gar*). In other words, the reason to flee is *"for [or 'because'] there will be a great tribulation"* (Matt 24:21) or, as Mark puts it, *"for [or 'because'] those days will be a time of tribulation"* (Mark 13:19). The parallel passage in Luke is phrased somewhat differently but is to the same effect. Luke 21:20–21 sets forth the context of those in Judea fleeing to the mountains *"when you see Jerusalem surrounded by armies."*[97]

Luke 21:22 states that the reason to flee is *"because [Greek = hoti] these are days of vengeance."*[98] That statement provides the theological explanation of the *"great tribulation"* referred to in Matthew and Mark. According to Pao and Schnabel, Jesus' statement that *"these are days of vengeance"* alludes to Hos 9:7 LXX, which "announces that 'the days of vengeance have come.'... This announcement belongs to Hosea's accusation that Israel has rejected Yahweh and rebuffed his prophet, the basis for his prophecy that God will punish the nation.... The reference to the coming days of vengeance as a 'fulfillment of all that is written'... not only refers to Deut. 28:64; Jer. 20:4–6; Zech. 12:3, which are alluded to in 21:24, but also echoes other OT oracles that announce punishment for Israel as a result of covenantal unfaithfulness."[99]

In other words, Luke is confirming what the context of the Olivet Discourse, and Jesus' prediction of the destruction of Jerusalem and the temple, had already established, namely, that Jerusalem and the temple would be destroyed because of God's rejection of Israel, as a result of its rejection of Jesus. Thus, the early church,[100] contemporary preterists,[101] and even dispensationalists[102] all see the destruction of Jerusalem in AD 70 as a judgment on Israel for rejecting Christ. Luke 21:23b confirms this. That verse begins with "for" (*gar*) and specifies that the wrath is on *"this people"* (i.e., first-century Israel).

Jesus' statement is correct

In the context of Israel and Jerusalem, Jesus' statement about the events of AD 70 being an unparalleled tribulation is factually correct. First-century Jewish historian Josephus details the savagery, slaughter, disease, famine, cannibalism, death of 1.1 million of the city's inhabitants, and enslavement of 97,000 more.[103] He concludes, "Neither did any other city ever suffer such miseries, nor did any age ever breed a generation more fruitful

---

97. The very fact that this "great tribulation" was a local event, as opposed to a worldwide, end-time event, is what enabled Jesus' followers to flee. See Schnabel, *40 Questions*, 79.

98. BDAG, *"hoti,"* 732, indicates that, in this context, *hoti* is a "marker of causality," often translated "because" or "since"; however, in some cases the word "for" recommends itself. Although BDAG does not specifically cite Luke 21:22 as an example, it is clear from the context that Luke's use of *hoti* is equivalent to Matthew's and Mark's use of *gar*.

99. Pao and Schnabel, "Luke," 376. With respect to other oracles that announce punishment of Israel for its covenantal unfaithfulness, see Lev 26:31–33; Deut 28:49–57; 32:35; 1 Kgs 9:6–9; Isa 34:8; Jer 5:29; 6:1–8; 7:8–15; 26:1–9; 46:10; 50:27; 51:6; Dan 9:26; Mic 3:12; Zech 11:6.

100. Tertullian, *An Answer to the Jews* 13; Eusebius, *Hist. eccl.* 3.6.32.

101. Gentry, "Exposition," 53–60.

102. Ice, "New Testament," 98, 105.

103. Josephus, *J. W.* 5.10.2–5; 6.3.3–4; 6.9.3.

in wickedness than this was, from the beginning of the world."[104] Carson adds, "There have been greater numbers of deaths—six million in the Nazi death camps, mostly Jews, and an estimated twenty million under Stalin—but never so high a percentage of a great city's population so thoroughly and painfully exterminated and enslaved as during the fall of Jerusalem."[105] Further, in a *theological* sense this was indeed the "great tribulation" for Israel because, as a result, "they no longer have a temple as required by their law."[106] The temple was the place of sacrifices; the significance of the destruction of the temple and, with it, the entire sacrificial system was profound: "This *tamid* [continual] sacrifice was symbolic . . . of the deity's presence among the people. No greater cultic calamity could be imagined than the loss of this sacrifice, since it symbolized the servering of the divine-human relationship (Dan 8:11)."[107] Gentry concludes, "The *covenantal significance* of the loss of the Temple stands as the most dramatic redemptive-historical outcome of the Jewish War."[108] Consequently, since AD 70 Judaism has not been able to be practiced as required by the OT.

The necessity of events following the "great tribulation"

Jesus' statement in Matt 24:21 requires a lengthy historical period *after* the *"great tribulation"* in order for his statement to make any sense. "That Jesus . . . promises that such 'great distress' is never to be equaled implies that it cannot refer to the tribulation at the end of the age; for if what happens next is the millennium or the new heaven and the new earth, it seems inane to say that such 'great distress' will not take place again."[109] Gentry adds, "The Lord is not referring to His Second Advent, or else we should wonder why His disciples should pray about fleeing from Judea (v. 16): what good would running to the hills be at the return of Christ? Why should 'winter' be a concern at that time?"[110] Consequently, the addition *"nor ever will"* at the end of Jesus' statement regarding the severity of the *"great tribulation"* implies that there will be subsequent tribulations after Jerusalem falls, "and in that respect the addition corresponds to 'the end is not yet' of [Matt 24:6; Mark 13:7]."[111]

Jesus' use of prophetic language

Jesus' language is typical of the prophetic language often found in biblical oracles of judgment and therefore is not necessarily to be taken literally. In connection with the tenth plague on the Egyptians, Exod 11:6 says, *"There shall be a great cry in all the land of Egypt, such as there has not been before and such as shall never be again."* Gentry comments: "Who would dare to say that *literally* there was not as great a lamentation during World

104. Ibid., 5.10.5.

105. Carson, "Matthew," 9:563.

106. Gentry, "Rebuttal," 189; see also Preston, *Like Father,* 154, 216, and sources cited therein.

107. Anderson, "Sacrifice and Sacrificial Offerings," 5:878.

108. Gentry, *Dominion,* 346–47, emphasis in original.

109. Carson, "Matthew," 9:563; see also Lane, *Mark,* 472; Schnabel, *40 Questions,* 40n.30.

110. Gentry, "Exposition," 53.

111. Beasley-Murray, *Jesus and the Last Days,* 419.

War II as there was during this one plague upon this one ancient nation? In addition, this verse states that Egypt will *never again* experience such a terrible event, which occurs hundreds of years before Christ. Yet the future Great Tribulation is supposed to be the worst ever for everyone—including Egyptians."[112]

Similar language is found elsewhere concerning catastrophic events. In speaking about the Babylonian captivity and the destruction of Jerusalem in 587/586 BC, Dan 9:12 says, *"Under the whole heaven there has not been done anything like what was done to Jerusalem."* In a prophecy regarding that same event, Ezek 5:9 uses language almost identical to Christ's in Matt 24:21: *"Because of all your abominations, I will do among you what I have not done, and the like of which I will never do again."* Ezek 7:5–6 goes on to call the Babylonians' taking of Jerusalem a *"unique disaster"* and says *"the end has come!"* Those passages talked about a "unique disaster" that would befall Jerusalem and never happen again. Nevertheless, Jesus used the *same* type of language about *another* judgment that would (and did) again fall on Jerusalem. Thus, although some might think that the *"great tribulation"* Jesus mentions is an end-time event, in reality it is not.

The "abomination of desolation" and "great tribulation" as foreshadows

Although the references to the *"abomination of desolation"* and the *"great tribulation"* relate to the events of AD 70, similar principles or foreshadowing may apply to events that will occur shortly before Christ returns, just as the prophesied actions of Antiochus Epiphanes in 167 BC foreshadowed the events of Titus and the Romans in AD 70. If that is true, however, one needs to keep in mind certain factors that bear on the proper interpretation of prophecy. Two such factors are discussed below.

Prophetic foreshadowing relates to principles or motifs

It is "extremely unlikely" that Jesus was making a "deliberate double reference . . . both to the fall of Jerusalem and to the sufferings of the end time and the Antichrist."[113] Nevertheless, beginning with Irenaeus (c. 130–200),[114] many scholars see the events of AD 70 as being a "type"[115] "parallelism,"[116] "symbol,"[117] or "adumbration [foreshadow; prefigure]"[118] of Antichrist and a future "great tribulation" just preceding the *parousia.*[119]

---

112. Gentry, "Exposition," 52. Schnabel similarly refers to Jesus' use of "hyperbolic language." Schnabel, *40 Questions,* 40n.30.

113. Hagner, *Matthew 14–28,* 712.

114. Irenaeus, *Haer.* 5.25.2; 5.30.2.

115. Ryle, *Expository Thoughts,* 313; Gentry, "Transition Text," n.p.

116. Nolland, *Luke 18:35–24:53,* 1008.

117. Carson, "Matthew," 8:492.

118. Bell, "Critical Evaluation," 224.

119. Full preterists deny that the events of AD 70 were a "type" or foreshadow of anything because, they contend, all biblical prophecy essentially is about covenantal transformation which was fulfilled in AD 70. Preston, *Like Father,* 296–308; Presson, *AD 70, passim.*

This is seen in various ways. First, both Jesus and the apostles specify that "tribulation" will characterize the entire time before the second coming.[120] Second, in Matt 24:21 and Mark 13:19, Jesus alludes to Dan 12:1 (*"a time of distress such as never occurred since there was a nation until that time"*) with respect to the destruction of Jerusalem. However, the *"time of distress"* in Dan 12:1 itself occurs "in the context of the final resurrection."[121] Third, thematically *"great tribulation"* in Matt 24:21 is connected with *"the great tribulation"* of Rev 7:14 and, more generally, with the beasts and events described in Daniel 7–8 and Revelation 6–18.[122]

All this is in keeping with the nature of prophetic discourse in which "end-time predictions commonly are connected by themes and key words rather than by a strict chronological order."[123] Thus, as Donald Hagner concludes, "Just as Jesus and the evangelist had no trouble applying the symbolism of Daniel to the fall of Jerusalem yet to occur, so may we perceive the fall of Jerusalem as an anticipation of the final judgment. The desolating sacrilege of [Matt] 24:15 and a time of indescribable suffering that is cut short only for the sake of the elect can easily suggest to us a time of future crisis that brings us to the brink of the eschaton."[124]

Future fulfillment cannot be "literal"

Because Matt 24:15; Mark 13:14 (*"abomination of desolation"*) and Matt 24:21; Mark 13:19 (*"great tribulation"*) have already been fulfilled in the events of AD 70, we cannot apply what Jesus says "literally" in every detail to any end-time tribulation. Although the events of AD 70 may foreshadow a period of increased tribulation shortly before Jesus comes again, by its very nature a "type" or "foreshadow" is not identical to its antitype or the event it foreshadows. Since Jesus' prophecy of *"great tribulation"* already has been fulfilled, we should not look for another *"great tribulation"* in which armies surround Jerusalem, there is an *"abomination of desolation"* in a new temple, people have to flee from Judea into the mountains, etc. Nothing in the text or context suggests an exact repetition of such events.[125]

120. Matt 24:9, 29; Mark 13:24; John 16:33; Acts 11:19; 14:22; 20:23; Rom 5:3; 8:35; 12:12; 2 Cor 1:4, 8; 2:4; 4:17; 6:4; 7:4; 8:2; Eph 3:13; Phil 4:14; Col 1:24; 1 Thess 1:6; 3:3, 7; 2 Thess 1:4, 6; Heb 10:33; Rev 1:9; 2:9–10.

121. Turner, "Structure and Sequence," 12.

122. The NT sees the "great tribulation" as having begun with Christ's own death. It will characterize the entire age before the *parousia,* as Christ indicated in the Olivet Discourse, although it probably will intensify shortly before the *parousia.* For more on this see chapter 11, particularly the section dealing with "the great tribulation" referred to in Rev 7:14.

123. Oropeza, *99 Reasons,* 195n.10.

124. Hagner, *Matthew 14–28,* 712–13.

125. Full preterist Don Preston repeatedly commits this hermeneutical error by making "all or nothing" arguments, i.e., that types must be repeated exactly in the anti-types or else historical events described in superlative do not foreshadow anything else: "If the events of AD 70 were typological of a future end of the age, then Christ will divorce and destroy the church, as an unfaithful bride that has become a harlot and will marry another bride—under (another) New Covenant." Preston, *AD 70,* 153; "Jesus said the events of AD 70 were the greatest that had ever been, or that ever would be (Matthew 24:21). So, how can the greatest events in history-past or future-foreshadow even greater events?" Ibid., 43; "Jesus said the events of AD 70 would be when 'all things that are written must be fulfilled' (Luke

Before Christ comes again, events that may occur on a worldwide basis will differ from the events of AD 70 because of different circumstances. We cannot use the reference to the *"abomination of desolation"* or the *"great tribulation"* that occurred in AD 70 to *specifically* predict what any end-time tribulation will look like. Craig Evans concludes by pointing us to the folly of trying to predict prophetic fulfillment by looking at the newspaper: "Christians today are tempted to match the details of the eschatological discourse to current events and happenings throughout the world. Proposed correspondences invariably prove inaccurate and sometimes occasion embarrassment. It is enough to be reminded that until the kingdom of God has come in its fullness, evil still poses a danger and may some day rise up in an unprecedented manifestation."[126]

The signs of the times: recapitulation (Matt 24:22–28; Mark 13:20–23)

Matt 24:22–28; Mark 13:20–23 appear to refer to the entire period before Christ comes again. Many connect Matt 24:22 with 24:21 (Mark 13:20 with 13:19) as the conclusion of the discussion begun in Matt 24:15; Mark 13:14 regarding the fall of Jerusalem. On the surface, that seems to be the most natural reading since Matt 24:22; Mark 13:20 begin with the Greek word *kai,* which normally is translated "and." However, there are several reasons why Matt 24:22; Mark 13:20 probably begins a new section (Matt 24:22–28; Mark 13:20–23) that covers the entire period until the second coming. Those reasons include the following:

(1) *Although the "kai" of Matt 24:22; Mark 13:20 could connect those verses to the prior section, Matt 24:21; Mark 13:19 themselves make a suitable ending to Matt 24:15–21; Mark 13:14–19.* The word "for" in Matt 24:21 and Mark 13:19 concludes Jesus' discussion of the events of AD 66–70 by giving the reason why people need to flee from Judea.[127]

(2) *The grammar of Matt 24:22; Mark 13:20 combines with the substantive context to show that the entire section deals with events of the entire inter-advent period ending with the second coming.* First, *kai* often has a contrastive or adversative effect.[128] The context, not the word itself, determines the meaning. Second, grammatically Matt 24:23 begins with "then" (Mark 13:21, *"and then"*), and Matt 24:24; Mark 13:22 begins with "for." Those verses therefore are linked with Matt 24:22; Mark 13:20. Consequently, to link Matt 24:22; Mark 13:20 with Matt 24:21; Mark 13:19 would also link Matt 24:23–24; Mark 13:21–22 with Matt 24:21; Mark 13:19. However, Matt 24:23–24; Mark 13:21–22 (and therefore Matt 24:22; Mark 13:20) are linked with what comes *after* the destruction of Jerusalem, namely, the events that culminate in the second

---

21:22). This means there could not be any additional eschatology beyond AD 70." Ibid., 49; Although Acts 1:11 says that Jesus will come back *"in just the same way as you have watched him go into heaven,"* the *"coming* described in Revelation 19 is *nothing like the going* of Acts 1!" Thus, Preston concludes, there will be no future, physical *parousia* of Christ. Preston, *Like Father,* 237.

126. Evans, *Mark 8:27–16:20,* 324.

127. Carson, "Matthew," 8:501–02.

128. See Matt 23:37; Mark 7:28; Luke 1:7; 4:23; 8:13; 15:16; 20:19; John 1:5, 11; 3:19; 5:40; Acts 9:26; 1 Cor 12:31b; Eph 4:26; 1 John 2:1, 4; 4:20; Rev 12:8, 16.

coming. "Verses 23, 24 [of Matthew] deal with deceivers and are similar to verses 5 and 11. Verses 23–26 provide the reason for the emphasis in verse 27, and verse 27 gives the reason why we are to give no credence to the pretensions mentioned in verses 23–26. Verse 27 deals obviously with the advent."[129]

(3) *The themes of persecution and false Christs are characteristic of the entire period before Christ comes again, not merely the time before AD 70.* The persecution or tribulation mentioned in Matt 24:22; Mark 13:20 also was mentioned in Matt 24:6–9; Mark 13:7–9, 12. The warnings against false Christs and being misled (Matt 24:23–26; Mark 13:21–22) also were given in Matt 24:4–5, 11; Mark 13:5–6. All of these things are characteristic of the entire period between Christ's two advents. This section ends with the second coming (Matt 24:27–28), just as the first section of the Discourse also concluded with "the end" (Matt 24:14; Mark 13:13).

(4) *Jesus describes the time period as "those days" which God will "cut short."* Jesus used *"those days"* to refer to the events surrounding the destruction of Jerusalem in AD 70 (Matt 24:19; Mark 13:17, 19; Luke 21:23) and also uses *"those days"* to refer to tribulation that will occur before the second coming (Matt 24:29; Mark 13:24). However, in Matt 24:22; Mark 13:20 Jesus adds the phrase *"those days will be cut short."* That added comment indicates that *"those days"* in Matt 24:22; Mark 13:20 include the entire period of time until the second coming (contrary to the more limited reference in Matt 24:19; Mark 13:17, 19; Luke 21:23). It indicates something worldwide in scope is occurring, not just a local phenomenon, because the basis on which the lives of God's people are saved is different in the two situations: in AD 70 people in Judea are urged to *"flee to the mountains"* in order to save their lives (Matt 24:16; Mark 13:14); before Christ comes again people are saved not by fleeing but by God's "cutting short" the days.[130] In other words, tribulation will characterize the entire period before Christ's return, and it will even worsen shortly before his second advent, but God will not allow the age to run its course, humanity to destroy itself, or his people to be eliminated from the earth.

(5) *The reference to "no life" being saved in Matt 24:22 and Mark 13:20.* The Greek phrase *pasa sarx* (lit., "all flesh," translated "no life" or "no one" in Matt 24:22; Mark 13:20) "normally refers to all mankind and is more sweeping than 'no one in Jerusalem.'"[131] Every use of "all flesh" in the Greek NT[132] describes all mankind, except 1 Cor 15:39 where the phrase is used in even a broader sense to describe all human and animal life. Thus, Matt 24:22; Mark 13:20 appear to begin a discussion of events that are worldwide, rather than limited to Jerusalem and Judea as was the case in Matt 24:16; Mark 13:14.

(6) *The reference to cutting the days short "for the sake of the elect" (Matt 24:22; Mark 13:20).* "The term 'elect' (in Matthew only at 22:14; 24:22, 24, 31; plus the variant at

---

129. Murray, "Interadventual Period," 388.

130. Contra Schnabel, *40 Questions,* 40–41.

131. Carson, "Matthew," 9:564.

132. Matt 24:22; Mark 13:20; Luke 3:6; John 17:2; Acts 2:17; Rom 3:20; 1 Cor 1:29; 15:39; Gal 2:16; 1 Pet 1:24.

20:16) most naturally refers to all true believers, chosen by God; so it is reasonable to assume that it does so here."[133] The *"cutting short those days for the sake of the elect"* was not required in AD 70 because, as mentioned above, the Christians had fled to safety. The nonbelieving Jews who remained in the city were no longer God's "elect" after their rejection of Christ.[134]

The second coming of Christ (Matt 24:27–31; Mark 13:24–27; Luke 21:25–28)

In describing his *parousia,* Jesus drew upon and synthesized a rich background of OT passages that talk about the coming of the Lord. For example, Ps 50:4–6 says that God comes in order to judge. He says, *"Gather My godly ones to Me"* (Ps 50:5).[135] Isaiah says, *"The Lord is about to come out of His place to punish the inhabitants of the earth"* (Isa 26:21). Associated with this are the resurrection of the dead (Isa 26:19), the blowing of the "great trumpet" (Isa 27:13), and the gathering together of God's people (Isa 27:13). T. Francis Glasson summarizes this OT picture as follows: "If we put together the various items, the picture that emerges is that the Lord will descend from heaven with the sound of a trumpet; he will be accompanied by hosts of angels; his people will be gathered; there will be resurrection and judgment. Anyone familiar with the NT will immediately recognize that this is precisely the picture presented in its pages of the Parousia of the Lord Jesus."[136]

The Son of Man will come like "lightning" (Matt 24:27–28)

Although Jesus here begins discussing his *parousia,* these verses are tied to his previous discussion of the signs that will characterize the inter-advent period. In Matt 24:23–26, he has been talking about the appearance of false Christs and false prophets. Now, in 24:27 he introduces his *parousia.* R. T. France shows how the grammar of the passage indicates the distinction between the events:

> The "for" which introduces this saying indicates how it fits into this context: "don't believe them, because. . ." In contrast with a so-called Messiah who has to be sought out in an obscure place and who needs authenticating signs to convince people of his claim, the *parousia* of the Son of Man will be as unmissable as a flash of lightning which blazes across the whole sky. The warning was perhaps prompted by the disciples' question in v. 3, which, while differentiating the *parousia* and the end of the age from "these things" (the destruction of the temple), has nevertheless suggested some association between the two events, probably supposing that the one cannot occur without the other. Not so, says Jesus. The time of the siege and capture of the city will be characterized by the claims and counterclaims of those who pretend to a messianic role, but the *parousia* of the Son of Man will need no such claims or proofs: everyone will see and recognize

133. Carson, "Matthew," 8:502; see also Payne, *Encyclopedia,* 487n.41.

134. See Matt 13:10–17; 21:18–22, 33–46; Mark 11:12–14, 20–24; 12:1–11; Luke 20:9–18.

135. It is possible that God is there addressing the angels.

136. Glasson, "Theophany and Parousia," 260.

it. . . . He is thus setting the *parousia* and the end of the age decisively apart from the coming destruction of the temple.[137]

Jesus' reference to "lightning" in Matt 24:27 may also imply judgment

Although the emphasis in 24:27 is on the sudden and unmistakable nature of the *parousia*, the reference to lightning probably also conveys the idea of judgment since that is how the word is consistently used both in the OT and NT. "The use of *brq* [Hebrew for lightning] in the OT relates to the theophanic [the manifestation of God to people] presence of Yahweh, usually in the context of divine judgment, retribution, or warfare."[138] W. Sibley Towner adds, "Lightning as a feature of the end of the age is almost the only use made of the imagery in the NT (see Matt 24:27; Luke 17:24; and esp. Rev. 4:5; 8:5; 11:19; 16:18), although the association with theophany is also reutilized (Matt. 28:3)."[139] Lightning as judgment is also used when Jesus speaks of Satan's fall in Luke 10:18.

Finally, lightning as judgment is indicated by the fact that lightning is associated with, if not identical to, *"fire from heaven"* which always indicates God's judgment: either his judgment on his enemies;[140] or his presence among his people and acceptance of their sacrifices.[141] Thus, in the OT the eschatological judgment of the *"day of the Lord"* is described in terms of fire.[142] Likewise, in the NT the judgment that accompanies the *parousia* is described in terms of fire.[143]

Jesus' reference to "vultures" (or "eagles") in Matt 24:28

Jesus' reference to "vultures" (or "eagles") in Matt 24:28 may imply the public nature of the *parousia*, or may imply judgment, or both (see also Luke 17:37). The statement is enigmatic. Hagner mentions the two most likely meanings:

> This proverb, rather more enigmatic than others in the Gospels, occurs also in Luke 17:37b, where it is spoken in response to the question "Where, Lord?" apparently concerning the location either of the one "taken" or the one "left." The imagery of flesh-eating birds is found elsewhere in the OT (Job 39:27–30; Hab 1:8) and NT (Rev 19:17–21). The most natural application of the imagery is to judgment, which may be the point of the proverb here. When the Son of Man comes, the judgment of the world will take place (cf. [Matt 24:]30, 39, 51; 25:30, 46). On the other hand . . . it may be that the proverb points primarily to the

137. France, *Matthew,* 917–18.

138. Koopmans, *"Brq,"* 769, citing Exod 19:16; Deut 32:41; 2 Sam 22:15; Job 20:25; Ps 18:14; 77:18; 97:4; 135:7; 144:6; Jer 10:13; 51:16; Ezek 21:10, 15, 28; Nah 2:4; 3:3; Hab 3:11; Zech 9:14.

139. Towner, "Lightning," 561.

140. Gen 19:24; 2 Kgs 1:10, 12, 14; Luke 9:54; 17:29; Rev 20:9. These are all the biblical instances when God sent fire from heaven. In Job 1:16 Satan sent fire from heaven; in Rev 13:13 the false prophet did.

141. 1 Kgs 18:30–39; 1 Chron 21:26; 2 Chron 7:1.

142. See Isa 66:15; Ezek 38:22; 39:6; Joel 2:3, 30; Zeph 1:18; 3:8; Mal 4:1.

143. See 2 Thess 1:6–8; 2 Pet 3:10; Rev 8:7–8; 14:18; 18:8; 20:8–9.

unmistakable character of the parousia. Thus, as surely as you know that where you see vultures gathered there is a carcass, so you will not be able to miss the coming of the Son of Man.[144]

"Immediately after the tribulation of those days" (Matt 24:29; Mark 13:24)

Jesus' reference to *"the tribulation of those days"* may refer back to the *"great tribulation"* of Matt 24:21; Mark 13:19, which deals with the destruction of Jerusalem in AD 70. Or, he may be referring to the tribulation that the church will face shortly before the *parousia* (i.e., *"the great tribulation"* of Rev 7:14). If the primary reference is to AD 70, then "immediately" suggests that the "tribulation" of which Jesus speaks began in AD 70 but then continues and includes the tribulation the church will face throughout the inter-advent period until the end of the age since the *parousia* did not, in fact, occur "immediately" after the "great tribulation" of AD 70. The parallel passage in Luke 21:24 helps to clarify that *"the tribulation of those days"* cannot be limited to the events of AD 70 but extends from then to the *parousia*. John Murray shows how Luke's account of the discourse supplements and clarifies Matthew's account:

> Luke includes an observation in Jesus' discourse not included in Matthew's account, and it belongs to what precedes Matthew 24:29, and must therefore be inserted. The observation given in Luke 21:24 is that 'Jerusalem will be trodden down by the Gentiles until the times of the Gentiles are fulfilled.' So, in view of this element, it is apparent that our Lord's delineation extended far beyond the destruction of Jerusalem and the events immediately associated with it. Hence the period of 'those days', in Matthew 24:29, must be regarded as the days that extend to the threshold of what is specified in verses 29–31.[145]

Further, even in Matt 24:29 itself Jesus simply talks about *"the tribulation of those days,"* not *"great tribulation,"* the phrase he had used in Matt 24:21. That language leads Murray correctly to infer that Jesus is speaking "inclusively and not restrictively," because "'those days' could properly be taken to mean the days preceding that of which Jesus now proceeds to speak, the days depicted already in verses 4–14, and 'the tribulation' not exclusively the 'great tribulation' of verse 21, but the tribulation which, according to the earlier part of the discourse, is represented as characterizing the interadventual period as a whole."[146] Jesus' reference to *"those days"* (v.29) and *"they will see"* (v.30) is akin to the language he uses in Matt 24:32–36 to distinguish the far event of *"that day,"* his *parousia*, from the near events of AD 70 that "you" and "this generation" will witness (see below). The definite article "the" before "tribulation" may suggest a particular tribulation, or a more specific manifestation of tribulation shortly before Christ returns, which is *analogous* to the *"great tribulation"* of AD 70. However, the definite article "the" in Matt 24:29

144. Hagner, *Matthew 14–28*, 707.

145. Murray, "Interadventual Period," 389. As Nolland puts it, Luke deals with a "worldwide version of a judgment for which that upon Jerusalem has been a microcosm. This universal judgment will usher in the coming of the Son of Man to whom the disciples will look for final deliverance." Nolland, *Luke 18:35–24:53*, 1007.

146. Murray, "Interadventual Period," 389.

need not necessarily have that effect. Rev 1:9 also uses the definite article "the" before "tribulation" but appears to refer only to the general suffering of believers, not a specific "tribulation."

The signs in the sky and on the earth (Matt 24:29; Mark 13:24–25; Luke 21:25–26)[147]

The signs may be figurative

The OT prophets frequently described political crises and regime changes metaphorically as cosmic upheavals or the overthrowing of creation itself. When Jesus refers to *"the sun being darkened, the moon not giving its light, and the stars falling"* in Matt 24:29; Mark 13:24–25; Luke 21:25–26, he is quoting from or alluding to several OT passages that use similar language for political events: Isa 13:10, 13 (the Medes' defeat of Babylon); Isa 34:4 (judgment against Edom); Jer 4:23–28 (judgment against Judah by Babylon); Ezek 32:7–8 (Babylon's defeat of Egypt); Amos 5:20; 8:9 (Israel's defeat by Assyria); Joel 2:10 (a great locust plague); Zeph 1:15 (Babylon's destruction of Jerusalem); Ps 18:7–15 (David's deliverance from Saul); Hag 2:6–7, 21–22 (encouragement to Zerubbabel to rebuild the temple). *"The roaring of the sea and of the waves"* (Luke 21:25) quotes or alludes to Isa 17:12–13 (an oracle concerning Damascus and tumult among the nations). Similar figurative language of physical or cosmic destruction is found at Judg 5:4; Ps 114:3–6; 144:5–7; Isa 5:25; 64:3; Mic 1:4–6; Nah 1:5; Hab 3:6–7, 10–12. Wright maintains, "This is simply the way regular Jewish imagery is able to refer to major socio-political events and bring out their full significance."[148] It is possible, therefore, that Jesus is using the figurative language which the prophets often employed to signify that his return will be the last and greatest "regime change" and manifestation of God.

The signs may be literal

On the other hand, the cosmic signs may be literal. "It is difficult to be sure how literally to take this, but there seems to be an escalation [in the signs] from [Luke 21:11–25]."[149] In light of that apparent escalation in the description of the cosmic signs, Carson concludes that the signs Jesus lists in Matt 24:29; Mark 13:24–25; Luke 21:25–26 "are probably meant to be taken literally, because of the climactic nature of the Son of Man's final self-disclosure."[150] That is consistent with the picture found in Isaiah 24 which, significantly,

147. Christ's language parallels John's description of the *parousia* and final judgment on an unrepentant world in Rev 6:12–14.

148. Wright, *Victory*, 361; see also Watts, "Mark," 225–27. Preterist interpreters cite the use of such language to conclude that Matt 24:29 "is stock-in-trade Old Testament prophetic language for *national disaster*. Our Lord, therefore, is not prophesying that bizarre astronomical events will occur; he is predicting that the judgment of God will soon fall decisively on the Jewish nation." Storms *Kingdom Come*, 265–66; see also Kik, *Eschatology*, 127–35; Gundry, *Dominion*, 347–48; DeMar, *Last Days*, 141–53; Mathison, *Postmillennialism*, 114; Preston, *Like Father*, 2–5, 8–12, 101, 220.

149. Nolland, *Luke 18:35–24:53*, 1007.

150. Carson, "Matthew," 8:505.

is part of Isaiah's "little apocalypse" (Isa 24:1—27:13). Isaiah describes God's coming universal judgment on, and reign over, the earth. In connection with that, the sun and moon no longer give their light since God himself will illuminate the restored creation when he appears (Isa 24:23; see also Isa 60:19–20). The same vision is found again in John's description of the New Jerusalem (Rev 21:23), which likewise is inaugurated at Christ's *parousia.*

This raises an interpretive question that is posed and answered by John Murray: "If we regard these occurrences as commotions and upheavals in the physical cosmos, how are we to reconcile such visible events with the uniform teaching of our Lord respecting the suddenness and unexpectedness of his advent? The answer is that the advent has its concomitants."[151] In other words, the cosmic signs occur unexpectedly in conjunction with the *parousia,* which itself occurs unexpectedly.

The cosmic signs themselves are *theologically* significant. Greg Beale explains that the signs reveal that the second coming entails judgment and renovation of the earth:

> If the earth is also to be destroyed literally, this is to demonstrate that the idolatrous earthly securities of the earth-dwellers will be destroyed. . . . Humanity has become perverted and has worshiped the creation (cf. Rom. 1:21–25; Rev. 9:20). Therefore, creation itself (sun, moon, stars, trees, animals, etc.) has become an idol that must be removed. The Bible repeatedly refers to the heavenly bodies as representing false deities worshiped by Israel and the nations (e.g., Deut. 4:19; 17:1–4; 2 Kgs. 23:4–5; Jer. 8:2; Ezek. 8:16; Amos 5:25–27; Acts 7:41–43). . . . The cosmic order of nature and of the luminaries (the course of the sun, moon, and stars) was seen as essential to the ongoing welfare of the world's existence. . . . . Hence, God judges the heavens by destroying its orderly movements in order to indicate that humanity has violated his moral order and is being judged.[152]

"The sign of the Son of Man" (Matt 24:30)

Matt 24:23–27; Mark 13:21–22 had indicated that the *parousia* will be a public, visible event which will leave no one in doubt when it occurs.[153] Christ's second coming will be almost the opposite of his first coming. In his first advent, Christ was announced only to shepherds; he was born in lowliness; he was a man of sorrows acquainted with grief, who was despised and rejected, betrayed and killed; as a result of which his followers can expect persecution. His second advent will be public, so that the entire earth will know;[154] it will be with power and great glory; he will judge the entire world; he will gather his elect from the four winds; and his followers will all be vindicated.

What the actual "sign" is remains difficult to say. The fact that Matt 24:30 begins with "then" makes it impossible to take the phenomena in the sky of 24:29 as the sign. Many hold that the only "sign" is the Son of Man himself appearing in the sky at his *parousia*

---

151. Murray, "Interadventual Period," 391.

152. Beale, *Revelation,* 402–04; see also Watts, "Mark," 225–26.

153. Murray, "Interadventual Period," 388–89; Blomberg, "Matthew," 87.

154. It will be even more luminous because the sun, the moon, and the stars will have ceased to shine.

(24:30).[155] The fact that v. 30 may be interpreted as people mourning *before* they see the Son of Man coming suggests that there is some sign other than the *parousia* itself.[156] Some have suggested that because in the OT when a "sign" is coupled with a trumpet (as in 24:31) the "sign" refers to a "standard" or "ensign."[157] "Theologically this means that the kingdom is being consummated. The standard, the banner of the Son of Man, unfurls in the heavens, as he himself returns in splendor and power."[158] The early church and some modern scholars identify the "sign" as the cross, which will be "a phenomenon or portent in the sky which will cause the tribes of the earth to mourn because it is the premonitory sign of the advent of the Son of man, the judge."[159] Beasley-Murray says, "The [sign] of the Son of Man most probably signifies the Shekinah glory on which he comes."[160] Regardless of its specific identity, the *"sign of Your coming"* (Matt 24:3) and the *"sign of the Son of Man"* (Matt 24:30) "both emphasize unmistakable visibility in the sky, as opposed to hiddenness in the desert or backrooms (cf. 26:64)."[161] Further, "It is probably not important to decide among these options, since in any event the sign does not enable anyone to recognize the 'signs of the times' until Christ is actually en route to earth."[162]

"Coming on the clouds of the sky with power and great glory" (Matt 24:30; Mark 13:26; Luke 21:27)

In the OT, clouds often symbolize the presence and glory of God.[163] They also have eschatological associations.[164] In describing his second coming, Jesus alludes to Dan 7:13–14: *"with the clouds of heaven one like the Son of Man was coming, and He came up to the Ancient of Days and was presented before Him. And to Him was given dominion, glory and a kingdom."* Preterists, of course, cite this as one reason why Jesus is not referring to his coming from heaven to earth at the end of time but of his ascension and enthronement in heaven,[165] the "sign" of his power being the destruction of Jerusalem in AD 70.[166]

155. See Gundry, *Matthew*, 488; Hendriksen, *Exposition*, 864.

156. Although Hendriksen says the view that "Christ's brilliant manifestation [itself] will be the sign that he is about to descend" . . . gains some support from the fact that . . . Mark and Luke leave out the word *sign*, and simply say, 'And then they shall see the Son of man coming in clouds with great power and glory.'" Hendriksen, *Exposition*, 864.

157. Glasson, "The Ensign," 299–300.

158. Carson, "Matthew," 8:505.

159. Higgins, "Sign of the Son of Man," 382.

160. Beasley-Murray, *Mark Thirteen*, 93.

161. Gundry, *Matthew*, 488.

162. Blomberg, *Matthew*, 362.

163. Exod 16:10; 19:9, 16; 24:15–16; 34:5; Lev 16:2; Num 10:34; 11:25; Ps 18:10–13; 97:2; 104:3; Isa 19:1.

164. Isa 4:5; Ezek 30:3; Dan 7:13; Zeph 1:15.

165. The word translated "sky" in Matt 24:30 is *ouranos*, which also may be translated "heaven." Likewise, preterists note that when that same verse says *"and then all the tribes of the earth will mourn,"* the word translated "earth" is *gē*, which also may be translated "land," i.e., the land of Israel. See DeMar, *Last Days*, 166–67.

166. See Wright, *Victory*, 361; Kik, *Eschatology*, 140–43; Chilton, *Paradise*, 100–103; DeMar, *Last Days*, 161–65; Mathison, *Postmillennialism*, 114; see also Preston, *Like Father*, 17.

However, a full-orbed understanding of Jesus' allusion to Daniel's reference to the Son of Man "coming up to" the Ancient of Days suggests that *both* Christ's ascension and his second coming are involved in fulfilling Daniel's prophecy. Goldsworthy explains this:

> The ascent of Jesus into the clouds [Acts 1:9] is followed by the angelic message that Jesus will return in like manner to his departure (Acts 1:11). . . . Jesus' being lifted into the cloud and the reference to his return in like manner point to the way the gospel structures the coming of the Son of Man. In Daniel 7 he comes in the clouds to God and receives the kingdom. This takes care of the ascension and the fact that some of Jesus' contemporaries would witness it [see Matt 16:28; Mark 9:1]. Daniel then tells how this kingdom becomes the possession of the saints of the Most High. This takes care of the "like manner" return of Jesus and the fact that the second coming is also spoken of in Daniel 7 terms.[167]

Carson adds, in the framework of NT eschatology:

> We may imagine Jesus the Son of Man receiving the kingdom through his resurrection and ascension, his divine vindication, so that now all authority is his ([Matt] 28:18). Yet it is equally possible to think of him receiving the kingdom at the consummation, when his reign or kingdom becomes direct and immediate, uncontested and universal. Unless one thinks of the location of the Ancient of Days in some physical and spatial sense, it is hard to imagine why Christ's approaching God the Father to receive the kingdom might not be combined with his returning to earth to set up the consummated kingdom. This interpretation goes well with the vivid context.[168]

"He will send forth his angels with a great trumpet and they will gather together His elect from the four winds" (Matt 24:31; Mark 13:27; Luke 21:26, 28)

In the parable of the wheat and the tares (Matt 13:24–30, 36–43) Jesus had said that, at the end of the age, "*The Son of Man will send forth His angels, and they will gather out of His kingdom all stumbling blocks, and those who commit lawlessness, and will throw them into the furnace of fire.*"[169] A similar image of "*one like a son of man . . . who sat on the cloud*" and reaped the earth in connection with angels is found in Rev 14:14–20, which also refers to the *parousia* and final judgment. Jesus' reference to "*a great trumpet*" probably is a quotation from Isa 27:13. The reference to "*the four winds*" probably is an allusion to Zech 2:6 and refers to the entire world (see also Jer 49:36). The reference to "gathering the elect" may allude to such OT "re-gathering of Israel after exile" passages as Deut 30:3–4; Isa 27:12–13, and the "gathering of His people for judgment" passage of Ps 50:5.[170]

---

167. Goldsworthy, *Whole Bible*, 50, 55–56. With respect to the "cloud(s)," the fact that apparently all of humanity will see him when Jesus returns (see Matt 24:30; Mark 13:36; 14:62; Luke 21:27; Acts 1:11) "seems to rule out a literal, geographically restrictive interpretation of the clouds." Schnabel, *40 Questions*, 253. The reference is directed to making the theological connection with Daniel's prophecy and the visible, public, and awesome nature of God's return to earth, rather than being a comment on the atmospheric conditions when that occurs. Ibid.

168. Carson, "Matthew," 9:568.

169. Matt 13:41–42; see also Matt 16:27; Mark 8:38; Luke 9:26.

170. See Blomberg, "Matthew," 87.

Jesus has, in effect, taken OT passages that in their original context dealt with Israel's return from exile,[171] and uses them as "types" that point to himself and the *parousia*. The parable of the wheat and the tares and Jesus' statements in Matt 16:27; Mark 8:38; Luke 9:26 concerning judgment are reflected in Luke's account of the Olivet Discourse, that when Christ comes he will bring both judgment on his enemies (Luke 21:26) and redemption for those who are his (Luke 21:28). Preterists are in accord with this basic outlook but relate it to the first century: the "judgment" is the destruction of Jerusalem in AD 70; the "redemption" (i.e., the "gathering of the elect") is the gospel messengers ("angels") who evangelize the nations after AD 70; the "great trumpet" is "the call of the gospel."[172]

The parable of the fig tree: "all these things" and "this generation" versus "that day and hour" (Matt 24:32–36; Mark 13:28–32; Luke 21:28–36)

In this portion of the discourse Jesus contrasts events that will happen in his own generation (the destruction of Jerusalem and the temple in AD 70) and his second coming (the timing of which is unknowable).[173] We see this contrast in several ways.

The parable of the fig tree (Matt 24:32–33; Mark 13:28–29; Luke 21:29–31)

The parable of the fig tree is related to the signs which culminated in the destruction of Jerusalem in AD 70 and has nothing to do with the founding of the modern nation of Israel in 1948, as some dispensationalists allege.[174] In context, the fig tree is linked with the things that are "near," which his disciples who were then alive (i.e., "you," "this generation") would be able to see.[175] The parallel passage in Luke shows positively that Jesus was not using the fig tree as a reference to modern Israel since in Luke 21:29 he says, *"Behold the fig tree and all the trees."* The fig tree in the the parable was simply a metaphor or easily understandable object lesson of what Jesus said was soon going to occur.[176]

171. Deut 30:3–4; Isa 27:12–13; Zech 2:6.

172. Chilton, *Paradise,* 103–05; DeMar, *Last Days,* 173–77.

173. Crispin Fletcher-Louis persuasively argues that in Jesus' statement *"Heaven and earth will pass away, but My words will not pass away"* (Matt 24:35; Mark 13:31; Luke 21:33), *"heaven and earth"* is not a reference to the end of the space-time universe, but to the temple. Fletcher-Louis, "Destruction of the Temple," 145–69.

174. E.g., Lindsey, *Late Great,* 53; MacDonald, *Believer's,* 1295–96.

175. Gary DeMar points out that not only the fig tree in this parable but "every instance of a leaves-only tree in the gospels is a sign of Israel's judgment, a judgment that came in A.D. 70." DeMar, *Last Days,* 402. In Matt 21:19; Mark 11:13–14 Jesus underlined the fact that the nation was facing imminent judgment by cursing a leaves-only fig tree. Ibid., 397–405.

176. Schnabel, *40 Questions,* 132.

"All these things" (Matt 24:33–34; Mark 13:29–30; Luke 21:28, 31–32)

Carson points out that if the phrase *"all these things"* includes "the celestial signs *and the Parousia itself* (vv.29–31), then vv.32–33 are illogical, because any distinction between 'all these things' and 'it is near' would be destroyed. . . . The more natural way to take 'all these things' is to see them as referring to the distress of vv.4–28, the tribulation that comes on believers throughout the period between Jesus' ascension and the Parousia."[177]

"This generation [Greek = genea]" (Matt 24:34; Mark 13:30; Luke 21:32)

Some take *"this generation"* to mean the generation living at the time of the second coming, or to mean "race," or the nation of Israel.[178] Although, as a dispensationalist, Thomas Ice thinks that *"this generation"* means the generation living at the time of the second coming, he admits, "Every other use of 'this generation' in Matthew (11:16; 12:41–42, 45; 23:36) refers to Christ's contemporaries."[179] Murray adds, "If race or people were intended in Matthew 24:34, one wonders why *genos* rather than *genea* had not been used. *Genos* would have conveyed the thought without any ambiguity."[180] *Genos* means "descendant, family, relatives, nation, people, class, kind."[181] It is used in the sense of race or nation in multiple passages.[182] Consequently, Carson concludes that *"this generation"* can "only with the greatest difficulty be made to mean anything other than the generation living when Jesus spoke. Even if 'generation' by itself can have a slightly larger semantic range, to make '*this* generation' refer to all believers in every age, or the generation of believers alive when eschatological events start to happen, is highly artificial."[183]

Additionally, given Jesus' announcement that the kingdom was at hand (Matt 4:17; Mark 1:15), coupled with his prophecy of the destruction of the temple, *theologically "this generation"* could *only* refer to the generation alive when Jesus was speaking. The theological significance of *"this generation"* in connection with Jesus' prophecy and mission is rarely commented on, but N. T. Wright clearly sees this and explains: "As a prophet, Jesus staked his reputation on his prediction of the Temple's fall within a generation;[184] if and

---

177. Carson, "Matthew," 8:507, emphasis in original.

178. Scofield, *New Scofield,* 1035n.1; MacDonald, *Believer's,* 1296.

179. Ice, "Rebuttal," 125.

180. Murray, "Interadventual Period," 392.

181. BDAG, *"genos,"* 194–95.

182. See, e.g., Mark 7:26; Acts 4:36; 7:19; 13:26; 18:2, 24; 2 Cor 11:26; Gal 1:14; Phil 3:5.

183. Carson, "Matthew," 8:507; see also Schnabel, *40 Questions,* 131. Neil Nelson discusses the major interpretive options for the meaning of "this generation." He concludes that throughout Matthew and in the Olivet Discourse, "this generation" primarily is used perjoratively as referring to "unbelieving, rejecting humanity, unresponsive to God and oblivious to the possibility of facing his judgment." Nelson, "This Generation," 383. He adds, "Matthew seems to have deliberately juxtaposed the phrase 'this generation' with his account of the days of Noah in 24:37–39 in order to echo the notorious generation of the flood (Gen 7:1 LXX). The flood generation is a type of 'this generation' that sees the end signs, just as the flood itself typifies the judgment that will occur at the *parousia*. 'This generation' in 24:34 represents a long line of unbelieving, unresponsive people from the time of Noah to the end of the age." Ibid., 383–84.

184. See Matt 21:33–45; 23:29–39; 24:1–2, 15–19, 32–34; Mark 12:1–12; 13:1–2, 14–19, 28–30; Luke 11:45–51; 13:34–35; 19:41–44; 20:9–19; 21:5–6, 20–24, 29–32.

when it fell, he would thereby be vindicated. . . . The generation that rejects Jesus must be the last before the great cataclysm. There can be no other, because if there were they would need another warning prophet; once the father has sent the son to the vineyard [Matt 21:33–46; Mark 12:1–12; Luke 20:9–19], he can send nobody else. To reject the son is to reject the last chance."[185]

Even though *"this generation"* refers to the generation of disciples who were then alive when Jesus was speaking, it is not correct to conclude that he believed the *parousia* would occur within his disciples' lifetime. Rather, Carson points out:

> All that v.34 demands is that the distress of vv.4–28, including Jerusalem's fall, happen within the lifetime of the generation then living. This does *not* mean that the distress must end within that time but only that 'all these things' must happen within it. Therefore, v.34 sets a *terminus a quo* [earliest limiting point] for the Parousia: it cannot happen until the events in vv.4–28 take place, all within the generation of A.D. 30. But there is no *terminus ad quem* [latest limiting point] to this distress other than the Parousia itself, and "only the Father" knows when it will happen (v.36).[186]

The contrast between the known and the unknown

Understanding *"this generation"* as the generation alive when Jesus spoke causes the remainder of the Olivet Discourse to cohere. B. J. Oropeza explains: "Once we understand 'this generation' to be first-century believers, it solves the problem of how the disciples were expected to be able to know when the time was near—even 'right at the door' (Mt 24:32–34)—but not able to know when Jesus would return as a thief in the night (Mt 24:36–44). The parable of the fig tree in Matthew 24:32–34 was told for those living in the first century regarding the destruction of the temple, but the thief-in-the-night lesson refers to Christ's return and is also given to subsequent generations."[187] Consequently, as Gentry adds, Jesus "clearly knows the time of the events leading to the destruction of the Temple in A.D. 70 . . . He tells His disciples that certain signs may come, but He knows full well that 'the end is not yet' (v. 6). He dogmatically asserts that these things will happen to 'this generation' (v. 34). Thus, He can positively assert 'behold, I have told you in advance' (v. 25)."[188]

On the other hand, with respect to his second coming, Jesus states that *"of that day and hour no one knows, not even the angels of heaven, nor the Son, but the Father alone"* (Matt 24:36). So different are the two sets of events that "our Lord in this discourse warns repeatedly that his coming would be unknown and would happen unexpectedly (cf. vss. 39, 42, 44, 50), and in Matt. 25:13 he uses the same expression as in 24:36, namely, 'ye do not know the day nor the hour.'"[189]

---

185. Wright, *Victory,* 362, 365.

186. Carson, "Matthew," 8:507.

187. Oropeza, *99 Reasons,* 93.

188. Gentry, "Transition Text," n.p.

189. Murray, "Interadventual Period," 395.

The contrast between "near" and "far"

Jesus said that the events leading up to the destruction of Jerusalem were "near" (Matt 24:32–33) and that *"this generation"* would witness them (Matt 24:34). On the other hand, when talking about his second coming in glory, Gentry points us to the considerably different language and examples that Jesus uses: "the reference is to a long delay: 'But and if that evil servant shall say in his heart, My lord delayeth his coming' (Matt. 24:48) 'While the bridegroom tarried, they all slumbered and slept' (Matt. 25:5). 'After a long time the lord of those servants cometh, and reckoneth with them' (Matt. 25:19). The designation 'far' is certainly a relative concept. However, when used in a context and in apposition to 'this generation' designates, its relativity is in strong contrast."[190]

"But of that day and hour no one knows" (Matt 24:36; Mark 13:32)

In this verse Christ contrasts *"all these things"* (i.e., the events leading up to and including the fall of Jerusalem in AD 70), which are "near" and which *"this generation"* will witness, with *"that day"* (i.e., his second coming in glory at the "end of the age") which *"no one"* will be able to predict. This contrast is clear for several reasons:

- *Grammatical indicators of a change of subject.* Matt 24:34–35; Mark 13:30–31 appear to conclude Jesus' preceding statement. Matt 24:36; Mark 13:32 begin with the Greek word *de* ("but"). *De* is "an adversative particle, which stresses a contrast between the previous material and that which follows."[191]

- *The different ways Jesus refers to people.* When he is talking about *"all these things"* Jesus addresses his disciples personally, using the second person plural pronoun "you" (three times in Matt 24:33–34), and speaks of *"this generation"* (Matt 24:34). However, when he speaks of his second coming Jesus speaks generally and in the third person (i.e., *"no one knows"* [Matt 24:36]). Jesus used that same distinction earlier in the discourse when he talked about the signs of the times that would begin to occur during the disciples' lifetime: *"you will be hearing of wars"* (Matt 24:6); *"they will deliver you to tribulation"* (Matt 24:9); *"when you see the abomination of desolation"* (Matt 24:15); *"pray that your flight will not be in the winter"* (Matt 24:20); *"if anyone says to you, 'Behold, here is the Christ'"* (Matt 24:23, 26). However, when he spoke of his second coming, he spoke generally and in the third person: *"then all the tribes of the earth will mourn"* (Matt 24:30); *"they will see the Son of Man coming"* (Matt 24:30); *"they will gather together His elect"* (Matt 24:31). These grammatical indicators show that "the disciples were expected to live to see the events leading up to the destruction of the temple in A.D. 70, spoken of in the parable of the fig tree, but they were not expected to see Christ's return."[192]

- *The technical meaning of "that day and hour."* John Murray makes the important point that in the NT *"that day"* is "a well-defined eschatological denotation to designate

190. Gentry, "Transition Text," n.p.

191. Jackson, "Matthew Twenty-Four," n.p.

192. Oropeza, *99 Reasons*, 91.

the day of the Lord, the last day (cf. Matt. 7:22; Luke 10:12; 21:34; 2 Thess. 1:10; 2 Tim. 1:12, 18; 4:8). So much is this the case, that the expression 'the day' has taken on a distinctly technical meaning (cf. Rom. 13:12; 1 Cor. 3:13; 1 Thess. 5:4; Heb. 10:23; 2 Pet. 1:19)."[193] Just as *"that day"* is a well-defined eschatological denotation to designate the eschatological last day or day of the Lord, so does "hour" stand for the second coming in Matt 24:44; Luke 12:39–40; John 5:25, 28; and Rev 3:3; 14:7, 15.[194] Murray discusses the significance of Jesus' reference to *"that day and hour"* in the context of Matt 24:36–37: "The identity of 'that day and hour' (vs. 36) is placed beyond question by verses 37–39. That Jesus was speaking of his advent in verse 36 is clearly indicated by the close connection at the beginning of verse 37: 'For as (*hōsper gar*) the days of Noah were'. He institutes a parallel to establish and enforce what is said to be unknown in verse 36. But in verse 37 it is 'the advent of the Son of man' that is in view, as also in verse 39. If he were not speaking of the day of his advent in verse 36, then the *hōsper gar* of verse 37 would lose its relevance."[195] The linkage of the "day" and the "hour" as a technical term for the second coming also is seen in Matt 24:50; 25:13 and Luke 12:46.

In short, Jesus is saying that his disciples in the first century would be able to tell when the temple was about to be destroyed, but no one will be able to predict when he will come again.

The second coming of Christ is totally unpredictable

Prophetic "signs" are not designed to enable one to calculate when or how the prophesied event will occur

Approximately 150 years ago, Charles Hodge observed, "Prophecy is very different from history. It is not intended to give us a knowledge of the future, analogous to that which history gives us of the past. This truth is often overlooked. We see interpreters undertaking to give detailed expositions of the prophecies of Isaiah, of Ezekiel, of Daniel, and of the Apocalypse, relating to the future, with the same confidence with which they would record the history of the recent past. Such interpretations have always been falsified by the event."[196] For example, many Hebrew Scriptures prophesied the coming of the Messiah. When Christ came, he "was indeed a king, but no such king as the world had ever seen, and such as no man expected; He was a priest, but the only priest who ever lived of whose

---

193. Murray, "Interadventual Period," 394–95; see also Moore, *The Parousia,* 100 ("'*That* day' carries Old Testament overtones [of the last judgment and *parousia*] which '*the* day' in modern usage does not").

194. Allen Kerkeslager argues that "every occurrence of 'hour' in Revelation refers to the parousia." Kerkeslager, "Day of the Lord," 5. In addition to the passages cited above, that is seen most clearly in those passages that talk about the resurrection of the righteous (Rev 11:11–13) and judgment of the unrighteous (Rev 11:13; 18:10, 17, 19) that accompany the *parousia*.

195. Ibid., 395.

196. Hodge, *Systematic Theology,* 3:790.

priesthood he was himself the victim; He did establish a kingdom, but it was not of this world."[197]

Hodge concludes by reminding us that even John the Baptist, who had introduced Jesus as the promised Messiah, later had doubts: "Though he believed that all the Old Testament prophecies about the Messiah would be fulfilled, he did not properly understand the *way* in which they would be fulfilled. . . . If believers like John the Baptist could have problems of this sort with predictions about Christ's first coming, what guarantee do we have that believers will not have similar difficulties with predictions about Christ's second coming? We are confident that all predictions about Christ's return and the end of the world will be fulfilled, but we do not know exactly how they will be fulfilled."[198]

It is impossible to predict even general time-frames for when the second coming will occur

The "signs of the times" are deliberately general and open-ended. Stephen Travis points out that they are not predictive of the end:

> Earthquakes, famine, political upheaval, false messiahs, persecution and gospel-preaching, and the fall of Jerusalem—these things are not the kind of events which will pinpoint a particular moment of history when the Son of Man will come. They are the kind of things which characterize the whole period between Jesus' first and second comings (though the fall of Jerusalem in A.D. 70 was of course a particular, 'one-off' event). Jesus warned his followers of them not so that they would know the date of the end, but so that they could understand the nature of the conflict which would surround them and thus be forearmed to endure it.[199]

Mark 13:10 (see also Matt 24:14) states that the gospel must be preached to all nations "first," or before the end occurs. As David Turner discusses, even this "is sufficiently vague so as to discourage undue speculation. How can anyone know with precision when this point of worldwide evangelism has been reached? Additionally, the words 'and then' (*kai tote*) do not necessarily mean that the end will come 'immediately after' (cf. [Matt] 24:29) worldwide evangelism."[200]

---

197. Ibid., 3:791.

198. Ibid., 3:132–33; see also Schnabel, *40 Questions*, 42–43.

199. Travis, *I Believe*, 92.

200. Turner, "Structure and Sequence," 9. This is also indicated in Rev 6:9–11 where, in heaven, martyrs ask, *"How long, O Lord . . . will You refrain from judging and avenging our blood on those who dwell on the earth?"* The answer is that *"they were told that they should rest for a little while longer, until the number of their fellow servants and their brethren who were to be killed even as they had been, would be completed also."* That answer, like Jesus' statement about preaching the gospel to the whole world, also answers the question "When will the end come?" But like Jesus' statement concerning the gospel, when the last believer will be martyred is completely unknown and cannot be calculated or predicted by anyone here on earth. See Johnson, *Triumph*, 126.

The presence of an "Antichrist" or "great tribulation" will not make it possible to predict when the second coming will occur

If some end-time "Antichrist" figure arises, the fact is that "we simply do not know how the final antichrist will arise or what form his appearance will take."[201] Although it appears that there will be increased persecution before the end, other passages indicate that most people will continue to go about their normal affairs of daily life. Thus, in Matt 24:38–39 Jesus compares his second coming to the days of Noah when people *"were eating and drinking, marrying and giving in marriage, until the day that Noah entered the ark, and they did not understand until the flood came and took them all away."* In Matt 24:40–41 he adds, *"Then there will be two men in the field; one will be taken and one will be left. Two women will be grinding at the mill; one will be taken and one will be left."*[202]

In Luke 17:28–30 Jesus similarly said, *"It was the same as happened in the days of Lot: they were eating, they were drinking, they were buying, they were selling, they were planting, they were building; but on the day that Lot went out from Sodom it rained fire and brimstone from heaven and destroyed them all. It will be just the same on the day that the Son of Man is revealed."* All of those statements suggest that most people will continue their normal recreation, social relationships, work, and other activities of daily life, right up until the time that Jesus comes. When he comes will not be predictable or calculable.

Jesus' reference to the "day" and "hour" do not permit us to predict even the general time period when he may return

The idea that because Jesus referred to *"that day and hour"* in Matt 24:36; Mark 13:32, we can at least predict the month, or year, or general time period when he will return is nonsense. First, as discussed above, *"that day and hour"* is a technical term that stands for the second coming itself, not a time reference contrasted with week, month, or year. Second, the whole thrust of Matt 24:36—25:46 is that his coming will be unexpected and unpredictable. Third, since Jesus himself and the angels of heaven do not know when that will be (Matt 24:36; Mark 13:32), how can any mere human being presume to know or predict when it will occur?

Finally, in Acts 1:7, when his disciples asked when he would restore the kingdom, Jesus replied, *"It is not for you to know the times or epochs which the Father has fixed by his own authority."* The Greek words for "times" or "epochs" are *chronos* and *kairos*. Oropeza discusses those words and their significance in connection with whether one will be able to predict when the *parousia* will occur. *Chronos* and *kairos*:

---

201. Hoekema, *Bible and Future,* 162. For a detailed discussion of this see chapter 10–The "Antichrist."

202. These passages (see also the parallel in Luke 17:34–36) stress the unexpectedness of Christ's second coming and the sharp separation of people that will occur at the *parousia*. "This separation occurs at the advent [not a supposed 'rapture' some years before the *parousia*], as is clear from the explicit reference to the advent in verses 37 and 39." Murray, "Interadventual Period," 395. "It is neither clear nor particularly important whether 'taken' means 'taken in judgment' (cf. v.39, though the verb 'took ... away' differs from 'taken' in vv.40–41) or 'taken to be gathered with the elect' (v.31)." Carson, "Matthew," 8:509.

cannot be reduced to the Greek words for "day" and "hour" (*hēmera* and *hōra*). Both words refer to time periods that could last many years. In Acts 1:21 the word *time* (*chronos*), which is commonly defined as a duration or span of time . . . refers to the entire three-and-a-half-year ministry of Jesus. It can also refer to a generation of forty years (Acts 13:18), or even an entire lifetime or longer (Acts 17:30; 1 Cor 7:39; 1 Pet 4:3). The word . . . *kairos* in Greek . . . can refer to a year (Rev 12:12–14; compare 12:6), a season or a few years (Lk 4:13; Acts 14:17; Gal 4:10; 6:9; Phlm 15), a former disposition or an entire lifetime (Mk 10:30; Rom 2:12; 8:18), or the entire New Testament era (Lk 21:24; Rom 3:25–26; 2 Cor 6:2; 1 Pet 1:10–11). In the Greek version of the Old Testament (called the Septuagint or LXX) *kairos* and *chronos* are connected together and refer to entire eras of successive kingdoms (Dan 2:21; compare 2:31–44). In Acts 1:7 Jesus clearly intended *times* and *dates* to mean much more than a few weeks or months. He is saying we cannot figure out the date of the end—period. Another way of rendering the combination of *times* and *dates* is this: "It is not for you to know the various epochs of history *[kairoi]*, nor yet how long they will last *[chronoi]*; for these are matters of God's own knowledge and disposal."[203]

The Olivet Discourse as a whole stresses faithful living because of the impossibility of knowing when Christ will return

Although the Olivet Discourse deals with the second coming, Jesus includes multiple practical imperatives. Travis discusses Mark's account of Jesus' discourse as follows: "Unlike Jewish apocalyptic writings, much of Mark 13 is cast in the form of commands. For example: 'Watch out' (verses 5, 9, 33). 'Don't be troubled' (verse 7). 'Do not worry' (verse 11). 'Be on your guard! I have told you everything ahead of time' (verse 23). 'Keep awake!' (verses 35, 37). This highlights the fact that Jesus's purpose is to encourage not speculation but watchfulness—to strengthen faith and forewarn his disciples what will be their lot as his followers."[204] Ford adds to this by noting how Christ framed his discourse verbally: "But what is present from beginning to end is the note of warning, the admonition to *be* right rather than merely to know or profess the right. The first and last words of Christ are *blepete* ["watch out"; "take heed"; "see": Mark 13:5, 9, 23, 33], and His imperatives throughout amount to nineteen. It is evident that His prophecy has primarily a moral pupose, as was the case also with most Old Testament predictions."[205]

Matthew's account of the discourse includes several parables: the thief in the night (Matt 24:42–44); the faithful and unfaithful slaves (Matt 24:45–51); the ten virgins (Matt 25:1–13); and the talents (Matt 25:14–30). Each one of these parables emphasizes that we will *not* know when the Lord will be returning:

- The "thief in the night" explicitly says, *"You do not know which day your Lord is coming"* (Matt 24:42; see also vv. 43–44);

---

203. Oropeza, *99 Reasons*, 42; see also Schnabel, *40 Questions*, 47–48.

204. Travis, *I Believe*, 92–93; see also Schnabel, *40 Questions*, 12.

205. Ford, *Abomination of Desolation*, 82.

- The "faithful and unfaithful slaves" states that the master *"is not coming for a long time"* (Matt 24:48), and the master will come *"on a day when he does not expect him and at an hour which he does not know"* (Matt 24:50);

- The "ten virgins" says, *"You do not know the day nor the hour"* (Matt 25:13);

- The "talents" speaks of the Lord going on a journey of indeterminate length (25:14) but which lasted *"a long time"* (Matt 25:19).

For the very reason that we do not know when the Lord will return we need to be alert, ready, prepared, and faithfully doing what we should be doing. Jesus says the same thing in Rev 16:15 (*"Behold, I am coming like a thief. Blessed is the one who stays awake"*; see also Rev 3:3). Jesus' commands to stay awake and remain faithful do not concern unbelievers, but believers. In other words, his coming will be unexpected by *everybody*—believers and unbelievers alike.

Dispensationalists often presume that certain "signs" enable us to calculate, at least in a *general* way, when Christ will return, e.g., the rebirth of Israel in 1948, which they think means that the second coming will be within one generation.[206] Or, they believe that the end-time tribulation will last precisely seven years (based on their [mis]understanding of Dan 9:24–27),[207] which would enable one to precisely calculate when Christ will return. For example, Hal Lindsey asserts, "According to Daniel's prophetic chronology, the minute the Israeli leader and the Roman leader sign this pact, God starts His great timepiece which has seven allotted years left on it. This event marks the beginning of the period of Biblical history previously noted as the Tribulation."[208] Or, the appearance of a political figure (Antichrist; a new "abomination of desolation") in a rebuilt temple in Jerusalem means that the second coming will be in three and a half years.[209]

In fact, "nowhere does the Bible hint of a seven-year tribulation period."[210] If what dispensationalists claim were true, then the entire point of Jesus' parables would be undermined. Such date-specific signs would mean that no one would be under any obligation to be alert or ready until those signs occurred. Accordingly, anyone who tries to predict the end by means of the Olivet Discourse invariably will be wrong, just as everyone in the past always has been wrong. Seven hundred years ago, Henry of Harclay (c. 1270–1317), chancellor of Oxford, realized that. He wisely and rightly cautioned that "any attempt to precisely calculate the time of the end was either erroneous or heretical. As he put it, 'All investigators of the end of the world, even if they were saints, were mistaken in their conjectures.'"[211] Blomberg adds that one could never use the events narrated in the discourse to predict when the end will occur because "once the temple was destroyed, everything was in place for Christ to come back. However, he has not done so yet, so we cannot predict when it will happen except to say that it will catch many by surprise

---

206. Lindsey, *Late Great,* 53–54; Whisenant, *88 Reasons,* 9; Higgins, *Manasseh Effect,* 31, 53, 77–79.
207. Ice, "Old Testament," 86.
208. Lindsey, *Late Great,* 152.
209. Ice, "Rebuttal," 135–38.
210. Jackson, "Daniel's Prophecy," 13.
211. McGinn, *Anti-Christ,* 167.

(24:37–42), and the rest of Jesus' sermon stresses faithful living so that Christians are ready whenever it takes place (24:43—25:46)."[212]

The whole subject of predicting when the end might come is not the reason why Jesus gave the discourse. Consequently, trying to predict the end from what Jesus said is using the discourse for a purpose Jesus did not intend. That amounts to taking it out of context. Whenever one takes Scripture out of context, one is bound to reach an erroneous conclusion. James Edwards concludes, "No one is either encouraged or commended for attempting to be an eschatological code-cracker. That is folly, for even the Son of Man is ignorant of the End [Mark 13:32]. The premium of discipleship is placed not on predicting the future but on *faithfulness in the present,* especially in trials, adversity, and suffering."[213]

212. Blomberg, "Matthew," 88.

213. Edwards, *Mark,* 386, emphasis in original.

9

The "Rapture": Pretribulational or Part of the Second Coming?

THE WORD "RAPTURE" IS derived from the Latin word *rapiemur* which is found in the Latin Vulgate Bible in 1 Thess 4:17 and is translated "caught up."[1] The two primary passages concerning the rapture are 1 Cor 15:50–54 and 1 Thess 4:13–18. The dispensationalist *New Scofield Reference Bible* calls 1 Thess 4:13–18 the "central passage" concerning the rapture of the church.[2] First Thess 4:13–18 and 1 Cor 15:50–54 deal with opposite sides of the same coin: in 1 Thessalonians the issue was whether dead believers would receive the same benefits as those who are alive at Christ's return; in 1 Corinthians the point was that, because flesh and blood cannot inherit the kingdom of God, believers who are alive at Christ's return must be transformed to participate in the kingdom.

Until dispensationalism was invented in the 1800s, all Christians understood that the church will be present during any end-time "tribulation" and that Christ's second coming will entail the resurrection of the dead and the rapture of living believers. Dispensationalism claims that there will be a pretribulational rapture of the church, which takes place seven years (or three and a half years for midtribulationists) before the second coming itself.[3] The reason for this, according to dispensationalism, is that "the tribulation concerns Israel, not the church."[4] As Travis points out, "The notion of spiriting the church away before the 'tribulation' derives not from any statement of scripture, but from the belief that Israel must go through the tribulation, and *therefore* the church cannot."[5]

In fact, all passages that deal with the issue make clear that the rapture and the second coming are not two events separated in time. The rapture occurs as part of the second

---

1. MacDonald, *Believer's,* 2038, 2046n.13; Bell, "Critical Evaluation," 2–3.

2. Scofield, *New Scofield,* 1292n.1.

3. Probably the most comprehensive examination of dispensationalism's pre-tribulational rapture doctrine is William Everett Bell, "A Critical Evaluation of the Pretribulation Rapture Doctrine in Christian Eschatology" (PhD Dissertation, New York University, 1967). It is available from UMI Dissertaion Services, 789 E. Eisenhower Parkway, PO Box 1346, Ann Arbor, MI 48106–1346; www.il.proquest.com.

4. Walvoord, *Rapture Question,* 62; see also Pentecost, *Things to Come,* 193, 197–98; Smith, *What the World,* 70; Higgins, *Manasseh Effect,* 51.

5. Travis, *I Believe,* 151.

coming which is after, not before, the tribulation.[6] The primary passages are discussed below.

1 Thessalonians 4–5

First Thessalonians 4–5 describes events (including the rapture) that occur as part of the second coming, not separate events that occur seven (or three and a half) years before the second coming.

1 Thessalonians 4–5 and the Olivet Discourse describe the same events

The Olivet Discourse is Christ's longest discussion of end-times, including what will happen in connection with the *parousia*. That discourse is probably a *source* of Paul's teaching on eschatology in 1 and 2 Thessalonians.[7] In the Olivet Discourse, Christ never speaks of a pretribulational rapture. However, in Matt 24:31 he does speak of the "gathering of the elect," which "can most readily be taken to refer to the gathering of the elect at the resurrection."[8] Thus, the one passage that directly correlates the "tribulation" with the "gathering of the elect" specifies that the "gathering," will be *after the tribulation* (Matt 24:29–31), not before. That Paul says the same thing in 1 Thessalonians 4–5 as Christ says in the Olivet Discourse is clearly seen in the following comparison:[9]

6. What is said in this chapter concerning dispensational pretribulationism equally applies to its variants midtribulationism and the pre-wrath rapture position. All variants of pretribulationism are forms of dispensational premillennialism. All follow the same hermeneutic grounded on Dan 9:24–27 (Daniel's "seventy weeks") which holds that there is a 2000+ year gap between the end of the 69th week and the beginning of the 70th; the 70th week is the last seven year period of history which will see the Great Tribulation. All these views are based on the same fundamental principle that the rapture is disconnected from the *parousia* itself, but is a separate, earlier, event. "Pre-wrath" advocate Marvin Rosenthal correctly states that "the Lord's coming is consistently portrayed as a singular event." Rosenthal, *Pre-Wrath*, 222. Nevertheless, he maintains that the Second Coming "includes the Rapture of the church, the outpouring of God's wrath during the Day of the Lord, and Christ's physical return in glory." Ibid., 221–22. Robert Van Kampen indicates that Christ actually makes four "comings": his coming for the church at the rapture; his coming to bring salvation to Israel at the end of Daniel's "seventieth week"; his coming with his angels to defeat Antichrist at Armageddon; and his coming with the church at the beginning of the millennium. Between the rapture and the church's return to earth with Christ at the beginning of the millennium a period of several years may ensue. Van Kampen, *The Sign*, 305–438; see critique at Showers, *The Pre-Wrath Rapture View*, 82–85. H. L. Nigro tries to correct this by saying that, when Christ comes to rapture his people, he *"remains on earth during the administration of the judgments of the Day of the Lord. When the armies see Him at the battle of Armageddon, He is simply manifesting Himself in the rightful role he assumed on arrival."* Nigro, *Before God's Wrath*, 198, emphasis in original. However, according to Nigro, the raptured believers themselves remain in heaven. Ibid., 206–208. Thus, however it is formulated, the pre-wrath position, like pre- and mid-tribulationism, in fact destroys the unity of the *parousia* by disconnecting the *parousia*'s entailments (resurrection, rapture, judgment, and renewal of the earth) from each other.

7. Waterman, "Sources of Paul's Teaching," 105–13.

8. Murray, "Interadventual Period," 391.

9. For another comparative table of 1 Thessalonians 4–5 and Matthew 24, see Schnabel, *40 Questions*, 100.

Event	1 Thessalonians 4–5	Matthew 24
1. Christ himself returns	4:16	24:30
2. From heaven	4:16	24:30
3. With a shout	4:16	24:30 (in power)
4. Accompanied by angels	4:16	24:31
5. With trumpet of God	4:16	24:31
6. Believers supernaturally gathered to Christ	4:17	24:31, 40–41
7. In clouds	4:17	24:30
8. Time unknown	5:2, 4	24:36, 42–44, 50
9. Will come as a thief	5:1–2	24:36
10. Unbelievers unaware of impending judgment	5:3	24:37–39
11. Judgment comes as travail upon expectant mother	5:3	24:8
12. Believers not deceived	5:4–5	24:42
13. Believers to watch	5:6	24:4, 33
14. Warning against drunkenness	5:7	24:49

William Everett Bell comments on the significance of the correspondence between the two passages:

> Not only are the principal features of Paul's account found also in Christ's Olivet discourse, but even the order is substantially the same. . . . It is difficult to see how any candid exegete can fail to see the obvious correspondence of the two accounts and thus conclude that Christ and Paul were speaking of the same event. . . . Indeed, the passage provides very little new information concerning the second advent, and that, of course, was not the purpose of the passage. It is universally acknowledged by expositors that the occasion for Paul's remarks was the inquiry of the Thessalonians concerning the future status of believers who had died. Would these recently-departed brethren share fully in the blessings of Christ's second coming? Paul assured them that death would be no hindrance to their participation in that event. Not only would they be raised from the dead (a fact already known), but they would be caught up ("raptured") simultaneously with those who remained alive. Therefore the only additional information afforded by the passage is some detail concerning the precise relationship of the dead to the living saints at Christ's coming.[10]

The primary images of 1 Thess 4:16–17 are clearly related to the second coming

Even pretribulationists agree that the second coming occurs after the tribulation.[11] Paul's description of the Lord's "descending from heaven" and believers being "caught up to

10. Bell, "Critical Evaluation," 250–51, 271–72.
11. Pentecost, *Things to Come*, 280; Ice, "New Testament," 95.

meet him" describe events relating to the second coming, not a "pretribulational rapture." The Lord's *"coming down from heaven"* (1 Thess 4:16) recalls, in a general way, the OT references to *"the day of the Lord"* when God will judge the wicked and save the righteous.[12] Jeffrey Weima notes that the *"trumpet of God"* (1 Cor 15:42; 1 Thess 4:16) in the OT functioned primarily "as a signal, marking in particular the visible appearance of God not only in the past (Exod. 19:13, 16, 19; 20:18), but especially at the future day of the Lord (Isa. 27:13; Joel 2:1; Zeph. 1:14–16; Zech. 9:14)."[13] Similarly, clouds are a sign of Christ's second coming.[14] The cloud image ultimately is derived from Dan 7:13, where Daniel had a vision and saw *"with the clouds of heaven one like a Son of Man was coming."* That passage from Daniel was quoted by Jesus in connection with his second coming. Given the consistent use of all these images in connection with the *parousia*, most standard popular and scholarly commentaries have no problem identifying the rapture described in 1 Thess 4:16–17 with the second coming described in Matt 24:29–31; Mark 13:24–27:

- *Matthew Henry's Commentary*: "Their ministration [i.e., the angels in Matt 24:31] will be ushered in with a great sound of a trumpet, to awaken and alarm a sleeping world. This trumpet is spoken of, 1 Co. 15:52, and 1 Th. 4:16."[15]

- *Africa Bible Commentary*: "Human history will move to a climactic end as the Lord of history returns *in clouds with great power and glory* ([Mark] 13:26). This awesome event is also described in Revelation 1:7 and 1 Thessalonians 4:13–18."[16]

- *Evangelical Commentary on the Bible*: "Paul now gives a thumbnail description of Christ's parousia: 'For the Lord himself will come down from heaven' ([1 Thess] 4:16). The Lord is none other than Jesus Christ. He, not man, ushers in the great event that marks the end of this age."[17]

- *New International Biblical Commentary*: "At the sound of the eschatological trumpet (cf. 1 Cor. 15:52; 1 Thess. 4:16), the angels will be sent to the four winds (cf. [Matt] 13:41, 49) to gather God's elect (for Old Testament parallels, cf. Zech 2:6 and Deut. 30:4). The scene depicted is clearly that of the return of Christ at the end of history as we know it."[18]

Grammatically 1 Thess 4:15–17 cannot represent an event different from the second coming

In 1 Thessalonians there are five references to the Lord's return: 1:9–10; 2:19–20; 3:12–13; 4:15–17; 5:23. Of those passages, 2:19–20; 3:12–13; 4:15–17; 5:23 us the word *parousia* with the definite article (i.e., *"the parousia"*), and 2:19, 3:13, and 5:23 contain the phrase *en*

12. See Isa 2:10–12; 13:6, 9; Ezek 7:19; 13:5; 30:3; Joel 1:15; 2:1, 11, 31; 3:14; Amos 5:18–20; Zeph 1:7–8, 14, 18; 2:2–3; Zech 14:1; Mal 3:2.

13. Weima, "1–2 Thessalonians," 880.

14. Matt 24:30; 26:64; Mark 13:26; 14:62; Luke 21:27; Rev 1:7; 14:14–16.

15. Henry, *Commentary*, 1743.

16. Cole, "Mark," 1194.

17. Ewert, "1–2 Thessalonians," 1081.

18. Mounce, *Matthew*, 227.

tē parousia (*"at the coming"*). Dispensationalists typically assign 1:9–10, 2:19–20, 4:15–17, and 5:23 to the pretribulational rapture but 3:12–13 to the second coming (because of the reference there to Jesus' coming *"with all His saints"*).[19] However, that is not grammatically possible.

In all four *"parousia"* passages (2:19–20; 3:12–13; 4:15–17; 5:23), the word for "coming" (*parousia*) is the same and the definite article is present. In Greek, when the definite article is used with a common noun (as it is with *parousia* here), it signifies something that is a matter of general knowledge or something that has been previously mentioned.[20] Pretribulationists use the terms *parousia* ("coming"), *apokalupsis* ("revelation"), and *epiphaeia* ("appearing") for *both* the pretribulational rapture and the second coming. Doing that "automatically excludes the use of the definite article [in 2:19–20; 3:12–13; 4:15–17; 5:23] in the sense of general knowledge . . . [since] 'the coming' can mean nothing specifically if there are two events which share the same designation."[21] Further, in 1 Thessalonians there is no previous mention that defines the specific meaning of *"the parousia"* in the context of that epistle. Therefore, there is no grammatical basis whatsoever to assign three uses of *"the parousia"* (2:19–20; 4:15–17; 5:23) to the pretribulational rapture and one (3:12–13) to the second coming.

That is all the more true with respect to 2:19, 3:13, and 5:23, because they all contain the same phrase, *en tē parousia* (*"at the coming"*). Nevertheless, pretribulationists assign 2:19 and 5:23 to the pretribulational rapture and 3:13 to the second coming. Bell points out, "There is no exegetical basis whatever for assigning these passages to the rapture rather than to the second coming."[22] Thus, in all the references to Christ's coming in 1 Thessalonians "there is not the slightest hint in the epistle that two separate and distinct comings are to be distinguished. The speaker remains the same, the audience remains the same, the general subject remains the same, and the specific terminology remains the same."[23]

In fact, when they are attacking the preterist idea of a non-bodily *"parousia,"* even pretribulationists admit that 1 Thess. 2:19; 3:13; 4:15; 5:23 *are all second coming passages*. For example, Stanley Toussaint states that, except when the word is used of someone other than Jesus, "In all the other cases *parousia* is used of the Lord's presence at His second coming (1 Cor. 15:23; 1 Thess. 2:19; 3:13; 4:15; 5:23; 2 Thess. 2:1, 8; James 5:7–8; 2 Pet. 1:16; 3:4, 12; 1 John 2:28)."[24] Thomas Ice not only quotes Toussaint's statement with approval,[25] but also quotes the *Theological Dictionary of the New Testament,* and states "TDNT describes *parousia* as a technical term 'for the "coming" of Christ in messianic glory.'"[26] Consequently, the pretribulational rapture doctrine is without any grammatical or exegetical basis at all.

---

19. Ice, "Rapture and Second Coming," 2.
20. Bell, "Critical Evaluation," 265.
21. Ibid., 266–67.
22. Ibid., 269.
23. Ibid., 267.
24. Toussaint, "A Critique," 476.
25. Ice, "Rebuttal," 147.
26. Ibid., 146, quoting Oepke, *"parousia,"* 5:859.

1 Corinthians 15

First Corinthians 15 is Paul's most detailed discussion of the resurrection, Christ's "coming," the rapture, and *"the end."*[27] Paul's discussion of these topics in 1 Cor 15:12–58 parallels his discussion of the same topics in 1 Thess 4:13–18:

Topic	*1 Thessalonians 4*	*1 Corinthians 15*
No hope without Christ & the resurrection	4:13	15:12–19
Christ rose and will bring the dead with him at his coming	4:14	15:20–28
At his coming, the living will be raptured/ transformed	4:15–17	15:50–54
Believers should be comforted/encouraged by this	4:18	15:58

These parallels of both content and structure indicate that both passages are the same in substance.[28]

First Cor 15:25–26 says that Christ *"must reign until He has put all His enemies under His feet. The last enemy that will be abolished is death."* First Cor 15:50–57 describes when Christ abolishes death. 15:50 says that *"flesh and blood cannot inherit the kingdom of God; nor does the perishable inherit the imperishable."* 15:53 goes on to state that the perishable must *"put on the imperishable, and this mortal must put on immortality."* That occurs at *"the last trumpet"* when *"the dead will be raised imperishable, and we will be changed"* (15:52). That event (the rapture) is linked with 15:54 which says, *"When this mortal will have put on immortality, then will come about the saying that is written, 'death is swallowed up in victory.'"* Andrew Lincoln states the obvious, "The clear temporal reference [to the events of 15:54] is to the parousia (cf. verse 52)."[29] Thus, *"the end"* (15:24) is coterminous with the abolition of death (15:26), which is when our mortal bodies are changed and *"put on immortality"* (15:52–54).

Those events all occur at Christ's "coming" (i.e., the *parousia*, 15:23). "The believer's victory over death is said in 1 Corinthians 15:54–55 to occur when believers receive resurrection bodies. This coincides with what is said in 1 Corinthians 15:23–26 to occur in conjunction with both the 'coming' of Christ and the 'end', when the believer's last enemy, death, will be overcome."[30] The rapture *cannot* happen before the tribulation because at the rapture death has been ended forever. In other words, the identity of the rapture in 1 Cor 15:50–54 with the second coming is confirmed in that the rapture occurs *"at the last trumpet"* (1 Cor 15:52) which will take place at the second coming *after* the tribulation (Matt 24:29, 31).

27. This passage is discussed in detail at Appendix 7: 1 Cor 15:20–57: The Resurrection, the *Parousia*, and the Millennium.

28. Joachim Jeremias has pointed out that the two passages express the same idea: "There [1 Thess 4:13–17] also we hear of the trump of God, there also we are told that the living and the dead in Christ share simultaneously in the parousia; there also the living have no precedence over the dead; there also the rising of the dead is rather mentioned first; there also Paul includes himself among the 'we' of those who are alive and remain unto the coming of the Lord; there also, finally, Paul is expecting that the union of the dead with Christ will take place only at the parousia." Jeremias, "Flesh and Blood," 153.

29. Lincoln, *Paradise Now*, 66.

30. Venema, *Promise*, 250.

Additionally, 1 Cor 15:54 quotes Isa 25:8, which talks about the beginning of God's eternal kingdom in which God *"will swallow up death for all time, and the Lord God will wipe tears away from all faces."* Isa 25:8 is again quoted in Rev 21:4. Rev 21:4 fulfills the prophecy of Isa 25:8 and relates to the establishment of God's eternal kingdom (the *"new heaven and new earth,"* Rev 21:1–4).[31] All these passages are consistent: the rapture is part of the second coming at the *end* of the tribulation; the second coming initiates a complex of events that include resurrection (and rapture), judgment, and the beginning of the eternal kingdom of God.

2 Thessalonians 1–2

Second Thessalonians 1–2 is an extended discussion concerning the second coming and *"our gathering together to him,"* which clearly is posttribulational, not pretribulational.

2 Thess 1:6–10 is posttribulational

Even pretribulationists agree that 2 Thess 1:6–10 concerns the posttribulational second coming of Christ.[32] At that time (and not before) Christ will do two things: (1) punish the ungodly who are persecuting Christians (1:6, 8–9); and (2) rescue Christians who are being persecuted and give them rest (1:7, 10). The "rest" or "relief" of 1:7 is contrasted with the "tribulation" or "affliction"[33] of 1:6. This passage is fatal to any view of a pretribulational rapture because: "Paul explicitly states that the hope of the Thessalonian believers is the glorious second advent of Christ, at which time they will receive rest from their afflictions. If the rapture, as an event separate from the second advent, is indeed 'the blessed hope' (Titus 2:13) of the Christian, this passage becomes inexplicable."[34]

2 Thess 2:1–2 and "our gathering together to him"

In 2 Thess 2:1–2 Paul states that *"our gathering together to him,"* which pretribulationists take as a reference to the rapture,[35] occurs at *"the coming"* of the Lord (2:1), which is *"the day of the Lord"* (2:2). Those events all must refer to the second coming since "the word 'gather together' (*episunago*) in Matthew 24:31 is the verb whose noun (*episunagoge*) is used in 2 Thessalonians 2:1 of our 'gathering together' unto the Lord at the Rapture."[36]

Further, 2:1 introduces a discourse concerning the "coming" (*parousia*) of Christ, i.e., the coming at which the church is raptured.[37] The only other time Christ's *parousia* is

31. See Beale and McDonough, "Revelation," 1151.

32. Pache, *Return*, 358; Hiebert, *Thessalonian Epistles*, 284–94; Feinberg, *Millennialism*, 289; Ice, "Rapture and Second Coming," 2.

33. Greek = *thlipsis*, the same word used in Matt 24:21, 29 for the "tribulation."

34. Bell, "Critical Evaluation," 275.

35. Ice, "Rapture and Second Coming," 2; MacDonald, *Believer's*, 2053.

36. Ladd, *Blessed Hope*, 73.

37. All standard translations of 2 Thess 2:1 translate the beginning of that verse as *"concerning the coming of our Lord"* (ESV; RSV; NKJV; NIV; NASB: *"with regard to the coming of our Lord"*). The Greek

mentioned in that discourse is in 2 Thess 2:8 (*"Then that lawless one will be revealed whom the Lord will slay with the breath of his mouth and bring to an end by the appearance of His coming [parousia]"*). Bell notes the fatal nature of 2 Thess 2:8 to pretribulationism:

> This description of the destruction of Anti-Christ by Christ Himself is an obvious reference to the glorious second advent and is so taken by all leading pretribulationists. But this identification, again, would seem to be fatal for pretribulationism. If Paul expressly sets out to inform the Thessalonians concerning certain aspects of the Lord's coming (*parousia*), which is identified as the rapture of the church, and then mentions the *parousia* again in the passage only in connection with the admittedly posttribulational *parousia* to destroy Anti-Christ, there can be no escaping the obvious identification of the two events as one and the same.[38]

The "restrainer" of 2 Thess 2:6–7

The "restrainer" who is *"taken out of the way"* (2 Thess 2:7) does not imply a pretribulational rapture. Pretribulationists identify the "restrainer" as the Holy Spirit who indwells believers (the church). They then wrongly claim that the church must be removed from the earth in order to take the restrainer *"out of the way."*[39]

The identity of the "restrainer"

The identity of the "restrainer" is not at all clear and has been identified in various ways. Even the grammar of "restrains" in 2 Thess 2:6–7 is difficult. "Paul first refers to this restraining influence in 2:6 as *to katechon* (a neuter participle meaning 'that which restrains') and then in 2:7 as *ho katechōn* (a masculine participle meaning 'the one who restrains')."[40] Thus, it is not clear whether the restrainer is an impersonal force or a personal entity. Desmond Ford lists seven characteristics of the "restrainer" that are apparent from 2 Thessalonians 2: it is a present force; it is a beneficent force; it is a law-abiding and

---

word for "concerning" is *huper*. BDAG states that, in this context, *huper* is a "marker of general content, whether of a discourse or mental activity, *about, concerning.*" BDAG, *"huper,"* 1031. It even cites this very verse as meaning "with reference to." Ibid. Dispensationalist William MacDonald recognizes the significance of that and states that if the meaning of *huper* is, indeed, "concerning," then "the passage seems to teach that the Rapture and the Day of the Lord are one and the same event, since the following verses clearly deal with the Day of the Lord." MacDonald, *Believer's,* 2053. Since that is fatal to pretribulationism, MacDonald and *The New Scofield Reference Bible* change the translation of *huper* from "concerning" to "by," in the sense of "on the basis of." Ibid.; Scofield, *New Scofield,* 1294. In other words, they contend that Paul is saying, "I appeal to you on the basis of the Rapture that you should not fear that you are in the Day of the Lord. The Rapture must take place first. You will then be taken home to heaven at that time and will thus escape the horrors of the Day of the Lord." MacDonald, *Believer's,* 2053. This amazing example shows the extent to which pre-existing dispensationalist theological presuppositions drive not only its exegesis of the text but even necessitate manipulation of the text.

38. Bell, "Critical Evaluation," 280–81.

39. Ryrie, *Holy Spirit,* rev. ed., 185; Walvoord, *Rapture Question,* 241–43.

40. Holmes, *1 and 2 Thessalonians,* 233.

law-upholding force; it has a divine time-mission; it is a power that actively withdraws; this power spans the ages; this power is very great and mighty.[41]

Michael Holmes notes that the following have been proposed as candidates for the restrainer: (1) the Roman Empire as personified in the emperor;[42] (2) the principle of law and order (personified in 2:7); (3) the Jewish state; (4a) Satan; (4b) a force or person hostile to God (taking the verb in the sense of "possess, occupy," or "hold sway"); (5a) God and his power; (5b) the Holy Spirit; (6) the proclamation of the gospel (the neuter participle) by Christians and especially by Paul himself (the masculine participle); (7) an angel who restrains evil until the gospel has been preached to all nations (see Mark 13:10).[43] The identity of the "restrainer" may represent a combination of forces and entities.[44]

Despite all of these suggestions, Holmes concludes that, other than a consensus that the restraining influence must be a force for good rather than evil, no suggestion has convinced "more than a minority of scholars, and none is free from difficulties."[45] The difficult grammar, veiled language, and uncertainty regarding contextual issues led Augustine to conclude, "I frankly confess I do not know what he means."[46] If one as eminent as Augustine was so uncertain as to Paul's precise meaning, perhaps modern interpreters likewise should exhibit reserve in their identification of the "restrainer."

Dispensationalism's own unique theology of the church is the only basis for its view of the "removal of the restrainer"

Dispensationalism alone sharply distinguishes Israel and the church.[47] Further, it holds the peculiar view that "the term *church* applies only to a certain body of saints, namely, the saints of this present dispensation."[48] Specifically, the church does *not* include "the elect in the tribulation period."[49] The reason for that is dispensationalism's belief that "the tribulation concerns Israel, not the church."[50]

Those false presuppositions drive the dispensational idea that the church will be removed from the earth—and with it the Holy Spirit—before the tribulation begins. Leading dispensationalist John Walvoord admits, "It is safe to say that pretribulationism

---

41. Ford, *Abomination of Desolation,* 216–17.

42. Those who take this view infer that Paul used veiled or cryptic language in describing the restrainer because "any allusion to the imperial power—especially to its prospective abolition—had best be as vague as possible lest the letter fall into the wrong hands." Bruce, "1 and 2 Thessalonians," 1163; see also Payne, *Encyclopedia,* 565.

43. Holmes, *1 and 2 Thessalonians,* 233–34.

44. See Storms, *Kingdom Come,* 535–36. Ford suggests that civil law that is dependent on the working of the Holy Spirit to move on people's hearts urging them to yield to the gospel (i.e., a combination of candidates 1, 2, 5, and 6, above) meets the requirements. Ford, *Abomination of Desolation,* 221.

45. Holmes, *1 and 2 Thessalonians,* 234.

46. Augustine, *Civ.,* 20.19. See also Schnabel, *40 Questions,* 160.

47. Ryrie, *Dispensationalism Today,* 159.

48. Walvoord, *Rapture Question,* 21.

49. Ibid., 37.

50. Ibid., 62; see also Pentecost, *Things to Come,* 193, 197–98; Smith, *What the World,* 70; Higgins, *Manasseh Effect,* 51.

depends on a particular definition of the church."[51] Dispensationalist Charles Ryrie acknowledges that that is the basis for the doctrine of the pretribulational rapture: "The distinction between Israel and the Church leads to the belief that the Church will be taken from the earth before the beginning of the tribulation (which in one major sense concerns Israel)."[52] The reason is that "the guaranteed indwelling presence of the Spirit in believers [i.e., in the church] *will necessitate the removal of the Spirit* when believers are raptured."[53]

Even assuming the Holy Spirit is the "restrainer," there is no logical reason why the church has to be raptured before the tribulation.

The dispensationalist and pretribulationalist understanding of the working of the Holy Spirit does not, in fact, render the removal of the Spirit necessary. Bell explains why:

> Even assuming the Holy Spirit to be the restrainer in II Thessalonians 2, the conclusion drawn by pretribulationists is a *non sequitur*. Walvoord himself, in his comprehensive work on the Holy Spirit, points out that the restraining ministry of the Holy Spirit is a work which has been going on since antediluvian times (Genesis 6:3) and is not to be thought of as a New Testament ministry alone. Since His permanent indwelling of believers did not begin until the day of Pentecost in Acts 2, it is obvious that His indwelling ministry is largely independent of His ministry in restraining sin. Therefore, if His restraining ministry should cease in the tribulation period (as pretribulationists posit) this would not necessarily affect His indwelling ministry. . . . Unless, then, the Holy Spirit's indwelling ministry specifically is mentioned as being withdrawn (which it is not, as Walvoord admits) there would seem to be no logical reason to assume that the removal of restraint—even that of the Holy Spirit—logically or Biblically necessitates the removal of the church.[54]

Bell's argument actually is stronger than he articulated it. The reason is that even pretribulationists acknowledge that the Holy Spirit continues to be present and active during the tribulation. Thus, John Walvoord admits that during the tribulation "the Holy Spirit is still omnipresent and still exercises some restraint, as the Book of Revelation makes plain in the protection of the 144,000."[55] Walvoord also states, "While the tribulation period is characterized by wickedness and apostasy, it will nevertheless be a period of great harvest of souls. In the light of these facts, it is essential that the Holy Spirit minister during this period. . . . Accordingly, it may be deduced that the Spirit of God will not only convict men of their need of Christ and reveal the way of salvation, but He will also regenerate those who believe."[56] He acknowledges that the Holy Spirit will fill and empower believers during the tribulation and holds open the possibility that the Spirit will even indwell be-

51. Walvoord, *Rapture Question*, 21.

52. Ryrie, *Dispensationalism Today*, 159.

53. Ryrie, *Holy Spirit*, 108, emphasis added; see also Travis, *I Believe*, 151.

54. Bell, "Critical Evaluation," 289–90. Bell's reference is to John Walvoord, *The Holy Spirit* (Wheaton, IL: Van Kampen, 1954).

55. Walvoord, *Rapture Question*, 243.

56. Walvoord, *Holy Spirit*, 228, 230.

lievers: "If believers are indwelt during the tribulation, however, it also would follow that they are sealed by the Spirit, the seal being His own presence with them. Even if the Spirit does not indwell all believers of this period, it is clear that some are filled with the Spirit and empowered to witness."[57] Charles Ryrie frankly admits that, during the tribulation, the Holy Spirit "will be present and active in the world; He will indwell and empower His people."[58] Given all that, the idea that it was necessary to remove the Spirit's presence *in the church* by means of a pretribulational rapture makes no sense.

Pretribulationism is self-contradictory regarding the Holy Spirit and the church in the tribulation

Pretribulationists admit that during the tribulation perhaps millions of people will become believers in Jesus Christ.[59] This means that the church would be removed from the earth *only to be immediately resumed and reconstituted* during the tribulation. However, *by definition,* believers in Jesus Christ (i.e., Christians; the church) are *indwelt with and led by* the Holy Spirit (John 14:16–17; Rom 8:9–17). Pretribulationists simply cannot account for the Holy Spirit in relation to this multitude of Christians. On one hand, they maintain, "Apparently the Spirit's work in believers during the Tribulation period will follow the pattern of His work in the Old Testament."[60] On the other hand, they admit that the Spirit "will *indwell* and empower his people" during the tribulation.[61] That makes those believers fully "the church."[62]

Nevertheless, dispensationalists implicitly deny that believers who live during the tribulation are the church. Instead, dispensationalists call them "tribulation saints."[63] However, if believers in Jesus Christ during the tribulation are not fully "the church," and

57. Ibid., 230–31.

58. Ryrie, *Holy Spirit,* rev. ed., 186, emphasis added.

59. Ryrie, *Holy Spirit,* 108.

60. Ryrie, *Holy Spirit,* rev. ed., 186.

61. Ibid., emphasis added.

62. The utter incoherence of dispensationalism is driven by its own unique definition of the church (discussed previously). As we have seen, dispensationalists admit that the Holy Spirit will be present and active during the tribulation, convicting people of their sins, regenerating, filling, and empowering them, just as He has done since the Day of Pentecost. Ryrie fully admits that the Holy Spirit will "indwell" believers during the tribulation. Here dispensationalism's peculiar definition of the church takes over. Ryrie says the Holy Spirit's "ministry of baptizing believers *into the body of Christ* will not occur then [during the tribulation]. The reason is simple: There will be no purpose for the baptism, for the body of Christ will be complete before the period begins. In addition, His work of restraining by indwelling believers *as the temple of God* will not carry over into the Tribulation, for the church will be raptured before the Tribulation begins." Ryrie, *Holy Spirit,* rev. ed., 187, emphasis added. It is impossible to understand what millions of believers in Jesus Christ during the tribulation are, if they are not the "body of Christ." It is also impossible to understand what Ryrie thinks the "indwelling" during the tribulation is or how it differs from the indwelling the Holy Spirit does now. Needless to say, there is not one hint anywhere in the Bible that believers during the tribulation have any different relationship among each other or with Christ than believers have now, or that believers who are indwelt by the Spirit just before the *parousia* are indwelt any differently from believers who are indwelt by the Spirit now. Dispensationalism's distinctions are incoherent and meaningless.

63. Walvoord, *Rapture Question,* 46; see also Pentecost, *Things to Come,* 263; Smith, *What the World,* 73–74.

do not fully have the Holy Spirit like believers before the tribulation, then much of the NT—including the promises of Jesus himself—would not apply to believers who happen to be alive during the very time when they need his promises and presence the most! Such incredible nonsense is, of course, nowhere hinted at anywhere in the Bible but is the necessary conclusion that dispensationalist pretribulationism leads to.

The "blessed hope" for which believers are to "watch," and which is the incentive for godly living, is the second coming, not a "pretribulational rapture"

Titus 2:13 and 2 Pet 3:12–13

Titus 2:13 urges Christians to be *"looking for the blessed hope and the appearing of the glory of our great God and savior, Jesus Christ."* Pretribulationists speak of the pretribulational rapture as *"the blessed hope."*[64] This passage, however, makes clear that the posttribulational second coming (*epiphaneia*) in "glory" is *"the blessed hope."* Grammatically, *"the blessed hope"* and *"the glorious appearing"* are "one and the same event, according to the rules of Greek syntax" because there is a "single definite article with two nouns in the same case, connected by the correlative *kai.*"[65] Indeed, all other passages that connect "glory" with Christ's "appearing," "coming," or "revelation," are manifestly postribulational second coming passages.[66]

Pretribulationists argue that Christians cannot "hope" or "look for" Christ's coming if the church first has to pass through the tribulation.[67] However, the only place other than Titus 2:13 where Christians are said to be *"looking for"* Christ's appearing is 2 Pet 3:12–13. Bell explains why 2 Peter 3 lays to rest the pretribulationist claim that Christians cannot hope or look for Christ's coming when they know they first must pass through tribulation:

> In [2 Pet 3:10], Peter describes the fiery dissolution of the present world, seen by pretribulationists at the close of the millennium. Then, immediately following in verses 11–12, he asks, "Seeing then that all these things shall be dissolved, what manner of persons ought ye to be in all holy conversation and godliness, look-ing for and hastening unto the coming of the day of God, wherein the heavens being on fire shall be dissolved, and the elements shall melt with fervent heat?" Here Peter exhorts Christians to holy living in the light of an event which must be at least 1,007 years away, according to pretribulational reckoning. . . . This passage also pierces through the thin pretribulational argument that a Christian cannot "look for" the coming of Christ if there are to be intervening events. Peter urges the Christians to "look for" the day of God, which has at least a thousand

---

64. Walvoord, *Rapture Question,* 74–75, 276; MacDonald, *Believer's,* 2141; Higgins, *Manasseh Effect,* 94–95.

65. Bell, "Critical Evaluation," 298.

66. See Matt 24:30–31; Mark 8:38; 13:26; Luke 9:26; 21:27; 2 Thess 1:9–10; 1 Pet 4:13; 5:1.

67. Walvoord, *Rapture Question,* 75; Smith, *Tribulation,* 33; Higgins, *Manasseh Effect,* 95.

years of intervening events between it and the present moment, according to pretribulationists.[68]

Believers are to "watch" and "be alert" for the second coming, not for a supposed pretribulational rapture

The passages that exhort Christians to "watch," "be awake," and be "alert,"[69] manifestly are talking about the second coming, *not* a rapture that will occur some years before the second coming. The Olivet Discourse, which largely concerns the second coming, concludes with multiple exhortations to "watch" and remain faithful.[70] "Watch" does not mean to look up at the sky but to be spiritually ready, i.e., "since one never knows when Christ will return, one should always live in readiness for that return."[71] The reason "is not that Christ might return before the disciples expected, i.e., at any moment, but that He might delay longer than they expected and thus they might become negligent and lose sight of the hope of His coming entirely."[72] Thus, the reason for Christ's exhortations to "watch" is the *exact opposite* of that given by pretribulationists. Ladd explains this:

> The reason for the exhortation to watch is not so much that Christ may come at any moment as it is that He may not come for some time. The central problem is the delay of the parousia. His return may not be until the second watch or even the third watch, late into the night. The point of the warning is that we cannot say that it will be soon; we do not know when. Therefore, we must always be ready, for we do not know when He will come. It is because of the *uncertainty* of the time, not its imminence, that we are to watch; and the idea again is of wakefulness rather than concentration of attention.[73]

68. Bell, "Critical Evaluation," 327–28.

69. E.g., Luke 12:35–40; Rom 13:11–12; Rev 3:3; 16:15.

70. Matt 24:42—25:30; Mark 13:33–37; Luke 21:34–36.

71. Hoekema, *Bible and Future,* 122.

72. Bell, "Critical Evaluation," 334.

73. Ladd, *Blessed Hope,* 116–17. Ladd also observes that the difference between those who watch and those who do not:

> is not between two classes of Christians—those who are worldly and separated, but between two classes of professing Christians—true servants and false servants. This is seen in the punishment meted out to those who did not watch: they are cut asunder and punished with the unfaithful [Luke 12:46]. *The delay of the master made no difference to the true servant;* he busied himself about his Lord's business. He was continually watching. But the master's delay induced the false servant to a sinful course of life. *The Lord's delay brought out the true character of his servants:* whether they were truly his servants or only professing to be servants when in reality they had no affection for their master.

Ibid., 117, emphasis in original.

Believers are to "hope" in the second coming, not in a supposed pretribulational rapture

Even pretribulationsists admit that multiple NT passages which offer comfort and hope for believers refer to the second coming not the "pretribulational rapture." Thus, Thomas Ice admits that 2 Thess 1:6–10 is a "second coming," not a "rapture," passage.[74] Yet that passage clearly offers the hope of repayment for and relief from afflictions suffered.[75] Similarly, the Olivet Discourse (another admittedly "second coming" passage)[76] promises the hope of relief from great persecution and suffering when the believers are gathered *"after the tribulation"* (Matt 24:29; Mark 13:24). Additionally, "The major point of the book of Revelation is that the believers who were suffering persecution at the hand of imperial Rome were to take hope and comfort from the fact that Christ would one day destroy the system and the city. It is simply not the teaching of the New Testament, then, that only an any-moment hope of Christ's coming can be of comfort to believers."[77]

The NT uses terms that describe the second coming of Christ *after* the tribulation—*apokalupsis* ("revelation"), and *epiphaneia* ("appearance")—as the objects of the believers' "hope." For example, 2 Thess 1:6–7 uses *apokalupsis* which, as mentioned above, manifestly occurs after the tribulation. In 2 Thess 2:8 Paul offers the hope that Christ will bring when he slays the man of lawlessness *"by the appearance [epiphaneia] of His coming."* That likewise manifestly occurs after the tribulation. Yet, in 1 Tim 6:14 Paul exhorts believers to *"keep the commandment without stain or reproach until the appearing [epiphaneia] of our Lord Jesus Christ."* As Ladd concludes, the Bible's use of *apokalupsis* and *epiphaneia* means that the second coming, which occurs after the tribulation, is not simply the occasion of judgment to be feared. Rather, for believers, *"It is also the day upon which the believer's hope is set when he will enter into the completed blessings of salvation at Christ's second coming."*[78]

Pretribulationism completely overturns the biblical doctrine of the second coming. It makes the "pretribulational rapture" the event of primary significance for the believer. That is extremely odd, since even pretribulationists acknowledge that *not one verse of Scripture* directly or explicitly says that there will even be a "pretribulational rapture."[79]

God has not appointed the church to "wrath," even though it will suffer during the tribulation

Nah 1:2 says, *"The Lord is avenging and wrathful. The Lord takes vengeance on His adversaries, And He reserves wrath for His enemies."* The Bible says that formerly we were children of

---

74. Ice, "Rapture and Second Coming," 2.

75. Recall Bell's statement earlier, "Paul explicitly states that the hope of the Thessalonian believers is the glorious second advent of Christ, at which time they will receive rest from their afflictions. If the rapture, as a separate event, is indeed 'the blessed hope' (Titus 2:13) of the Christian, rather than the second advent, this passage becomes inexplicable." Bell, "Critical Evaluation," 275.

76. Ice, "Rapture and Second Coming," 2.

77. Bell, "Critical Evaluation," 326–27.

78. Ladd, *Blessed Hope,* 69, emphasis in original.

79. Ice, "Rapture and Second Coming," 2.

wrath like other unbelievers (John 3:36; Eph 2:3; 5:6–10) but have been saved from God's wrath and will be delivered from the wrath to come (Rom 5:9; 1 Thess 1:10; 5:9). Most verses that talk about God's wrath "refer primarily to God's wrath in the final judgment. But the Great Tribulation will, in one of its aspects, be the outpouring of the divine wrath upon a rebellious and sinful civilization. It is the out-reaching of final judgment just before the end comes. It is in fact the beginning of that judgment."[80] Pretribulationists claim that the church will be removed from the earth before the great tribulation (which they view as a seven year period—the "seventieth week of Daniel"—based on their interpretation of Dan 9:24–27) so that it will not experience God's wrath.[81] The "pre-wrath" rapture view accepts the dispensational interpretation of Daniel's "seventy weeks" but holds that the Great Tribulation begins at the middle of Daniel's "seventieth week" and is then cut short by Christ's coming from heaven to rapture his church; he then pours out his wrath on the unrepentant remainder of humanity.[82] However, no verse actually says that the chuch will leave the earth in order to avoid God's wrath.

Promises to save the church from God's wrath (Rom 5:9; 1 Thess 5:9; Luke 21:34–36)

Promises such as *"we shall be saved from the wrath of God"* (Rom 5:9), *"God has not destined us for wrath"* (1 Thess 5:9), and the exhortation to remain faithful *"that you may have strength to escape all these things that are about to take place"* (Luke 21:34–36) do not imply that the church will be removed from the earth before God pours out his wrath. The context of all those passages is God's eternal wrath in judgment after the tribulation. The contrast in Rom 5:9 and 1 Thess 5:9 is between "wrath" and "salvation." That contrast demands the meaning of *eternal* wrath because "salvation" clearly is eternal salvation, not "salvation" from temporary tribulation. Both Luke 21:34–36 and 1 Thess 5:9 are explicitly in the context of *"that day"* (Luke 21:25–28, 34), *"the day of the Lord"* and *"the day"* (1 Thess 5:2, 4), all of which refer to the second coming of Christ which *follows* the tribulation.[83] First Thess 5:4 does not say that the church will be absent from the world when that day occurs, but that the day will not overtake Christians *"like a thief"* if they remain *"alert and sober"* (1 Thess 5:4–6). The point Paul is making is that the *"day of the Lord,"* i.e., the *parousia,* will "overtake *all* like a thief in the night, but as long as the Thessalonians were living godly lives they had nothing to fear."[84] Indeed, the juxtaposition of *"the day of the Lord"* and *"the day"* with the exhortation to *"be alert and sober"* demonstrates that the church *will be present* on earth when the *parousia* occurs.[85]

---

80. Ladd, *Blessed Hope,* 122.

81. Scofield, *New Scofield,* 1356n.2; Smith, *Tribulation,* 4–6; Walvoord, *Rapture Question,* 160.

82. Rosenthal, *Pre-Wrath,* 108–13.

83. See Ewert, "1–2 Thessalonians," 1082; Murray, "Interadventual Period," 394–95.

84. Oropeza, *99 Reasons,* 22; see also Ewert, "1–2 Thessalonians," 1082–83.

85. See Payne, *Encyclopedia,* 561–62.

Rev 3:10 and the promise to "keep you from the hour of testing"

Rev 3:10 promises that Jesus will *"keep you [the church of Philadelphia] from the hour of testing."* That does not imply that the church of Philadelphia (or the church in general) is going to be removed from the earth before the tribulation.

The verb "keep you from" does not imply physical removal

In Greek, the wording is "I will *keep you out of [tērēsō ek]* the hour of trial." That language neither asserts nor requires bodily removal before a coming trial. The only other place in the Bible where precisely the same words are used is John 17:15. In that verse, Jesus specifically asked his Father *not* to take his disciples out of the world. Instead, Jesus prayed that the Father would *"keep them* [the disciples] *from* [lit., *'out of'—tērēsēs ek*] the evil [one]." It is clear that "Jesus prays for the disciples' preservation from the power of Satan, even though they would remain *in* the 'world,' the sphere of Satan's activity."[86]

Douglas Moo notes that all other passages that have the same wording, subject, and object as Rev 3:10 contradict the "pretribulational rapture" view: "In only three other verses in the New Testament does *tēreō* ('keep') have God or Christ as its subject and believers as its object: John 17:11, 12, 15. In each case, *spiritual preservation* is clearly intended."[87] Ladd also observes, "A similar thought occurs in Galatians 1:4, where we read that Christ gave himself for our sins to deliver us from (literally, 'out of,' *ek*) this present evil age. This does not refer to a physical removal from the age but to deliverance from its power and control."[88] Mounce concludes, "The hour of trial is directed toward the entire non-Christian world, but the believer will be kept from it, not by some previous appearance of Christ to remove the church bodily from the world, but by the spiritual protection he provides against the forces of evil."[89]

Schuyler Brown summarizes the majority view of Rev 3:10: "As a reward for its faithful perseverance Christ promises the church of Philadelphia (and all faithful Christians) his special protection in the hour of universal tribulation which is to precede his return. For Christians this tribulation, besides being a threat to their physical safety, will also be a further test of their faith, which, by the Lord's help, they will be able to withstand. For the enemies of the church, however, whether Jews or gentiles, it will come as the deserved punishment for their wickedness."[90] Even pretribulationist Wilbur Smith concludes that this verse does not speak of a pretribulational rapture: "Though so worthy, this church was nevertheless to know a time of severe trial. Note carefully that the word is **trial** here, not *tribulation*. But in the trial the believers were to be divinely kept (see Jn 17:15)."[91]

---

86. Moo, "Posttribulation Rapture Position," 197.

87. Ibid., 197–98.

88. Ladd, *Blessed Hope,* 85.

89. Mounce, *Revelation,* 103.

90. Brown, "Hour of Trial," 314.

91. Smith, "Revelation," 1504, emphases in original.

The significance of the fact that the promise was made only to the church of Philadelphia

The promise in Rev 3:10 was given to a specific local church: the church in Philadelphia. "If the tribulation was not to come in the lifetime of the recipients, the promise would seem to be rather meaningless to them. . . . Wherein lies the value of the promise to Philadelphia specifically, then?"[92] The statement to the church in Philadelphia cannot imply a pretribulational rapture of the whole church since Philadelphia was only one of the seven churches to whom the book of Revelation was written. "Since the other six churches are not promised such a deliverance, this would seem to imply some kind of partial rapture position, which is strongly condemned by pretribulationists."[93]

Finally, to escape the persecution it faced in the first or second century, the church in Philadelphia was *not* in fact removed from the earth. Consequently, even if Philadelphia is viewed as representative of all the churches, Rev 3:10 cannot legitimately be interpreted to mean a supernatural removal from the earth since that is *not* what was meant concerning the *very church to which it was written.*

"The hour"

There are two plausible views concerning the meaning of *"the hour"* in Rev 3:10:

(1) *"The hour of trial which is about to come upon the whole world, to test those who dwell on the earth"* may refer to tribulation, affliction, and persecution that will precede the *parousia*. In that case, *"The hour of trial* from which the Lord is to preserve these Christians is not the 'time' during which the judgments of God are on the earth, but the trials themselves. *Cf.* Mk. 14:35, where 'hour' represents the horrors of the cross and its attendant circumstances."[94]

(2) *"The hour"* may refer to the *parousia* itself and the judgments of God that will accompany it and will fall on those who oppose Christ (i.e., on *"those who dwell on the earth"*). In that case, the promise "to be 'kept out of the hour of testing' refers to the assumption of the church into heaven at the 'hour' of the parousia."[95] The major arguments for this position are:

- "Every occurrence of 'hour' in Revelation refers to the parousia. . . . 'hour' was already a term used of the moment of the parousia in the Synoptic tradition, and 3:2–3 demonstrates that the author used this tradition. . . . Because the

---

92. Bell, "Critical Evaluation," 304.

93. Ibid., 307. Pretribulationist Chuck Smith apparently holds to a partial rapture position. In commenting on Rev 3:10 Smith states, "Here is a definite promise that this church would escape the Tribulation. I must concur that at least *part* of the Church will face the Great Tribulation. The unrepentant of the church of Thyatira, who will not turn from their spiritual fornication, will go through the Tribulation and miss the Rapture." Smith, *Tribulation*, 19.

94. Beasley-Murray, "The Revelation," 1286. A related view is that *"the hour of trial"* refers to "the wrath of God from which believers are eternally delivered." Ngundu, "Revelation," 1553. These constitute the majority position.

95. Kerkeslager, "Day of the Lord," 1.

other 10 uses of 'hour' in Revelation refer to the parousia, it appears quite likely that the use of 'hour' in 3:10 also refers to the parousia."[96]

- "The purpose of 'the hour of testing' is to test 'those who dwell upon the earth,' a phrase which is consistently used in Revelation to refer to the ungodly opponents of the churches. The thrust of the verse is decidedly against all attempts to make it refer to a period in which God's people are 'tested.'"[97]

- "The promise of 3:10 is paralleled by the explicit parousia promise of 3:11. The purpose of 3:11 is to give temporal poignancy to what is already a parousia promise in 3:10."[98]

The death of faithful Christians during the tribulation does not mean that they have experienced God's wrath

"The Israelites were in Egypt during the visitation of the plagues upon the Egyptians but they were sheltered from the worst of these plagues which befell the Egyptians. In a similar way it is possible that the Church may find herself on earth during the period of the Tribulation but will by divine protection be sheltered from the sufferings entailed by the outpouring of the bowls of wrath and thus be delivered from the wrath to come."[99] In the book of Revelation "When the breaking of the sixth seal was followed by signs of the end, men cried out in terror, 'The great day of . . . wrath has come, and who can stand before it?' (6:17). The answer to this question is now given [beginning in Rev 7:1]. Those whom God has sealed will be safely preserved from the outpouring of divine wrath, even though they suffer martyrdom."[100]

Several passages in Revelation indicate that the wrath of God and plagues sent by God will be on unbelievers only.[101] On the other hand, "Protection from the wrath of God does not imply deliverance from the wrath of man."[102] Indeed, dispensationalists hold that the 144,000 of Rev 7:4–8 (whom they contend are Jewish witnesses for Christ who will be martyred during the "great tribulation") will "have protection from God's wrath, but not from the beast's animosity."[103] Thus, even on dispensational pretribulationist presuppositions, Christians will be present during the period of God's wrath, and even be killed, yet not experience God's wrath. Consequently, there is no basis to contend that the church must be raptured before the tribulation in order to not experience God's wrath.

The suffering and death of Christians during the tribulation will be a testing, refining, and demonstration of their faith, not a sign of God's wrath against them.[104] There is

96. Ibid., 5, 7, 10.

97. Ibid., 7.

98. Ibid., 10.

99. Ladd, *Blessed Hope,* 84.

100. Ladd, *Commentary,* 110.

101. Rev 6:15–17; 7:3; 9:4, 20–21; 11:17–18; 14:9–20; 16:1–19; 19:15.

102. Hoekema, *Bible and Future,* 170; see also Ladd, *Blessed Hope,* 127; Thomas, "Classical Dispensationalist View," 218, 220.

103. Thomas, "Classical Dispensationalist View," 218, 220.

104. See Rev 6:9–11; 7:13–17; 11:7–12; 12:10–17; 13:7; 14:12–13; 17:14; 20:4.

an almost paradoxical relationship between God's wrath, the world's evil, and the church's suffering and triumph: "As God exerts his wrath upon the evil world in the form of the seals, trumpets, and bowls, the world retaliates with its own vengeance against Christ's followers. God allows the dragon for this short period (Mark 13:20) to 'conquer' the saints (Rev. 13:7). . . . However, these very tribulations are the victory of the church (Rev. 12:11) and of God (7:10)."[105]

Summary of the relationship between the church, God's wrath, and the tribulation

The issue of the relationship between tribulation, suffering, and God's wrath is an important one. It is important because, throughout the entire history of Christianity, in all parts of the world, Christians have been persecuted and have suffered for their faith.[106] The theology that says one generation of Christians will escape all tribulation and suffering by being removed from the earth is unprecedented. Ladd explains:

> It would be contrary to the entire history of God's dealings with His people both in the Old and New Testament dispensations if God should in the consummation of the age reverse Himself to do something He has never previously done, namely, to protect His people from the hostility of an evil age. . . . Throughout the history of the Christian Church, God has permitted His people to suffer again and again at the hands of civil governments and rulers who were hostile to the things of God and therefore became instruments in the hands of the prince of evil. Jesus Himself prophesied that throughout the course of the age, His disciples would experience tribulation and death; they would be hated by all nations for

---

105. Osborne, *Revelation*, 325.

106. Pretribulationism's doctrine of the pretribulational rapture implies, at minimum, that the last generation of people who are *not* raptured and who therefore endure great tribulation *are* subject to the wrath of God. In this respect pretribulational theology is much like Job's three friends who assumed that there was a direct 1:1 relationship between doing good and being rewarded and doing bad and being punished. Job's friends assumed that, since Job was suffering, he had to have sinned and was being punished for that sin (see Job 4:7–11; 8:1–22; 11:1–20). That same attitude was shown by Jesus' disciples who assumed that a man's blindness had to be the result either of his own or his parents' sin (John 9:1–2). As the entire book of Job makes clear, and as Jesus clarified in John 9:3, the theological presupposition that there is a 1:1 relationship between suffering and experiencing God's wrath is untrue.

Pretribulationism is, of course, internally inconsistent on this point. Some pretribulationists like Robert Thomas acknowledge that at least some believers "have protection from God's wrath, but not from the beast's animosity." Thomas, "Classical Dispensationalist View," 218, 220. The fact that there will be believers in Christ during the tribulation undercuts the entire basis for the pretribulationist position: "tribulational saints" (as pretribulationists call them) *are believers;* they suffer and die; yet *they* are *not* subject to the wrath of God; therefore, it is *not necessary* to claim that the church must be removed from the earth in order to escape the wrath of God. The same is true of the pre-wrath position. According to that view, non-raptured people will "become believers after the rapture." Nigro, *Before God's Wrath,* 33. Pre-wrath commentator Charles Cooper states, "Those saved after the Rapture will not experience God's wrath just as those before the coming of God's wrath will not experience it (Rev. 9:4). However, those saved after the Rapture will continue to face the persecution of Antichrist just as each generation saved before the Rapture potentially might face it." Cooper, "The Prophetic Pillars," 7. Since the martyrs after the rapture are not subject to the wrath of God even though they will suffer and die while he pours out his wrath on the earth, there is no necessity for the pre-wrath rapture at all, since the basis for the pre-wrath position itself is defeated.

His name's sake (Matt. 24:9). Because of the character of the age, Jesus promised that in the world His disciples would have tribulation (Jn. 16:33). It is indeed the divine order that "through many tribulations it is necessary for us to enter into the kingdom of God" (Acts 14:22). . . . Why should God do something for the Church at the end of the age when He has never done it before? Granted that the Great Tribulation and the sufferings which will be inflicted by the Antichrist will be more fearful than anything previously experienced, yet they are not different in kind from all the tribulation and persecution of the ages. . . . God will not deliver His people *from* such tribulation, but He will preserve them *in* it. Jesus assured His disciples of this fact. Even though they are put to death, not a hair of their head would perish (Lk. 21:16–18). Physical death, bodily suffering is not to be feared, fearful as it is, by those who have been redeemed by the suffering and death of Christ. Martyrdom has ever been a mark of faithfulness to Christ. . . . Why should it be any different at the end?[107]

The pretribulational distinction between the rapture and the second coming is based on bad hermeneutics and exegesis

Pretribulationsists typically contrast the rapture and the second coming, as follows:[108]

Rapture	*Second Coming*
1. Translation of all believers	1. No translation at all
2. Translated saints go to heaven	2. Translated saints return to earth
3. Earth not judged	3. Earth judged and righteousness established
4. Imminent, any-moment, signless	4. Follows definite predicted signs including tribulation
5. Not in the Old Testament	5. Predicted often in Old Testament
6. Believers only	6. Affects all men
7. Before the day of wrath	7. Concluding the day of wrath
8. No reference to Satan	8. Satan bound
9. Christ comes for His own	9. Christ comes with His own
10. He comes in the air	10. He comes to the earth
11. He claims His bride	11. He comes with His bride
12. Only His own see Him	12. Every eye shall see him
13. Tribulation begins	13. Millennial Kingdom begins

Meaningless distinctions based on the pretribulational presuppositions themselves

All of the supposed distinctions above are "essentially meaningless contrasts between the rapture and the second coming which serve simply to restate the pretribulational

107. Ladd, *Blessed Hope*, 127–29.

108. Ice, "Rapture and Second Coming," 3; see also MacDonald, *Believer's*, 2050.

position."[109] These supposed "contrasts" amount to nothing more than the logical fallacy of "begging the question," i.e., assuming the conclusion as the premise of the argument. In other words, pretribulationism assumes in advance at least two things: "(1) the assumption in advance that there are indeed two separate and distinct future comings of Christ, catalogued by predetermined standards, and (2) the assumption that every passage dealing with the second coming of Christ must contain all of the information contained in every other passage, or else run the risk of being construed as a separate event."[110] However, "it is unreasonable to expect the Biblical writers or spokesmen to touch on every aspect of a subject every time it is mentioned. No hermeneutical system demands this."[111]

For example, premillennialists (including pretribulationists) see the binding of Satan (Rev 20:1–3) as occurring just after the second coming; pretribulationists see no mention of Satan's being bound in connection with the rapture, so they assume that the rapture and the second coming are two separate events (see contrast 8, above). "Even a casual study, however, will reveal that Revelation 20 is the only passage in the entire Bible dealing with the binding of Satan (unless Matthew 12:29 be included, but this would be irrelevant for the present point anyhow) and thus the contrast is meaningless."[112] Tim Warner points out the logical prerequisite necessary in order for different descriptions or accounts of a phenomenon to constitute descriptions or accounts of two different phenomena: "Merely looking for differences in two accounts does not indicate that they are referring to different things or events UNLESS the accounts are *mutually exclusive*. That is, if the details of one account are impossible to harmonize with the details of another account, only then can it be said with any certainty that the accounts are describing two different things or events."[113]

Dispensationalism's methodology of pretribulational "contrasts" forces contrasts between passages which even pretribulationists admit are "second coming" passages

William Everett Bell applies pretribulationism's own methodology to passages that deal with the second coming:

> Using [pretribulationists'] own methodology, it would be a simple matter to "prove" that the second advent described in Revelation 19 is not the same second advent described in Revelation 1:7, for example, (although [dispensationalist John] Walvoord and pretribulationsists generally insist that they are the same):

(1) At the second advent in Revelation 19, Satan is bound and cast into the abyss, while at the second advent in Revelation 1:7 Satan is not bound.

(2) At the second advent in 1:7, Christ comes in the clouds, while at the second advent in chapter 19, He does not come in the clouds.

---

109. Bell, "Critical Evaluation," 345.

110. Ibid., 346.

111. Ibid., 243.

112. Ibid., 346.

113. Warner, "Rapture & Second Coming," n.p.

(3) The dead are resurrected at the second advent in chapter 19, but no mention of a resurrection is found in 1:7.

(4) At the second advent in chapter 19, Anti-Christ is destroyed, while at the second advent in 1:7, Anti-Christ is not destroyed.

(5) The second advent of chapter 19 initiates the millennium, but no mention of any millennium is found in 1:7. . . . This type of argument could be carried on indefinitely from the two passages until dozens of supposed "distinctions" were noted. . . . Such arguments, if expanded slightly, could be used to "prove" three, four, five, or almost any number of future comings of Christ. Such arguments, then, are completely irrelevant to a serious study of the nature and time of the second advent and serve to influence chiefly those who are impressed more with the quantity than the quality of the arguments.[114]

Dispensationalism's methodology of pretribulational contrasts forces contrasts between two "rapture" passages

Tim Warner applies pretribulationism's own methodology to passages that deal with the "rapture" of the church:

> Let's do a similar test on two passages that we all agree are "rapture" passages, 1 Cor. 15:50–54 & 1 Thess. 4:13–18. . . . Both passages speak of the same coming. In 1 Cor. 15, the resurrection of the body and changing of the living saints into incorruptible bodies are explicitly mentioned. Yet, there is no hint of the 'translation' (catching up) of the saints, described in 1 Thess. 4. There are other notable differences as well. 1 Thess. 4 mentions the descent of the Lord, and the shout of Michael, neither of which are mentioned in 1 Cor. 15. Using Ice's argument from silence, we would be forced to conclude that 1 Cor. 15 is speaking of a different coming than 1 Thess. 4![115]

Christ's coming "for" his church and coming "with" his saints

Christ's coming "for" his church and coming "with" his saints (contrast 9, above) does not indicate two separate events but different aspects of a single event. First Thess 4:14–17 links the Lord's coming "with" his saints (4:14) and coming "for" his saints (4:15–17). The fact that the coming "for" and coming "with" the saints are different parts of the same event is seen when one considers the Greek word for "meet"—*apantēsis*—in 1 Thess 4:17 (*"we who are alive and remain will be caught up . . . to meet the Lord in the air"*). "When a dignitary paid an official visit or *parousia* to a city in Hellenistic times, the action of the leading citizens in going out to meet him and escorting him on the final stage of his journey was called the *apantēsis*."[116]

114. Bell, "Critical Evaluation," 346–48.

115. Warner, "Rapture & Second Coming," n.p.

116. Bruce, "1 and 2 Thessalonians," 1159; see also Wright, *Resurrection*, 217–18; Ewert, "1–2 Thessalonians," 1081; Longman and Reid, *Warrior*, 173–74.

The word is used in exactly that sense the only two other times it appears in the NT: Matt 25:6 and Acts 28:15–16. Matt 25:6 is a parable (the bridegroom and the virgins) that pertains to the second coming. In that passage the bridegroom is on the way to the wedding feast and is met by the virgins. He does not reverse directions. Instead, the virgins reverse directions and accompany him to the wedding feast. In Acts 28:15–16 Paul was headed to Rome. He was met by some Roman believers at the Three Inns. When they met, Paul did not reverse directions. Instead, the believers reversed directions and accompanied Paul into Rome. Additionally, this description of the rapture and the raptured people returning with Jesus to the earth "echoes Jesus' first triumphal entry, when the crowd came out from Jerusalem to meet their King, only to return with him to his royal city (Matthew 21:8)."[117]

When Christ returns there will be a meeting in the air. Since they do not stay in midair, someone has to reverse directions: either Christ or the raptured saints. The pretribulational rapture theory would have Christ himself reverse directions and go back to heaven which is exactly the *opposite* of the biblical pattern. If that were the case, there would be no need for Christ to have left heaven at all. Consistent with the only two other uses of *apantēsis* in the NT, it is the *saints* who reverse directions and accompany Christ to the earth at his second coming.

Ladd clarifies why the rapture and the second coming need not be separated:

> The second coming of Christ will be a coming which is at the same time a coming *for* His saints and a coming *with* them. The Rapture of the Church is essentially an indication of the transformation of living believers into their glorious resurrection bodies without passing through death. They are caught up from the earth to be with the Lord and thus enter into the new realm of their glorified existence along with the resurrected dead. Thereafter they shall ever be with the Lord, and they accompany him as he continues on to the earth. There is no ground whatsoever to assume that there must be a considerable interval of time between the Rapture and Christ's coming with His Church.[118]

The "pretribulational rapture" is read into biblical texts because of dispensationalist presuppositions themselves

The dispensationalist doctrine of the pretribulational rapture is not based on exegesis of the biblical texts but is read into the biblical texts because it is demanded by the dispensationalist system itself. Dispensationalists fail to recognize that NT writers "are capable of writing about a single event in a variety of ways."[119] Instead, they take the same terms and arbitrarily apply them sometimes to their supposed pretribulational rapture and sometimes to the admittedly posttribulational second coming, *even within the same context.*[120]

---

117. Sittema, *Meeting Jesus,* 144.

118. Ladd, *Blessed Hope,* 91.

119. Travis, *I Believe,* 152.

120. For example, Thomas Ice applies "coming" (*parousia*) to the rapture in 1 Thess 2:19; 4:15; 5:23; 2 Thess 2:1, and "coming" (*parousia*) to the second coming in 1 Thess 3:13; 2 Thess 2:8. Ice, "Rapture and Second Coming," 2.

Dispensationalism's use of the same terms to denote two separate ideas shows that its pre-existing theology is driving its exegesis, not (as should be the case) exegesis determining theology. Bell makes this clear:

> A close study of the classification of passages by leading pretribulationists reveals clearly that the basis for classification is theological, not exegetical. If the passage deals with the second coming as a hope for believers, it is usually (but not consistently) classified as the rapture. If the passage seems to involve judgment upon unbelievers and the world, it is usually (but not consistently) classified as the second coming. Usually little or no exegesis is required, seemingly, to classify the usages. Sometimes a passage refers to the hope of believers and the judgment of unbelievers, and this causes some consternation among pretribulationists, who frequently place a question mark after the reference to indicate their uncertainty, e.g., II Thessalonians 2:1, II Peter 3:4. The fact that leading pretribulationists frequently disagree among themselves (and even with themselves) on the question demonstrates the subjectivity of the method.[121]

The problem of which passages to classify as "rapture" passages and which to call "second coming" passages arises from dispensationalism's underlying false assumption that there are *two*, not one, future comings of Christ. That false assumption is necessitated by dispensationalism's equally false rigid dichotomy between Israel and the church. Bell astutely observes, "Since dispensationalists approach all scripture with the basic *a priori* [i.e., something assumed in advance; not based on prior study or examination] distinction between Israel and the church with its resulting pretribulation rapture, no scripture can be allowed to teach differently, however plain its meaning. This, of course, is deductive rather than inductive study, and is a flagrant begging of the question."[122]

Applying the same terms to both the rapture and the second coming can only be sustained hermeneutically if the rapture and second coming *are part of the same event*. Travis states, "It is in fact impossible to sustain the distinction between two comings. The same technical terms—'coming', 'revelation', 'appearing'—are used in the New Testament to describe Jesus's coming to gather his people and his coming for judgment. . . . And passages such as 2 Thessalonians 1:5–10 and Matthew 24:36–44 show clearly enough that judgment and salvation are part of a single event."[123]

No scriptural passage mentions *two* future comings of Christ and *clearly distinguishes them*. *No passage* says that there will be a rapture before the tribulation. *No passage* says that only the saints will see Jesus at the rapture or that there will be a tribulation after the rapture. *No passage* says that translated saints go to heaven or stay there for seven (or three and a half) years after the rapture. *Multiple passages* (in fact, *every passage that discusses Christ's return*) talk about Christ's coming in the *singular*. The only fair conclusion from the biblical data is that dispensationalism's separation of the rapture from the second coming is imaginary. The only reasonable conclusion is that the rapture is part of a complex of events that will occur at the Second Coming of Christ, which itself will occur after, not before, the tribulation

---

121. Bell, "Critical Evaluation," 269–70.

122. Ibid., 235–36.

123. Travis, *I Believe*, 152.

Pretribulationism divides the church into "first class" and "second class" Christians and thereby reverses what Christ accomplished on the cross

The NT is very clear that there are not different "classes" of Christians: there is neither Jew nor Gentile, but we are all equally *"one new man"* in Christ;[124] we are all equally "living stones," a "holy temple," and a "holy priesthood."[125] Pretribulationism is incompatible with those fundamental spiritual truths and, in effect, reverses what Christ accomplished on the cross. The reason why is discussed by William Everett Bell, who concludes by observing the ironic and almost perverse effect to which pretribulationism leads:

> The question is simply this: are not the so-called "tribulation saints" also saved by the death of Christ? If so, why should they be permitted by God to undergo a period of persecution which is unthinkable for the church to undergo? The only possible answer to this question is that the "tribulation saint," although saved by faith in Christ, is nevertheless not so privileged as the "church saint" and thus can be permitted to suffer tribulation that would not be permitted for the church. . . . It is difficult to understand how two sinners, both depraved and saved only by the grace of God through the atonement of Christ, can achieve such widely differing positions of favor—the one totally immune from any such suffering as that pictured in the tribulation period, the other apparently quite eligible for it. It would seem that this position clearly implies that only "church saints" are "first-class" saints, the saints of other ages being "second-class" or even "third-class" saints.[126] [Dispensationalist Dwight] Pentecost admits something of the kind—even in the New Jerusalem, stating that Christians make up the bride of Christ, but Old Testament saints find their place only as servants.[127] Here is seen the ultimate result of the Israel-church dichotomy. Although dispensationalists like to think of themselves as the champions of Israel and the protectors of Israel's promises, which must not be appropriated by the church,

124. Gal 3:28; Eph 2:11–16; Col 3:9–11.

125. 1 Cor 3:16; 2 Cor 6:16; Eph 2:19–22; 1 Pet 2:4–5.

126. This same problem is inherent in the pre-wrath position with respect to those believers who are raptured and those who become believers after the rapture.

127. The problem is not just with Dwight Pentecost but is inherent in dispensationalism. Thus, dispensationalist Chuck Smith, commenting on the "great multitude" of Rev 7:9–15, says, "I do not believe that this 'great multitude' is the Church." Smith, *What the World,* 73. According to Smith, they are Christians but happened to become believers in Jesus Christ after the church had been raptured. They even "refused to take the mark of the beast and refused to bow to the Antichrist or to his image" and "kept their testimony and the faith of Jesus Christ" to the point of being martyred for Christ. Ibid., 74. Nevertheless, Smith states, "Notice that, though this 'great multitude' is brought into the heavenly scene, they aren't brought into the same position as the Church. . . . They're before the throne of God serving Him day and night. The Church, on the other hand, is not in heaven as a servant. The Church is there as the Bride of Christ, married to Him. We [but apparently not they] shall live and reign with Jesus Christ." Ibid. Similarly, Smith thinks the 144,000 of Rev 14:1–5 are "Orthodox Jews who, sometime after the rapture of the Church, come to the realization that Jesus Christ was indeed the Messiah" and "will be bearing witness of Jesus Christ." Ibid., 127. His dispensationalism leads him to the following conclusion: "They do follow the Lamb wherever He goes. The Church is the Bride of Christ and she is with the Lamb and shall ever be with the Lamb. The 144,000 don't have as great a place in heaven as the body of Christ. So, I have no desire to be one of them. God has chosen a better place for me as a part of the Bride of Christ." Ibid., 129.

etc., the end result is seen to be just the opposite. The final end of dispensational interpretation exalts the church but lowers Israel and the saints of other ages to a lesser level and regards them as less favored and less privileged than the church, even into eternity. It is only this totally unscriptural view of the subordinate and inferior nature of "non-church saints" . . . that can support the current argument [i.e., dispensationalist pretribulationism], and therefore the argument must be set aside as invalid.[128]

128. Bell, "Critical Evaluation," 336–38.

10

The "Antichrist"

CONTRARY TO MUCH POPULAR opinion, the term "antichrist" (Greek = *antichristos*) is not found in the book of Revelation but appears only in 1 John 2:18, 22; 4:3; 2 John 7. Nevertheless, "when the title does occur for the first time, the matter is not discussed as a novelty. Evidently the concept was old, even if the term were new."[1] Thus, John says that *"you heard that antichrist is coming"* (1 John 2:18).

Hoekema relates that "anti" has different, though related, meanings: "The original meaning of the Greek prefix *anti* is 'instead of' or 'in place of.' On this basis *antichristos* means a substitute Christ or a rival Christ. Since, however, the antichrist as depicted in the New Testament is also the sworn adversary of Christ, we may combine both ideas: the antichrist is both a *rival* Christ and an *opponent* of Christ."[2] This dual nature of Antichrist is expressed as early as the *Didache* (c. 70–110), which talks about "the deceiver of the world" who will "commit abominations the likes of which have never happened before" and humanity's passing through a "fiery test" in which many will fall away but others will endure in their faith and be saved.[3]

In addition to 1 and 2 John, the major NT passages that are usually seen as referring to "Antichrist," although they do not explicitly use that term, are the *"man of lawlessness"* in 2 Thess 2:3–12 and the "beasts" of Rev 11:7; 13:1–18; 14:9; 15:2; 16:2, 10, 13; 17:3–17; 19:19–20; 20:10. Those passages appear to be reworkings of OT and extra-biblical depictions of an eschatological opponent of God's Messiah.

---

1. Ford, *Abomination of Desolation,* 162.

2. Hoekema, *Bible and Future,* 157; see also McGinn, *Anti-Christ,* 4 ("The fundamental nature of the evil represented by Antichrist has been expressed primarily through the polarity of dread and deception," i.e., Antichrist is both a persecutor of Christianity and the church and a perverter of Christianity and the church).

3. *Didache* 16.4–5. Interestingly, the *Didache* viewed Antichrist as a future phenomenon even though it was written *after* the destruction of Jerusalem in AD 70 (and probably was written by those who had lived through the events of AD 70). It therefore stands in contrast to the view of preterists who believe all the passages that may deal with the subject of Antichrist were fulfilled by AD 70. E.g., Preston, *AD 70, passim.*

Person versus personification

"A survey of the historic teachings about the antichrist brings two main lines of thought to the fore: (1) that the antichrist is a power or movement; and (2) that the antichrist is a human person at the end of history."[4] Both views arose early in church history.[5] Although all the Bible's passages must be synthesized to form a good understanding of "Antichrist," the primary NT passage that suggests an end-time individual is the *"man of lawlessness"* of 2 Thessalonians 2. The primary NT passages that suggest a power or entity that transcends the individual are the descriptions of the "beasts" in Revelation.[6]

There is also a third dimension to Antichrist: an "internal," spiritual dimension, without individual, institutional, political, or military associations.[7] That theological or spiritual aspect of Antichrist is the thrust of 1 and 2 John (the only times the word "antichrist" is actually used). Many people are so interested in what may happen in the future, externally, that they do not realize that Antichrist in this third (perhaps most important) sense *already is present* among or even in us (1 John 2:18) and *has been present* since John wrote his epistle.

Antichrist as a person

Grant Osborne is typical of those who take the "Antichrist as person" view: "While the beast sums up the beasts of Daniel, he is also the fulfillment of the 'little horn' of Daniel, Antiochus Epiphanes. . . . The description of the two beasts in [Revelation] 13 fits an individual rather than an empire, and the rest of the NT expects a person, from Mark 13:14 ('he is standing') to 2 Thess. 2 ('the man of lawlessness') to the 'many antichrists' of 1–2 John, who are individual false teachers, as proleptic of the final Antichrist (1 John 2:18)."[8] The majority of those who see Antichrist as a person view him as a human agent influenced or possessed by the devil; a minority view him as the devil incarnate.[9]

In Jewish apocalyptic writing "Antichrist" figures are always Gentiles.[10] Irenaeus (c. 130–200)[11] and his follower Hippolytus (c. 170–236)[12] first proposed that Antichrist would be a person from the tribe of Dan based on Jer 8:16 and the absence of Dan from the list of tribes in Rev 7:4–8.[13] David Aune lists the major characteristics of Antichrist

---

4. Berkouwer, *Return of Christ*, 261; see also Johnson, *Triumph*, 190n.12.

5. See Johnson, "Revelation," 521–22, 529; McGinn, *Anti-Christ*, 78. The most comprehensive historical survey of views concerning Antichrist is Bernard McGinn, *Anti-Christ: Two Thousand Years of the Human Fascination with Evil* (New York: HarperSanFrancisco, 1994).

6. Schnabel suggests that the two lines of thought are compatible: Antichrist can be both a system and a leader of that system. See Schnabel, *40 Questions*, 176.

7. Johnson, *Triumph*, 190n.12; McGinn, *Anti-Christ*, 64–65, 76–77.

8. Osborne, *Revelation*, 495.

9. McGinn, *Anti-Christ*, 2, 49, 282n.4.

10. Bauckham, "List of Tribes," 100.

11. Irenaeus, *Haer.* 5.30.2.

12. Hippolytus, *Treatise on Christ and Antichrist* 14.

13. Gen 49:17; Lev 24:10–11; Deut 33:22; Judg 18:11–31; 1 Kgs 12:28–29 have also been used throughout history to suggest that something is suspicious or evil about the tribe of Dan and to show

in Christian literature, from Irenaeus to the early fourth century, as follows: "(1) he is the agent of Satan, (2) he is a deceiver, (3) he performs false signs and wonders, (4) he is extremely evil, (5) he persecutes the people of God, (6) he has excessive pride, and (7) he claims divine honors."[14]

Antichrist as a personification

Personification

Personification is a form of metaphor in which a non-human (God, an animal, an object, an idea, or other abstract notion) is described as if it were human or had its own person-hood. For example, God is described as having hands (Isa 49:16) and eyes (Hab 1:13); rivers are told to "clap their hands" (Ps 98:8); hills "hear" and mountains "listen" (Mic 6:1–2). Wisdom is personified as a woman in Prov 1:20 "Mammon" (i.e., wealth) is personified as a god in Matt 6:24 and Luke 16:13. Death and Hades are personified in Rev 20:14. "When principles are viewed as persons, they must be spoken of as persons; and it will surely not be urged that death and Hades are persons because it is said of them, in [Rev 20:14], that they 'were cast into the lake of fire.'"[15] Similarly, "that Paul speaks of the antichrist [in 2 Thess 2:3–10] in 'personal' terms does not decide the issue; for this was also John's mode of presentation [in 1–2 John], yet John clearly spoke of an antichrist [indeed, of 'the antichrist'] already present."[16]

Further, the Bible always uses the term "beast" to describe empires, not individuals. The description of the "beast" in Revelation 13 is drawn from Daniel 7, which describes four empires as four different beasts. The fourth beast in Dan 7:7–8, 11–12, 19–25 refers to the Roman Empire, not an individual. Nevertheless, the fourth beast is spoken of in "personal" terms.[17] Consequently, the use of personal pronouns to refer to the "beasts" of Revelation is not determinative of whether Antichrist is a person.[18]

Antichrist as the personification of evil

Given the apparently trans-historical, trans-individual, and ultimately theological descriptions, the "beasts" or "Antichrist" may, in fact, be *personifications* of evil and

---

that Antichrist will arise from that tribe. McGinn, *Anti-Christ*, 296n.12.

14. Aune, *Revelation 6–16*, 753, citations omitted.

15. Milligan, *Revelation*, 331.

16. Berkouwer, *Return of Christ*, 270.

17. Although a Bible translation may say *"its body"* [Dan 7:11] and *"its claws"* [Dan 7:19], the literal Hebrew is *"his body"* and *"his claws."*

18. Rev 19:20 states that the "beast" and the "false prophet" are *"thrown alive into the lake of fire."* The fact that they are thrown alive into the lake of fire but everyone else is killed with the sword which came from the mouth of Christ (Rev 19:21) indicates that the beast and the false prophet are *not* individual human beings, but symbolize "institutional structures by which human civilizations and cultures oppose God, his truth and his church. If the beast and false prophet portrayed mere human beings, there would be no reason for Christ to spare them the first death (physical death) before casting them into the second death, the lake of fire (20:14)." Johnson, *Triumph*, 278.

anti-Christian social-political-religious systems and institutions. As such, Antichrist may be manifested in different ways at different times and places throughout history, including (but not limited to) a final manifestation shortly before Christ returns. Tyconius (c.?–390) and Augustine (354–430) held this view.[19] Augustine referred to others who also did.[20] The following commentators are representative of the "Antichrist as personification of evil" view:

- *William Tyndale*:

  Antichrist is not an outward thing, that is to say, a man that should suddenly appear with wonders, as our fathers talked of him. No, verily; for Antichrist is a spiritual thing; and is as much to say as, against Christ; that is, one that preacheth false doctrine, contrary to Christ. Antichrist was in the Old Testament, and fought with the prophets; he was also in the time of Christ and the apostles, as thou readest in the epistles of John and of Paul to the Corinthians and Galatians, and other epistles. Antichrist is now, and shall (I doubt not) endure till the world's end. But his nature is (when he is uttered, and overcome with the word of God) to go out of the play for a season, and to disguise himself, and then to come in again with a new name and new raiment.[21]

- *Stephen Smalley*: "The beast is a symbol of the perpetual deification of secular authority. Even more, he represents the powers of evil which lie behind the kingdoms of this world, and which encourage in society, at any moment in history, compromise with the truth and opposition to the justice and mercy of God."[22]

- *Desmond Ford*: "The pictures in John's Apocalypse of the varied manifestations of Antichrist embody the characteristic features found in Daniel, Mark, and 2 Thess. 2. . . . Antichrist is a genus as well as a specific figure, and all who oppose by cruelty, or counterfeit by subtlety Christ and His church, come under this head."[23]

- *Alan Johnson*: "The description John gives of the beast from the sea does not describe a mere human political entity such as Rome. Rather, it describes in archetypal language the hideous, Satan-backed system of deception and idolatry that may at any time express itself in human systems of various kinds, such as Rome. Yet at the same time John also seems to be saying that this blasphemous, blaspheming, and blasphemy-producing reality will have a final, intense, and, for the saints, utterly devastating manifestation."[24]

- *William Milligan*: "The beast is . . . the spirit of the world, partly in its secularising influence, partly in its brute force, in that tyranny and oppression which it exercises against the children of God."[25]

---

19. McGinn, *Anti-Christ*, 76–77.

20. Augustine, *Civ.*, 20.19.

21. Tyndale, *Doctrinal Treatises*, 42.

22. Smalley, *Revelation*, 337.

23. Ford, *Abomination of Desolation*, 310.

24. Johnson, "Revelation," 525.

25. Milligan, *Revelation*, 297.

The "Antichrist within"

In addition to individual (Antichrist as a person) and corporate or collective (Antichrist as the personification of evil as actualized in anti-Christian social-political-religious systems and institutions), there is a third view of Antichrist. Beginning with Origen (c. 185–254), continuing with Tyconius (c.?–390) and Augustine (354–430), and developed thereafter, Antichrist also has had an "internalized" identification, i.e., Antichrist is the personification of deception, heresy, pride, hypocrisy, and the omnipresent "internal spirit of denial of Jesus that could be found in the heart of any Christian" who denies Christ by deeds even while professing belief.[26] This view is based on such texts as 1 John 2:18–19, 22; 4:3 and 2 John 7. This "Antichrist within" is present both within the church as a whole and within each Christian individually.[27]

John's descriptions of Antichrist in 1 John and 2 John

The issue of person versus personification is reflected in John's ambiguous use of the term "antichrist." In 1 John 2:18 (*"you heard that antichrist is coming"*), *antichristos* appears to be a person who will come in the future; however, that is not entirely clear since no definite article ("the") is used before the word "antichrist."[28] John's other descriptions make clear that "Antichrist" is not limited either to one person or to some future manifestation. In 2:18 John states, *"Even now many antichrists have appeared."* John then says, *"They went out from us, but they were not really of us"* (2:19). Thus, "Antichrist" is equated with all false teachers and was actually present in John's day.

First John 2:22 says, *"Who is the liar but the one who denies that Jesus is the Christ? This is the antichrist, the one who denies the Father and the Son."* In that verse, as Hoekema puts it, "the antichrist is thought of as a person, since the definite article is used with the word. But he is thought of as a person who is already present in John's day—in fact, as one who stands for a group of persons."[29] Hence, John's use of the term "antichrist" appears to be a personification to describe anyone who denies the truth of Christ.

First John 4:3 adds to the description: *"Every spirit that does not confess Jesus is not from God; this is the spirit of the antichrist, of which you have heard that it is coming, and now it is already in the world."* Even though the definite article is used with "antichrist," and both the future coming and current presence are referred to, "John speaks of antichrist only in impersonal terms."[30] Second John 7 states, *"Many deceivers have gone out*

---

26. McGinn, *Anti-Christ*, 64–65, 76–77, 81, 248, 279. This was also indicated by Polycarp in *To the Philippians* 7:1.

27. First John 2:19 says that the antichrists *"went out from us."* In his homily on 1 John 2:18–23 Augustine commented, "If before they went out they were not of us, then there are many within, many who haven't gone out but are antichrists even so. . . . I say it so that no one in the Church may be an antichrist. . . . All of us ought to question our own consciences about whether we are antichrists." Leinenweber, *Love One Another*, 26.

28. Joel McDurmon also points out that "John does not say that antichrist 'is coming in the future,' he simply reminds his listeners that 'antichrist comes.' The verb here is in the present tense, not a participle and not future." McDurmon, *Jesus v. Jerusalem*, 184–85.

29. Hoekema, *Bible and Future*, 157.

30. Ibid.

into the world, those who do not acknowledge Jesus Christ as coming in the flesh. This is the deceiver and the antichrist." In all of these passages, the emphasis is not on the person but on the heretical *beliefs* and *teaching* concerning Jesus Christ. G. C. Berkouwer therefore concludes, "The central meaning of the antichrist, according to John, is the great lie, the denial that Jesus is the Christ."[31]

Riddlebarger summarizes John's treatment of Antichrist:

> First, John argues that Antichrist is not some mysterious individual who is only and finally revealed in the last days. In fact, John says just the opposite. Whatever (or whoever) the Antichrist is, it (or he or she as the case may be) was already present at the time of John's writing. . . . The very presence of Antichrist is clearly an indication that the last hour has indeed already come. And since Antichrist was present in John's own lifetime, we can only conclude that we have been in the last hour since John composed his epistle. . . . [Second,] John indicates that there is not merely one Antichrist, but a series of such enemies of Jesus Christ. . . . So it is quite erroneous to contend that Antichrist is limited to a specific individual, totally unknown to Christians until his revelation immediately before Jesus Christ's return. . . . In other words, one of John's purposes in writing these epistles is to warn all Christians who worry that Antichrist is still to come in the last hour that, on the contrary, many Antichrists have already come, and so it is indeed *already* the last hour. . . . [Third,] John's focus is squarely upon the heretical nature of these individual Antichrists and their false doctrine. . . . Antichrist is any heretic who denies the full humanity or deity of Christ! He was already present when John wrote his first epistle, and John warns us that he will be present throughout the life of the church. . . . [T]he primary thrust is doctrinal (the Antichrist is primarily a false teacher) and only incidentally political and economic (i.e., people being prevented from buying and selling).[32]

John is the only biblical writer to actually use the term "antichrist," and his descriptions of Antichrist in 1 and 2 John are considerably different from most popular contemporary conceptions of Antichrist. John never speaks of "*the* Antichrist" as an evil end-time individual at all. Gary DeMar summarizes, "Antichrist is simply any belief system [or those who espouse it] that disputes the fundamental teachings of Christianity, beginning with the person of Christ. These antichrists are 'religious' figures. The antichrist, contrary to much present-day speculation, is not a political figure, no matter how *anti-* (against) Christ he may be."[33] This should be borne in mind when considering the identity and nature of any purported "Antichrist." Most popular depictions of "Antichrist," however, draw heavily, if not exclusively, from Paul's description of the "*man of lawlessness*" in 2 Thessalonians 2 and the "beasts" of Revelation rather than from John's actual descriptions of "antichrist(s)." It is to those other passages we now turn.

---

31. Berkouwer, *Return of Christ*, 265.
32. Riddlebarger, "The Antichrist," 5–6.
33. DeMar, *Last Days*, 269.

Antichrist seen in parallels between Daniel, 2 Thessalonians 2, and Revelation

The prophecies of Daniel

The prophecies in Daniel are based in history but thematically appear to extend to the end of the age. Daniel uses apocalyptic imagery in referring to "beasts," a "little horn," and a "despicable person." The "beasts" of Dan 7:1–7, 15–23 are kings or, more specifically, kingdoms. The *"little horn"* of Dan 7:7–8, 20–25; 8:9–26 and the *"despicable person"* of Dan 11:21–37 appear to refer to Antiochus Epiphanes (c. 215–164 BC), ruler of the Seleucid Empire, whose defiling of the Jerusalem temple and attempt to outlaw the practice of Judaism led to the Maccabean Revolt beginning in 167 BC.[34] He was actually Antiochus IV, but took the name "Epiphanes" (which means "manifest") "because he regarded himself as a god manifest in human flesh."[35]

Antiochus was one important component of a greater world-historical, geopolitical scheme laid out in Daniel 7. In Daniel 7, the four beasts represent four successive kingdoms and are parallel to the four parts of the statue in Nebuchadnezzar's dream in Daniel 2. Consequently, most interpret the first beast as Babylon, the second as Medo-Persia, the third as Greece, and the fourth as Rome during which God will inaugurate his messianic kingdom (Dan 2:44; 7:21–22).[36] The vision also appears to describe the disintegration of the Roman Empire (Dan 2:42; 7:24), the rise of other powers, including that which many interpret as Antichrist (7:8, 25), and the destruction of all such powers when a "Son of Man" comes with the clouds of heaven (2:44; 7:13–14, 26–27).

Tokunboh Adeyemo maintains, "History has no record of ten such kings [7:24], nor has it recorded the rise of something equivalent to the little horn (7:7, 8, 20–25). Furthermore, since no other animal rose from the sea after the fourth beast, its dominion seems to be open-ended (extending to and including contemporary history) until the beast is slain and destroyed by the Ancient of Days (7:11, 22, 26). Thus the final act of the drama involving the fourth beast lies in the future, a position that is scripturally corroborated by the end-time prophecies of the NT (Rev 13; 17; Matt 24; 2 Thess 2)."[37]

That Daniel's vision extends beyond Antiochus is indicated in Daniel 8, in which Gabriel tells Daniel that the vision pertains to *"the time of the end"* (8:17), *"the appointed time of the end"* (8:19), and *"many days in the future"* (8:26). Similarly, Dan 11:35 refers to the *"end time"* and *"the appointed time,"* and Dan 11:40 refers to *"the end time."* Dan 12:1–2 speaks of a general resurrection and final judgment and concludes by saying that the vision is to remain sealed *"until the end of time."*

34. Adeyemo, "Daniel," 1004, 1009; Beasley-Murray, "Interpretation of Daniel 7," 44–45, 53; Payne, *Encyclopedia*, 371–72, 377–78; McGinn, *Anti-Christ*, 14; Scofield, *New Scofield*, 908n.4, 910n.1, 3. Adeyemo, Payne, and Scofield do not believe that Antiochus is in view in Daniel 7, although they agree that he is in view in Daniel 8 and 11. They contend that strictly an end-time Antichrist figure is in view in Daniel 7. Whether or not Antiochus is in view in Daniel 7, the customary reapplication of prophetic themes, language, and imagery to similar events beyond the original historical referent would allow for a wider application than simply to Antiochus.

35. Metzger, *Introduction*, 132.

36. See VanGemeren, "Daniel," 593, 596–97; Adeyemo, "Daniel," 994–95, 1002–3; Payne, *Encyclopedia*, 370.

37. Adeyemo, "Daniel," 1003.

Reapplication of Daniel's prophecies in 2 Thessalonians 2 and Revelation

Just as Jesus in the Olivet Discourse applied Daniel's *"abomination of desolation"* references to the events of AD 70, so Paul in 2 Thessalonians 2 and John in Revelation apply Daniel's themes and imagery to Antichrist. In the literature of late inter-testamental Judaism there appear to have been two types of eschatological "Anti-Messiah" figures: a political-military tyrant from outside the community who oppresses the people and a false teacher from inside the community who deceives the people. The two are combined in the *"man of lawlessness"* (2 Thess 2:3–12) but are separated in the two "beasts" of Revelation 13.[38]

Daniel and the *"man of lawlessness"* of 2 Thess 2:3–12

In 2 Thess 2:4 Paul's description of the *"man of lawlessness"* is drawn from Dan 11:36, which generally is seen as a depiction of Antiochus Epiphanes, and from such passages as Dan 8:9–14; 9:26–27; 11:31, 45; 12:11, which also usually are taken to refer to Antiochus and his depredations.[39] C. Marvin Pate lists several points of comparison between the *"man of lawlessness"* of 2 Thess 2:3–12 and the figures described in Daniel: "(1) like the beast in Daniel 7:8; 11:35–36, the man of lawlessness arrogates to himself divine status, even to the point of occupying the temple of God (cf. 2 Thess. 2:4 with the desecration of the temple described in Dan. 11:31); (2) both are characterized as being lawless (*anomias,* 2 Thess. 2:3; *anomountes,* Dan. 11:32); (3) both are revealed at a propitious time (*apokalupthēnai kairō,* 2 Thess. 2:6; *apokalupthēnai kairou,* Dan. 11:35)."[40]

Paul also saw an ongoing connection between the first century and the end-time: *"In his time he [the 'man of lawlessness'] will be revealed. For the mystery of lawlessness is already at work"* (2 Thess 2:6–7). Beale discusses this: "The reason Paul uses the word 'mystery' in verse 7 is that he understands the Antichrist prophecy from Daniel as beginning to be fulfilled in the Thessalonian church in an enigmatic manner not clearly foreseen by Daniel. . . . Paul sees that, though this fiend has not yet come so visibly as he will at the final end of history, he is *nevertheless* 'already at work' in the covenant community through his deceivers, the false teachers."[41]

Daniel and the *"beasts"* of Revelation

The description of the "beast" of Rev 13:1–7 is primarily drawn from Daniel 7. The *"beast coming up out of the sea"* is from Dan 7:2–3. The *"ten horns"* are based on Dan 7:7, 20, 24. Rev 13:1–2 turns Daniel's lion, bear, leopard, and "dreadful and terrifying" beast, which in Daniel represented four successive world empires, into one. However, in Revelation the image of the beast also draws from Daniel's descriptions of the "little horn" and Antiochus. Thus, Alan Johnson notes that, according to Rev 13:2, "this beast had 'on each head

---

38. See Osborne, *Revelation,* 494; Schnabel, *40 Questions,* 153.

39. See Weima, "1–2 Thessalonians," 887. As Schnabel states, Antiochus "became the 'prototype' for the supreme opponent of God on earth." Schnabel, *40 Questions,* 155.

40. Pate, *End of the Ages,* 226.

41. Beale, *Temple,* 286–87.

a blasphemous name.' This prominent feature is repeated in 17:3 (cf. 13:5–6). Arrogance and blasphemy also characterize the 'little horn' of Daniel's fourth beast (7:8, 11, 20, 25) and the willful king of Daniel 11:36. John alludes to the vision of Daniel but completely transforms it."[42] Both Daniel's little horn (Dan 7:21) and Revelation's beast (Rev 13:7) wage war against the saints and overcome them.

These connections were made early in church history. The *Epistle of Barnabas* (c. 70–131) quotes Dan 7:7–8, 24 in referring to "the last stumbling block [who] is at hand."[43] Justin Martyr (c. 100–165) refers to "he whom Daniel foretells would have dominion for a time, and times, and an half [Dan 7:25], is even already at the door."[44] Irenaeus (c. 130–200) identifies Antichrist as the "little horn" of Dan 7:8, the "lawless one" whom Christ will slay (2 Thess 2:8), and the first beast of Rev 13:1–8.[45]

Comparison of Daniel 7, 8, 11; 2 Thessalonians 2; and Revelation 13, 19

The following table shows the connections:

Dan 7:7–27 (4th beast & little horn)	Dan 8:9–26 (little horn)	Dan 11:21–45 (the despicable person)	2 Thess 2 (man of lawlessness)	Rev 13, 19 (the two beasts)
Extremely strong; greater than the others: 7:7, 17, 19–20	Exceedingly great; very mighty, but not by his own power: 8:9–10, 24; Prospers and performs his will: 8:24	He will accomplish what his fathers never did, and will do as he pleases: 11:24, 36	Is in accord with the activity of Satan, with all power: 2:9	The dragon gave him his power, throne, and great authority; authority over all people: 13:2–4, 7
Utters great boasts: 7:8, 11, 20; Speaks out against the Most High: 7:25	Magnifies himself: 8:4, 8, 11, 25; Opposes the Prince of princes: 8:25; Removes the regular sacrifice, throws down the sanctuary, and tramples the holy place; is the transgression that causes horror: 8:11–13	Enraged at the holy covenant: 11:28, 30; Exalts and magnifies himself above all gods; speaks out against God, and shows no regard for God: 11:36–37 Does away with the regular sacrifice; sets up the abomination of desolation: 11:31	Opposes and exalts himself above every so-called god or object of worship; shows himself to be God: 2:4; Takes his seat in the temple of God: 2:4	Speaks arrogant words and blasphemies: 13:5–6; Is worshiped: 13:4, 8, 12; 19:20

42. Johnson, "Revelation," 525.

43. *Barn.* 4:3–6.

44. Justin Martyr, *Dial.* 32.

45. Irenaeus, *Haer.* 5.25, 28, 30.

Dan 7:7–27 (4th beast & little horn)	Dan 8:9–26 (little horn)	Dan 11:21–45 (the despicable person)	2 Thess 2 (man of lawlessness)	Rev 13, 19 (the two beasts)
Devours, crushes, and tramples others: 7:7, 19; Wages war against the saints, overpowers them and wears them down: 7:21, 25	Tramples down some of the host of heaven and stars: 8:10; Will destroy to an extraordinary degree, including the holy people: 8:24–25	Will kill many, including the faithful: 11:32–35, 44	Man of lawlessness; son of destruction: 2:3	Makes war against the saints and overcomes them: 13:7, 15; 19:19
	Insolent and skilled in intrigue, shrewd, and will cause deceit to succeed: 8:23, 25	Seizes the kingdom by intrigue; speaks lies; uses smooth words to turn people to godlessness: 11:21, 27, 32	Acts with all deception: 2:10	Deceives the earth-dwellers: 13:14; 19:20
			Does signs, and false wonders: 2:9	Performs great signs: 13:13
Authority for time, times, and half a time: 7:25	Tramples the holy place for 2,300 evenings and mornings: 8:14	Will prosper until the indignation is finished: 11:36		Is given authority for 42 months: 13:5
His dominion is taken away and destroyed forever; his body is given to burning fire at the coming of a Son of man: 7:11, 13–14, 22, 26–27	Will be broken without human agency: 8:25	His end will come at the appointed time: 11:35, 45	Will be slain by the breath of the Lord's mouth at his coming 2:8	Seized and thrown into lake of fire at Lord's coming: 19:20

Antichrist seen in parallels between the Olivet Discourse and 2 Thessalonians 2

Several parallels between the Olivet Discourse and 2 Thessalonians 2 suggest a connection between the *"abomination of desolation"* of AD 70 (Matt 24:15) and the end-time *"man of lawlessness"* (2 Thess 2:3).[46] Both appear in passages that have as their theme the end of the age and the *parousia* of Christ:[47]

46. Preterists certainly would agree with these parallels; preterism views the *"man of lawlessness"* as an historical figure in the period of time before AD 70. See DeMar, *Last Days*, 273–311; Gentry, *Dominion*, 386–92.

47. For parallels between the restraint, revealing, and destruction of the *"man of lawlessness"* and the

Topic	Matthew 24	2 Thessalonians 2
1. Warning not to be deceived or disturbed	24:4, 6	2:1–3
2. Times of deception	24:5, 11, 23	2:10–12
3. Apostasy	24:10	2:3
4. Lawlessness and evil	24:6–10, 12	2:7, 9–10, 12
5. Lack of love	24:10, 12	2:10
6. False Christs/Man of lawlessness	24:5, 11, 23–24, 26	2:3
7. Abomination of desolation/Son of destruction	24:15	2:3
8. In the holy place/In the temple of God	24:15	2:4
9. Signs and false wonders	24:24	2:9
10. Second Coming of Christ	24:27, 29–30	2:1–2, 8
11. The elect are safe and will be gathered	24:22, 31	2:1, 13
12. "I have told you"	24:25	2:5, 15

The connection between the events described in the Olivet Discourse and an end-time Antichrist was made early in Christian history. *Didache* 16 (c. 70–110), which has many close ties to Matt 24:4–44, speaks of "the deceiver of the world [who] will appear as a son of God." Paul saw a connection between the *"man of lawlessness"* who *"will be revealed"* (2 Thess 2:6) and the *"mystery of lawlessness"* which *"is already at work"* (2 Thess 2:7). In the Olivet Discourse Jesus spoke of the *"abomination of desolation"* in the context of the events of AD 70. Consequently, instead of seeing that as a "type" or "foreshadow" of an end-time Antichrist, consistent with Paul's treatment of the *"man of lawlessness,"* it may be better to say that "the Roman invasion [of AD 70] was a *manifestation* of Antichrist, though a manifestation which was to swell into greater dimensions, eventually enshrining supernatural events."[48]

The activities of the "man of lawlessness" in 2 Thess 2:3–12[49]

The "apostasy" (2 Thess 2:3)

The word "apostasy" (Greek = *apostasia*) can refer to a political or a religious crisis or revolt. However, in both the Septuagint[50] and the NT[51] it always refers to a religious falling away from the faith. A "falling away" assumes a "prior turning to" God. The immediate context of "apostasy" in 2 Thess 2:3 is Paul's mention of deception in the church (2 Thess 2:1–2). Additionally, in 2:3 apostasy "is conjoined with the 'man of lawlessness', and in

---

binding, release, and destruction of Satan at the *parousia,* see below, chapter 11, the section *"The binding and release of Satan before the parousia and his destruction at the parousia are parallel to the restraint, revealing, and destruction of the 'man of lawlessness' in 2 Thess 2:6–12."*

48. Ford, *Abomination of Desolation,* 187n.120.

49. See the discussion in chapter 9 regarding the "restrainer" of 2 Thess 2:6–7.

50. The Greek OT: Josh 22:22; 2 Chron 29:19; Jer 2:19.

51. Acts 21:21; see also the verb form in 1 Tim 4:1; Heb 3:12.

verses 8–12 deception and departing from the faith also appear in conjunction with 'the lawless one'. . . . [This suggests that verses 3–4] refer to a future apostasy throughout the worldwide church and the Antichrist's influence in the church."[52] The parallel with Dan 11:30–45 suggests the same thing.[53]

Vos observes that according to 2 Thess 2:3–12, Antichrist's activity "lies fundamentally in the sphere of religious and moral seduction. He proceeds, not by applying violence, but through estranging and leading astray his followers from the truth of the Gospel. Of political organization and activity . . . nothing is said by the Apostle in so many words."[54] Paul's description of the *"man of lawlessness"* thus echoes John's description of "Antichrist."

The "temple of God" (2 Thess 2:4)

The "temple of God" is not a past or future Jewish temple building

Some, beginning with Hippolytus (c. 170–236),[55] have held that Antichrist would rebuild the physical Jewish temple in Jerusalem. However, the reference to the *"temple of God"* cannot be referring to a physical Jewish temple.[56] First, Paul is writing to Christians, not Jews, and "2 Thessalonians 2:3 appears not to be talking about an 'apostasy' from the faith in geographically conceived Israel."[57] Second, in 2 Thessalonians 2 Paul does not mention either the destruction of the existing temple or the construction of a future temple building, nor does he assume that a future temple building is a necessity. Consequently, the self-deification of the *"man of lawlessness"* cannot plausibly have been thought (particularly by Paul's original readers) to take place in such a restored temple building.[58] Third, according to 1 Thess 2:14–16 "Paul believed that national Israel as the chosen people of God had come to its end. Presumably, the end of Israel's temple also would have been included in Paul's understanding since Christ had predicted its destruction (e.g., Luke 21:6, 32). This means that Paul did not view Israel's temple as 'the temple of God' *even before* its actual destruction in AD 70, and it is unlikely that he uses this phrase in verse 4 to refer to 'the temple of God' as the same kind of Israelite temple directly preceding the lawless one's entry into it."[59] Finally, because the temple and its sacrifices have been fulfilled and

---

52. Beale, *Temple*, 272. A few dispenationalists have the idiosyncratic view that the "apostasy" refers to the "pretribulational rapture" of the church. See Higgins, *Manasseh Effect*, 107–09; see also Pentecost, *Things to Come*, 204, 332, who interprets "apostasy" as "departure," which he says could be either "a departure from the faith or a departure of the saints from the earth."

53. See Beale, *Temple*, 273–74; Vos, *Pauline Eschatology*, 111–12.

54. Vos, *Pauline Eschatology*, 122–23.

55. Hippolytus, *Treatise on Christ and Antichrist* 6.

56. Contra Schnabel, *40 Questions*, 160–1, 258, who thinks that 2 Thess 2:4 relates to Titus and the Romans in the temple in AD 70.

57. Beale, *Temple*, 274.

58. Schnabel, *40 Questions*, 149.

59. Beale, *Temple*, 279; see also Storms, *Kingdom Come*, 530.

superseded in Christ,[60] even if a temple is rebuilt in Jerusalem it would be an idol temple. It could not be the *"temple of God."*[61]

The *"temple of God"* refers to the church

James Sweeney makes the important point that in 1–2 Corinthians "Paul was able to refer to believers in the 50s AD, *while the Jerusalem temple was still standing,* as the temple of God indwelt by the Spirit."[62] Thus, in God's eyes the Jerusalem temple had already been replaced even before it was physically destroyed by the Romans in AD 70.

In 2 Cor 6:16—7:1, after comparing the church to a temple, Paul concludes by saying, *"Therefore, having these promises."* The promises from which he quotes in 2 Cor 6:16–18 include Lev 26:11–12, 2 Sam 7:14, and Ezek 37:27, where God promised to build a house and establish David's throne forever, be a father to him, and establish his sanctuary and dwelling place forever with his people. By referring to those promises in the context of calling the church *"the temple of the living God"* (2 Cor 6:16), Paul is saying, "The fullest realization of God's covenant, the eternal and abiding presence of God, binding his people to himself and himself to them forever: these are the promises that are fulfilled in the church—we *are* a temple of the living God."[63] In his commentary on 2 Thess 2:4, John Calvin observed, "Paul places Antichrist nowhere else than in the very sanctuary of God. For this is not a foreign, but a domestic enemy, who opposes Christ under the very name of Christ."[64] Indeed, "Paul's normal use of the word *naos* [Greek for 'sanctuary' or 'temple'] is with reference to the Christian church [see 1 Cor 3:16–17; Eph 2:20–22]."[65]

The actual phrase *"temple of God"* is found ten times in the NT other than in 2 Thess 2:4.[66] In all those other passages that phrase refers to the church. In Matt 26:61 Jesus' reference probably was to the temple of his own body.[67] If the reference was to the then-existing temple building, it was only as a physical "type" or foreshadow of Christ and his people as the true temple.[68]

Early in its history, the church saw Paul's *"man of lawlessness"* as coming from within the church, not ouside of it. Beale comments, "The earliest source in line with the understanding that the 'man of lawlessness' will deceptively infiltrate the church as the 'temple of God' is the *Epistle of Barnabas* 4 (mid-nineties AD), which appeals to the Dan. 7 prophecy of the end-time tyrant and associates him with 'the works of lawlessness' and 'the age of lawlessness', and equates the church with the temple (see also *Barnabas* 6 and 16 for

60. Matt 5:17; Mark 14:58; John 2:18–22; 2 Cor 3:12–16; Gal 3:23—4:7; Heb 4:14—5:10; 7:1—10:22.

61. As Augustine pointed out, "the apostle would not call the temple of any idol or demon the temple of God." Augustine, *Civ.,* 20.19.

62. Sweeney, "Jesus, Paul, and the Temple," 629, emphasis in original. See 1 Cor 3:9, 16–17; 6:19; 2 Cor 6:16. "The dating of 1 Corinthians in the fifth decade of the first century is not greatly debated." Ibid., 629n.116.

63. Clowney, "Final Temple," 186.

64. Calvin, "Second Epistle to the Thesalonians," 330–31.

65. Ford, *Abomination of Desolation,* 211.

66. Matt 26:61; 1 Cor 3:16, 17a, 17b; 2 Cor 6:16a, 16b; Rev 3:12; 7:15; 11:1, 19.

67. Nixon, "Matthew," 848; see John 2:19–21.

68. Beale, *Temple,* 275–76.

the church as the temple)."[69] Early theologians such as Jerome (c. 331–420) and John Chrysostom (c. 347–407) similarly held that the "temple of God" in 2 Thess 2:4 referred to the church.[70]

He "takes his seat" in the temple of God (2 Thess 2:4).

"Taking his seat" is a metaphor for assuming or usurping authority. F. F. Bruce notes, "Had they said, 'so that he takes his seat on the throne of God,' few would have thought it necessary to think of a literal throne; it would simply have been regarded as a graphic way of saying that he plans to usurp the authority of God. This is what is meant by the language actually used here, although the sacral associations of *naos* imply that he demands not only the obedience but also the worship due to God alone."[71]

The "beasts" of Rev 11:7; 13:1–18; 14:9; 15:2; 16:2, 10, 13; 17:3–17; 19:19–20; 20:10

A comparison of the descriptions and activities of the "beasts" of Revelation

The following table lists the descriptions and activities of the "beasts" in Revelation:

Rev 11:7	*Rev 13:1–8*	*Rev 13:11–18*	*Rev 16:10–16*	*Rev 17:3–17*	*Rev 19:19–20*
Ascends from the abyss.	Ascends from the sea: 1	Ascends from the earth: 11		Ascends from the abyss: 8	
	Has 10 horns, 7 heads: 1	Has 2 horns like a lamb: 11		Has 10 horns (=kings), 7 heads (=mountains =kings): 3, 9–10	
	Blasphemous names on his heads: 1			Full of blasphemous names: 3	

---

69. Ibid., 284n.41.

70. See McGinn, *Anti-Christ*, 74, 300n.65.

71. Bruce, *1 and 2 Thessalonians*, 169; see also Storms, *Kingdom Come*, 529n.4.

	Speaks arrogant words and blasphemies: 5–6	Speaks like a dragon and deceives earth-dwellers: 11, 14	Unclean spirits come out of beast's & false prophet's mouth: 13		
	Earth-dwellers amazed, follow, & worship the beast: 3–4, 8	Makes earth-dwellers worship 1st beast: 12, 14		Earth-dwellers will marvel at the beast: 8	
Fights, defeats, & kills the 2 witnesses	Fights saints & overcomes them: 7	Authority to give breath to image of 1st beast & kill those who do not worship beast's image: 15	Unclean spirits from beast & false prophet assemble kings of the world for war against God: 13–14	Beast & kings assemble for war against the Lamb: 14	Beast & kings assemble for war against rider of white horse & his army: 19
				The Lamb will overcome them: 14 Beast will go to destruction: 8	Beast & false prophet seized & thrown into lake of fire: 20

The OT uniformly uses the imagery of "beasts" to signify forces of evil, world empires, and the satanic influence behind the evil and empires

Although many people apply the "beast" imagery to a supposed end-time individual, the Bible always applies beast imagery to empires, forces, and entities that transcend the individual. In addition to the "beasts" of Daniel 7, the OT contains several other references to "beasts" as epitomizing evil empires.[72] Hence, Sam Storms concludes that the "beast" of Revelation 13 "is primarily corporate in nature, rather than personal."[73]

At the same time, as Johnson notes, "the national entities were inseparably identified with the archetypal reality of the satanic, idolatrous systems represented by the seven-headed monster (Leviathan, Rahab, and the dragon) so that the beast represented, not the political power, but the system of evil that found expression in the political entity."[74] That connection is seen by a comparing the "dragon" of Rev 12:3–4, 7—13:1 and the "beast" of Rev 13:1–10. The dragon (i.e., the devil) is described as being red and as having seven heads and ten horns (Rev 12:3). Likewise, the beast is described as scarlet (Rev 17:3)

72. Ps 74:13–14; 87:4; 89:10; Isa 27:1; 30:7; 51:9; Jer 51:34; Ezek 29:3; 32:2–3.

73. Storms, *Kingdom Come,* 478.

74. Johnson, "Revelation," 525.

and has seven heads and ten horns (Rev 13:1; 17:3). This comparison clearly shows the identification between ungodly world empires and the satanic "power behind the throne." The dragon has diadems on his heads (Rev 12:3) and the beast has diadems on his horns (Rev 13:1). Beale observes, "That the dragon had diadems on his heads (12:3) and the beast now has them on his horns shows that the dragon has the ultimate rule and mandates his will through the beast."[75]

The characteristics of the "beast" may reflect aspects of first-century Rome and its emperors

Several aspects of the "beast" reflect the first-century Roman context in which John wrote. Stephen Smalley notes the claims to divinity by Roman emperors reflect the blasphemous names on the heads of the beast: "The titles of blasphemy on the seven heads of the beast may allude to the honorific designations given to Roman emperors in the first century AD, in order to support their wish to be venerated as divine within the cult of Caesar. The imperial coinage of the time bore eloquent testimony to this desire; and, at their deaths, Julius Caesar, Augustus, Claudius and Vespasian were declared by the Senate to be 'divine' (*divus*). . . . All this may suggest that the beast of Rev. 13.1 symbolizes the Roman Empire, the unjust oppressor of the Christian Church."[76] Preterists identify the "beast" from the sea with Rome, as epitomized by Nero.[77]

The "beast" of Revelation transcends first-century Rome and its emperors

Although the depiction of the "beast" in Revelation may be anchored in first century Rome, its meaning and relevance point beyond the situation that Christians faced in that time and place. John's combining Daniel's four beasts into one suggests that the beast transcends any one historical empire.[78] That is confirmed by the OT which "uses *the same sea monster image* to represent successive evil empires spanning hundreds of years."[79] Johnson concludes that the identification of the sea beast and the dragon—the oppressive empire with the satanic power behind it—"helps us see that the beast itself is not to be identified with any one historical form of its expression or with any one institutional aspect of its manifestation. In other words, the beast may appear now as Sodom, Egypt, Rome, or even Jerusalem and may manifest itself as a political power, an economic power, a religious power, or a heresy (1 John 2:18, 22; 4:3)."[80]

75. Beale, *Revelation*, 684.

76. Smalley, *Revelation*, 336.

77. Chilton, *Paradise*, 175–81; DeMar, *Last Days*, 255–59.

78. Resseguie, *Revelation of John*, 182, 191; this is paralleled in John's description of "Babylon the great" in Revelation 17–18 as being based on first-century Rome but as transcending the Roman Empire. See the discussion of Babylon the great in chapter 11, below.

79. Beale, *Revelation*, 686, emphasis in original. "Rahab" is a synonym for Egypt in Ps 87:4 and for Babylon in Jer 51:34. See also Johnson, *Triumph*, 188–89.

80. Johnson, "Revelation," 525; see also Storms, *Kingdom Come*, 488; Rushdoony, *Thy Kingdom*, 170 ("The beast, symbol of human government and empire, of anti-Christian states and cultures generally, represented the Roman Empire of St. John's day, and all other anti-Christian orders. The beast represents

The description of the "beast" from the sea (Rev 13:1–10) is a parody of Christ

Like the *"man of lawlessness"* of 2 Thess 2:3–12, the most important aspect of the beast of Revelation is not political or economic but is theological. Rev 13:5–6; 17:3 stress the beast's arrogance and blasphemies. That the beast is truly "Antichrist"—the great theological counterpart to Christ and all that Christ represents—is seen in the many parallels between Christ and the beast. Both Christ and the beast: (1) Have swords;[81] (2) Have horns;[82] (3) Are slain, with the same Greek word (*sphagizō*) used to describe their deaths;[83] (4) Rise to new life, with the same Greek word in 2:8 and 13:14 (*ezēsen*) used to say that they *"came to life"*;[84] (5) Are given authority;[85] (6) Wear many diadems;[86] (7) Have a throne;[87] (8) Have authority over "every tribe, tongue, people, and nation";[88] (9) Have followers who have their names written on their foreheads;[89] and (10) Receive universal worship.[90]

Additionally, the description of the beast as the one who *"was and is not and is to come"* (Rev 17:8) parallels the description of God as the one *"who is and who was and who is to come"* (Rev 1:4, 8; 4:8). In contrast with each other, the beast has blasphemous names written on his heads (Rev 13:1; 17:3); Christ has a name written on him which no one knows except himself (Rev 19:12). Those who have the Lamb's name written on their forehead have been purchased (Greek = *agoradzō*) from the earth (Rev 14:1, 3); those who do not have the beast's name written on their forehead are not able to buy (*agoradzō*) on the earth (Rev 13:17).[91]

---

the totality of all such empires in the ancient world, and all to come. Its seven heads and ten horns emphasize totality."). John does with the "beast" what he does elsewhere in the book: he sees the forces at work in his world and both universalizes them and exposes their true and deepest significance. John sees what most people do not, namely, although we may not overtly "worship the beast" (Rev 13:8), if Jesus Christ is not our true Lord then at the level of our most fundamental identity we are, indeed, "earth-dwellers" who do, in fact, worship the beast. He is revealing the ultimate stakes involved in our relationship with our society and culture.

81. Compare Rev 1:16; 2:12, 16; 19:15, 21 and 13:10.

82. Compare Rev 5:6 and 13:1, 11.

83. Compare Rev 5:6 and 13:3, 8.

84. Compare Rev 2:8, 5:6, 9; 13:8 and 13:3, 12.

85. Compare Rev 2:27; 5:1–9 and 13:2, 14.

86. Compare Rev 13:1 and 19:12.

87. Compare Rev 13:2 and 3:21.

88. Compare Rev 5:9; 7:9 and 13:7.

89. Compare Rev 13:16–17 and 14:1.

90. Compare Rev 5:8–14 and 13:4, 8.

91. The "mark of the beast" (Rev 13:16–17; 14:9–11), like God's seal on the church (Rev 7:3), is not an "outward tattoo or insignia on the body but rather a symbol of the beast's ownership and control of his followers' thoughts (forehead) and deeds (right hand)." Johnson, *Triumph*, 196. The beast's mark and God's seal are "made visible in peoples' norms, values, and beliefs." Resseguie, *Revelation of John*, 136.

The beast from the earth (Rev 13:11–17)

The second beast "is also a parody of the messianic Lamb of 5:6 and has an ironic relation with that Lamb. It, too, is a lamb with horns [Rev 13:11]."[92] The second beast has primarily a religious role and later is called *"the false prophet"* (Rev 16:13; 19:20; 20:10). This beast parallels the *"man of lawlessness"* with respect to satanic influence (Rev 13:11; 2 Thess 2:9), signs (Rev 13:13–15; 2 Thess 2:9), deception (Rev 13:14; 2 Thess 2:10), and worship (Rev 13:12, 15; 2 Thess 2:4). Preterists identify the beast from the earth (the "false prophet") as the "Jewish religious leaders who sought to seduce Christians" before AD 70.[93] Others see this beast as the "imperial cult" of ancient Rome which now transcends Rome or as "religious deception."[94]

Beale summarizes the essential nature and role of this second "beast":

> Whereas the true prophet was to lead people to worship God, this prophet leads them to worship the state. This beast may take many forms and may at times even be equated with the state, as well as well as with false prophets in the church (as in 2:2, 14–15, 20–24). That manifestations of the beastly false prophet occur in the church is also suggested by the OT, where false prophecy almost always takes place within the covenant community. This is reinforced by Christ's prophecy that false prophets and messiahs would arise in the believing community itself (Matt. 24:5, 11 and parallels). Jesus also likened false prophets to beasts and foretold that "false prophets" would "come . . . in sheep's clothing but are inwardly ravenous wolves" (Matt. 7:15). The image of a wolf in lamb's clothing suggests a traitor within the fold of the church. . . . Whereas the first beast speaks loudly and defiantly against God, the second beast makes the first beast's claims sound plausible and persuasive. . . . Therefore, it takes a discerning Christian to detect the evil inherent in the second beast.[95]

The fatal head wound and recovery of the beast (Rev 13:3, 12, 14)

The beast's fatal head wound

The word for the beast's "wound" in Greek is *plēgē*, which is usually translated "plague." Everywhere else in Revelation that word signifies a divinely inflicted judgment or punishment.[96] Rev 13:14 adds that the beast's fatal head wound was inflicted by the "sword."[97] In

---

92. Beale, *Revelation*, 707. When Rev 13:11 says that this second beast has *"horns like a lamb and he spoke as a dragon,"* the reference clearly is not to *any* lamb and dragon but to *the* Lamb and Dragon. As Schüssler Fiorenza says, the second beast "exercises the power of the Lamb while it preaches the message and speaks the language of the Dragon." Schüssler Fiorenza, *Revelation*, 84.

93. Chilton, *Paradise*, 181; see also DeMar, *Last Days*, 259–60.

94. Johnson, *Triumph*, 196, 338; see also Schüssler Fiorenza, *Revelation*, 86. The interaction between religion and the state is seen in that the second beast both enforces religious worship of the first beast (Rev 13:5) and also enforces economic loyalty to the first beast (Rev 13:6–7). See Schnabel, *40 Questions*, 197.

95. Beale, *Revelation*, 707–08.

96. See Rev 9:18, 20; 11:6; 15:1, 6, 8; 16:9, 21; 18:4, 8; 21:9; 22:18.

97. Most English translations of Rev 13:3 are misleading in that they translate the Greek *hōs*

Revelation the sword frequently refers symbolically to the divine judgment of the Messiah.[98] The reference to the sword also echoes Isa 27:1 which says, *"In that day the Lord will punish Leviathan the fleeing serpent with His fierce and great and mighty sword, even Leviathan the twisted serpent; and He will kill the dragon who lives in the sea."*

All of those references point to the true meaning of the *"fatal wound"* suffered by the beast: "Everywhere in the book the only sufficient conqueror of the beast and the dragon is the slain Lamb, together with the faithful saints (Rev 12:11; 19:19–21). Furthermore, it is the event of the life and especially the crucifixion, resurrection, and exaltation of Jesus that dealt this death blow to the dragon and the beast (Rev 1:5; 5:9; 12:11). This same thought is paralleled by other NT teaching (Luke 10:17–24; 11:14–22; John 12:31–33; Col 2:15)."[99] Consequently, the fatal "plague" by the "sword" in Rev 13:3, 12, and 14 "cannot be describing a literal death and resurrection of some historical [or future] person."[100]

The recovery of the beast

All of the parallels between the first "beast" and Christ, and the parallel positions within the covenant community between the second "beast" and the *"man of lawlessness,"* highlight the essentially theological or spiritual nature of "Antichrist." In other words, all of the political, economic, and social issues raised by governments and cultures confront us with the fundamental question: Where does my primary loyalty lie—with Christ or with the world? That same issue, in a different form, is raised by the beast's fatal head wound and his recovery. Richard Bauckham observes, "The parallel between the 'death' and 'resurrection' of the beast and the death and resurrection of Jesus Christ poses the issue of what is truly divine. Is it the beast's apparent success which is worthy of religious trust and worship? Or is the apparent failure of Christ and the martyrs the true witness to the God who can be ultimately trusted and may alone be worshipped?"[101]

---

esphagmenēn to suggest that the beast only "seemed" (ESV; NIV; RSV; "as if," NASB; NKJV) to be slain. Schnabel states, "The comparative particle *hōs* does not express a condition. The genitive expression *hē plēgē to thanatou* in the second part of 13:3, often translated as 'mortal wound,' is epexegetical (or descriptive): the 'wound' involved 'death,' which means the beast died as the result of a wound inflicted by a sword (13:14)." Schnabel, *40 Questions,* 177n.7.

98. Rev 1:16; 2:12, 16; 19:15, 21.

99. Johnson, "Revelation," 526.

100. Beale, *Revelation,* 689.

101. Bauckham, *Climax of Prophecy,* 452. Despite the parallel, Beale notes the fundamental difference between the resurrection of the beast and the resurrection of the Lamb: "The Lamb really did conquer the defeat of death by resurrection, but the beast's continued existence is not a reversal of his actual defeat." Beale, *Revelation,* 689. Indeed, Rev 17:8 says that the beast comes up out of the abyss only to *"go to destruction."*

The number of the beast: 666 (Rev 13:18)

Nero and the use of gematria

Gematria is a mystical method of interpreting Scripture by substituting numbers for letters in certain words or names. It is sometimes used to try to figure out who Antichrist is. The most popular version of this is based on the Nero *redivivus* ("Nero returned to life") myth that was circulated in the first century, i.e., Emperor Nero really had not died but had escaped to Parthia in the East and would return with a huge army subduing all opposition.[102] If the words "Caesar Nero" are transliterated into Hebrew, they have the numerical value of 666.[103] Therefore, some scholars believe that John identifies Nero as the beast.[104]

Gematria fails as a method of identification

However appealing the Nero idea is to some, gematria ultimately fails as a method of identifying Antichrist. First, to attempt a literal calculation of some individual's name is contrary to the symbolic way in which numbers are used in Revelation and other apocalyptic literature. Second, there are many names, both ancient and modern, that come to 666 when subjected to gematria.[105] Even the word "beast," when transliterated into Hebrew, comes to 666.[106] As far back as the second century, Irenaeus recognized the same thing: "It is therefore more certain, and less hazardous, to await the fulfillment of the prophecy, than to be making surmises, and casting about for any names that may present themselves, inasmuch as many names can be found possessing the number mentioned; and the same question will, after all, remain unsolved."[107]

The problem is deeper than the multiple spurious identifications of Antichrist based on gematria over the last two thousand years. The real problem is the use of gematria itself. Its use is akin to magic or the occult. Beale points out why the method itself is not what John had in mind: "There is no evidence of any other number in the book being used in such a way. All the numbers have figurative significance and symbolize some spiritual reality and never involve any kind of literal gematria calculation. . . . If a Hebrew or Greek

---

102. Minear, *New Earth*, 248–50; McGinn, *Anti-Christ*, 45–54, 65–67. Richard Bauckham, *Climax of Prophecy*, 384–452 has done an exhaustive study of John's use of the Nero's return myth, including the historical records, John's use of the Jewish Sybylline Oracles and the Christian apocalypse the Ascension of Isaiah, and a detailed study of the significance of numbers. He states, "The legend of Nero's return proved useful to John because he could adapt it to the needs of his prophetic vision of the triumph of the kingdom of God over the Roman Empire's pretensions to divine rule." Ibid., 450–51.

103. Resseguie, *Revelation of John*, 189. Nero, of course, was the first Roman emperor to systematically persecute the church. He was called a "beast" by several Greek authors. Schnabel, *40 Questions*, 190.

104. See Chilton, *Paradise*, 180–81; DeMar, *Last Days*, 260–61. Schnabel, however, observes that John could not have been identifying Nero as the "final" Antichrist since Nero died in AD 68, whereas John wrote Revelation several years after that. Schnabel, *40 Questions*, 190.

105. See Beale, *Revelation*, 720–21; DeMar, *Last Days*, 231–38.

106. Resseguie, *Revelation of John*, 191.

107. Irenaeus, *Haer.* 5.30.3; see also Schüssler Fiorenza, *Revelation*, 16.

gematria system of literal computation were being used exceptionally here, then John would have alerted his readers by writing something like 'and the number of his name *in Hebrew* (or *Greek*) is 666.'"[108] This suggests that such a calculation method will *never* yield the correct interpretation and that John's reference to 666 was never intended to promote the use of gematria at all.

The transcendent nature of evil

Because the beast appears to transcend historical individuals and empires, the number of the beast likewise probably transcends historical individuals and empires. That is indicated in two ways.

The "number of [a] man" (Rev 13:18)

The Greek phrase *"number of a man"* does not have a definite article (i.e., the word "the") before "man." Consequently, it "can be translated generically as 'a number of man' (i.e., a number of humanity), or nongenerically, referring to an individual, 'a number of a person' (i.e., a specific individual)."[109] The "generic" sense of the "number of man" in Rev 13:18 is indicated by its closest biblical parallel—Rev 21:17. In that verse an angel was measuring the wall of New Jerusalem *"according to human measurements."* The word "human" in 21:17 does not have the definite article in front of it. The phrase "human measurements" obviously does not indicate the measurement of or by a specific person. Rather, it has a generic meaning.[110]

The parallel between Rev 13:18 and 21:17 also is seen in how they *contrast*. In 13:18 "man" or "human" is identified with the beast; in 21:17 "man" or "human" is identified with an angel. Bauckham states, "The parallel and contrast surely suggest that whereas the beast is humanity debased, the new Jerusalem represents humanity exalted to the position of the angels."[111] Beale therefore concludes that most likely "the omission of the article in 13:18 indicates the general idea of humanity, not some specific individual who can be discerned only through an esoteric method of calculation. Therefore, in both verses *anthrōpou* [the Greek word for 'man'] is a descriptive or qualitative genitive, so that the phrase here should be rendered 'a human number' (so RSV) or 'a number of humanity.' It is a number common to fallen humanity."[112]

The significance of the number 666

Beale discusses the significance of the contrast between the use of "six" and "seven" throughout Revelation: "The number seven refers to completeness and is repeated

---

108. Beale, *Revelation*, 721.

109. Resseguie, *Revelation of John*, 189.

110. Ibid., 189–90.

111. Bauckham, *Climax of Prophecy*, 398.

112. Beale, *Revelation*, 724.

throughout the book. But 666 appears only here. This suggests that the triple sixes are intended as a contrast with the divine sevens throughout the book and signify incompleteness and imperfection. . . . The triple repetition of sixes connotes the intensification of incompleteness and failure that is summed up in the beast more than anywhere else among fallen humanity."[113] Or, as Resseguie puts it, 666 is the epitome of "humanity's bestial traits."[114] Milligan summarizes the idea like this, "The number six was held to signify inability to reach the sacred point and hopeless falling short of it. To the Jew there was thus a doom about the number six even when it stood alone. Triple it; let there be a multiple of it by ten and then a second time by ten until you obtain three mysterious *sixes* following one another, 666; and we have represented a potency of evil than which there can be none greater, a direfulness of fate than which there can be none worse."[115] In the second century Irenaeus arrived at a similar conclusion. He held that 666 signifies "a summing up of the whole of that apostasy which has taken place during six thousand years."[116]

Concluding comments regarding Antichrist

The relevance of Antichrist for our own time: faithfulness and discernment

Unfortunately, the history of Christianity, almost from its beginning, has been littered with attempts to identify Antichrist. Nero (or the Roman Empire), a Jew from the tribe of Dan, Muhammad (or Islam), the pope (or the papacy, or the Roman Catholic Church), Peter the Great, Napoleon III, Mussolini, Mikhail Gorbachev, Henry Kissinger, and a host of others have been put forward as the Antichrist.[117] Thus, the dispensationalists' "remarkable ingenuity in adapting their message to current historical fears, especially since the 1960s,"[118] has been matched by literalists throughout history.

At least three related factors appear to be responsible for this: (1) "The apocalyptic mentality has always found historical change ripe material for the application of biblical prophecy";[119] (2) People manifest "eagerness to heighten the importance of a contemporary event by using heightened rhetoric ('This week's game of the century!')";[120] and (3) "The tendency to demonize one's opponents, especially in times of unusually threatening conflict, has been a major engine in Antichrist's ongoing career."[121]

---

113. Ibid., 721–22.

114. Resseguie, *Revelation of John,* 190.

115. Milligan, *Revelation,* 235.

116. Irenaeus, *Haer.* 5.28.2.

117. McGinn, *Anti-Christ,* 46–49, 52, 61, 85–87, 102, 143–213, 233–38, 246, 256, 260; see also MacDonald, *Believer's,* 2054. Oropeza lists reasons why several current world figures are not the Antichrist. Oropeza, *99 Reasons,* 148–58.

118. McGinn, *Anti-Christ,* 257.

119. Ibid., 242; see also Stout, *New England Soul,* 253 ("Millennial rhetoric was evanescent and event-centered; it could arouse in times of crisis, but it could not supply the terms for day-to-day living in time of peace"); Wilson, "American Civil War," 399 ("Millennialsim thrives on dramatic events").

120. McGinn, *Anti-Christ,* 157.

121. Ibid.; see also ibid. at 151.

Behind the specific and sometimes fanciful identifications of Antichrist, however, lies an element of truth. That is, just as Christ's rule extends throughout this entire age, so the evil activities of the devil and his servants extend throughout the same time.[122] All the descriptions of Antichrist indicate a present, ongoing aspect in addition to a future, final manifestation. That suggests that the "spirit of antichrist" has been and will continue to be actualized in many times, places, and manners. Although many people speculate about what a "final" Antichrist may look like, that is not what the church is called to do. Hoekema reminds us, "We simply do not know how the final antichrist will arise or what form his appearance will take. In our day of rapid change, such a person could rise up in a very short time. In the meantime, we must always be alert to the presence of antichristian forces, movements, and leaders in our own day, as one of the continuing signs that we are living 'between the times.'"[123]

When Jesus appeared, he forced his contemporaries to make a choice, here articulated by N. T. Wright: "What does loyalty to Israel's god mean for a Palestinian Jew faced with the announcement that the long-awaited kingdom is now at last appearing? Jesus' zealous contemporaries would have said: Torah provides the litmus test of loyalty to Israel's god and to his covenant. Jesus said: what counts is following me."[124] The same issue still faces us today. John's imagery and the parallels he makes between Christ and the beast confront us with that choice and force us to deal with the questions: What is my first or ultimate priority? What is most important to me: Christ or the world, its institutions, and all that it has to offer? That issue is driven home by the fact that the dragon, the beast from the sea, and the beast from the land constitute a trinity competing with the Father, the Son, and Holy Spirit: "As the Son receives authority from the Father ([Rev] 2:27; 3:21), so the sea beast receives authority from the dragon, and as the Spirit glorifies the Son (John 16:14), so the second beast does with respect to the first beast (Rev. 13:12–15)."[125]

When John in Rev 13:18 refers to the need for wisdom and understanding in connection with the identification of the beast, he is not telling us to identify some particular person. Rather, John is calling us to understand and resist those beliefs, values, and forces within society that are demanding our allegiance in place of Christ. Resseguie concludes: "In its debased, fallen form humanity demands allegiance to its own self-serving values, norms, and beliefs. When that happens, humans and human institutions become bestial. The call for wisdom and understanding is also an exhortation to understand evil's deceptive nature and to resist the ideologies that support it.[126]

The purpose of Antichrist

According to 2 Thess 2:8–12, God uses Antichrist for his own purpose: to test human beings in order to reveal their true loyalties. Larry Harper describes this: "Those who have no 'love of the truth' will be taken in by his delusion and will thereby be left without

122. See Beale, *Revelation*, 691.

123. Hoekema, *Bible and Future*, 162.

124. Wright, *Victory*, 381.

125. Beale, *Revelation*, 729; see also Torrance, *Apocalypse Today*, 113.

126. Resseguie, *Revelation of John*, 191.

excuse. 'The cause of his advent' is, put simply, God's desire to sift all mankind to separate the wheat from the chaff, the wheat from the tares."[127] In his discussion of Antichrist and the apostasy, Irenaeus said the same thing:

> Throughout all time, man, having been molded at the beginning by the hands of God, that is, of the Son and of the Spirit, is made after the image and likeness of God: the chaff, indeed, which is the apostasy, being cast away; but the wheat, that is, those who bring forth fruit to God in faith, being gathered into the barn. And for this cause tribulation is necessary for those who are saved, that having been after a manner broken up, and rendered fine, and sprinkled over by the patience of the Word of God, and set on fire [for purification], they may be fitted for the royal banquet. As a certain man of ours said, when he was condemned to the wild beasts because of his testimony with respect to God: "I am the wheat of Christ, and am ground by the teeth of the wild beasts, that I may be found the pure bread of God."[128]

The sovereignty of God over both Satan and Antichrist

Paul's discussion of the *"man of lawlessness"* reveals that ultimately God is in charge of what is happening. He is working out his purposes through the *"lawless one"* whom *"the Lord will slay with the breath of His mouth and bring to an end by the appearance of His coming"* (2 Thess 2:8). God is the one who sends *"a deluding influence so that they will believe what is false, in order that they may all be judged who did not believe the truth, but took pleasure in wickedness"* (2 Thess 2:11–12). Similarly, with the "beasts" of Revelation God is in ultimate control: He is sovereign over Satan and his minions;[129] the authority granted the forces of evil is only temporary (see Rev 12:6, 12; 13:5); and the beast, the false prophet, the dragon, and their followers are permitted to arise and prosper for a season, only to be eternally destroyed by Christ.[130]

Consequently, we may not understand why God acts as he does, but we can have confidence that even the worst evils human beings and Satan can devise are subject to God's orchestration and are part of his overall plan: *"For God has put it in their hearts to execute His purpose by having a common purpose, and by giving their kingdom to the beast, until the words of God will be fulfilled"* (Rev 17:17).

---

127. Harper, *The AntiChrist*, 17n.35.

128. Irenaeus, *Haer.* 5.28.4.

129. See Rev 6:1–3, 5, 7, 9, 12; 9:1–2; 11:2–3; 13:5, 7; 20:1–3, 7.

130. See Rev 14:18–20; 17:8; 18:1–2, 21; 19:11–21; 20:9–10, 14–15. See also Osborne, *Revelation*, 492–93; Beale, *Revelation*, 695.

11

The Book of Revelation

Genre

VIRTUALLY ALL INTERPRETERS RECOGNIZE that Revelation comprises three genres: letter (epistle); prophecy; and apocalyptic.[1] The genres have been merged or mixed together. Therefore, as Beale puts it, "the most preferable view is that Revelation is 'a prophecy cast in an apocalyptic mold and written down in a letter form' in order to motivate the audience to change their behavior in the light of the transcendent reality of the book's message."[2]

Letter (epistle)

C. Marvin Pate outlines the epistolary framework of the book as follows: "Revelation is encased by an epistolary framework (1:4–8 and 22:10–21). . . . The prescript (1:4–8) contains the typical epistolary components—sender, addressees, greetings, and the added feature of a doxology. The postscript (22:10–21), in good ancient letter form, summarizes the body of the writing, as well as legitimates John as its divinely inspired composer."[3] The significance of Revelation's being a letter is that the book was written to be relevant and understandable to its first-century recipients.[4] Therefore, people who say that Revelation is a "secret code" that only applies to events that take place just before the second coming of Christ, thousands of years after the first century, are incorrect.[5]

---

1. Osborne, *Revelation,* 12; see also Carson and Moo, *Introduction,* 714–16.

2. Beale, *Revelation,* 39.

3. Pate, "Introduction," 12.

4. Johnson, *Triumph,* 27; see also Schnabel, *40 Questions,* 13–14. In this respect Revelation clearly contrasts with the Jewish apocalyptic book of *1 Enoch* in which the author states that he "saw a Holy vision in the Heavens, which the Angels showed to me. And I heard everything from them, and I understood what I saw: *but not for this generation, but for a distant generation that will come.*" *1 Enoch* 1:2, emphasis added.

5. Stylianopoulos, "I Know," 31 ("A literal reading of Revelation as a code book for deciphering

Prophecy

Both at the beginning and end of the book John calls Revelation a book of "prophecy."[6] Other passages talk about prophets or people prophesying.[7] This does not mean that Revelation is all about the future. For example, Rev 10:11 and 11:3 both use the word "prophesy." However, in both cases the term indicates proclaiming the word, righteous acts, and judgments of God, as opposed to "predicting the future."

We must recall the essential nature of biblical prophecy, i.e., oracles of judgment and oracles of salvation, designed to change people's behavior. That also is true of Revelation.[8] The fact that the entire book focuses on the present, was intended to be relevant to John's first-century audience, and is designed to affect the behavior of the readers, may be inferred from the fact that both at the beginning (Rev 1:3) and at the end (Rev 22:7) the reader is urged to "heed" the words of the prophecy.[9] Thus, as with all biblical prophecy, the prophetic element of Revelation discerns God's nature and purpose in the present circumstances of the churches, sees how God's ultimate purpose relates to the present situation, and calls for a response by the people.[10]

Apocalyptic

The first word of the book, *apokalupsis* (apocalypse; revelation), indicates the book's apocalyptic genre.[11] The essential meaning is to "reveal, disclose, bring to light, make fully

---

maps in history is a distortion and betrayal of its message"). Richard Bauckham notes that the popularized fundamentalist-dispensationalist interpretation of Revelation essentially misunderstands the genre of prophecy itself: "Conversely, fundamentalist interpretation, which finds in biblical prophecy coded predictions of specific events many centuries later than the prophet, misunderstands prophecy's continuing relevance by neglecting to ask what it meant to its first hearers." Bauckham, *Theology*, 152–53.

6. Rev 1:3; 22:7, 10, 18, 19.

7. Rev 2:20; 10:7; 11:3, 6, 10, 18; 16:6; 18:20, 24; 19:10; 22:6, 9.

8. See Schüssler Fiorenza, "Apokalypsis and Propheteia," 109 ("Rev proves to be a genuine expression of early Christian prophecy. . . . Whereas early Christian homily focuses on the interpretation and exposition of Scripture and tradition, early Christian prophecy announces judgment or salvation."). David Aune's analysis of the "seven letters to the seven churches" (Revelation 2–3) reveals that "the prophetic speech form which the central section of the seven proclamations most resembles is the salvation-judgment oracle, a development of postexilic Israelite prophecy." Aune, *Prophecy in Early Christianity*, 277; see also Ulfgard, *Feast and Future*, 13; Schüssler Fiorenza, *Revelation*, 46–47; Schnabel, *40 Questions*, 13.

9. See also Schnabel, *40 Questions*, 72, who also cites Rev 2:7, 11, 17, 29; 3:6, 13, 22; 13:9; 22:10 to the same effect.

10. See Bauckham, *Theology*, 148–49. The fact that the book of Revelation was designed to be understood by John's first-century audience is indicated by Rev 22:10 which says, *"Do not seal up the words of the prophecy of this book, for the time is near."* That is in contrast to Dan 8:26 where Daniel is told to *"keep the vision secret, for it pertains to many days in the future."*

11. It is important to note that, as with epistolary and prophetic literature, "apocalyptic literature does not just focus on coming events, but gives warning and comfort in the present situation as well." Ulfgard, *Feast and Future*, 11n.46.

known."[12] That is confirmed by the highly visionary and symbolic nature of the entire book.[13]

The essence of the book is symbolic

Revelation as a whole, beginning with Rev 1:1's use of *sēmainō* ("communicate by symbols") and *deichnumi* ("show"), together with the repeated introductory formula "I saw" or similar expressions,[14] denote the fact that the general nature of the book is symbolic, not "literal" or didactic.[15] The use of *sēmainō* in Rev 1:1 is an allusion to Daniel 2:28–29, 45 and means "symbolize."[16] The fact that Revelation is being communicated by symbols (which, in fact, fill the book) has important hermeneutical implications. Beale states that, in light of the explicitly symbolic nature of the book, "the dictum of the popular approach to Revelation—interpret literally unless you are forced to interpret symbolically—should be turned on its head. Instead, . . . the preceding dictum should be reversed to say 'interpret symbolically unless you are forced to interpret literally.' Better put, the reader is to expect that the main means of divine revelation in this book is symbolic."[17]

The sources of apocalyptic symbolism

John uses symbols because he saw visions that could not be expressed in words alone. Although many of Revelation's symbols may be esoteric (at least to us), the sources for interpreting them are not. John's primary sources for the imagery he uses are the OT, inter-testamental literature, and the Greco-Roman world of his own day, with which his first-century readers were familiar.[18] The extent of Revelation's dependence on the OT for its symbols is seen in the fact that Revelation contains approximately 630 allusions to the OT alone.[19] Consequently, to understand John's imagery we must look, not to political and other events of our day, but to the literature and socio-political situation of John's day.

---

12. BDAG, *"apokaluptō," "apokalupsis,"* 112.

13. A good three-part series of audio lectures by D. A. Carson concerning the nature and function of apocalyptic, with special emphasis on the book of Revelation, entitled "Preaching Apocalyptic," is available at: http://resources.thegospelcoalition.org/library?utf8=%E2%9C%93&query=carson+preaching+apocalyptic.

14. Rev 4:1; 12:1–3; 13:1–3; 14:1; 17:1–3, 20:1.

15. Beale, *Revelation,* 973; see also Schüssler Fiorenza, *Revelation,* 40.

16. Beale, "Purpose of Symbolism," 54.

17. Ibid., 55; see also Johnson, *Triumph,* 7. Kistemaker concurs, "For an apocalyptic book that is filled with symbolism a figurative explanation is not only sound exegesis, it is even desired." Kistemaker, "Temple," 441.

18. Osborne, *Revelation,* 17.

19. *UBS4,* 891–900. See also *UBS4,* 900–901 for additional allusions to biblical apocrypha and Jewish apocalyptic literature.

The nature of apocalyptic symbolism

"Apocalyptic pictures are not meant to be photographs of objective facts; they are often symbolic representations of almost unimaginable spiritual realities."[20] That is one reason why, as Dennis Johnson tells us, prophets often "describe their visions in cautious and ambiguous similes . . . lest we forget the limited capacity of human experience and language to convey heavenly reality."[21]

Different symbols may refer to the same thing but give us different perspectives or points of view on that subject; in Rev 4:1 heaven is pictured as a throne room, and in Rev 6:9 it is pictured as a temple. Ladd states, "It is precisely the fluidity of apocalyptic thinking which makes this possible. . . . In fact, God does not sit upon a throne; he is an eternal Spirit who neither stands or sits or reclines. The picture of God seated upon his throne is a symbolic way of asserting the kingship and sovereignty of the Deity."[22] Similarly, Christ is portrayed both as a lion (Rev 5:5) and as a lamb (Rev 5:6). Throughout the book, the church is described in different ways, often in ways that seem difficult to understand.[23] Symbols may also be multi-layered. For example, in Rev 17:1–4 John sees a woman who is a harlot; 17:8 says that she is *"the great city, which reigns over the kings of the earth"*; 17:5 calls her *"Babylon the great."* Babylon itself is not limited to a single city but is symbolic of a worldwide socio-economic and religious culture or civilization.[24]

Additionally, "paradox is central to the symbolism."[25] Thus, a recurrent pattern throughout the book is that "things are not what they appear to be." For example, the church at Philadelphia has *"little power"* (Rev 3:8); however, *because* of that fact Christ will make those of the "synagogue of Satan" come and *"bow down at your feet, and make them know that I have loved you"* (Rev 3:9). On the other hand, the church at Laodicea says, *"I am rich, and have become wealthy, and have need of nothing"*; however, the reality, according to Christ, is that they are *"wretched and miserable and poor and blind and naked"* (Rev 3:17). Throughout the book, Christians are depicted as being attacked and overcome by the forces of Satan and evil;[26] yet paradoxically, it is their very deaths, because of their faithfulness to the gospel, that reveal their victory.[27]

---

20. Ladd, *Commentary,* 102; see also Johnson, *Triumph,* 2 (the visions and symbols reveal the "invisible realities and forces that drive and therefore explain the course of observable historical events").

21. Johnson, *Triumph,* 216n.24 (e.g., *"there was something resembling a throne, like lapis lazuli in appearance"* [Ezek 1:26]; *"I saw something like a sea of glass mixed with fire"* [Rev 15:2]).

22. Ladd, *Commentary,* 102.

23. See below, the section "The church in Revelation."

24. Johnson, *Triumph,* 62–63.

25. Ibid., 9.

26. E.g., Rev 11:7; 13:7.

27. E.g., Rev 6:9–11; 12:11; 20:4–6.

Guidelines for interpreting symbols in Revelation

Some symbols are interpreted in Revelation itself

Seven stars are the angels of the seven churches (1:20); seven lampstands are the seven churches (1:20); seven lamps of fire are the seven Spirits of God (4:5, i.e., the Holy Spirit);[28] bowls of incense are prayers of the saints (5:8); the great dragon is Satan (12:9); the saints' fine linen, bright and clean, is the righteous acts of the saints (19:8). When the book itself defines some of the symbols, then whenever these symbols appear later in the book they likely mean the same thing as previously defined. The two lampstands in Rev 11:4 are an example of this, i.e., since the "two witnesses" of Rev 11:3 are said to be "two lampstands" (Rev 11:4), and lampstands previously have been defined as churches (Rev 1:20), the "two witnesses" likely are not individuals but symbolize the corporate church in its prophetic and witnessing role.[29]

Other symbols show continuity with other books of the OT or NT

Although John's images are based in the common world of the first-century readers, those images are not merely historical references. Richard Bauckham points out why: "Because John's images are images designed to penetrate the essential character of the forces at work in his contemporary world and the ultimate issues at stake in it, to a remarkable extent they leave aside the merely incidental historical features of his world."[30] That principle is seen in John's treatment of the OT. John, like all biblical prophets, interprets what had been written before for a new age and new circumstances. The primary integrating point is the first coming of Jesus Christ, which profoundly altered the theological landscape. As a result of the significance of Christ, although the images drawn from the OT remain recognizable, Dennis Johnson points out that "they are modified and recombined into new configurations—as we would expect, since the sacrifice and resurrection of the Lamb have brought the warfare of the ages to a new phase and theater of operations."[31] Given the new redemptive-historical situation and Christian context of Revelation, such OT entities and images as the temple, altar, and incense have been given new meanings.[32]

---

28. See below, concerning the use of numbers in Revelation.

29. Beale, "Purpose of Symbolism," 55–56. See also the discussion regarding the "two witnesses" below.

30. Bauckham, *Theology*, 156.

31. Johnson, *Triumph*, 13; see also Bauckham, *Climax of Prophecy*, 209; Bauckham, *Theology*, 144–45; Schüssler Fiorenza, *Revelation*, 31.

32. See, e.g., Rev 5:8; 6:9; 8:3–4; 21:22. Michel Gourgues notes the "essential difference" between Revelation and Jewish apocalyptic writings: "while in the Jewish apocalyptic writings the advent of the Messiah is expected at the end of time, in Revelation the Messiah has already come and is already reigning in heaven." Gourgues, "Thousand-Year Reign," 679, citing Rev 3:21; 5:12; 11:15; 14:14; 17:14; 19:16.

Those symbols that are not explicitly defined in the book need to be interpreted according to the context, the major idea that John is conveying, and the general purpose of prophetic symbolism

Osborne reminds us that the overarching *theological* significance of the symbols is paramount: "It is likely that God has chosen esoteric symbols from the common store of apocalyptic symbols in the first century in order to *turn the reader away from exactly what he is going to do and toward the theological meaning* of how he is going to do it. We do not know what is going to happen behind the picture of locust plagues, meteor showers, volcanic eruptions, and horrible storms. Some may happen literally, many will not. It is important to realize that we know no more about the second coming than Jesus' Jewish disciples did about the first."[33]

For example, Rev 16:16 (see also 20:9) refers to gathering the ungodly for war at a place called Har-Magedon. Milligan asks:

> Why Har-Magedon? There was, we have every reason to believe, no such place. The name is symbolical. It is a compound word derived from the Hebrew and signifying the mountain of Megiddo. We are thus taken back to Old Testament history, in which the great plain of Megiddo, the most extensive in Palestine, plays on more than one occasion a notable part. In particular, that plain was famous for two great slaughters, that of the Canaanitish host by Barak, celebrated in the song of Deborah [Judges 5], and that in which King Josiah fell [2 Chron 35:22]. The former is probably alluded to, for the enemies of Israel were there completely routed.[34]

Thus, the reference to Har-Magedon is not asserting that there will be a final physical battle at a particular (non-existent) mountain, plain, or camp, but is drawing a *theological connection* to show what will happen to all of Christ's enemies.[35]

Further, in interpreting Revelation's symbolism we must always bear in mind the moral and ethical purpose behind all prophecy, including apocalyptic: to get God's people to see spiritual reality from God's point of view and then respond to his will and purpose. Håkan Ulfgard, in dicussing the symbolism of Revelation's seals, trumpets, and bowls, says that "the function of this apocalyptic-prophetic writing is to *comfort* the readers in view of a persecution that has already begun and that will be even more accentuated, and to *challenge* them to endurance."[36] Beale adds, "Symbolic warnings shock true believers

---

33. Osborne, *Revelation*, 16, emphasis added.

34. Milligan, *Revelation*, 272; see also Schnabel, *40 Questions*, 233, 237.

35. Meredith Kline argues, for contextual and grammatical reasons, that "Har-Magedon" should really be transliterated as *"Har Mō'ed"* ("Mount of Assembly"). That would suggest that Har Magedon is Mount Zion and that the Har Magedon battle is the Gog-Magog crisis of Ezekiel 38–39, which is described or alluded to in Revelation 16:12–16; 19:11–21; 20:7–10 as the climactic effort to destroy the church that is terminated by Christ's *parousia*. Kline, "Har Magedon," 207–22. In Revelation, Mount Zion is used typologically to refer to "the church as the earthly expression of the heavenly Mount Zion." Johnson, *Triumph*, 235. Preterists likewise understand the symbolic nature of the Megiddo imagery but apply it to the destruction of Jerusalem in AD 70. See DeMar, *Last Days*, 317–19.

36. Ulfgard, *Feast and Future*, 29.

out of their spiritual laziness in going along with the sinful status quo of the unbelieving majority."[37]

Two common and important examples of the nonliteral use of language in Revelation

Numbers in Revelation

"Numbers are used in apocalyptic literature as symbols of ideas. This has been clearly demonstrated by comparative studies within the literature."[38] Their symbolic use in apocalyptic literature, including Revelation, is "flexible."[39] The four major numbers from which most of the other numbers in the book derive are 4, 7, 10, and 12. Osborne states that, although some consider numbers in Revelation as literal, "it seems more likely that the numbers in the book are meant symbolically, as was common in ancient apocalypses. Each of the numbers tends to signify wholeness or completeness throughout Scripture. . . . This does not mean that no number can be literal. There were of course twelve tribes and twelve apostles, but even that number was chosen by God for theological reasons."[40]

For example, Christ initially is seen as *"one like a son of man . . . and His eyes [implicitly two, as with men] were like a flame of fire"* (Rev 1:13–14). In Rev 5:6 Christ appears as *"a Lamb standing, as if slain, having seven horns and seven eyes."* Seven, as a number of fullness or completion, connotes Christ's omnipotence ("seven horns") and omniscience ("seven eyes" = fullness of vision).[41] In these examples we see the symbolic and flexible use of numbers characteristic of the apocalyptic genre.[42]

Time references in Revelation

Bauckham infers, "Since the 'one hour' of the reign of the ten kings with the beast (17:12) could not conceivably be intended literally, we should not expect any of the time periods in Revelation to be literal."[43] Similarly, the "ten days" of tribulation (Rev 2:10) clearly is not meant literally. As with so much else in the book, John is making *theological* connections, not giving us a precise, chronological "history written in advance."

In the middle of the book we see a time period that recurs, phrased in different ways: *"forty-two months"* (11:2; 13:5); *"twelve hundred and sixty days"* (11:3; 12:6); *"time, times, and half a time"* (12:14). These time periods are figurative, not literal.[44] They all

37. Beale, "Purpose of Symbolism," 59.

38. Summers, "Revelation 20," 180.

39. Johnson, *Triumph*, 15.

40. Osborne, *Revelation*, 17.

41. See Schüssler Fiorenza, *Revelation*, 60.

42. See also Schnabel, *40 Questions*, 61–4. Schnabel remarks, "This numerical symbolism suggests that unless there is a clear indication to a literal interpretation, the numbers in John's Apocalypse should be understood to have a symbolic meaning." Ibid., 63.

43. Bauckham, *Climax of Prophecy*, 449.

44. See Osborne, *Revelation*, 17–18. Schnabel notes that if those time periods were to be taken literally, and if the church knew when the literal time period begins, then Christians could calculate when the end would come. Since that is contrary to Jesus' many statements that the end is unknowable, the

stem from or are variants of times stated in Dan 7:25; 9:27; 12:7, 11–12. The time references in Daniel originally applied to the three and a half years of Antiochus Epiphanes's depredations against Israel until the success of the Maccabean revolt. In typical prophetic fashion, however, the inter-testamental Jewish writings took this time period to signify "a general time of trial for believers, as a time associated with Israel's Babylonian captivity, or as the period that must pass before Israel's final redemption."[45] John is taking that three-and-a-half year time period in its archetypal sense of a time of severe testing until God gives his people final relief and is applying it to the church. Rev 12:5–6 shows that this period of testing began at Christ's resurrection and ascension. It will end with his return in glory at the *parousia*.[46]

There is more to the "three and a half years" than simply an undetermined length of time that extends from Christ's ascension until the *parousia*. That is seen in how John has structured the time periods. The time of the Gentiles trampling the "holy city" (11:2) = the time of prophesying of the "two witnesses" (11:3) = the time the "woman" is in the wilderness (12:14). The *"forty-two months"* (11:2; 13:5), *"twelve hundred and sixty days"* (11:3; 12:6), and *"time, times, and half a time"* (12:14) are all different ways of referring to the same period, but the different ways of phrasing this time period indicate different perspectives or theological emphases. In their order of appearance and significance, they are arranged chiastically: the *"forty-two months"* focus on the church's enemies and their aggression against the church; whereas the *"twelve hundred and sixty days"* and *"time, times, and half a time"* focus on the church's witness and protection by God, as follows:[47]

> A. *42 months*: The "holy city" is trampled by the nations (Rev 11:1–2).
> B. *1260 days*: The "two witnesses" prophesy and cannot be harmed (Rev 11:3–6).
> B'. *1260 days [as expanded by "time, times, and half a time"]*: The "woman" is nourished and protected in the wilderness (Rev 12:6, 13–16).
> A'. *42 months*: The "beast" blasphemes and makes war against the "saints" (Rev 13:5).

"literal" interpretation cannot be correct. See Schnabel, *40 Questions*, 83; see also above, chapter 8, the section "The second coming of Christ is totally unpredictable."

45. Beale, *Revelation*, 565, citations omitted; see also Carson, "This Present Evil Age," 25–27; Storms, *Kingdom Come*, 483 (these time periods "are all *theological*, not chronological, designations. They have in view the *kind* or *quality* of time, not its duration."). Beale also suggests that the period of "forty-two" months is an allusion to Elijah (Luke 4:25; Jas 5:17) and Israel's wandering in the wilderness which involved forty-two encampments. Beale, *Revelation*, 565–68.

46. "These periods showing harmony in duration and extent appear to refer to an undetermined length that extends from Jesus' ascension to his return." Kistemaker, "Temple," 438; see also Beale, *Revelation*, 566–67; Beale and McDonough, "Revelation," 1119; Resseguie, *Revelation of John*, 30–31; Schüssler Fiorenza, *Revelation*, 75.

47. See Johnson, *Triumph*, 172; see also Silva, *NIDTTE*, 4:673 (These passages all "refer to the same period, the age of the church, which is one of prophetic witness and at the same time one of persecution. In the light of eternity it is a comparatively short amount of time, although when expressed in terms of days it may seem lengthy"); Bauckham, *Climax of Prophecy*, 401 (42 and 1260 are both "rectangular" numbers, i.e., the sum of successive even numbers, "to designate this ambiguous period in which the beast and the saints oppose each other," as opposed to "triangular" numbers, i.e., the sum of successive numbers, including 666 which represents the beast, and "square" numbers, i.e., the sum of successive odd numbers, including 144 which represents the saints).

Suffering and safety, trial and testimony, alienation and nourishment are all bound up in these descriptions of the time of testing of the church.[48] Through it all, these descriptions also demonstrate God's sovereigny over the church, Satan, suffering, and evil.

Interpretive approaches

Important questions regarding the book of Revelation are: To what extent is the book related to the first century (i.e., the time when it was written and the circumstances and audience to which it was addressed)? To what extent is it related to the period just before Jesus comes again? And to what extent is it trans-historical or principiant (i.e., deals with principles that apply throughout history, without specifically referring to particular historical events)? Different answers to these questions have led to five main interpretive approaches to the book.[49]

The preterist approach

The preterist approach contends that the book relates to the events in the first century. John is telling the churches how to cope with oppression and how God would deliver them from their oppressors. There are two basic variants of the preterist approach: The primary preterist position is that Revelation "is not concerned with either the scope of world history or the end of the world, but with events that were in the near future to St. John and his readers. . . . The Book of Revelation is a 'covenant lawsuit,' prophesying the outpouring of God's wrath on Jerusalem. It is a prophecy of the period known in Scripture as 'the Last Days,' meaning the last days of the covenantal nation of Israel, the forty-year 'generation' (Matt. 24:34) between the Ascension of Christ (A.D. 30) and the Fall of Jerusalem to the Romans (A.D. 70). It foretells events that St. John expected his readers to see very soon."[50] The second form of preterist interpretation holds that Revelation is a prophecy of the triumph of the church over its enemies: unbelieving Israel and the Roman Empire.[51]

---

48. Ibid., 183.

49. Beale, *Revelation*, 44–49 and Johnson, *Triumph*, 351–63 provide succinct overviews of the major interpretive schools. Gregg, *Revelation: Four Views*, is a parallel commentary (preterist, historicist, futurist, and idealist [spiritual]) of the entire book of Revelation.

50. Chilton, *Vengeance*, 51–52; see also Preston, *Like Father*, 17–18, 230.

51. Chilton, *Vengeance*, 165–66; Bahnsen, *Victory*, 9–22. C. Marvin Pate has recently argued that the seal judgments of Revelation 6 contain an "already, but not yet" aspect: they point back to the fall of Jerusalem in AD 70, but they also were forecasting the future fall of the Roman Empire which, he believes, in John's mind was coterminous with the *parousia*. Pate, "Revelation 6," 45–55.

Strengths of the preterist approach

The greatest strengths of this approach are the seriousness with which it takes the historical setting in which John wrote, the seven churches to whom he actually wrote, and the time references at the beginning and end of the book.[52]

Weaknesses of the preterist approach

WHEN THE BOOK OF REVELATION WAS WRITTEN

The preterist version which sees Revelation as being fulfilled in AD 70 can only be valid if the book was written before AD 70. Strong arguments have been made for that position.[53] Nevertheless, based both on internal and external evidence, the consensus of most scholars, both historically and today, is that the book was written during the reign of Domitian, around AD 95.[54]

THE TIME REFERENCES

The time references, beginning in Rev 1:1 (*"the things which must soon take place"*), are derived from Dan 2:28–29, 45. In Rev 1:1 John substituted "quickly" for Daniel's *"in the latter days."* Beale discusses the significance of John's substitution of wording: "quickly" in this context "connotes neither the speedy manner in which the Daniel prophecy is to be fulfilled nor the mere possibility that it could be fulfilled at any time, but the definite, imminent time of fulfillment, which likely has already begun in the present. . . . John's substitution of ['quickly'] implies his expectation that the final tribulation, defeat of evil, and establishment of the kingdom, which Daniel expected to occur distantly 'in the latter days,' would begin in his own generation, and, indeed, that it had already begun to happen."[55]

John's time references link the present and the future. They show that the principles about which he writes already are present and active. They are consistent with the "already, but not yet" nature of the kingdom and with the "signs" Jesus gave in the Olivet Discourse, which occurred in principle in his own generation yet allow the consummation to occur at an unpredictable time in the future.[56]

THE ESCHATOLOGICAL AND UNIVERSAL ASPECTS OF REVELATION

Perhaps the greatest problem with the preterist approach is that it does not take seriously the eschatological and universal aspects of Revelation. Preterism makes *Israel* the subject

---

52. I.e., Rev 1:1, 3; 2:10, 16; 3:10; 22:7, 10, 12, 20.

53. Gentry, *Before Jerusalem Fell*; Noe, "An Exegetical Basis," 781–84.

54. Beale, *Revelation*, 4–27.

55. Ibid., 181–82.

56. Full preterists, of course, contend that the signs not only were fulfilled in principle but were fulfilled in their entirety by AD 70.

of God's judgment in Revelation. However, Revelation's depiction of the "beasts" comes largely from Daniel 2 and 7.[57] Daniel's beasts describe four *world empires*, which also are the subject of God's ultimate judgment and the substitution of his own kingdom (Dan 2:34–35, 44–45). Further, Daniel 2 and 7 both contemplate *universal* judgment, not merely a local judgment such as occurred in AD 70.[58] The preterist view of Rev 19:11–21—that Christ divorces his unfaithful wife (Israel) and takes a new bride (the church)[59]—also does not correlate with that passage's apocalyptic context of universal judgment.[60]

Similarly, Rev 1:7 says that when Christ comes *"all the tribes of the earth will mourn over Him."* To limit that to mean "all the tribes of the *land* [of Israel]" when Christ came in judgment on Jerusalem in AD 70 is to ethnically, geographically, and temporally "obscure the passage's allusion to God's promise of international blessing to and through Abraham (Gen. 22:18). The circle of mourners will include not just Israel but also the Gentile nations."[61] Indeed, when Revelation later refers to *"every tribe"* (which corresponds to *"all the tribes"*) it clearly is referring to a multi-ethnic, multi-national multitude of the faithful (5:9; 7:9), or of rebels against Christ (11:9; 13:7).

Again, Rev 3:10 talks about an *"hour of testing"* that will come upon *"the whole world, to test those upon the earth."* The word translated "world" is the Greek *oikoumenē*, which refers to the entire earth and all its inhabitants or, sometimes, to the Roman Empire.[62] The word translated "earth" is *gē*, which refers to the entire earth or, sometimes, to some portion of it, such as the land of Israel.[63] Johnson remarks on the significance of the two Greek words in this context: "The interchangeability of *gē* and *oikoumenē* is one indication of the inadequacy of the preterist interpretation that limits Revelation's prophecies of judgment to the devastation of Jerusalem and the 'land' of Judea, culminating in 70."[64] The preterist version that sees Revelation fulfilled with the fall of the Roman Empire faces a similar problem. Ladd states, "While the Rome of John's day embodied antichristian tendencies, the portrait of Antichrist in Revelation 13 is far larger than historical Rome."[65] The final judgment simply was not fulfilled in the fall of Rome in the fifth century.

Preterism not only misses the universal scope of the judgment, but misses the universal scope of God's plan to renew creation to a state of perfect righteousness. It overlooks the symbolism of the New Jerusalem as a Holy of Holies and how the new heavens and new earth reverse and surpass the forces set in motion in Genesis 1–3 and thus are the

---

57. See above, chapter 10–The "Antichrist."

58. See Beale, *Revelation*, 44–45.

59. See Gentry, "A Preterist View," 80–81.

60. See Payne, *Encyclopedia*, 624n.150.

61. Johnson, *Triumph*, 52–53; contra Mathison, *Postmillennialism*, 261n.10; Preston, *Like Father*, 94, 314n.36. In this regard, since Rev 1:7 speaks of the mourners as *"those who pierced Him,"* it is important to remember that it was the Romans (gentiles), not the Jews, who actually "pierced" Jesus. In a greater sense, however, we *all* sent Christ to the cross and pierced him. Christ bore the sins and died for people of every "tribe, tongue, nation, and people" of the earth (Rev 5:9; 7:9). Hence, to limit the reference in Rev 1:7 to Israel is to miss the universal culpability of humanity and the universal atoning work of Christ.

62. BDAG, *"oikoumenē,"* 699.

63. Ibid., *"gē,"* 196.

64. Johnson, *Triumph*, 88n.35.

65. Ladd, *Commentary*, 9.

consummation of God's worldwide historical plan and drama going all the way back to Eden (see below). As Mark Stephens puts it, "John pushes the boundaries of his eschatology much further than many of Israel's prophets, by universalizing the results. For John, the 'end' was not simply the land of Israel, nor the people of Israel. His eschatological resolution embraces peoples from every tribe (Rev 7:9; 21:3), and the 'land' which is impacted is the entire earth. Furthermore, John's vision is a vision of eternity, as opposed to a vision of long life (see, for example, Isa 65:17–25)."[66] In a practical sense, therefore, all preterist views reduce the book largely to an historical account that has little relevance to the church since at least the fifth century, and which provides no hope concerning the future.

The historicist approach

This approach views Revelation as a symbolic prophecy of the entire history of the church, from its beginning until the *parousia*. The book's various symbols designate different historical movements and events in the Western world and the Christian church, such as the Goths, Muslims, the medieval papacy, the Reformation, etc.[67]

A variant of that approach sees the "seven letters to the seven churches" (Revelation 2–3) as describing the history of the entire church age in seven eras epitomized by the seven churches. Dispensationalist Chuck Smith, for example, sees the church at Ephesus as epitomizing the early church until the death of John (c. AD 99); Smyrna represents the church from the second through the fourth centuries; Pergamum is the beginning of the church-state system under Constantine and incipient Roman Catholicism; Thyatira is the Roman Catholic Church of the Middle Ages; Sardis represents the church of the Protestant Reformation; Philadelphia is the faithful church in the last days; and Laodicea is the apostate church in the last days.[68] That view was quite popular in the nineteenth century, particularly among dispensationalists, although it had adherents going back to the Middle Ages.

Strengths of the historicist approach

This approach takes seriously the historical setting in which John wrote and the fact that Revelation is applicable and relevant for all periods of church history until Christ returns.

Weaknesses of the historicist approach

Most historicists tend to view the literary order of the *visions* of the book as the chronological order in which certain events occur *in history* and tend to ignore the evidence of recapitulation in Revelation.[69] The historicist approach in general and the "seven

---

66. Stephens, *Annihilation or Renewal*, 259.

67. Ibid., 11; Beale, *Revelation*, 46.

68. Smith, *What the World*, 24–36; see also Scofield, *New Scofield*, 1353n.4; Ironside, *Great Parenthesis*, 123–24; Pentecost, *Things to Come*, 153; MacDonald, *Believer's*, 2355.

69. See below, the section "Structure: progressively parallel; not strictly chronological."

churches" variant have fallen out of favor largely because they are both subjective and arbitrary.[70] Typical of the criticisms of historicism are the following:

- *Ladd*: "There are no fixed guidelines as to what historical events are meant."[71]

- *Milligan*: "No one has been able to prepare a chronological scheme making even an approach to general acceptance. The history of the church cannot be portioned off into seven successive periods marked by characteristics to which those noted in the seven epistles correspond."[72]

- *Schaff*: "In regard to the number and length of the periods [of church history, represented by the seven churches] there is, indeed, no unanimity; the less, on account of the various denominational differences establishing different points of view, especially since the sixteenth century."[73]

- *Beale*: Historicism "tries to identify historical movements too specifically and limits prophecies of the Apocalypse to Western church history, leaving aside the worldwide church" and "such a projection of future history would have had little relevance to the first-century readers of Revelation."[74]

- *Payne*: "Advocates of the historical school of interpretation always seem to discover the climax of prophecy in their own day—a sure proof of the illegitimacy of this approach."[75]

The futurist approach

Futurists essentially take Rev 4:1—22:5 as depicting the "tribulation period" and its aftermath (i.e., the future period of time immediately before and after the *parousia*). There are essentially two futurist views which correspond to the two main premillennialist views: more moderate futurism corresponds to historic premillennialism; more extreme futurism corresponds to dispensationalist premillennialism.[76] Because moderate futurism does not make the sharp distinction between Israel and the church, it does not see a "pretribulational rapture" as implicit in Revelation. While it sees the bulk of the book as concentrating on the end of history, it does not see the visions of the book as necessarily

70. Thomas, "Chronological Interpretation," 323–27; Thomas, *Revelation 1–7*, 507–11; Osborne, *Revelation*, 105; see also Hamstra, "An Idealist View," 131. Interestingly, as if to prove one of the major criticism's of the historicist approach (i.e., that historicism is subjective and arbitrary), John Higgins, a pastor in the same denomination as Chuck Smith, contends that Sardis is not the church of the Protestant Reformation but was "the 'Renaissance' church" of the Middle Ages and the Enlightenment that introduced secular humanism into the church. Higgins, *Manasseh Effect*, 74–75. Further, he sees Philadelphia as the Reformation church which still continues today but is ending and will be followed by "the last age" (Laodicea) which is now emerging. Ibid.

71. Ladd, *Commentary*, 11.

72. Milligan, *Discussions*, 269.

73. Schaff, *History*, 1:14.

74. Beale, *Revelation*, 46.

75. Payne, *Encyclopedia*, 593.

76. Ladd, *Commentary*, 12.

indicating the chronological sequence of events that will transpire.[77] On the other hand, dispensationalists believe that the church is raptured at or before Rev 4:1 and is not present until 19:7 (where it is seen in heaven). Rev 4:1—19:7 is said to focus exclusively on the Israel of the future and chronologically describe the seven-year tribulation. Antichrist will make himself known and will begin the "great tribulation" against the 144,000 Jews who have converted to Christ and against others who do not support his rule.[78] After that will come the *parousia,* a literal millennium, judgment on unbelievers, and the new heaven and new earth (Rev 19:11—22:21).

Strengths of the futurist approach

The greatest strength of this approach is that it recognizes that Revelation does deal with events just before, at the time of, and after Christ's *parousia.*

Weaknesses of the futurist approach

Most futurists incorrectly view the *literary order* of the book's *visions* as the *chronological order* in which certain events occur *in history.*[79] Additionally, futurism renders virtually the entire book of Revelation irrelevant for John's original audience in the first century. Gentry correctly states that futurism "has to reinterpret phenomena in John's day to make them fit modern times. It overlooks the claims of the nearness of the events in Revelation."[80] The dispensationalist version of futurism further renders the book irrelevant to the church since it claims that the church will be "raptured" into heaven and will not experience any of the events on earth depicted in Rev 4:1—22:5. Finally, futurism, particularly in its dispensationalist form, often leads to speculation that is divorced from the first-century and church-centered context of the book. As a result, the relevance, power, and theological significance of the book's imagery are lost.

The idealist approach

Whereas both historicism and futurism tend toward specific and speculative identification of Revelation's images with particular historical (or presumed future) events, the opposite is true in idealism. The idealist approach sees Revelation as a symbolic portrayal of the conflict between good and evil, the kingdom of God and the powers of Satan.[81] Johnson comments, "In general, the idealist view is marked by its refusal to identify any of the images with specific future events, whether in the history of the church or with regard

---

77. Ibid.; see also Beale, *Revelation,* 47.

78. See Osborne, *Revelation,* 21; MacDonald, *Believer's,* 2361; Smith, *Tribulation,* 17–21; Smith, *What the World,* 39–40, 68–75, 120–24.

79. See below, the section "Structure: progressively parallel; not strictly chronological."

80. Gentry, "A Preterist View," 92; see also Johnson, *Triumph,* 20 ("Interpretations of the visions that lie completely beyond the original readers' frame of reference are suspect").

81. Ladd, *Commentary,* 11–12; Beale, *Revelation,* 48.

to the end of all things."[82] Strict idealism focuses on the trans-historical principles that the symbols represent. Accordingly, the beast represents satanic evil wherever it occurs in opposition to the church, and the seals, trumpets, and bowls represent God's judgment on evil throughout history.

Strengths of the idealist approach

Idealism, more than any other approach, correctly recognizes that theology and symbolism are central to Revelation. It sees that the book deals with issues and teaches principles that are relevant to the entire life of the church from the first century to the second coming.

Weaknesses of the idealist approach

The primary weakness of "pure" idealism is its failure to connect any of the prophecies of the book with history, either past, present, or future, although the book itself appears to do so from time to time.[83] "The problem with this alternative is that it holds that Revelation does not depict any final consummation to history, whether in God's final victory or in a last judgment of the realm of evil."[84]

Summary of the above four approaches

One might schematically and summarily critique the above views along the axes of relevance for the church today and hope for ultimate resolution in the future as follows:[85]

	Preterism	*Historicism*	*Futurism*	*Idealism*
Relevance	1st century—Yes After 1st century—No	Yes	1st century—Yes (chapters 2–3 only) After 1st century—No Just before *parousia*—Yes	Yes (in principle, but not historically)
Hope	No	Yes	Yes	No

82. Johnson, "Revelation," 410.

83. See Osborne, *Revelation*, 20.

84. Beale, *Revelation*, 48. Ironically, this is also a problem with full preterism which sees Revelation 21–22 as a description not of the final consummation but of the church. It sees the church age as "endless." Preston, *Like Father*, 54–55. Thus, according to full preterism, there is no end to sin, oppression, or death. Ibid., 262–63, 266; Preston, *AD 70*, 22.

85. To clarify the "No" answers: On the "Relevance" axis, the preterist view of Revelation makes the book not directly relevant for the church today because it contends that only the church of the first century (or up to the fifth century at most) was being addressed; since futurism contends that the church is raptured at Rev 4:1 and the vast bulk of the book (Rev 4:1—22:5) only pertains to Israel and the seven years before the *parousia*, that view likewise renders the vast bulk of the book irrelevant for the church today. On the "Hope" axis, all preterist views give no hope for the future because they see Revelation essentially as history that ended in AD 70 or at the latest with the fall of Rome in the fifth century; pure idealism and full preterism give no hope for the future because they do not view the book as depicting any future consummation.

The eclectic approach

Each of the above approaches has certain strengths but also weaknesses. Consequently, most Evangelical and Reformed interpreters utilize various aspects of all the approaches in interpreting the book of Revelation.[86] This fifth alternative approach may be described as "modified idealism" or "eclecticism."[87] This approach is consistent with biblical prophecy and apocalyptic in general: prophecies based on specific events result in themes and principles that apply throughout history; the prophets take prophecies relating to one event, time, and place, and rework and apply them to other events, times, and places; specific events often serve as examples or paradigms for later events or principles. The following commentators elaborate this:

- *Witherington*: "John's Revelation is on target for his Asian audience, but the symbols he uses are flexible enough that they could and would be appropriately used to address many another situation of crisis in church life."[88]

- *Milligan*: "As on so many other occasions, [John] starts from what is limited and local only to pass in thought to what is unlimited and universal. His Jerusalem, his Babylon, is not the literal city. She is 'the great harlot that sitteth upon many waters;' and 'the waters which thou sawest,' says the angel to the Seer, 'are peoples, and multitudes, and nations, and tongues [Rev 17:1, 5, 15].'"[89]

The principles of idealism, utilized in the eclectic approach, provide practicality for the faith and life of the church from the first century to the *parousia*. However, the eclectic approach recognizes that Revelation does more than set forth ongoing principles; it describes both first-century events and also the consummation of the ages. Consequently, this approach provides ultimate hope for believers. This is the approach that will be presented here.

The situation of the late first-century churches

"The book of Revelation reflects conflict among Christians, conflict between Christians and Jews, and conflict between Christians and the representatives of Rome. The work attempts to interpret these conflicts and to resolve them in accordance with its own perspective."[90]

The kingdom and the culture

Revelation raises a fundamental question faced by many Christians: Since God is sovereign and Christ already has inaugurated his kingdom, why is the culture so pagan and we suffer? First-century Greco-Roman religion was linked to various cultural, social,

---

86. See, e.g., Beale, *Revelation*; Johnson, *Triumph*; Osborne, *Revelation*; Smalley, *Revelation*.
87. Beale, *Revelation*, 48–49.
88. Witherington, *Revelation*, 25.
89. Milligan, *Revelation*, 295.
90. Yarbro Collins, "Book of Revelation," 400.

economic, and political practices. Christians therefore were faced with sometimes difficult choices concerning when to acquiesce to the prevailing practices and when and how to resist.[91] Those same issues, of course, confront Christians today.

There were at least three religious factors facing the churches in the first century that had legal implications. First, in Roman society, the different trade guilds all had their own patron gods. The effect of those patron gods is indicated by Beale:

> Apparently, a significant group among the Asia Minor churches did not think it a grave sin to show open expression of loyalty to such trade guild deities. This was especially the case when they were expected to pay their "dues" to trade guilds by attending annual dinners held in honor of the guilds' patron deities. Homage to the emperor as divine was included along with worship of such local deities. For the culture in general these expressions of loyalty were part of being patriotic.... Refusal to show gratefulness to these gods was bad citizenship.[92]

Second, the churches were facing the rise of emperor worship.[93] This had both religious and social implications, as Witherington mentions: "John's revelation comes to him at a time when the imperial cult was increasingly being used as the social glue to bind each major Asian city, but also the province, together.... Texts such as Rev. 13.4; 15–16; 14.9–11; 15.2; 16.2; 19.20; 20.4, which refer or allude to worship of the Beast, likely reflect the impact of the emperor cult on John and other early Christians."[94]

Third, as was discussed in connection with the Olivet Discourse, the legal vulnerability of the churches was exacerbated by a changed legal status of Christianity in relation to Judaism after AD 70. In light of that changed legal status, it is possible that some Jewish leaders informed local officials that Christians were not a sect of Judaism and therefore were not entitled to practice their religion outside of Palestine where Christianity originated. In any event, Revelation reflects that opposition to Christianity derived not only from the Roman state but also from Judaism (Rev 2:9; 3:9).

The issue of persecution

Related to the issue of the kingdom and culture is the issue of persecution. Although in the last years of his reign Nero systematically persecuted Christians in Rome itself, "there is no evidence that during the last decade of the first century there occurred any open and systematic persecution of the church."[95] Nevertheless, Revelation indicates that by the end of the first century the churches in Asia were experiencing at least sporadic instances of persecution (Rev 1:9; 2:10, 13). John may be foreseeing that existing trends in

91. See Beale, *Revelation,* 28.

92. Ibid., 30.

93. Yarbro Collins comments, "The imperial cult was a ubiquitous and impressive phenomenon in the regions in which the seven cities of the book of Revelation were located." Yarbro Collins, "Book of Revelation," 395–96. There were eighty imperial temples in the sixty cities of Asia Minor; the cult was also celebrated in the theatre and the stadium; the emperor was regularly associated with the gods and sometimes presented as a god himself, including his depiction as a god on coins. Ibid., 396.

94. Witherington, *Revelation,* 25; see also Schüssler Fiorenza, *Revelation,* 54.

95. Ladd, *Commentary,* 8.

society will lead to increased persecution in the future.[96] Thus, Revelation is replete with examples that both warn believers of coming persecution and exhort them to be faithful witnesses to death.[97]

Internal problems

As the letters to the seven churches (Revelation 2–3) make clear, "the problems which directly confronted the churches of John's time, and shaped the contents of Revelation, arose from *within* his community, and not merely from beyond it."[98] Those problems included: lack of love (2:4); false teaching (2:14–15); immorality based on false teaching and false prophecy (2:20–21, 24); spiritual deadness, lack of faithfulness, lack of perseverance (3:1–4); lukewarmness and pride (3:15–17).

Purposes and themes

As we observe the situations of the first-century churches and consider Jesus' analysis of those churches in Revelation 2–3, we will see parallels to the trials we face and issues we confront today. The purposes and themes of the book help orient us to the book and give us an overall grasp of what it is all about. These purposes and themes are interrelated and have been expressed in various ways. The following are representative.

To explain to the church how God is dealing with the world

Wilbur Smith has highlighted an important aspect of Revelation's structure and the significance of that structure:

> Many scenes of this book are located in heaven, while the judgments themselves take place on this earth; and the scenes in heaven always precede the earthly events to which they are attached. . . . I have always felt that there are two great truths to be drawn from this phenomenon. First, what is about to take place on earth, though unknown to man and unexpected by him, is fully known to those in heaven. . . . Secondly, what is to take place on earth is under the complete control and direction of heaven, so that we may safely say, judging from this book, as well as from other prophetic books in the Scripture, that everything that takes place on this earth only fulfills the Word of God.[99]

Walter Elwell similarly states:

> The purpose of Revelation is ultimately to explain to the church how God is dealing with the world. . . . A fundamental theme that runs through Revelation is that life and history can be observed from two points of view. We may look at the problems, persecution, sufferings, evil, and distress that surround us and

---

96. Stylianopoulos, "I Know," 25.
97. See, e.g., Rev 3:10; 6:9–11; 7:13–17; 11:3–12; 12:1–17; 13:7; 17:14; 19:7–10; 20:4–6.
98. Smalley, *Revelation*, 4.
99. Smith, "Revelation," 1497.

become discouraged; or we may look beyond that to the glorious eternal realities that also surround us—God, Christ, the saints of old, the angels, the throne of God, the music, color, sound, and beauty of heaven, the New Jerusalem with its streets of gold, and the victory already won. The choice is ours; both perspectives are true.[100]

John is explaining through visions and symbols that God is fulfilling his eternal plan. As Richard Bauckham states, the point of the book is "not so much to enable them [the seven churches to whom John was writing] to foresee the future as to enable them to see their present from the perspective of the future."[101] It might not appear obvious to us in this world that God is fulfilling his plan. However, as Dennis Johnson succinctly puts it, "One of the key themes of the book is that things are not what they seem."[102]

A call to perseverance in the struggle with the powers of evil

Alien cultural values, sporadic persecution, legal and social vulnerability, and pressure from both the state and Jews would have tempted Christians to compromise their faith and practice. Revelation makes clear that, from the first century to the *parousia,* there will be evil and attempts to suppress the witness of the church. God's plan includes martyrdom for many of his people. Therefore, God's people are to remain faithful despite hardship and keep the words of the prophecy that are written in the book (Rev 1:3; 22:7). R. Fowler White states, "Like Jesus' initial kingship, the church's kingship consists now in conquering by maintaining her faithful witness in the face of trials (e.g., 2:9–11, 13; 3:8; 12:11); in overcoming the powers of evil (e.g., 6:8 in relation to 6:9–11); in subduing sin in her members' lives (see chaps. 2–3); and in beginning to rule over death and Satan by identification with Jesus (cf. 1:5–6, 18). The church's endurance, then, is part of the process of conquering."[103] Elisabeth Schüssler Fiorenza summarizes, "John seeks to move [his audience] to control their fear, to renew their commitment, and to sustain their vision."[104]

To comfort and encourage Christians because Christ is victor

Revelation demonstrates that God is sovereign over all of history, over all evil, and is orchestrating the events of history to glorify his name and bring about a glorious, eternal conclusion for his people. As Sam Hamstra tells us, Revelation "shows us a God of love and power, who triumphs sovereignly over all his and our enemies. Human history, as we know it, will culminate when Satan suffers eternal defeat and the bridegroom embraces

100. Elwell, "Revelation," 1200–01.

101. Bauckham, *Theology,* 167.

102. Johnson, *Triumph,* 9.

103. White, "Agony, Irony," 175.

104. Schüssler Fiorenza, *Revelation,* 37. Schüssler Fiorenza concludes that the Greek word *hupomonē* (patience; perseverance; steadfastness), which is found at Rev 1:9; 2:2, 3, 19; 3:10; 13:10; 14:12, is a primary Christian virtue throughout the book. The reason is that "Christian existence is determined by the conjunction of oppressive eschatological tribulations with the Christian claim to share in the divine empire and royal power of God, which requires consistent resistance and steadfast perseverance." Schüssler Fiorenza, *Revelation,* 51.

his bride. The church will enjoy eternal joy and peace with Jesus."[105] William Hendriksen summarizes this important theme as follows:

> In the main, the purpose of the book of Revelation is to comfort the militant Church in its struggle against the forces of evil. It is full of help and comfort for persecuted and suffering Christians. To them is given assurance that God sees their tears (7:17; 21:4); their prayers are influential in world affairs (8:3, 4) and their death is precious in His sight. Their final victory is assured (15:2); their blood will be avenged (19:2); their Christ lives and reigns for ever and for ever. He governs the world in the interest of His Church (5:7, 8). He is coming again to take His people to Himself in "the marriage supper of the Lamb" and to live with them for ever in a rejuvenated universe (21:22). . . . Throughout the prophecies of this wonderful book Christ is pictured as the Victor, the Conqueror (1:18; 2:8; 5:9ff.; 6:2; 11:15; 12:9ff.; 14:1; 15:2ff.; 19:16; 20:4; 22:3). He conquers death, Hades, the dragon, the beast, the false prophet, and the men who worship the beast. *He* is victorious; as a result, so are *we*, even when we seem hopelessly defeated.[106]

Structure: general considerations

The complexity, unity, and importance of structure

The more one studies the book of Revelation the more one is impressed by the intricacy of its design. Dennis Johnson comments, "The interconnections in Revelation may be so complex that one structural outline cannot do it full justice. Here we may have not a two-dimensional jigsaw puzzle but a three-dimensional Rubik's cube."[107] Despite its literary complexity, Richard Bauckham's study of Revelation reveals that it is "actually one of the most unified works in the New Testament. . . . Revelation was evidently designed to convey its message to some significant degree on first hearing (cf. 1:3), but also progressively to yield fuller meaning to closer acquaintance and assiduous study."[108]

This structural design is important for our understanding the book, especially given its apocalyptic and symbolic nature. Ranko Stefanovic summarizes the importance of the structure of the book for understanding its content: "It appears that the rich structural design of the book of Revelation was well planned by the inspired author. This design is, thus, very significant for understanding the sweeping thematic progression of the book. It warns the reader against studying and interpreting a passage or section in isolation from the rest of the book. Any interpretation of the text must be in agreement with the general purpose of the book as a whole."[109]

---

105. Hamstra, "An Idealist View," 127.

106. Hendriksen, *More Than Conquerors*, 7–8.

107. Johnson, *Triumph*, 35.

108. Bauckham, *Climax of Prophecy*, 1n.1, 1.

109. Stefanovic, "Finding Meaning," 43; see also Schüssler Fiorenza, *Revelation*, 32.

Repetition of phrases and ideas

Part of Revelation's complex, unified literary structure is revealed in its pattern of the repetition of phrases and ideas. Several phrases and ideas recur, often in widely separated passages, and sometimes in slightly varying form. Bauckham points out, "These repetitions create a complex network of textual cross-reference, which help to create and expand the meaning of any one passage by giving it specific relationships to many other passages."[110] One reason for the repetition of key phrases may be because John was writing for *hearers* as well as for readers (Rev 1:3). "In a text intended for oral performance the structure must be indicated by clear linguistic markers."[111]

Repetition of phrases and ideas helps tie the book together and reinforce its basic message

Phrases, substantive ideas, and promises to the church are introduced at the beginning of the book and find their fulfillment at the end of the book:

1:1; 22:6: "to show to His servants"	2:7, 11, 17, 26; 3:5, 12, 21; 21:7: "who overcomes"
1:1; 22:6: "things which must soon take place"	2:7; 22:2, 14: "the tree of life"
1:1; 22:6, 16: Jesus sends his angel	2:10–11; 20:6; 21:4: deliverance from the "second death"
1:2; 19:10; 20:4: "the testimony of Jesus"	2:16; 3:11; 22:7, 12, 20: "I am coming quickly"
1:3; 22:7: "blessed is he . . . who heeds"	2:17; 19:12: A name "no one knows"
1:3; 22:7: "the words of the prophecy"	2:23; 20:12; 22:12: "according to . . . deeds"
1:3; 22:10: "the time is near"	2:27; 19:15: "He will rule them with a rod of iron"
1:4; 22:16: "the seven churches"	2:28; 22:16: "morning star"
1:6; 20:6: "priests of God"	3:4, 5, 18; 19:8, 14: clean, white garments
1:8; 21:6; 22:13: "the Alpha and the Omega"	3:5; 20:12, 15; 21:27: "book of life"
1:8; 21:22: "the Almighty"	3:12; 21:22: temple
1:14; 2:18; 19:12: eyes "like a flame of fire"	3:12; 22:4: God's name on overcomers
1:16; 2:16; 19:15: sword from Christ's mouth	3:12; 21:2, 10: New Jerusalem comes from heaven
1:17; 22:13: "the first and the last"	3:21; 20:4: overcomers sit on thrones
1:18; 20:14: "death and Hades"	

---

110. Bauckham, *Climax of Prophecy*, 22.

111. Ibid., 3; see also Schüssler Fiorenza, *Revelation*, 40.

Repetition of phrases and ideas reinforces theological parallels and contrasts John wants his readers to see

Rev 17:1—19:10 and Rev 21:9—22:9 parallel each other. They both deal with cities that are portrayed as women: "In 17:1—19:10 he sees the harlot of Babylon and her fall; in 21:9—22:9 he sees the bride of the Lamb, the New Jerusalem, which comes down from heaven. Together these two sections form the climax towards which the whole book has aimed: the destruction of Babylon and her replacement by the New Jerusalem."[112] Consequently, both sections begin and end almost identically

17:1–3: *"Then one of the seven angels who had the seven bowls . . . came and spoke with me, saying, 'Come here, I will show you' . . . And he carried me away in the Spirit."*	21:9–10: *"Then one of the seven angels who had the seven bowls . . . came and spoke with me, saying, 'Come here, I will show you' . . . And he carried me away in the Spirit."*
19:9b–10: *"And he said to me, 'These are true words of God.' Then I fell at his feet to worship him. But he said to me, 'Do not do that; I am a fellow servant of yours and your brethren who hold the testimony of Jesus; worship God.'"*	22:6–9: *"And he said to me, 'These words are faithful and true . . . And when I heard and saw, I fell down to worship at the feet of the angel who showed me these things. But he said to me, 'Do not do that. I am a fellow servant of yours and of your brethren the prophets and of those who heed the words of this book. Worship God.'"*

The subtlety of the book's structure is seen in that the main enemies of God and his people make their principal appearances in this order: Death and Hades (6:8); the dragon (12:3); the beast and false prophet (13:2; 13:11 [discounting the anticipatory reference in 11:7]); Babylon (17:1 [discounting the anticipatory reference in 14:8]). Their destruction is in the reverse order, creating a chiastic arrangement: Babylon (18:1–24); the beast and false prophet (19:20); the dragon (20:10); Death and Hades (20:14).[113]

Basic structure of content

Many commentators see a basic two-part structure of the content of the book: chapters 1–11 and 12–22. These two major sections can be seen as unfolding the messages of the two books (scrolls) of Revelation: the sealed book of 5:1–5, whose message is unfolded in 6:1—11:9; and the "little book" of 10:2, 8–10, whose message is unfolded in 12:1—21:8.[114] Hendriksen further comments on the content of the two halves of the book: "The first major division (chapters 1–11) reveals the Church, indwelt by Christ, persecuted by the world. But the Church is avenged, protected and victorious. The second major division (chapters 12–22) reveals the deeper spiritual background of this struggle. It is the conflict

---

112. Bauckham, *Climax of Prophecy*, 4–5.

113. Beale observes, "This reversal points further to a lack of concern for chronological sequence in the Apocalypse. The four foes are eliminated simultaneously, as is evident from the repetition of the wording and OT allusions in the descriptions of their defeat (e.g., 'gather together for the battle' [16:14; 19:19; 20:8])." Beale, *Revelation*, 812.

114. McGinn, *Anti-Christ*, 50.

between the Christ and the dragon in which the Christ, and therefore His Church, is victorious."[115]

Basic literary structure

There have been many proposed literary structures of Revelation. Ralph Korner summarizes the bases of the different proposals:

> Some proposals have used implicit indicators as structural organizers. Some examples of this approach involve chiasm, intercalation, reiteration and encompassing. Other suggestions have emphasized the use of explicit textual indicators such as: "in the Spirit"; "what is now and what will take place later"; "come and see"; "earthquake"; and, of course, the number "7." Regarding the use of the number 7, some scholars propose an overall septenary outline for the Apocalypse within which is included the explicit references to the 7 Churches, the 7 Seals, the 7 Trumpets and the 7 Bowls.[116] Some outlines with less than seven major sections provide a septenary structure only for each major textual section. And, finally, some have combined the two above approaches resulting in an overall septenary outline for the Apocalypse within which is incorporated a sevenfold structure for a number of those self-same sections.[117]

Representative structural outlines

One reason why commentators have proposed different structures for the book is that both substantive theological content and literary markers must be taken into account. Some commentators give primacy to content, while others may give greater weight to literary factors. The following represent some of the more well thought-out models of the book's structure.

a. *G. K. Beale*[118]

1:1–20: Prologue

2:1—3:22: The letters to the seven churches: Christ encourages the churches to witness, warns them against compromise, and exhorts them to hear and to overcome compromise in order to inherit eternal life.

4:1—5:14: God and Christ are glorified because Christ's resurrection demonstrates that they are sovereign over creation to judge and to redeem.

115. Hendriksen, *More Than Conquerors,* 23; see also Payne, *Encyclopedia,* 594.

116. Revelation's pattern of seven plagues (seals-trumpets-bowls) appears to be based on Leviticus 26. Beale, *Revelation,* 803; Johnson, *Triumph,* 223. "As in Leviticus, and as throughout Revelation, the number of seven judgments is figurative for many severe judgments and does not refer to a literal seven woes." Beale, *Revelation,* 803. There are factors that militate against many of the book's proposed seven-part structures, some of which seem "forced." Johnson, *Triumph,* 35–41; see also Schüssler Fiorenza, *Revelation,* 73.

117. Korner, "And I Saw," 160–62, citations omitted.

118. Beale, *Revelation,* x–xvi.

6:1—8:5: The seven seals

8:6—11:19: The seven trumpets

12:1—15:4: Deeper conflict

15:5—16:21: The seven bowl judgments: God punishes the ungodly during the inter-advent age and consummately at the last day because of their persecution and idolatry

17:1—19:21: Final judgment of Babylon and the beast

20:1-15: The millennium is inaugurated during the chuch age as God limits Satan's deceptive powers and as deceased Christians are vindicated by reigning in heaven. The millennium is concluded by a resurgence of Satan's deceptive assault against the church and the final judgment.

21:1—22:5: The new creation and the church perfected in glory.

22:6-21: Conclusion

b. *Introductory sanctuary scene model*[119]

Prologue (1:1–8)

1. Introductory scene (1:9–20)

The seven churches (2:1—3:22)

2. Introductory scene (4:1—5:14)

The seven seals (6:1—8:1)

3. Introductory scene (8:2–6)

The seven trumpets (8:7—11:18)

4. Introductory scene (11:19)

The wrath of the nations (12:1—15:4)

5. Introductory scene (15:5–8)

The wrath of God (16:1—18:24)

6. Introductory scene (19:1–10)

The final judgment (19:11—20:15)

7. Introductory scene (21:1–8)

The New Jerusalem (21:9—22:5)

Epilogue (22:6–21)

c. *A chiastic [ideas are repeated in inverted order] model*[120]

A. Prologue (1:1–8)

---

119. Paulien, "Role of the Hebrew Cultus," 248. Note that all the introductory scenes are visionary or are explicitly set in heaven and employ OT cultic imagery. Stefanovic, "Finding Meaning," 32 slightly modifies this.

120. Stefanovic, "Finding Meaning," 38–40.

  B. Promises to the overcomer (1:9—3:22)

   C. God's work for man's salvation (4:1—8:1)

    D. God's wrath mixed with mercy (8:2—9:21)

     E. Commissioning John to prophesy (10:1—11:18)

      F. Great controversy between Christ and Satan (11:19—13:18)

     E'. Church proclaims the end-time gospel (14:1-20)

    D'. God's final wrath unmixed with mercy (15:1—18:24)

   C'. God's work for man's salvation completed (19:1—21:4)

  B'. Fulfillment of the promises to the overcomer (21:5—22:5)

 A'. Epilogue (22:6-21)

d. *Richard Bauckham*[121]

 1:1-8: Prologue

 1:9—3:22: Inaugural vision of Christ and the churches including seven messages to the churches

 4:1—5:14: Inaugural vision of heaven leading to three series of sevens and two intercalations:

 6:1—8:1; 8:3-5: Seven seals, numbered 4+1+(1+intercalation)+1

 8:2; 8:6—11:19: Seven trumpets, numbered 4+1+(1+intercalation)+1

 12:1—14:20; 15:2-4: The story of God's people in conflict with evil

 15:1; 15:5—16:21: Seven bowls, numbered (4+3) without intercalation

 17:1—19:10: Babylon the harlot

 19:11—21:8: Transition from Babylon to the New Jerusalem

 21:9—22:9: The New Jerusalem the bride

 22:6-21: Epilogue

e. *William Hendriksen*[122]

 1. Christ in the midst of the lampstands (1:1—3:22)

 2. The vision of heaven and the seals (4:1—7:17)

 3. The seven trumpets (8:1—11:19)

 4. The persecuting dragon (12:1—14:20)

 5. The seven bowls (15:1—16:21)

 6. The fall of Babylon (17:1—19:21)

 7. The great consummation (20:1—22:21)

---

121. Bauckham, *Climax of Prophecy*, 21–22.
122. Hendriksen, *More Than Conquerors*, 16–18.

f. *Elisabeth Schüssler Fiorenza*[123]

A. 1:1–8: Prologue and Epistolary Greeting

 1:1–3: Title

 1:4–6: Greetings

 1:7–8: Motto

B. 1:9—3:22: Rhetorical Situation in the Cities of Asia Minor

 1:9–10: Author and Situation

 1:11–20: Prophetic Inaugural Vision

I. 2:1—3:22: Prophetic Messages to Seven Communities

C. 4:1—9:21; 11:15–19: Opening the Sealed Scroll: Exodus Plagues

 4:1—5:14: Heavenly Court and Sealed Scroll

II. 6:1—8:1: Cosmic Plagues: Seven Seals

III. 8:2—9:21; 11:15–19: Cosmic Plagues: Seven Trumpets

D. 10:1—15:4: The Bitter-Sweet Scroll: "War" against the Community

 10:1—11:14: Prophetic Commissioning

 12:1—14:5: Prophetic Interpretation

 14:6—15:4: Eschatological Liberation

C'. 15:5—19:10: Exodus from the Oppression of Babylon/Rome

IV. 15:5—16:21: Cosmic Plagues: Seven Bowls

 17:1–18: Rome and Its Power

 18:1—19:10: Judgment of Rome

B'. 19:11—22:9: Liberation from Evil and God's World-City

 19:11—20:15: Liberation from the Powers of Evil

 21:1–8: The Liberated World of God

 21:9—22:9: The Different Cosmopolis of God

A'. 22:10–21: Epilogue and Epistolary Frame

 22:10–17: Revelatory Sayings

 22:18–21: Epistolary Conclusion

Structure: progressively parallel; not strictly chronological

In order to understand how Revelation is put together and what it means we must understand that the book is not simply a chronological narrative. Stephen Travis emphasizes

---

123. Schüssler Fiorenza, *Revelation*, 35–36. The Roman numerals indicate explicitly numbered seven-series.

the crucial point that in Revelation "the fact that the *visions* follow in sequence is not necessarily a reason for believing that they represent a continuous *historical* sequence."[124] Prophetic books (e.g., Isaiah) frequently record visions or prophecies in a different order from the order in which they are actualized history. Similarly, prophetic books (e.g., Daniel) frequently include different visions that repeat or recapitulate the same events from different perspectives.

Revelation draws heavily from such OT books as Isaiah, Ezekiel, and Daniel. Beale discusses the significant *structural* similarity between Revelation and Daniel:

> Daniel's structure of five synonymously parallel visions (chs. 2, 7, 8, 9, 10–12) may be the most influential on the structure of Revelation, since Daniel is used so much in the book and is used to signal the broad structural divisions of the Apocalypse.... Daniel's five parallel visions are supplemental perspectives about the same general period of the future; it would be unexpected for a book like Revelation to model itself on Daniel's parallel structure and yet have its parallel sections not also pertain to the same general period of the future.[125]

In light of the above, most commentators see the book's different sections as being essentially parallel to each other: the same substantive events may be repeated in different visions (using different imagery) and in different literary units. These parallel sections encompass the entire church age; they overlap both temporally and thematically (i.e., recapitulate each other); and they conclude with the end of the age, the *parousia*, the judgment, and the new heavens and new earth. Even though they recapitulate each other, the parallel sections show some chronological and thematic progression, i.e., earlier in the book the end is reached, but the end assumes greater focus and becomes more exhaustively described in later parallel accounts. William Hendriksen first called this "progressive parallelism" because the different sections of the book are "arranged in an ascending, climactic order. There is progress in eschatological emphasis. The final judgment is first *announced* then *introduced* and finally *described.* Similarly, the new heaven and earth are described more fully in the final section than in those which precede it."[126] This is the view taken by Victorinus of Pettau (died c. 304), Bishop of Poetovio (modern Ptuj, Slovenia), author of the earliest complete commentary on Revelation that has come down to us.[127]

---

124. Travis, *I Believe*, 142; see also Johnson, *Triumph*, 32, 43, 129, 140, 146, 163, 215; Schnabel, *40 Questions*, 67–68, 274.

125. Beale, *Revelation*, 135–36.

126. Hendriksen, *More Than Conquerors*, 36.

127. Bruce, "Earliest Latin Commentary," 352–53. In chapter 8 of his commentary, regarding the relationship of the trumpets and bowls, Victorinus states: "The '*trumpet*' is the word of power. And although there is a repetition of scenes by the *bowls*, this is not spoken as though the events occurred twice. Rather, since those events that are future to them have been decreed by God to happen, these things are spoken twice. And therefore, whatever he said rather briefly by way of the trumpets he said more completely by way of the bowls. Nor ought we to pay too much attention to the order of what is said. For the sevenfold Holy Spirit, when he has passed in revue the events to the last time, to the very end, returns again to the same times and supplements what he had said incompletely. Nor ought we inquire too much into the order of the Revelation. Rather, we ought inquire after the meaning, for there is also the possibility of a false understanding." Victorinus, "Commentary," 8.2. This same recapitulation view was applied by Tyconius in his influential commentary on Revelation (now lost to us), written about AD 385. See Yarbro Collins, "The Book of Revelation," 388.

Progressive parallelism is clearly seen in how the seals in Revelation (Rev 6:1–17; 8:1–5) parallel Christ's Olivet Discourse and end with a description of the end of the age. Similarly, the trumpets (Rev 8:6—9:21; 11:15–19), the woman and the dragon (Rev 12:1—14:20), and the bowls (Rev 16:1–21) all are parallel and end with a description of the end of the age:[128]

Matt 24 (Olivet Discourse)	Rev 6/8:5 (Seals)	Rev 12–14 (Woman & Dragon)	Rev 8–9/11 (Trumpets)	Rev 16 (Bowls)
Wars: 24:6 Int'l unrest: 24:7 Earthquakes: 24:7 Famine: 24:7 Persecution: 24:9 False Christs: 24:23	Wars: 6:3–4 Int'l unrest: 6:3–4 Famine: 6:5–6 Persecution: 6:9–11 False Christ: 6:1–2	War: 12:7; 13:7 Earth woe: 12:12 Sea woe: 12:12 River: 12:15 Persecution: 12:13 False god: 13:4, 12–14	Earth: 8:7 Sea blood: 8:8–9 Rivers & springs: 8:10 Euphrates: 9:14	Earth: 16:2 Sea blood: 16:3 Rivers & springs: 16:4 Euphrates: 16:12
Sun dark: 24:29 Moon dark: 24:29 Stars fall: 24:29 Powers of heaven shaken: 24:29	Sun dark: 6:12 Moon: blood: 6:12 Stars fall: 6:13 Earthquake; heaven shaken: 6:12, 14		Sun dark: 8:12 Moon dark: 8:12 Star falls: 8:10 Stars dark: 8:12 Earthquake: 11:13	Sun scorches: 16:8 Throne of beast: dark: 16:10
Son of Man & cloud: 24:30 Angels gather: 24:31	God's & Lamb's wrath: 6:16–17 Loud voice: 7:2 Thunder: 8:5 Sounds: 8:5 Lightning: 8:5 Earthquake: 8:5	God's wrath: 14:10 Son of Man & cloud: 14:14 Loud voice: 14:15 Angels reap: 14:17–20	God's wrath: 11:18 Loud voices: 11:15 Thunder: 11:19 Sounds: 11:19 Lightning: 11:19 Earthquake: 11:19 Hail: 11:19	God's wrath: 16:19 Loud voice: 16:17 Thunder: 16:18 Sounds: 16:18 Lightning: 16:18 Earthquake: 16:18 Hail: 16:21

Different views of the extent of chronological movement versus recapitulation among the seals-trumpets-bowls

There is some disagreement among commentators concerning the extent to which the seals, trumpets, and bowls overlap. One complicating factor is mentioned by Johnson: "Just as the vision genre sometimes compresses vast historical eons into symbolic images that pass like the twinkling of an eye (see Rev. 12:1–5, which spans redemptive history from Genesis 3 to Acts 1), so also a split-second in time may be expanded in visionary

---

128. For another comparative table of the seals-trumpets-bowls, see Schnabel, *40 Questions*, 51–2. For another comparative table of the signs Jesus lists in the Olivet Discourse and the seals, see ibid., 70.

descriptions and simultaneous climactic events presented as successive, in order to help hearers to see different facets of Christ's victory."[129]

Those who think the seals, trumpets, and bowls are sequential in time typically cite: (A) the order of the plagues differ; (B) their intensity increases from one-quarter of humanity in the seals (6:8), to one-third in the trumpets (9:15), to universality in the bowls (16:1–11); (C) the absence (in the bowl series) of "interludes or delays which impede the advance of the trumpet cycles toward their climax";[130] and (D) the bowls are described as being *"the last, because in them the wrath of God is finished"* (15:1).[131]

Robert Thomas sees the seals, trumpets, and bowls as being essentially, but not entirely, chronological. As he sees it, they have a "telescopic" relationship in which the bowl judgments are contained in and "issue from the last of seven trumpet judgments which, in turn, result from the seventh of seven seal judgments."[132]

On the other hand, Elisabeth Schüssler Fiorenza draws a demarcation between the fifth seal and what follows. She sees the first five seals as preparatory, as opposed to the sixth-seventh seals, trumpets, and bowls, which she sees as the final, cosmic-cataclysmic events of the "great day of the Lord."[133]

Then again, Dennis Johnson appears to view the bulk of the seals and trumpets not as sequential but as overlapping throughout this age.[134] His demarcation essentially is between the trumpets and the bowls. He views only the seven bowls as indicating the final judgment, but essentially agrees with Thomas that they are "contained within and elaborat[e] on the seventh trumpet and the sixth seal."[135]

Others see progression of events in Revelation not as strictly chronological or historical but as representing a *literary* progression.[136] In other words, the relationship between the seals, trumpets, and bowls is primarily thematic. Recapitulation is the occasion for new emphases.[137] Beale, for example, contends that the bulk of the bowls recapitulate

129. Johnson, *Triumph*, 176.

130. Ibid., 36.

131. See Beale, *Revelation*, 116–21; Resseguie, *Revelation of John*, 56–59; Smith, "Revelation," 1515–16; Thomas, "Classical Dispensationalist View," 191–93; Johnson, *Triumph*, 36–37, 46–47, 223n.4. Futurists, particularly dispensationalists, see Rev 4:1—20:15, including the seals, trumpets, and bowls, as predicting the *historical order* of events that will happen only during the "tribulation" that will occur shortly before Christ's second coming and not as applying at all to the events of history during the "church age" which, in their view, ends with the pretribulational rapture of the church. E.g., Smith, *What the World*, 39–41, 55. Even such commentators, however, recognize that Revelation, to a large extent, recapitulates itself. Ibid., 135.

132. Thomas, "Analysis of the Seventh Bowl," 73; see also Thomas, "Structure of the Apocalype," 52, 66; MacDonald, *Believer's*, 2351. As a dispensationalist, Thomas sees all of the seals, trumpets, and bowls as occurring only in the end-time shortly before the *parousia*, after the church has been raptured.

133. Schüssler Fiorenza, *Revelation*, 65, 71, 93.

134. Johnson, *Triumph*, 122, 146, 223.

135. Ibid., 223n.4.

136. Resseguie, *Revelation of John*, 59.

137. Greg Beale explains this as follows: "The observation of the wider effect of the succeeding plague series conforms well with the contention of recapitulationists that there is a thematic progressive intensity among the three septets. This ascending thematic movement, whose increasing, climactic force builds as the book advances, can be pictured in the form of a conical spiral. In fact, this same increasing, thematic intensity is observable within each of the three plague series, where the seventh element of

the seals and trumpets throughout this age, all having a common ending (the final judgment). He states, "There is not a one-to-one correspondence between each corresponding trumpet and bowl. But they are similar enough to be considered parts of the same overall program of divine judgments occurring during the same general period."[138] In his view, the first five seals, six trumpets, and five bowls cover the time between Christ's resurrection and the *parousia*; the last two seals, seventh trumpet, and last two bowls depict the last judgment.[139]

The progressively more intense descriptions of the "earthquake" in Rev 8:5; 11:19; 16:18–21 and the cosmic destruction in Rev 6:12–17 and 20:11 are thematic, not chronological

Revelation's use of the earthquake is drawn from the OT, which describes the quaking of the earth when God manifests himself. Often in such cases earthquakes are part of the quaking of the entire cosmos when God appears. That occurred on Mount Sinai and on other occasions in the past.[140] The OT further states that such quaking will occur in the future "day of the Lord."[141] Significantly, in the Olivet Discourse Christ used the same kind of language to describe his second coming.[142] That background provides the context for interpreting Rev 4:5; 8:5; 11:19; 16:18–21; 6:12–17; and 20:11:[143]

4:5: *lightning and sounds and thunder*
8:5: *thunder and sounds and lightning and an earthquake*
11:19: *lightning and sounds and thunder and an earthquake and great hail*
16:18–21: *lightning and sounds and thunder and a great earthquake . . . and great hail*

6:14: *The sky was split apart . . . and every mountain and island were moved out of their places*
16:20: *every island fled away, and the mountains were not found*
20:11: *earth and heaven fled away, and no place was found for them*

Richard Bauckham explains the significance of the above table:

---

each (sometimes including the sixth) reach a universal, climaxing crescendo after the preceding plagues have been said to have had only fractional effect. . . . [This] explains, for example, why the bowls can be synonymously parallel with the trumpets and yet have a wider effect and can be described in somewhat different ways." Beale, *Revelation*, 127–30.

138. Ibid., 810. He sees the "seven last plagues" in 15:1 as referring "not to trials occurring after the seals and trumpets at the very end of history but to the bowls coming last after the seals and trumpets in the sequence of formal sevenfold visions seen by the seer. They are 'last' in that they complete the thought revealed in the preceding woe visions. This means that the bowl judgments need not represent what occurs after the series of judgments described in chs. 6–14. The bowls go back in time and explain in greater detail the woes throughout the age, culminating in the final judgment." Ibid. Schnabel appears to have a similar view. He sees the seals, trumpets, and bowls (as well as the signs Jesus enumerated in the Olivet Discourse) all as recapitulating history, from the first century to the beginning of God's new world. Schnabel, *40 Questions*, 67–69, 258.

139. Beale, *Revelation*, 810.

140. See Exod 19:18; Judg 5:4–5; 2 Sam 22:8–16; Pss 18:7–15; 68:8; 77:16–18; 114; Isa 64:3; Hab 3:3–15.

141. Isa 13:13; 24:18–23; 34:4; Joel 2:10; Mic 1:3–4; Nah 1:5–6.

142. Matt 24:29–30; Mark 13:24–25; Luke 21:25–26.

143. For another comparative table of Rev 4:5; 8:5; 11:19; 16:18–21 see Schnabel, *40 Questions*, 242.

The formula, whose core is an allusion to the Sinai theophany [Exod 19:16], is expanded by the addition of an extra item in 8:5 and 11:19, while in 16:18–21 the earthquake and hail are described at some length. In 4:5 the formula describes a theophany confined to heaven, which in the latter instances becomes a theophany resulting in judgment on earth. Thus the formula serves to anchor the divine judgments of chapters 6–16 in the initial vision of God's rule in heaven in chapter 4. It also creates a particular kind of relationship between the three series of seven judgments. The judgments of the seventh seal-opening, the climax of the first series, described by this formula in 8:5, encompasses the whole course of the judgments of the seven trumpets, and similarly the judgment of the seventh trumpet, described by this formula in 11:19b, encompasses the whole series of the bowl judgments, climaxing in the final, fullest elaboration of the formula in 16:18–21. Thus the formula indicates that it is the same final judgment which is reached in the seventh of each of the three series. With each of the first two sevenths we attain a preliminary glimpse of the final judgment, which the following series then approaches again from closer range, as it were. . . . Two passages remain to be considered. Both 6:12–17 and 20:11 are explicitly passages in which the earthquake accompanies the theophany of God the Judge. Moreover in these two cases John employs the tradition of the cosmic quake, in which the heavens as well as the earth flee from God's presence. The first passage echoes several Old Testament descriptions of the Day of the Lord. The second seems to include the notion of the destruction of the old cosmos to be replaced by the new (cf. 21:1).[144]

Rev 6:14 (*"every mountain and island were moved out of their places"*), 16:20 (*"every island fled away, and the mountains were not found"*), and 20:11 (*"earth and heaven fled away, and no place was found for them"*) are all clearly parallel, virtually identical, descriptions that can only describe the same event: the destruction of the earth at the end of the age, God's judgment at the *parousia*. The reference in 6:14 to *"every mountain and island"* parallels 16:20. Both 16:20 and 20:11 say that every island (16:20), or earth and heaven (20:11), *"fled away."* They both use the same word, including even the same person and tense, for *"fled away"* (*pheugō*). Both passages add that the mountains (16:20), or earth and heaven (20:11), were not *"found."* Again, both passages use the same word for not being found (*heuriskō*). The events described in all those passages must refer to the *parousia* because they *cannot happen twice.* J. Webb Mealy observes, "John's insistent point, from ch. 6 on, has been that no one on earth survives the parousia. . . . Taken at face value, the upheavals of chs. 6 and 16 are just as fatal as those of Rev. 20.11."[145] Consequently, from chapter 6 on, the book must be recapitulative, not a chronological narrative.[146]

---

144. Bauckham, *Climax of Prophecy,* 8, 208.

145. Mealy, *After the Thousand Years,* 160; see also at 158–62, 194; Schnabel, *40 Questions,* 277. Schüssler Fiorenza similarly observes that 6:12–14 "can only be understood in apocalyptic terms to mean the final dissolution of the whole world." Schüssler Fiorenza, *Revelation,* 64. After quoting Rev 16:20, Rist and Hough conclude, "[The result of the great earthquake is] doubly astounding since this had already occurred as far back as 6:14b as one result of the opening of the sixth seal. This repetition is just one of the indications that the different series of plagues are not actually to be considered as following one upon the other, but are probably to be regarded as differing versions of the same series of eschatological woes preparing the way for the end of this world and age." Rist and Hough, "Revelation of St. John," 488.

146. Rev 6:12–17 and 7:3 also provide a clear example of the fact that the order of the visions John

The repeated pattern of judgment shows that Revelation is not a single, chronological narrative, but is structured in progressively parallel sections

There is a recurrent pattern of judgment throughout Revelation. The judgments follow a characteristic pattern: they originate in heaven but their main effects are on the earth. Later descriptions are intensified and add details to the earlier descriptions of the same event. In addition to the seals-trumpets-bowls, this pattern also appears elsewhere. Andrew Steinmann describes this:

> In 14:14–20 there is a double harvest of the earth. . . . The pattern is similar to the seventh seal, trumpet and bowl. The judgment originates in heaven, but its main effects—especially punishment—are felt on earth. A new element is introduced, however: Not only is the judgment on the earth depicted, but also the blessings of the saints who were taken out of the world in the first judgment are depicted. This pattern is repeated in 19:1–21. . . . The judgment originates in heaven, and its consequences are played out on the earth. Here, however, the blessings-of-the-saints theme introduced in the two-harvest judgment is expanded in the "marriage feast" where the blessedness of the saints at the final judgment is not merely implied but explicitly depicted. There remains one final judgment scene, that of 20:9—22:5. . . . The pattern is the same as the other judgments. It is initiated in heaven, but the judgment's consequences are felt on earth. In addition, as in chap. 19 there is an expanded section on the blessings for the saints, in this case in the new Jerusalem.[147]

The repeated references to the "wrath" of God demonstrate recapitulation

Rev 6:17 says, *"The great day of their wrath has come, and who is able to stand?"* That is, of course, a rhetorical question, the answer to which is "no one" (at least among unbelievers). That question and answer "enhances the universal, consummate nature of the scene."[148] Rev 11:18 is similar: *"Your wrath came, and the time came for the dead to be judged . . . and to destroy those who destroy the earth."* Rev 14:10 similarly speaks of *"the wine of the wrath of God, which is mixed in full strength in the cup of His anger."* It introduces a two-fold harvest-vintage scene that can only occur at the end of the age: "The first (vv. 14–16) represents a harvest, a reaping of souls, and apparently a gathering in of the redeemed. . . . The second one [14:17–20], which is not a harvest but a vintage scene [the angel *"gathered*

---

had *cannot* represent the chronology of the events in history that they symbolize. In 7:3 an angel says that the earth is not to be harmed until the bond-servants of God have been sealed. However, 6:12–17 had depicted the destruction of the earth and sky at the "last day." Consequently, 7:3 must precede 6:12–17 in *history* even though it follows 6:12–17 in the sequence of visions.

147. Steinmann, "Tripartite Structure," 77–78. "All agree that the dominant themes from 6:1 to 20:15 are, in order of importance, judgment, persecution, and salvation/reward and that these themes are intensified as the book progresses. . . . At least one probable reason for the intensification is to emphasize the reality of the three motifs of judgment, persecution, and salvation for a confused church living in the midst of compromise and doubt." Beale, *Revelation*, 144–45.

148. Beale, *Revelation*, 124. "The 'great day' of 6:17 is also probably equivalent to 'the great supper of God' in 19:17–18, where virtually the same classes of people listed in 6:15 are mentioned as being destroyed by Christ's final judgment (as in 6:15, and similarly in 16:14; note also 'the kings of the earth' in 19:19; for the same episode cf. 20:8–10)." Ibid., 401.

the clusters from the vine of the earth, and threw them into the great wine press of the wrath of God"], must depict the gathering of the unbelieving and wicked ones of the earth."[149] Rev 19:15, a clear second coming passage, again refers to *"the wine press of the fierce wrath of God,"* thus connecting it to 14:19–20. Rev 16:19 uses the same image of God's wrath as 14:10 when it speaks of *"the cup of the wine of His fierce wrath."* The context in all of these passages—as indicated by the repeated references to "wine" and God's "wrath"—can only be the consummation and final judgment.

The descriptions of God and Christ demonstrate progressive parallelism

God and Christ are described in Rev 1:4, 8, and 4:8 as the one *"who is and who was and who is to come."*[150] In Rev 11:17 and 16:5 God and Christ are addressed directly as the one *"who are and who were."* The references to *"and who is to come"* are omitted. The reason for the change is that the sounding of the seventh trumpet in 11:15 and the third bowl in 16:4 announce or anticipate the coming of the kingdom, judgment, and reign of God and Christ.[151] Those descriptions of God are parallel descriptions of the coming of God and Christ and show progression prior to his coming.

Repeated expressions of singing and rejoicing in heaven demonstrate progressive parallelism

In Rev 11:17, a heavenly scene of praise and worship following the vindication of the "two witnesses," the twenty-four elders proclaim, *"O Lord God, the Almighty, . . . You . . . have begun to reign."* In Rev 19:6 the great multitude in heaven similarly proclaims *"the Lord our God, the Almighty, reigns."* The same word (Greek = *basileuō*) is used for "reign" in both cases. In both cases the verbs are in the aorist active indicative tense. Johnson discusses the significance of this: "The aorist tense of this verb signals the initiation of God's rule, the establishment of his redemptive and eschatological kingdom in its full and final phase."[152]

In Rev 15:3–4, a parallel passage of praise and rejoicing in heaven, the redeemed *"sang the song of Moses, the bond-servant of God, and the song of the Lamb."* This song draws heavily on the OT "songs of Moses" (Exod 15:1–18; Deut 32:1–43) as well as other OT passages such as Ps 86:8–10; 111:1–3; Isa 66:23; Jer 10:7. These songs all show the fulfillment of the "new song" sung by the twenty-four elders in Rev 5:9–10 in which they recounted the Lamb's sacrificial death, made the redeemed to be a kingdom and priests, and enabled the redeemed to reign upon the earth.

---

149. Smith, "Revelation," 1514. Rev 14:14–20 also uses imagery from Christ's explanation of the parable of the wheat and the tares (Matt 13:24–30, 36–43) in which he explained that *"the harvest is at the end of the age; and the reapers are angels"* (Matt 13:39).

150. In Rev 17:8, a similar threefold description is reapplied to the beast (who *"was, and is not, and is about to come up out of the abyss and go to destruction"*) "to mock the beast." Beale, *Revelation*, 864.

151. Johnson, *Triumph*, 54n.12; Bauckham, *Climax of Prophecy*, 32.

152. Johnson, *Triumph*, 262, 262n.32, 263n.33.

Following the overthrow of Babylon the great, in Rev 19:1–6 the multitude in heaven rejoices over God's having *"avenged the blood of His bond-servants"* (Rev 19:2). That is reminiscent of the "song of Moses" (Deut 32:1–43) which concludes by saying that God *"will avenge the blood of His servants"* (32:43). Further, in Rev 19:6 the heavenly multitude repeats the sentiments expressed in Rev 11:17, saying, *"Hallelujah! For the Lord our God, the Almighty, reigns."* All of these songs depict different visions of the defeat of evil, the vindication of the saints, and the concomitant rejoicing in heaven at the fulfillment of God's plan, his triumph, and his reign. The connections among these passages again demonstrate the progressively parallel structure of the book: Rev 11:17 arises strictly in the context of judgment; Rev 15:3–4 reveals the vindication of the saints as a result of the judgment; and Rev 19:6 points forward by referring to the bride of Christ (19:7–8), the New Jerusalem, which is elaborated by 21:1—22:5.

Repeated expressions of finality demonstrate progressive parallelism

Rev 10:7 (when the angel is about to sound the seventh trumpet) states, *"The mystery of God is finished."* Rev 15:1 (when the angels are about to pour the bowls) similarly states, *"the wrath of God is finished."* In both cases the Greek *etelesthē* ("is finished") precedes the "mystery of God" and the "wrath of God." Placing the verb in that position in both cases emphasizes "the finality and completion of God's plan."[153] Similarly, Rev 16:17 says, *"A loud voice came out of the temple from the throne, saying, 'It is done.'"* In parallel fashion, Rev 21:6 says, *"Then He said to me, 'It is done.'"* Those parallels also show the "progressively" parallel nature of the book: Rev 10:7 arises during an interlude of the trumpet judgments; Rev 15:1 is just prior to the last of the "seven plagues" (the bowl judgments); Rev 16:17 occurs when the seventh bowl is poured out; and Rev 21:6 is said when New Jerusalem descends from heaven.

Rev 1:19 and the structure of the book

Dispensationalists take the view that the church is raptured and not even present on earth, but only in heaven, after Rev 3:22. They base their view on Rev 1:19, which they see as establishing a three-part structure to the book: *"the things which you have seen"* (which they interpret to be the vision of Christ in Rev 1:1–18); *"the things which are"* (which they interpret to be the seven churches of Rev 2:1—3:22, which they then interpret to refer to the "church age" ending at the pretribulational rapture of the church), and *"the things which will take place after these things"* (which they interpret to be the things which take place after the rapture of the church).[154] That view is not sustainable for several reasons:

---

153. Ibid., 162n.9.

154. Smith, *Tribulation*, 17–20; Smith, *What the World*, 1, 17–18; Thomas, "Classical Dispensationalist View," 186–87; MacDonald, *Believer's*, 2354, 2361.

Begging the question

The dispensationalist view *assumes in advance* that the church is raptured before the tribulation because that is demanded by dispensationalism itself. That, of course, is the fallacy of *petitio principii* or "begging the question" (i.e., taking for granted or assuming the very thing that needs to be proven). As was discussed above in chapter 9, the "pretribulational rapture" is not a biblical idea. Further, such an idea is not mentioned anywhere in Revelation.[155]

Rev 1:19 is not designed to establish a three-part chronological structure for events that take place in history

Beale discusses the first two phrases of Rev 1:19 (*"the things which you have seen"* and *"the things which are"*) in connection with their greater context:

> First, "things that you have seen" in 1:19 probably does not refer only to the initial vision in 1:12–18 and therefore to a part of the book that deals with the past in distinction to parts that deal with the present and the future, referred to in the subsequent phrases in 1:19. It refers, rather, to the book's entire vision ("what you see," the aorist tense of *eides* indicating not the time of the vision but its totality). This likelihood is substantiated by the observation that v 19 does not stand alone but is part of an overall section (vv 9–20) that is best viewed as a commissioning narrative, so that "write what you see" is merely a repetition of the command in 1:11 to record all the visions of the book. Second, "things that are" probably refers not only to the present as described in chs. 2–3 but to references to the present throughout the book. In fact, it may not be a temporal reference at all, but an allusion to the figurative nature of the book that needs to be interpreted (accordingly, some translate *ha eisiv* as "what they [the pictorial visions] mean.")[156]

The third phrase, *"after these things,"* does not mean "after the things of the church are completed."[157] Rather, Rev 1:19 (along with 1:1; 4:1; and 22:6) alludes to Dan 2:28–29, 45. That context is important because Dan 2:29 uses the phrase *"after these things"* (Greek = *meta tauta*) as equivalent to the phrase *"in the latter days"* (Dan 2:28). As such, when John uses the same phrase in Rev 1:19, the time period to which it refers includes the

---

155. Amazingly, even though the "pretribulational rapture" is foundational for the dispensationalist interpretation of Revelation, leading dispensationalist spokesman John Walvoord admits that "the main problem with the Book of Revelation is that there is no clear mention of the rapture of the church from Revelation 4 through Revelation 18. Here again, the massive fact that a book presenting great detail concerning the events leading up to the second coming of Christ should omit completely any hope of the rapture of the church for the tribulation saints must be faced." Walvoord, *Rapture Question*, 260. See also Mounce, *Revelation*, 119n.7 ("the very discussion of a 'rapture of the church' lies outside of John's frame of reference. He knows nothing of such a 'rapture.'").

156. Beale, *Revelation*, 162–63.

157. As, for example, Chuck Smith takes it. Smith, *Tribulation*, 17–20; Smith, *What the World*, 1, 17–18.

entire period from Christ's first coming until the establishment of the new heavens and new earth.[158]

"The things which are" and "the things which will take place after these things" are connected and are not capable of complete separation

Both *"the things which are"* and *"the things which will take place after these things"* describe the *content* of the one "revelation" that Jesus Christ gave to John (Rev 1:1–2). As such, the "seven letters to the seven churches" (Revelation 2–3) concern the churches' present circumstances but also make promises with respect to the future. Similarly, many of the events of Revelation 4–22 take place throughout history and transcend history. Thus, a simple and definable "past-present-future" chronological structure of Revelation is not correct.

The church in Revelation: introduction

Dispensationalists also base their view that the church is not present throughout the bulk of the book on the fact that "the word *church,* so prominent in chapters 2 and 3, does not occur again until 22:16."[159] Again, that view *assumes in advance* that the church is raptured before the tribulation because that is demanded by dispensationalism itself. That view is not sustainable for several reasons.

The absence of the word "church" proves nothing at all

First, William Everett Bell makes the obvious point that "the word 'church' (*ekklēsia*) as a denotation of the body of Christ as a whole does not appear at all in the book. The only usage of the word in the book is to apply to a particular local church or to 'the churches.' . . . Since the terminology is not used in the book at all, it should be obvious that the absence of the corporate 'church' in some of the chapters can be no more significant than its absence in the book as a whole."[160] Second, the word "church" is not used in John's visions describing the people of God *in heaven* where dispensationalists say the church *is* located after Rev 3:22. Even Rev 19:7–9, which refers to the *"marriage supper of the Lamb,"* does not use the word "church" but calls the church the "bride" and the "saints." Third, several Gospels and Epistles also do not use the word "church" but clearly are talking to and about the church.[161]

---

158. Beale, *Revelation,* 159; see also above, chapter 4, the section "Christ's first coming and the 'last days.'" The words *meta tauta* occur eight other times in the book of Revelation (4:1; 7:1; 7:9; 9:12; 15:5; 18:1; 19:1; 20:3). The phrase indicates "the order in which John saw the visions but not necessarily the historical order of their occurrence as events." Beale, *Revelation,* 316–17.

159. Walvoord, *Revelation,* 103; see also Scofield, *New Scofield,* 1356n.1; MacDonald, *Believer's,* 2051.

160. Bell, "Critical Evaluation," 318–19.

161. *Ekklēsia* does not appear in the gospels of Mark, Luke, and John. It also does not appear in the epistles of 2 Timothy, Titus, 1 Peter, 2 Peter, 1 John, 2 John, and Jude.

The entire book concerns the church

Both John's introduction (Rev 1:1–4) and his concluding reference to the church in Rev 22:16 (*"I, Jesus, have sent My angel to testify to you these things for the churches"*) make clear that the *entire book* concerns the church. Goldsworthy states, "Revelation 1:4 tells us that the whole of the book is addressed to these churches, and that fact alone means that the letters [i.e., Revelation 2–3] are not intended to stand alone and apart from the whole book."[162] In Rev 22:16 where Jesus says *"I have sent My angel to testify to you these things,"* the subject of the angel's testimony is the entire book, not just some part of it.

The dispensationalist interpretation that the church is absent from the book after chapter 3 is amazingly far-fetched. As Bell puts it, the idea that "in the consummating book of the New Testament, directed specifically to seven historical local churches facing severe persecution and needing desperately some hopeful words from the apostle, John instead directs only three chapters to them and spends the remainder of his time compiling a lengthy eschatological handbook concerning events which were to take place on the earth after the church is removed . . . reveals its shallowness and its failure to deal with the contents of the book in any meaningful way."[163]

The importance in Revelation of the use of OT figures to describe the church

At the very outset of the book (Rev 1:6) John says, *"He has made us to be a kingdom, priests to His God and Father."* That is applying to the church the language of Exod 19:5–6, which originally had applied to OT Israel (see 1 Pet 2:5, 9). Rev 5:9–10 uses similar language and also refers to *"every tribe and tongue and people and nation."* Milligan notes the significance of this: "As the language used here of these *men of every tribe, and tongue, and people, and nation,* when they are said to have been made *a kingdom and priests unto our God,* is the same kind as that of [1:6], we seem entitled to conclude that, even from its very earliest verses, the Apocalypse has the universal Church in view."[164]

The application in Revelation of OT figures for the nation of Israel to the church has important implications for understanding the book and seeing the central place the church has in it. Desmond Ford explains this:

> The whole trend of the book, from the introductory reference to the Christian churches in Asia under Jewish sanctuary symbolism, to the final vision of the New Jerusalem, testifies to the fact that in the thinking of the seer, the Christian church has taken the place of literal Israel. . . . If the things of Israel are now applied to the Christian church they must thereby automatically have a world-wide application rather than merely a local. The true Israel is scattered throughout every nation, and similarly Babylon also has become world-wide. The seven lampstands point to a world-wide body of believers, but the original seven-branched candlestick resided in a Palestinian holy place. Throughout this book John takes

---

162. Goldsworthy, *Whole Bible,* 217.
163. Bell, "Critical Evaluation," 317.
164. Milligan, *Revelation,* 82.

materials from the visions of the Old Testament prophets originally couched in a local setting, and he applies them to world-wide events.[165]

The church in Revelation: major figures and symbols

Since the book of Revelation is *"the Revelation of Jesus Christ"* (Rev 1:1), Christ's body, the church, is present throughout the book. It is described in various symbols in virtually every chapter. John assumes the NT truth that, "as the body of Christ, it is to be expected that the body will share the experience of the Head."[166] Thus, throughout the book we see the church experiencing both the suffering, and the vindication and triumph, of Christ. The following are the major symbols used to describe the church throughout the book of Revelation:

The "bond-servants" (Rev 1:1; 2:20; 7:3; 11:18; 19:5; 22:3, 6)

Every reference to "bond-servants" (Greek = *doulos,* often translated "slave" or "servant") in Revelation (except 15:3 where the term is used of Moses) undeniably refers to Christians (i.e., the church). In fact, every time the term is applied in the NT to believers living after Jesus' resurrection, it applies to Christians, not Jews. In Rev 7:3 "bond-servants" is another way of describing the 144,000 of 7:4. Since nowhere in the NT is the term "bond-servants" used to distinguish "Jewish believers" from regular Christians of any background, it should be taken the same way, as applying to the church, in 7:3.[167]

The seven churches (Rev 2:1—3:22)

The seven churches were real, historical churches in the Roman province of Asia (modern Turkey). The letters to the seven churches show that the church is the true Israel of God. The distinction between outward, physical Israel and inner, spiritual Israel is clear from the references in 2:9 and 3:9 to *"those who say they are Jews and are not, but are a synagogue of Satan."* In other words, "there are men who are actually and outwardly Jews—literal Israel—but in reality they are not true Jews—spiritual Israel—but follow the ways of Satan rather than God."[168]

Although they are addressed to specific, historical situations in the different churches, the seven messages have universal import.[169] They address issues and problems that are common to all churches and set forth principles valid in all churches.[170] The "seven letters" have a common purpose: "The entire sequence is a literary composition designed

---

165. Ford, *Abomination of Desolation,* 257, 258.

166. Ibid., 259.

167. For more on the 144,000, see below.

168. Ladd, *Commentary,* 116; see also Mathison, *Postmillennialism,* 145, 153.

169. A good, non-technical introduction to the the seven letters to the seven churches is John Stott, *What Christ Thinks of the Church* (Wheaton, IL: Harold Shaw, 1990).

170. Osborne, *Revelation,* 105; Payne, *Encyclopedia,* 595n.23.

to impress upon the church universal the necessity of patient endurance in the face of impending persecution."[171] Consequently, virtually all commentators view the seven churches as representative of churches throughout history until the second coming.[172] Even dispensationalists now agree that the seven churches "typify local churches of all locations and all times" until Christ returns.[173] Several linguistic and contextual factors within Revelation suggest that the seven churches of Revelation 2–3 were selected to typify or apply to the universal church:

- *"The seven churches."* The early church regarded the number "seven" as indicating fullness or completeness. Hence, the "seven" churches signify the universal church.[174] Additionally, Milligan notes that in Rev 1:4 the definite article ("the") before "seven churches" is an indication that the seven churches were designed to have universal applicability: "John addressed himself not to seven, but to 'the seven churches which are in Asia,' as if there were no more churches in the province. More, however, there certainly were. . . . Their number—seven—must thus be regarded as typical of unity, and the seven churches as representative of the one universal church."[175]

- *Write in "a book" (or scroll).* The fact that the seven messages to the seven churches are to be written on only one book or scroll (Rev 1:11) is significant. Hamstra says, "The fact that there is only one scroll, instead of seven, confirms that the book is for the entire Christian Church."[176]

- *To "the churches."* The way Jesus ends each message to the seven churches in Revelation 2–3 demonstrates that each message is not limited to that individual church but also is applicable to the wider church. The reason is that, even though each of the "seven letters" is addressed to a particular church, the end of each letter is to the churches as a whole, i.e., *"He who has an ear, let him hear what the Spirit says to the churches"* (2:7, 11, 17, 29; 3:6, 13, 22).

- *Fulfillment of promises at the end of the book.* What is promised to the seven churches in Rev 2:1—3:22 finds its fulfillment later, particularly at the end of the book. That indicates the continued presence of the church throughout the book and the representative nature of the seven churches.[177]

---

171. Mounce, *Revelation,* 65.

172. E.g., Milligan, *Discussions,* 269; Stott, *What Christ Thinks,* 8; Osborne, *Revelation,* 105. Preterists, of course, see the seven churches only historically since they believe that Revelation points to and is fulfilled in the events of AD 70.

173. Thomas, "Chronological Interpretation," 327; see also Thomas, "Classical Dispensationalist View," 216.

174. Aune, *Revelation 1–5,* 130; see also Johnson, *Triumph,* 14; Schüssler Fiorenza, *Revelation,* 53.

175. Milligan, *Revelation,* 28–29.

176. Hamstra, "An Idealist View," 101.

177. See above concerning the repetition of phrases and ideas as tying the book together and reinforcing its basic message.

The "saints" (Rev 5:8; 8:3–4; 11:18; 13:6–7, 10; 14:12; 16:6; 17:6; 18:20, 24; 19:8; 20:9)

Everywhere else the NT uses the word "saints" it manifestly is referring to Christians (the church).[178] Most of the images in Revelation picture the "saints" on earth.[179] Others picture them in heaven.[180] That is consistent with the rest of the NT, which establishes a connection between the church on earth and the church in heaven. For example, Phil 3:20 tells us *our citizenship is in heaven.* Eph 2:6 affirms that the church is *raised up with Him, and seated with Him in the heavenly places* (see also Col 3:1). As in Rev 14:1 where the 144,000 are *standing on Mount Zion* with the Lamb, so in 13:6–7 the saints on earth also are *"those who dwell [or 'tabernacle'] in heaven."*

In Revelation the connection between the saints on earth and the saints in heaven is seen in at least two ways: in persecution and defeat; and in ultimate victory. The saints on earth are oppressed "because loyalty to their heavenly citizenship demands disobedience to their earthly citizenship."[181] Nevertheless, although they are oppressed on earth, the saints' spiritual connection with the heavenly realm remains active and effective. In both Rev 5:8 and 8:3–4 censers (incense bowls) symbolize *the prayers of the saints.* In 8:5 an angel fills the censer with the fire of the altar and throws it to earth. Johnson points out, "The imagery is powerful: Christians' prayers are integral to the downfall of the gospel's enemies."[182]

Those "purchased . . . from every tribe and tongue and people and nation [who have been made] a kingdom and priests to our God" (Rev 5:9–10)

The "new song" of Rev 5:9–10 is a song of victory and redemption. Those who have been purchased out of every tribe, tongue, people, and nation, now constitute a kingdom and priests.[183] The reference to *"kingdom and priests"* is drawn from the promises given to Israel in Exod 19:6 and Isa 61:6. Andrew Bandstra mentions two significant points concerning Revelation's use of those texts: "(a) First of all, the verbs of both of these OT texts are future tenses—they contain God's promises to His people for the future. By affirming that Jesus has made us to be a kingship and priests, the author clearly sees Christ's redemptive actions as a *fulfillment* of those promises of God. (b) Second, the promises made to 'the house of Jacob,' or 'the people of Israel' [Exod 19:3] or 'those mourning in Zion' [Isa 61:2–3] are in Revelation seen to be fulfilled in the Christian church."[184]

With respect to their *"reign upon the earth"* (Rev 5:10), both the present (*"they reign"*) and the future tense (*"they will reign"*) are supported by good textual evidence.

178. See Matt 27:52; Acts 9:13, 32, 41; 26:10; Rom 1:7; 8:27; 12:13; 15:25, 26, 31; 16:2, 15; 1 Cor 1:2; 6:1, 2; 14:33; 16:1, 15; 2 Cor 1:1; 8:4; 9:1, 12; 13:13; Eph 1:1, 15, 18; 2:19; 3:8, 18; 4:12; 5:3; 6:18; Phil 1:1; 4:22; Col 1:2, 4, 12, 26; 1 Thess 3:13; 2 Thess 1:10; 1 Tim 5:10; Phlm 5, 7; Heb 6:10; 13:24; Jude 3.

179. Rev 5:8; 8:3–4; 11:18; 13:7, 10; 14:12; 16:6; 17:6; 18:24; 20:9.

180. Rev 13:6; 18:20; 19:8.

181. Beale, *Revelation*, 697.

182. Johnson, *Triumph*, 142.

183. For more on "purchased" see below at "The 144,000 (Rev 7:4–8; 14:1–5)."

184. Bandstra, "Kingship and Priests," 16. This is also affirmed in 1 Pet 2:5, 9; Rev 1:6.

The present is probably to be preferred since, as Beale observes, Rev 5:9–10 appears to describe "an inaugurated fulfillment of the prophesied kingdom of the saints and 'son of man' in Daniel 7 and by the fact that 1:5b–6a, which views the saints as a *present* kingdom, is developed in 5:9b–10a. . . . Both 1:5–6 and 5:9–10 make explicit that the creating of saints as a kingdom is a direct result of Christ's redemptive death, so that it is probable that this kingdom began immediately after this death."[185] In other words, "The saints who are now crushed on earth are already recognized in heaven as those to whom dominion belongs, and stand even now before the throne of the Most High."[186]

The martyrs (Rev 6:9–11)

Some hold that the martyrs are OT saints, largely because of the "absence of the stock phrase 'the testimony of Jesus' in Rev. 6:9"[187] and the fact that they had not obtained their white robes until Rev 6:11.[188] Nevertheless, the context makes it far more likely that the martyrs represent Christians, although perhaps including OT saints.

First, the context in Revelation concerns the church and the persecution of Christians for the testimony of Jesus.[189] Second, Ladd articulates an important aspect of the broader NT context of martyrdom as it relates to Christians individually and to the church as a whole: "One of the repeated emphases of the entire New Testament is that it is the very nature of the church to be martyr people. When Jesus taught that a man to be his disciple must deny himself and take up his cross (Matt. 10:38; 16:24), he was not speaking of self-denial or the bearing of heavy burdens; he was speaking of the willingness to suffer martyrdom. The cross is nothing less than an instrument of death. Every disciple of Jesus is in essence a martyr; and John has in view all believers who have suffered."[190] Therefore, Beale concludes that while it is possible that only literal martyrs are in mind, it is "more likely 'slain' is metaphorical and those spoken of represent the broader category of all saints who suffer for the sake of their faith. . . . The only other place in the Apocalypse where deceased believers are exhorted to 'rest' appears to be addressed to all saints in general who persevere by 'keeping the commandments . . . and their faith' and 'die in the Lord' (14:12–13)."[191]

As to not explicitly saying *"of Jesus"* after *"the testimony"* in Rev 6:9, some ancient manuscripts do include the phrase *"of the Lamb"* after *"because of the testimony."*[192] In any event, the testimony *"of Jesus"* is implied from Rev 1:2, 9. Further, Rev 12:11, which

185. Beale, *Revelation,* 362–63; see also Bandstra, "Kingship and Priests," 17–20.

186. Hooker, *Son of Man,* 29. For more on this see below, the section "The paradoxical nature of 'overcoming.'" Even if the future reading of Rev 5:10 is preferred, it would be assuring believers that the condition brought about by entering into a saving relationship with Christ will be a lasting one. "The future reading then means a promise, seen from the point of view of present accomplishment." Ulfgard, *Feast and Future,* 63n.269.

187. Mealy, *After the Thousand Years,* 85n.1.

188. Milligan, *Revelation,* 98–102.

189. See Rev 1:9; 2:9; 2:13; 3:10, and virtually everything from Rev 7:1—20:10.

190. Ladd, *Commentary,* 104; see also Bauckham, *Theology,* 155; Milligan, *Revelation,* 102, 192.

191. Beale, *Revelation,* 390–91.

192. Ibid., 391.

obviously refers to Christian martyrs, likewise speaks only of *"the word of their testimony,"* which is equivalent to *"the testimony of Jesus"* (12:17). Finally, receiving white garments is a heavenly reward for the faithful.[193]

The "144,000" (Rev 7:4–8; 14:1–5)

Most agree that the 144,000 of Rev 7:4–8 and Rev 14:1–5 represent the same group.[194] There are two main views about the identity of the 144,000:

(1) They are a group of ethnic Jews who have become believers in Jesus Christ during the tribulation shortly before the *parousia*. The identification of the 144,000 with ethnic Israel is based on taking the number and the tribal identities literally and on the dispensational presupposition that the church has been raptured before the sealing of the 144,000 occurs.[195]

(2) The other main view (which we believe is the correct one) is that "under a Jewish figure, they include all the followers of Christ, or the universal Church."[196] This is consistent with Revelation's use of OT figures to describe the church (see above) and the purpose of the book as a whole: to inform, exhort, and comfort the church. It is also consistent with the theme of the sections of the book in which the 144,000 are found (i.e., Rev 6:1—8:5 and 12:1—14:20), both of which deal with the church's facing persecution.

There are several exegetical reasons why the 144,000 constitute the church as a whole and not Jews or Jewish Christians:

The 144,000 are the same as the "bond-servants" of Rev 7:3

The term for "bond-servant" (Greek = *doulos*) "is never used exclusively of Jewish Christians anywhere else in the book, but always refers to believers in general."[197] In fact, the entire NT makes very clear that in Christ *"there is no distinction between Greek and Jew, circumcised and uncircumcised"* (Col 3:11; see also Gal 3:28). Christ *"made both groups into one and broke down the barrier of the dividing wall . . . so that in Himself He might make the two into one new man"* (Eph 2:14, 16).

Singling out ethnic Israelites for special favor is contrary to the entire thrust of the gospel, the NT, and Revelation in particular. Stephen Smalley discusses this:

193. Rev 3:4, 5, 18; 6:11; 7:9, 14; 19:8, 14.

194. E.g., Beale, *Revelation*, 733; Ladd, *Commentary*, 114–17, 190; MacDonald, *Believer's*, 2371.

195. Pate, "Progressive Dispensationalist View," 164–65; Thomas, "Classical Dispensationalist View," 196–97; MacDonald, *Believer's*, 2364. Gentry similarly believes that these are ethnic Jews who became believers but, as a preterist, believes that this occurred before AD 70. Gentry, "A Preterist View," 56–57.

196. Milligan, *Revelation*, 117. Ladd puts it similarly, "by the 144,000 John means to identify spiritual Israel—the church." Ladd, *Commentary*, 114. See also Beale, *Revelation*, 412–23; Hamstra, "An Idealist View," 106–07; Hendriksen, *More Than Conquerors*, 110–11; Ngundu, "Revelation," 1559; Schüssler Fiorenza, *Revelation*, 67.

197. Beale, *Revelation*, 413; see also Ulfgard, *Feast and Future*, 73.

Nowhere else in the Apocalypse is any distinction drawn between Jewish and Gentile Christians. In Rev. 2–3, Christ walks among every part of the seven Asiatic churches, which were made up . . . of both former Jewish *and* former Gentile members. The sealed scroll of Rev. 5.1—8.1 contains the judgemental and salvific purposes of God for his whole world and his entire Church. . . . The praises of God which ring through the drama of Revelation, and culminate in the vision of the holy city of the new Jerusalem (Rev. 21–22), are offered by all the saints of God, whatever their ethnic and religious background; and they all wear the same whitened robes (3.4, 5, 18; 6.11; 7.9, 13).[198]

Sealing on the forehead (Rev 7:3) corroborates that the entire church is sealed inasmuch as there is no indication of any limit among believers of those who are sealed.[199] The universal sealing of the whole church is confirmed by Rev 7:1 in which four angels standing at *"the four corners of the earth"* hold back *"the four winds of the earth"* until the sealing is done. The reason why that confirms the sealing of the whole church is stated by Smalley: "Those demonic tempests are universal, and not particular, in nature; they affect potentially all creation, not just a part of it, and all Christians, not simply a privileged group of believers."[200]

The primary OT background to the sealing of the church in Rev 7:3 probably is Ezek 9:3–10, where God commanded an angel to mark the foreheads of all those who sighed and groaned over the abominations of Jerusalem; they would be spared during the judgment of the city. Milligan comments that just as "preservation of the faithful in the midst of judgment on the wicked is the theme of the Old Testament vision . . . in like manner it is the theme of this vision of St. John."[201]

The sealing of the 144,000 contrasts with Satan's sealing his followers

Being sealed on their foreheads shows God's ownership and is equivalent to having the name of Christ and God *"written on their foreheads"* (Rev 14:1; 22:4). It contrasts with the sealing that Satan does of his followers. The "mark" of the beast on the forehead of unbelievers (Rev 13:16–17; 14:9–11) is identified with the beast's name.

In Revelation all human beings are identified with one of two camps: the world or the church; all belong either to Christ or to the beast. Consequently, since Satan puts a seal on all of his followers (13:16–17; 14:9–11), God correspondingly seals all of his followers.[202] The universality of the sealing is confirmed by Rev 20:4 which speaks of *"those who had not worshiped the beast or his image, and had not received the mark on their forehead."*

198. Smalley, *Revelation*, 187

199. See Morris, *Revelation*, 111. Ulfgard points out, "These people are to be sealed in order to escape the wrath of God announced in 6:16f, not in order to escape the wrath of anti-divine powers. The sealing of 7:4–8 is thus clearly intended for the whole Christian people of God." Ulfgard, *Feast and Future*, 72.

200. Smalley, *Revelation*, 188.

201. Milligan, *Revelation*, 114. Beale notes, "The context of Ezekiel 9, which provides so much of the background here, knows of no distinction between major groups of the faithful, but distinguishes only true believers from unbelievers." Beale, *Revelation*, 413. The sealing also is akin to the marking of the door with the blood of the lamb at the time of the exodus from Egypt (Exod 12:1–13).

202. Beale, *Revelation*, 413.

That is not referring to an ethnically-based group of people. Rev 22:4 likewise talks about those who have *"His name . . . on their foreheads"* and clearly refers to all Christians.

The seal primarily implies spiritual protection. Although they may suffer and be martyred for their faith, since they bear the seal and name of Christ, not the mark of Satan and the beast, they can remain faithful to death and are protected from God's wrath in the judgment. This applies to all Christians regardless of ethnic background. If the sealing here is only of a select group of Christians [i.e., Jewish believers only, as some commentators maintain] then, because nowhere else in Revelation does such a sealing take place, it follows that the remaining members of the church are *not* sealed and protected.[203]

The description of the tribes of Israel (Rev 7:4–8) indicates that the universal church, not just Jewish believers, is in view

The NT shows the church to be the true, spiritual Israel.[204] In Revelation, even before chapter 7, Christians have been depicted as true Israel. Exod 19:6 is applied in Rev 1:6 and 5:10 to the church; Dan 7:18, 22 in Rev 5:9; Isa 62:2 and 65:15 in Rev 2:17 and 3:12; Isa 43:4; 45:19; 49:23; and 60:14 in Rev 3:9.[205] Ladd concludes that since "John distinguishes between literal and spiritual Israel, it would be possible for him to speak of the twelve tribes of Israel and by doing so to designate those who are true Jews—the church. And he indicates this intention [in Rev 7:4–8] by listing the twelve tribes in a form not identical with empirical Israel."[206]

Several aspects of the list of the tribes in Rev 7:4–8 are highly unusual: (1) The tribe of Dan is missing. (2) Manasseh is present but Ephraim is missing. (3) Joseph has been substituted for Ephraim, but that would create a duplication because Joseph would include both Ephraim and Manasseh since Joseph was their father. (4) The order of the tribes does not correspond to any listing in the OT: Gad, Asher, and Naphtali—who were sons of handmaids—are listed ahead of all the other sons except Judah (who is listed first) and Reuben.[207] (5) The tribes themselves were no longer in existence as a result of the Assyrian exile in 722 BC, the fall of Jerusalem in AD 70, and mixed marriages.[208]

Christopher Smith cogently demonstrates how John has adapted the conventional listings of the tribes to portray the church as the new Israel:

> Judah is elevated to the head of the list because Christ, the head of the church, was descended from this tribe. . . . The *promotion* of the handmaids' sons typifies the inclusion of the Gentiles in the new covenant[209] . . . Reuben is not displaced,

203. Smalley, *Revelation,* 186, 188; Schüssler Fiorenza, *Revelation,* 66; see Rev 9:4.

204. See above, chapter 3, regarding "Christ's first coming and the fulfillment of the OT eschatological prophecies concerning Israel."

205. See Beale, *Revelation,* 418.

206. Ladd, *Commentary,* 116. Jas 1:1 reflects this: James was writing to Christians but addressed his book *"to the twelve tribes who are dispersed abroad."*

207. Ibid., 114–15. Ladd observes, "John's list agrees with no known list of the enumeration of the twelve tribes of Israel," and concludes, "when interpreted literally, *these twelve tribes do not represent actual Israel."* Ibid., emphasis in original.

208. See Schüssler Fiorenza, *Revelation,* 67.

209. Elsewhere Smith comments, "what better explanation is there for the change he makes here

however. As the first-born, he represents believing Israelites, those who, like the first-born in the Old Testament, "belong to the Lord" (Exod. 13.2). . . . Dan specifically is excluded, as many commentators have suggested, because of that tribe's longstanding association with idolatry [and apostasy], and because of the Jewish tradition that the antichrist would come from the tribe of Dan.[210]

Contextual details confirm that the 144,000 from the "tribes of Israel" in Rev 7:4–8 represent a Jewish figure to symbolize the church. The details of the vision suggest that this is a vision of heaven—the true heavenly reality of the church (see Eph 2:6; Rev 20:4). John hears the noises of heaven (Rev 14:2), and the 144,000 are singing *"a new song before the throne and before the four living creatures and the elders"* (Rev 14:3; see also Rev 5:8–10). Heb 12:18, 22 state that Christians *"have come to Mount Zion and to the city of the living God, the heavenly Jerusalem."*[211] The church's already having *"come to Mount Zion"* is reflected in the 144,000 of Rev 14:1 who are *"standing on Mount Zion."* They contrast with those who *"dwell on the earth,"* who are all the followers of the beast (Rev 13:8, 12, 14). The descriptions in both Revelation 13 and 14 are intended to be all-inclusive. To contend that the 144,000 only includes a segment of believers destroys the contrast John is making between the residences of the people in Revelation 13 and those in Revelation 14.[212]

The 144,000 of Rev 14:1–5 are parallel to all the redeemed of Rev 5:9

In Rev 14:3–4 the 144,000 are those *"purchased from the earth"* and those who have been *"purchased from among men . . . for God."* In Rev 5:9 the Lamb *"purchased for God men from every tribe and tongue and people and nation."* The parallel between the two is so close that both groups mentioned as "purchased" likely are identical. Beale draws the obvious conclusion: "This would mean that the 144,000 in 14:1–3 are not some small remnant of ethnic Israelites but another way of speaking of the larger remnant of humanity living during the church age whom Christ has redeemed from throughout the world."[213] That is consistent with the other NT uses of "purchased" people (1 Cor 6:20; 7:23; Greek = *agorazō*). In those other passages Christ likewise purchased Christians in general (i.e., the church).[214]

---

than an attempt to depict the admission to privilege of those born low." Smith, "The Tribes of Revelation 7," 217.

210. Smith, "Portrayal of the Church," 114–15; see also Smith, "The Tribes of Revelation 7," 213–18.

211. Elsewhere the NT views Israel's salvation on Mount Zion as having been fulfilled in Christ and the church. Compare Joel 2:28–32 and Acts 2:16–21; Ps 2:6–9 and Acts 13:33; Heb. 1:1–5; Rev. 2:26–27; 12:5.

212. This universal division of all people into two competing groups is discussed below in the "Overview of major ideas and sections," particularly in the subsection "The contrast between the churches and the 'earth-dwellers.'"

213. Beale, *Revelation*, 412.

214. Second Pet 2:1, the last verse where Christ is said to have "purchased" people, appears to be a case in which Peter used phenomenological language since he is referring to *"false teachers among you . . . even denying the Master who bought them."* In other words, "he described the false teachers as believers because they made a profession of faith and gave every appearance initially of being genuine believers." Schreiner, *1, 2 Peter, Jude*, 331. Even that passage confirms that whenever Christ truly purchases people,

In Rev 14:1–5 the 144,000 are described as virgins

Here, again, one must beware of falling into the trap of interpreting apocalyptic imagery literalistically, as Payne does when he describes the 144,000 as "dedicated Christian youth."[215] Nowhere else does the Bible view sexual relations within marriage as sinful. If the image of Rev 14:4 is taken literally and is *not* a symbolic representation of all believers, then John would be requiring celibacy and being male for the whole church. That, of course, is contrary to everything else in the NT.[216]

The issue of Rev 12:1—14:20 is the persecution of the church by Satan and the world system. Even though believers may be killed (13:7, 15), 14:1 shows the faithful believers standing with the Lamb on Mount Zion. In other words, just as the Lamb triumphed over Satan through his death, so do his people who follow in his footsteps (14:4).[217]

"The word 'chaste' (or 'virgins') can refer to the spiritual condition, not only to physical relations."[218] The prophets repeatedly compare idolatry and unfaithfulness to God with sexual immorality.[219] Jesus compared rejection of him to adultery.[220] Jas 4:4 extends the concept of spiritual adultery beyond specific idolatries or acts by calling people "adulteresses" who have *"friendship with the world,"* or even *"wish to be a friend with the world."* On the other hand, *all* Christians are called to be betrothed to Christ as *"a pure virgin"* (2 Cor 11:2). That idea is carried forward in Revelation in the image of the church as the bride (Rev 19:7–9; 21:2, 9).

In the specific context of the 144,000, John speaks of the idolatrous worship of the beast or consorting with Babylon the great as sexual immorality.[221] We already have seen the juxtaposition of chapters 13–14 in terms of where those who follow the beast reside (they *"dwell on the earth"*), compared to where those who follow the Lamb reside (they are *"standing on Mount Zion"*). The Lamb and the beast themselves are also juxtaposed in Revelation 13–14 which, again, highlights the contrast between the two. In 14:1 we see the true Lamb; in 13:11 we see the false lamb. The contrast highlights the fact that all people follow either one or the other of the two "lambs." Thus, it is obvious that the 144,000 are not "dedicated Christian youth" or any other subset of the church; the 144,000 is a figure for the church as a whole. Consequently, as Ladd concludes, they are "virgins and undefiled in the sense that they have refused to defile themselves by participating in the fornication of worshiping the beast but have kept themselves pure unto God."[222]

---

he purchases the church in general, not a special class of people.

215. Payne, *Encyclopedia,* 612.

216. See Beale, *Revelation,* 738; Schüssler Fiorenza, *Revelation,* 88.

217. Bauckham sees the reference to virgins as belonging to the image of an army: "The followers of Christ are symbolized as an army of adult males who, following the ancient requirement of ritual purity for those who fight in holy war (Deut. 23:9–14; 1 Sam. 21:5; 2 Sam. 11:9–13; 1QM 7:3–6), must avoid the cultic defilement incurred through sexual intercourse. This ritual purity belongs to the image of an army: its literal equivalent in John's ideal of the church is not sexual asceticism, but moral purity." Bauckham, *Theology,* 78; see also Yarbro Collins, "Book of Revelation," 405–8; Johnson, *Triumph,* 202–3.

218. Ladd, *Commentary,* 191.

219. E.g., Isa 57:3; Jer 2:7—3:10; Ezek 23:48–49.

220. Matt 12:38–39; 16:1–4; Mark 8:38.

221. Rev 13:4, 6, 8, 11–18; 14:8; 17:2, 4: 18:3, 9; 19:2.

222. Ladd, *Commentary,* 191.

"144,000" is symbolic, not literal

Most commentators agree that the number 144,000 is symbolic.[223] Gentry says, "In Revelation perfectly rounded thousands all appear to be symbolic."[224] Smith expresses the symbolic import of the number 144,000: "The number 144,000 is much better explained by its symbolic import—12 x 12 x 10 x 10 x 10 expressing completion in a salvific, covenant sense—than as a literal census of a Jewish remnant."[225] Beale concludes by describing the probable basis of the 144,000:

> The square of twelve may be merely the number of the tribes of Israel multiplied by itself or, more likely, the twelve tribes multiplied by the twelve apostles. Ch. 21 confirms this suggestion, where the names of the twelve tribes and of the twelve apostles form part of the figurative structure of the heavenly city of God. . . . If Gentile believers are clearly identified together with "the twelve tribes of the sons of Israel" as part of the new Jerusalem (21:12, 14, 24; 22:2–5), then it is not odd that John should refer to them together with Jewish Christians in 7:4 as "the twelve tribes of the sons of Israel." This receives confirmation from the prior observation that the "sealing" of 7:2–3 is equivalent to believers receiving a "name." And it is clear that one of the names written on Gentile Christians, in addition to the names of God and Christ, is "the name of the new Jerusalem" (3:12), which is a virtual reference to all Christians as "new" Israel.[226]

The "great multitude" (Rev 7:9–17; 19:1, 6)

The primary issue regarding the "great multitude" is whether it is a different group from the 144,000 or is equivalent to the 144,000 seen from a different perspective. Those who think that the 144,000 are Israelite believers hold that the "great multitude" consists of Gentiles converted by the 144,000 Jewish Christians during the "great tribulation"[227] or are martyrs from all ethnic backgrounds.[228] The bases for those beliefs include the fact that the 144,000 are on earth, are specifically enumerated, and are drawn from the "twelve

---

223. E.g., Beale, *Revelation*, 416–23; Osborne, *Revelation*, 310–12; Smalley, *Revelation*, 184–88; Resseguie, *Revelation of John*, 136–38.

224. Gentry, "A Preterist View," 56.

225. Smith, "Portrayal of the Church," 116.

226. Beale, *Revelation*, 417.

227. Pate, "Progressive Dispensationalist View," 165; MacDonald, *Believer's*, 2364–65.

228. Payne, *Encyclopedia*, 610–11; see also Johnson, "Revelation," 484. The "pre-wrath" rapture view and, for different reasons, Luter and Hunter place the rapture of the church at this point and see the "great multitude" as the church in heaven for some period of time before the *parousia*. See Luter and Hunter, "Overlooked," 6–7, 14–15. However, Stylianopoulos points out that Rev 7:9–17 cannot be talking about a rapture because Rev 18:4 "addresses the saints who are still on earth, calling them to an alternative life distinct from that of pagan society symbolized by Rome. Revelation is not at all concerned with the concept of rapture. On the contrary, one of its main themes is that the saints on earth are God's witnesses on earth through suffering up to the final eschatological events." Stylianopoulos, "I Know," 23n.22. Ulfgard adds, "To say that they have left tribulation behind is not primarily a way of saying that they have died [or been raptured!], but that they have been liberated from the realm of evil and brought into a new dimension of existence, life before God." Ulfgard, *Feast and Future*, 102.

tribes of Israel," whereas the "great multitude" is in heaven, could not be counted, and come *"from every nation and all tribes and peoples and tongues"* (Rev 7:9).[229]

However, the symbolic nature of the number 144,000 and the theological designation of the church as the true Israel indicate that "what some have seen as contrasts [between the groups described in 7:4–8 and 7:9–17] may actually be designed to complement each other and show the continuity of the first group with the second."[230] Christopher Smith adds that "there is no difficulty in seeing the church as both earthly and heavenly at the same time. It is only the assumption that the 144,000 symbolizes a different group that prevents it from having a double location."[231] The fact that the "great multitude," like the 144,000, represents the entire church is seen in the following ways:

The relationship between the 144,000 and the "great multitude" parallels the relationship of the Lion and the Lamb in Rev 5:5–6

There is a significant parallel between the description of the church in chapter 7 and the description of Christ in chapter 5. In both cases John uses a "hearing-seeing" pattern, and in both cases that which is identified is identified by two different symbols. Thus, in Rev 5:5 John "hears" one of the elders talk of Christ as *"the Lion that is from the tribe of Judah."* However, in 5:6 John "saw," not a Lion, but *"a Lamb standing, as if slain."* The Lamb *is* the Lion, not someone or something else. John employs that same method of identification in chapter 7 by identifying the church first by what he "heard" (the 144,000) and then by what he "saw" (the great multitude). Bauckham notes, "The two images depict the same reality. They are parallel to the two contrasting images of Christ in 5:5–6."[232]

This double form of identification has theological significance in that it reveals different aspects of the church, just as "Lion" and "Lamb" reveal different aspects of the person and work of Christ. Resseguie elaborates this:

> One point of view—what he hears [7:4]—is the inner reality or theological perspective. The other point of view—what he sees [7:9]—is the outward reality. On the one hand, John hears a symbolic number that represents the complete number of those who belong to God [i.e., God's true Israel]. . . . On the other hand, John sees a multitude from every tribe and nation and language and people (7:9). . . . This is the outward reality: the Israel of God includes all who follow the Lamb, both Jews and Gentiles.[233]

---

229. Pate, "Progressive Dispensationalist View," 165–66; see also Resseguie, *Revelation of John,* 137; Smalley, *Revelation,* 185.

230. Johnson, "Revelation," 484.

231. Smith, "Portrayal of the Church," 16.

232. Bauckham, *Theology,* 76. Contrary to the position adopted here, that the 144,000 from the "twelve tribes of Israel" is a Jewish figure for the true "spiritual Israel" (the universal church), Bauckham is of the view that the 144,000 are Jewish followers of Christ, and the great multitude are followers of Christ from all the nations. Bauckham, *Climax of Prophecy,* 216.

233. Resseguie, *Revelation of John,* 137–38.

Ulfgard adds, "While 7:4–8 (in an audition and from an earthly perspective) gives the symbolic number 144,000 to those who will be saved through God's protective sign, 7:9–17 (in a heavenly perspective) visualizes their security and comfort in God."[234]

A similar "hearing-seeing" (or "seeing-hearing") pattern to describe the same thing is found throughout Revelation. Thus, in Rev 9:13–16 John heard the angel blowing the sixth trumpet and what that entailed; in 9:17–21 he saw in a vision what occurred as part of the same reality he had just heard. In Rev 14:1 John saw the Lamb and the 144,000 on Mount Zion; he then heard the same reality described in 14:2–5. In Rev 15:2 he saw the overcomers standing on the sea of glass; in 15:3–4 he heard what was sung by that same group. In Rev 17:1–6 John saw the "great harlot"; in 17:7–18 he heard the angel state the identification and description of the same reality he had just seen. In Rev 21:1–2 John saw New Jerusalem coming down out of heaven; in 21:3–4 he heard a voice from heaven describing its significance.

Just as the 144,000 identifies the church as true, spiritual Israel, so does the phrase "a great multitude which no one could count"

The phrase *"a great multitude which no one could count"* (Rev 7:9) evokes the promise in the Abrahamic Covenant that God would *"greatly multiply your descendants [lit. 'seed'] so that they will be too many to count."*[235] The NT repeatedly explains that the Abrahamic Covenant, and specifically the promise to multiply Abraham's seed, is fulfilled in Christ and the church.[236] Therefore, Beale rightly concludes, "The multitudes in Rev. 7:9 are the consummate fulfillment of the Abrahamic promise and appear to be another of the manifold ways in which John refers to Christians as Israel."[237]

The use of "a great multitude" elsewhere in Revelation

Rev 19:1 and 6 are the only other occasions when the phrase *"a great multitude"* is used in the book. In both cases it obviously refers to the entire church, not just a segment of it. On all three occasions in the book when *"a great multitude"* is found, the same Greek phrase (*ochlos polus*) is used.

The "temple" and "holy city" (Rev 11:1–2)

There are different views on the meaning of the temple and the holy city, which (as with most of John's imagery) fall into two large classes: "literal" views and "figurative or symbolic" views.[238]

---

234. Ulfgard, *Feast and Future*, 105.

235. Gen 16:10; see also Gen 13:16; 15:5; 22:17; 26:4; 32:12.

236. See John 8:31–58; Rom 4:11–18; 9:6–8; Galatians 3–4.

237. Beale, *Revelation*, 427.

238. There have been a number of different proposed identifications of temple and the holy city. Five of them are surveyed in Reader, "The Riddle," 407–14.

The temple and holy city as literal

Preterists view the temple as the literal, historical temple in Jerusalem that was destroyed in AD 70.[239] The reference in Rev 11:2 to the outer court being *"given to the nations; and they will tread under foot the holy city for forty-two months"* is seen as being derived from Christ's prediction in Luke 21:24 regarding the siege and fall of Jerusalem by the Romans.[240] On the other hand, dispensationalist and some other futurist views project Revelation 11 into the period immediately preceding Christ's *parousia*. Both the temple and the altar are taken as referring to a literal, restored temple in the literal "holy city" of Jerusalem. "Those who worship in it" are seen as believing ethnic Jews.[241]

Both "literal" positions have little regard for the *purpose* of the book (which is relevant and directed to the church from the first century to the *parousia*); the *structure* of the book (in which progressively parallel sections recapitulate the challenges facing the church during all periods of history); or the *symbolic nature* of the book (in light of which "the dictum of the popular approach to Revelation—interpret literally unless you are forced to interpret symbolically—should be turned on its head"[242]). In this regard, G. B. Caird makes the perhaps counter-intuitive point (at least to "literalist" minds) that, when we take Revelation's apocalyptic genre seriously, "It is hardly too much to say that, in a book in which all things are expressed in symbols, the very last things the temple and the holy city could mean would be the physical temple and the earthly Jerusalem. If John had wanted to speak about them, he would have found some imagery to convey his meaning without lapsing into the inconsistency of literalism."[243]

The temple as figurative

The actual phrase *"temple of God"* is found eleven times in the NT.[244] Every other time that phrase is used it refers to the church.[245] Consequently, the "temple" is best understood as figurative or symbolic of the church. Additionally, there are good contextual and theological reasons within Revelation itself why the "temple" of Rev 11:1–2 cannot be a literal physical building, but symbolizes the church.

First, the Greek word for "temple" here is *naos. Naos* never refers to a physical, earthly temple any other time it is used in Revelation. In Revelation, *naos* refers either

---

239. Gentry, "A Preterist View," 65–67; see also Mathison, *Postmillennialism,* 145, 151; Bahnsen, *Victory,* 18.

240. Payne, *Encyclopedia,* 616; Bahnsen, *Victory,* 18–19.

241. Thomas, "Classical Dispensationalist View," 198; MacDonald, *Believer's,* 2367; Smith, *What the World,* 99–100; see also Ladd, *Commentary,* 149–51.

242. Beale, "Purpose of Symbolism," 55

243. Caird, *St. John the Divine,* 131.

244. Matt 26:61; 1 Cor 3:16, 17a, 17b; 2 Cor 6:16a, 16b; 2 Thess 2:4; Rev 3:12; 7:15; 11:1, 19.

245. In Matt 26:61 Jesus' reference probably was to the temple of his own body (see John 2:19–21). Nixon, "Matthew," 848. If the reference was to the then-existing temple building, it was only as a physical "type" or foreshadow of Christ and his people as the true temple. Beale, *Temple,* 275–76. Some people contend that the reference to the "temple of God" in 2 Thess 2:4 is to a future physical temple building. See chapter 10 above for reasons why that reference is to the church.

to God's existing heavenly temple[246] or to the future New Jerusalem where God and the Lamb are the temple.[247] In Rev 3:12 the promise to the overcoming saints is that they will be made *"a pillar in the temple of My God."*[248] Since overcomers are promised to be made parts of God's temple, it is not surprising that their identity as the temple is confirmed in Rev 11:1–2 even while they are on earth.[249]

Second, the symbolic nature of the language of Rev 11:1–2 and identification of the "temple" with the church are reinforced by the fact that John is told to "measure" not only the temple and the altar but also *"those who worship in it."* "Measuring" the temple comes from Ezek 40:2–5; Zech 2:1–5. Throughout the Bible, "measuring" is not merely a physical act to determine the size of something but has theological significance. Milligan says, "To measure expresses the thought of preservation, not of destruction. . . . When God therefore measures, He measures, not in indignation, but that the object measured may be in a deeper than ordinary sense the habitation of His glory."[250] God is not interested in preserving physical buildings, since he *"does not dwell in houses made by human hands"* (Acts 7:48). Rather, he is interested in preserving his people, the church, which *is* his temple.[251]

Third, Rev 13:6 is consistent with identifying the temple as the church by telling us that the beast blasphemes *"His [God's] name and His tabernacle, that is, those who dwell in heaven."* Thus, in 13:6 the "tabernacle" and *"those who dwell in heaven"* are equated, just as the "temple" and God's people are equated in 11:1.[252] That identity is corroborated by the fact that both the "forty-two months" and the "1260 days" of Rev 11:1–2, when seen in their context throughout Revelation, are, respectively, references to the persecution of, and God's protection of, the church.[253]

The holy city as figurative

Jerusalem was called the "holy city" in the OT and through the time of Jesus' ministry on earth.[254] However, after Jesus' resurrection and ascension Jerusalem is no longer called

246. Rev 7:15; 11:19; 14:15, 17; 15:5–6, 8; 16:1, 17.

247. Rev 3:12; 21:22. New Jerusalem itself is a figure that *primarily* refers to God's *people,* not a place. See below for more regarding this.

248. Even "literalists" take that promise symbolically. See Schnabel, *40 Questions,* 12.

249. Similarly believers, while still on earth, nevertheless are said to be "raised" and "seated" with Christ in "heavenly places" (Eph 2:6). Further, Christ, in heaven, so identifies with his people on earth that he said to Saul of Tarsus, "Saul, Saul, why are you persecuting *Me?*" (Acts 9:4).

250. Milligan, *Revelation,* 169. "Measuring as preservation" is another reason why either the first-century temple building or a proposed future temple building cannot be in view here. The reason is that in the Olivet Discourse Christ predicted the *destruction* of the temple, not its preservation. See Reader, "The Riddle," 410. A future temple building cannot be in view here for the additional reason that that would be a return to the "shadows" of the OT system, which Christ has forever fulfilled, abolished, and superseded. See Heb 4:14—5:10; 7:1—10:22.

251. See 1 Cor 3:9, 16–17; 2 Cor 6:16—7:1; Eph 2:21; 1 Pet 2:5; Rev 3:12; see also Rev 13:6.

252. Johnson notes that the NASB's use of the words "that is" between *"those who dwell in heaven"* and *"His tabernacle"* equates the two and "accurately reflects the implication of the Greek grammar." Johnson, *Triumph,* 166n.12.

253. See above, the section on "Genre" regarding the time references in Revelation.

254. E.g., Neh 11:1, 18; Isa 48:2; Matt 4:5; 27:53.

the "holy city." In Revelation, "holy city" is used only four times: here, and in 21:2, 10; 22:19 where it refers to the New Jerusalem, which is equated with the redeemed, the bride of Christ, the church. Kistemaker concludes, "The holy city is the spiritual Jerusalem of the saints."[255]

The outer court

The *"outer court"* is tied to the *"holy city"* in Rev 11:2. Thus, what is said about the *"holy city"* also applies to the *"outer court."* Many see *"the court which is outside the temple"* as a reference to those who outwardly belong to the church but are not true believers.[256] However, "in what follows in ch.11 there is no mention of apostates or compromisers, only a contrast of true witnesses with those who persecute them."[257] Therefore, the "outer court" likely suggests the outer experience of the church that faces persecution, as opposed to the inner, spiritual safety of the church which has been "measured" and is protected by God. Again, this imagery is another way of viewing the same reality, the church, from different points of view.[258]

The identification of the "outer court" with the outward, physical state of the church and the hardship it suffers, as opposed to its inward, spiritual security in Christ, is consistent with John's description of the church throughout Revelation: the church follows in the footsteps of Christ; it may suffer and die transiently and physically, but it triumphs spiritually and eternally. Caird explains:

> Like the seal which was set on the foreheads of God's servants, the measuring of the temple betokens an inner security against spiritual dangers. But the angel's orders are to leave the outer court exposed, because God does not offer to the church security from bodily suffering or death. It is his intention that they should remain outwardly vulnerable to the full hostility of their enemies, secure only in their faith in the crucified and risen Lord. The one thing he guarantees is that his witnesses shall have free scope to prophesy; for to prophesy is to die the death of a martyr.[259]

This view also correlates with Revelation's picture of the church as the "holy city": during "this age" the church is "measured" (i.e., is known and protected spiritually by God), but its "outer court" is not measured, and so it and the "holy city" will be *"tread under foot . . . for forty-two months"* (i.e., throughout "this age" the church, although protected spiritually, is subject to physical persecution in the world). With the *parousia* and the "age to come," however, the "holy city" *in its entirety* is "measured" (Rev 21:15–17). In other words, in the consummation, the church not only is protected spiritually but now is no longer subject to any physical persecution. This dual picture also is consistent with the "already, but not yet" nature of the kingdom. Revelation's imagery is thus coherent

---

255. Kistemaker, "Temple," 437; see also Bauckham, *Climax of Prophecy,* 172.

256. Hendriksen, *More Than Conquerors,* 127; Milligan, *Revelation,* 174–75; Reader, "The Riddle," 411.

257. Beale, *Revelation,* 560.

258. See Resseguie, *Revelation of John,* 161; Bauckham, *Climax of Prophecy,* 272.

259. Caird, *St. John the Divine,* 132; see also Johnson, *Triumph,* 166–69.

with the rest of the NT's view of the church. To take such images as the "temple," "holy city," and "outer court" as physical entities, or as distinguishing believing Jews from non-believers, would actually destroy the amazingly coherent inter-relationship of Revelation's own symbology as well as the coherence of Revelation with the rest of the NT.

The "two witnesses" (Rev 11:3–12)

As with most of the symbols in the book, the "two witnesses" have been the subject of a variety of interpretations.[260] However, there are two primary clusters of interpretation: (1) Literalists view the "two witnesses" as literal individuals, either the reincarnation of "Elijah and Moses [who] are God's messengers who will represent the Jewish Christian community at the end of history"[261] or "two actual historical eschatological personages who will be sent to Israel to bring about her conversion."[262] (2) The better view sees the "two witnesses" as a symbol for the entire church, particularly in its role as a faithful witness.[263] The reasons for identifying the two witnesses with the church are as follows:

The symbolism behind the two witnesses is broader than Moses and Elijah

Rev 11:6 certainly alludes to Elijah (see 1 Kgs 17:1) and Moses (see Exod 7:14—12:32). The reference to *"fire flow[ing] out of their mouth and devour[ing] their enemies"* (11:5) is closely based on Jer 5:14. The resurrection of the two witnesses (11:11)—*"the breath of life came into them"* and *"they stood on their feet"*—is taken from Ezek 37:5, 10. The fact that the symbolism behind the two witnesses in Rev 11:3–11 transcends Moses and Elijah indicates that the two witnesses themselves transcend Moses and Elijah (or individuals like Moses and Elijah).

The attributes of Moses and Elijah are applied collectively

While the role of the church-as-witness in 11:3–12 is modeled on Moses and Elijah, the "two witnesses" "do not function as two individual entities, but only as one entity—always in unity and in absolute union."[264] For example, 11:5 says *"fire flows out of their mouth."* That statement cannot be "literal" and alone is sufficient to indicate that these are not individual human beings. Further, the word "mouth" is singular. Similarly, 11:8 refers to their *"dead body"* (the Greek is singular), not "bodies." Thus, the "two witnesses" are treated as one collective entity not two individuals.

---

260. See Strand, "Two Witnesses," 127n.3.

261. Pate, "Progressive Dispensationalist View," 169; see also Smith, *What the World,* 103–4 (Elijah and either Moses, Enoch, or Zerubbabel).

262. Ladd, *Commentary,* 154; see also Pentecost, *Things to Come,* 305–8.

263. Hendriksen, *More Than Conquerors,* 129; Payne, *Encyclopedia,* 617; Beale, *Revelation,* 573; Johnson, *Triumph,* 171.

264. Strand, "Two Witnesses," 130. "That these prophets are not two individuals comes from observing that the powers of both Moses and Elijah are attributed to *both* the two witnesses equally, and not divided among them." Beale, *Revelation,* 575.

The "two witnesses" theme throughout the book of Revelation

Kenneth Strand observes, "The book of Revelation places a pervasive emphasis on 'two witnesses' that constitute a unity in their divine activity—namely, 'the word of God' and 'the testimony of Jesus Christ.'"[265] Therefore, as Andrew Steinmann concludes, "This close identification of the twofold witness with the saints demonstrates that the two witnesses in the third scene of the sixth trumpet should be understood as the assembly of the saints, the Church."[266]

The two witnesses are "the two olive trees and the two lampstands" (Rev 11:4)

In Zech 4:12–14, from which this image is drawn, the two olive trees are identified as *"the two anointed ones who are standing by the Lord of the whole earth."* Yoilah Yilpet gives us the important context of Zechariah which is behind the identification of the "two witnesses" as "two olive trees." In Zechariah, "these two anointed ones were Joshua and Zerubbabel, who served as high priest and governor in the kingly line. Later, these two offices would be combined in the Messiah who is both priest and king ([Zech] 6:13; Ps 110:4; Heb 7)."[267]

That imagery is carried forward in Revelation. Rev 1:6; 5:10; 20:4, 6 identify the church as a kingdom of priests who will reign with Christ. "Lampstands" earlier have been identified as the seven churches (Rev 1:12, 20; 2:1). Since the seven lampstands are churches, so are the two lampstands. With respect to the difference between the "seven" and the "two," Bauckham synthesizes John's use of this imagery: "If the seven lampstands are representative of the whole church, since seven is the number of completeness, the two lampstands stand for the church in its role of witness, according to the well-known biblical requirement that evidence be acceptable only on the testimony of two witnesses (Num 35:30; Deut 17:6; 19:15; cf. Matt 18:16; John 5:31; 8:17; 15:26–27; Acts 5:32; 2 Cor 13:1; Heb 10:28; 1 Tim 5:19). They are not part of the church, but the whole church insofar as it fulfills its role as faithful witness."[268]

The witnesses prophesy for three and a half years (Rev 11:3)

The two witnesses prophesy for three and a half years (11:3), the same length of time "the holy city" is trampled (11:2), "the woman" is in the wilderness (12:6, 14), and "those tabernacling in heaven" are blasphemed and attacked (13:6). Those texts are all symbols of the church as a whole. Beale reminds us that "the period of three and a half years is based on Dan. 7:25; 12:7, 11 (and perhaps Dan. 9:27), which prophesies a time of tribulation for Israel *as a community*."[269] Rev 11:3 is consistent with that pattern. It is another image

---

265. Strand, "Two Witnesses," 134; see Rev 1:2, 9; 6:9; 20:4; cf. 12:17; 14:12.

266. Steinmann, "Tripartite Structure," 75.

267. Yilpet, "Zechariah," 1081.

268. Bauckham, *Climax of Prophecy*, 274.

269. Beale, *Revelation*, 574, emphasis in original; see also above, the section "Time references in Revelation."

that brings out a nuance or aspect of the church as the true Israel. Further, since the three and a half years is not a literal three-and-a-half year period of time, but is a symbolic representation of the time from Christ's death and resurrection until the *parousia*,[270] the "two witnesses" could not possibly be individual human beings.

The beast "will make war with them" (Rev 11:7–10)

One does not *"make war"* against individuals. The beast's *"making war"* against the two witnesses and "overcoming" them is based on Dan 7:21, where the horn of Daniel's fourth beast *"wages war"* against the saints and "overpowers" them. In Daniel's context, the war is not against individuals but is against God's people as a whole (Dan 7:18, 22–27).

Rev 11:8 also tells us that, after they are killed, their bodies will lie in *"the great city."* Every other reference to *"the great city"* in Revelation is to "the harlot, Babylon the great."[271] As indicated in 11:8–9, "the great city encompasses all who dwell upon the earth, who give allegiance to the beast."[272] Thus, "Babylon the great" is not merely a single city but a worldwide socio-economic-religious culture or entity that is opposed to God and Christ.[273] Consequently, the "two witnesses" likewise are a figure for another world-wide socio-economic-religious entity, the church.

Further, Rev 11:7, 9–10 are clearly parallel to 13:1–2, 7–8:

11:7, 9–10: *"the beast that comes up out of the abyss will make war with them, and overcome them and kill them . . . Those from the peoples and tribes and tongues and nations will look at their dead bodies . . . And those who dwell on the earth will rejoice"*	13:7–8: *"And it was given to him [i.e., the beast that comes up out of the sea, 13:1–2] to make war with the saints and to overcome them, and authority over every tribe and people and tongue and nation was given to him. All who dwell on the earth will worship him"*

The "beast" that comes up out of the abyss is the same as the "beast" that comes up out of the sea. The *"peoples and tribes and tongues and nations"* of those who rejoice at the death of the two witnesses and those who worship the beast correspond to each other; they are the counterpart of the church which has been redeemed out of every *"tribe and tongue and people and nation"* (Rev 5:9; 7:9). Those who *"dwell on the earth"* are set in opposition to the church as a whole.[274] The conclusion is inescapable: Rev 11:7, 9–10 is a parallel description of the same event recorded in Rev 13:1–2, 7–8.[275] That further compels the conclusion that the "two witnesses" of Rev 11:3–12 is a picture of the universal church.

270. Kistemaker, "Temple," 438; Johnson, *Triumph,* 189; Beale and McDonough, "Revelation," 1119; Resseguie, *Revelation of John,* 30–31.

271. Rev 16:19; 17:18; 18:10, 16, 18, 19, 21.

272. Johnson, *Triumph,* 173.

273. For more on this see below, the section "Rev 17:1—19:10: Final judgment of Babylon."

274. See later in this chapter for further discussions of these points.

275. There is one nuance to this comparison. Rev 11:7–13 appears to relate to events that take place at the end of history. As was mentioned above in the section "Time References in Revelation," the 42 months (Rev 11:2) and 1260 days (Rev 11:3) refer to the entire period of the witness of the church that began with Christ's resurrection and ascension. Rev 11:7, however, relates to events *"when they have finished their testimony."* The *"three and a half days"* (11:9, 11) contrast with the 1260 days, and the section ends with the *parousia* (see the next section in the main text). While Rev 13:7 may likewise have special application to the period at the end of history, the principles stated in that chapter apply to all of

The resurrection of the two witnesses (Rev 11:11–13)

This description is taken from Ezek 37:5, 10. There are two main views concerning the resurrection and ascent of the "two witnesses": it is a figure for the church's ultimate vindication; or it is a description of the actual resurrection of believers at the *parousia*. Beale articulates the first view: "The ascent of the witnesses figuratively affirms a final, decisive deliverance and vindication of God's people at the end of time. This figurative understanding is enforced by the Ezekiel prophecy, which uses nonliteral resurrection language to speak of Israel's restoration from captivity. . . . John applies Ezekiel's words to the restored church because he sees its members finally released from their earthly pilgrimage of captivity and suffering. This demonstrates that they are God's true people (cf. Ezek. 37:12–13)."[276]

On the other hand, the resurrection could be the literal resurrection and rapture of the church at Christ's return. Ezek 37:5, 10 is part of Ezekiel's prophecy of the dry bones that, in a vision, he sees re-animated to life. The image certainly conveys the idea of resurrection, not simply vindication. Whether Rev 11:12 signifies vindication or literal resurrection is of little moment, since final vindication entails resurrection and *vice versa*.

Further, this passage parallels Revelation 20. *"When they have finished their testimony"* (Rev 11:7) parallels *"after these things"* (Rev 20:3) and *"when the thousand years are completed"* (Rev 20:7). The *"three and a half days"* (Rev 11:11) of the beast's triumph over the "two witnesses" is consistent with the *"short time"* Satan is given to *"deceive the nations"* and bring worldwide opposition against the saints (Rev 20:3, 7–9). In Rev 20:9–10, Satan and his minions are destroyed at the *parousia*, at which resurrection and judgment occur (Rev 20:11–15). That similarly is indicated here by the fact that the resurrection occurs *"in that hour"* in which also *"there was a great earthquake"* (Rev 11:13). The "hour" suggests Christ's second coming and the judgment it entails.[277] The "earthquake" also is a motif indicating the *parousia* and God's judgment of the earth.[278]

The "woman" and "her children" (Rev 12:1–17)

As was mentioned earlier in this chapter, Revelation 12 is a central passage in the book. It recapitulates the history of the church and its conflict with Satan beginning at least with the first coming of Christ, if not before. The picture of the woman in 12:1 is from Gen 37:9. Ladd describes and synthesizes the major views of the identity of the woman:

---

history since Christ's resurrection and ascension. As was discussed in chapter 10, the "beasts" of Revelation 13 represent anti-Christian governments, societies, and cultures that began with ancient Rome but exist throughout history. That is seen in Rev 13:5 which says that *"authority to act for forty-two months was given to [the beast]."* Rev 13:7, unlike Rev 11:7, does not specify that the *"war with the saints"* takes place only after certain events have been completed, and the discussion of the activities of the beast in Revelation 13 does not end with a description of the *parousia*. Thus, in principle, the beast is *always* at war with the saints, although that warfare will intensify at the end of history.

276. Beale, *Revelation*, 597.

277. See Rev 3:3; 14:7, 15 and the section in chapter 9, "Rev 3:10 and the promise to keep you from the hour of testing."

278. This has been discussed above in the section "Structure: progressively parallel; not strictly chronological."

The central feature of this heavenly woman is that she is the mother of the Messiah (vs. 2). Some commentators think she represents Mary, the mother of the Lord; others Israel, the people who gave birth to Messiah. It is true that Isaiah 66:7 pictures Zion as being in travail to give birth to the new redeemed Israel (see Isa. 26:17; Mic. 4:10); but this heavenly woman is mother both of Messiah and of the actual church on earth (her 'offspring,' vs. 17). Therefore, it is easier to understand the woman in a somewhat broader sense as the *ideal* Zion, the heavenly representative of the people of God (Isa. 54:1; 66:7–9).[279]

The woman *"gave birth to a son"* (12:5), who obviously is Christ. The dragon (Satan, 12:9) *"went off to make war with the rest of her children,"* who are specifically described as those *"who keep the commandments of God and hold to the testimony of Jesus"* (12:17). That can only be the church, since only Christians meet that description.[280]

The "harvest" (Rev 14:15–16)

The gathering of the grapes for the wine press of God (Rev 14:17–20) clearly refers to the judgment of the ungodly at the end of the age.[281] Some see the reaping of the harvest (Rev 14:15–16) as representing another account of the same judgment of the ungodly in order to emphasize "the severity and unqualified nature of the punishment."[282] On the other hand, others (probably the better view) hold that the grain harvest is the redemption of the godly (the church), in distinction to the judgment of the ungodly, for the following reasons:

(1) Just as the references to wine in Rev 14:8, 10 prefigure the "wine press" metaphor of 14:19–20, so the "first fruits" of 14:4 prefigures the grain harvest metaphor of 14:15–16.

(2) The grain harvest takes place in only one action: reaping (no threshing or winnowing is said to take place); therefore, it is not parallel to the grape harvest which takes place in multiple actions: gathering, throwing, and treading.

(3) Regarding eschatological consummation, reaping in the NT is always a positive image of bringing people into the kingdom (Mark 4:29; John 4:35–38), not of judgment on the ungodly.[283]

---

279. Ladd, *Commentary*, 167; see also Carson, "This Present Evil Age," 19–20; Caird, *St. John the Divine*, 149. Beale adds, "That the woman represents the old and new covenant community is apparent from the remainder of the chapter, where her 'seed' is not only Christ but also the community of his followers (so vv 6, 11–17). Since the whore of ch. 17 symbolizes the unbelieving community, so here the contrasting figure of the righteous woman must represent the believing community." Beale, *Revelation*, 630. The church, i.e., true Israel, the New Jerusalem, is called *"our mother"* in Gal 4:26.

280. This is another example of the apocalyptic use of two different symbols to describe the same entity. The messianic community, the true Israel, the ideal Zion (i.e., the Old and New Covenant church as a whole) is first described as a mother, but then (at least the New Covenant church) is described as her own "children."

281. Such imagery for God's judgment is drawn from Isa 63:1–6; Lam 1:15; see also Rev 19:15.

282. Beale, *Revelation*, 774–75.

283. Bauckham, *Climax of Prophecy*, 290–96; Johnson, *Triumph*, 209–12.

The victors over the beast (Rev 15:2–4)

This scene pictures the victorious "overcoming" church mentioned by Christ in Rev 2:7, 11, 17, 26; 3:5, 12, 21. The scene's setting and imagery are linked to the scenes in Rev 4:6 (*"sea of glass"*) and 5:9 (the song praising the Lamb). That reinforces the idea of the overcoming church pictured in heaven.

The "standing" of the saints may suggest resurrection. The verb for "stand" used here (*histēmi*) is not typically used for resurrection.[284] However, it is used of Christ's *"standing at the right hand of God"* in Acts 7:55–56, of the Lamb's standing in Rev 5:6, of the great multitude's standing before the throne in Rev 7:9, and of the two witnesses' "standing" in Rev 11:11 after they had been dead for three and a half days. All such uses of *histēmi* certainly denote victory and vindication if not also resurrection (or victory and vindication *as evidenced by* resurrection).

That the universal church is being referred to also is indicated by the songs sung. Rev 15:3 first mentions the "song of Moses," which refers back to the song of victory sung after the exodus from Egypt (Exod 15:1–21). However, Milligan notes that the song sung by the victors "is not that of Moses only, the great centre of the Old Testament Dispensation; it is also *the Song of the Lamb,* the centre and the sum of the New Testament. Both Dispensations are in the Seer's thoughts, and in the number of those who sing are included the saints of each, the members of the one Universal Church."[285]

The "called and chosen and faithful" (Rev 17:14)

Here the church is clearly identified, since the people referred to are *"those who are with Him [the Lamb]."* Further, they are described as the *"called and chosen [elect] and faithful."* Everywhere else in the NT, after Christ's resurrection, when those words describe people, they are used to describe Christians (the church).[286]

"My people" (Rev 18:4)

"My people" can only be those who are united with and faithful to the Lord (i.e., the church). John's exhortation to *"come out of her, my people"* is yet another example of an inter-textual allusion. The statement alludes to Isa 48:20; 52:11; Jer 50:8; 51:6, 9, 45.[287] In

---

284. On the other hand, *anistēmi*, which is derived from *histēmi*, frequently is used for resurrection. See Matt 12:41–42; 17:9; 20:19; Mark 8:31; 9:9–10, 31; 10:34; 12:23, 25; 16:9; Luke 9:8, 19; 11:31–32; 16:31; 18:33; 24:7; John 6:39, 40, 44, 54; 11:23, 24; 20:9; Acts 2:24, 30, 32; 3:26; 13:33, 34; 17:3; 31; Rom 14:9; 1 Thess 4:14, 16.

285. Milligan, *Revelation,* 261, emphasis in original.

286. *"Called"*: Rom 1:1, 6, 7; 8:28; 1 Cor 1:1, 2, 24; Jude 1.
"Chosen [elect]": Matt 20:16; 22:14; 24:22, 24, 31; Mark 13:20, 22, 27; Luke 18:7; Rom 8:33; 16:13; Col 3:12; 2 Tim 2:10; Titus 1:1; 1 Pet 1:1; 2:4, 9; 2 John 1, 13.
"Faithful": Matt 24:45; 25:21, 23; Luke 12:42; 16:10; 19:17; John 20:27; Acts 10:45; 16:1, 15; 1 Cor 4:2, 17; 7:25; 2 Cor 6:15; Eph 1:1; 6:21; Col 1:2, 7; 4:7, 9; 1 Tim 1:12; 3:1; 4:3, 10, 12; 5:16; 6:2; 2 Tim 2:2; Titus 1:6; 1 Pet 5:12; 3 John 5; Rev 2:10, 13.

287. In 2 Cor 6:16–17 Paul similarly paraphrased Isa 52:11 in exhorting believers to remain pure. In that passage he also called the chuch the *"temple of God"* (cf. Rev 11:1, 19). Since 2 Corinthians was

all of those passages, the context concerned literal Babylon. So here, as Johnson says, like the warnings in the letters to the seven churches (Revelation 2–3), this verse "is addressed to professing Christians who were being seduced by Satan through the wiles of the queen prostitute to abandon their loyalty to Jesus."[288]

The "bride" (Rev 19:7–9; 21:2, 9; 22:17)

As he has done throughout the book, in his image of the bride, John has taken an OT image relating to the restoration of Israel[289] and has applied it to the church. In Rev 21:9 the New Jerusalem is described both as *"the bride"* and *"the wife of the Lamb."* John does that to elaborate the nature of the relationship between Christ and his people. Celia Deutsch elaborates, "The specification of the woman as bride evokes the notion of newness and ardor, and the reference to Jerusalem as wife suggests enduring fidelity and fruitfulness. Thus, in designating the New Jerusalem as bride and wife, John is telling us of the city's beauty, and the intimacy and fruitfulness of the relationship between God and the redeemed in the apocalyptic age. Moreover, the appearance of similar language in [Rev 19:7, 9; 21:9; 22:17] indicates that that relationship has already begun in the historical community."[290]

The bride of Christ contrasts with the harlot of the world

The wording of Rev 17:1 and 21:9 are parallel. The Bride is clothed *"in fine linen, bright and clean; for the fine linen is the righteous acts of the saints"* (Rev 19:8). The "Mother of Harlots" is dressed as a harlot, *"clothed in purple and scarlet, and adorned with gold and precious stones and pearls, having in her hand a gold cup full of abominations and of the unclean things of her immoralities"* (Rev 17:4; 18:16). The bride is exalted (Rev 21:9—22:5); the harlot is destroyed (Rev 17:1—19:6).

The "marriage supper of the Lamb" is contrasted with "the great supper of God"

All who are invited to the *"marriage supper of the Lamb"* are *"blessed"* (Rev 19:9);[291] at the *"great supper of God,"* all who oppose Christ are killed and eaten (Rev 19:17–21).

---

written in approximately AD 56, it is possible that John knew of it. Regardless of that, John's use of *"come out of her"* shows the common practice among the apostles to identify OT themes and phrases and apply them to the church.

288. Johnson, "Revelation," 567.

289. See Isa 49:18; 61:10; 62:5.

290. Deutsch, "Transformation of Symbols," 112–13. Revelation shows us the lengths to which Christ will go to prepare and sanctify his bride so that she is *"made ready . . . for her husband"* (Rev 21:2; see also Eph 5:25–27). The beauty and radiance of the church as the bride of Christ illustrate C. S. Lewis's statements that "there are no *ordinary* people," and "the dullest and most uninteresting person you can talk to may one day be a creature which, if you saw it now, you would be strongly tempted to worship." Lewis, *Weight of Glory,* 18–19.

291. This fulfills both the OT prophecy of Isa 25:6 and Christ's "messianic banquet" prophecies of Matt 8:11; 22:1–10; 26:29; Mark 14:25; Luke 13:29; 14:16–24; 22:16, 18, 29–30.

The "armies" (Rev 19:14)

There are different views concerning the identity of the "armies" of Rev 19:14. The two main views are that they represent angels or that they represent redeemed believers (i.e., the church, perhaps in concert with angels). In Rev 12:7 angels waged war with the dragon and his armies. Elsewhere in the NT, angels are said to accompany Christ at the *parousia* and participate in the execution of the final judgment.[292]

The better view is that the heavenly armies of Rev 19:14 include the saints, not merely angels. That is seen by comparing Rev 19:13–15 with the important parallel passage of Rev 17:14 which:

> supports the identification of the armies as the saints, not angels, because there it is saints who accompany Christ, and there also Christ is called "Lord of lords and King of kings" (as in 19:16). The "white, pure linen" worn by the armies . . . is appropriate both for angels (15:6; Dan. 10:5; 12:6; Ezek. 9:2) or saints (19:8). But in the Apocalypse, with one exception (15:6), only saints wear white garments (3:4–5, 18; 4:4; 6:11; 7:9, 13–14). The saints here and in 17:14 take part in the final judgment only in that their testimony is the legal evidence condemning their oppressors (for such an understanding of a witness that judges see Matt. 12:41–42 par.; Rom. 2:27).[293]

Mealy notes additional inter-textual references within Revelation which indicate that the armies of 19:14, at minimum, include the church: "The robe dipped in blood (Rev. 19.13) recalls 7.14, in which the robes of the saints attending Christ's parousia were described as washed and made white in the blood of the Lamb. . . . The sharp sword (Rev. 19.15) correlates with the warning to the church at Pergamum in 2.16. . . . The reference to Christ ruling the nations with a rod of iron (Rev. 19.15) closely echoes the words of 2.26–27, in which Christ promises the church in Thyatira that the overcomer will participate with him in his role as ruler and judge at the parousia."[294]

Those sitting on the thrones (Rev 20:4–6)

Virtually all commentators agree that the church (or its representatives, the martyrs) is being described in this passage. The parallels between this scene and the scene in Rev 6:9 indicates that these are heavenly, not earthly, thrones.[295] That the scene is in heaven, not

---

292. See Matt 13:40–42; 16:27; 24:30–31; 25:31–32; Mark 8:38; Luke 9:26; 2 Thess 1:7; Jude 14–15.

293. Beale, *Revelation*, 960; see also Johnson, *Triumph*, 274; Bauckham, *Climax of Prophecy*, 237; Schüssler Fiorenza, *Revelation*, 78.

294. Mealy, *After the Thousand Years*, 221–22.

295. Regarding the parallels between Rev 20:4–6 and Rev 6:9, see below on Rev 20:1–15, the section "The timing of the 'thousand years.'" On the other hand, J. Marcellus Kik states, "Throne is a figure of speech indicating the reign of the saint. . . . The thrones stand for the saints' spiritual dominion within himself and over the world. Through the grace of Christ they reign in life over the flesh, the world, and the devil. . . . He reigns over sin because sin has no dominion over him. He reigns over Satan who cannot touch him. He reigns over the world because of Him who has overcome the world. . . . Thus these thrones are not literal and material. . . . Rather they are the thrones occupied by the saints on earth during the period of [the] thousand years." Kik, *Eschatology*, 210, 213. Kik notes that in Rev 20:4 the words *sat, given, worshipped, received,* and *reigned* all are in the aorist tense. He concludes, "Since they are all in

on the earth, also is apparent from the fact that, as Onesimus Ngundu tells us, "all of John's forty-seven references to 'a throne' or 'thrones' in Revelation locate the throne in heaven, except for Satan's throne (2:13) and that of the beast (13:2; 16:10)."[296] Even the thrones of Satan and the beast are "not earthly but located in a spiritual dimension."[297]

The Greek of the passage is irregular. It is therefore difficult to say whether one group of people is being described in different ways, or more than one group is being described. Yarbro Collins describes the ambiguity:

> The text is ambiguous on the issue of participation in this messianic reign. If *hoitines* ["those"] retains its classical sense, it would refer to a wider circle than the martyrs referred to in the *tōn pepelekismenōn* ["who had been beheaded"] clause. Thus participation would seem to be open to all faithful Christians. But *hoitines* in NT Greek most often functions just like the ordinary relative, so the *hoitines* clause may be a further qualification of "the souls of those who had been beheaded." Thus participation would be limited to the martyrs. . . . Although it is not clear whether the thousand-year reign was limited to the martyrs, at least it is clear that they are singled out for special emphasis. The first resurrection and the exercise of kingly power with Christ are blessings by which those who share the fate of Jesus with regard to his death are also enabled to share in his glorious destiny.[298]

In light of the ambiguous Greek, Ladd observes, "Some commentators see three groups in this passage: the saints in general (those who sat in the thrones), the martyrs (those beheaded), and the living saints (those who had not worshipped the beast nor received its mark)."[299] Others see this heavenly court as also including angels, since in Rev 4:4 those sitting on thrones appear to be angels.[300]

---

the same tense they must refer to the same time. That is, the time of not worshipping the beast and not receiving his mark is the same time as that of sitting on thrones and living and reigning with Christ." Ibid., 228. R. Fowler White adds, "To say in [Rev] 20:6 that those who take part in the first resurrection will reign with Christ is to say that they will do so first on earth before they die and then in heaven after they die." White, "Death and the First Resurrection," 13. In a private communication with the author, White likewise cited the aorist tense of the verbs, stating, "As Augustine taught, the first resurrection *precedes the martyrs' bodily death and delivers them to it.* To put this in terms of the text itself, the martyrs were slain because they had *not worshiped the beast or his image, and* had *not received the mark on their forehead and on their hand, and* had *come to life and* had *reigned with Christ for a thousand years.* The aorist verbs here should be translated consistently as referring to events preceding the martyrs' death."

296. Ngundu, "Revelation," 1675; see also Gourgues, "Thousand-year Reign," 679.

297. Beale, *Revelation,* 999.

298. Yarbro Collins, "Political Perspective," 251.

299. Ladd, *Commentary,* 265.

300. See below in the "Overview of major ideas and sections" regarding Rev 4:4. There is also debate concerning whether the scene described in Rev 20:4–6 takes place before or after the *parousia.* In that respect, Rev 20:4–6 is one of the most disputed passages in the entire Bible. This passage is elaborated both below in the "Overview of major ideas and sections" and in Appendix 2: The Millennium: An Amillennial Synthesis of the Biblical Data. For our current purposes it is sufficient to see that Rev 20:4–6 is yet another picture of the church.

The "camp of the saints and the beloved city" (Rev 20:9)

Neither the "camp" nor the "city" is to be taken as a literal camp or city. They, like the many other figures we have seen, figuratively and symbolically describe the church. The *"beloved city"* (i.e., the church) contrasts with the *"great city"* (i.e., Babylon, the worldwide anti-Christian, religious-cultural entity). Additionally, the *"camp of the saints"* and the *"beloved city"* are the same, not different. As we saw above and will below, the New Jerusalem is equated with the *"holy city"* which is equated with believers (the church). Rev 3:12 further identifies all believers (i.e., *"he who overcomes"*) with *"the city of My God"* (i.e., the New Jerusalem). The *"beloved city"* cannot be different from the *"holy city"* or *"the city of My God,"* which is the New Jerusalem, i.e., the believers, the overcomers, *"the camp of the saints."* These are all overlapping metaphors that are equated with the church.[301]

The equation of the *"camp of the saints"* with the *"beloved city"* shows in another way that the worldwide church is being described. In 20:9 the NASB and ESV say that Gog and Magog came up on *"the broad plain of the earth."* The NKJV and NIV translate that phrase as *"the breadth of the earth."*[302] Gundry therefore observes, "To come against this city or camp, Gog and Magog had to spread out 'over the breadth of the earth.' So the city did not seem to be confined to one spot. It was the saints themselves wherever they lived on earth."[303]

"His people(s)" (Rev 21:3)

This verse is the culmination of a recurrent statement throughout the Bible (with some variations): *"I will be their God, and they will be my people."*[304] The OT passages speak of the special relationship between God and his people. The exilic and post-exilic prophets use this phrase to speak of a restored Israel. The NT takes this same language and applies it to God's new, true, restored Israel—the church. Revelation culminates this by applying it forever to the "holy city," the "New Jerusalem," the "bride," the "wife of the Lamb" (Rev 21:2, 9–10), i.e., the transformed and glorified people of God—the church.[305]

In the statement *"I will be their God, and they will be my people,"* all the OT and NT passages use the singular "people." In Rev 21:3, however, a significant number of early manuscripts use the plural "peoples" rather than the singular "people."[306] If that is the case, John makes the change from "people" to "peoples" to "make obvious that prophecies

---

301. See Kistemaker, "Temple," 437; Bauckham, *Climax of Prophecy,* 172; Beale, *Revelation,* 1027.

302. In a footnote the NASB notes that the phrase literally is *"breadth of the earth."*

303. Gundry, "New Jerusalem," 256–57. Contra Schnabel, *40 Questions,* 227, who sees this as a reference to the Abyss.

304. Gen 17:8; Exod 6:7; 29:45; Lev 26:12; Jer 7:23; 11:4; 24:7; 30:22; 31:1, 33; 32:38; Ezek 11:19–20; 14:10–11; 36:28; 37:23, 27; Hos 2:23; Zech 8:8; 13:9; Rom 9:25–26; 2 Cor 6:16; Heb 8:10; Rev 21:3.

305. The statement in Rev 21:3 that *"the tabernacle of God is among men"* was foreshadowed in Rev 7:15 which says that God *"will spread his tabernacle over them"* (i.e., over the "great multitude"—the church). That cross-reference confirms that the universal church is in view in both passages.

306. *UBS4* finds that "peoples" is the preferred reading. *UBS4,* 881.

originally focusing on Israel have been fulfilled in 'every tribe, tongue, people, and nation' (see 5:9; 7:9)."[307]

The "New Jerusalem" (Rev 21:1—22:15)

As we have seen with many of John's other symbols and images, there are two main camps regarding the interpretation of the "New Jerusalem": literalists and non-literalists. Literalists interpret New Jerusalem as a literal description of an actual physical city. However, *"the bride, the wife of the Lamb"* (Rev 21:9), which obviously is the church, is equated with the city in Rev 21:2, 10. Further, Gundry observes that the descriptions of the New Jerusalem are more "personal than topographical."[308] God's eternal plan has always been to dwell in a holy place with his holy people.[309] This plan finds its consummation in the New Jerusalem. Consequently, Ortlund states, "The dwelling of God with man *in the form of a city* may . . . suggest the perfect social union of the redeemed with one another as God's final and eternal answer to the successive societal failures littering the course of human history."[310]

That the names of the twelve apostles are said to be the "foundation" of the wall of the city again suggests that more than just geography is being described: "Noteworthy is the observation in 21:14 that the apostles are part of the foundation, whereas the tribes are part of the gates in the wall built on the foundation. One might have expected the opposite portrayal since Israel preceded the church in redemptive history. But the reversal figuratively highlights the fact that fulfillment of Israel's promises has finally come in Christ, who, together with the apostolic witness to his fulfilling work, forms the foundation of the new temple, the church, which is the new Israel."[311] Given all this, New Jerusalem primarily appears to be a metaphor for God's people and his relationship with them rather than a description of the geography that will exist after Christ comes again.[312]

---

307. Beale, *Revelation*, 1047; see also Gundry, "New Jerusalem," 257; Johnson, *Triumph*, 305n.2. Beale adds, "Zech. 2:10–11 anticipates Rev. 21:3 in its interpretation of the same prophecies concerning God's final communion with his people, foreseeing an ethnic expansion of the boundaries of true Israel by identifying 'many nations' as 'my people,' a term always used elsewhere in the OT for Israel." Beale, *Revelation*, 1047.

308. Gundry, "New Jerusalem," 256.

309. See Goldsworthy, *According to Plan*, 76; Alexander, *From Eden*, 29 ("God is interested in making the whole earth his residence by filling it with holy people").

310. Ortlund, *God's Unfaithful Wife*, 166n.73.

311. Beale, *Revelation*, 1070.

312. New Jerusalem is the description of the consummate, eternal state that will be ushered in with Christ's *parousia*. As such, its significance is multivalent. It includes the restoration of the earth and physical cosmos. See below in the "Overview of major ideas and sections" for a more detailed explanation of this. As was the case with those seated on the thrones in Rev 20:4–6, for present purposes the meaning of the symbol of New Jerusalem at minimum includes depicting the eternal state of the church *as a "holy city"* and is not merely a description of the physical appearance or geography of the eternal *"new heaven and new earth."* R. Fowler White puts it like this, "The saints appear as the holy city (cf. [Rev] 3:12), while the new heavens and earth emerge as the eternal dwelling place of God and man." White, "On the Hermeneutics," 61.

Overview of major ideas and sections[313]

Several aspects of the major ideas and sections of Revelation have already been discussed above in chapter 10–The "Antichrist" (the "beasts" of Revelation) and in this chapter regarding "Genre" (regarding numbers and time periods in Revelation), "Structure: general considerations," "Structure: progressively parallel; not strictly chronological" (particularly parallels of the seals-trumpets-bowls and the multiple descriptions of the *parousia* and final judgment), and "The church in Revelation: major figures and symbols (the multiple depictions of the church)." As we go through the major sections of Revelation, please refer back to those prior discussions as those aspects of the book will not be repeated. Other important aspects of the major sections of the book are below.

Rev 1:1–20: prologue

John promises blessing to those who read, hear, and heed the words of the book (Rev 1:3). Even in the introduction, the focus is on Christ (Rev 1:5–8, 13–18).

The *"seven Spirits who are before His throne"* (Rev 1:4; see also 3:1; 4:5; 5:6) probably is a figurative reference to the Holy Spirit. The Holy Spirit clearly is one[314] yet is referred to as *"the seven Spirits"*[315] which, in Rev 5:6, are equated with the Lamb's "seven eyes." The "seven eyes" and "seven Spirits" have been adapted from Zech 3:8–9; 4:1–10.[316] In Zech 3:9, the "seven eyes" are related to an inscription that deals with God's removing the iniquity from the land. In Zech 4:2, 10, the "seven lamps" and "seven eyes" are associated with God's Spirit. Beale and McDonough comment, "John has interpreted the 'seven eyes' in Zechariah as Yahweh's Spirit and has identified both as a possession of the Lamb. It is only by the Spirit of Yahweh's 'Servant the Branch [Zech 3:8], the messianic lamb, that iniquity has been removed from the world (Zech. 3:9) and resistance to the kingdom overcome (cf. Zech. 4:6–7)."[317] The reference to *"seven* Spirits" suggests the fullness of the Spirit.

---

313. Good audio expositions of the book of Revelation that can be listened to or downloaded for free are available online by: Arturo Azurdia at: http://www.monergism.com/thethreshold/articles/onsite/azurdia_revelation.html; G. K. Beale at: http://resources.thegospelcoalition.org/library?f%5Bbook%5D%5B%5D=Revelation&f%5Bcontributors%5D%5B%5D=Beale%2C+G.K.&page=2&sort=contributors; D. A. Carson at: http://resources.thegospelcoalition.org/library?f%5Bbook%5D%5B%5D=Revelation&f%5Bcontributors%5D%5B%5D=Carson%2C+D.+A.&sort=contributors; John Fesko at: http://www.genevaopc.org/audio/fesko-lectures/72-revelation-lecture-series.html; Jonathan Menn at: http://www.eclea.net/sermons.html#revelation (both audio and written transcripts); and Kim Riddlebarger at: http://www.christreformed.org/kim-riddlebarger/#Revelation (audio), and http://kimriddlebarger.squarespace.com/downloadable-sermons-on-the-bo/ (written transcripts).

314. Rev 2:7, 11, 17, 29; 3:6, 13, 22; 22:17; see also Eph 4:4.

315. Rev 1:4; 5:6; or "sevenfold Spirit," NIV note.

316. The "seven Spirits" may also have been adapted from Isa 11:2 which speaks of *"the Spirit of the Lord . . . the spirit of wisdom and understanding, the spirit of counsel and strength, the spirit of knowledge and the fear of the Lord."*

317. Beale and McDonough, "Revelation," 1102; see also Bauckham, *Theology*, 110–15.

Rev 2:1—3:22: the letters to the seven churches

Even in the first century, the churches were experiencing the signs Christ had warned about in the Olivet Discourse, including persecution by Jews,[318] persecution in general including death,[319] false prophets,[320] falling away from the faith,[321] and love growing cold.[322] In this section, Christ encourages the churches to witness and warns them against compromise in order that they may inherit eternal life.

The ethical nature of the prophecies to the churches

The "seven letters to the seven churches" is a key section in the book. They consist entirely of Christ's words to the churches, which alone makes them important. They provide exhortations, warnings, and promises that play out throughout the rest of the book and are fulfilled at the end of the book. Håkan Ulfgard notes, "The 'letters' to the seven churches also have the character of a public, prophetic message. Their words of comfort or threat are not directed at the distant future, but speak directly into the lives of the readers/listeners, challenging them to identify themselves with the 'symbolic universe' outlined in John's visions, and to act accordingly."[323]

Part of the prophetic-ethical strategy of the seven messages is to highlight the contrast between "present and eschatological reality." Richard Bauckham explains:

> The Bride is the New Jerusalem, which comes down out of heaven from God (21:2), the church at the consummation of history. The Bride is the church which the Lamb, when he comes, will find ready for his marriage, arrayed in the fine linen of righteous deeds (19:7–8). The Bride is the church seen from the perspective of the *parousia*. Very different were the churches addressed in the Apocalypse. The 'soiled clothes' of the Christians at Laodicea (3:17) contrast with the pure linen of the Bride. The general unpreparedness for the Lord's coming at Ephesus, Pergamum, Sardis (3:17) contrasts with the Bride's ardent prayer for the Bridegroom's coming (22:17). The contrast is not really between the faithful and the unfaithful within the churches. . . . The contrast is rather between present and eschatological reality, between the churches as they are and the churches as they must become if they are to take their place at the eschatological nuptial banquet.[324]

That same contrast should impel us to assess the present state of our own churches and lives in light of the coming eschatological reality.

---

318. Compare Mark 13:9 and Rev 2:9–10; 3:9.

319. Compare Matt 24:9 and Rev 2:9–10, 13.

320. Compare Matt 24:5, 11, 23–26 and Rev 2:2, 6, 14–15, 20–24.

321. Compare Matt 24:10 and Rev 2:14, 20–24; 3:1–3, 15–17.

322. Compare Matt 24:12 and Rev 2:4.

323. Ulfgard, *Feast and Future,* 13; see also Schüssler Fiorenza, *Revelation,* 47; Aune, *Prophecy in Early Christianity,* 277.

324. Bauckham, *Climax of Prophecy,* 167.

The contrast between the churches and the "earth-dwellers"

The phrase *"those who dwell on the earth,"* or variants of that phrase, repeatedly occurs throughout the book.[325] The phrase always has a negative meaning. It indicates that, at their essence, unbelievers approach life from a worldly perspective and mindset; they are *of* the world in addition to being *in* the world (cf. John 17:14–18). As such, they follow the ways of the world and fall under God's condemnation.

By contrast, in Revelation the church always belongs to heaven regardless of where its members may reside physically.[326] Throughout Revelation, *all* of humanity ("*every tribe and people and tongue and nation*") is seen as being a member of one of two, mutually opposing, camps: the world,[327] or the church;[328] those who dwell on the earth,[329] or those who are citizens of heaven;[330] those who worship the beast,[331] or those who worship the Lamb;[332] those who bear the mark of the beast,[333] or are those who are sealed by God;[334] those whose names have not been written in the book of life,[335] or those whose names have been written in the book of life;[336] those who are part of the "great city,"[337] or those who are part of the "beloved city."[338] There is no "neutral" or third alternative.[339] Therefore, believers should approach life from a heavenly perspective and mindset (Phil 3:20); although they are *in* the world they should not be *of* it (John 17:13–19). The entire book of Revelation provides the heavenly perspective of the true significance of what is occurring on earth so that believers can be conformed to the image of Christ (Rom 8:29).

The paradoxical nature of "overcoming"

In Rev 2:7, 11, 17, 26; 3:5, 12, 21 Christ gives promises to the one who "overcomes." The Greek for "overcome" or "conquer" is *nikaō*. That same term also is used in Rev 12:11, 15:2, and in Rom 8:35–37. The use of *nikaō* in Revelation indicates a paradoxical notion

---

325. Rev 3:10; 6:10; 8:13; 11:10; 13:8, 12, 14; 14:6; 17:2, 8.

326. Johnson, *Triumph*, 147; see also Luter and Hunter, "Overlooked," 3–8.

327. Rev 11:9; 13:7; 14:6; see also 17:15.

328. Rev 5:9; 7:9.

329. Rev 3:10; 6:10; 8:13; 11:10; 13:8, 12, 14; 14:6; 17:2, 8.

330. Rev 6:9, 11; 7:9–10; 11:12; 12:10; 14:1–3; 15:2–4; 19:1–9, 14; 20:4–6.

331. Rev 13:3, 4, 8, 12, 15; 14:9, 11; 19:20.

332. Rev 4:8–11; 5:9–14; 6:9; 7:9–17; 11:15–18; 12:11, 17; 14:4, 12; 15:2–4; 17:14; 19:5–9; 20:4; 21:9; 22:3.

333. Rev 13:16–17; 14:9, 11; 19:20.

334. Rev 7:3; 9:4; 14:1; 22:4.

335. Rev 13:8; 17:8; 20:15.

336. Rev 3:5; 21:27.

337. Rev 11:8; 16:19; 17:18; 18:10, 16, 18, 19, 21.

338. Rev 20:9.

339. See Schüssler Fiorenza, *Revelation*, 84, 130; see also Stott, *What Christ Thinks*, 8–9; Luter and Hunter, "Overlooked," 8; Stylianopoulos, "I Know," 26. In the second half of the book we see this dualism expressed through the contrast of three vivid images involving animals, women, and cities: Beast—Lamb; Harlot—Bride; Babylon the great—New Jerusalem.

of "overcoming" that is modeled on Christ's own overcoming of Satan and death. For example, Rev 1:5–6 describes Christ's redemptive work. R. Fowler White points out, "That the victory of Christ took place at his death is clear from John's reference to his blood (1:6). Without at all denying the victory in Christ's resurrection, the irony of victory in Christ's death is palpable."[340] The paradoxical nature of Christ's overcoming likewise is portrayed in Revelation 5. Greg Beale observes, "He conquered death by being raised from the dead. But the present victorious effect of the Lamb's overcoming resides not only in the fact that the Lamb continues to 'stand' but also in the fact that it continues to exist as a *slaughtered* Lamb. . . . That is, Christ as a Lion overcame by being slaughtered as a Lamb, which is the critical event in chap. 5."[341]

The church follows in her Master's footsteps. Revelation is saying that "like Jesus' initial kingship, the church's kingship consists now in conquering by maintaining her faithful witness in the face of trials (e.g., 2:9–11, 13; 3:8; 12:11); in overcoming the powers of evil (e.g., 6:8 in relation to 6:9–11); in subduing sin in her members' lives (see chaps. 2–3); and in beginning to rule over death and Satan by identification with Jesus (cf. 1:5–6, 18). The church's endurance, then, is part of the process of conquering."[342] We see this same paradoxical notion of "overcoming" in Rev 11:7; 13:7 where the beast is said to "overcome" the saints by causing their physical suffering and death. Nevertheless, Christ and the saints are said to "overcome" the dragon, the beast, and all their agents *"because of the word of their testimony, and they did not love their life even when faced with death"* (12:11; see also 15:2; 17:14). White concludes, "Perseverance in faith despite persecution *is* victory for the church in history."[343]

Rev 4:1—5:14: the throne, the book (scroll), and the Lamb

In this section, God and Christ are glorified because Christ's resurrection demonstrates that they are sovereign over creation to judge and to redeem. "The 'book' is best understood as containing God's plan of judgment and redemption, which has been set in motion by Christ's death and resurrection but has yet to be completed."[344] Schüssler Fiorenza states, "The central theological question of chapters 4–5 as well as of the whole book is: Who is the true Lord of this world?"[345]

---

340. White, "Agony, Irony," 172; see also Bauckham, *Climax of Prophecy,* 214–15; Beale, *Revelation,* 352.

341. Beale, *Revelation,* 352.

342. White, "Agony, Irony," 175; see also Bauckham, *Climax of Prophecy,* 228–29, 235, 237; Bauckham, *Theology,* 149–50; Johnson, *Triumph,* 194; Stylianopoulos, "I Know," 22, 23n.22, 26, 29. Bandstra discusses the same idea in connection with the present "reign" of the church as *a kingdom and priests* (Rev 5:10). See Bandstra, "Kingship and Priests," 22–25.

343. White, "Agony, Irony," 168; see also Beale, *Revelation,* 269–71;Schüssler Fiorenza, *Revelation,* 124.

344. Beale, *Revelation,* 340.

345. Schüssler Fiorenza, *Revelation,* 58.

There are significant parallels between these two chapters and Daniel 7:

Event	Daniel 7	Revelation 4–5
1. Introductory vision phraseology	Dan 7:9	Rev 4:1
2. Throne(s) set in heaven	Dan 7:9a	Rev 4:2a
3. God sitting on a throne	Dan 7:9b	Rev 4:2b
4. God's appearance on the throne	Dan 7:9c	Rev 4:3a
5. Fire before the thone	Dan 7:9d–10	Rev 4:5
6. Heavenly servants surrounding the throne	Dan 7:10b	Rev 4:4b, 6b–10; 5:8, 11, 14
7. Book(s) before the throne	Dan 7:10c	Rev 5:1–5
8. The book(s) opened	Dan 7:10c	Rev 5:2–5, 9
9. A divine figure receives authority to reign forever	Dan 7:13–14a	Rev 5:5b–7, 9a, 12–13
10. The kingdom's scope: "all peoples, nations, and tongues"	Dan 7:14a	Rev 5:9b
11. The seer's emotional distress on account of the vision	Dan 7:14	Rev 5:4
12. The seer's reception of counsel from a heavenly servant	Dan 7:16	Rev 5:5a
13. The saints given divine authority to reign over a kingdom	Dan 7:18, 22, 27a	Rev 5:10
14. Concluding mention of God's eternal reign	Dan 7:27b	Rev 5:13–14

Those parallels indicate the following four basic ideas:

(1) John intends chs. 4–5 to depict the fulfillment of the Daniel 7 prophecy of the reign of the "son of man" and of the saints, which has been inaugurated by Christ's death and especially his resurrection, that is, his approach to the throne to receive authority.

(2) The combination of such scenes as Isaiah 6 and Ezekiel 1–2 with the predominant scene from Daniel 7 expresses a judgment nuance in the vision, since these scenes all serve as introductions to announcements of judgment. . . . More precisely, these OT scenes present a vision of God's cosmic reign and dominion that issues first in judgment, followed by redemption. This is the theological background of Revelation 4–5 and subsequent chapters.

(3) The idea of judgment is also connoted by the image of the "book," which has been described in language from Ezekiel 2, Isaiah 29, Daniel 7, and Daniel 12. Each of these contexts has the central idea of judgment, but again together with ideas of salvation or blessing.

(4) The Daniel 7 idea of a kingdom in which all peoples will serve the "son of man" (Dan 7:14) and God (7:27b) is seen by John as fulfilled in the church. Yet the church is also the fulfillment of the Danielic reign of the saints of Israel.[346]

346. Beale, *Revelation,*, 368–69. See ibid., 314–15 with respect to the above table.

The twenty-four elders (Rev 4:4, 10; 5:8; 11:16; 14:3; 19:4)

Many view the twenty-four elders as representing the entire OT and NT church, combining the numbers of the twelve patriarchs and the twelve apostles.[347] However, in Rev 5:8–10, 11:16–18, and 14:1–3 there appears to be a distinction between the twenty-four elders and the redeemed.[348] Further, in Rev 5:8 and 7:13–14 (cf. 8:3), elders perform angelic functions and reveal matters to John. Consequently, although they are associated with the chuch, they do not appear to be identical to the church.[349]

The book (scroll) sealed with seven seals (Rev 5:1–4)

There are several theories concerning the identity of the sealed book. Some suggest that the book is the disclosure of the names of the redeemed. However, Caird observes that "by opening the scroll the Lamb does not merely disclose its contents, but puts them into operation," and "there is no suggestion here or elsewhere in the book that John's purpose was to reveal the identity of the redeemed."[350] Others contend that the book is the OT. However, the description of the scroll is drawn from Ezek 2:9—3:3. Therefore, to view the book or scroll as the OT "overlooks John's dependence on Ezekiel . . . and it does not explain why the death of Christ should be the indispensable qualification for opening the scroll."[351]

Kenneth Gentry correctly notes the dependence on Ezekiel and observes that the point of Ezekiel's vision was "judgment on Israel."[352] As a preterist, he contends the scroll is "God's divorce decree against his Old Testament wife for her spiritual adultery."[353] In the OT, God indeed talked about such a divorce (see Isa 50:1; Jer 3:8). In AD 70, "the final and conclusive destruction of the temple accomplishes this."[354] However, by concentrating on the events of AD 70, the preterist view misses the far broader story of Revelation. It also fails to see how Revelation transforms and universalizes OT ideas.

Another view is that the book is the revelation of those coming events which John has been charged to communicate. However, Christ won the right to open the scroll by his death on the cross. Caird states:

> There is no very obvious reason why, having won the right in A.D. 30, he should have postponed the exercise of it until A.D. 95. The natural assumption is that the opening of the scroll, by which its contents are both revealed and put into effect, follows immediately on the victory by which he acquired the right to open it. This means that from John's standpoint some at least of the contents are already past; and for confirmation of this we need only turn to the vision introduced by

347. Milligan, *Revelation*, 69; Hendriksen, *More Than Conquerors*, 85.

348. Ladd, *Blessed Hope*, 97–98.

349. See Ladd, *Commentary*, 73–75; Beale, *Revelation*, 322; Johnson, *Triumph*, 99–100.

350. Caird, *St. John the Divine*, 71.

351. Ibid., 72.

352. Gentry, "A Preterist View," 51.

353. Ibid., 51–52.

354. Ibid., 52; see also Preston, *AD 70*, 165–72.

the breaking of the fifth seal, in which John looks back on a past martyrdom as well as forward to a future one.[355]

The best view, therefore, is articulated by Caird that "the content of the scroll is God's redemptive plan, foreshadowed in the Old Testament, by which he means to assert his sovereignty over a sinful world and so to achieve the purpose of creation. John proposes to trace the whole operation of this plan from its beginnings in the Cross to its triumphal culmination in the New Jerusalem."[356]

The Lion who is a Lamb (Rev 5:5–6)

In our previous discussion of the different symbols of the church in Revelation, we discussed the "hearing-seeing" pattern of identification.[357] Just as Revelation has a paradoxical notion of "overcoming," so Rev 5:5–6 presents a paradoxical identification of Christ as both a military conqueror and a sacrificial victim. Bauckham explains that in the contrast between what he hears (Rev 5:5) and what he sees (Rev 5:6), John:

> first evokes the idea of the Messiah as the Jewish nationalistic military conqueror and then reinterprets it by means of the notion of sacrificial death for the redemption of people from all nations (cf. 5:9–10). . . . By placing the image of the sacrificial victim alongside those of the military conqueror, John forges a new symbol of *conquest* by sacrificial death. . . . He [Jesus] has won a victory, but by sacrifice, not military conflict, and he has delivered God's people, but they are from all nations, not only Jews. The continuing and ultimate victory of God over evil which the rest of John's prophecy describes is the outworking of his decisive victory won on the cross.[358]

Rev 6:1—8:5: the seven seals

In this section, Christ exercises his role as king and judge by using evil heavenly forces to inflict trials on people throughout the time before his return to purify believers or punish unbelievers. Although Christians are persecuted, the last judgment is God's ultimate response to the saints' prayer in 6:10 that he avenge their blood.

The four horsemen (Rev 6:1–8)

On their face, the first four seals unleash four individual "horses," upon each of which sits an individual rider.[359] Nevertheless, Milligan begins by stating the perhaps obvious point that "not one of the four riders is a person. Each is rather a cause, a manifestation of certain truths connected with the kingdom of Christ when that kingdom is seen to be, in

355. Caird, *St. John the Divine*, 71–72

356. Ibid., 72; see also Beale, *Revelation*, 340.

357. See the discussion of the "great multitude" of Rev 7:9–17, above.

358. Bauckham, *Climax of Prophecy*, 214–15.

359. The personal, singular "he" or "him" is used of each of the riders.

its own nature, the judgment of the world. Even war, famine, and death and Hades, which follow, are not literally these things. They are simply used, as scourges of mankind, to give general expression to the judgments of God."[360]

In addition to identifying these "four horsemen of the apocalypse," there is also the issue of *when* the horsemen are unleashed. Some think that the horsemen are unleashed only shortly before Christ's second coming. However, the context of the passage demonstrates otherwise. Revelation 6 is intimately connected with Revelation 5. Revelation 5 provided that the Lamb (Christ) alone was worthy to *"open the book"* (Rev 5:4, 8) and *"break the seals"* (Rev 6:1, 3, 5, 7, 9, 12; 8:1), based on what he did *on the cross* (Rev 5:5–6, 9). Consequently, Rev 6:1–8 describes destructive forces that were unleashed as a result of Christ's death on the cross and his concomitant resurrection and ascension.

The identification of the seals as being inaugurated with the death, resurrection, and ascension of Christ, as opposed to being events that only occur shortly before the *parousia*, is confirmed by the parallel between the "signs" Jesus gave in the Olivet Discourse, which characterize the entire period between Christ's first advent and the second coming, and the events listed in Rev 6:1–14:

Olivet Discourse (signs)	Revelation 6 (seals)
Matt 24:5, 11, 23–24; Mark 13:6, 22 (false Christs)	corresponds to 1st seal (6:2)
Matt 24:6–7, 12; Mark 13:7–8; Luke 21:10 (wars and rumors of war)	corresponds to 2nd seal (6:4)
Matt 24:7; Mark 13:8; Luke 21:11 (famine)	corresponds to 3rd seal (6:6)
Matt 24:22; Mark 13:12, 20; Luke 21:24 (death); Luke 21:11 (plagues)	corresponds to 4th seal (6:8)
Matt 24:9; Mark 13:9, 13; Luke 21:12, 16–17 (believers persecuted & killed)	corresponds to 5th seal (6:7–10)
Matt 24:29; Mark 13:24–25; Luke 21:25 (signs in the sky & heavens)	corresponds to 6th seal (6:12–14)

Although the events of the first four seals may occur one after another, it is more likely that they occur simultaneously since: (1) the fourth seal appears to summarize the first three; and (2) Ezek 14:12–21; Zech 6:1–8; and the Olivet Discourse on which Rev 6:1–8 is based portray such events as occurring simultaneously.

Just as Revelation 4–5 raised the question "Who is the true Lord of this world?" Christ's receipt of the book (scroll) and his breaking of its seals answers that question. By receiving the book and breaking its seals, Christ demonstrates that he is the reigning Lord, exercising sovereignty over the world and all that happens in it.[361] That Christ is the ultimate cause of the judgments is seen in the fact that Christ's breaking the seals is the basis of the command to the horsemen to "come" (Rev 6:1, 3, 5, 7). The major OT

360. Milligan, *Revelation*, 89. Although perhaps self-evident, Milligan's point needs to be borne in mind in connection with identifying other apparently "personal" actors in Revelation (e.g., the "two witnesses" of Revelation 11; the "woman" of Revelation 12; the beast from the sea of Revelation 13; and the beast from the earth [i.e., the "false prophet"] of Revelation 13). As we have seen earlier in this chapter and in chapter 10–The "Antichrist," all of these actors are personifications of collective entities.

361. Rev 1:5, 13–14; 2:26–28; 3:21; 5:1–4 show that Christ already has begun his messianic kingship. See also Matt 28:18; Acts 2:32–36; Eph 1:18–22 which all attest that he is reigning now as messianic king.

passages behind Rev 6:1–8 likewise have God as the ultimate cause of the judgments (see Zech 6:1–8; Ezek 14:12–21). This is important for what follows in the rest of the book: even in oppression, plagues, and death, Christians should be able to recognize that Christ is sovereign.[362] That Christ ultimately is in charge gives Christians confidence and hope. Such trials test, prove, and refine the faith of believers while, at the same time, acting as punishments on those who reject Christ and persecute the church.

The rider of the white horse (Rev 6:1–2)

The identity of the first horseman has caused considerable debate. The issue is whether he is a positive or a negative rider.

THE WHITE HORSEMAN AS POSITIVE

Ngundu states the "white horseman as Christ" view and describes its major problems: "Some commentators[363] have identified the rider as Jesus Christ, but the problem with this view is that since the Lamb is the one opening the seals in heaven, he cannot also be one of the riders. Moreover, theologically it would be inappropriate to have an angelic being, a creature, command Christ, the Creator, to do things (6:1)."[364]

The second "white horseman as a positive force" view is stronger than seeing the first horseman as Christ himself. Several commentators conclude, "The rider is not Christ himself but symbolizes the proclamation of the gospel of Christ in all the world."[365] This view is based on the fact that the fourteen times it is used elsewhere in the book "white is always a symbol of Christ, or of something associated with Christ, or of spiritual victory."[366] Also, "the same basic structure of thought appears in the Olivet Discourse and in the Revelation: a time of preliminary troubles marked by evils in human society and in nature (the seven seals) . . . there is, however, in the preliminary evil period one positive note . . . 'the gospel must first be preached to all nations' (Mark 13:10)."[367] Further, the bow is often used as a symbol of divine victory,[368] and elsewhere in Revelation Christ is seen wearing crowns (Rev 14:14; 19:12) and "conquering" (Rev 3:21; 5:5; 17:14)

---

362. Schüssler Fiorenza, *Revelation*, 61. The authority of the four horsemen are in the form of "divine passives, i.e., *"it was given to him"* (Rev 6:2); *"it was granted"* (Rev 6:4); *"authority was given to them"* (Rev 6:8). The power given to the horsemen not only is given to them by heavenly authority but is subject to divinely-appointed limits (see Rev 6:6, 8).

363. E.g., Irenaeus, *Haer.* 4.21.3; Hendriksen, *More Than Conquerors*, 93–96.

364. Ngundu, "Revelation," 1557.

365. Ladd, *Commentary*, 99; see also Milligan, *Revelation*, 89–90.

366. Ladd, *Commentary*, 98.

367. Ibid., 98–99.

368. Ps 45:4–5; Isa 41:2; 49:2–3; Hab 3:9, 13; Zech 9:13.

THE WHITE HORSEMAN AS NEGATIVE

Other commentators hold that it is more likely that the rider on the white horse, like the riders on the other three horses, is a symbol of Antichrist and the forces of evil. Reference to a personal Antichrist, however, appears to be problematic. Smalley, for example, states, "As with the personal equation of the first rider with Christ, the inclusion of Antichrist here breaks the sequence of otherwise impersonal causes which are mentioned during this scene in Rev. 6."[369]

Therefore, the "white horseman as evil" view is strongest when identifying the white horseman as false Christs, false prophecy, or the forces of evil in general, rather than as Antichrist *per se*. Alan Johnson mentions the major arguments in favor of that position:

> Support for the identification of the white horse with the Antichrist and his forces is the parallelism with the other three horses, which are instruments of judgment. The references in 19:11–16 to the rider on the white horse as "Faithful and True" and of whom it is said that "with justice he judges and makes war" may stand in contrast to the rider in 6:2 who is not faithful or true and who wages war for unjust conquest. . . . Again, the "bow" would most naturally be connected with the enemy of God's people (Ezek 39:3; cf. Rev. 20:7–8).[370] Finally, the parallelism to the Olivet Discourse shows that the first events mentioned are the rise of "false Christs and false prophets" (Matt 24:24).[371]

Additionally, the four horse-drawn chariots of Zech 6:1–8 clearly are an OT source behind the four horsemen of Rev 6:1–8. In Zechariah, the four horse-drawn chariots are all of the same nature. Further, the fourth horseman ("Death," with "Hades" following him, Rev 6:7–8) appears to be the result or summary of the activities of the prior horsemen. If so, then the first horseman, like the other three, must be evil. On balance, therefore, the "white horseman as evil" appears to be the stronger position.

The martyrs (Rev 6:9–11)

As with the first four seals, martyrdom (the fifth seal) is an event which characterizes the entire period until Christ's return. This passage is of crucial importance in understanding the book, since the rest of the book, in essence, represents and illustrates the answer to the martyrs' prayer in Rev 6:10.[372] The martyrs epitomize the paradoxical nature of the believers' victory over Satan, the "beast," the forces of evil, and the world. The paradoxical or counter-intuitive nature of the martyrs' victory is discussed by Bauckham:

> When the beast puts the martyrs to death, who is the real victor? The answer, in Revelation, depends on whether one sees the matter from an earthly or a heavenly perspective. From the earthly perspective it is obvious that the beast has

369. Smalley, *Revelation*, 150.

370. John's first-century audience probably would have understood the "bow" as an allusion to the Parthians, and possibly the Babylonians, who were known, and feared, as mounted archers. Schüssler Fiorenza, *Revelation*, 63; Johnson, *Triumph*, 119–20.

371. Johnson, "Revelation," 473.

372. The martyrs' prayer, *"How long, O Lord?"* echoes Habakkuk's cry (Hab 1:2–4) when his own people were being oppressed, justice was perverted, and Israel was faced with the might of Babylon.

defeated the martyrs (11:7; 13:7). . . . The apocalyptic visions, however, reveal that from a *heavenly* perspective things look quite different. From this perspective the martyrs are the real victors. To be faithful in bearing the witness of Jesus even to the point of death is not to become a helpless victim of the beast, but to take the field against him and win. John can depict the triumph of the martyrs only in scenes set in heaven, because it requires the heavenly perspective—established when the slaughtered Lamb is first seen triumphant before the throne of God (5:6)—to make their triumph apparent, but the heavenly perspective is destined to prevail on earth at the parousia (19:11–21). . . . The martyrs conquer not by their suffering and death as such, but by their faithful *witness* to the point of death (cf. 12:11). Their witness to the truth prevails over the lies and deceit of the devil and the beast. For those who reject this witness, it becomes legal testimony *against* them, securing their condemnation. This negative function of witness . . . entails also a positive possibility: that people may be won from illusion to truth.[373]

The prayer of the martyrs and its answer (Rev 6:10–17)

The prayer of the martyrs and its sequellae are unique in Revelation, as John Heil points out, "In a book imbued with references to worship, the opening of the fifth seal in [Rev 6:9–11] contains the only example of a prayer of supplication and its answer."[374] As such, this prayer "exemplifies the prayer of the holy ones [in Rev 5:8]," and "with regard to the succeeding context, the souls' prayer sets the agenda for the remainder of the book."[375]

God's immediate answer to the martyrs in Rev 6:11 serves to warn the "servants" to whom the book is addressed (Rev 1:1) that, like the "fellow servants" (6:11) and brothers of the souls under the altar, they can expect to be killed for the word of God and testimony of Jesus Christ. At the same time, "they are assured that God will eventually judge and vindicate them, so that they can hope to share in the white robes and heavenly rest of the souls who have gone before them."[376]

The judging of *"those who dwell on the earth"* and the vindication of the church, which answer the martyrs' prayer, are seen at various points in the remainder of the book. In Revelation 6 itself, the answer to the prayer of 6:10 is explicitly seen at 6:12–17. The context of the martyrs' prayer of 6:10, and God's telling the martyrs to wait until the number of their fellow servants to be killed was complete (6:11), shows that what is depicted in 6:12–17 must be the final judgment.[377] As Beale points out, "the calamitous scene in 6:12–17 assumes that the persecution of all Christians who are to be persecuted has finally

373. Bauckham, *Climax of Prophecy,* 235, 237.

374. Heil, "Fifth Seal," 220.

375. Ibid., 242.

376. Ibid., 221–22.

377. Preterists, on the other hand, cite the fact that the people say to the mountains, *"Fall on us"* (Rev 6:16) as evidence that "this passage is not speaking of the End of the World, but of *the End of Israel* in A.D. 70." Chilton, *Veangeance,* 198. The reason is that the original context of the statement is Hosea's prophecy against Israel (Hos 10:8) which Jesus quoted on the way to his crucifixion (Luke 23:28–30), specifically referring to the coming destruction of Jerusalem which happened in AD 70. Ibid., 198–99.

run its course and that all that remains is to execute final punishment on the persecutors, which strikes the very last note of world history. Consequently, this passage cannot deal with preparousia judgments of unbelievers during an extended tribulation period, since they have not yet finished persecuting the saints at that point."[378]

Because of the progressively parallel nature of the book, every scene of judgment on the ungodly and vindication of the believers is an answer to the prayer of the martyrs in Rev 6:10. Rev 7:9 depicts an answer to their prayer, as it shows *"a great multitude which no one could count . . . standing before the Lamb . . . and palm branches were in their hands, and they cry out with a loud voice, saying 'Salvation to our God who sits on the throne, and to the Lamb.'"*[379] Rev 14:3 shows the 144,000 singing a new song before the throne. Rev 15:2–4 similarly shows *"those who had been victorious over the beast . . . standing on the sea of glass, holding harps of God, and they sang the song of Moses . . . and the song of the Lamb."* Those images all show the vindication of the saints as the answer to the martyrs' prayer.

In Rev 16:3–6, the prayer is shown to be answered in the judgment of the earth-dwellers. The prayer's mention of God's avenging *"our blood"* is directly alluded to: Rev 16:3–4 states that the second and third bowls poured by the angels turn the sea, rivers, and springs into "blood." Rev 16:6 concludes, *"For they poured out the blood of the saints and prophets, and You have given them blood to drink. They deserve it."* Likewise, in the judgment of Babylon (Rev 18:21–24), verse 24 says that *"in her was found the blood of the prophets and of saints and of all who have been slain on the earth."* When they are rejoicing over the judgment of Babylon, the multitude in heaven specifically rejoice over the fact that God *"has avenged the blood of His bond-servants on her"* (Rev 19:2). That is a direct answer to the martyrs' prayer in 6:10 in which they asked *"How long, O Lord . . . will You refrain from judging and avenging our blood on those who dwell on the earth?"* The Greek word for "avenge" (*ekdikeō*) appears in Revelation only in 6:10 and 19:2, thus connecting the two passages.

The great tribulation (Rev 7:14)

This is the only place in the Bible where the phrase *"the great tribulation"* occurs. In the Olivet Discourse (Matt 24:21), Jesus referred to *"great tribulation"* (without the definite article "the") in connection with the destruction of Jerusalem in AD 70. The images are drawn from Dan 12:1 which speaks of *"a time of distress such as never occurred since there*

378. Beale, *Revelation*, 396. As noted earlier, the language of Rev 6:12–17 parallels the description of the final judgment found at Rev 16:18–21 and 20:11. The imagery is drawn from such OT passages as Ps 76:7; Isa 2:10; 13:10; 34:4; Jer 4:23–26; Ezek 38:20; Hos 10:8; Nah 1:2–6; Hag 2:6; Mic 3:2.

379. In Rev 6:11, God told the martyrs to rest until the full number of their brethren who also were to be killed had been completed. That is the exact situation dealt with in Revelation 7. Ulfgard, *Feast and Future*, 32–33; Bauckham, *Climax of Prophecy*, 229n.55; Steinmann, "Tripartite Structure," 71–72. Schüssler Fiorenza sees Rev 7:1–8 as the answer to the question raised in 6:17, "Who is able to stand?" (i.e., "Who can survive the wrath of God and the Lamb?"), whereas 7:9–17 points to those who have endured to the end and therefore participate in eschatological salvation. Schüssler Fiorenza, *Revelation*, 67–68. The views of all of these commentators are consistent. The only people who can stand (Rev 7:9) and survive God's wrath are those who have been washed in the blood of the Lamb (7:14). Yet, those "standing" and surviving God's wrath have become the "full number" of martyrs (6:11), as God had said would happen. Ibid., 69. In all these scenes, the underlying, fundamental question again is raised: "Who is the true Lord of the world?" And, more personally, "Who is *my* true Lord?"

was a nation until that time." The only other time the phrase *"great tribulation"* occurs is in Rev 2:22 when Christ tells the church at Thyatira that he will throw those who commit adultery with Jezebel into *"great tribulation."* The use of the article ("the") in 7:14 suggests that this is the eschatological distress or tribulation prophesied by Daniel.

Although the emphasis may be on the final war waged by the dragon and his followers against the church, this eschatological distress is not limited to a brief period shortly before the *parousia.* Smalley states that "the 'great ordeal' survived by the redeemed does not occur exclusively at the end of history. The time of judgement has already been set in motion in John's day, and may overtake believers as well as unbelievers (cf. 2.22) at any time, until the end of time. It is a present reality, and not only a future certainty, which can assume the form of persecution (2.2–3), famine (6.5–6), imprisonment (2.10) and even death (2.13; 6.9)."[380] Smalley concludes, "The ecclesial vision of Rev. 7:9–17 refers to a company of the faithful which includes martyrs, but embraces *all* believers."[381]

That also is suggested by Rev 1:9 and the broader context of the NT's understanding of tribulation and suffering. In Rev 1:9, John calls himself *"your brother and fellow partaker in the tribulation and kingdom."* In other words, John's conviction is that the tribulation has already begun in his own day. As Heinrich Schlier puts it, "From the standpoint of the triumphant Church all the affliction of this present time is set in the light of the [great tribulation] which has already opened."[382] This suggests an "already, but not yet" nature of the tribulation, similar to that of the kingdom: since we are in "the last days" as a result of Jesus' atoning sacrifice, the tribulation has already begun; however, we can anticipate an extreme form of that tribulation shortly before Christ returns.[383]

"They have washed their robes and made them white in the blood of the Lamb" (Rev 7:14)

"Being placed in the blood makes the blood the instrument by which the whitening takes place."[384] The NT gives a radical explanation of how tribulation and suffering demonstrate that the blood of Jesus whitens a person. In Col 1:24 Paul says his own sufferings on

380. Smalley, *Revelation,* 196.

381. Ibid.

382. Schlier, *"thlibō, thlipsis,"* 143–45. The gospels and epistles of Paul, Peter, and Jude all portray the church as experiencing the eschatological drama of tribulation, which characterizes this entire age and is not simply a phenomenon that occurs shortly before the *parousia.* That is, of course, consistent with what Christ himself predicted in the Olivet Discourse and elsewhere. For discussions of this see Allison, *End of the Ages,* 36–39, 49, 57–66, 115–41; Mattill, "Way of Tribulation," 531–46; Schüssler Fiorenza, *Revelation,* 68.

383. Ulfgard notes that the reference in Rev 7:14 to the *"blood of the Lamb"* in connection with the *"great tribulation"* points back to the pattern of the exodus: just as Israel was saved from Egypt through the blood of lambs, so the "great multitude" owes its salvation to the blood of the Lamb. However, when these ideas are combined in Revelation, there is a difference: "the evil time does not preceded God's victory but follows it. The eschatological era inaugurated by Christ means the beginning of both judgment and salvation. Tribulation is simultaneous with victory according to John's Christian awareness, i.e., Christian existence is at the same time a sharing of royal dignity in front of God and a suffering in the world. . . . Both conditions result from the eschatological turning-point of the ages in the Easter event." Ulfgard, *Feast and Future,* 80.

384. Porter, *Idioms,* 158.

behalf of the church are *"filling up what is lacking in Christ's afflictions."* In 2 Cor 4:8–12 he also explains that the suffering of believers is *"carrying about in the body the dying Jesus"* so that, paradoxically, *"the life of Jesus also may be manifested in our mortal flesh."* Likewise, in Rev 7:14 and elsewhere in Revelation, those who have experienced tribulation, suffering, and death for the sake of Christ have demonstrated their radical identification with him. They have borne witness, both verbally and in their own bodies, to the suffering and death that he endured. They have, by their faithfulness through suffering, demonstrated that their faith was real. Their suffering has purified them. They have been conformed into Christ's image (Rom 8:29) because, like Christ, they have been *"obedient to the point of death"* (Phil 2:8). Because Christ is totally righteous, total commitment to Christ *is* righteousness and results in totally pure garments (see Rev 19:8).

Similarly, Rev 12:11 states that *"they overcame him [Satan] because of the blood of the Lamb and because of the word of their testimony, and they did not love their life even when faced with death."* Bauckham explains, "The victory does not consist in their mere death as such, but in their faithful witness to the point of death (cf. 2:13; 11:7), maintaining the witness of Jesus (12:7; 19:10), following in the path of Jesus whom Revelation 1:5 calls 'the faithful witness'. The value of their witness is derivative from his, it is maintaining his witness, and so the victory of their faithful witness as far as death is derivative from his victory."[385] Again we see Revelation's paradoxical view of overcoming and victory. Just as Jesus the Lamb triumphed through his sacrificial death (Rev 5:6, 9), so the victory of God's people is of the same kind as the Lamb's: faithfulness even to the point of martyrdom.

The connection of Revelation 7 and 12 also shows us how John is depicting the church as the new, true Israel. We see this in at least two ways. First, the white-washed robes of Rev 7:14 echo Exod 19:10, 14 where the people of Israel in the wilderness following the exodus had to *"wash their garments"* to prepare for God's presence on Mount Sinai. In Revelation, "the multitude in their white-washed robes are depicted as a true congregation of God analogous to Israel at Sinai."[386] Second, Rev 12:6, 14 speak of the woman fleeing to the "wilderness" where she was "nourished." That likewise recalls Israel's wilderness wanderings when God sustained the nation for forty years. The feast of tabernacles celebrated that event.[387] In Rev 7:9, the great multitude is seen standing before the Lamb with palm branches in their hands. Palm branches were particularly associated with the feast of tabernacles (Lev 23:40). Just as the palm branches were used to celebrate God's protective presence among his people in the wilderness, so "in the Christian reinterpretation of the Bible they tell the readers/listeners that they share the same experience with Christ."[388] Given that connection, the great multitude's crying out *"salvation to our God"* (Rev 7:10) may allude to Ps 118:25. That psalm was recited at the feast of tabernacles, and the *lulav* (palm branches) were waived at that point.[389]

---

385. Bauckham, *Climax of Prophecy,* 228–29.

386. Ulfgard, *Feast and Future,* 84.

387. Exod 23:16; 34:22; Lev 23:33–43; Num 29:12–38; Deut 16:13–15.

388. Ulfgard, *Feast and Future,* 90.

389. Ibid., 91. This connection is strengthened by the fact that when Jesus entered Jerusalem for the last time, the people *"took the branches of the palm trees and went out to meet Him"* (John 12:13). In Rev 7:9–10 the great multitude is also *"standing . . . before the Lamb"* with palm branches in their hands. The Greek word for "palm trees" is *phoinix.* In the NT it occurs only in John 12:13 and Rev 7:9.

Rev 8:6—11:19: the seven trumpets

In the first six trumpets (Rev 8:6—9:21), God responds to the saints' prayer in Rev 6:10 by using angels to bring judgments on the persecutors of the church. In 10:1–11, John is recommissioned to prophesy about God's plan for bringing in the consummation of the kingdom. In 11:1–13, God's decree ensures his presence with his people and their effective witness, despite their persecution. In the seventh trumpet (11:14–19), God brings final judgment and establishes the consummated kingdom.

The trumpet judgments (Rev 8:6—9:21; 11:15–19)

In typical prophetic fashion, in the OT the exodus plagues had been broadened to apply to Israel in its land (Amos 4:10) and to Israel in exile (Deut 28:27–60). In the trumpets of Revelation, the exodus plagues are again seen typologically. Now they apply to the entire world:

1st trumpet (hail) (8:7)	corresponds to 7th plague (Exod 9:22–25)
2nd and 3rd trumpets (water to blood) (8:8–11)	correspond to 1st plague (Exod 7:20–25)
4th trumpet (darkness) (8:12)	corresponds to 9th plague (Exod 10:21–23)
5th trumpet (locusts) (9:1–11)	corresponds to 8th plague (Exod 10:12–15)

The trumpets also parallel the exodus judgments in that, just as Israelites were not affected by the plagues but only the Egyptians,[390] so Christians, but not unbelievers, are protected from the trumpet judgments (Rev 9:4). In Revelation this does *not* mean that these judgments do not affect Christians. Christians may suffer *physically* in the same ways as non-Christians suffer during these judgments, but the basis and nature of the judgments are different for Christians and non-Christians. Milligan explains, "The judgments of the Trumpets are judgments on the world. The Church, it is true, may also suffer from them, but not in judgment. They may be part of her trial as she mixes with the world during her earthly pilgrimage. Trial, however, is not judgment. To the children of God it is the discipline of a Father's hand. In the midst of it the Church is safe, and it helps to ripen her for the fullness of the glory of her heavenly inheritance."[391]

The first six trumpets parallel the first five seals. However, the focus is different: "whereas the first five seals focused on the trials through which believers must pass, now the focus in the first six trumpets is on judgments that unbelievers, both inside and outside the visible church, must endure."[392] The seventh trumpet parallels the sixth and

---

390. Exod 7:18, 21, 24; 8:3–4, 8–9, 11–12, 21–23, 29–31; 9:3–7, 10–11, 14, 23–26; 11:4–7.

391. Milligan, *Revelation*, 155–56. That is the same phenomenon we saw in Rev 7:14. Tribulation and suffering for Christ test, prove, and purify our identification with Christ in his own suffering and death. That is exactly what was predicted by Christ in the Olivet Discourse and in such passages as Matt 10:16–39 and John 15:18–25. Dispensationalists, who think that the church will be raptured before any of these events occur and will have a "ring-side seat" to observe the sufferings of others, do not seem to have any conception of the Christian's radical identification with Christ in his suffering or the paradoxical nature of both Christ's victory and ours.

392. Beale, *Revelation*, 472–73.

seventh seals. They all describe the *parousia* which brings with it the final judgment and the beginning of the consummated kingdom.

A "FALLEN STAR" IS GIVEN THE KEY TO THE "BOTTOMLESS PIT" OR "ABYSS" (REV 9:1–2, 11; 11:7; 17:8; 20:1, 3)

In Revelation, the image of the "abyss" or "bottomless pit" appears seven times.[393] It is the abode of locust-demons [evil spirits] and their king (9:1–11); the beast rises from it (11:7; 17:8); it is where Satan is bound (20:1–3).[394] The *"star from heaven which had fallen to the earth"* (9:1) corresponds to Satan's being *"thrown down to the earth"* (12:9, 10, 13) and to Christ's statement, *"I was watching Satan fall from heaven like lightning"* (Luke 10:18). "This 'fallen star' is the contrast and counterpart of Him who is 'the bright, the morning star [Rev 22:16]', and who 'has the keys of death and of Hades [Rev 1:18].'"[395] The fallen angel is "given" the key to release the locusts from the abyss. That is a "divine passive." In other words, "only by God's permission can [the evil spirits] be released to bring destruction to the earth (9:1–11; 20:1–3)."[396]

The opening of the abyss in Rev 9:2 may, counter-intuitively, correspond with the "binding of Satan" in Rev 20:1–3, *not* with the "loosing" or "releasing" of Satan in 20:3, 7. The reason is that the events of Rev 9:1–12 are not events that occur only immediately before the *parousia* but clearly are preliminary. More important theologically is the fact that the demons who are released in 9:1 cannot oppress believers but only those *"who do not have the seal of God on their foreheads"* (9:4). Beale observes that, similarly, "the locking up of the 'abyss' in 20:1–3 may convey the idea that Satan and his hordes cannot be on the loose to deceive those 'who did not receive the mark [of the beast] on their foreheads [20:4]'. 9:1–10 and 20:1–3 are synchronous and portray those whom Satan is permitted to deceive and those whom he is not permitted to deceive."[397]

LOCUSTS FROM THE BOTTOMLESS PIT (REV 9:1–12)

The "locusts" are demonic in character. That is indicated by the facts that they dwell in and arise from the abyss as does the beast (see Rev 11:7; 17:8); their king is "the angel of the abyss" whose names mean "destruction" (Abaddon) or "destroyer" (Apollyon; Rev 9:11); and their actions are to torment and hurt people (Rev 9:5, 10).

While the locusts parallel the eighth plague of Egypt, the primary imagery appears to be drawn from the book of Joel. Joel speaks of a great locust plague (Joel 1:4). The locusts in Joel have the appearance *"like the appearance of horses, and like war horses."*[398] They came with the sound of chariots.[399] They are associated with the darkening of the sun,

393. Rev 9:1, 2, 11; 11:7; 17:8; 20:1, 3.

394. See also Luke 8:31; 2 Pet 2:4.

395. Milligan, *Revelation*, 148.

396. Moo, "The Sea," 157n.22; see also Beale, *Revelation*, 492–93.

397. Beale, *Revelation*, 986. See below regarding the connection of the locusts with deception.

398. Joel 2:4; compare Rev 9:7.

399. Joel 2:5; compare Rev 9:9.

moon, and stars[400] and herald the coming day of the Lord and the judgment that comes with it.[401] The demonic "locusts" are not permitted to harm believers, since believers have been sealed (Rev 9:4). That demonstrates Christ's ultimate authority over Satan and all of the evil that the book of Revelation depicts.

The "five months" of Rev 9:5, 10 should not be taken literally since, as discussed earlier, most if not all of the numbers and time periods elsewhere in the book are not literal. Milligan concludes that the "five months" is "more in accordance with the style of the Apocalypse to regard that particular period of time as simply denoting that the judgment has definite limits."[402]

The Euphrates (Rev 9:13–14; see also 16:12)

To "literalize" the Euphrates would depart from sound principles of exegesis when dealing with a book of visions and metaphors.[403] The Euphrates "is simply a symbol of judgment; and the four angels which had been bound at it, but were now loosed, are a token—four being the number of the world—that the judgment referred to, though it affects but a third part of men, reaches men over the whole surface of the globe."[404] The number "four" as indicating the world is seen in the fact that the earth is said to have "four corners" (Rev 7:1; 20:8) and "four winds" (Rev 7:1).[405] The reference to the Euphrates anticipates the sixth bowl where the Euphrates again is mentioned.[406] That connection suggests that this trumpet likely covers the entire inter-advent period and and finds its culmination in the sixth bowl.

The "200,000,000" (Rev 9:15–16)

Although many Bibles translate the number of the horsemen as 200,000,000, that is not accurate. The actual wording in the Greek is *dismuriades muriadōn* ("double myriad of myriads" or "twice ten thousand times ten thousands"). Beale describes the significance of this:

> Without exception, *murias* ("ten thousand") designates an incalculable immensity wherever it is used without any numerical adjective. In the LXX the plural also has a figurative connotation of an innumerable, indefinite host [e.g., Gen 24:60; Lev 26:8; Num 10:36; Deut 32:30; 33:2, 17; 1 Kgs 18:7–8; Ps 3:6; Dan 7:10;

400. Joel 2:10; compare Rev 9:2.

401. Joel 2:1, 11, 30–32.

402. Milligan, *Revelation*, 147.

403. Johnson, *Triumph*, 151.

404. Milligan, *Revelation*, 151. The Euphrates as representing judgment draws on such OT references as Isa 7:20; 8:7–8; Jer 13:1–11; 46:1–26, where the Euphrates symbolized or was associated with Assyria and Babylon whom God used to bring judgment on sinful Israel, Judah, and Egypt.

405. "Revelation makes greater use of an alternative fourfold division of creation: earth, sea, (rivers and) springs, heaven (8:7–12; 14:7; 16:2–9). These four parts of creation are respectively the targets of the judgments of the first four trumpets (8:7–12) and the first four bowls (16:2–9)." Bauckham, *Climax of Prophecy*, 31.

406. See discussion below in connection with Rev 16:12.

Mic 6:7]. . . . The use of the double plural *muriades muriadōn* ("ten thousands of ten thousands") in Rev. 5:11 in referring to an innumerable host confirms the same figurative use of the almost identical double plural here. The prefix *dis-* ("twice") intensifies the figurative aspect of innumerability. Therefore, a figurative meaning is demanded by a literal translation of the number, since its plural forms leave it too indefinitely stated to be calculated precisely.[407]

Attempts by some dispensationalists to take the number literally and apply it to the modern Chinese army are foolish.[408] That is particularly evident given the description of the "horses" and riders in 9:17–19 which cannot possibly be taken literally.

The identity and purpose of the horsemen (Rev 9:17–21)

Most commentators take the "horses" and their riders to be demonic, similar to the "locusts" of 9:1–11. Boxall is representative:

> As befits their demonic origin, these horses have the same hybrid nature as the locusts (Joel's vision of the Day of the Lord has influenced both: e.g., Joel 2:4–5; cf. Ezek. 38:14–16). Their heads are like lions' heads (again perhaps a parody of the true messianic Lion: 5:5; cf. 9:8), and their tails were like serpents, with heads by which they inflicted harm (cf. the scorpion-like tails of the locusts at 9:10, which also cause harm; at 12:9 Satan will be identified as the ancient serpent). The heads on the tails are probably to be envisaged as serpent-heads biting their victims.[409]

The ultimate purpose of the horsemen relates to redemption: either to bring humanity to repentance;[410] or to confirm humanity in its idolatry and sin from which it does not repent (Rev 9:20–21)—and if there is no repentance, then there will be judgment. That leads Steinmann to conclude that the horsemen are not demonic but are a figure for Christians as witnesses in the world: "They bring a message of spiritual death to those who will not repent. That they share some of the features of the demonic scorpions of the fifth trumpet (breastplates, cf. 9:7, 17; powerful tails, 9:7, 19) reveals that the world sees them as demonic, as Jesus was viewed on occasion (cf. Matt 12:22–30; Mark 3:23–27; Luke 11:14–23)."[411]

If both the locusts and horsemen are demonic, then the picture most likely shows them following in the footsteps of their ultimate father, who was *"a murderer from the beginning . . . a liar and the father of lies"* (John 8:44). Beale maintains that the locusts and horsemen do not depict modern warfare but figuratively depict *deception*. Although that may seem counter-intuitive, he states, "The combination of serpents (9:19) and

---

407. Beale, *Revelation,* 509.

408. See Lindsey, *Late Great,* 84–87; Walvoord, *Revelation,* 166; see also Smith, *What the World,* 120 (*"the kings from the east"* of Rev 16:12 are the armies of China, Japan, and India); Pentecost, *Things to Come,* 331 (*"the kings from the east"* are a "great opposing Gentile force that will be composed of the coalition of nations in Asia").

409. Boxall, *Revelation,* 148.

410. Stylianopoulos, "I Know," 23n.23.

411. Steinmann, "Tripartite Structure," 74.

scorpions (vv 3, 5, 10) reflects a broader linkage in biblical and ancient thought, where the combination was metaphorical for judgment in general and deception or delusion in particular."[412] Thus, the demons deceive and harden the earth-dwellers in their rejection of Christ, their idolatry, and their sin.

Rev 9:20 indicates that the basic or root sin of mankind is idolatry which manifests itself in such practices as murder, sorcery, immorality, and theft (Rev 9:21).[413] Idolatry results from deception and turning from the truth to a lie. The entire scene echoes the song of Moses in Deuteronomy 32. There, God warns Israel against idolatry,[414] compares the fruit of idolatry to the *"venom as serpents,"*[415] and says that he will send against them *"the teeth of beasts"* and *"the venom of crawling things."*[416]

If the horsemen symbolically depict Christian witness, the result is the same. The fire from their mouths (Rev 9:17) is akin to the fire that comes out of the mouths of the "two witnesses" in Rev 11:5. The actions of the horsemen are called "plagues" (Rev 9:18, 20); the two witnesses had the power to bring "plagues" on the earth (Rev 11:6). The fact that the demonic locusts could not kill, but the horsemen can, suggests to Steinmann that "Satan can harm the soul but that Christians through the preaching of God's word of judgment on the unrepentant can wield God's power of divine judgment that kills the soul."[417]

Ironically, therefore, whether the horsemen are demonic or are Christian witnesses is not particularly significant in light of their activities and purpose. Even if they are demons, we must remember that it was Christ who broke the seals thereby releasing the horses and horsemen in Rev 6:1–8; it is God who authorized the release of the locusts in 9:1; it is God who gives authority to the beast to make war with the saints and overcome them in 13:7; and it is God who will release Satan in Rev 20:3, 7. So, either way, ultimately it is God who authorizes the release of the horses and horsemen in 9:13–14 to accomplish his purposes.

We see God's superintending hand in the activities of the horsemen in that the horsemen have *"fire and brimstone"* that proceeds *"out of their mouths"* (Rev 9:17–18). The "mouths" suggest the speech of the horsemen: either deception that seduces mankind into idolatry (if the horsemen are demons), from which mankind does not repent; or the testimony of the believers (if the horsemen are Christian witnesses), which proves not to lead to mankind's repentance. The *"fire and brimstone"* is a clear Scriptural phrase signifying God's judgment.[418] It also is used in Revelation to describe the second death, the eternal "lake of fire" into which Satan, the beast, the false prophet, and all those whose names are not written in the book of life will be thrown as a result of God's judgment on their idolatry and sin.[419]

412. Beale, *Revelation,* 515; see Num 21:6; Deut 8:15; Ps 58:3–6; see also Luke 10:17–19; see also Johnson, *Triumph,* 151.

413. See Boxall, *Revelation,* 149.

414. Deut 32:21; compare Rev 9:20.

415. Deut 32:33; compare Rev 9:19.

416. Deut 32:24; compare Rev 9:17–19.

417. Steinmann, "Tripartite Structure," 74.

418. See Gen 19:24; Deut 29:23; Ps 11:6; Isa 30:33; 34:8–9; Ezek 38:22; Luke 17:29.

419. Rev 14:10; 19:20; 20:10; 21:8.

Rev 21:8 demonstrates its connection with 9:20–21 by repeating that idolaters, murderers, sorcerers, and immoral persons will be in the lake that burns with fire and brimstone. As if to cement that connection, 21:8 ends its list of those who are subject to the second death by mentioning "all liars" (i.e., those who follow the path of idolatry by turning from the truth to a lie). Thus, either directly or indirectly, the horsemen are the instruments of God's judgment. The fact that they have the power to kill (9:18, 20), whereas the locusts earlier in the chapter did not (9:4–6), indicates the "sealing" of God's judgment for idolatry (i.e., if the idolater does not have God's seal of protection [9:4], upon death his eternal spiritual state is sealed or made certain).

Regardless of the identity of the horsemen, therefore, John's interest in Revelation 9 primarily is *theological,* not physical. He is using vision and symbolism not to talk about the torment or even death of the body *per se* but to highlight the torment and death of body and soul that will ensue if believers fall back in their commitment to Christ. As Jesus said, *"Do not fear those who kill the body but are unable to kill the soul; but rather fear Him who is able to destroy both soul and body in hell"* (Matt 10:28). The entire chapter is a highly graphic way of keeping the central issue—Where or with whom does our allegiance lie?—before us.

The little book [scroll] (Rev 10:2, 8–10)

The little book of Revelation 10 is closely associated with, if not identical to, the book (scroll) of Revelation 5, for the following reasons:

(1) Both books are opened.

(2) Both are held by Christ (as the Angel of the Lord in ch. 10).[420]

(3) Christ is likened to a lion (5:5; 10:3).

(4) Both are allusions to the scroll of Ezekiel 2.

(5) Both are associated with a "strong angel" who "cries out."

(6) God is called the one who "lives forever and ever" (5:13; 10:6).

(7) Both books are directly related to the end-time prophecy of Daniel 12.

(8) In both visions someone approaches a heavenly being and takes a book out of the being's hand.

(9) In both visions John's prophetic commission includes nearly identical language in reference to the voice speaking from heaven (4:1; 10:8).

(10) Both scrolls concern the destiny of "peoples, nations, tongues, and tribes/kings" (5:9–10; 10:11).[421]

---

420. The similarities of "another strong angel" (Rev 10:1–3) to Christ cause some (e.g., Beale, *Revelation,* 522–26) to conclude that he is Christ. That identification "is rejected by most scholars because in the Apocalypse Christ never elsewhere appears as an angel." Mounce, *Revelation,* 201. Most, therefore, conclude that he is simply an angel like the "strong angel" of Rev 5:2 or "another angel" of Rev 8:3. E.g., Hendriksen, *More Than Conquerors,* 123–24; Johnson, *Triumph,* 157–59).

421. See Beale, *Revelation,* 527; see also Johnson, *Triumph,* 159–60.

The great city (Rev 11:8)

In Rev 11:8, John first mentions *"the great city"* which "mystically" or "spiritually" is identified as *"Sodom and Egypt, where also their Lord was crucified."* That would appear to identify *"the great city"* as Jerusalem. However, elsewhere in Revelation *"the great city"* is consistently used to identify "Babylon the great."[422] At this point, we need to recall what apocalyptic genre and symbolism entail and John's overall purpose in writing. Bauckham reminds us, "We need to realize that the Spirit's identifications are not simple allegories, but define present situations seen in eschatological perspective. . . . The story is set in Jerusalem because Jerusalem's treatment of the prophets and especially of Jesus is paradigmatic: this is what those who bear the witness of Jesus may expect from the world. Any and every city in whose streets the corpses of the witnesses lie is *thereby* identified, its character seen in the Spirit, as Sodom and Egypt."[423]

Do the ungodly truly repent before the parousia (Rev 11:13; see also 6:14–17; 9:20–21; 16:11)?

After the death of the "two witnesses," they went up to heaven *"and their enemies watched them . . . and the rest were terrified and gave glory to the God of heaven"* (Rev 11:12–13). Opinion is divided concerning whether that represents true repentance or not.

GIVING GLORY TO GOD AS ACKNOWLEDGING HIS SOVEREIGNTY BUT NOT AS TRUE REPENTANCE

The great earthquake and the context of the final judgment

In this very passage, Rev 11:11–12 depicts the vindication and/or resurrection of the church at the end of time while those who watched are called *"their enemies."* Given this context and designation, the actions of the "enemies" in 11:13 cannot represent true repentance and conversion. Additionally, the OT background for the "great earthquake" appears to be Ezek 38:19. There, when Gog comes against Israel, the great earthquake is part of the manifestation of God's presence when he comes in final judgment. Gog and Magog of Ezekiel 38–39 are likewise used in Revelation as part of the *parousia* and final judgment (Rev 20:8–9). As noted earlier, the "earthquake" motif is used throughout Revelation, including Rev 11:13, as a manifestation of the final judgment. W. Reader points out that the mass conversion of 90 percent of the depraved world at the end of history is an idea "found nowhere else in the book. It contradicts the idea that those saved are a limited

---

422. Rev 16:19; 17:18; 18:10, 16, 18, 19, 21; see also Rev 14:8; 17:1, 5; 18:2; 19:2. See Reader, "The Riddle," 407–14. Preterists identify *"the great city"* and "Babylon the great" as Jerusalem. Mathison, *Postmillennialism,* 152–54; Preston, *Like Father,* 102–03, 167–69, 327n.129. The specific nature and identity of Babylon the great is discussed below at "17:1—19:10: final judgment of Babylon."

423. Bauckham, *Climax of Prophecy,* 172. The fact that the great city is "mystically" and "spiritually" identified as Jerusalem itself is a verbal clue that the focus is not on literal Jerusalem.

group (7:1–15; 14:1–5; 18:4) and cannot be harmonized with the repeated statement that the plagued world remained impenitent (9:20f; 16:9, 11, 21)."[424]

Giving glory to God

Although "giving glory to God" usually signifies true worship, it does not always indicate that. In some cases it indicates the response of unbelievers who acknowledge God's sovereignty without necessarily having repentant and regenerate hearts.[425] An example is Nebuchadnezzar in Dan 2:46–47. There, the king recognized God's sovereignty and paid homage to Daniel. However, such acknowledgement was only temporary. It was followed in Daniel 3 by the attempt to force Daniel and others to worship a golden idol on pain of death. So in Rev 11:13, those who acknowledge God's sovereignty remain unbelievers.[426]

GIVING GLORY TO GOD AS TRUE REPENTANCE

Contrasting responses

On the other hand, Rev 14:6–7 the angel who proclaims the gospel calls for a two-step process of repentance, *"fear God, and give Him glory."* The repentance of Rev 11:13 is consistent with what the angel calls for and is inconsistent with the response of the people seen in 16:9. In 16:9, the people cursed God and did not give Him glory; in 11:13, the people acted consistent with the angel's charge in 14:7, i.e., *"the rest were terrified"* and *"gave glory to the God of heaven."*[427] Bauckham suggests that this response stems from those in 11:13 being convinced of the truth of the testimony of the "two witnesses" because they "perceive the martyrs' participation in Christ's triumph over death" as a result of the resurrection of the two witnesses.[428] Thus, true repentance may be in view.

Fear; glory; God of Heaven

While "fear" may or may not signify reverence toward God,[429] when it is coupled with giving glory to God it is likely to have the positive meaning of worship.[430] Further, in Revelation, "to give glory to God" always "refers positively to giving God the worship which is due to him (4:9; 14:7; 16:9; 19:7)."[431]

---

424. Reader, "The Riddle," 413.

425. See Josh 7:19; 1 Sam 6:5; Acts 12:23.

426. See Beale, *Revelation*, 603–04.

427. See Resseguie, *Revelation of John*, 166.

428. Bauckham, *Climax of Prophecy*, 281; see also Schüssler Fiorenza, *Revelation*, 79.

429. Compare Rev 1:18; 14:7; 15:4; 19:5 with 1:7; 2:10; 18:10, 15.

430. See Bauckham, *Climax of Prophecy*, 278.

431. Ibid., 278–79.

The mission of the church, regardless of the results

The martyrdom of the "two witnesses" is another instance of the paradoxical nature of Christian witness. *"Following the Lamb wherever He goes"* (Rev 14:4) may lead to death and apparent defeat in this world but, as with Christ's own crucifixion, is the means by which God triumphs over sin and evil. Bauckham believes that the believers' faithful witness to death is the manner in which the ungodly nations will be brought to repentance and faith.[432] On the other hand, if a mass conversion of unbelievers does not occur before Christ's return, the witness of Christian martyrdom still is necessary and important: it proves their faith to be genuine, which is vital for their own everlasting well-being;[433] and it provides evidence for God's condemning and judging the unbelieving world.[434] Regardless of the number of conversions that result from such witness, Bauckham concludes with the important observation (which also should be an exhortation to us) that "the delay of the *parousia* is filled with the mission of the church."[435]

Rev 12:1—15:4: the woman, the dragon, and the beast

The visions of Revelation 12–14 begin with the birth (12:1, 4–5)[436] and ascension (12:5) of Christ and may even reach back to the Garden of Eden (12:9). It is at these points when the conflict between the woman and the dragon or serpent began and was most basic and acute. John's visions in this section extend to the *parousia* and judgment (14:14–20) and the vindication and glorification of God's people (15:2–4). As Hendriksen noted earlier, beginning in Revelation 12 we receive an explanation of the deeper spiritual background of the struggle of the church with the forces of evil.[437]

---

432. Bauckham, *Climax of Prophecy,* 279–83. Schüssler Fiorenza sees that the "rhetoric of judgment" in Revelation expresses hope for the conversion of the nations in response to the witness of believers. That indicates that John is advocating "a theology of justice rather than a theology of hate and resentment." Schüssler Fiorenza, *Revelation,* 79.

433. See, e.g., Rev 6:9, 11; 7:9–17; 11:11–12; 15:2–4; 20:4–6.

434. Beale, *Revelation,* 960; see also Johnson, *Triumph,* 274; Bauckham, *Climax of Prophecy,* 237; Schüssler Fiorenza, *Revelation,* 78.

435. Ibid., 33.

436. Although on its face Rev 12:1–5 appears to refer to the birth of Christ, G. B. Caird makes the plausible point that Rev 12:5 actually is referring not to Christ's birth but to his death on the cross and the resurrection and ascension the cross entailed. The reason is that 12:5 is alluding to Ps 2:7–9. "In the psalm it is not at his birth but at his enthronement on mount Zion that the anointed king is addressed by God, 'You are my son; today I have begotten you', and is given authority to smash all the nations with an iron bar (Ps. ii. 7–9). A king's birthday is the day of his accession." Caird, *St. John the Divine,* 149; see also Rom 1:3–4; Allison, *End of the Ages,* 72–73. As Longman and Reid point out, this not only makes sense of the allusion to Ps 2:7–9 but also "explains the otherwise inexplicable leap from nativity to ascension." Longman and Reid, *Warrior,* 183. Contextually that also makes sense inasmuch as Rev 12:5 leads immediately to the casting down of Satan in 12:7–12, an event that occurred as a result of what Christ accomplished on the cross.

437. Hendriksen, *More Than Conquerors,* 23. Similarly, Rev 13:1–10 provides a much fuller explanation of Rev 11:7.

Rev 11:3–13 and 12:1—15:4 "portray essentially the same point in different imagery."[438] Both passages show the powers of evil making "war" against the church.[439] In both cases the church is protected.[440] In both cases the church is vindicated and is seen in heaven.[441] In both cases its persecutors are judged.[442]

Isa 26:16—27:1 may stand behind Revelation 12. In Isaiah, Israel is depicted as a woman in labor who cries out in pain;[443] there is the promise of resurrection;[444] God's people are hidden and protected for "a little while";[445] and God punishes the "serpent," the "dragon."[446]

The defeat and casting down of the dragon (Rev 12:7–12)

The "dragon" is identified as *"the serpent of old who is called the devil and Satan"* (Rev 12:9)

THE DRAGON'S (SATAN'S) DEFEAT OCCURRED AT THE CROSS

Bauckham notes, "The defeat of the Dragon (12:7–9) is doubtless the same event as the victory of the Lamb (5:5–6), and both are to be historically located in the death and resurrection of Jesus Christ (continued in the witness and martyrdom of his followers 12:11)."[447] Hence, Caird states, "Michael's victory is simply the heavenly and symbolic counterpart of the earthly reality of the Cross."[448]

The context of Revelation 12 also makes clear that Satan's being *"thrown down"* is not an event that occurred before history began or an event that will occur just before the end of history. Rev 12:5–6 connect Christ's resurrection and ascension with the woman fleeing into the wilderness. Rev 12:9, 11, 13–14 similarly connect the expulsion of Satan with the *"blood of the Lamb"* and the flight of the woman. Dennis Johnson explains, "Since the immediate sequel to the dragon's expulsion is its pursuit of the woman and her flight into the wilderness (vs. 13–14), the first vision guides us to interpret the expulsion of the dragon and its angelic allies as referring not to a primeval rebellion that antedated the fall of humanity but to the victory and ascent of the woman's child."[449]

---

438. Bauckham, *Climax of Prophecy,* 273n.52.

439. Rev 11:7; 12:17.

440. Temporally in Rev 11:3–7; geographically in 12:6, 14–16.

441. Rev 11:11–12; 14:13–16; 15:1–4.

442. Rev 11:13–19; 14:7–11, 17–20.

443. Compare Isa 26:16–17 and Rev 12:1–2. For the contrast between the woman of Revelation 12 and the harlot of Revelation 17–18, see below concerning Babylon the great.

444. Compare Isa 26:19 and Rev 12:5.

445. Compare Isa 26:20 and Rev 12:6, 14.

446. Compare Isa 27:1 and Rev 12:7–9. See Rissi, *Time and History,* 35–37; Court, *Myth and History,* 112; Allison, *End of the Ages,* 72–73; Beale, *Revelation,* 632.

447. Bauckham, *Climax of Prophecy,* 186.

448. Caird, *St. John the Divine,* 154; see also Ladd, *Commentary,* 172. Early in church history, Papias indicated the same thing. Papias, *Fragment* 24.

449. Johnson, *Him We Proclaim,* 388.

"Having great wrath, knowing that he has only a short time" (Rev 12:12) indicates the same thing, as Milligan describes: "This period of time is not to be looked at as if it were a brief special season at the close of the Christian age, when the wrath of Satan is aroused to a greater than ordinary degree because the last hour is about to strike. The *great wrath* with which he goes forth is that stirred in him by his defeat through the death, resurrection, and ascension of our Lord. It was roused in him when he was 'cast into the earth,' and from that moment of defeat therefore the 'short season' begins."[450] This is consistent with the fact that Christ's first coming began the "last days"; hence, in this context, Satan's "short time" is equivalent to the "last days."[451]

Satan's fall in Rev 12:10 (*"now . . . the accuser of our brethren has been thrown down"*) corresponds to John 12:31 (*"now the ruler of this world will be cast out"*).[452] Beale explains that, in John 12, Jesus says that his being "lifted up" on the cross means that "the inaugurated judgment of the devil is to be executed decisively. These parallels confirm further that the imagery in Rev. 12:7–10 explains the significance of Christ's death and resurrection and does not refer to events in the distant future."[453]

The nature of Satan's defeat

Caird makes the interesting observation, "In the book of Job one of the angels in the heavenly court is called the Satan (with the definite article), because he holds an appointment as accuser or prosecutor in the lawcourt of God [Job 1:6–12]. . . . Satan appears again as accuser in the visions of Zechariah, where the high priest Joshua is on trial [Zech 3:1–7]."[454]

The "casting down" of Satan appears to relate in significant part to his ability to accuse the brethren as well as to deceive the nations (Rev 12:10). Satan has only one fatal accusation he can make against people: unforgiven sin. At the cross, Jesus took that ability of Satan *"out of the way, having nailed it to the cross"* and thereby *"disarmed the rulers and authorities"* (Col 2:14–15). What Christ accomplished on the cross, therefore, significantly affected Satan's ability to accuse the saints. Beale cogently discusses this: "In the light of Rev. 12:11, the accusations of v 10 appear to be directed against the illegitimacy of the saints' participation in salvation. . . . The death and resurrection of Christ have banished the devil from this privilege formerly granted him by God, because Christ's death was the penalty that God exacted for the sins of all those who were saved by faith. . . . Therefore, the devil no longer had any basis for his accusations against the saints, since the penalty that they deserved and that he pleaded for had at last been exacted in Christ's death."[455]

The result for believers is an important change in status and security, even though it may not appear so to the naked eye. Hence, part of the reason why John wrote the entire

---

450. Milligan, *Revelation*, 209–10.

451. See above, chapter 4, the section "Christ's first coming and the 'last days.'"

452. The Greek verbs used in the two passages are similar, forceful words, derived from the same root: John 12:31—*ekballō* ("drive out; expel"); Rev 12:10—*kataballō* ("throw down; strike down").

453. Beale, *Revelation*, 660. See also below at 20:1–3 regarding the "binding of Satan."

454. Caird, *St. John the Divine*, 154.

455. Beale, *Revelation*, 659. See also Rom 3:21–26; 8:1, 33–34, 38–39.

book of Revelation is to make clear to believers that "things are not what they seem."[456] External hardships are no indication of God's disfavor or of spiritual insecurity. Beasley-Murray clearly grasps this in connection with the casting down of Satan in Rev 12:7–12:

> Two things are in mind here. First, that Satan has no place in heaven represents an important victory won for man, since Satan is no longer able to accuse man before God, which suggests that God will no longer listen to accusations against his people, for they are forgiven. Secondly, Satan's defeat in heaven signifies that his power has been broken in the affairs of man in history, so that even if he does intensify his efforts to control the nations and destroy the work of God, the extent of his influence is limited (he has for example no power over the Church), and his days are numbered (vv. 13ff.).[457]

The sea and the abyss (Rev 12:12; 9:1–2, 11; 11:7; 13:1; 17:8; 20:1, 3; 21:1)

Rev 12:12 says, *"Woe to the earth and the sea, because the devil has come down to you."* Whereas 12:9 had said that the devil had been *"thrown down to the earth,"* it appears from 12:12 that he also was thrown down to the sea. The sea often is associated with chaos and evil.[458] Just as the beasts of Dan 7:2–8 arose out of the sea, so the beast of Rev 13:1 arose out of the sea. The OT portrays the sea as the abode of evil sea monsters, although God is sovereign over the sea and its inhabitants.[459] The sea as chaos and evil is further indicated by Rev 21:1 which says that in the new heavens and new earth *"there is no longer any sea."* That means "the sea as the source of satanic evil opposing God's throne has been eliminated and replaced by the river of redemption, which has its source in the throne [Rev 22:1]."[460]

The sea appears to be synonymous with the abyss. Jonathan Moo states that this identification of the sea and the abyss "is made clear at 11:7 and 17:8, where the same beast that comes up from the sea at 13:1 is described as having come up from the *abussos* [abyss]."[461] Consequently, Satan's being *"thrown down to the earth"* (12:9) and *"coming down to the earth and the sea"* (12:12) are parallel to his being *"thrown into the abyss"* (20:1–3).[462]

---

456. Johnson, *Triumph*, 9.

457. Beasley-Murray, *Revelation*, 202. "This understanding of Satan's fall from heaven is comparable to that of [Luke 10:17–20]. . . . That is, the devil's fall means that the salvation of Jesus' followers is secure from Satanic threat, and their power over demons is an initial indication of the devil's defeat and their salvific security." Beale, *Revelation*, 660.

458. See Beale, *Revelation*, 789; Schüssler Fiorenza, *Revelation*, 83. See also Schnabel, *40 Questions*, 279 for different meanings the term "sea" encompasses in Revelation.

459. Job 38:8–11; Ps 74:12–15; 89:9–10; 104:5–9; Prov 8:27–29; Isa 27:1; 51:9–10; Ezek 32:2.

460. Beale, *Revelation*, 328.

461. Moo, "The Sea," 156.

462. That confirms that Satan's being bound and *"thrown into the abyss"* in Rev 20:1–3 occurred in connection with Christ's first coming and is not an event that takes place after his *parousia*. See also below at 20:1–3 for more on the relationship between the "casting" (12:9) and the "binding" (20:3) of Satan.

The death, but paradoxical victory, of the saints (Rev 12:11; 13:7)

In Rev 13:7 it says that authority was *"given to"* the beast to make war against the saints and overcome them. That is a "divine passive" (i.e., the authority was granted to the beast by God, much like God gave Satan authority over Job in Job 1:12; 2:6). That tells us, as Resseguire puts it, "God is in control and the war against the saints does not further the beast's aims but rather thwarts them. Evil is conquered by the saints' testimony—even their testimony unto death. Christ conquers by his death on the cross, and it is the pattern of the saints also (12:11)."[463]

Rev 15:5—16:21: the seven bowl judgments

In this section, God punishes the ungodly during the inter-advent age and brings final judgment at the last day because of their persecution and idolatry. As we saw earlier in tabular form,[464] the plagues of the trumpets and bowls occur in the same order and involve: (1) the earth; (2) the sea; (3) rivers; (4) the sun; (5) the realm of evil; (6) the Euphrates; and (7) the final judgment of the world with "lightning, sounds, thunder, earthquake, and great hail." At this point, we must again recall that Revelation is *not* a chronological narrative. As with the seals and trumpets, the bowls are not necessarily sequential but may be simultaneous. Thus, concerning the sixth bowl (darkness), Milligan points out, "We are told of *their pains and of their sores*. But pains and sores are not an effect produced by darkness. They can, therefore, be only those of the first bowl, a conclusion confirmed by the word 'plagues' instead of plague [16:9]."[465]

As was true with the trumpets, the bowl judgments draw upon the imagery of the exodus plagues:

1st bowl (sores) (16:2)	corresponds to 6th plague (Exod 9:8–11)
2nd and 3rd bowls (water into blood) (16:3–6)	correspond to 1st plague (Exod 7:20–25)
5th bowl (darkness) (16:10–11)	corresponds to 9th plague (Exod 10:21–23)
6th bowl (frogs) (16:12–16)	corresponds to 2nd plague (Exod 8:2–9)
7th bowl (hail) (16:17–21)	corresponds to 7th plague (Exod 9:22–26)

The sixth and seventh bowls (Rev 16:12–21)

The sixth and seventh bowls are connected. The sixth bowl prepares the world for the final war against God; the result occurs at the seventh bowl, which is the *parousia*. The focus on Satan, the "gathering for war" of the world against God and his people, and the complete and final defeat of God's enemies, show that sixth and seventh bowls correspond to Rev 20:7–10 (and also parallel 19:17–21). Milligan indicates the probable reason why the seventh bowl is poured out on the air: "The seventh or last Bowl is poured out into the

---

463. Resseguie, *Revelation of John*, 185.

464. See above, the section "Structure: progressively parallel; not strictly chronological."

465. Milligan, *Revelation*, 268, emphasis in original.

air, here thought of as the realm of that prince of this world who is also 'the prince of the power of the air' [Eph 2:2]."[466]

That the church is present during this time is apparent from Rev 16:15 which says, *"Behold, I am coming like a thief. Blessed is the one who stays awake and keeps his clothes, so that he will not walk naked and men will not see his shame."* Just as we earlier saw the connection between the seals and the Olivet Discourse, here we see the same connection between the bowls and the Olivet Discourse. *"I am coming like a thief"* repeats Christ's warning to the church in Matt 24:43 and Rev 3:3. *"Blessed is the one who stays awake"* repeats Christ's exhortations to the church in Matt 24:42–44, 45–51; Matt 25:1–13, 14–30 that we need to be alert, ready, prepared, and faithfully doing what we should be doing.

The drying up of the Euphrates to prepare for the kings of the east (Rev 16:12)

As with so much else in Revelation, the imagery of the sixth bowl is based on historical precedents which are then used typologically. The drying up of the Euphrates and the kings from the east appear to draw on God's judgment of Babylon, which itself followed the pattern of the drying up of the Red Sea and the Jordan River at and following the exodus.[467] Isaiah and Jeremiah had prophesied that judgment on Babylon would include the drying up of the Euphrates.[468] The prophecies were fulfilled by Cyrus's diversion of the water (see Isa 44:27–28). That allowed Cyrus's army to enter Babylon unexpectedly and defeat it.[469] Cyrus, his princes and kings, were "from the east."[470]

Beale describes how John takes the fall of historical Babylon and typologically universalizes it in Revelation:

> As at the exodus and especially at the fall of historical Babylon, the drying up of the Euphrates again marks the prelude to the destruction of latter-day Babylon. And just as Babylon has been universalized and become symbolic,[471] so the Euphrates cannot be a literal geographical reference to the Euphrates in modern Iraq, Syria, and Turkey but must be figurative and universal, despite those who contend that the reference is literal. This is indicated by 17:1, where the Babylonian harlot "sits on many waters," which is another way of referring to "the Euphrates and its water" (16:12). The "many waters" of 17:1 are figuratively interpreted as "peoples and multitudes . . . and nations and tongues" in 17:15. . . . Therefore, the drying up of the Euphrates' waters is a picture of how the multitudes of Babylon's religious adherents throughout the world become disloyal to Babylon [see 17:15–18]. Disenchantment with Babylon is a prelude to Babylon's judgment, and the final judgment itself.[472]

There is dispute concerning the identity of *"the kings of the east."*

---

466. Ibid., 273.

467. See Exod 14:21–22; Josh 3:16; 4:23.

468. Isa 11:15; 44:27–28; Jer 50:38; 51:36.

469. Beale, *Revelation*, 827.

470. Isa 41:2, 25; 46:11; Jer 50:41; 51:11, 28.

471. See discussion of Babylon below.

472. Beale, *Revelation*, 828.

The "kings of the east" as unbelievers

The majority sees the *"kings of the east"* as "a figurative universalization of not only Baby-lon and the Euphrates River but also of Cyrus and his allies, 'the kings from the rising of the sun,' who are interpretively escalated into 'the kings of the whole inhabited earth' (16:14; cf. 18:18)."[473] A similar view, expressed by Ladd, is that "the kings of the east—the pagan hordes—join forces with the kings of the whole (civilized) world to do battle with Messiah, for it is clearly the eschatological 'battle on the great day of God the Almighty' (vs. 14)."[474]

The "kings of the east" as believers

Others see the *"kings of the east"* in positive terms. The reasons are stated by Desmond Ford, who notes that the word for "east" (Greek = *anatolē*, which also means "rising" or "the position of the rising sun") was a familiar symbol for the Messiah in NT times: "It pointed to something or Someone of heavenly origin. Elsewhere the Apocalypse used the term in this manner [Rev 7:2], and it is hardly likely that a book so carefully written should change the meaning of this symbol in the later chapter. . . . The 'kings of the east' may be intended as a direct contrast to the 'kings of the whole world' mentioned in the same paragraph, and could represent heavenly beings who come to deliver the saints, as the Median kings from the east came with Cyrus to deliver Israel of old from Babylon."[475] Since the sixth bowl is the preparation for the final battle and the *parousia*, the *"kings of the east"* may therefore refer to the heavenly armies that accompany Christ in Rev 19:11–16.

Rev 17:1—19:10: final judgment of Babylon

As has been seen elsewhere throughout Revelation, humanity consists of two, and only two, types or groups: those who are committed to Christ and those who are not. Babylon epitomizes the system and worldview of everything and everyone that is not Christ's. The world's system appears all-powerful but contains the seeds of its own destruction. God's judgment on the ungodly economic, cultural, and religious system of the world leads to the establishment of God's consummated reign (Rev 19:6) and the union with his people (Rev 19:7–9). Rev 13:4 raised the question, *"Who is able to wage war with him [the beast]?"* That is answered in Rev 17:14: the Lamb and those who are with him (*"the called and chosen and faithful"*) will overcome the beast because the Lamb is *"Lord of lords and King of kings."* In yet another recapitulated image, the saints are vindicated, the blood of the martyrs is avenged, and the prayer of Rev 6:10 is answered.

---

473. Ibid.

474. Ladd, *Commentary*, 213.

475. Ford, *Abomination of Desolation*, 268.

Babylon the great, the mother of harlots (Rev 17:1–5, 9, 15, 18) in its first-century context

Most commentators identify Babylon as Rome, based on the reference to the seven hills (Rev 17:9).[476] The Greek word which the NIV translates as "hills" is the plural of *oros* which, as BDAG puts it, is "a relatively high elevation of land that projects higher than a *bounos* ('a minor elevation, hill')."[477] Consequently, most translations (e.g., ESV, NASB, NKJV, RSV) translate the term as "mountains" rather than "hills." Although the allusion probably is to Rome, the use of *oros* in 17:9 suggests that "Babylon the great" transcends historical Rome since Rome's hills are actually of very minor elevation even compared to the hills of Palestine.[478] Indeed, the fact that John uses the name "Babylon the great" rather than "Rome" indicates that he is not limiting his identification to the then-existing Roman state or society.[479] While John uses Roman power, economy, and culture as the historical backdrop for his depiction of Babylon the great,[480] Rome is seen as a paradigm or "type." Specifically, Rome/Babylon is depicted as a *corrupting influence* on people (i.e., it is a "harlot").[481]

There are two major sources for John's depiction of Babylon the great: Jeremiah's oracle against historical Babylon (Jeremiah 50–51), and Ezekiel's oracle against Tyre (Ezekiel 26–28).[482] Richard Bauckham's extensive study of this portion of Revelation has led him to conclude that what is in view here primarily is a two-fold corruption: first, cultural and economic exploitation and corruption; and second, religious corruption.[483] They are, of course, related: Jesus frequently warns believers about the fact that the lure of riches can turn one's head, choke the word in one's life, and thereby become one's new, true Lord.[484] Paul does the same thing.[485]

---

476. E.g., Bauckham, "Economic Critique," 52; Schüssler Fiorenza, *Revelation*, 97; Beale, *Revelation*, 869–70.

477. BDAG, *"oros,"* 724.

478. "The altitude of the central part of Rome ranges from 13 metres (43 ft) above sea level (at the base of the Pantheon) to 139 metres (456 ft) above sea level (the peak of Monte Mario)." "Rome," *Wikipedia*, n.p.

479. Schüssler Fiorenza, *Revelation*, 89.

480. Bauckham sees the depiction of Babylon the great as Roman civilization riding on the back of Roman military power. Bauckham, "Economic Critique," 52.

481. Babylon is called the *"Mother of Harlots"* (Rev 17:5). That is figurative language to indicate "that which allures, tempts, seduces and draws people away from God." Hendriksen, *More Than Conquerors*, 167. Such allurement reveals that people's primary commitment and loyalty is to the world. Schnabel, *40 Questions*, 208.

482. Allusion also is made to the shorter oracles against Babylon and Tyre found among the OT prophets (Babylon: Isa 13:1—14:23; 21:1–10; 47; Jer 25:12–38; Tyre: Isaiah 23). Bauckham, "Economic Critique," 54. In alluding to these OT oracles but reinterpreting them to apply to the Rome of his day and beyond the Rome of his day, John is standing in the line of biblical prophets, and Jesus himself, who took the inspired words of the prophetic tradition and gave them new meaning and application.

483. Bauckham, "Econcomic Critique," 47–90; See also Schnabel, *40 Questions*, 209.

484. E.g., Matt 6:19–24; 13:7, 22; 19:16–30; Mark 4:7, 18–19; 10:17–25; Luke 8:7, 14; 12:13–21; 16:13.

485. E.g., Col 3:5–6; 1 Tim 3:3; 6:6–11.

The images of the harlot, drawn from the OT oracles concerning Tyre (Isa 23:15–18; Ezekiel 26–28), primarily relate to the first of these two forms of corruption:

> The reference there is obviously to the vast trading activity through which the city of Tyre had grown rich. Tyre's commercial enterprise is compared with prostitution because it is association with other nations for the sake of profit. . . . In other words, Rome is a harlot because the associations with the peoples of her empire are for her own economic benefit. . . . Rome offered the Mediterranean world unity, security, stability, the conditions of prosperity. But in John's view these benefits are not what they seem: they are the favors of a prostitute, purchased at a high price.[486]

The list of cargoes (Rev 18:12–13)

Bauckham has compared Ezekiel's account of Tyre's trade in Ezek 27:12–25 with John's account of Rome's trade and concludes that Ezekiel's account was an accurate portrayal of Tyre's trade in the sixth centry BC and John's list of cargoes is an accurate list of Rome's imports in the first century AD.[487]

John completes his list of cargoes in 18:13 by referring to slaves. Slavery was the basis of Rome's economic system. Yet the way John phrases the mention of slaves as part of Babylon the great's cargoes is profoundly theological:

> That John gives both the common term for slaves in the slave markets ["bodies"] and a scriptural description of slaves ["souls of people"] must mean that he intends a comment on the slave trade. He is pointing out that slaves are not mere animal carcasses to be bought and sold as property, but are human beings. But in this emphatic position at the end of the list, this is more than just a comment on the slave trade. It is a comment on the whole list of cargoes. It suggests the inhuman brutality, the contempt for human life, on which the whole of Rome's prosperity and luxury rests.[488]

Those who mourn for Babylon (Rev 18:3, 9–11, 14–19)

In Revelation 18, John observes that three classes of people lament the destruction of Babylon the great: *"the kings of the earth"* (18:9); *"the merchants of the earth"* (18:11); and *"every shipmaster, passenger, sailor, and all who make their living by the sea"* (18:17). Bacukham concludes, "These are precisely the people who themselves benefited from

---

486. Bauckham, "Economic Critique," 54–56; see also Johnson, *Triumph,* 228.

487. Bauckham, "Economic Critique," 59. This is another example of the reapplication of OT prophecies and prophetic themes. Elsewhere Bauckham points out that, unlike ancient Babylon, Tyre had been notable not for its political empire but for its economic empire. Consequently, "it is to focus his indictment of Rome for her *economic* exploitation and his pronouncement of judgement on Rome for *this* aspect of her evil, that John reapplies to Rome Ezekiel's oracle against Tyre. . . . It shows us how prophecy, whether in the Old or the New Testament, can be both very specific in its condemnation of societies contemporary with the prophet, but also paradigmatic and so available for reapplication to later societies guilty of similar evils." Bauckham, *Bible in Politics,* 92.

488. Bauckham, "Economic Critique," 79.

Rome's economic exploitation of the Empire. What they lament is the destruction of the source of their own wealth."[489]

Babylon is not limited to Rome but is universal

Although the context of Revelation 17–18 may have been the social, economic, political, and religious circumstances of his own day, John's apocalypse far transcends Rome. Although there are some identifying first-century markers ("seven hills"; the list of cargoes), "they are sufficiently few to make the reapplication of the images to comparable situations easy."[490] This is seen in the language John uses. In his description of Babylon as a *"great harlot"* and the *"mother of harlots,"*[491] John stands in a long line of prophets who employ the language of illicit sexual relations to condemn economic injustice, cultural corruption, and religious faithlessness.[492] For example, Isa 23:1–18 condemns Tyre as a harlot for its commercial trade practices. Ezekiel condemns Jerusalem as a harlot for its idolatry, cultural corruption, and economic injustice (Ezek 16:1–59). The entire book of Hosea is a graphic portrayal of Israel's "harlotry" in its use of its money and resources (Hos 2:5–9), its idolatry (Hos 2:11–13; 4:11–13; 13:1–2), and its general cultural corruption (Hos 4:1–2, 7–8, 14; 10:13).

Further, John constantly speaks in "universal" terms: the expected trial *"is about to come upon the whole world"* (Rev 3:10); the beast has authority *"over every tribe and people and tongue and nation"* and *"all who dwell on the earth will worship him"* (Rev 13:7–8); the kings *"of the whole world"* are gathered for the final battle (Rev 16:14); Babylon corrupts and deceives *"all the nations"* (Rev 14:8; 18:3, 23) and is guilty of the blood *"of all who have been slain on the earth"* (Rev 18:24).[493]

Just as the beast of Rev 13:1–2 combines all of the features of the four beasts of Dan 7:3–8 into one, so Babylon the great combines in itself all of the evils of the two great evil cities (Babylon and Tyre) on which it is prophetically based. Thus, Babylon is not an individual city, or even an individual empire, but appears to be a worldwide entity. It may be seen as "the ultimate seductive expression of secular wrongdoing,"[494] or "the final manifestation of the total history of godless nations . . . who will seduce all the world to worship that which is not God,"[495] or material seduction and fallen human culture.[496] Indeed, "John's Babylon is the final climax of the enterprise begun at Babel (= Babylon) in

489. Bauckham, *Bible in Politics*, 97. John's perspective, of course, is not that of the people of the *earth* and the *sea* (Rev 18: 9, 11, 17) but is that of *heaven* (18:20). From his perspective, the fall of Babylon is cause for rejoicing and the worship and praise of God (18:20; 19:1–6).

490. Bauckham, *Theology*, 156.

491. Rev 17:1, 5; see also Rev 17:2, 4, 15; 18:3, 7, 9.

492. "Harlotry and fornication are metaphors for economic exploitation, social tyranny, political compromise, and religious assimilation with the dominant culture." Resseguie, *Revelation of John*, 218.

493. Similarly, the *"many waters"* on which the great harlot Babylon sits (Rev 17:1) are explicitly defined to be *"peoples and multitudes and nations and tongues"* (Rev 17:15); cf. Rev 5:9; 7:9 where the church is drawn *"from every tribe and tongue and people and nation."*

494. Smalley, *Revelation*, 427.

495. Ladd, *Commentary*, 222.

496. Johnson, *Triumph*, 17, 246, 268–69n.2, 339.

Genesis 11: the agelong human enterprise of organizing human society in opposition to God. . . . In other words, it transcends its original reference and becomes a symbol of the whole history of organized human evil whose fall will be the end of history."[497]

In his portrayal of Babylon the great, John is again confronting his audience with the choice between the beast or the Lamb, the world or the church, those who dwell on the earth or those who are citizens of heaven, because Babylon is the "anti-kingdom"— the alluring, all-encompassing alternative to the kingdom of God.[498] Thomas Torrance concludes, "Ostensibly Babylon is a world-wide civilization and culture, magnificent in her science and arts and commerce, but it is drugged with pride and intoxicated with its enormous success. At the same time it is a strange mingling of world power and religion, of paganism and Christianity, which becomes the greatest hindrance to the Christian Gospel. Its inner mystery is revealed at last as the great dominion of Satan that desires to entrench itself forever in the creation of God, in sharp antagonism to the dominion that supervenes upon the world from above, the Kingdom of God."[499]

The spiritual nature of Babylon

As mentioned above, there are two aspects to Babylon the great's corruption of humanity: the cultural-economic and the religious. According to Milligan, the religious aspect of Babylon the great's corrupting influence may be inferred from an OT referent: "In conjunction with the fact that Babylon is a harlot [Rev 17:5], destruction by fire [Rev 18:8] leads us directly to the thought of the spiritual, and not simply the civil, or political, or commercial, character of the city. According to the law of Moses, burning appears to have been the punishment of fornication only in the case of a priest's daughter [Lev 21:9]. . . . The conclusion to be drawn is that Babylon is a spiritual city."[500]

Throughout the Bible, the language of harlotry, sexual immorality, and infidelity are equated with *spiritual* infidelity (i.e., forsaking God to pursue other gods and ungodly practices).[501] Desmond Ford points out, "While it is true that Scripture uses the harlot

497. Bauckham, *Bible in Politics*, 93. Babylon the great's transcending historical Rome and representing the universal seduction of the world is consistent with the reference to the "seven kings of which one is an eighth" in Rev 17:9–11. Bauckham states that this may be "a reflection of the Hebrew idiom, the 'graded numerical saying,' which uses two consecutive numbers in parallel. In some cases this idiom indicates that the enumeration is illustrative rather than exhaustive (Prov 6:16; 30:15, 18, 21, 29), but when the numbers seven and eight are used in this way, they seem to indicate an indefinite but adequate number (Eccl 11:2; Mic 5:4[5]). . . . This usage may confirm what we would be justified in suspecting in any case: that John's numbers seven and eight are not to be taken literally, as defining how many Roman emperors there will actually be before the parousia, but as symbolizing all the evil, antichristian emperors there can be before their excess of evil brings its own destruction." Bauckham, *Climax of Prophecy*, 405.

498. John is thus challenging Christians to critique their own societies. As Bauckham says, "Any society whom Babylon's cap fits must wear it. Any society which absolutizes its own economic prosperity at the expense of others comes under Babylon's condemnation." Bauckham, *Theology*, 156; see also Schnabel, *40 Questions*, 211–12.

499. Torrance, *Apocalypse Today*, 115.

500. Milligan, *Revelation*, 309, 310.

501. See, e.g., Jer 3:6–10; Ezek 16:15–22; Hos 2:2; 4:12; Mal 2:13–16; 1 Cor 6:15–18; Jas 4:4; Rev 2:18–22; 14:8; 17:1–5; 18:1–3; 19:1–2. See also Schnabel, *40 Questions*, 209.

symbol for cities such as Tyre and Nineveh [to indicate economic and cultural corruption] it is much more frequently applied to the apostatizing people of God."[502] Ford discusses the literary background of the "harlot" symbolism John uses for Babylon the great:

> "Harlot" and not "adulteress" *is* the most appropriate figure, for the emphasis is upon the many lovers and the wages gained. The literary origin of the symbolism in Rev. 17 is to be found in Jer. 2:33–34 and 3:1–11, where Judah is a harlot (Jer. 2:20) with a sign upon her forehead (Jer. 3:3), who causes transgression in others (Jer. 2:33), and "on whose skirts is found the lifeblood of the guiltless poor" (Jer. 2:34). She is clothed in crimson (Jer. 4:30) and golden ornaments. Her lovers will despise her (Jer. 4:30) and seek her life. . . . *Pornē* [prostitute; whore] is used in the LXX [Greek OT] at least fifty times to describe the spiritual fornication of Israel and Judah.[503]

Babylon the great's religious and spiritual corruption was present in the nature of first-century Rome's civil religion. Bauckham discusses this:

> From John's Jewish Christian perspective, the political religion of Rome was the worst kind of false religion, since it absolutized Rome's claim on her subjects and cloaked her exploitation of them in the garb of religious loyalty. Thus, for John, Rome's economic exploitation and the corrupting influence of her state religion go hand in hand. . . . In John's perspective, the evils of Rome came to a head in her persecution of Christians, because here Rome's self-deification clashed with the lordship of the Lamb to which the Christian martyrs bore witness and so what was implicit in all of Rome's imperial policies here became explicit.[504]

One aspect of this religious corruption may also have been the cooperation between first-century Judaism and Rome. Some commentators identify the harlot with unfaithful Israel, especially Jerusalem.[505] "The description in [Rev 17:6; 18:24] of the harlot's killing the martyrs is distinctly reminiscent of Jesus' accusations against Jerusalem (Mt 23:29–39). . . . When John speaks of the beast turning on the harlot and destroying her [Rev 17:16–18], he in all probability alludes to the divine judgment that befell Jerusalem for cooperating with the imperial cult."[506]

As was true with respect to cultural-economic corruption, the religious corruption of Babylon the great is not limited to first-century Rome. As Ford states, John was not primarily interested in the current political and economic situation *per se,* although he was fully aware of it. Rather, "To him Babylon is essentially religious and personifies the whole world's apostasy from God. . . . John saw more than just Rome, and . . . was particularly

---

502. Ford, *Abomination of Desolation*, 270.

503. Ibid., 270, 304n.159.

504. Bauckham, "Economic Critique," 57–58.

505. McDurmon, *Jesus v. Jerusalem*, 2; Chilton, *Paradise*, 187–88 (Jerusalem is the harlot; her being pictured as "sitting on the beast" [Rev 17:3] represents "her dependence upon the Roman Empire for her national existence and power").

506. Pate and Haines, *Doomsday Delusions*, 43; see also Beale, "Purpose of Symbolism," 63 ("The wicked religious-economic culture of the evil Roman world system is the focus in Revelation 17, and the apostate church and unbelieving Israel are included with it, inasmuch as they have become a part of the sinful world system"); Campbell, "Antithetical Feminine-Urban Imagery," 100n.78 ("For John and his readers steeped in prior revelation, 'Babylon' was Jerusalem barely disguised").

concerned with the final apostasy which will have as its centre the issue of the relationship to God rather than political matters. Furthermore, he was writing to professing Christians, not for unbelieving citizens of Rome. Therefore, he intends by his portrayal to admonish the flock, lest its members be led by Antichrist into spiritual fornication."[507]

Babylon the harlot is the counterpart to the pure woman of Rev 12:1

The universal nature of Babylon the great is seen in its contrast with the woman of Revelation 12. Ford states, "As the woman of Rev. 12 obviously is a figure for the people of God in all times, so the woman in Rev. 17 encompasses the rebels of every era. But as John particularly applies the bride eschatologically [see Rev 19:7–8; 21:2, 9], so with the harlot. Paul had spoken of [the apostasy] and Babylon to John summarizes the rebellion spoken of by the apostle to the Gentiles. Babel had originated in rebellion, and thus it will end."[508]

The table below shows how the woman, the ideal Zion, the heavenly representative of the people of God (Rev 12:1–2, 5–6, 13–17), is contrasted with "the great harlot" of Revelation 17–18:

The Woman of Revelation 12	*The Great Harlot of Revelation 17–18*
Clothed with the sun (12:1)	Clothed with purple & scarlet (17:4; 18:16)
The moon is under her feet (12:1)	Sits on many waters (17:1, 15)
Wears a crown of 12 stars (12:1)	Adorned with gold, precious stones, & pearls (17:4; 18:16)
Gave birth to a son (12:5)	Is the mother of harlots (17:5)
Fled into the wilderness (12:6, 14)	Lives sensuously with the kings and merchants of the earth (17:2; 18:3, 9)
Is sustained by God (12:6, 14)	Is carried by the beast (17:3, 7)
Is persecuted by the dragon (12:13, 15)	Is drunk with the blood of the saints (17:6; 18:24)

Babylon is the counterpart of the New Jerusalem

Both Babylon and the New Jerusalem are symbolic. The fact that Babylon is described both as a woman and a city, and the New Jerusalem likewise is described both as a woman and a city (Rev 21:2), shows not only their universal nature but also the connection of culture, economics, and religion: they mutually interact, and all determine and reveal one's

---

507. Ford, *Abomination of Desolation,* 269, 304n.159. The spiritual nature of the harlot has led some commentators to view Babylon as the prophets viewed faithless Israel: "Babylon is not the Jerusalem only of 'the Jews.' She is the great Church of God throughout the world when that Church becomes faithless to her true Lord and King. . . . Babylon is the world in the Church." Milligan, *Revelation,* 295–96. However, "Babylon is never called *moichalis,* 'adulteress'; always *porne,* 'harlot'. Hence, Babylon was never the Lamb's wife." Hendriksen, *More Than Conquerors,* 167n.3. Further, the references to merchants, cargoes, shipmasters, and sailors in Rev 18:11–19 do not harmonize well with a false church but better describe Babylon as the world-city. Ibid., 167n.1. Babylon as Rome and Babylon as the false church have elements of truth, but both ideas are too limited.

508. Ford, *Abomination of Desolation,* 269.

true loyalties. Resseguie summarizes this comparison of Babylon the great and the New Jerusalem: "Babylon, the city of this world, the place of exile and alienation for Christians, is the spiritual capital for those who are earthbound, whose point of view is from below (that is, from this world). The earthbound includes not only those outside the church but also those within. Babylon is where the 'inhabitants of the earth' dwell and the followers of the beast make their home. Yet Babylon is not only the home of the earth's inhabitants; it is also where Christians live, although it cannot be called their home."[509]

The parallels between Babylon and New Jerusalem show the seductive nature of the world and its values; the contrasts show that the world and its values ultimately are deadly:[510]

Babylon (Revelation 17–18)	New Jerusalem (Revelation 21–22)
Introduction	*Introduction*
Approach of the angel (17:1)	Approach of the angel (21:9)
Invitation: "Come, I will show you" (17:1)	Invitation: "Come, I will show you" (21:9)
Translation of seer by angel (17:3)	Translation of seer by angel (21:10)
To a wilderness (17:3b)	To a high mountain (21:10)
Opening of the vision (17:3)	Opening of the vision (21:10b)
Comparisons	*Comparisons*
Dressed in fine linen, purple, and scarlet (17:4; 18:16)	Dressed in fine linen, bright and clean (19:8)
Adorned with gold (17:4; 18:16)	Made of pure gold (21:18, 21)
Adorned with jewels (17:4; 18:16)	Brilliance is like crystal-clear jasper (21:11); city wall is jasper (21:18); foundation of city wall is adorned with every kind of precious stone (21:19–20)
Adorned with pearls (17:4; 18:16)	Twelve gates are twelve pearls (21:21)
Contrasts	*Contrasts*
The great harlot (17:1)	The bride, the wife of the Lamb (21:2, 9)
Dwelling place of demons (18:2)	Dwelling place of God (21:3, 22)
A name written on her forehead (17:5)	God's name written on its citizens' foreheads (22:4)
Her followers are not in the book of life (17:8)	Its citizens are in the Lamb's book of life (21:27)
Holds a golden cup full of abominations and unclean things of her immorality (17:4); a prison of unclean spirits and unclean birds (18:2)	Nothing unclean will enter it (21:27)
Her wine makes the nations drunk (17:2; 18:3)	The water of life is given freely, and the tree of life brings the healing of the nations (21:6; 22:1–2)

509. Resseguie, *Revelation of John*, 35.

510. The parallels and contrasts between Babylon and New Jerusalem are explored in great detail in Campbell, "Antithetical Feminine-Urban Imagery," 81–108.

Babylon (Revelation 17–18)	New Jerusalem (Revelation 21–22)
Corrupts & deceives the nations; the kings of the earth committed immorality with her (17:2; 18:3, 9, 23)	The nations will walk by its light; the kings of the earth will bring their glory into it (21:24, 26)
God's people are called to come out of Babylon (18:4)	God's people are called to enter New Jerusalem (22:14)
Doomed to destruction (17:16–17; 18:8–23)	The saints will reign forever and ever (22:5)

"Come out of her, my people" (Rev 18:4)

In connection with the church in Revelation, we earlier noted the allusion to Isa 48:20; 52:11; Jer 50:8; 51:6, 9, 45 as the background for John's exhortation to *"come out of her, My people."* Theodore Stylianopoulos makes the perhaps obvious point that, in John's first-century context, John's command or exhortation "is not for physical withdrawal but for a distinctly countercultural way of life in the midst of Greco-Roman society."[511]

Since Babylon the great transcends first-century Rome, John's exhortation applies at all times and places to Christians who always are at the risk of seduction by the allure of the world's many charms. Onesimus Ngundu emphasizes this: "Even in its OT setting, this was no mere warning to leave the city of Babylon. John, like the OT prophets, is exhorting God's people to shun the charms and snares of the prostitute city. Babylon exists wherever there is idolatry, prostitution, self-glorification, self-sufficiency, pride and complacency, reliance on luxury and wealth, and violence against life (18:4–8, 24). Believers are to separate themselves from all forms of Babylon. While they still have to live and work in the world, they also need to claim a distinctive identity and to develop habits of resistance that will enable witness to take place."[512]

The judgment of Babylon is patterned on the judgment of historical Babylon (Rev 18:1–24)

In connection with the sixth bowl (Rev 16:12), we saw how God's judgment in Revelation is patterned in part on the destruction of historical Babylon. Now, Rev 18:7 quotes Isa 47:7–8 concerning Babylon's sensuality. However, the comparison between historical Babylon and the world's Babylon the great of Revelation 18 is not limited to that one quotation. Revelation 18 uses Isaiah 47 something as a template to pronounce God's judgment on Babylon the great for its pride, sensuality, sorceries, and ungodliness, just as God similarly judged historical Babylon. The following table shows the similarities between the two Babylons:

---

511. Stylianopoulos, "I Know," 26. "None of John's first readers lived in the city of Rome. The command is for the readers to *dissociate* themselves from Rome's evil, lest they share her guilt and her judgment." Bauckham, "Economic Critique," 84–85.

512. Ngundu, "Revelation," 1572.

Historical Babylon—Isaiah 47	Babylon the Great—Revelation 18
Calls herself a queen, not a widow (47:7–8)	Calls herself a queen, not a widow (18:7)
Thinks she is secure (47:8, 10)	Thinks she is secure (18:7)
Glorifies herself (47:8, 10)	Glorifies herself (18:7)
Sensual (47:8)	Sensual (18:3, 9)
Uses sorcery (47:9, 12–13)	Uses sorcery (18:23)
Sinful (47:10)	Sinful (18:4–5)
Judgment will come suddenly (47:9, 11)	Judgment will come suddenly (18:8, 10, 17)
Will burn (47:14)	Will burn (18:8–9, 18)
Those who slept with her cannot save her (47:15)	Those who slept with her cannot save her (18:3, 9–19)

Beale summarizes the correspondence between the two Babylons:

> As elsewhere in Revelation, the pride and fall of historical Babylon is taken as a typological pattern of the hubris and downfall of the worldwide Babylonian system at the end of history. As with old Babylon, latter-day Babylon sees herself as a mother to all her inhabitants, whom she nourishes. She has complete confidence that she will never be without the support of her children. As with the Babylonian nation, latter-day Babylon's political and economic security will be removed suddenly. And her proud confidence in such security will be revealed as without foundation and as a delusion (as in Isa. 47:9–11; Jer. 50:31–32). Such confidence is self-idolatry, which must be judged. The church must beware of trusting in economic security lest its members be judged along with the world.[513]

Rev 18:1—19:6: the judgment on Babylon

Rev 18:1—19:6 has an interconnecting structure:

> 18:1–3: An angel pronounces judgment on Babylon
> 18:4–20: A voice from heaven predicts the fall of Babylon
> 18:21–24: An angel pronounces judgment on Babylon
> 19:1–6: Voices in heaven praise God for the fall of Babylon*

* See Bauckham, *Climax of Prophecy*, 338–43. For similar structural outlines see Beale, *Revelation*, 891.

Although Rev 18:6 might be taken as giving Babylon twice the punishment she deserves, the references to "double" and "twice" are idiomatic Hebrew expressions for "equivalent" retribution.[514] That is confirmed by Rev 18:7 which says, *"To the degree that she glorified herself and lived sensuously, to the same degree give her torment and mourning."*

---

513. Beale, *Revelation*, 903.

514. Kline, "Double Trouble," 171–79; see also 1 Tim 5:17; Ladd, *Commentary*, 238 ("punishment in full measure"); Beale, *Revelation*, 900–902.

Rev 19:11–21: the second coming of Christ

In this section, Christ reveals his sovereignty and faithfulness to his promises when he comes again to bring judgment on all those who have opposed him and oppressed his people. In keeping with the progressively parallel structure of the book, the *parousia* or its effects have been mentioned or described at Rev 1:7; 6:12–17; 8:1–5; 11:11–19; 14:14–20; 16:17–21; 19:1–6 (the *parousia* or its effects will also be described at 20:7–10, 11–15; and 21:1–2). Revelation 19 symbolically describes the *parousia* in detail. The events of Revelation 19 are clearly linked with previous *parousia* passages. Mealy describes these connections:

> In Revelation 19, preceding the revelation of Jesus on a white horse, John de- scribes a triumphal liturgy before the throne of God, which has affinities both with the scene of 7.9–12 and with that of 11.15–17. Praises are offered to 'God who sits on the throne' because of the justice of his judgment in the overthrow of Babylon (19.1–3); and then, as in 16.17, 'A voice came from the throne'. . . . The first sentence [19:5] clearly harks back to Rev. 11.18, where the parousia was predicted as the time for God's reward to be given to 'Thy bond-servants the prophets and to the saints and to those who fear Thy name, the small and the great'. Similarly, the giving of praise to God because he has taken up his escha- tological reign (v. 6) points back to 11.15–17. . . . In Revelation 19, the throne of God is shown for the third time [19:1–6] (cf. 7.9–17; 11.15–18) to denote the parousia not only as an occasion of wrath, but also one of rejoicing. It all depends on what group of people is facing the throne.[515]

As the *parousia* itself begins, John sees *"heaven opened"* (Rev 19:11) which harks back to previous *parousia* and judgment passages.[516] The consummate nature of this scene is indicated in that the only weapon involved in the warfare being described is, *"From His mouth comes a sharp sword"* (Rev 19:15).[517] Ladd notes, "The idea goes back to creation. God created the worlds by his word. He spoke and it was done. This creation was mediated through the living word, Christ (John 1:3; Heb. 1:2). The judgment of the old order will also be mediated through the word of Christ."[518] Jesus' name, *"King of kings and Lord of lords"* (Rev 19:16), indicates his ultimate rulershsip over all other authorities.[519]

The *parousia* entails both the vindication of the righteous and the judgment of the unrighteous. The *parousia* also is described both as a courtroom proceeding and as a battle or war.

The parousia as vindication of the righteous

When Jesus returns he will come, symbolically, not on a donkey (see John 11:13–15) but on *"a white horse"* along with his armies *"on white horses"* (Rev 19:11–14). In ancient Rome, victorious generals in major wars sometimes had a public "triumph" in which they

515. Mealy, *After the Thousand Years*, 156.

516. Rev 6:14; 11:19; 15:5; cf. 4:1.

517. See also Rev 1:16; 2:12; Isa 11:4; 49:2; Heb 4:12.

518. Ladd, *Commentary*, 255.

519. The same description was earlier applied to him in inverted order in Rev 17:14.

entered Rome in a chariot pulled by four white horses with their victorious army following behind them.[520] The color white thus suggests victory.

White also conveys the ideas of righteousness, holiness, and vindication. Beale explains:

> Throughout the Apocalypse "white" has represented a reward for purity or purity itself, resulting from persevering faith tested by persecution [3:4–5]. . . . 19:7–8 has refined this idea by understanding "white" garments not only as representing righteousness but also as a reward of *vindication* for those who have persevered through persecution. Vindication is probably included in most of the earlier uses of "white" (e.g., the Son of man and the saints stand vindicated by God after their faithful witness is rejected by the world and they are persecuted: 1:14; 2:17; 3:4–5; 4:4; 6:11; 7:9, 13; 14:14). In particular, in 14:14 and 20:11 "white" conveys ideas of not only divine holiness and purity but also juridical vindication of truth through judgment. Likewise, the white color of the horse here suggests the same idea of vindication in introducing the following judgment scene, especially because of its close connection to vv 7–8 and especially to the "white linen" of v 14, which also contains the idea of vindication.[521]

As we have seen throughout Revelation, God's identifying with and vindicating his people follows the pattern of his identifying with and vindicating Christ: believers will suffer, die, and appear defeated in this world, but their faithfulness to death results in their eternal victory and vindication.[522]

The parousia as judgment of the unrighteous

In addition to vindicating the righteous, the *parousia* entails the judgment of the unrighteous. Rev 19:15–21 concentrates on the *parousia* as judgment on the unrighteous.

The judgment at the parousia as both a battle and a courtroom proceeding

In describing the *parousia*, Rev 19:11 says, *"In righteousness He judges and wages war."* That is consistent with the picture throughout the Bible of God's judgment at his coming as both a court of law and a war or battle. VanGemeren explains this: "The imagery of trial and war is a metaphorical expression of God's rule. He rules in his judgments and in his battles. In his wrath, he vindicates his name, but he also vindicates all who belong to him and who trust in him for protection and deliverance."[523]

---

520. Ramsay, "Triumphus," 1163–67.

521. Beale, *Revelation*, 950.

522. Rev 2:9–10, 13; 6:9–11; 7:9–17; 11:7–13; 12:11; 14:1–5, 13; 17:14; 18:20–24; 19:1–9; 20:4–6.

523. VanGemeren, *Interpreting*, 220. Mealy and Schnabel rightly see Rev 20:7–10 and 20:11–15 as dual depictions of the judgment, one as a battle and one as a courtroom proceeding. See Mealy, *After the Thousand Years*, 180; Schnabel, *40 Questions*, 290. As discussed above in chapter 7, however, I believe their exegesis of important aspects of those passages is incorrect.

The Judgment of the Lord as a Court of Law

In the OT, God's judgment is depicted in courtroom terms, as VanGemeren describes:

> The Lord's coming may be compared to a court scene. In his court Yahweh is the *prosecutor, witness,* and *judge.* He is the sovereign judge seated above his creation: "But the Lord is in his holy temple; let all the earth be silent before him" (Hab. 2:20; see Zeph. 1:7). When he comes, he will assemble all nations and "enter into judgment against them" (Joel 3:2). He brings charges (Hos. 4:1–3), serves as witness for the prosecution (Jer. 29:23; 42:5; Mic. 1:2), condemns, and executes the verdict. The bases of the accusation and condemnation are human arrogance, the rejection of his kingdom, and a selfish and greedy lifestyle [Mal 3:5].[524]

In the NT, we see the judgment described in courtroom terms in Matt 12:39–42 (Luke 11:29–32); Matt 25:31–46; Acts 10:42; 17:31; Rom 14:10; 1 Cor 4:4–5; and 2 Cor 5:10. In Revelation, the judgment-as-courtroom-proceeding explicitly appears at Rev 11:18 and 20:11–15. In Revelation 19, the judgment-as-courtroom theme is suggested by the metaphor *"His eyes are a flame of fire"* (Rev 19:12). That indicates Christ's role as divine, all-seeing judge. It is also seen in Rev 2:18–23 where, by the same metaphor, Christ's all-seeing eyes pierce through the exterior to the interior[525] of the church of Thyatira and the prophetess Jezebel and her followers. The result is vindication and reward of the faithful and judgment of the unfaithful.

The Judgment of the Lord as a Battle or War

In the battle theme, "Yahweh is the *Divine Warrior,* who comes to establish order out of chaos, anarchy, and autonomy of the kingdoms of humankind. The warrior vents his wrath against all opposition in his realm [Isa 13:13]. In his wrath he comes with vengeance, likened to war and a bloodbath [Jer 46:10]."[526] Vos elaborates this:

> The setting is martial; the background that of a fierce battle and a decisive victory. In the Old Testament this is for a long time the prevailing mode of representation, though from Daniel and the Psalms onward the formal forensic picture becomes increasingly in evidence, without, however, entirely superseding the other. In the martial judgment there is no apparatus of records kept and examined, and no verdict solemnly pronounced on the basis of these. . . . There is one peculiar feature about this execution of judgment . . . the immediateness of its effect. This is best illustrated by the description of the disposal of the "Man-of-Sin" [2 Thess 2:8]; it is brought about by the breath of the mouth of Christ, by the mere manifestation of His coming. Plainly this feature was borrowed from [Isa 11:4]. In Isaiah it is simply one of the illustrations of the prophet's conception of the instantaneousness of Jehovah's supernatural working particularly in judgment.[527]

---

524. Ibid., 219.

525. He *"searches the minds and hearts"* (Rev 2:23).

526. VanGemeren, *Interpreting,* 220.

527. Vos, *Pauline Eschatology,* 262–63.

In Revelation, the judgment-as-battle appears at Rev 6:12–17; 11:18; 14:17–20; 16:14–21; 17:14; 18:17–24; 19:11–21; 20:7–10. In Revelation 19, the reference to Christ's riding on a white horse (19:11) and his "armies" also following on white horses (19:14) indicate the *parousia*-and-judgment-as-war theme.[528] That is made explicit in Rev 19:17–21. In 19:17, *"the great supper of God"* parodies the *"the marriage supper of the Lamb"* (19:9). That connection is seen in that both Rev 19:9 and 19:17 contain the same phrase, *eis to deipnon* ("to the supper"). As Beale notes, "the link implies that judgment is but the other side of the coin of salvation."[529]

Rev 20:1–15: the binding of Satan; the reign of the saints; the judgment of Satan; and the final judgment

The "thousand years" or "millennium" is the period between Christ's first coming until shortly before his second coming. During that period, God limits Satan's deceptive powers and deceased Christians are vindicated by reigning in heaven.[530] The period is concluded by a resurgence of Satan's deceptive assault against the church. That, in turn, is concluded by the *parousia* and the final judgment.

Although there are four paragraphs or subsections in Revelation 20 (20:1–3, the binding of Satan; 20:4–6, the reign of the saints; 20:7–10, the final destruction of Satan and his forces; and 20:11–15, the last judgment), those really are subsets of two larger sections: events before the *parousia* (20:1–6); and events connected with the *parousia* (20:7–15).

The events recorded in Rev 20:1–15 do not follow chronologically from where 19:21 left off. Instead, following the progressively parallel structure of the book, Revelation 20 recapitulates history from Christ's first coming to the *parousia* and final judgment, adding new details and emphases.[531] Milligan points out, *"The overthrow of Satan,* and not the reign of a thousand years, is the main theme of the first ten verses of the chapter."[532] Satan is Christ's greatest adversary. In Revelation 19, John described the end of the beast and false prophet. It is therefore proper that the end of Satan (the "power behind the throne") be emphasized separately in this chapter.

---

528. See Schnabel, *40 Questions*, 236, 288.

529. Beale, *Revelation*, 965. The image of flesh-eating birds gorging on the dead (19:17–21) is drawn primarily from Ezek 39:4, 17–20. It is "the application of an ancient curse formula" that reflects "an ancient means for hurting and humiliating an enemy even after death." Aune, *Revelation 17–22*, 1067–68; see Gen 40:19; Deut 28:26; 1 Sam 17:44, 46; 1 Kgs 14:11; 16:4; 21:24; 2 Kgs 9:10; Job 39:27–30; Jer 7:33; 15:3; 16:4; 19:7; 34:20; Hab 1:8; Matt 24:28; Luke 17:37.

530. An aspect of this reign begins on the earth. See Kik, *Eschatology*, 41–49; Appendix 2: The Millennium: An Amillennial Synthesis of the Biblical Data.

531. See Appendix 2: The Millennium: An Amillennial Synthesis of the Biblical Data for the reasons why chapter 20 recapitulates chapter 19 instead of following it chronologically and for further discussion of the "thousand years," the "two resurrections," and the reign of the saints (Rev 20:4–6).

532. Milligan, *Revelation*, 336, emphasis in original.

The binding of Satan (Rev 20:1–3): symbolic language

Beale begins our discussion of Revelation 20 by reminding us of the danger of "literalism" when John is writing about spiritual truths in an apocalyptic genre: "It is wrong to picture the devil being 'cast out of the earth' in some spatial sense, so that he is no longer present on the earth. This would be to take the 'abyss' in an overly literalistic manner. Rather, like 'heaven' throughout the Apocalypse, it represents a spiritual dimension existing alongside and in the midst of the earthly, not above it or below it (as with, e.g., the heavenly sphere in 2 Kgs. 6:15–17 and the Satanic sphere in Eph. 6:10–17; cf. 2 Cor. 10:3–5)."[533]

Beale's point is highlighted when we consider the language John uses in 20:1–3. "Satan is not a literal dragon who can be bound with a physical chain or locked away in a physical pit."[534] To hold to a "literal" thousand years requires, to be consistent, that the "key" and "chain" held by the angel in Rev 20:1 are a physical key and chain and that the "abyss" of Rev 20:3 is an actual pit in the earth which has a physical lock and physical "seal."[535] That, of course, is not what is intended by such language. Satan is a spiritual, not a physical, being. The language John uses is figurative or symbolic.

There is another important aspect to John's language concerning the "binding" of Satan and its relationship to how this appears in history, namely, John is employing "epic idiom" to describe God's victory over the dragon.[536] After surveying multiple biblical examples of the use of epic idiom, White states, "In each and every case . . . the monster's fate in the epic idiom is only analogous, not identical to its fate in history. This will be so whether they find the evil animal to have been captured or slain. In all such cases, the fate of the dragon represents the truth that the effort of God's enemies to resist his creative and redemptive work in heaven and earth is itself effectually resisted by God whether through temporal or final means."[537] He concludes that "the fate of the dragon in Rev 20:1–3 is *analogous but not identical* to the fate of Satan in history. Stated differently, while the dragon is captured and confined in the epic imagery and plot of John's vision, Satan is not captured and imprisoned in history. Rather, like the serpentine dragons of Babylon and of the darkness and deep, Satan is deposed from his role as deceiver of the world nations."[538]

533. Beale, *Revelation*, 987. The different views of the binding of Satan have been stated above in chapter 7–The Millennium; see also above in this chapter at 8:6—11:19 and 12:1—15:4 regarding the casting down of the dragon, the sea, the bottomless pit, and the abyss.

534. Johnson, *Triumph*, 283. Dispensationalist Chuck Smith appears to believe that the the abyss is, indeed, a literal hole in the ground. He states, "The *abyssos* is literally a shaft. Somewhere upon the surface of the earth there is a shaft. The entrance to this shaft leads down into the heart of the earth where Hades exists. Hades is often translated 'hell' in the Bible. Hell does exist. It's in the center of the earth." Smith, *What the World*, 83.

535. Waltke, "Kingdom Promises," 273; Jackson, "Examining," n.p.

536. White, "On the Hermeneutics," 62. What John is doing is borrowing "imagery and plot from pagan cosmogenic myth . . . so that Elohim the true Creator was depicted in combat with the anti-creative dragon, serpent, or sea. In fact, we should state the matter differently: precisely by calling attention to the mythic traditions in their reformulations of creation and redemption, the monotheistic writers of Scripture were 'demythologizing' those traditions." Ibid., 61. This is similar to what John did earlier in Revelation 13 and 17 in appropriating and transforming the Nero *redivivus* legend and how he, like other NT prophets and writers, frequently reappropriated the images of OT prophecies for his own purposes and circumstances.

537. Ibid., 62.

538. Ibid., 63, emphasis added.

The binding of Satan occurred at Christ's first coming

The first issue is *when* did this "binding" occur? Premillennialists contend that the binding occurs after the *parousia*. All others agree that the binding occurred in connection with Christ's first coming. Both the NT and contextual clues within Revelation itself make clear that Satan's binding occurred in connection with Christ's first coming. Hoekema tells us why: "Is there any indication in the New Testament that Satan was bound at the time of the first coming of Christ? Indeed there is. When the Pharisees accused Jesus of casting out demons by the power of Satan, Jesus replied, 'How can one enter a strong man's house and plunder his goods unless he first binds the strong man?' (Matt. 12:29). Interestingly enough, the word used by Matthew to describe the binding of the strong man is the same word used in Revelation 20 to describe the binding of Satan (the Greek word *deō*)."[539]

Jesus' own words in John 12:31 correspond to Rev 20:3: John 12:31 (*"Now is the time for judgment on this world; now the ruler of this world will be cast out* [Greek = *ekballō*]"); Rev 20:3 (*"He threw* [Greek = *ballō*] *him into the abyss"*). Consequently, the NT often talks of Satan's judgment, fall, limitation, and defeat in connection with Christ's first coming and during this age.[540]

Jesus' giving his disciples the Great Commission (Matt 28:18–20) reflects this new state of affairs. Gentry discusses this: "The earthly political authority to which Satan arrogantly laid claim, by which he oppressed the nations, and which he offered to Christ [Matt 4:8–9; Luke 4:5–6; Eph 2:1–2] was righteously won by Christ's glorious redemptive labor. . . . We should remember that the Great Commission opened with this noble declaration: 'All authority has been given to Me in heaven and on earth' (Matt. 28:18b). That authority encompassed heaven and earth and is 'above every name that is named [Eph 1:21; Phil 2:9–10; 1 Pet 3:22].'"[541]

The binding of Satan in Rev 20:1–3 is parallel to the casting down of Satan in Rev 12:7–12

Grenz states, "The Apocalypse itself also gives evidence to the correctness of this interpretation [that Satan's binding occurred at Christ's first coming], for the twelfth chapter, which forms the center of the book, depicts Christ's coronation as bringing about the ejection of Satan from heaven."[542] In other words, the binding of Satan in Rev 20:1–3 is parallel to Satan's being *"thrown down to the earth"* (Rev 12:9) and coming down to the earth and the sea (Rev 12:12).[543] William Shea notes the fact that the same four names for Satan (*"the*

---

539. Hoekema, *Bible and Future,* 228–29. Statements of the early church fathers concerning the binding of Satan during this present age are collected in Hill, *Regnum Caelorum,* 260–64.

540. For other verses on the "casting" theme see Matt 12:28; Mark 3:22–23; 9:38; 16:17; Luke 9:49–50; 10:18; John 12:31; Acts 5:16; 16:16–18; 19:11–12; 2 Pet 2:4.

For other verses on the more general theme of the limiting of Satan see Matt 12:29; Mark 3:24–27; John 16:11; 17:15; Acts 26:18; Rom 8:33, 38–39; 16:20; 1 Cor 15:25; Eph 1:20–23; 3:8–12; 6:10–16; Col 1:13; 2:10, 15; Heb 2:14; Jas 4:7; 1 Pet 3:21–22; 1 John 2:13; 3:8; 4:3–4; 5:18; Jude 6.

541. Gentry, *Greatness,* 58, 94.

542. Grenz, *Millennial Maze,* 162.

543. See previous discussion in connection with Revelation 12.

dragon, the serpent of old, who is the devil and Satan") "occur in the same order in both passages of the Greek text [12:9; 20:2], and these two passages are the only places in the entire book where this series as a whole is applied to him. This unique parallel between these two passages provides some evidence of an intent to connect the two narratives."[544] The parallels between the two chapters are consistent with the recapitulatory nature of the entire book. As with the many other inter-textual cross-references throughout the book, the parallels between chapters 12 and 20 indicate that they depict the same events from different perspectives, to bring out different nuances or emphases.[545]

The parallels between Revelation 12 and 20 are reflected in the following table:

Rev 12:7–12	*Rev 20:1–6*
Angels' evil opponent is *"the great dragon . . . the serpent of old who is called the devil and Satan"* (12:9)	Angels' evil opponent is *"the dragon, the serpent of old, who is the devil and Satan"* (20:2)
Satan cast to earth [and the sea] (12:9; 12)	Satan cast into the abyss (20:3)
Satan *"knows that his time is short"* (12:12)	Satan to be *"released for a short time"* (20:3)
Satan's fall results in the kingdom (12:10–11)	Satan's fall results in the kingdom (20:4–6)
The saints' kingship is based not only on Satan's fall but on Christ's victory and their faithfulness to *"the word of their testimony"* even to death (12:11)	The saints' kingship is based not only on Satan's fall but on their faithfulness *"of their testimony of Jesus and because of the word of God"* even to death (20:4)

The scenes of the woman and the dragon (Rev 12:1–17) and the binding and release of Satan (Rev 20:1–3) are also consistent with the scene of the two witnesses and the beast (Rev 11:3–12). All three scenes use different imagery to picture the same time period and same events (the spiritual protection of the church despite the opposition to it and its suffering in this world): the two witnesses are divinely protected until they have finished their testimony; the woman is protected in the wilderness; Satan is bound for a thousand years to prevent him from deceiving and gathering the nations to destroy the church.[546]

Nevertheless, the "binding" of Rev 20:3 is not identical in all respects to the "casting" of Rev 12:9, but is an aspect of it. The reason is that Satan will be "loosed" from his "binding" (i.e., from the restrictions that have been placed on his ability to "deceive the nations") for a short time before Christ returns (Rev 20:3, 7). On the other hand, "the victory [Christ] won over Satan was won once and for all."[547] Satan will never again ascend to the place, status, or authority he had before he was "cast down" by what Christ accomplished on the Cross.

544. Shea, "Parallel Literary Structure," 45.

545. Two different emphases that should be noted are: (1) The "short time" in Rev 12:12 and 20:3 are different: in Rev 12:12 the "short time" is the entire period from Christ's resurrection and ascension to the *parousia*, whereas the "short time" in 20:3 only is the end of that period, shortly before the *parousia*. (2) Satan's deceptive activity referred to in Rev 12:9 and 20:8 likewise are different: the former occurs throughout the period from the ascension to the *parousia*, whereas the latter occurs only for a short time before the *parousia* and also is not subject to the restrictions now placed on Satan. See the next two sections in the main text for further discussion of these points.

546. Johnson, *Triumph*, 286–87; see also ibid. at 44–45.

547. Ladd, *Commentary*, 263.

The purpose of the binding of Satan

Satan has been an active agent in the world since Adam and Eve in the Garden of Eden (Gen 3:1–13). Jesus called him the *"father of lies"* (John 8:44), and he *"deceives the whole world"* (Rev 12:9–10). Nevertheless, the scope of his deceptive authority has been significantly limited, his power has been decisively broken, and his ultimate defeat has been definitely ensured.[548] Satan's binding at Christ's first coming is a relative, not absolute, curtailment of his activities for a specific purpose during a specific time.[549] Satan is bound *"so that he would not deceive the nations any longer"* (Rev 20:3). Gentry elaborates this: "In Old Testament times only Israel knew the true God (Ps. 147:19-20; Amos 3:2; Luke 4:6; Acts 14:16; 17:30). But Christ's incarnation changed this as the gospel began flowing to all nations (e.g., Isa. 2:2–3; 11:10; Matt. 28:19; Luke 2:32; 24:47; Acts 1:8; 13:47)."[550] John Sittema adds that Jesus' ascension "marked his triumphal enthronement, and with it, the binding of Satan 'so that he can no longer deceive the nations.' This is the necessary corollary to Pentecost languages [Acts 2:1–11] that would enable the kingdom's advancement to the ends of the earth (see Luke 11:20–21)."[551] Paul states this in Acts 26:18 where he says that Christ sent him to the Gentiles *"to open their eyes so that they might turn from darkness to light and from the dominion of Satan to God, that they may receive forgiveness of sins and an inheritance among those who have been sanctified by faith in Me."*

Rev 20:7–8 also clarifies the nature of this binding since v. 7 picks up where v. 3 leaves off.[552] Rev 20:3 states that Satan is bound *"so that he would not deceive the nations any longer, until the thousand years were completed."* Verses 7–8 then say, *"When the thousand years are completed, Satan will be released . . . and will come out to deceive the nations . . . to gather them together for the war."* Johnson highlights the significance of 20:7–8 on the meaning of 20:3:

> Although it is true throughout history that Satan, the ancient serpent, "deceives the whole world" (Rev. 12:9), in this vision a specific deception to obtain a specific objective is in view. We see this objective when, at the end of the thousand years, the dragon is released and comes out "to deceive the nations which are in the four corners of the earth, Gog and Magog, to gather them together for the

---

548. Peter O'Brien notes the significance of Christ's triumph over Satan for believers now: "Christ's triumph over the powers has 'already' occurred ([Eph] 1:21). Because of believers' union with him in his resurrection and exaltation ([Eph] 2:5, 6), they no longer need to fear the powers. The fruits of Christ's victory have 'not yet' been fully realized. However, those in him possess all the resouces needed to resist the influence and attacks of the devil and his hosts (cf. [Eph] 6:10–20)." O'Brien, *Ephesians*, 33.

549. Even though he disagrees about the timing of the "binding," premillennialist Ladd agrees that the binding of Satan "is a symbolic way of describing a curbing of his power and activity; it does not mean complete immobility. His incarceration in the abyss does not mean that all of his activities and powers are nullified." Ladd, *Commentary*, 262.

550. Gentry, "A Preterist View," 83; see also Johnson, *Triumph*, 287–88. Beale puts it similarly, "During the age when Christ 'builds his church . . . the gates of hell will not prevail over' the church's growth because 'the keys of the kingdom' have been given to the church to overcome Satan's deception against it (Matt. 16:18–19)." Beale, *Revelation*, 987.

551. Sittema, *Meeting Jesus*, 86n.3.

552. Schüssler Fiorenza correctly points out, "Although the chapter *formally* divides into three divisions, with 20:7–10 as part of the vision beginning in 20:4ff, *contextually* 20:7–10 brings to conclusion 20:1–3." Schüssler Fiorenza, *Revelation*, 106.

war" (20:8). . . . In light of this explanation of the aim behind the dragon's deception (20:8), his binding during the thousand years prevents Satan from gathering
the nations in a worldwide conspiracy to blot out the church.[553]

The releasing of Satan (Rev 20:3, 7)

Rev 20:7 states, "*When the thousand years are completed, Satan will be released from his
prison.*"[554] Beale describes the scenario the Bible depicts when Satan is released shortly
before Christ comes again:

> Throughout the time between Christ's first and second comings, Satan will not
> be able to deceive any of "the full number" (6:11) of those purchased by Christ
> because they have been "sealed." When "the full number" has been gathered in,
> then the devil will be permitted to deceive the majority living at the end of his-
> tory, causing them not only to be blinded to the truth of Christ but also to seek
> to annihilate Christ's followers. . . . At the end of the age, persecution by deceived
> multitudes will break out against the church, such that it would vanish were it not
> for God's intervention on its behalf (so also Mark 13:19–22; Matt. 24:21–24).[555]

This context helps us see the difference between the "short time" Satan is given following his release in Rev 20:3 and the "short [or 'little'] time" he had when cast to the
earth in Rev 12:12. The short time of Rev 20:3 is the very last stage of the time Satan had
in Rev 12:12.[556]

553. Johnson, *Triumph,* 284–85; see also Hoekema, *Bible and Future,* 228. The fact that the church
has not been destroyed but has spread to include people *"from every tribe and tongue and people and nation"* of the world (Rev 5:9) is the "analogous but not identical" historical manifestation of John's vision
of Satan's binding, discussed above by White. See White, "On the Hermeneutics," 66n.41.

The language of Rev 20:3, 7–9 makes clear the specific purposes of the "binding" of Satan, i.e., preventing him from stopping the spread of the church throughout the world and preventing him from
leading a worldwide conspiracy to destroy the church. However, we have seen earlier that, as a result
of Christ's first coming, Satan's power also has been limited in other ways: he no longer has access to
heaven, he no longer is able to accuse believers, and he no longer has control over believers since they
have been transferred from his dominion to that of Christ; hence, believers can *"resist the devil and he
will flee from you"* (Jas 4:7).

554. "Released" is a "divine passive," which indicates that it is God who authorizes it. Resseguie,
Revelation of John, 248.

555. Beale, *Revelation,* 986–87.

556. See Beale, *Revelation,* 993. The Greek wording of the two verses is different: Rev 12:12 = *oligon
kairon*; Rev 20:3 = *mikron chronon.* The words essentially are synonymous. However, Zodhiates notes a
difference regarding the words for "time": *Chronos* "perceives time quantitatively as a period measured
by the succession of objects and events and denotes the passing of moments. Another word, *kairos* . . .
considers time qualitatively as a period characterized by the influence or prevalence of something."
Zodhiates, *Complete Word Study,* "*chromos,*" 1487. That distinction is consistent with the way Revelation uses the phrase "short time": in Rev 12:12 the "short time" (*kairos*) denotes that, qualitatively, the
period following Satan's being cast to the earth is the time characterized by his influence or prevalence
on the earth; in Rev 20:3 the "short time" (*chronos*) denotes that, quantitatively, Satan's remaining time
of influence will soon end.

The binding and release of Satan before the parousia and his destruction at the parousia are parallel to the restraint, revealing, and destruction of the "man of lawlessness" in 2 Thess 2:6–12

The binding of Satan now, but his release shortly before the *parousia*, is consistent with 2 Thess 2:6–12 where *"the mystery of lawlessness is already at work,"* but *"the one whose coming is in accord with the activity of Satan"* currently is restrained. When the restraint *"is taken out of the way . . . the lawless one will be revealed."* In fact, both Revelation 20 and 2 Thessalonians 2 are parallel in multiple respects, including the essential order of the events they describe.

2 Thess 2:6–12	*Rev 20:1–15*
Man of lawlessness (MOL) is currently restrained (2:6–7)	Satan is bound by an angel (20:1–3)
Restrainer will be taken out of the way (2:7)	After the "1000 years" Satan will be released (20:3, 7)
MOL will be revealed & come in accord with Satan (2:8–9)	Satan will come out (20:8)
MOL will deceive those who perish (2:8–12)	Satan will deceive the nations & gather them together for the war (20:8–9)
MOL will be slain at Christ's coming (2:8)	Satan will be destroyed [at Christ's coming] (20:9–10)
Those who did not believe the truth & took pleasure in wickedness will be judged (2:12)	The dead will be judged; those whose names are not in the book of life will be thrown into the lake of fire (20:11–15)

Sydney Page highlights the parallels between the two passages:

> Both passages speak of a restriction that prevents a major outbreak of evil for a limited period of time but that will eventually be removed, with the result that there will be a period of heightened opposition to God that will be brought to an end by divine intervention. Besides having this basic sequence of events in common, Revelation 20 and 2 Thessalonians 2 exhibit a number of similarities of detail. The overarching sovereignty of God is emphasized in both accounts. . . . Both accounts also highlight the role of deception in connection with this eschatological rebellion. . . . Not only do the two passages have the theme of deception in common, but in both Satan occupies a prominent position in relation to it. In Revelation he is presented as the one who deceives, and in 2 Thess 2:9 he is seen as the real force behind the lawless one's program of deception. Finally, there is a significant similarity between the Johannine and Pauline conceptions of how the rebellion is terminated. . . . But the resemblance is even closer than this, for in [2 Thess 1:7–9] Paul, like John, associates the return of Christ with fire and the execution of final judgment on the enemies of God.[557]

Those parallels demonstrate that the events of both passages end (not begin) at the *parousia*.

---

557. Page, "Revelation 20," 40–41.

The reign of the saints (Rev 20:4–6)

Because the overthrowing and permanent destruction of Christ's greatest adversary is the main theme of Rev 20:1–10, no specifics are given concerning the nature of the "thousand years" other than the summary fact that the saints *"sat on [thrones], and judgment was given to them"* (20:4). Premillennialists place this scene *after* the second coming of Christ, think that the "first resurrection" is the resurrection of believers at the *parousia*, and maintain that *"the rest of the dead"* who *"come to life"* refers to the resurrection of everyone, believers and unbelievers alike, a thousand years years after the *parousia*. Amillennialists hold that the "thousand years" is a figurative description of the current time, after Christ's resurrection but *before* the second coming. They contend that the "first resurrection" refers to Christians' new life in and union with Christ,[558] Christ's resurrection in which believers spiritually participate,[559] or the Christians' translation to heaven upon their physical death.[560] *"The rest of the dead"* who *"come to life"* refers to the unbelievers who were not participants in the "first resurrection" but whose only resurrection is the bodily resurrection that takes place at the *parousia*.[561]

The timing of the "thousand years"

Hoekema points out:

> That the millennial reign described in verses 4–6 occurs before the second coming of Christ is evident from the fact that the final judgment, described in verses 11–15 of this chapter, is pictured as coming after the thousand-year reign. Not only in the book of Revelation but elsewhere in the New Testament the final judgment is associated with the second coming of Christ. (See Revelation 22:12 and the following passages: Mt. 16:27; 25:31–32; Jude 14–15; and especially 2 Thess. 1:7–20.) This being the case, it is obvious that the thousand-year reign of Revelation 20:4–6 must occur *before* and *not after* the second coming of Christ.[562]

---

558. Augustine, *Civ.*, 20.6–10; White, "Death and the First Resurrection," 22; Shepherd, "Resurrections," 36–38; Venema, *Promise*, 331–36.

559. Hughes, "First Resurrection," 315–18.

560. Kline, "First Resurrection," 366–75.

561. Beale, *Revelation*, 1013–14; White, "Death and the First Resurrection," 10–11. For more detailed discussions of all these issues see Beale, *Revelation*, 991–1017 and Appendix 2: The Millennium: An Amillennial Synthesis of the Biblical Data.

562. Hoekema, "Amillennialism," 160; see also above, chapter 5–The Eschatological Significance of Christ's Second Coming. Waldron adds, "If Rev. 20:11–15 is regarded as chronologically subsequent to Rev. 20:1–10 (as it is by premillennialists [e.g., Thomas, *Revelation 8–22*, 581]) then the analogy of faith (which clearly teaches that the general judgment occurs at Christ's second coming) demands that the '1000 years' and 'little season' precede the second coming." Waldron, "Preterism," n.p.

The reign of the saints as a *current*, not future, phenomenon is consistent with the rest of Revelation and the NT, which picture the church currently as raised with Christ in heaven.[563] For example, Rev 20:4b clearly parallels Rev 6:9:[564]

Rev 6:9	*Rev 20:4b*
I saw (*eidon*) under the altar	I saw (*eidon*)
the souls (*tas psuchas*)	the souls (*tas psuchas*)
of those who had been slain	of those who had been beheaded
for the word of God (*dia ton logon tou theou*) and the witness (*kai dia tēn marturian*) they had borne.	for their witness to Jesus (*dia tēn marturian Iēsou*) and for the word of God (*kai dia ton logon tou theou*)

In short, "The opening verses of the chapter declare the cosmic victory won by Christ at his first advent. Verses 4–6 speak of the resultant victory of his faithful witnesses, despite apparent defeat, whether that victory be in the heavenly realm of the intermediate state or the earthly realm of Christian living."[565] Thus, "When saints are translated to heaven at death they join Christ on his judicial throne to rule over the enemy in inaugurated fulfillment of the promise given to 'overcomers' in 3:21 and 2:26–27, though these promises will also reach complete fulfillment at the final resurrection of the saints."[566]

The final destruction of Satan and his forces (Rev 20:7–10)

THE BATTLE OF REV 20:7–10 IS THE SAME AS THE BATTLE OF REV 16:14–16 AND 19:17–21 WHICH OCCURS IN CONNECTION WITH THE PAROUSIA

Premillennialists see the battle of Har-Magedon (Rev 16:14–16) and the battle of Rev 19:19–21 as two descriptions of the same event which occurs in connection with the *parousia*.[567] However, they see the battle of Rev 20:7–10 as another similar battle that takes place after the *parousia* and after Christ has reigned on the earth in perfect righteousness for a thousand years.[568] That idea contradicts the very nature of the second coming which entails resurrection, judgment, and renewal of the earth, and begins the *"age to come"* in which there will forever be no more sin or evil. Grenz comments:

> Another difficult dimension of the premillennial chronology is its conception of the ultimate victory of Christ. According to Paul, the final enemy of Christ is death, and the Lord destroys this last foe at the resurrection of the believers (1 Cor 15:25–26, 50–55 [which occurs as part of the *parousia*]). . . . Because of

563. See Eph 2:5–6; Phil 3:20; Heb 12:18–24; Rev 1:6; 5:9–10; 6:9–11; 7:9–17; 13:6; 14:1–4; 15:2–4. Statements of the early church fathers concerning the reign of the saints with Christ as having a celestial setting in the present age are collected in Hill, *Regnum Caelorum*, 264–68.

564. The following table and wording are from Gourgues, "Thousand-year Reign," 680.

565. Grenz, *Millennial Maze*, 163.

566. Beale, *Revelation*, 996; see Matt 19:28; Luke 22:30; 1 Cor 6:2–3.

567. E.g., Ladd, *Commentary*, 256–57.

568. Ibid., 269–70.

their loyalty to the premillennial doctrine, they teach that death is not destroyed until the end of the millennial reign. The premillennial chronology, therefore, places the final victory of Christ a full thousand years after the resurrection and thus a thousand years after the event that Paul declares marks the triumph of the Lord.[569]

In addition to the effect Christ's second coming has in eliminating sin and death, the context of Revelation itself reveals that the battle of 20:7–10 is the same as that of 16:14–16 and 19:17–21.[570] All three passages draw on the Gog-Magog prophecy of Ezekiel 38–39. Meredith Kline discusses the interrelationship of Ezekiel 38–39; Rev 16:14–16; 19:17–21; and 20:7–10. He details how Revelation indicates they must all be referring to the same battle that occurs at the time of the *parousia*:

> The war (*polemos*) of Rev 20:8 is certainly "the war of the great day of God, the Almighty," the battle of Har Magedon described in 16:14–16. In each case it is the war to which Satan, the dragon, gathers the nations of the whole world. . . . The relationship of Rev 20:7–10 to Ezekiel 38–39, obvious enough from the adoption of the Gog-Magog terminology in Revelation 20, is also evidenced by a set of basic similarities: the marshaling of hordes from the four quarters of the earth (Ezek 38:2–7, 15; 39:4; Rev 20:8); the march of the gathered armies to encompass the saints in the city of God, center of the world (Ezek 38:7–9, 12, 16; Rev 20:9); the orchestration of the event by God (Ezek 38:4, 16; 39:2, 19; Rev 20:3, 7); the timing of the event after a lengthy period in which God's people were kept secure from such a universal assault (Ezek 38:8, 11; Rev 20:3); the eschatological finality of the crisis (Ezek 39:22, 26, 29; Rev 20:10ff.); and the fiery destruction of the evil forces (Ezek 38:22; 39:6; Rev 20:9–10). Just as clearly, the Gog-Magog prophecy of Ezekiel 38–39 is a primary source drawn on by Rev 16:14–16; 19:17–21 and other Apocalyptic prophecies of the final conflict. Prominent in these passages is the major feature that marked the dependence of Rev 20:7–10 on the Ezekiel prophecy—namely, the universal gathering of the enemy armies (Rev 16:14–16; 17:12–14; 19:19; and compare 6:15 with Ezek 39:18–20), including too the historical setting of that event at the close of the world-age (Rev 6:12–17; 11:7–13; 16:16–17 [cf. 17:10–14]; 19:15–21), following an era in which it is given to the Church to fulfill its mission of gospel witness (11:3–7; cf. 12:6, 14). . . . It therefore follows that the thousand years that precede the Gog-Magog crisis of Rev 20:7–10 precede the Har Magedon-*parousia* event related in the other passages. Har Magedon is not a prelude to the millennium, but a postlude. Har Magedon marks the end of the millennium. And that conclusion spells the end of premillennialism.[571]

Since Revelation as a whole has a progressively parallel structure, in this recapitulation of the final destruction of Satan and his forces we see a subtle development of the ideas that had previously been discussed in chapters 16 and 19: "In Rev.16.14 the worldly

---

569. Grenz, *Millennial Maze*, 143–44.

570. This has already been mentioned above in connection with the discussion of the progressively parallel structure of the book and will be looked at again in Appendix 2: The Millennium: An Amillennial Synthesis of the Biblical Data.

571. Kline, "Har Magedon," 218–20. Since the battle depicted in Ezekiel 38–39 is against Israel, the allusion to Ezekiel in Rev 20:8 demonstrates that the church is the new, true Israel.

rulers are mustered for the battle, by demonic spirits, on the Day of the Lord; in 19.19 the beast, with the rulers of the earth and their armies, wages war against the Messiah and his followers; while in 20.8 the Satan himself assembles innumerable and hostile nations from the four corners of the earth . . . to do battle with God's people on the earth and in heaven (20.9)."[572] In other words, the culminating picture of this event reveals Satan to be the "power behind the throne" who directs both the demons and the beast.

It may seem "natural" to view the events of Rev 20:7–10 as a physical battle between Satan and his followers and the church involving the physical weapons of war. Support for the "physical" aspect of warfare between the world and the church is found in Matt 24:22 which says, *"Unless those days had been cut short, no life would have been saved; but for the sake of the elect those days will be cut short"* (see also Mark 13:20). However, that probably is not, in fact, the focus of the passage. In commenting on this passage, J. Marcellus Kik points out:

> The language is so vivid that it is hard for us to realize this is not a battle of arms—of sword and gun. Our Lord clearly indicates that the battle for Christianity is not fought with carnal sword. It is a battle between the true Gospel and the false Gosel. It is a battle of truth against error. . . . It is not a war against flesh and blood "but against principalities, against powers, against spiritual wickedness in high places" [Eph 6:12]. . . . There will undoubtedly be persecution. The enemy may use physical violence. But the main weapons will be in the realm of the spirit.[573]

We need to recall that throughout the book of Revelation, the emphasis has been on the issues of who is one's true Lord and remaining faithful to death. We saw that the most important aspect of Babylon the great was her spiritual corruption, not her political or economic corruption. The same was true with respect to "Antichrist"—the Bible's emphasis is on his/its spiritual nature, not political or economic issues. Thus Christ's primary concern regarding his return is, *"When the Son of Man comes, will He find faith on the earth?"* (Luke 18:8) As we also have seen, God's judgment is frequently depicted as a battle or war, and when God sends *"fire from heaven"* (Rev 20:9) it always indicates his judgment.[574] Consequently, Rev 20:9–10 and the other passages in the book that appear to describe God's dramatically terminating a physical battle against the saints may in fact be figurative or symbolic descriptions of the final judgment itself that occurs in connection with Christ's *parousia*.

Satan is "thrown into the lake of fire . . . where the beast and the false prophet are" (Rev 20:10)

Premillennialists contend that the beast and false prophet have been in the lake of fire for a thousand years before the devil is cast there. Most English translations appear to imply this by saying that Satan is thrown into the lake of fire *"where the beast and the false prophet are"* (NASB; NKJV), or *"were"* (ESV; RSV), or even *"had been thrown"* (NIV). In

---

572. Smalley, *Revelation*, 513.

573. Kik, *Eschatology*, 238, 240–41.

574. See chapter 8, the section *"Jesus' reference to 'lightning' in Matt 24:27 may also imply judgment"* for the passages in which God sends fire from heaven.

fact, the judgment of Satan, the beast, and the false prophet are simultaneous, not sequential. The judgment in Rev 20:10 is a recapitulation of the judgment in Rev 19:20, with the additional reference to Satan, since the defeat of Satan is the focus of Rev 20:1–10.

The Greek grammar of this clause is ambiguous and most naturally supports the simultaneous, recapitulation view, not the sequential judgments view. Andrew Steinmann explains why:

> 20:10 should be seen as a recapitulation of the judgment in 19:20 with the addition of Satan's judgment. 20:10 literally reads: "And the devil who had deceived them was thrown (*eblēthē,* aorist passive indicative) into the lake of fire and sulfur, where both the beast and the false prophet. . . . and they will be tormented day and night forever and ever." The ellipsis of a verb governing "beast" and "false prophet" requires the translator to supply one in English. Most translators supply "where the beast and the false prophet were/are"—as if the two judgments are sequential, not synonymous. But the ellipsis of a third-person-plural form of *einai* is rare (BDF 71). A more common form of ellipsis would be the omission of a verb coinciding with the preceding verb. Thus the most natural translation of 20:10 would be: "And the devil who had deceived them was thrown into the lake of fire and sulfur where the beast and the false prophet were thrown" (cf. NIV). (Note: "Were thrown" [aorist] = at the same time, not "had been thrown" [pluperfect] = prior to the time when the devil was thrown in.).[575]

The last judgment (Rev 20:11–15)

"John has already set the precedent for the idea that the same judgment can be viewed first as a battle/confrontation, and then as a courtroom scene. . . . The scene of 20.11–15 invites understanding as a restatement, using different imagery, of the final judgment just narrated in 20.7–10."[576] Thus, while Rev 20:7–10 and 20:11–15 both describe the final judgment, each description has its own emphasis. Shea lists those emphases: "The earlier of the two emphasizes the destruction of the devil and his agents, perhaps because the whole narrative of Rev 20 began with him as its subject. Then the closing scene which follows places its emphasis upon God as the judge, who presents his final judgment at this time."[577] The fact that 20:11 states *earth and heaven fled away, and no place was found*

---

575. Steinmann, "Tripartite Structure," 77–78n.18; see also Beale, *Revelation,* 1030 (Satan, the beast, and the false prophet can all be seen "as thrown into the fire at the same time whether the elided [i.e., omitted] verb is 'are cast' or 'were cast' [the latter of which would be identical to the preceding verb in regard to the devil]"). Additionally, because Rev 20:7–10 recapitulates Rev 19:17–21, it is highly unlikely that Satan is cast into the lake of fire ages after his cohorts have been sent there. Beale deals with a possible objection to that: "Some think that for 20:10 to recapitulate the events associated with the demise of the beast and false prophet we would need more explicit language, something like 'After the battle of Gog and Magog, Satan was thrown into the lake of fire *along with* the beast and false prophet.' But this is not a necessary expectation, especially since the style of recapitulation in the OT prophetic literature is not characterized by such explicitness, nor are the recapitulations elsewhere in Revelation so characterized." Beale, *Revelation,* 1028.

576. Mealy, *After the Thousand Years,* 177, 179.

577. Shea, "Parallel Literary Structure," 49.

for them" both recapitulates prior depictions of the final judgment[578] and sums up the creation-changing nature of the *parousia* and the judgment that occurs in connection with it.[579]

THE FINAL JUDGMENT OCCURS AS A PART OF THE EVENTS ENTAILED BY THE PAROUSIA

There is a clear correspondence between Rev 20:11–15 and 1 Cor 15:20–54. In 1 Cor 15:26 Paul said, *"The last enemy that will be abolished is death."* Rev 20:14 says that *"death and Hades were thrown into the lake of fire."* Page states, "The symbolic description of the destruction of Death and Hades [at the eschatological judgment] corresponds to Paul's statement in 1 Cor 15:26. . . . For both John and Paul the last scene in the drama of redemption before the inauguration of the eternal state is the elimination of death."[580] That occurs in connection with the *parousia* (see 1 Cor 15:50–54). As we have seen, the Gospels, Epistles, and Revelation tell a coherent story: the *parousia* entails resurrection and judgment; it is the dividing point between *"this age"* and the *"age to come."*

JUDGMENT OF UNBELIEVERS ONLY OR OF ALL PEOPLE?

Some people, primarily dispensationalists, think that there are multiple, distinct judgments in the NT: the judgment of the "nations" to see who will enter the millennial kingdom (Matt 25:31–46); a separate judgment of believers before the "judgment seat of Christ" to receive their rewards (2 Cor 5:10); and the "great white throne" judgment of Rev 20:11–15 which they think applies only to unbelievers.[581] Others see Rev 20:11–15 as the general judgment of all people, believers and unbelievers alike.[582] Although the emphasis in this passage may be on unbelievers, all people are included, since, as previously discussed,[583] the Bible indicates that there is only one general judgment of all people. Ladd summarizes, "The final issue of the judgment of the nations is not the millennial kingdom but is either eternal life or eternal punishment (Matt. 25:46). This is clearly the final judgment which decides the eternal destiny of men. The judgment seat of Christ is also the judgment seat of God before which all believers must stand (Rom. 14:10)."[584]

In keeping with the progressively parallel nature of the book, Rev 20:11–15 is an elaboration of the judgment that already was mentioned, although not described, at Rev

---

578. Rev 6:12–14; 11:13; 16:17–21.

579. See Matt 24:29; Mark 13:24–25; Luke 21:25–26; Acts 3:19–21; Rom 8:17–25; 2 Pet 3:3–15.

580. Page, "Revelation 20," 42.

581. E.g., Scofield, *New Scofield*, 1036–37n.2, 1375n.1; Thomas, "Classical Dispensationalist View," 223; MacDonald, *Believer's*, 1299; Smith, *What the World*, 193. Non-dispensationalist premillennialist Eckhard Schnabel also sees the judgment of Rev 20:11–15 as pertaining only to unbelievers. Schnabel, *40 Questions*, 226.

582. E.g., Hendriksen, *More Than Conquerors*, 196; Ladd, *Commentary*, 271; Ngundu, "Revelation," 1576. Some, while holding that there is only one general judgment of all people, contend that Rev 20:11–15 *describes* only the judgment of unbelievers. Johnson, "Revelation," 589–90; Milligan, *Revelation*, 357.

583. See chapter 5–The Eschatological Significance of Christ's Second Coming.

584. Ladd, *Commentary*, 271.

11:18. Beale points out that the statement *"the dead were judged"* shows that Rev 20:11–15 "is an expansion of the earlier brief account of final punishment in 11:18 ('the time [came] for *the dead to be judged*'). 11:18 also focuses on judgment of the wicked, but includes 'the reward' for God's 'servants the prophets and the saints and those fearing' God."[585]

The wording of Rev 20:11–15 (i.e., *"the great and the small"*), when compared with the limitations or qualifications of that phrase when it is used elsewhere in Revelation, leads to the conclusion that all people, believers and unbelievers, are being judged. Thus, in Rev 11:18 and 19:5 *"the small and the great"* refers to *all believers,* and in Rev 13:16 and 19:18 *"the small and the great"* refers to *all unbelievers.* On the other hand, as David Brown points out, "in the passage before us, the only party to whom 'the small and great' belong—as far as appears—is *'the dead.'* Are we not irresistibly led, then, to conclude that the meaning intended is, the dead—universally, or at least indiscriminately?"[586]

In its reference to the "books," Rev 20:12 alludes to Dan 7:10; 12:1–2. The allusion to those two Danielic passages again indicates the all-inclusive nature of the judgment in Rev 20:11–15. Beale and McDonough explain why: "The point of the books in Dan. 7 is to focus on the evil deeds of the end-time persecutor of God's people, for which the persecutor(s) would be judged. The book in Dan. 12:1 also concerns the end time, but it is an image of redemption. Those written in the book will be given life, but those excluded from the book will suffer final judgment (12:1–2). These two Daniel prophecies are depicted to find realization at the time of the last judgment."[587]

Finally, the NT makes clear that all people must appear before the judgment seat of God.[588] Rev 3:5 specifically refers to believers in the book of life (see also Rev 13:8). Nowhere else in Revelation besides 20:11–15 does the judgment-as-courtroom-proceeding *with the book of life* appear. Beasley-Murray comments on this: "[Rev] 3:5 assumes that the believer in Christ will appear before the tribunal of God for judgment, exactly as in this scene. If the Church is excluded from the last judgment, it can only be because it has already appeared before God in judgment. John himself gives no hint that such an event has taken place. It is wiser to recognize that John teaches that all must submit to the judgment of God, saints and sinners alike."[589] Because the judgment of Rev 20:11–15 applies to believers as well as to unbelievers, the preliminary mention in 3:5 of believers' names not being erased from the book of life is thereby tied up and fulfilled.

The nature of the judgment

Rev 20:12 states that people are judged *"according to their deeds."* We cannot work our way to heaven or do enough "good deeds" to justify our acquittal in God's judgment; we are saved only by God's grace through faith in Christ.[590] Nevertheless, as Ngundu summarizes:

---

585. Beale, *Revelation,* 1033; see also Johnson, *Triumph,* 298.

586. Brown, *Christ's Second Coming,* 200; see also Beale, *Revelation,* 1033.

587. Beale and McDonough, "Revelation," 1150.

588. E.g., Rom 14:10; 2 Cor 5:10; Heb 9:27.

589. Beasley-Murray, *Revelation,* 301.

590. John 3:16–18; 6:28–29; Rom 2:16–17; 10:8–13; Gal 3:1–14; Eph 2:8–9.

Works are an index of the spiritual condition of a person's heart. . . . The judgment will reveal whether or not people's loyalties have been with God and the Lamb or with God's enemies. John's theology of faith and its insuperable relation to works is the same as that of Jesus Christ (John 5:29), Paul (Rom 2:6–8) and James (Jas 2), and that is why another book, the *book of life,* seems to be decisive (20:12, 15; 3:5; 13:8; 17:8; 21:27). Those who have their names in the Lamb's "book of life" will also have records of righteous deeds. The opposite will also be true. The imagery reflects the delicate balance between grace and sin.[591]

Beale concludes, "The 'life' granted the saints in association with the book comes from their identification with the Lamb's righteous deeds, and especially his death, which means likewise that they are identified with his resurrection life (cf. 5:5–13). They do not suffer judgment for their evil deeds because he has already suffered it for them: he was slain on their behalf (so esp. 1:5 and 5:9). The Lamb acknowledges before God all who are written in the book (3:5) and are identified with his righteousness and death."[592]

Rev 21:1—22:5: the new heaven and new earth: the New Jerusalem

In this section, the new creation and the church are perfected in glory. The word for "new" (Rev 21:1–2, 5; also in 2 Pet 3:13) is *kainos.* Richard Trench explains the meaning of *kainos* in this context: "*Kainos* refers to something new in *quality* and is contrasted with that which has seen service—the outworn, the exhausted, or that which is marred through age. . . . Thus, in the kingdom of glory, everything will be new: 'the new Jerusalem' (Rev. 3:12; 21:2), the 'new name' (2:17; 3:12), 'a new song' (5:9; 14:3), 'a new heaven and new earth' (21:1; cf. 2 Pet. 3:13), 'all things new' (Rev. 21:5)."[593] Consequently, Wilbur Smith concludes that "this passage does not teach that the heavens and earth are now brought into existence for the first time, but that they possess a new character."[594]

591. Ngundu, "Revelation," 1576. Because what one does is the index of the spiritual condition of the heart, what we do reveals what our beliefs truly are. Therefore, at the final judgment all people will be judged, and receive reward or suffer loss, "according to their deeds" (Ps 62:12; Prov 24:12; Eccl 12:13–14; Jer 17:10; Obad 15; Matt 6:5–6, 16–18; 16:27; 25:14–30; Luke 12:47–48; John 5:28–29; Rom 2:1–6; 12:19; 1 Cor 3:8, 11–15; 2 Cor 5:10; Gal 6:7–8; Eph 6:8; Col 3:25; Heb 10:26–27; 1 Pet 1:17; 2 Pet 2:20–22; Jude 14–15; Rev 2:23; 14:13; 20:11–13; 22:12). In particular, because all people have been made in the "image of God" (Gen 1:26–27; 5:1–3; 9:6; Eph 4:24; Col 3:10; Jas 3:9), and how we treat God's image shows what we really think of him, how we treat people in this life will be a primary basis for our final judgment, both for reward and punishment, because that reveals our real relationship with Jesus (Matt 6:1–4; 10:42; 24:45–51; 25:31–46; Mark 9:41–42; Luke 6:35; 12:33, 41–48; 14:13–14; 16:1–9; Rom 2:1–6; 1 Tim 6:18–19; 2 Tim 4:14; Heb 6:10; 1 Pet 5:1–4).

592. Beale, *Revelation,* 1037. The fact that the "life" given in connection with the "book of life" is based on the saints' identification with the life and death of the Lamb becomes especially clear when we note two other, more complete, descriptions of the "book of life." In Rev 13:8 it is called *"the book of life of the Lamb who has been slain."* In Rev 21:27 it is called *"the Lamb's book of life."*

593. Trench, *Synonyms,* 233–34.

594. Smith, "Revelation," 1521; see also Osborne, *Revelation,* 729–30.

Is the new heaven and new earth present or future?

Preterists, some postmillennialists, and some idealists contend that in the New Jerusalem "we have essentially a picture, not of the future, but of the present; of the ideal condition of Christ's true people, of His 'little flock' on earth, in every age. The picture may not yet be realized in fullness; but every blessing lined in upon its canvas is in principle the believer's now, and will be more and more his in actual experience as he opens his eyes and his heart to receive."[595] Thus, Christ's giving the *"water of life"* (Rev 21:6) relates to His promises in John 4:13–14; 7:37–39 to give believers, in the present, *"living waters."* The reference to *"the nations"* (Rev 21:24) is taken literally to be unconverted nations, as is the reference to the "unclean" (Rev 21:27), which "must be supposed to be alive upon the earth after the New Jerusalem has appeared."[596] That position has the merit that, in principle, the New Jerusalem does exist now. Christians' citizenship is in heaven (Phil 3:20); already we have come to Mount Zion, the heavenly Jerusalem (Heb 12:22).[597]

On the other hand, as was suggested above in the section "Interpretive approaches," although Revelation emphasizes the principles that apply to believers now and in all eras, it does more than that: it also gives us the account of the end of this age and the beginning of the age to come. The description of the new heavens and new earth as the future eternal state is a necessary counterpart to Revelation's earlier descriptions of the end of history. Rev 17:1—19:6 describes the overthrow of the harlot city of the world and the rejoicing that occurs in heaven as a result. Rev 19:11–21 describes the *parousia*. Rev 20:1–15 recapitulates the church age, ending with the judgment at the *parousia*. Those passages indicate that there is an end of history. One of John's purposes in writing the book was, as Beasley-Murray puts it, to "inspire in his readers the faith that the empire of the Antichrist and his minions is destined to be replaced by the rule of Christ and his saints. He could not but believe that the overthrow of the harlot-city and the Antichrist would be followed by the establishment of the bride-city in the rule of the Christ."[598] If Rev 21:1—22:5 does *not* describe in visionary form the age to come, then we would have *no* description of the age to come at all but would be left at the point of the final judgment. In a book that is designed in part to culminate God's story and bring to conclusion the entire Bible, that is unlikely.

In this final part of the book, therefore, every visible and invisible threat to all of God's people, both spiritually and physically, is eliminated: all past hurts, sorrows, and regrets are wiped away, and all is made new. There is no longer any injustice, sin, or discord, but perfect holiness, joy, and harmony reign among people and between people and God. This is not merely an idealization of the "already" of the kingdom but is a visionary

595. Milligan, *Revelation*, 373; see also Kik, *Eschatology*, 20–21; Chilton, *Paradise*, 203–09; Mathison, *Postmillennialism*, 157–58.

596. Milligan, *Revelation*, 373; see also Kik, *Eschatology*, 20–21; Preston, *Like Father*, 266.

597. Although the focus of the New Jerusalem is a vision of the *"age to come,"* it also has an ethical purpose in that it depicts *in principle* what our life in Christ should look like now: "The whole description of the city in 21:9—22:5 is eminently appropriate to the concept of the kingdom of Christ revealed in this world." Beasley-Murray, *Revelation*, 316; "What we find here in Revelation 21:1—22:5 is a description of the redeemed universe of the future as foreshadowed by the redeemed Church of the present." Hendriksen, *More Than Conquerors*, 197.

598. Beasley-Murray, *Revelation*, 315.

depiction of the "not yet" of the kingdom. Consequently, the majority view sees Rev 21:1—22:5 as referring to what will happen in the future, beginning with the *parousia*.

The events described in Rev 21:1–4 take place at the parousia

Rev 21:3 describes Christ's return to the earth. In doing so, it uses the phrase *"the tabernacle of God is among men."* The Greek word for "tabernacle" is *skēnē*. This is important, because it both links the *parousia* with Christ's first coming and, at the same time, shows how the *parousia* fulfills the Jewish hopes of God's coming to dwell with them. G. R. Beasley-Murray explains:

> The Jews looked for a return of the *Shekinah* in the kingdom of God. Greek-speaking Jews were conscious that the term *Shekinah* has the same consonants as the Greek *skēnē* [tabernacle], and this enabled them to associate with *skēnē* the conceptions of the *Shekinah*. A notable example of this occurs in John 1:14, 'The word became flesh and pitched its tent (Greek *eskēnōsen,* from *skēnē*) among us, and we beheld his glory.' In the incarnate Lord the hope of the return of God in his *Shekinah* glory was fulfilled. This same revelation of divine glory reaches its consummation in our text.[599]

The significance of the *parousia* for God's people extends beyond the fact that now *"the tabernacle of God is among men"* (Rev 21:3). God's people are described as a bride (Rev 19:7–8; 21:2, 9) and a city, the New Jerusalem.[600] The symbolism of the bride and the city "depict fundamentally the same thing, namely, God's people in fellowship with their Redeemer."[601] In Rev 19:7–8 the bride *"made herself ready"*; in 21:2 she is seen *"coming down out of heaven from God."* Beasley-Murray concludes, "John clearly wishes to indicate that the bride will appear in splendour along with the bridegroom, and that the marriage supper will then be celebrated."[602]

Rev 21:1—22:5 fulfills the NT promises that Christ's second coming brings with it the restoration of creation

The new earth is an integral aspect of God's redemptive program. The need for a redeemed creation stems from the fall of mankind and the "curse" which affected all of creation (Gen 3:14–19). Hoekema discusses this: "God now sent his Son into this world to redeem that creation from the results of sin. The work of Christ, therefore, is not just to save certain individuals, not even to save an innumerable throng of blood-bought people. The total work of Christ is nothing less than to redeem this entire creation from the effects of sin."[603]

---

599. Ibid., 311.

600. In Rev 21:2, 9–10 the bride is explicitly equated with the city.

601. Beasley-Murray, *Revelation,* 316.

602. Ibid., 315. Mealy lists six other reasons to demonstrate that the descent of the New Jerusalem in Rev 21:1–6 occurs at the *parousia,* not a thousand years after the *parousia*. Mealy, *After the Thousand Years,* 223–25.

603. Hoekema, *Bible and Future,* 274–75. The redemption of creation had been promised in Acts

Earlier we saw that Christ's *parousia* entails the destruction or cleansing of the present world.[604] That the descent of the New Jerusalem—i.e., the restoration of creation—occurs as part of the complex of events of the *parousia* is indicated in Rev 21:1 which states that *"the first heaven and the first earth passed away."* The redeemed creation described in Rev 21:1—22:5 is not merely an idealized picture of *"this age."* Rather, the *"new heavens and new earth"* are "new," i.e., new in *quality.* They are not like the *"first earth"* or the *"first things"* which have *"passed away"* (Rev 21:1, 4). Consequently, Rev 21:4 says that, in the new earth, *"there will no longer be any death; there will no longer be any mourning, or crying, or pain."* Rev 22:3 adds, *"There will no longer be any curse."*

Those facts rule out premillenialism and preterism since both hold that sin and death are still in effect after the second coming.[605] Because the renewal of creation at Christ's second coming includes the removal of death, mourning, crying, pain, and the curse, of necessity there no longer can be any sin. Consequently, the idea that there will be a massive sinful rebellion a thousand years after Christ returns cannot possibly be correct.

The parousia and judgment: negative and positive aspects

Although the judgment described in Rev 20:11–15 included both the righteous and the unrighteous, the focus there was on the judgment of the ungodly who are thrown into the *"lake of fire."* Rev 21:1—22:5 likewise depicts the negative aspect of the judgment entailed by the *parousia,* but different imagery is used. Beasley-Murray explains, "The lake of fire signifies not extinction in opposition to existence, but torturous existence in the society of evil as opposed to life in the society of God. For which reason John is able to represent the same reality by the very different symbol of life outside the city (21:27) in contrast to life inside the city (21:24ff.), the separation being effected by the city's wall (21:14)."[606]

In Rev 21:1—22:5, while negative effects of the *parousia* and judgment are mentioned, the references to those who are excluded from the New Jerusalem are almost stated as asides. Instead, the emphasis is on the positive effects of the *parousia.* Most of Revelation 21–22 recounts the elimination of all suffering and death, the healing of the nations, the presence of God and the Lamb, and the great glory, light, and life of the new, eternal kingdom. Mealy discusses one subtle aspect of the "positive" emphasis of the *parousia* that, again, shows the progressively parallel nature of the book:

> In Rev. 21.6, the Enthroned One announces that 'It is done' (literally, 'They are done' [*gegonan*]). This echoes the equivalent phrase that was heard from the throne upon the outpouring of the seventh and final bowl of God's wrath in 16.17 (*gegonen*). If the significance of the cry 'It is done' in the context of the seventh bowl was to signal the fulfillment of the parousia as the judgment of the world, then perhaps the positive 'They are done' here refers to the completion of both sides of the eschatological transition to God's kingdom, both negative and

---

3:19–21; Rom 8:17–25; 2 Pet 3:3–15.

604. See above, chapter 5, the section "Christ's second coming brings with it the destruction or cleansing of the present world and the restoration of creation."

605. See the critiques of premillennialism, new creation millennialism, and preterism in Chapter 7.

606. Beasley-Murray, *Revelation,* 304.

positive. As 21.4 affirms, 'The first things have passed away'. Yet not only has the old been judged and removed, but the new has been established in its place.[607]

Rev 21:1—22:5 fulfills what was promised to believers earlier in the book

Earlier, when discussing the repetition of themes, phrases, and promises to the church, we noted how Rev 21:1—22:5 fulfills the promises made to the church in the first three chapters of the book. Similarly, in Rev 7:16-17 believers were promised that they would no longer hunger or thirst, the Lamb would *"guide them to springs of the water of life,"* and *"God will wipe away every tear from their eyes."* Those promises likewise are fulfilled in Rev 21:4; 22:1-2. Additionally, all of the instances of persecution, oppression, and evil committed against the church throughout the entire book now are reversed. The church finds everlasting compensation—indeed, more than compensation—in the new world of the New Jerusalem. As Schüssler Fiorenza puts it, "Not oppressive rulership and subordination but the life-giving and life-sustaining power of God characterizes God's eschatological reign and empire."[608]

Rev 21:1—22:5 fulfills Isa 65:17—66:24

The only places in the OT where a *"new heavens and a new earth"* are referred to are in Isa 65:17 and 66:22. Isa 65:18-19; 66:10, 13, 20 also speak about a restored Jerusalem. As he has done throughout Revelation, John draws on OT imagery but universalizes and reinterprets it to apply to God's new, true people—the church. The parallels between Isaiah 65-66 and Revelation 21-22 indicate that John is describing the consummated kingdom after the *parousia.*[609] Indeed, the parallel between Revelation 21 and Isaiah 65 reveals that *"New Jerusalem"* is equivalent to the *"new earth."* In Isa 65:17-18 *"Jerusalem"* appears to be equal to the *"new heavens and new earth."* Similarly, John describes *"a new heaven and a*

---

607. Mealy, *After the Thousand Years,* 225.

608. Schüssler Fiorenza, *Revelation,* 113.

609. John gives the authoritative and inspired meaning of Isaiah's reference to the *"new heavens and new earth"* (see also 2 Pet 3:13). One implication of this is that Isaiah's statement in Isa 65:20 about a youth dying at the age of one hundred *cannot* be taken literally and *cannot* be referring to a temporary thousand-year "millennium." The reason is that John is talking about the *eternal state* after the *parousia* in which *"there will no longer be any death"* (Rev 21:4). Isa 65:19 itself states that *"there will no longer be heard in her [Jerusalem] the voice of weeping and the sound of crying."* Arthur Lewis pointedly asks, "How could parents in that day have any joy or hope, knowing that their children will die when they reach the age of one hundred?" Lewis, *Dark Side,* 37. Isaiah's reference to a youth dying at one hundred years of age is an example of "prophetic idiom," i.e., the OT prophets speak of Messiah's eternal kingdom using the language and limited frame of reference of their own physical, Israelite context. However, the NT repeatedly makes clear that Israel was simply a physical "type" or "shadow" of vastly greater realities. Thus, the OT language of a youth living to age one hundred is physical, typological language that points to resurrection life—eternal life—for God's people in the eternal state. See Irons, "Prophetic Idiom"; see also Lewis, *Dark Side,* 37 ("Isaiah often saw the future reign of the Lord in limited and metaphoric terms"). Postmillennialist Greg Bahnsen takes the "death at age 100" in Isa 65:20 literally but contends that Isaiah is talking about a time in which "because of the blessing of God on His people, life spans will be so extended that dying at 100, you are considered dying as a child [i.e., the 'golden age' postmillennialists believe will occur in history before the *parousia*]." Bahnsen, *Victory,* 58.

new earth" (Rev 21:1) but then immediately describes "*the holy city, New Jerusalem*" (Rev 21:2–3, 10—22:5) because the New Jerusalem *is* the new heaven and new earth.[610]

The references in Rev 21:24–27 and 22:2, 14 to the "nations," "nothing unclean," and "entering the city" are figurative portrayals of the perfect righteousness of the new creation

Rev 21:24–27 is figurative language. The kings and nations are not separate from or outside the city but are another way of describing the nature of the city. Gundry points out:

> "Bring into it [i.e., into the city (Rev 21:24)]" is spatial language, but the meaning is non-spatial, just as the dimensions of the city are spatial but their meaning non-spatial. . . . The meaning of "bring into it" has to do with the glory and honor of the saintly nations of kings that make up the city, not with unsaintly traffic from countryside into city. . . . To enter the city is to help make it up—and there is nothing about leaving it once the glory and honor have been brought in.[611]

Rev 21:24–27; 22:14 mean that only those whose names are written in the Lamb's book of life will be able to enter the new heaven and new earth at all, because Rev 20:15 says, "*If anyone's name was not written in the book of life, he was thrown into the lake of fire.*"[612]
Martin Kiddle states

> *The nations* are the redeemed, who belong spiritually but not racially to the twelve tribes. Did not Christ redeem 'men from every tribe and tongue and people and nation'? Very well, *that* is how Christians must read these old prophecies: *they are the nations.* Similarly, the *kings of the earth* . . . (so we must infer) are the martyr monarchs, who reigned as the successors of the heathen rulers (cf. xx. 4–6); or perhaps all loyal Christians, of whom the heavenly hosts cried out: *they shall reign on earth* (v. 10).[613]

Here again we must keep in mind a key purpose of John's writing: the vices John lists in Rev 21:8, 27; 22:11, 15 and his statements about entering the city (Rev 21:24–26; 22:14) or not being able to enter the city (Rev 21:27; 22:15) both warn believers not to betray their faith and values and exhort them to live steadfast lives of faithfulness, since the glorious end is so clearly in sight.[614]

---

610. See Beale, *Temple*, 368; Levenson, *Creation and the Persistence*, 89–90, 107.

611. Gundry, "New Jerusalem," 264. See also Rev 3:12 where Jesus promises that the one who overcomes will be made a pillar in the temple of God "*and he will not go out from it anymore.*"

612. See also Rev 21:7–8 which states that only "*he who overcomes will inherit these things*" whereas those who practice sin and evil "*will be in the lake of fire.*" Rev 21:27 makes the same point but uses different imagery: "*nothing unclean, and no one who practices abomination and lying, shall ever come into it [i.e., into the city].*" This again shows that preterism's literal interpretation of Rev 21:24–27 is misguided. See Preston, *Like Father*, 266.

613. Kiddle, *Revelation*, 439, emphasis in original; see also Gundry, "New Jerusalem," 263. Both descriptions (nations and kings) relate facets of God's people and life with him in the eternal state. In the same way, in Revelation 12 the woman and her children were both metaphorical ways of speaking of the same entity, the church. Again, in Rev 19:7–9 the church is spoken of both as the bride at the marriage supper and also as the guests at that same supper.

614. Beale, *Revelation*, 1102; Schüssler Fiorenza, *Revelation*, 110; Boxall, *Revelation*, 308.

Rev 21:24–26 alludes to Isaiah 60. Isaiah 60 speaks of glorified Zion. Isa 60:3 says that in glorified Zion *"nations will come to your light."* Rev 21:24 similarly says, *"The nations will walk by its [New Jerusalem's] light."* Isa 60:11 says, *"Your gates will be open continually; they will not be closed day or night."* Rev 21:25 similarly says, *"In the daytime (for there will be no night there) its [New Jerusalem's] gates will never be shut."* Isa 60:20 (see also Isa 60:19) says, *"Your sun will no longer set, nor will your moon wane; for you will have the Lord for an everlasting light."* Rev 21:23 similarly says, *"The city has no need of sun or of the moon to shine on it, for the glory of God has illumined it, and its lamp is the Lamb."* Isa 60:21 says, *"Then all your people will be righteous; they will possess the land forever."* Rev 21:27 similarly says, *"Nothing unclean, and no one who practices abomination and lying, shall ever come into it, but only those whose names are written in the Lamb's book of life."* [615] Isa 60:3–14 says that the kings of the nations will come and bring their wealth to Zion. Rev 21:24–26 similarly says, *"The kings of the earth will bring their glory into [New Jerusalem]"* and *"they will bring the glory and the honor of the nations into it."* These comparisons show how, as he has done throughout the book, John has taken OT passages and prophecies relating to Israel, and has redefined and reapplied them to the everlasting, universal church. [616]

Rev 22:1–2 says that the "tree of life" which is along the river formed by the "water of life" is for the "healing of the nations." The image of the water of life healing the nations does not imply, as preterists believe, that in the New Jerusalem "there remain diseased nations in need of healing." [617] Instead, it is "prophetic idiom" which illustrates what is then stated in Rev 22:3, that *"there will no longer be any curse"* (see also Rev 21:4).

The New Jerusalem is the consummation of God's eternal plan to dwell in a holy place with his holy people

God's goal throughout biblical history has been to fill every part of his creation with his presence. Beginning at the Garden of Eden, God desired to make the entire earth his dwelling place that he would share with his holy people. Because of sin, God's glory could not dwell completely in the old creation. Although God had walked in the Garden with Adam and Eve (Gen 3:8), because of their sin he drove them out of the Garden (Gen 3:23–24). God then progressively revealed his special presence on the earth among his people in the tabernacle and in Solomon's temple, which served as *"a copy and shadow of the heavenly things."* [618]

615. As Kiddle points out, "The gates are ever open, but only for righteous men. They are never shut, because there is no night to fear, and no evildoers may approach the eternal radiance." Kiddle, *Revelation*, 440.

616. See Kiddle, *Revelation*, 439–40. The phrase *tēn doxan kai tēn timēn* ("the glory and honor") of Rev 21:26 appears elsewhere in Revelation only in 4:9, 11 and 5:12, 13. In those passages it refers to the praise of God and the Lamb by the living creatures, twenty-four elders, and angels in heaven. Accordingly, whereas the ungodly nations formerly gave everything they had to Babylon the great, now, in contrast, the reference to "glory and honor" in Rev 21:26 shows the wholehearted worship, praise, and submission to God by all nations, for all eternity, throughout the entire new heaven and new earth. See Beale, *Revelation*, 1096; see also Gundry, "New Jerusalem," 264; Smalley, *Revelation*, 559.

617. Johnson, *Triumph*, 321; contra Preston, *Like Father*, 266..

618. Heb 8:5; see also Ps 78:69; Heb 8:1—10:1.

God then inaugurated the final stage of his presence in the person of Jesus Christ. Through the Holy Spirit's indwelling the church, his presence is now spread over the entire world. The time of the "shadows" of man-made temples has been completed, and the time of the new, true temple—his actual presence in Christ and the church—has come. However, although the true spiritual reality to which the OT tabernacle and temple pointed has been inaugurated, it has not yet been consummated. That consummation will occur when Christ returns to the earth. When he does, all creation will be redeemed (Rom 8:15–25).

When sin is forever eliminated from creation, the entire world (i.e., the *new heaven and new earth*") will be an Eden-like garden/city/temple—the perfect container for God's glorious presence. No longer will God's presence be housed in a physical building. Instead, the Lord God Almighty and the Lamb will fill, not just a portion of creation, but all of it (Rev 21:22). That is why the center of the vision is the earth—heaven coming *to the earth*.[619] In other words, "the 'new heaven' and the 'new earth' will be a single reality, characterized by the full, immediate presence of God among his people."[620]

The measuring of the city

The "measuring" of the city (Rev 21:15–17) contrasts with the measuring of the temple, altar, and worshippers, but leaving out the outer court, in Rev 11:1–2. As a result of that measuring, the church was spiritually protected but physically was subject to persecution and oppression. "Here the entire city is measured as another token of its complete safety from every enemy that formerly threatened its holiness and happiness."[621]

New Jerusalem as a Holy of Holies

The perfect holiness of the New Jerusalem is seen by the fact that the New Jerusalem is a Holy of Holies:

- Just like the Holy of Holies (1 Kgs 6:16–20; 2 Chron 3:8), the city is a perfect cube (Rev 21:16).[622]

---

619. See Schüssler Fiorenza, *Revelation*, 109.

620. Schnabel, *40 Questions*, 280.

621. Johnson, *Triumph*, 312. The measurements should not be taken "literally" as if they were the measurements of a physical city but are clearly symbolic, based on multiples of the number 12. See Johnson, *Triumph*, 312–13. As Gundry stated with respect to people "coming into" the city, this is "spatial language, but the meaning is non-spatial." Consequently, "it is false to infer that the city covers 144,000,000 square stadia of earth but not the whole earth or that the 144,000 Israelites do not encompass the innumerable multitude." Gundry, "New Jerusalem," 264. John's purpose is not primarily to describe a "place." Rather, "He is describing eternally secure peoples." Ibid., 260.

622. Schüssler Fiorenza raises the additional possibility that since, as we saw above, John has compared and contrasted Babylon and the New Jerusalem, his description of New Jerusalem as being "*laid out as a square*" (Rev 21:16) may be picturing "God's city as the anti-image of Babylon." Schüssler Fiorenza, *Revelation*, 111. The reason is that, in his famous *History*, Greek historian Herodotus (c. 484–425 BC) had written regarding historical Babylon that "the shape of the whole [was] square." Herodotus, *History*, 1:178. Further, the dimensions of ancient Babylon were multiples of twelve ("each face measures one hundred and twenty furlongs"), just as New Jerusalem's dimensions are all multiples of twelve. Ibid. While depicting the New Jerusalem as the Holy of Holies is clearly John's primary point, this possible

- Just as the Holy of Holies was overlaid with pure gold (1 Kgs 6:16–20; 2 Chron 3:8), *"the city was pure gold, like clear glass"* (Rev 21:18).

- Just as the Holy of Holies was the special place of God's presence and glory, the city is now the place of God's presence and glory (Rev 21:22–23; 22:1, 3–5).

- Only the Holy of Holies, not other sections of Israel's temple (i.e., the holy place and the outer courtyard), is found in Revelation 21. Thus, God's special presence, which formerly was limited to the Holy of Holies, now encompasses all of his new creation.

On the other hand, the New Jerusalem consummates and surpasses the Holy of Holies with respect to our access to God.

- Only the high priest could enter the Holy of Holies, and he had to offer sacrifices for his own sin and the sins of the nation (Lev 16:1–28). In the New Jerusalem, all of God's people are without sin and will serve the Lord and reign forever and ever (Rev 21:7–8, 27; 22:3–5).

- The high priest could only enter the Holy of Holies one day per year, on the Day of Atonement (Lev 16:29–31). In the New Jerusalem, we not only will have direct access to God, but we will *always* be in his immediate presence (Rev 21:3–4, 22–23; 22:3–5).

- On the Day of Atonement the high priest had to offer incense which formed a thick cloud that covered the mercy seat so that he could not see God's glorious appearance, or he would die (Lev 16:13; see Exod 33:20). In the New Jerusalem, all of God's people will *"see his face"* (Rev 22:4).

Rev 22:6–21: epilogue[623]

The epilogue of the book is consistent with the rest of the book and with prophecy in general. Prophets spoke oracles of judgment and oracles of salvation to warn the people and exhort them to change their ways and return or stay faithful to the Lord. Revelation specifically was written to inform, exhort, comfort, and encourage the churches. Beale therefore observes:

> These final verses especially tie in to the introduction in 1:1–3: both identify the book as a consummation from God (using the same wording from Dan. 2:28–29, 45); both focus on John as a "witness" to the revelation that he has been given; and both speak of the revelation as a "prophecy" communicated to "hearers." . . . This conclusion shows that the purpose of the whole book is to induce holy obedience among God's people so that they might receive the reward of salvation. . . . The repeated exhortations to holiness are the main point of the epilogue, since they are supported by the exclamations about Christ's coming. No fewer than eight of the final fifteen verses underscore the book's intention to encourage

---

allusion to historical Babylon demonstrates the multivalence, depth, and subtlety of Revelation.

623. Although most commentators assume that in Rev 22:6 the angel who showed John New Jerusalem is speaking, in 22:7 the speaker clearly is Christ Himself. That increases the possibility that it is Christ who is speaking in 22:6 and throughout much of chapter 22. See Schüssler Fiorenza, *Revelation,* 114.

obedience either through exhortations to obedience, through promised blessings for holy living, and through warnings of judgment for unholy living.[624]

Revelation ties together and completes the entire Bible

The new creation of Revelation links with the original creation of Genesis

The last two chapters of Revelation clearly are linked, often by contrast, with the first three chapters of Genesis as follows:

Genesis	*Revelation*
"In the beginning God created the heavens and the earth" (Gen 1:1)	*"I saw a new heaven and a new earth"* (Rev 21:1)
"The darkness He called night" (Gen 1:5)	*"There will be no night there"* (Rev 21:25; 22:5)
"The gathering of the waters He called seas" (Gen 1:10)	*"There is no longer any sea"* (Rev 21:1)
"Let there be lights in the expanse of the heavens . . . to give light on the earth" (Gen 1:14–15)	*"The city has no need of the sun or of the moon to shine on it"* (Rev 21:23; 22:5)
"In the day that you eat from it you will surely die" (Gen 2:17)	*"There will no longer be any death"* (Rev 21:4)
"The man and his wife hid themselves from the presence of the Lord God" (Gen 3:8)	*"God Himself will be among them . . . they will see His face"* (Rev 21:3; 22:4)
"I will greatly multiply your pain in childbirth" (Gen 3:16)	*"There will no longer be any . . . pain"* (Rev 21:4)
"Cursed is the ground because of you" (Gen 3:17)	*"There will no longer be any curse"* (Rev 22:3)

Sam Hamstra comments on the contrasts between what was begun in Genesis and what is completed in Revelation:

> In Genesis God created the heaven and the earth; in Revelation we read of a new heaven and earth (21:1). In Genesis the luminaries are called into being; in Revelation the glory of the Lord lights the city [21:23; 22:5]. In Genesis we read of the cunning power of Satan; in Revelation the devil is bound and hurled into the lake of fire (20:10). In Genesis we read of paradise lost; in Revelation paradise is restored. Genesis describes the divorce of humankind as Adam and Eve run from God; in Revelation the redeemed enjoy the intimate fellowship of marriage to the Lamb [19:7–9; 21:2–4; 22:4]. In Genesis nature threatens the security and hurts humanity; in Revelation nature sustains and comforts people [22:1–2]. In Genesis the tree of life is protected by an angel lest anyone eat its fruit; Revelation restores humanity's access to the fruit (22:14). This obvious correlation between the first and last books of the Bible illustrates the fulfillment of the first messianic prophecy (Gen. 3:15) and God's faithfulness to the covenant (Rev. 21:3).[625]

624. Beale, *Revelation*, 150.

625. Hamstra, "An Idealist View," 123. T. Desmond Alexander adds, "The very strong links between Genesis 1–3 and Revelation 20–22 suggest that these passages frame the entire biblical meta-story."

The new creation of Revelation surpasses the original creation of Genesis

Jonathan Moo concludes our survey of Revelation by discussing the potentialities of the pre-consummate creation, how those potentialities played out in history, and how God has brought the cosmos to an even greater glory than the original creation:

> The fact that there is no more sea or night in the new heaven and new earth [Rev 21:1, 25] suggests an allusion to the first creation since in both instances these elements are in some way subjugated, divided or restrained. . . . It is as if the first creation, while good in itself, had had the potential to develop in two directions: if humankind fulfilled its role and lived in harmony with God and the rest of creation, the latent powers of chaos represented especially by the sea and darkness would be forever within the scope of human dominion and would become perhaps sources of creative energy and delight—just as they were for God, for whom even Leviathan could be a plaything.[626] But if the covenant between God and his creatures was broken and human beings allied themselves with the serpent and its realm, the forces of chaos would be let loose and the sea become a thing of terror, an abode of evil and an instrument of judgement. Scripture may be largely a record of humankind opting for this latter path, but John's intent is to assure the churches that they have not therefore been abandoned to a world of sorrow, pain and mourning. Instead, the triumph of the "Lamb that was slain" means that the creator's fidelity to his creation—hinted at in the rainbow around the throne [Rev 4:3], sign of the Noahic covenant—is expressed finally through nothing less than the renewal of the cosmos, an event in which the world is brought beyond any threat of future rebellion or sin.[627]

Alexander, *From Eden*, 10.

626. See Job 41:1–7; Ps 74:14; 104:24–26.

627. Moo, "The Sea," 166–67.

12

The Importance of Eschatology

The study of eschatology is a worthy Christian endeavor. Its significance to the Christian worldview is evident in the large role it plays in Scripture, which holds priority in the developing of a truly Christian worldview. It is also crucial to the development of a distinctly Christian philosophy of history, which is fundamental to the Christian understanding of the here and now. In addition, eschatology significantly impacts the Christian's cultural endeavors because it sets before the Christian the foreordained pattern of the future.[1]

Views of the end of time—and even the absence of such views—have much to tell us both about society's perceptions of the meaning of history and about its understanding of evil. They may also help reveal something about society's self-understanding. . . . Apocalyptic symbols are not merely images to be pondered; they are also stimuli to action. Even the earliest apocalypses combined a literal sense of a divinely predetermined plan for history with an insistence on the necessity for choice within history.[2]

The theological importance of eschatology

Eschatology helps to integrate and tie together our overall theology

THE BIBLE TELLS A coherent, unfolding story from Genesis to Revelation. The biblical storyline has an inner unity, and Jesus Christ is at the heart of that story.[3] An important part of the biblical story is its consummation. Our eschatology exposes whether our theology as a whole is consistent or inconsistent with the rest of the biblical structure and story. For example, the primary role that dispensationalism gives the nation of Israel and the secondary role it gives the church in eschatology is fundamentally inconsistent with the

---

1. Gentry, *Dominion*, 25–26.

2. McGinn, *Anti-Christ*, 2, 278.

3. Luke 24:25–27, 44–47; John 5:39–40, 46; Acts 3:18, 24; 10:43; 26:22–23; Rom 1:1–4; Heb 1:1–2; 1 Pet 1:10–12.

entire biblical storyline. Premillennialism of either the historic or dispensational variety is inconsistent with the "two-age" eschatological structure of the NT and with what the *parousia* signifies and entails. Full preterism also is inconsistent with the nature of the *parousia*. Postmillennialism is inconsistent with the radical, pervasive, and intractable nature of indwelling human sin, both individually and structurally. Eschatology, therefore, is important both for systematic theology (i.e., analyzing major Christian doctrines by themselves) and also for biblical theology (i.e., analyzing the overall, progressively-revealed biblical storyline from beginning to end).

Sound eschatology is a source of hope and expectation

Most Christians, in most places, throughout most of history, have experienced hardship and persecution. That is still true today. Jesus and the apostles said that tribulation will characterize the entire time before the second coming.[4] In this vital area sound eschatology is important. "Preterism consistently carried out empties the New Testament of hope for the modern believer. If the rapture of the living saints, the resurrection of the dead saints, the coming of Christ are already past realities, if all prophecy is really fulfilled, then upon what do we base our hope for the future?"[5] On the other hand, dispensationalism offers a false hope based on its belief that the last generation of Christians living before Christ returns will be removed from the earth in order to avoid tribulation and persecution.

In contrast with such views, the early disciples looked for the hope of the second coming. Their attitude was different from modern preterists or dispensationalists because their eschatology was different from preterism or dispensationalism. They did not expect to avoid suffering but knew they were being purified by suffering.[6] The early Christians could long for Christ's coming with a pure conscience, knowing that "everything that brings it closer must be a cause of encouragement. . . . Indeed as they themselves are caught up in the times of turmoil and distress, their reaction should be exactly the opposite to that which would be natural under such burdens: they should stand erect and raise their heads because their final deliverance draws near [Luke 21:28]."[7] Having a sound eschatology enables modern believers to have the same hope and expectation the early disciples had.[8]

---

4. Matt 5:10–12; 24:6–9, 22, 29; Mark 13:7–9, 12, 20, 24; John 15:18–20; 16:33; Acts 11:19; 14:21–22; 20:23; Rom 5:3; 8:35–39; 12:12; 2 Cor 1:4, 8; 2:4; 4:8–11, 17; 6:4; 7:4; 8:2; 12:10; Eph 3:13; Phil 4:14; Col 1:24; 1 Thess 1:6; 3:3, 7; 2 Thess 1:4, 6; 2 Tim 3:12; Heb 10:33; 1 Pet 4:12–16; Rev 1:9; 2:9–10.

5. Waldron, "Preterism," n.p.

6. *Barn.* 4:3–5; *Shepherd of Hermas, Vision* 2.2.6–8; 4.1.1—4.3.6; *Didache* 16:1–8; Justin Martyr, *Dial.* 110; Irenaeus, *Haer.* 5.25.1–26.1; 5.28.4; 5.30.4; 5.35.1; Tertullian, *Res.* 22, 25, 27, 41.

7. Nolland, *Luke 18:35—24:53,* 1007.

8. This was demonstrated in the life of Christian martyr Dietrich Bonhoeffer. While he was imprisoned by the Nazis during World War II, Bonhoeffer wrote that he found the books of Psalms and Revelation to be "unexpectedly helpful." Bonhoeffer, *Letters and Papers,* 128. By contrast, he observed that his fellow prisoners who did not have a Christian worldview compartmentalized their lives and lapsed into superstition or fatalism in their attempts to deal with the stress of prison life and the fear engendered by air raids. Ibid., 231, 310–11.

Throughout much of history, most people, including most Christians, have been illiterate. Oral and visual transmission of the faith therefore has been particularly important. Since eschatology is an important part of the biblical story, it should not be surprising that "apocalyptic writings, such as the book of Revelation, Ezekiel, and the 'synoptic apocalypse' (Matt. 24:4–36; Mark 13:5–37; Luke 21:8–36) exerted a significant influence in early Christian art."[9] In their study of apocalyptic themes in the monumental and minor art of early Christianity, Herrmann and van den Hoek found that, in their visions of paradise and the second coming, the early Christian artists were very selective in their borrowings from apocalyptic texts. Such selectivity was purposeful:

> Scenes of punishment and disaster were completely avoided. Biblical apocalyptic texts are terrifying and promise a dreadful fate to all but the most faithful and pure, but this frightening message is not what is communicated by apocalypses in early Christian art. The intention comes out explicitly in the inscriptions of mosaics at S. Pudenziana in Rome and the Monastery of the Stonecutters in Thessaloniki. The texts underline that God is there to be viewed, he is present in the building, and he brings salvation. The message could hardly be more comforting. Apparitions from threatening visions were used to illustrate prophecies of peace. Apocalyptic texts have been mined to extract material for images of a benevolent God in heaven and returning to earth. Apostles, saints, bishops, and churches are presented as parts of a system that mediates between heaven and earth and that offers safety, hope, and joy to the faithful individual. In the terrifying world of the late Roman Empire and the early Middle Ages, carefully crafted apocalyptic works of art were intended to provide the viewer with gratification and freedom from anxiety.[10]

As the work of these early artists attests, eschatology is not divorced from life. It is practical and can provide hope and comfort in ways that other means, including others aspects of theology, cannot.[11]

Sound eschatology strengthens the teaching ministry of the church

Second Tim 3:16–17 declares, "*All Scripture is inspired by God and profitable for teaching, for reproof, for correction, for training in righteousness; so that the man of God may be adequate, equipped for every good work.*" Paul "*did not shrink from declaring to you the whole purpose [or counsel] of God*" (Acts 20:27). To not have a well-thought-out eschatology that is consistent with the rest of our theology means that much of the Bible will remain a mystery. However, to be able to teach and preach from all sections of the Bible, including the eschatological parts, will help produce well-grounded, well-rounded, deeper Christians.

9. Herrmann and van den Hoek , "Apocalyptic Themes," 33.

10. Ibid., 80.

11. See Travis, *I Believe*, 209–50.

Sound eschatology strengthens the life of the church

In many churches today, eschatology essentially is ignored. In other churches, and among various popular "prophecy experts," eschatology is amazingly misunderstood and misused. James Edwards comments on the effects of this dual problem: "This unfortunate set of circumstances—both its abuse and its subsequent neglect—has weakened the church rather than strengthened it. If we dispense with eschatology, then the purpose and destiny of history fall into the hands of humanity alone. No one, I think, Christian or not, takes solace in that prospect. Unless human history, in all its greatness and potential as well as its propensity to evil and destructiveness, can be *redeemed,* human life is a futile and sordid endeavor."[12]

Sound eschatology shows us that the kingdom already has been inaugurated but has not yet been consummated. It "asserts that history is meaningful because it is directed toward an end, a goal that lies at its conclusion and gives meaning to the whole"[13] This understanding of history affects how Christians live and their attitude toward their lives: "the Christian has tasted the goodness of the eternal kingdom and even now participates in the reign of God. For this reason the disciple is called to offer joyful obedience to the God of the future. At the same time, the church has not entered into the fullness of God's universal rule. Therefore, the community of the faithful must avoid all triumphalism."[14]

Sound eschatology helps us see our situation in true perspective: see our enemies in their true light; see our redeemer and king in his true glory; and see ourselves in our true beauty.[15] Consequently, eschatology helps Christians avoid despair when they see evil rampant in the world, helps Christians endure and remain faithful when they suffer and are tempted to compromise, and helps Christians bear witness to the gospel in any circumstance. Eschatology gives Christians the confidence that comes from a high view of God's sovereignty because they understand that God has declared *"the end from the beginning, and from ancient times things which have not been done, saying 'My purpose will be established, and I will accomplish all My good pleasure'"* (Isa 46:10). That enables Christians to live out their faith, act as God's instruments to redeem people, and not allow things to remain as they are.[16]

Eschatology, evangelism, and Christian social action: introduction

"The longing that things *ought not to be* as they are, and *cannot be allowed* to remain as they are, is essentially an eschatological longing."[17] Eschatology (although perhaps unacknowledged), therefore, is the source or basis of discontent with existence as it is. But eschatology is more than that: it is the stimulus to act on our discontent with existence as it is. Because eschatology, including apocalyptic books such as Revelation, has the two-fold

12. Edwards, *Mark,* 402.

13. Grenz, *Millennial Maze,* 200.

14. Ibid., 201.

15. Johnson, *Triumph,* 337–43.

16. As OT prophecy was fulfilled in Jesus Christ, God proved his word true. Just as he fulfilled his promises in the past, so God will fulfill his promises in the future. See Schnabel, *40 Questions,* 315.

17. Edwards, *Mark,* 402, emphasis in original.

nature of true biblical prophecy (i.e., oracles of judgment and oracles of salvation), by its very nature it demands a behavioral response on the part of its hearers.[18] That necessarily affects how we are to live. Indeed, the language, images, and ideas of eschatology have been powerful weapons across the centuries in the quest for justice and social change. Revelation has inspired hymns and art, has been the book of martyrs and visionaries, and has acted as a prophetic critique of the church, the state, and the culture.

At the heart of Christianity is its dual concern for winning converts (evangelism) and dealing with poverty, injustice, and bad social conditions (social activism)

We all know of, and many experience, the great and wonderful things that exist in this world. Those things include both the material (e.g., technological advances in all areas, medical care unimaginable one hundred years ago) and the immaterial (e.g., love, knowledge, beauty). On the other hand, everyone knows of the radical nature of evil in the world that corrupts everything, both material and immaterial. Rampant evil, corruption, and decay warp material things, social structures, relationships (among individuals, groups, and with the environment), and warp each individual human heart. As Aleksandr Solzhenitsyn put it, "If only there were evil people somewhere insidiously committing evil deeds, and it were necessary only to separate them from the rest of us and destroy them. But the line dividing good and evil cuts through every human being."[19] This leads to the universal realization that things are not the way they should be. That realization is, as Edwards observed above, at root, theological and eschatological. The theological reasons both for the heights of humanity's achievements and goodness and the depths of human depravity and evil were succinctly summarized by Francis Schaeffer: "Why is he [man] so wonderful and yet so flawed? Who is man? Who am I? Why does man do these things that make man so unique, and yet why is man so horrible? Why is it? The Bible says that you are wonderful because you are made in the image of God, but that you are flawed because at a space-time point of history man fell."[20]

For Christians, the eschatological discontent expressed by James Edwards entails certain obligations. Christians are not merely to bemoan what is wrong with the world. Rather, because they have been given a new heart (Ezek 36:26), the mind of Christ (1 Cor 2:16), the Holy Spirit (John 14:17; Rom 8:1–17), and the word of God,[21] they are now God's agents of change in and for the world. Stephen Travis puts it like this:

> If the coming of God's rule in Jesus's ministry meant fighting disease and bondage to evil, working against divisions in society and commercial exploitation, his followers are not at liberty to abandon such demands in preference for something else. We are certainly not free to concentrate on 'spiritual' concerns to the neglect of what Jesus called 'the weightier matters of the law'—justice, mercy

18. Green, *How to Read*, 129–30; Schüssler Fiorenza, *Revelation*, 103, 129–30.

19. Solzhenitsyn, *Gulag Archipelago*, 75.

20. Schaeffer, *Escape*, 1:219.

21. Luke 8:11, 15, 21; John 8:31; 17:14; Acts 4:29–31; Rom 15:18; 1 Thess 2:13; 2 Tim 3:16–17; Heb 4:12; Jas 1:22.

and honesty (Matthew 23:23). . . . [On the other hand,] the winning of people to Christian discipleship must never be made subservient to the search for a better society. . . . In the quest for a better society the need for better people, transformed by the grace of Christ, is paramount. . . . We dare not give people only 'the food that spoils', essential though that is. We must lead them also to 'the food that lasts for eternal life, the real and 'living bread which came down from heaven' (John 6:27, 51).[22]

The hope that our eschatology brings necessarily translates into practical involvement with the world, i.e., dealing with poverty, injustice, and bad social conditions. That demonstrates the reality of our faith which, in turn, facilitates evangelism.[23] James Boice reports, "Lord Shaftesbury, the great English social reformer and mature Christian, said near the end of his life, 'I do not think that in the last forty years I have ever lived one conscious hour that was not influenced by the thought of our Lord's return.' In this case, the expectation of meeting the Lord face to face was one of the strongest motivations behind his social programs."[24] Edward Schillebeeckx perceptively adds:

> Christian faith in a post-terrestrial future can only be seen to be true if this eschatological hope shows itself capable of bringing mankind a better future here and now. Who could believe in a God who will make everything new "later" if it is in no way apparent from the activity of those who hope in the One who is to come that he is already beginning to make everything new *now*—if in fact it is not apparent that this eschatological hope is able *now* to change the course of history for the better? . . . It will have to be clear from the concrete practice of Christian life that God [in fact] manifests himself as the one whose power can bring about the new future.[25]

These dual concerns were affirmed by the international, inter-denominational Lausanne Covenant of 1974:

---

22. Travis, *I Believe*, 236, 245.
23. See Green, *How to Read*, 131–34.
24. Boice, *Foundations*, 456.
25. Schillebeeckx, *God the Future*, 183–84.

5. *Christian Social Responsibility*	6. *The Church and Evangelism*
We affirm that God is both the Creator and the Judge of all people. We therefore should share his concern for justice and reconciliation throughout human society and for the liberation of men and women from every kind of oppression. Because men and women are made in the image of God, every person, regardless of race, religion, colour, culture, class, sex or age, has an intrinsic dignity because of which he or she should be respected and served, not exploited. Here too we express penitence both for our neglect and for having sometimes regarded evangelism and social concern as mutually exclusive. Although reconciliation with other people is not reconciliation with God, nor is social action evangelism, nor is political liberation salvation, nevertheless we affirm that evangelism and socio-political involvement are both part of our Christian duty. For both are necessary expressions of our doctrines of God and man, our love for our neighbour and our obedience to Jesus Christ. The message of salvation implies also a message of judgment upon every form of alienation, oppression and discrimination, and we should not be afraid to denounce evil and injustice wherever they exist. When people receive Christ they are born again into his kingdom and must seek not only to exhibit but also to spread its righteousness in the midst of an unrighteous world. The salvation we claim should be transforming us in the totality of our personal and social responsibilities. Faith without works is dead. (Acts 17:26, 31; Gen. 18:25; Isa. 1:17; Psa. 45:7; Gen. 1:26, 27; Jas. 3:9; Lev. 19:18; Luke 6:27, 35; Jas. 2:14–26; Joh. 3:3, 5; Matt. 5:20; 6:33; II Cor. 3:18; Jas. 2:20)	We affirm that Christ sends his redeemed people into the world as the Father sent him, and that this calls for a similar deep and costly penetration of the world. We need to break out of our ecclesiastical ghettos and permeate non-Christian society. In the Church's mission of sacrificial service evangelism is primary. World evangelization requires the whole Church to take the whole gospel to the whole world. The Church is at the very centre of God's cosmic purpose and is his appointed means of spreading the gospel. But a church which preaches the cross must itself be marked by the cross. It becomes a stumbling block to evangelism when it betrays the gospel or lacks a living faith in God, a genuine love for people, or scrupulous honesty in all things including promotion and finance. The church is the community of God's people rather than an institution, and must not be identified with any particular culture, social or political system, or human ideology. (John 17:18; 20:21; Matt. 28:19, 20; Acts 1:8; 20:27; Eph. 1:9, 10; 3:9–11; Gal. 6:14, 17; II Cor. 6:3, 4; II Tim. 2:19–21; Phil. 1:27)

The power of eschatological rhetoric as a motivator for social change

All cultures mold their subjects into their own image. The successful, the rich, the powerful tend not see this or, if they see it, do not wish to change it because their success, wealth, and power are derived from conformity to the dominant cultural ideology. Even those who do not have great worldly success, wealth, or power tend to be conformed to the ideology of the world and the dominant culture. In his survey of the flow of history and culture, *How Then Shall We Live?*, Francis Schaeffer notes, "As the more Christian-dominated consensus weakened, the majority of people adopted two impoverished values: *personal peace* and *affluence*."[26]

This set of values is not limited to the West. Personal peace and affluence are not necessarily bad values. Yet they (or any other set of values we may espouse) force us to ask the question: Are they *Christ's* values? Any values or priorities, although good in themselves, if turned into ultimate values or priorities, become forms of idolatry. Such values are centered in the well-being of the self for this earthly life alone. As such, they (along with

26. Schaeffer, *How Then*, 5:211, emphasis in original.

success, wealth, power, or virtually any other set of values) cause us not to critique the prevailing worldview but to become complacent with injustice, oppression, inhumanity, and structural evils,[27] as long as our own well-being is reasonably intact.

On the other hand, eschatology, particularly a book like Revelation, "offers a different way of perceiving the world which leads people to resist and to challenge the effects of the dominant ideology."[28] This alternative vision of the world is strongly theocentric—indeed, Christ-centered. Richard Bauckham states, "In the end it is only a purified vision of the transcendence of God that can effectively resist the human tendency to idolatry which consists in absolutizing aspects of this world. The worship of the true God is the power of resistance to the deification of military and political power (the beast) and economic prosperity (Babylon)."[29] Such a view provides the basis to confront oppression, injustice, and inhumanity. As Theodore Stylianopoulos says, "Revelation is above all a call for justice, a cry for the kingdom, a prayer for the disclosure of God's rule on earth as it is in heaven."[30] Likewise, Revelation provides the basis for us to critique the church itself which, far too often in history, has demonstrated that it has "left its first love" and attached itself to supporting the state, the dominant culture, and the world.[31] In these ways, the book of Revelation and eschatology in general confront us with the fundamental issues we saw recurring throughout Revelation: Where do my primary loyalties lie and who is my true Lord? Our responses to our own culture and to the world's ideologies and influences demonstrate our answers to those questions.

In commenting on Rev 18:24, Bauckham notes "the sense of solidarity it voices between the Christian martyrs and all the other innocent victims of Rome. If John urges his churches to dissociate themselves from the political and economic power-structures of Rome, this is not to turn them into an inward-looking sectarian group, concerned only with their own fate. It is rather because, in their prophetic witness to the world, these followers of the Lamb, himself a victim of Rome, cannot be allied with the murderers but must witness against the murderers."[32] Response frequently has come from the op-

27. Schüssler Fiorenza says, "Revelation consistently speaks of the power of Satan in national, political, and cosmic terms (13:7; 18:3, 23; 20:3). Satan deceives the nations and not merely individuals into sinful actions (20:7–8). Revelation's notion of ultimate evil is best understood today as *systemic evil* and *structural sin*." Schüssler Fiorenza, *Revelation*, 87, emphasis in original.

28. Bauckham, *Theology*, 159. Elsewhere Bauckham states, "Those who imagine early Christianity as a quietist and apolitical movement should study the book of Revelation." Bauckham, *Bible in Politics*, 101.

29. Bauckham, *Theology*, 160. In this regard, T. Desmond Alexander, in commenting on the rivalry between the USSR and the USA in the latter half of the twentieth century, observes that "in resisting communism Christians may have been deceived into thinking that capitalism is the church's ally. Yet, if we want to identify the greatest enemy of the Christian faith, we must look closely at Babylon and observe its obsession with consumerism. There is nothing that stands more effectively as a barrier to people knowing God than the desire for wealth that comes through capitalism." Alexander, *From Eden*, 183.

30. Stylianopoulos, "I Know," 28.

31. Schüssler Fiorenza observes, "Whereas mainline Christianity has often co-opted or neutralized Revelation's political-religious language and vision by identifying God's empire with the institutional church or with the interior salvation of the soul, messianic-prophetic Christian movements have again and again affirmed Revelation's visions of salvation as a vision of total well-being and freedom from oppression. They have read it as promising liberation from oppressive ecclesiastical structures and from the destructive domination of those who have power in the world." Schüssler Fiorenza, *Revelation*, 128.

32. Bauckham, *Bible in Politics*, 101.

pressed and the disadvantaged. They often realize what the rich and powerful do not: that the dominant culture in any land has within it the seeds, and bears the marks, of Babylon the great. Elisabeth Schüssler Fiorenza observes, "Oppressed and disadvantaged Christians read Revelation contextually as political-religious typology that speaks to their own situation. Latin American or South African liberation theologies cherish Revelation's political world of vision for its prophetic indictment of exploitation and oppression as well as its sustaining vision of justice."[33] An example of this is the insurrection led by John Chilembwe in January 1915 in Nyasaland (modern Malawi) against the British colonial authorities against the injustices and exploitation of the colonial system. Chilembwe himself was a Baptist minister. Philip Jenkins writes, "Almost certainly he was drawing heavily on Baptist apocalyptic ideas."[34] Schüssler Fiorenza gives three other notable examples of such a perspective and witness drawn from the eschatology of Revelation: "In his *Letter from a Birmingham Jail*, Martin Luther King, Jr., echoes the language and images of Revelation when interpreting experiences and hopes in the struggle for the civil rights of African-Americans; Allan Boesak's commentary *Comfort and Protest* contextualizes Revelation in the struggle against apartheid in South Africa; and Daniel Berrigan penned his reflection on Revelation, *Nightmare of God*, while imprisoned for his activities in support of anti-nuclear-war protests."[35]

Eschatological language, images, and ideas often have proven to be powerful tools for analyzing contemporary events and motivators for action. With respect to the concept of Antichrist, for example, Bernard McGinn discusses the difference between "Antichrist *language*" and "Antichrist *application*." Antichrist language is using the term "Antichrist" or its equivalents "only as a weapon to smear opponents, paying no attention to the general course of salvation history."[36] This has been done throughout history, often on both sides of the same issue. Antichrist application, on the other hand, "occurs when a conscious and concerted effort is made to understand historical events, recent and contemporary, in the light of the Antichrist legend as part of an apocalyptic view of history."[37]

33. Schüssler Fiorenza, *Revelation*, 7.

34. Jenkins, "Chilembwe's rising," 45. The revolt was crushed but "left behind a legacy of nationalist and Africanist sentiment. Chilembwe today is Malawi's greatest national hero. His face appears on Malawi's currency, and every January 15 the nation celebrates John Chilembwe Day." Ibid.

35. Schüssler Fiorenza, *Revelation*, 11. The opposite phenomenon, from the "other side of the coin," was seen during the American Civil War (1861–1865). Paul Harvey reports, "Southern Christians, faced with the overwhelming fact of racial slavery, were less enthusiastic about millennial visions of an American society cleansed of sin. Southern evangelicalism was oriented to the private, to reforming individual behavior rather than assuming the critic of the social order." Harvey, "Southern Redemption," 170.

Here we see the fundamental questions posed by Revelation raised yet again: Where do my primary loyalties lie? Who or what is my true functional Lord that is molding and motivating my attitudes and behaviors? People can only answer those questions for themselves, but they need to be aware that their socio-economic circumstances confront them with such questions nonetheless. That is not to say that only those who oppose the state, the successful, the wealthy, and the powerful, necessarily are correct. Tremendous amounts of unspeakable evil have been done in the name of opposing the successful, the wealthy, the powerful, and the privileged—witness, for example, the French Revolution and every communist revolution. The issues are one's motivation and who is one's real Lord: Jesus, or someone or something else.

36. McGinn, *Anti-Christ*, 120.

37. Ibid., 120–21. It should be noted that, although some people believe that apocalyptic application

For example, in the fifteenth century, Antichrist rhetoric "functioned as an integral part of a broad apocalyptic appeal" by radical Hussites to galvanize peasants and some city dwellers to overthrow the existing social and religious order.[38] During the Reformation, the potentially revolutionary nature of Protestantism was "seen to lie in the changes called for in church and society when the authority of the Holy Scripture supplants that of reigning church tradition."[39] Because of the invention of the printing press, pamphlets, both written and illustrated, proved to be of great importance in furthering the Protestant message.[40] Eschatological and apocalyptic themes often were employed. One important early pamphleteer was Heinrich von Kettenbach. Steven Ozment states, "Kettenbach drew no fewer than forty-nine contrasts between the 'anti-Christlike' behavior of the pope and the biblical ministry of Jesus—perhaps the most popular tactic of early Protestant propaganda, both pictoral and written. In heated apocalyptic language, he urged pious German knights to take up arms against chapters, cloisters, and abbacies, all 'plunderers of the bodies, souls, honor, and goods' of kings and noblemen."[41] The same was true during the Peasants' Revolt in Germany during the sixteenth century.[42] Antichrist rhetoric also exploded during the English Civil War of the seventeenth century, which McGinn concludes "was arguably the last major political event, in western Europe at least, in which Antichrist beliefs played a significant role."[43]

Apart from Antichrist language and application, eschatological language and motifs have proven to be important in other ways, particularly in times of crisis and social change. For example, in American history, Roger Williams founded the state of Rhode Island and was a pioneer of religious toleration and rights for native Americans. McGinn notes that "it is often forgotten that he arrived at these forward-looking views on the basis of a deeply apocalyptic theology of history."[44] America's first-generation Puritan ministers such as John Cotton expounded the book of Revelation and tied it to the mission of the colonists in New England to "add incentive and urgency to New England's special mission."[45] Harry Stout observes that "millennial speculations and predictions also played a supporting role in arousing public support for war [the French and Indian War of 1754–1763]."[46]

Although prior to the outbreak of the American Revolution in 1775 millennial rhetoric played no significant part in justifying opposition to England's policies, Stout

---

and motifs were an important ground for support of the first crusade in the eleventh century, that was not the case. Ibid., 121; see also McGinn, *Visions,* 88–89.

38. McGinn, *Anti-Christ,* 185–87.

39. Ozment, *Protestants,* 47.

40. Ibid., 45–46. Ozment states that "Protestant authors produced perhaps as many as ten thousand different titles by 1550." Ibid., 46.

41. Ibid., 48.

42. McGinn, *Anti-Christ,* 213–17.

43. Ibid., 225. Charles Reagan Wilson adds, "By the late 1640s, more extreme millennial sectarians, such as the Fifth Monarchists, shocked mainstream Protestant reformers by calling Presbyterianism—of all things—the Beast of Revelation. Each event of the Civil War promoted more extreme language, moving well beyond the desires of middle-class reformers." Wilson, "American Civil War," 398.

44. McGinn, *Anti-Christ,* 239.

45. Stout, *New England Soul,* 48–49.

46. Ibid., 246.

finds, "With the onset of war, however, it played a vital role in affirming that the struggle was more than a constitutional dispute; it was part of a foreordained plan to establish a new order for the ages that would prevision, in civil and religious forms, the shape God's millennial kingdom would eventually assume in the fullness of time."[47] Interestingly, just as in 1639–40 John Cotton had used the account of the woman flying to the wilderness (Rev 12:14) to encourage his New Englanders to be steadfast in their mission to make New England a model of true faith against "Popish Superstition and Idolatry," so in 1776 Samuel Sherwood used the same text to maintain that the beast who was trying to destroy the church was not limited to the Roman Empire, or Roman Catholicism, but included "all enemies of Christ's church and people," specifically, George III and England.[48]

Again, in the American Civil War (1861–1865), most Northern clergy viewed the war in apocalyptic terms, as God's instrument for ushering in the millennium.[49] African Americans in particular, according to Charles Wilson, "expressed concrete millennial hopes for the war. The Day of Jubilee seemed so dramatic an expectation that blacks developed premillennial visions, seeing their freedom perhaps as the beginning of a new kingdom brought on in an awful conflagration."[50]

Perhaps America's most popular song of that era, and most important battle song, "The Battle Hymn of the Republic" by Julia Ward Howe, first published in 1862, is saturated with Scripture and eschatology. The first stanza and chorus go:

> Mine eyes have seen the glory of the coming of the Lord:
> He is trampling out the vintage where the grapes of wrath are stored;
> He hath loosed the fateful lightning of His terrible swift sword:
> His truth is marching on.
> (Chorus)
> Glory, glory, hallelujah!
> Glory, glory, hallelujah!
> Glory, glory, hallelujah!
> His truth is marching on.

The first line is based on Christ's statements in the Olivet Discourse concerning the second coming. "Trampling out the vintage where the grapes of wrath are stored" is based on Rev 14:18–20; 19:15 and the apocalyptic text of Isa 63:3. The "fateful lightning" derives from the lightning that emanates from the throne of God that accompanies the

---

47. Ibid., 307.

48. Ibid., 48–49, 308–9.

49. Chesebrough, *God Ordained*, 88–89; Wilson, "American Civil War," 399.

50. Wilson, "American Civil War," 399. Even the South saw the war in millennialistic terms, although the Southern version (at least the *white* Southern version, not that of the slaves) allowed for slavery in the looked-for millennium. Chesebrough, *God Ordained*, 226–27. This recalls to one's mind Shakespeare who said in *The Merchant of Venice*, "The devil can cite Scripture for his purpose." I.iii.99; see Matt 4:1–11; Luke 4:1–13. That is not to denigrate the southerners as devils. Lincoln perceptively and charitably stated in his speech on the Kansas-Nebraska Act, "They are just what we would be in their situation." Lincoln, *Speeches and Writings*, 315. However, this example highlights the fact that people can and do use eschatological language (and Scripture in general) to advance their own agendas, not God's. That is just another way of putting the primary underlying issue: Who really is our Lord? Who or what is primary to us? Who or what is setting our agenda: Christ and his word; or ourselves, our culture, and our circumstances?

parousia.[51] His "terrible swift sword" draws on Rev 19:15 and Isa 27:1. Thus, apocalyptic imagery is powerful visually, in writing, and when set to music. It moves people. It has been employed in support of good causes and bad—which should cause those using eschatological language, themes, and images to reflect on why and how they are using them, since eschatology is an important part of the word of God. But eschatology should not be ignored.

The differences between the various eschatological views suggest that, to the extent that Christians act consistent with their beliefs, eschatology may affect evangelism, social action, and other practical aspects of Christian living

"Most human beings act from a complex tangle of motives, impulses, and values; absolute consistency is rare."[52] A person's view of eschatology is *one* influence why someone acts the way he does. Of course, other theological, secular, political, economic, relational, and personal factors motivate people to act in different ways. Nevertheless, it is reasonable to assume that eschatology is important. Travis mentions the logic of eschatology vis-à-vis social change: "to regard the kingdom as wholly future or a wholly other-worldly phenomenon normally leads to a conservative attitude towards social change, and to a narrow view of the church's mission in terms of rescuing individuals out of a fallen world. By contrast, those who stress that the kingdom of God is already at work in the world are likely to argue for radical social change and for a view of mission which refuses to limit its scope to the spiritual deliverance of individuals out of the world into the safety of the church."[53] In fact, there are clear historical correlations between Christians' eschatological views and how they live their lives, particularly with respect to evangelism and social action.

Eschatology, evangelism, and Christian social action: postmillennialism

The basic outlook of postmillennialism toward history and humanity's future

Grudem summarizes postmillennialism's basic outlook on history as follows, "The primary characteristic of postmillennialism is that it is very optimistic about the power of the gospel to change lives and bring about much good in the world."[54] Today, most preterists are postmillennial in their eschatology and thus share the same essentially optimistic philosophy of history.[55]

---

51. Rev 4:5; 8:5; 11:19; 16:18.
52. Boyer, *When Time,* 302.
53. Travis, *I Believe,* 49–50.
54. Grudem, *Systematic Theology,* 1111; see also Grenz, *Millennial Maze,* 184.
55. Pate, "Introduction," 23.

Historical trends: social engagement; a focus on this world; the rise of the "social gospel"

Partial preterist and postmillennialist Kenneth Gentry states that the eschatological theme of the victory of the gospel "is most influential in promoting a full-orbed Christian witness and Bible-based social activism."[56] As a result of postmillennialism's essentially optimistic view of the divine power of the Spirit now at work through the church, Stanley Grenz concludes:

> Postmillennialists tend to focus their attention on the present situation, finding in it only a few, albeit challenging, impediments to the full realization of the blessed society. And they are hopeful that the soon overcoming of these remaining problems might just mark the dawning of the reign of God. At its best, then, the postmillennial world view leads to engagement in the world. . . . It is no historical accident that by and large the great thrusts toward worldwide evangelistic outreach and social concern in the modern era were launched by a church imbued with the optimism that characterizes postmillennial thinking.[57]

For example, the Puritans were mostly postmillennialists. Their eschatology affected their attitude toward their mission as they left Europe and settled in the "New World." Avihu Zakai explains that the Puritans "believed themselves sent by God's divine providence into exile in America to establish Christ's Kingdom upon the stage of the world. This divine plan would eventually transform the world into the Kingdom of God. They confidently expected their own rigorous adherence to God's Word would lead to the millennial rule of Christ, and, consequently, to the establishment in New England of the utopian New Jerusalem described in the Book of Revelation."[58]

Eschatological thinking continued to exert its influence in America long after the Puritans were gone. Grenz states, "Perhaps nowhere was this American Christian utopianism speaking the language of the Apocalypse more pronounced than in the antislavery movement. . . . When victory came, postmillennial optimism anticipated a new day for the nation. . . . But the victory over slavery did not result in the millennial era. Other evils remained in the land. As a result, the postmillennial spirit with its visions of a Christianized society fostered other reformist movements—women's suffrage, temperance and even the social gospel."[59]

The influence of eschatology on one's broader theology is seen in the rise of Christian liberalism and the "social gospel" movement of the latter half of the nineteenth century. Postmillennialism tends to stress the continuity between the things of this age and the millennium. The tendency of postmillennialists to identify with contemporary society augmented the rise of theological liberalism and the more secular orientation of the social gospel movement. Proponents of the social gospel felt that "social transformation rather than individual conversions [was] considered the sign of the kingdom."[60] By Christian-

---

56. Gentry, *Dominion*, 16.

57. Grenz, *Millennial Maze*, 185.

58. Zakai, "Theocracy in Massachusetts," 23.

59. Grenz, *Millennial Maze*, 58.

60. Erickson, *Christian Theology*, 1214; see also Grenz, *Millennial Maze*, 185–86, 188.

izing the social order and economic structure, the hope was that discrimination, injustice, and war would wither away. Those hopes were largely overturned by World Wars I and II and postmillennialism declined, although, as noted earlier, it has staged something of a comeback in recent years.

Historical trends: a resurgence of postmillennial activism from the left and right

Liberation theology

In the 1970s, from the left side of the political spectrum, liberation theology arose among South American peasantry. Its insistence on changing unjust social and economic structures echoed the social gospel movement of the nineteeth and early twentieth centuries and amounted to a "reassertion of the optimistic world view of the older postmillennialism."[61] Liberation theology arose largely within Roman Catholicism (since much of South America is Roman Catholic) but also included Protestant contributions. Despite certain criticisms, in general the Roman Catholic hierarchy has recognized "the positive aspects of liberation theology, especially with reference to the poor and the need for their liberation, as forming part of the universal heritage of Christian commitment to history."[62]

Christian Reconstructionism

Postmillennialism has also been expressed in recent theologically conservative movements. Grenz states, "Among Pentecostals this rebirth of postmillennialism has carried the banner of the 'kingdom now' theology. Perhaps more significant, however, has been the politically conservative social-theological movement, which emerged in the 1970s and 1980s under the banner of 'Christian reconstructionism,' or 'dominion theology.'"[63] Christian reconstructionists "claim that our God-ordained obligation includes enforcing obedience in society to the divine law revealed in the Bible. In fact, the goal of reconstructionists is nothing less than the establishment of 'a Christian Republic, where God's law rules.'"[64]

Paul Boyer notes a distinction between postmillennialists of the latter nineteenth and the latter twentieth centuries: "While postmillennialists of an earlier day had focused on issues of social justice, the Reconstructionists were more interested in imposing their own (they saw it as Christ's) stern morality on the world."[65] Boyer's observation concerning the liberal emphasis on social justice and the conservative emphasis on individual morality is interesting and astute. That phenomenon is not limited to postmillennialists. We will see it recur in rather extreme form when we look at dispensational premillennial-

---

61. Grenz, *Millennial Maze*, 193.
62. Boff and Boff, *Liberation Theology*, 77.
63. Grenz, *Millennial Maze*, 194.
64. Ibid., 82.
65. Boyer, *When Time*, 303.

ists. The dichotomy between the emphasis on social justice and individual moral behavior indicates that *both* sides of the divide have truncated theologies. The Bible has much to say about social justice *and* morality. This issue obviously transcends eschatology. But the historical correlation between eschatological views and an emphasis or de-emphasis of various social, political, and moral positions suggests the importance of eschatology as an influence on one's overall social-political-moral worldview.[66]

Environmentalism

Janel Curry-Roper has done a study of the relationship between eschatological views and one's attitude toward the environment. She found that modern reconstructionist postmillennialists hold that "the earth is to be treated with respect because it is under the sovereignty of God. . . . Their land ethic, however, seems closely, if woodenly, strapped to Old Testament law as represented in the Hebrew Scriptures. . . . This limitation keeps these postmillennialists from a full and mature elaboration of a viable land ethic."[67]

Eschatology, evangelism, and Christian social action: premillennialism

The basic outlook of premillennialism (especially dispensational premillennialism) toward history and humanity's future

Premillennialsim, especially dispensational premillennialism, has an almost opposite outlook on history compared to postmillennialism. It displays a basically pessimistic view concerning history and our role in its culmination.[68] In other words, all the efforts of Christians in the world will not lead to the reformation of society. Rather, Antichrist will arise. The kingdom will not come gradually through the church but will be inaugurated by the cataclysmic event of the second coming.

Historical trends: dispensationalist social disengagement

Boyer, who noted the difference between the social and moral emphases among liberal and conservative postmillennialists, also observes the historical influence of dispensational premillennialism on social activism: "Logically, the premillennial outlook seemed to imply passivity, since society's evils and injustices merely bore out the prophesied degeneracy and wickedness of the present age. And, indeed, from John Darby's [dispensationalism's originator in the 1830s] day on, a vast body of premillennialist writing warned against the lure of social activism. . . . Through the Depression and World War II, prophecy writers emphasized the uselessness of human efforts at social betterment: regardless

---

66. One could, of course, also argue the reverse, i.e., that one's pre-existing social-political-moral worldview is shaping or coloring one's eschatology. At minimum, we must be aware of the clear correlation between the two.

67. Curry-Roper, "Contemporary Christian Eschatologies," 164.

68. Grenz, *Millennial Maze*, 185.

of what governments and uplift organizations might do, war, suffering, and conflict were bound to grow worse."[69]

Several studies of dispensational premillennialism have shown that its view of society has significantly affected how its followers engage the world and its problems.[70] Richard Lovelace, for example, recounts that "[one] factor in the breakup of evangelical social concern was a monolithic shift in eschatology which occurred in the latter half of the nineteenth century. Up to this point premillennial, postmillennial and amillennial evangelicals had been united in working and praying toward spiritual, cultural and social renewal. . . . The whole momentum of Dispensational theology moved toward a form of premillennialism which was evangelistically active but socially passive."[71]

Marginalization of the disadvantaged

Dispensationalist premillennial eschatology has contributed to the marginalization of the disadvantaged: "Historian R. Laurence Moore has interpreted the entire course of U.S. fundamentalism as a process by which economically disadvantaged people who might otherwise have challenged the status quo were instead neutralized by their premillennial eschatology, so that their activist impulses, never robust, 'grew weaker as the years passed.'"[72] Unfortunately, that attitude of social passivity is still found among well-known dispensationalists. It is particularly acute when people think that the church is going to be raptured within a few years. B. J. Oropeza reports, "According to Jack Van Impe, 'One who honestly feels that Christ may come at any moment is not involved with this world.' This is diametrically opposed to the spirit of Jesus, who makes helping one's neighbor the criterion for one's entrance into the kingdom of God (Mt 25:31–46; compare Luke 10:25–41; 16:19–31)."[73]

Environmentalism

One example of this social disengagement is the environment. In her study of eschatology and the environment, Curry-Roper found:

> Dispensationalism maintains that the present general direction of history is toward societal and ecological deterioration. The only hope for societal structures is the return of Christ. . . . Little can be done at present. Satan has the upper hand and humankind can only hope and pray for the end to come. . . . Dispensationalism uses information on environmental pollution, concern over the environmental impact of nuclear weapons, and so on, to show how proph-

---

69. Boyer, *When Time*, 298.

70. The most comprehensive study of dispensationalism's approach to evangelism, social activism, and political action, with an emphasis on the importance of the nation of Israel, is Timothy Weber, *On the Road to Armageddon: How Evangelicals Became Israel's Best Friend* (Grand Rapids: Baker Academic, 2004).

71. Lovelace, *Dynamics*, 376–77; see also Truesdale, "Last Things First," 117–18; Weber, *Living in the Shadow*, 215–16; Bloch, *Visionary Republic*, 131; Dayton, *Evangelical Heritage*, 126–28.

72. Boyer, *When Time*, 300.

73. Oropeza, *99 Reasons*, 174; see also Jas 2:15–17.

ecy is being fulfilled, and thus it fosters no active, stewardly response—only idle waiting. Furthermore, dispensational premillennialism is not itself a motivating force for action; rather it has to be purposely set aside in order to justify ecologically responsible action. What, then, is the meaning of Christ's return for the natural world in dispensationalism? The earth seems to have no place in the future—heaven is sought after, not earth. The earth is not a significant part of the redemption plan that began with Christ's resurrection. No theology of the earth exists in contemporary dispensational premillennial thought. The earth is destroyed or perhaps inherited by Jews while Christians inherit heaven. . . . Since heaven, not the earth, is to be inherited by believers upon Christ's return, the present natural world is of little theological consequence.[74]

Professor Al Truesdale similarly wrote that dispensationalism "makes it religiously unnecessary and logically impossible to engage in the long-range commitments to the environment required by a truly serious attitude of ecological stewardship."[75] In his article concerning the impact of eschatology on ecology, Truesdale added, "It is logically impossible and morally contradictory both to embrace this creation as inviolable and at the same time reject it as hopelessly doomed and excluded from God's future. . . . Until evangelicals purge from their vision of the Christian faith the wine of pessimistic dispensationalist premillennialism, the Judeo-Christian doctrine of creation and the biblical image of stewardship will be orphans in their midst. These doctrines will be unable to yield their rich potential for environmental ethics."[76]

Historical trends: moral and political concerns

Reactionary moralism

Dispensational premillennialist social and political engagement, at least in the United States, has largely focused on moral issues such as opposing abortion, pornography, homosexuality, suggestive rock music, and sex and violence on television. Unfortunately, as D. A. Carson comments, "much of this cultural engagement is reactive: fundamentalists spot directions being taken by the broader culture that they feel are immoral or dangerous and adopt strategies to confront them and if possible overturn them. At the risk of generalization, they are reasonably effective at combating what they do not like in the culture even while exhibiting relatively little interest in the ways one should support the culture, working into the worlds of art and music."[77]

In his study of American premillennialism from 1875–1982, Timothy Weber arrived at a similar conclusion: "Some premillennialists assume political and social responsibility.

74. Curry-Roper, "Contemporary Christian Eschatologies," 161–63, 166–67.

75. Truesdale, "Last Things First," 116.

76. Ibid., 118. Guth, Green, Kellstedt, and Smidt, in their analysis of several surveys of clergy, religious activists, political party contributors, and the general public, arrived at similar conclusions. They found that, overall, "conservative [i.e., dispensationalist premillennial] eschatology remains a powerful influence in virtually all samples," and "the complex of ideas in dispensational theology—and not just Biblical literalism—may well condition fundamentalists, Pentecostals, and other evangelicals against active conern with environmental policies." Guth et al., "Faith and the Environment," 374, 377.

77. Carson, *Christ and Culture*, 209.

Naturally, their participation in politics is highly discriminatory. Premillennialists are very selective about what they become involved in. Their approach tends to be individualistic, moralistic, and short-term. That is, they usually refuse to get involved in long-term projects for social transformation."[78] The reason likely flows from the fact that dispensationalism essentially has only a negative view of culture in general; it has not integrated its eschatology into a coherent theology that embraces all areas of life.

Pro-Israel politics

Dispensationalists view the founding of the state of Israel in 1948 to be the "paramount prophetic sign" in history.[79] They have "made Israel the center of their prophetic teaching."[80] The dispensationalist view of Israel clearly influences political opinions. One example of this is a national telephone survey conducted in 2002 of 801 randomly selected Americans concerning their attitudes toward American policy in the Middle East. It found that fundamentalist Christians (in addition to Jews) were the most staunchly pro-Israeli. "The particular questions on which fundamentalists are most distinctive suggest that premillennial dispensationalism is at work among fundamentalists, causing them to see the conflict between Palestinians and Israelis through very different lenses than other Americans."[81] While dispensationalists are not the only ones to support Israel, what is different about dispensationalists is "their deterministic, non-moral approach [i.e., their beliefs that Israel is the elect and that Jewish history is predetermined by God and foretold in prophecy; therefore, Israel's actions need not be evaluated on the basis of moral law] and their eagerness."[82]

Dispensational dualism

Not all dispensationalist premillennialists, of course, are disengaged from society. Leading dispensational premillennialists such as Hal Lindsey and the late Jerry Falwell became politically active in the 1980s. However, as Weber analysed the bases of both men's political prescriptions in relation to their eschatology, he arrived at essentially the same conclusion for both of them: Lindsey "never demonstrates how his diagnosis of and prescription for American political and social life has anything to do with biblical prophecy. His observations and remedies come out of right-wing political ideology and have nothing to do with premillennialism per se. . . . Though his premillennialism led him in one direction, his political commitments led him in another."[83] Likewise, "Falwell is not going against his premillennialist principles. He is merely setting them aside or keeping them separate from his politics, where other values and commitments take precedence."[84]

78. Weber, *Living in the Shadow,* 236; see also Weber, *On the Road,* 56.

79. Lindsey, *Late Great,* 43; see also Wilson, *Armageddon Now,* 132.

80. Weber, *Living in the Shadow,* 209; see also Sizer, *Zion's Christian Soldiers,* 10–19, 40–129.

81. Mayer, "Christian Fundamentalists," 706; see also Sizer, *Zion's Christian Soldiers,* 11–12.

82. Wilson, *Armageddon Now,* 141, 143; see also Weber, *Living in the Shadow,* 204–11.

83. Weber, *Living in the Shadow,* 219–20.

84. Ibid., 221.

Politically active dispensationalists Ed Dobson and Ed Hindson wrote, "Just as there are many passages that describe the end times, there are scores of passages that outline Christian responsibilities in this world. We take both sets of passages seriously. The Bible says that we should be ready for the second coming and that we should be good citizens—the salt of the earth. We do not view those missions as contradictory or mutually exclusive. We will work to better the world because the Bible tells us to, and we will await Christ's return because the Scripture says it will happen."[85] Similarly, moderate dispensationalist Billy Graham said, "We must do what we can, even though we know that God's ultimate plan is the making of a new earth and a new heaven."[86]

Those statements reveal a profound dualism concerning the relationship between dispensationalist eschatology and social action. In other words, dispensationalist eschatology is *divorced* from real life in the here-and-now. Thus, Dobson and Hindson see "two sets" of biblical passages—one on eschatology and one on how to live—but the former has nothing to do with the latter. Such dualism is consistent with Boyer's findings that "most [dispensational] premillennialists vigorously denied that their eschatology led them [to withdraw] from the world around them" but insisted "that their beliefs *did* offer a broad scope for activism—*in the religious arena.*"[87]

That is exactly the response of dispensational premillennialist popularizer Hal Lindsey. In his huge bestseller, *The Late Great Planet Earth,* Lindsey made many predictions, including open persecution of "real Christians," internal chaos from student rebellions and Communist subversion that would cause the United States to cede its power to Western Europe, "a growing desire around the world for a man who can govern the entire world," and geometrically increasing population growth and social problems.[88] Timothy Weber asks, "But what does Lindsey expect premillennialists to *do* about these predictions? His suggestions are religious, not political. Like premillennialists in the past, Lindsey's purposes are overwhelmingly evangelistic and spiritual. . . . Lindsey advises his readers to submit to the Holy Spirit's direction in their lives, read the Bible regularly, and, in the knowledge that the rapture may occur at any moment, take the gospel to others before it is too late."[89]

Those responses confirm Curry-Roper's conclusion: "This view of history and supposed lack of power reinforce a dualistic worldview in which the soul and those things

85. Dobson and Hindson, "Apocalypse Now," 21

86. Graham, *Approaching Hoofbeats,* 196.

87. Boyer, *When Time,* 300, emphasis in original.

88. Lindsey, *Late Great,* 180–86.

89. Weber, *Living in the Shadow,* 215. Donald Dayton observes an historical trend that is consistent with Hal Lindsey's response to perceived social problems: "One of the most striking contrasts between pre-Civil War revivalists [who were predominantly postmillennial in their eschatology,] and those after the war [who were predominantly premillennial and dispensationalist] is that the former founded liberal arts colleges while the latter established Bible schools. To the post-war premillennialist the liberal arts college involved too much affirmation of the cultural values of this world and took time away from the crucial task of getting a minimal knowledge of the Bible before rushing into the inner cities or the mission fields to gather as many souls as possible before the imminent return of Christ." Dayton, *Evangelical Heritage,* 127–28. Dayton parenthetically notes an ironic sequel to this: "One sign of how little premillennial eschatology really influences the practice of contemporary Evangelicals—in spite of the popularity of Hal Lindsey's best-selling interpretations of it—is seen in the fact that over the last generation many of these Bible schools have been gradually transformed into liberal arts colleges!" Ibid., 128.

'spiritual' belong to God while the remainder is 'of the world' and not redeemable. . . . If the New Testament has nothing to say about things not explicitly mentioned, then Christian faith and ethics are limited to personal piety. This restriction allows the balance of one's activities to be left untouched by redemption."[90] Historical data, therefore, seem to confirm that dispensational premillennialism is not part of a truly coherent biblical theology of all of life. The emphasis is on personal piety. Individual dispensationalists may be as active in the social realm as postmillennialists, amillennialists, and historic premillennialists. But if they are so engaged, it is *in spite* of their eschatology rather than *because* of it.

Historical trends: personal evangelism

"While dismissing social reform, premillennialists strongly endorsed missionary work."[91] Evangelism remains a strong concern of dispensational premillennialists today. Several international missions organizations were founded and remain led by dispensationalists. However, dispensationalist eschatology affects the *manner* of evangelism. Boyer reports that dispensationalism's founder, John Nelson Darby, after outlining his end-time scenario, wrote, "This is the evil which is coming, and the world ought to be warned of it, because some may be salutarily frightened at the thought, and led to consider the Word of God."[92] Prophecy's primary value, agreed James Brookes in 1870, was "as a motive to repentance."[93] Consequently, Dwight Wilson reports that, throughout dispensationalism's history, "every conceivably possible prophetic fulfillment," as indicated by geopolitical events, particularly those involving Israel, has been exploited by dispensationalists "for the sake of their prime objective: evangelism. The doomsaying cry of 'Armageddon Now!' was an effective evangelistic tool of terror to scare people into making decisions for Christ and to stimulate believers to 'witness for Christ' to add stars to their heavenly crowns before it was everlastingly too late."[94] Timothy Weber, in his recent study of dispensationalism's influence on evangelism and social action, concluded, "But dispensationalists' understanding of the missionary mandate was different from that of other evangelicals. . . . The church's duty was evangelistic, by which premillennialists meant the widespread and rapid spreading of the gospel to unbelievers, not Christianization, which included the gradual transformation of social, political, and educational instutions along Christian lines."[95]

The dispensationalist approach to evangelism was demonstrated by the Jesus People Movement of the 1960s–1970s, in which many thousands of young people came to faith in Christ. David Di Sabatino did a major study of that movement. One of his findings was:

> The fervent belief in the imminent Second coming of Christ fostered an unshakeable apocalypticism among the majority of Jesus People. Though the Bible states that "no man knoweth the day nor the hour," most Jesus People believed

90. Curry-Roper, "Contemporary Christian Eschatologies," 161–62.
91. Boyer, *When Time*, 97.
92. Ibid., 300.
93. Ibid.
94. Wilson, *Armageddon Now*, 218.
95. Weber, *On the Road*, 60.

that the "rapture" (which would snatch all the Christian believers up to heaven before the end of the world) would occur within their lifetime. . . . Since the last days were quickly approaching, a sense of urgency towards the fate of those still unevangelized developed. Street-corner witnessing efforts were girded by a "turn or burn" mentality. Those that did not accept their message of hope through Jesus Christ were forthrightly told that their choice would exclude them from the "rapture of the church," that they would be damned to hell. . . . [Because of their eschatology] the Jesus People did not readily embrace social amelioration as one of their dominant themes.[96]

Dispensationalist eschatology therefore tends to separate evangelism from a holistic approach to life. Evangelism is focused on getting people to make a "decision for Christ." Little tends to be done to disciple believers to apply their faith. Faith tends to be applied only in the religious arena (e.g., going to church, personal devotions, prayer, Bible study), not in the social arena as well (e.g., the arts, righting injustice, cultural renewal).

Although dispensational premillennialists have been active in personal evangelism, they have done so in spite of their doctrine, rather than because of it

The dispensational doctrine of the "pretribulational rapture" actually "robs the Church of one of the most dynamic incentives for world-wide evangelization."[97] The reason, Ladd states, is that "according to the usual pretribulational interpretation, Matthew 24:14 ["*The gospel of the kingdom shall be preached in the whole world as a testimony to all the nations, and then the end will come*"] does not belong to the Church but to the Jewish remnant which will be brought into existence after the Rapture of the Church to be a witness for God to the nations after the Church has been taken away."[98] Dispensationalist Thomas Ice admits that, according to dispensationalism, "the prophecy of [Matt] 24:14 awaits a future fulfillment, specifically during the future Tribulation."[99] Dispensationalist popularizer Hal Lindsey says that the preaching of the gospel to the whole world (Matt 24:14; Mark 13:10) will be fulfilled by the 144,000 of Rev 7:4–14, whom he claims will be "144,000 Jewish Billy Grahams turned loose on this earth—the earth will never know a period of evangelism like this period. These Jewish people are going to make up for lost time. They are going to have the greatest number of converts in all history."[100]

Such ideas are unbelievable, as Travis points out: "In effect, dispensationalism diminishes the role of the Christian church. It assigns the great commission (Matthew 28:18–20) not to the church but to the Jewish remnant after the rapture of the church. It thus expects the Lord to achieve *after* his coming the work which he has in fact committed

96. Di Sabatino, "Jesus People," 140–42.

97. Ladd, *Blessed Hope*, 146.

98. Ibid., 147.

99. Ice, "Rebuttal," 135.

100. Lindsey, *Late Great*, 111. Lindsey does not seem to notice that nothing is said in the text of Rev 7:4–14 about evangelism at all. See Schnabel, *40 Questions*, 86n.4.

to the church *now,* and for which he has promised the Holy Spirit's power."[101] Thus, the logical consequence of dispensationalism's peculiar doctrines actually is to discourage evangelism since "pretribulationsim sacrifices one of the main motives for world-wide missions, viz., hastening the attainment of the Blessed Hope [i.e., the second coming of Christ]."[102] Any theology that, if logically and consistently acted upon, tends to discourage evangelism and social engagement cannot be biblical.

Eschatology, evangelism, and Christian social action: amillennialism

The basic outlook of amillennialism toward history and humanity's future

Between postmillennial optismism and premillennial pessimism lies amillennialsim. Grenz summarizes what he terms the "realistic" outlook of amillennial eschatology:

> No golden age will come to humankind on earth, except perhaps as the partial triumph now enjoyed by the church in the midst of tribulation. . . . The result is a world view characterized by realism. Victory and defeat, success and failure, good and evil will coexist until the end, amillennialism asserts. . . . Both unchastened optimism and despairing pessimism are illegitimate, amillennialism declares. The amillennialist world view calls the church to "realistic activity" in the world. Under the guidance and empowerment of the Holy Spirit the church will be successful in its mandate (postmillennialism); yet ultimate success will come only through God's grace (premillennialism). The kingdom of God arrives as the divine action breaking into the world (premillennialism); yet human cooperation brings important, albeit penultimate, results (postmillennialism). Therefore, the people of God must expect great things in the present; but knowing that the kingdom will never arrive in its fullness in history, they must always remain realistic in their expectations.[103]

Historical trends: building the kingdom one-step-at-a-time

Historically, most mainstream denominations have been essentially amillennial in their eschatology. Much of the work of founding schools, hospitals, and social service agencies has been carried out under their auspices. By its very nature, amillennial eschatology tends to avoid the excesses of over-identification with or absorption by the world to which some postmillennialists are prone and the withdrawl from the world to which some dispensationalist premillennialists are prone. The amillennialist attitude is well-captured by the following historical example: "At the meeting of the Connecticut Assembly in 1780 there was a sense of approaching judgment, of the world coming to an end. Outside, there was a threatening roll of thunder. The Speaker said, 'Either this is the end of the world or

---

101. Travis, *I Believe,* 154.

102. Ladd, *Blessed Hope,* 146.

103. Grenz, *Millennial Maze,* 186–87.

it is not. If it is not, we should proceed with the business. If it is, I prefer to be found doing my duty.'"[104]

Historical trends: environmentalism

In her study of Christian eschatologies and environmentalism, Curry-Roper joined amillennialism and historic premillennialism together "because they are very similar in their hermeneutic, view of prophecy, view of the kingdom of God, and thus expectations of the future."[105] She found that "amillennialism and historic premillennialism have been the most productive of these three main traditions in writings about the environment and mankind's relationship to it."[106] According to her analysis, the amillennial view regarding the environment and other matters requiring social action may be summarized as follows:

> With the aid of the Holy Spirit, Satan can be beaten back—evidence of the power of God in this age—but he cannot be totally subdued until the return of Christ. . . . This faith in Christ's return motivates amillennialists and historic premillennialists to work towards healing in areas affected by the fall—healing of the divisions between person and person, mankind and nature, and among organisms within the natural realm. It is a call to exhibit rightly dominion—to be an example of substantial healing to the world. . . . Nature is included in mankind's call to heal because of God's concern and power over all. . . . Christians are called to work at this restoration in order to give evidence of the future universal restoration of this very earth that will take place when Christ returns. In this way earth retains its geographic dimension yet has transcendental connotations also.[107]

---

104. Travis, *I Believe*, 219.

105. Curry-Roper, "Contemporary Christian Eschatologies," 164. R. S. Beal Jr.'s defense of premillennialist environmentalism confirms Curry-Roper's view. Beal (a premillennialist) disputes Al Truesdale's claim that (dispensationalist) premillennialism is inconsistent with environmentalism. Beal bases his claim that premillennialists exhibit environment concern on three grounds: (1) Because God places great value on his creation, Christians should also; (2) The rule of life for Christians is "the principle of totally unselfish, wholly giving love"; and (3) "At the return of Christ the earth will be renovated, restored, brought into a new and greater splendor" but will not be burned up or destroyed. Beal, "Can a Premillennialist," 172–77. Beal's first two arguments are not drawn from eschatology but from other biblical commands or concerns (see the discussion of "dispensational dualism," above). His third argument is based on eschatology but is a decidedly *non-dispensational* view of the destruction/renewal of the earth. Thus, while he provides reasons for premillennialists to demonstrate concern for the environment, Beal does not actually answer Truesdale's contention (and thereby implicitly confirms) that *dispensational* premillennialism is, in fact, inconsistent with environmentalism.

106. Curry-Roper, "Contemporary Christian Eschatologies," 164.

107. Ibid., 164–65, 167, citations omitted. Her analysis is confirmed in that amillennialists, along with a few historic premillennialists, have been in the vanguard of writing about the proper Christian view of the environment and ecology. The most important early such work was Francis Schaeffer's *Pollution and the Death of Man*, published in 1970. Truesdale gives a brief summary of the evangelical response to the environmental crisis in his article. Truesdale, "Last Things First," 117.

Eschatology, evangelism, and Christian social action: conclusion

In her study, "Contemporary Christian Eschatologies and Their Relation to Environmental Stewardship," Janel Curry-Roper stated, "I believe that eschatology is the most ecologically decisive component of a theological system. It influences adherents' actions and determines their views of mankind, their bodies, souls, and world-views."[108] Both in the past and present, eschatological views have significantly affected believers' strategies of evangelism and social action (or social passivity). We need to be aware of these historical tendencies. Such awareness is particularly important if our own eschatological view inclines us either to withdraw from active engagement with the world and its problems or inclines us to overestimate our own ability and influence.

We also can draw on the insights and emphases of eschatological positions we reject. Grenz concludes:

> The millennial views all have important points to make concerning this eschatological living [during the "already, but not yet" of the kingdom of God]. . . . The optimism of postmillennialism derives from two foundational truths. First, in the final analysis, God is sovereign over history and is actively engaged in bringing his sovereign goal to pass. . . . But second, this same God has invited us—through Christ has even *commissioned* us—to participate in the advance of the divine reign. . . . Premillennialism reminds us that ultimately it is God, and not our feeble actions, who is the hope of the world. Finally, amillennial realism lifts our sights above the merely historical future to the realm of the eternal God. It reminds us that the kingdom of God is a transcendent reality that can be confused with no earthly kingdom prior to the final transformation of creation. . . . Because of the cosmic dimensions of the vision of corporate eschatology, our ultimate goal is not a golden age on earth, whether preceding or following the return of Christ. Rather, we await with eager anticipation a glorious eternal reality, the new heaven and new earth.[109]

By understanding eschatology, we can have a well-integrated theology that enables us to live authentic Christian lives with confidence and hope. Such lives will demonstrate the present reality of the kingdom while we look forward to the final consummation in all its glory.

---

108. Curry-Roper, "Contemporary Christian Eschatologies," 159.
109. Grenz, *Millennial Maze*, 212–14.

The Four Basic Millennial Views

Four Views[1]	Postmillen-nialism[2]	Amillennialism	Historic Premillen-nialism	Dispensational Premillinialism[3]
Herme-neutics	Historical, grammatical and literary.	Historical, grammatical and literary.	Historical, grammatical and literary.	Historical, grammatical and literary. Tends to favor literal over literary.
Second Coming	Happens after the millennium – hence the prefix post.	Happens after the millennium. Differs with postmill in the nature of the Kingdom.	Happens before the millennium – hence the prefix pre. Differs from dispensational premill by teaching the rapture of the church after the tribulation.	Happens before the millennium – hence the prefix pre. Differs from historic premill by teaching the rapture of the church before the tribulation.
Timing of the King-dom	Kingdom came in 1st century (Matt 3:2; 4:17; 10:7; 12:28; Luke 17:21; and Col 1:13).	Kingdom came in 1st century (Matt 3:2; 4:17; 10:7; 12:28; Luke 17:21; and Col 1:13).	Kingdom came in 1st century (Matt 3:2; 4:17; 10:7; 12:28; Luke 17:21; and Col 1:13).	Earthly kingdom will be established during the future millennium after the second return of Christ. Progressive Ds are willing to say that it was inaugurated in the 1st century.

Nature of the Kingdom	The kingdom is Spiritual in nature. Its effects will gradually affect and visibly dominate all of society.	The kingdom is Spiritual in nature. Its effects cannot be appreciated by carnal eyes, nor comprehended by the unregenerate human intellect (John 18:28–38; 1 Cor 1:18; 2:14). For example, the religious leaders saw the miracles of Jesus; they could not deny them, but attributed them to Beelzebul (Matt 12:24–29).	The kingdom is now established and will be visibly dominate during the future millennial reign of Christ.	The second coming establishes the Kingdom suddenly and cataclysmically. All will feel its effects.
Christ's Reign in the Kingdom	Christ reigns now from heaven. his kingdom will continue to rule until "He has put all enemies under His feet" (1 Cor 15:25)	Christ reigns now from heaven over all things.	Christ reigns now from heaven over all things.	Christ reigns over believers and will reign over the earth with a rod of iron after his second coming. Progressive Ds are willing to admit that Jesus Christ is now reigning in an "already" aspect of the Davidic kingdom and that his reign will be visibly demonstrated on earth worldwide in the "not yet" aspect during the millennium
Description of the Millennium	We are in the millennium now. The millennium will slowly and progressively become a "golden age."	The millennium is the intermediate state and is a literary figure for "completeness of exaltation, security and blessedness" (Warfield). Some amills say the millennium incorporates regeneration (Augustinian view). There will be ups and downs to the influence of the Gospel on earth.	The millennium is future. Christ will reign on earth as a visible King.	The millennium is future. Christ will reign on earth as a visible King.

Dura-tion of the Millen-nium	A prolonged period of time, greater than 1000 years.	A period of more than a thousand years and descriptive of the saints rule with Christ in heaven during the intermediate state.	Can be a prolonged period of time. Some see it to be a literal 1000 years	A literal 1000 years.
Satan's binding & current status	At Christ's death and resurrection, Satan was bound; meaning his ability to deceive the nations was restricted, thus opening the door for worldwide evangelism.	Some amills agree with postmills at this point. However, the binding of Satan in Rev 20:2 specifically refers to Satan's inability to deceive the nations, Gog and Magog (Rev 20:7–9)	Satan is bound after the second coming.	Satan is bound after the second coming.
Great Tribu-lation	Culminated in AD 70	Some believe the Great Tribulation culminated in AD 70 (preterist). Others believe that the Great Tribulation persists until Christ's second coming.	Future 3.5-year period immediately preceding the second coming.	Future 3.5-year period immediately preceding the second coming. Typically believes the church will be raptured before the great tribulation.
Anti-christ	Antichrist is not future but present (1 John 2:18; 4:3) Antichrist is not simply an individual but a multitude (1 John 2:18; 4:3) Antichrist is not so much a person as it is a Christological heresy (1 John 2:22; 2 John 7)	Some believe that there will be a future Antichrist. Others would agree with the postmillennial view of Antichrist.	A future Antichrist (specific individual) will inflict persecution on Christians before the rapture.	A future Antichrist (specific individual) will become the world dictator and persecute both Jews and Christians. He will reach his dominant political position after the rapture

Rapture	The rapture occurs at the end of the millennium when believers who have just been raised from the dead, together with believers who have just been transformed are caught up in the clouds to meet the Lord in the air (1 Thess 4:13–18).	The rapture occurs at the end of the millennium when believers who have just been raised from the dead, together with believers who have just been transformed are caught up in the clouds to meet the Lord in the air (1 Thess 4:13–18).	Posttribula-tion: asserts that the living believers will be raptured at the second coming of Christ, after the tribulation and before the millennium. There are four categories of posttribula-tionists: (a) classic, (b) semi-classic, (c) futur-ist and (d) dispensational.	Pretribulation: rapture of the church will take place before the seven year tribulation foretold in Dan 9:24–27. The church is exempt from God's wrath (1 Thess 1:10) and therefore the great tribulation. Typically argue that the "absence" of the word church in Rev 4–18 indicates the church has been raptured.
The Temple	The temple and the sacrificial system have been done away with by the sacrifice of Jesus (Dan 9:24–27). The New Testament does not teach that the temple will be rebuilt in Jerusalem.	The temple and the sacrificial system have been done away with by the sacrifice of Jesus (Dan 9:24–27). The New Testament does not teach that the temple will be rebuilt in Jerusalem.	The temple and the sacrificial system have been done away with by the sacrifice of Jesus.	The Jewish temple and sacrificial system will be reinstated (Dan 9:24–27; cf. 2 Thess 2:4; Rev 11:1, 2).
Israel	The prophecies and prom-ises to Israel are fulfilled in the Church. Ethnic Jews will ultimately be converted over time through the preaching of the Gospel.	The prophecies and promises to Israel are fulfilled in the Church. Some ethnic Jews will be converted through the preaching of the Gospel; perhaps on a large scale.	The prophe-cies and promises to Israel are fulfilled in the Church. There will be a fu-ture salvation of Israel.	The OT prophecies regarding Israel will be fulfilled during the millennial period when Christ reigns from earthly Jerusalem. Progressive Ds are be-ginning to acknowledge that the church is the first-stage partial fulfill-ment of OT prophecies.

Israel & the Church	The Church is spiritual Israel. It is "the Israel of God." There is neither Jew nor Greek; all are one in Christ.	The Church is spiritual Israel. It is "the Israel of God." There is neither Jew nor Greek; all are one in Christ.	The Church is spiritual Israel. It is "the Israel of God." There is neither Jew nor Greek; all are one in Christ.	Israel and the Church are separate and distinct people in the plan of God. Progressive Ds no longer view Israel and the church as representing two different purposes and plans of God. Both are seen as sharing in the same messianic kingdom of salvation history.
The Church	Church is understood as those called by God out of the world, who in every age have believed the promise(s) of God that the seed of the woman would crush the head of the serpent (cf. Jer 31:31–34). Over time and through tribulation the Church will grow and flourish (Isa 11:9).	Church is understood as those called by God out of the world, who in every age have believed the promise(s) of God that the seed of the woman would crush the head of the serpent (cf. Jer 31:31–34). The Church will continue to hold forth the Word of Life until the Consummation Coming.	Church is understood as those called by God out of the world, who in every age have believed the promise(s) of God that the seed of the woman would crush the head of the serpent (cf. Jer 31:31–34). The Church will continue to hold forth the Word of Life until the second coming when Christ comes to establish his millennial kingdom.	Classics made a sharp distinction between Israel and the church where each represented two different purposes in the plan of God (church is a parenthesis). Progressive Ds are beginning to acknowledge that the church is the first-stage partial fulfillment of OT prophecies.
Historic Expectation[4]	Optimistic. Says that what is holding back the Golden Age of Gospel dominance is the church's unfaithfulness. Cultural mandate will be fulfilled (Gen 1:28).	Optimistic. There will always be true believers, but their witness will not always be believed. Some amills are more optimistic than others. Although it is often overlooked by amills, I believe the cultural mandate will be fulfilled (Gen 1:28).	There will always be true believers, but their witness will not always be believed. Tend to be more pessimistic as history is leading to the Great Tribulation.	There will always be true believers but their witness will not always be believed. Tend to be more pessimistic.

The Hope of the Church	The conversion of the nations through Gospel preaching and the work of the Holy Spirit. Following this, Christ's return and the Consummation (Titus 2:11–14).	Conversion of the elect. Christ's personal, visible, glorious return, which will usher in the Consummation (Titus 2:11–14; Rev 19:11–21).	The personal, visible, glorious return of Christ to establish the millennial kingdom (Titus 2:11–14; Rev 20:1–6) followed by the new heavens and the new earth.	The personal, visible, glorious return of Christ to establish the millennial kingdom (Titus 2:11–14; Rev 20:1–6) followed by the new heavens and the new earth.
Key Texts in Revelation	Rev 19:15, 21 [Gospel Victory]	Rev 12:11; 20:4–6 [intermediate state]	Rev 20:1–10 [millennial kingdom chronologically follows second coming in 19:11–21]	Rev 1:19 [structure of book]; 4:1 [rapture]; 20:1–10 [millennial kingdom chronologically follows second coming in 19:11–21]
Key Concept	Victory! The earth will be full of the knowledge of the LORD as the waters cover the sea (Isa 11:9).	Everyone who wants to live a godly life in Christ Jesus will be persecuted (2 Tim 3:12). Gospel "victory" is defined as overcoming the world, the flesh and the devil (Rev 12:11; 15:2).	Messiah will reign in the future millennium from the earthly Jerusalem (Isaiah 60–62).	OT prophecies regarding the Jewish people will be fulfilled in a literal way. Messiah will reign in the future millennium from the earthly Jerusalem (Isaiah 60–62).
Achilles Heel	Rev 19:15, 21 describes "execution" and not conversion. Postmillennialists define Gospel "victory" differently from Scripture, especially the Apocalypse (Rev 5:5, 6; 12:11; 15:2–4; cf. 2 Tim 3:10–12; Heb 12:1, 2).	If recapitulation is not a principle of Revelation then the amillennial view will be essentially invalidated. If it can be proved that 20:4–6 describes the reign of Christ on earth then amill is done.	If recapitulation is true at certain points in Revelation, then the view is invalidated (i.e., Har-Magedon in 16:13–16; 19:17–21; 20:7–10). If it can be shown that the "first resurrection" of 20:4–6 is not physical then this view is done.	If recapitulation is true at certain points in Revelation, then the view is invalidated (i.e., Har-Magedon in 16:13–16; 19:17–21; 20:7–10). If it can be shown that the "first resurrection" of 20:4–6 is not physical then this view is done.

Adher-ents	Daniel Whitby, A.A. Hodge, Charles Hodge, B.B. Warfield, Loraine Boettner, J. Marcellus Kik, Christian Re-constructionists (fn. 2)	Augustine, Geerhardus Vos, Herman Bavinck, Louis Berkhof, John Murray, Cornelius Van Til, William Hen-driksen, Leon Morris, Anthony Hoekema, Ro-man Catholicism	Irenaeus, Henry Alford, J. Oliver Bus-well, Francis Schaeffer, George E. Ladd, James M. Boice, Mil-lard Erickson	See fn. 3.

1. This appendix is reproduced verbatim as it appeared on the website, http://www.christchurchre-formed.com/revelationbibleoutlines/Chart.pdf, with the permission of the church that posted it. It no longer appears to be available online. The following information was set forth in the original note 1, and the remaining footnotes also are as they appeared on the original document. These tables are adapted from Jack Van Deventer, "Comparison of the Four Millennial Views," *Credenda Agenda*, Vol.10, No. 3, pp. 38–39 and H. Wayne House, *Charts of Christian Theology & Doctrine*, pp. 133–138

2. The most common type of postmillennialism today is theonomic postmillennialism (represented by: Rousas Rushdoony, Greg Bahnsen, Gary North, Kenneth Gentry, Gary DeMar).

3. There are different camps of dispensationalism: (1) "Classical or Scofieldian Dispensationalists" (represented by J.N. Darby, L.S. Chafer, C.I. Scofield), (2) "Essentialist/revised or Normative Dispensa-tionalists" (represented by Zane Hodges, Dwight Pentecost, Charles Ryrie and John Walvoord) and (3) "Progressive Dispensationalists" (represented by Craig Blaising [Joseph Emerson Brown professor of Christian theology at Southern Baptist Theological Seminary and formerly at Dallas Seminary], Darrell L. Bock [Research Prof of NT at Dallas Theological Seminary], Robert L. Saucy [distinguished prof. of systematic theology at Talbot School of Theology], Marvin Pate, Kenneth Barker, David Turner)

4. All four views believe that history will end "on a sour note" with Satan deceiving the nations and gathering Gog and Magog against the camp of the saints (Rev 20:7–10).

While the four basic millennial positions are highly nuanced, the views can be boiled down to two basic issues: (1) *chronology*—i.e., when does the millennium occur and is the church a part of it? and (2) *the nature of the kingdom of God*—Is there a golden age of Gospel victory (postmillennialism)? Will Jesus literally set up a throne in earthly Jerusalem (premillennial-ism)? Is the kingdom something that can only be seen by faith (amillennialism)?

The Millennium:

An Amillennial Synthesis of the Biblical Data

THE AMILLENNIAL POSITION BEST accords with the biblical data. This conclusion is based on the overall structure of biblical eschatology and the structure and language of Revelation 20.

The Structure of Biblical Eschatology

Scripture sets forth a clear, consistent, comprehensive eschatological interpretive grid that rules out premillennialism. That structure is the doctrine of the "two ages" (Greek: *aiōn; "age"):* "this age" and the "age to come."[1]

The Nature of the "Two Ages"

The terminology of the two ages "pervades the New Testament, is homogeneous and provides us with a truly structural concept for biblical eschatology. It means the same thing—assumes the same, basic structure—wherever it is used."[2] There are multiple places in the New Testament where this terminology or a distinctive part of it is used. Two features distinguish this age from the age to come. First, this age and the age to come are *qualitatively different.* This age is temporal; the age to come is eternal. This age is characterized by sin, death, marriage, and all that accompanies life in this body; the age to come is characterized by holiness and new, resurrected life.[3]

Second, the two ages *comprehend all of time,* and the age to come *immediately succeeds* this age. In Matt 12:32, Jesus states that whoever speaks against the Holy Spirit shall not be forgiven "either in this age, or in the age to come." Vos points out, "The very name 'coming aion' is not merely expressive of futurity, but also carries within itself the element of direct successiveness. Were this otherwise, then the entire closely-knit scheme

---

1. The two-age structure of biblical eschatology is discussed in greater detail in the main text, chapter 4–Interpreting Biblical Eschatology in Light of its Overall Structure.

2. Waldron, "Structural Considerations," n.p.n.3.

3. See Riddlebarger, *Amillennialism,* 82–83.

intended to comprehend all happenings in the universe from beginning to end would fall to pieces, because of the lacking link in the middle. To say that a sin will not be forgiven either in this age or in the age to come could never have served as a formula for absolute unforgivableness *ad infinitum*, Matt. xii. 32, if there were conceivable a gap between the two aions."[4] To the same effect is Eph 1:21 which says that Christ is above "*all rule and authority and power and dominion, and every name that is named, not only in this age but also in the one to come.*"

The Overlap of the Two Ages: the "Already" and the "Not Yet"

With the first coming of Christ, the powers of the age to come, which is the age of restoration and God's manifest presence and rule, have "invaded" this age and have been "tasted" by his people.[5] Waldron explains:

> The age to come is the age of the resurrection (Luke 20:34–36). The resurrection has already begun (1 Cor. 15:23). *The age to come* is the age of the reign of God and his Christ. This reign has already begun (Heb. 2:5; cf. 2 Cor. 4:4 and Eph. 2:2). As *this age* is the age of the old creation, so *the age to come* is the age of the new creation. Yet in a sense the new creation has already been inaugurated (2 Cor. 5:17; Gal 6:15).[6]

As a result of Christ's first coming, this age is in its "last days."[7] Although the kingdom of God and reign of Christ have been inaugurated and realized in principle (the "already" of the kingdom), they have not yet been fully manifested but await a future consummation in all their glory (the "not yet" of the kingdom).[8]

The overlapping of the two ages and the "breaking in" of the age to come into this age explains why the Bible constantly assumes a "two-stage" character of salvation: "Justification (Romans 5:1; Matthew 12:37), adoption (Romans 8:14–16 with v. 23 of the same chapter and also Galatians 4:4–6 with Eph. 4:30), and redemption (Ephesians 1:7 with 4:30) with many other of the biblical realities associated with salvation can be spoken of both as past realities and future blessings. This is so because *the age to come* which brings salvation unfolds itself in two stages. There is an overlapping of *this age and the age to come*."[9] Similarly, some of Jesus' parables, such as the parable of the wheat and the tares (Matt 13:24–30, 36–43) and the parable of the dragnet (Matt 13:47–50), speak of the dual nature of the kingdom: currently, good and evil co-exist, but there will come a time of harvest and the separation of good from evil.

4. Vos, *Pauline Eschatology*, 25–26

5. Heb 6:5; see Ladd, "Revelation 20," 173: "The binding of Satan is a work of God's Kingdom in Christ; because of it, the blessings of the eschatological Kingdom, the powers of the Age to Come, may be experienced while we still live in the old age"; see also Wright, *Resurrection*, 332.

6. Waldron, "Structural Considerations," n.p.

7. Acts 2:17; Heb 1:2; Jas 5:3; 1 Pet 1:20; 1 John 2:18; Jude 18.

8. E.g., Hoekema, *Bible and Future*, 13–22; Venema, *Promise*, 12–32; Vos, *Pauline Eschatology*, 38 (helpful diagram).

9. Waldron, "Structural Considerations," n.p.

A specific time exists when "this age" will end and the "age to come" will be fully consummated in all its glory. "The Scriptures explicitly tell us that the line of demarcation between these two ages is our Lord's second advent."[10] All of the biblical passages that deal with the second coming (i.e., the *parousia*) speak of only one coming, or one day, at the end of this age.[11] The *parousia* entails three things:

(1) *Resurrection* of all people, the just and the unjust alike (Dan 12:2; Matt 13:30, 39–42, 48–50; 25:31–32; Luke 17:22–37; John 5:25–29; Acts 24:14–15; Rev 20:11–15);

(2) *Judgment*—rewards for the righteous and punishment for the unrighteous (Matt 7:21–23; 10:32–33 (Mark 8:38); Matt 13:24–30, 36–51; 16:27; 24:42–51; 25:10–13, 14–30, 31–46; Luke 12:35–48; 17:22–37; 19:12–27; 21:26–28; John 5:25–29; Acts 17:31; Rom 2:5–16; 14:10–12; 1 Cor 4:5; 2 Cor 5:10; 2 Thess 1:6–10; 2 Tim 4:1; Heb 6:2; Jas 5:7–9; 2 Pet 3:7–13; Rev 11:18; 14:14–20; 19:11–21; 20:11–15; 22:12); and

(3) *The restoration of creation* (Acts 3:19–21; Rom 8:17–25; Heb 1:10–12, 2 Pet 3:3–13).

The Bible gives no hint of two separate comings and judgments separated by a thousand years.

A clear indication that there is one resurrection and one judgment of both the righteous and the wicked is found in Jesus' teaching in Matt 12:39–42 (Luke 11:29–32) where he says that the men of Nineveh *"will stand up with this generation at the judgment, and will condemn it because they repented,"* and *"the Queen of the South will rise up with this generation at the judgment, and will condemn it, because she came from the ends of the earth to hear the wisdom of Solomon."* "Stand up" is the future middle indicative of *anistēmi*, from which the noun *anastasis* (resurrection) is derived. "Rise up" is the future passive indicative of *egeirō* and so literally means "will be raised up."[12] These are the primary words signifying resurrection in the NT. "At the judgment" and "this generation" "both have eschatological content. The scene painted presupposes a universal judgment for it involves the Ninevites and the Israel of Jesus' time, as well as the queen of the South."[13] Thus, we see the redeemed and the unredeemed from different times and places being resurrected together (i.e., *"with* this generation") at the time of the judgment, with the redeemed playing a part in the judgment of the unredeemed.[14] Further, "the judgment" is

---

10. Riddlebarger, *Amillennialism*, 85; see also Venema, *Promise*, 90–95 ("the return of Christ marks the close of the present age"). See main text, chapter 5–The Eschatological Significance of Christ's Second Coming, for a more detailed discussion of the significance and effects of the *parousia*.

11. Heb 9:28 says that Christ *"will appear a second time,"* not "a second and third time." In fact, in John 5:28–29 Jesus says that there will be *"an* [i.e., one] *hour,"* not two separate hours, when the resurrection of, and eternal rewards and punishments to, both the just and the unjust will occur. Christ could not "come" again after his *parousia* in any event since, even by premillennialist reckoning, he will be on earth following his "second coming."

12. "Both verbs can mean 'will rise up', but in the present context the passive form of the second invites the sense 'will be raised up [by God]'." Nolland, *Matthew*, 512; see also France, *Matthew*, 487n.2, 492n.17.

13. Davies and Allison, *St. Matthew*, 2:358.

14. In addition to denoting resurrection, to "stand up" (*anistēmi*) and "rise up" (*egeirō*) can also mean to appear as a witness in court. See Mealy, *The End*, 150–52 for biblical examples of this. Here the words are being used in both senses.

a noun, and includes the definite article, which specifies that there is only one judgment (as opposed to an indefinite "will rise up *in judgment*").[15]

Premillennialism is Not Compatible with the Bible's "Two-Age" and "Already, But Not Yet" Eschatological Structure

For a premillennial "millennium" to work there must be some form of continued "overlap" between "this age" and the "age to come" even after Christ's second coming. Evil must continue to exit with good; unredeemed, natural, sinful, and mortal people must co-exist with resurrected, sinless, immortal people. However, that flies in the face of the above passages which consistently describe Christ's second coming as entailing the end of the age; the resurrection of both the redeemed and the unredeemed, the judgment of both the righteous and the wicked, and the re-creation of the earth.[16]

---

15. Holleman comments, "The idea here is that the unrighteous generation of Jesus' time will be convicted by the righteous generations of former times, since the latter repented and believed while Jesus' generation did not. In order to judge, the people of Nineveh will rise [*anastēsontai*], i.e., they will share in the eschatological resurrection. The relationship assumed here between resurrection and judgement is traditional: it is often said that people will be raised to be judged." Holleman, *Resurrection and Parousia*, 81–82.

16. Daniel Wallace, a dispensational premillennialist, acknowledges that "amillennialists have had a superior exegesis" of such passages as Matthew 24–25 (the Olivet Discourse), 2 Thessalonians 1, and 2 Peter 3, which show the eternal state ushered in at Christ's second coming. Wallace, "New Testament Eschatology," n.p. Wallace attempts to overcome this by appealing to the doctrine of "progressive revelation." The appeal to "progressive revelation"—i.e., the idea that Rev 20:2–7 merely supplements the rest of NT revelation concerning eschatology by adding a "new detail" (the thousand-year gap between the second coming and final judgment/beginning of the age to come)—fails for several reasons: (1) What is at issue is the meaning (and timing) of the "thousand years" of Rev 20:2–7. To assume that this is a literal period of time after the *parousia begs the very question at issue*. (2) John cannot have added any "new" data in Revelation 20 because, both in his Gospel and in Revelation, he consistently pictures the second coming as entailing exactly what the two-age model and the rest of Scripture describe it as involving, namely, the resurrection and judgment of both the righteous and the unrighteous on the last day of this age. Thus, in John 5:28–29 he records that "an hour" (not two or more) is coming in which "all" (not some) who are in the graves will rise to life or condemnation. In John 6:39–40 he records that Jesus will raise "every" believer (not some) to life "on the last day," and in John 12:48 he records that Jesus will likewise judge all unbelievers "on the last day." In Revelation itself, John records the same thing. In Rev 22:12 he records Jesus saying that he is "coming" quickly to render to "everyone" (not some) according to what he has done. (3) "Progressive revelation" is a legitimate appeal in cases where it augments, but does not fundamentally contradict, other Scriptural revelation. In this case, however, the premillennial interpretation of Rev 20:2–7 fundamentally contradicts multiple passages throughout the NT concerning the nature of the two ages and the nature of the second coming and all that it entails. As such, the premillennial interpretation of Revelation 20 is not a legitimate instance of "progressive revelation" at all. (4) The premillennial interpretation of Revelation 20 is *substantively wrong* because it is *methodologically backwards* (i.e., it is used by premillennialists as the "tail that wags the dog"). Keith Mathison observes, "Premillennialism interprets the clearer texts of Scripture in light of the less clear text. The symbolic passage in Revelation 20 is made the touchstone for end-time chronology, despite the many passages throughout the rest of Scripture which indicate that Jesus was given the messianic kingdom at His first advent. . . . When a difficult text like Revelation 20 is interpreted in such a way that it conflicts with a large number of clearer texts, then we are forced to conclude either that Scripture contradicts itself or that the interpretation is wrong." Mathison, *Postmillennialism*, 176, 263n.4; see also Vos, *Pauline Eschatology*, 226

Appendix 2

Premillennialism contradicts the Bible's "two-age" eschatological structure

Premillennialism is inherently incapable of placing the "millennium" *anywhere* consistent with the Bible's two-age structure. Waldron summarizes the fatal nature of the Biblical doctrine of the two ages to any idea of post-*parousia* provisional or temporary "millennium":

> Where in the two-age structure can the millennium be placed? Shall it be put in this age or in *the age to come*? The fact is that it fits into neither age. Why does it not fit in *this age*? Because the millennium occurs after Christ's second coming. Why does it not fit in *the age to come*? Because no wicked men in an unresurrected condition remain in that age. When we remember that there is no intermediate period between the two ages and no other period beside the two ages, no place for premillennialism remains.[17]

Premillennialism contradicts the unity of the *parousia*, the one general resurrection, and the one general judgment

The idea of two physical resurrections separated by a thousand years also contradicts multiple passages concerning the *unity* of the general resurrection with the "day" or "hour" of the Lord and the voice, shout, and trumpet that herald the resurrection. David Brown points out, "It is quite true that the words 'day' and 'hour' in Scripture . . . are often equivalent to *time* or *period;* yet always as meaning the *definite* or *fixed* period of the thing spoken. . . . The *unbroken continuousness* of it . . . is essential to the very propriety of the language."[18] In other words, it is not the *length of time* that the word "hour" marks but the unity of the *period* and the *action* occurring in it. Thus, Dan 12:2 and John 5:28–29 both speak of the simultaneous resurrection of the righteous and the wicked; the righteous are raised to life and the wicked to judgment (damnation).

On the other hand, the premillennialist view "is in no sense *one unbroken resurrection*-hour. For . . . all the righteous are to rise together *before* the millennium, and the wicked are to rise in a body not even at the *end* of the millennium—not within the millennial 'hour' at all, therefore—but *at the end of another period to succeed the millennium;* a period which, though it be called 'a little season' (Rev. xx. 3), relative to 'the thousand years,' may, according to that way of reckoning, extend over two or three hundred years."[19]

Additionally, John 5:28–29, 1 Cor 15:51–52 and 1 Thess 4:16 speak of the resurrection occurring with a "voice," "shout," and "trumpet." Since the voice/shout/trumpet announces the resurrection, it must either raise both the righteous and the wicked together, which is the natural meaning of what the Bible says, or it must be uttered *twice*: "it must sound, that is, before the millennium to raise the righteous, and, after a silence of more than a thousand years, it must sound again to raise the wicked. Can anything more unnatural be forced upon the simple and majestic words of our Lord? No: The trumpet-sound is *one*."[20]

---

17. Waldron, "Structural Considerations," n.p.
18. Brown, *Christ's Second Coming,* 191, emphasis in original.
19. Ibid., 192, emphasis in original.
20. Ibid., 193, emphasis in original.

Premillennialism contradicts the Bible's description of the nature of existence after the second coming

Premillennialism entails the belief that people in natural bodies and resurrected people will co-exist. However, none of the passages detailing the two ages hint of glorified and natural people co-existing. That idea contradicts the very nature of the second coming which ends "this age" and begins the "age to come," when the temporal has passed away and there are no marriages or sexual relationships.[21] Further, inherent in premillennialism is the idea that sin and death continue to exist after the second coming. That likewise is contradicted by the qualitative difference between the two ages and the triumphal consummation of history by Christ at the second coming:

> The most serious problem to be faced by all premillenarians is the presence of evil in the millennial age. . . . The last day has already come, and our Lord has raised his own and sent those who are not his into the fires of eternal judgment. There simply cannot be people in unresurrected bodies on the earth after our Lord's return, for the wheat has already been separated from the weeds (Matt. 13:37–43), the sheep have already been separated from the goats (Matt. 25:31–46), and the elect have already been gathered from the four corners of the earth by the angelic host (Matt. 24:30–31).[22]

Christ's second coming will inaugurate the eternal state (the "age to come"), not a penultimate and temporary state (the "millennium"). Premillennialism turns the second coming, which is the climax of this age, into an anti-climax.[23] Consequently,

21. See chapters 4 and 5 in the main text regarding the nature of the two ages and the significance of the second coming. J. Webb Mealy's new creation millennialism does not entail this problem.

22. Riddlebarger, *Amillennialism,* 86–87. The extent of this problem is discussed in greater detail in the critique of historic premillennialism in the main text, chapter 7–The Millennium. As was also discussed in that chapter, J. Webb Mealy's new creation millennialism does not solve this problem.

23. Garlington remarks, "Therefore, we must take exception to those chiliastic [premillennialist] schemes which confuse this pattern by placing more emphasis on the (supposed) penultimate rather than ultimate stage of the work of Christ." Garlington, "Reigning," n.p.

The attempt by dispensationalists to salvage their system by maintaining that the "day of the Lord" means the entire period from the second coming to the end of the "millennium" a thousand years later (Pentecost, *Things to Come,* 231) is without exegetical basis. That certainly is not the "literal" meaning of any of the passages that refer to the day of the Lord. Rather, that idea is based simply on the *a priori* presuppositions of dispensational premillennialism in order to make their scheme fit a passage such as 2 Pet 3:3–13. Such an "expanded" notion of the "day of the Lord" results in a forced and unnatural understanding of 2 Peter 3:3–13 for several reasons, as Waldron explains:

> Our objection is not that the *Day of the Lord* is literally a day of 24 hours, it is rather based on the following considerations: (1) Verse 10 would have to read not "in which" but "at the end of which." The natural significance of 2 Peter 3:10 is, however, that when Christ comes the world is immediately (not 1000 years later) destroyed. (2) This understanding contradicts the clear implication of the passage that the destruction of the *Day of the Lord* is swift destruction. The analogy of the flood implies (v. 6) swift destruction (Matt. 24:37–44; Luke 17:22–27). The analogy of the thief (v. 10) implies swift destruction (Matt. 24:42, 43; 1 Thess. 5:2f.). A destruction that takes place over a period of 1000 years is anything but swift and sudden. (3) This theory ignores the fact that in the New Testament and in 2 Peter 3:3–13 the *day of the Lord* is a synonym for the *parousia.* To affirm that the *day of the Lord* lasts over 1000 years is analogous to affirming the same with reference to the *parousia*—a ludicrous thought. Verse 9 makes plain that the alternative to repentance before the *parousia* is perishing. This, a 1000 year *parousia* or day of the Lord does not account for. (4) The analogy between the flood and the day of the Lord undermines this

premillennialism's view of the *parousia* is seriously inadequate. Vos rightly concludes, "The *parousia* taken as an event with Paul is catastrophic. Of a development within the limits of the concept, or a duplication or triplication of the event there is nowhere any trace. It is a point of eventuation, not a series of successive events. . . . To conceive of Paul as focusing his mind on any phase of relative consummation, and as tying up to this the term '*parousia*,' inevitably would involve his relegating the eternal things to a rank of secondary importance."[24]

Premillennialism contradicts the two-stage ("already, but not yet") nature of the kingdom of God

The premillennial view of a post-*parousia* "millennium" flies in the face of those passages that describe the kingdom as having a two-stage nature: an inaugurated ("already") stage, and a consummated ("not yet") stage. This is seen when we compare Christ's parable of the wheat and the tares (Matt 13:24–30, 36–43), 1 Cor 15:20–28, and Revelation 20, all of which address the nature of the kingdom. The following table makes this graphically clear:

The Coming Of The Kingdom	
Matthew 13	
Messiah Sower Mixed Kingdom	Messiah Harvester Perfected Kingdom
1 Corinthians 15	
Christ Resurrected; enthroned Reign of Conquest	Christ's *Parousia*; resurrected Consummate State
Revelation 20	
Satan Bound Reign of Christ (1000 Years)	Satan Burned New Heavens and Earth

Waldron explains:

> The significance of this comparison of Matthew 13, 1 Corinthians 15, and Revelation 20 is striking in its graphic rebuttal of a premillennial interpretation of Revelation 20. The coming of Messiah as sower and then harvester in Matthew 13 marks respectively the inauguration and consummation of the kingdom. The resurrection of Christ as firstfruits and then those who are Christ's at his coming marks respectively the inauguration and consummation of the kingdom in 1 Corinthians 15. In precisely the same way the binding and burning of Satan marks the inauguration and consummation of the millennial kingdom in

---

theory. The day of the Lord like the flood is a catastrophic event not an age-long period of time.

Waldron, "General Judgment," n.p. See also Bauckham, "Delay of the *Parousia*," 23 ("There is actually no parallel [in contemporary Jewish or Christian literature] to the idea that the day of judgment would last a thousand years, and it is difficult to see how it could fit into the eschatology of 2 Peter 3").

24. Vos, *Pauline Eschatology*, 76.

Revelation. The plain implication is that Satan's binding is coincident with the coming of Christ as sower and His resurrection as firstfruits, while [h]is burning is coincident with His second coming as harvester to resurrect His people.[25]

Beale concludes, "Just as the Devil's captivity is limited to a thousand years [(Rev 20:1–3), but is then thrown into the lake of fire forever (Rev 20:10)], the saints intermediate reign [Rev 20:4–6] is likewise limited, but is followed by a consummate stage of reigning in eternity."[26] Only the amillennial view is consistent with both the "two ages" and the "already, but not yet" nature of the kingdom. Premillennialism cannot account for either and is inconsistent with both.

Revelation 20

Premillennialists of all camps agree that the only place in the entire Bible which explicitly, if not also implicitly, speaks about a "millennium" (the "thousand years") is Rev 20:2–7.[27] Since Revelation 20 is the sole exegetical pillar of premillennialism, the premillennialist "must prove that Revelation 20 teaches a future millennium and that no other interpretation is possible. If there is another feasible interpretation of this passage, then premillennialism is left without its central exegetical pillar."[28] The amillennial view of Revelation 20 not only fits the Bible's "two-age" and "already, but not yet" framework but also gives a "logical, consistent, penetrating, and relevant interpretation of [Revelation 20] itself."[29]

Revelation 20 recapitulates, rather than follows, the events of Rev 19:11–21

Premillennialists must view the events of Revelation 20 as chronologically following, rather than recapitulating, those of Rev 19:11–21. The book of Revelation as a whole, however, demonstrates a "progressively parallel" recapitulative structure.[30] Even dispensationalists concede that one characteristic feature of the book is the fact that related events do not follow a chronological order but later passages recapitulate and amplify earlier depictions of the same event.[31] For example, dispensationalists agree that Revelation 12–19 recapitulates the events of Revelation 4–11.[32] Consequently, there can be no

---

25. Waldron, "Eschatological Kingdom," n.p.

26. Beale, *John's Use,* 377.

27. Blaising and Bock, *Progressive Dispensationalism,* 273 (progressive dispensationalists); Ladd, "Revelation 20," 167 (historic premillennialist); Mounce, *Revelation,* 367 (historic premillennialist); Wallace, "New Testament Eschatology," n.p. (classic dispensationalist).

28. Waldron, "Eschatological Kingdom," n.p.

29. Ibid.

30. Hendriksen, *More Than Conquerors,* 16–23; Hoekema, *Bible and Future,* 223–26; Beale, *Revelation,* 121–51. See the main text, chapter 11, particularly the section "Structure: progressively parallel; not strictly chronological."

31. Even adamant dispensationalist Chuck Smith states, "There is one aspect of the book of Revelation that sometimes makes it difficult to understand or follow—the related events do not always follow a chronological order. Many times John will describe the overall scene and then return to fill in the details and amplify some of the earlier descriptions." Smith, *What the World,* 135.

32. Pentecost, *Things to Come,* 187–88; see also Mueller, "Recapitulation," n.p.

objection *in principle* to the amillennial view that Revelation 20 recapitulates the period covered by Rev 19:11–21. The following factors show that Revelation 20 does, in fact, recapitulate Rev 19:11–21.[33]

The theme of angelic ascent and descent

Rev 20:1 begins with the descent of an angel from heaven to bind Satan for "a thousand years." Throughout Revelation, when an angel is said to ascend or descend and begin a new vision sequence, "without exception it introduces a vision either suspending the temporal progress of a preceding section to introduce a synchronous section [10:1] or reverting to a time anterior to the preceding section [7:2 and 18:1]."[34] The angel's descent in 20:1 therefore is consistent with the prior pattern of angelic ascent or descent if the events of Revelation 20 recapitulate Rev 19:11–21 but is inconsistent with that pattern if Revelation 20 chronologically follows the events of Rev 19:11–21.

The discrepancy between Rev 19:11–21 and Rev 20:1–3, 8

In Rev 19:11–21, Christ triumphs over and destroys all nations that are opposed to his kingdom. The language of Christ's victory is complete, final, and total. If Revelation 20 is read chronologically, it is senseless to speak of binding Satan in order to prevent his deceiving the nations since the nations which were formerly deceived by Satan have been completely vanquished. The language of Revelation 19 is too absolute to allow for rebellious survivors. Mealy points out, "The sense of these words [Rev 19:20–21] is as plain as it is consistent with the pattern leading up to them: no one on earth survives the confrontation with the returning Christ."[35]

White adds that the premillennialists' attempt to solve the problem by claiming that the nations of 20:3 are survivors of the battle of 19:19–21[36] "is transparently gratuitous, for it derives its force, at least in part, from the very point in question, viz., whether the order in which the visions of 19:11–20:3 are presented reflects the sequence in which the events depicted there will occur in history."[37] He concludes, "Any historical relationship among the visions must be *demonstrated* from the *content* of the visions, not simply *presumed* from the *order* in which John presents them."[38]

That same criticism applies to premillennialist attempts to solve the problem by claiming that only "armies," not "nations," were killed and that the survivors are "earthdwellers who supported but were not a part of the army."[39] The language of the passage is all-comprehensive and permits no exceptions. Rev 16:14 speaks of gathering "*the kings of*

---

33. These factors, except the last one, "the destruction of death," are based on Venema, *Promise*, 305–15; White, "Reexamining," 319–44; White, "Making Sense," 539–51; Beale, *John's Use*, 359–71.

34. Beale, *Revelation*, 975.

35. Mealy, *After the Thousand Years*, 91; see also Schnabel, *40 Questions*, 237.

36. E.g., Mounce, *Revelation*, 363

37. White, "Reexamining," 323–24.

38. Ibid., 324.

39. Osborne, *Revelation*, 702.

the whole world" for the battle. Rev 19:18–21, in progressively parallel fashion, adds detail and speaks of "kings and armies." It then specifically defines those kings and armies to include *everyone* who does not worship the Lamb: "kings" and "commanders" and *"mighty men"* and *"horses and those who sit on them"* and *"all men, both free men and slaves, and small and great"* (v. 18), and the "beast" and the *"kings of the earth and their armies"* (v. 19), and the *"false prophet"* (v. 20), and *"the rest"* (v. 21). That is consistent with Rev 20:8 which likewise describes the opponents of Christ at the final battle in all-inclusive terms: *"the nations which are in the four corners of the earth, Gog and Magog . . . the number of them is like the sand of the seashore."* The all-inclusive nature of the dead is indicated by Rev 19:21 which says that the dead are *"killed with the sword which came from the mouth of Him who sat on the horse."* Rev 19:15 describes the purpose of the "sword" as being *"so that with it He may strike down the nations"* (not just "kings" or "armies").[40]

The universal, all-inclusive nature of this battle and judgment is also seen in Rev 19:18 which describes those involved as *"small and great."* That description (along with *"free men and slaves"*) is based on Rev 13:16 which describes the *"false prophet"* as causing "all" people to be given the *"mark of the beast."* Thus, consistent with the rest of Revelation, all of humanity is pictured as having either the mark of the beast or the seal of the Lamb.[41] That the picture of "the great supper of God" in Rev 19:17–21 includes all of humanity and not just a portion of it is corroborated in that the same *"small and great"* language (in reverse order, *"the great and the small"*) is used in Rev 20:12 to describe the all-inclusive nature of the "Great White Throne Judgment." White concludes, "In other words, the discrepancy consists in this: it makes no sense to speak of protecting the nations from deception by Satan in 20:1–3 after they have just been both deceived by Satan (16:13–16, cf. 19:19–20) and destroyed by Christ at his return in 19:11–21 (cf. 16:15a, 19)."[42]

The use of Ezekiel 38–39 in these visions

Rev 19:17–18 quotes from the Gog-Magog conflict in Ezek 39:17–20. In Rev 20:7–10, which describes the great warfare that will conclude the millennium, John again draws

---

40. "Nations" obviously is an all-inclusive term that encompasses all individuals as well as nation-states. Thus, the premillennialists' attempt to distinguish "armies" from "nations" or "people who supported he armies but were not actual soldiers" is nonsensical and contrary to the thrust of the entire passage. That is seen clearly in Rev 20:8 where the "nations" are deceived and are *"like the sand of the seashore."* When the fire from heaven "devoured them" (20:9), obviously all *individuals* were devoured, not just political or other entities. Premillennialists do not attempt to distinguish individuals from nations in 20:8–9. That implicitly shows that the attempt to distinguish survivors, or supporters, from armies in 19:19–21 is illegitimate.

41. See Johnson, *Triumph*, 285–86n.31. The reference to *"free men and slaves"* is significant for another reason. Schnabel points out, "In antiquity, only free people fought in armies, not slaves. . . . This means that Revelation 19:17–21 does not describe an actual military battle between armies but the confrontation between the followers of the Beast and (the followers of) Jesus Christ." Schnabel, *40 Questions*, 226; see also ibid., 237, 288. Thus, both Mounce's "survivors of the battle" and Osborne's "supporters but not actual soldiers" views are wrong exegetically for the reasons stated above but also are fundamentally wrong hermeneutically because they are based on the flawed hermeneutic of "literalism" when interpreting apocalyptic literature.

42. White, "Reexamining," 321.

from the Gog-Magog conflict of Ezekiel.[43] The premillennial scheme has the identical language and imagery from the same episode of a single prophecy described by Ezekiel, but has such identical language and imagery refer to two different episodes in history, separated by a thousand years. A far more plausible reading is that the visions of Revelation 19 and 20 describe the same event as parallel descriptions of the same historical period.[44]

"The battle" (or "the war") of Rev 19:19 and 20:8

Rev 16:14, 19:19, and 20:8 all describe an end-time conflict in which Christ is triumphant and the rebellious nations are defeated. Each time it is described as "the battle" (or "the war"). The use of the definite article ("the") in Rev 16:14, 19:19 and 20:8 suggests that this battle represents the final and conclusive defeat of Christ's enemies. The "article of previous reference" in Rev 20:8 "tells us that John is referring to something of which he has already spoken. This previous reference is to 'the battle' mentioned in 19:19 and 16:14–16."[45] Since in 16:14 and 19:19 the battle takes place in close association with Christ's second coming, "this clear reference of 20:8 to the battle of 19:19 and 16:14–16 makes clear that the time period in view immediately precedes the second coming."[46] Rev 16:14; 19:19; and 20:8 are the *only* uses of *polemos* ("battle") accompanied by the article in Revelation, which is a firm indication that 20:8 is repeating the previous accounts of the final battle of 16:14 and 19:19.[47]

Further, the language used to describe the nations' revolt and campaign against Christ is virtually identical in all these accounts. Rev 16:12–16; 19:19–20; and 20:8 have in common not only the same language for the gathering together the forces for the battles but also the idea that the gathered forces have been deceived into participating. That corroborates that "Satan's deception of the nations in 20:8 'to gather them together for the war' is the same event as the deception of the nations in 16:12–16 and 19:19."[48] It is therefore more likely that the battle of Rev 19:19 and 20:8 are parallel accounts of the same event rather than 20:8 being a new conflict and victory for Christ a thousand years after a similar conflict and victory that occurred at Christ's second coming.

That Revelation 16, 19, and 20 all describe the same "battle" is also seen in the fact that the same Greek verb (*synagō*) is used in 16:14, 16; 19:17, 19; and 20:8 to describe the "gathering" of the forces.[49] Those are the only places in the entire book where *synagō* is used. That is not by accident.

43. Compare Rev 20:8 with Ezek 38:2; 39:1, 6; and Rev 20:9 with Ezek 38:22; 39:6.

44. For comprehensive discussions of Ezekiel 38–39 in relation to Revelation 19–20, see Beale, *Revelation*, 976–80; Beale, *John's Use*, 361–67.

45. Waldron, "Eschatological Kingdom," n.p.

46. Ibid.

47. White, "Reexamining," 328–29. That is particularly clear since on other occasions (Rev 9:7, 9; 11:7; 12:7, 17; 13:7) *polemos* had been used without the article to refer to warfare in general. See Johnson, *Triumph*, 233n.13, 277n.14.

48. Beale, *Revelation*, 980.

49. See Johnson, *Triumph*, 277n.13.

The end of God's wrath

Rev 15:1 declares that with the outpouring of the seven bowls *"the wrath of God is finished."* The last of the seven bowls of wrath was poured in Rev 16:17–21. In 16:17 a loud voice came from the throne of heaven saying *"it is done."* The completion of God's wrath is recapitulated by the parallel vision of Rev 19:11–21.[50] To read Revelation 19 and 20 as historically consecutive, as premillennialists do, would mean that God's wrath would not be completed as Rev 15:1 says but that God would continue to have and pour out his wrath a thousand years later, after Christ's reign during the millennium.

The cosmic destruction of Rev 19:11–21 and 20:9–11

Rev 6:12–17; 16:17–21; 19:11–21; and 20:9–11 all describe the shaking of the cosmos that accompanies the coming of Christ and his exercise of judging the nations. In Rev 6:12–14; 16:18–20; and 20:11, the cosmic destruction is explicit. In Rev 19:11–21 it is implicit by virtue of the reference to God's "wrath" (19:15; compare 6:16; 16:19) and the fact that "in 19:19–21 John resumes and concludes the plot line he began but dropped in 16:12–16."[51] Heb 12:26–27 says that the "shaking" of the earth at Christ's *parousia* is the last instance of such shaking. It makes no sense to say that the shaking of the cosmos at Christ's second coming will be followed by a further shaking of the cosmos at the end of the millennium. That imagery also ties the battle with Gog and Magog (Ezekiel 38–39) to this last battle at the time of Christ's *parousia*, since Ezek 38:18–23 explicitly says that in the Gog and Magog battle of "that day," the mountains will be *"thrown down"* and all creatures and *"all the men who are on the face of the earth will shake at My presence."* It is therefore incredible to maintain, as premillennialists do, that these passages describe two different events, separated by a thousand years.

The abolition of death

First Cor 15:25–26 states that Christ *"must reign until He has put all His enemies under His feet. The last enemy that will be abolished is death."* That constitutes *"the end, when He hands over the kingdom to the God and Father"* (1 Cor 15:24). Rev 19:11–21 describes the *parousia* of Christ and the concomitant death and destruction of "the rest," the "small and great." Rev 20:7–9 similarly pictures the destruction and death of the nations who gathered together for "the war" against Christ and his church *"when the thousand years are completed."* The question therefore is: When is death abolished—at Christ's *parousia* or a thousand years thereafter?

Paul answers the question of when Christ abolishes death in the context of 1 Corinthians 15 when he describes the consummation in vv. 50–57. He begins in v. 50 by saying that *"flesh and blood cannot inherit the kingdom of God; nor does the perishable inherit the imperishable."* He then states when the perishable will *"put on the imperishable, and this mortal must put on immortality"* (v. 53; see also v. 51). That occurs at *"the last trumpet"*

---

50. Rev 19:15 specifically refers to Christ's treading *"the wine press of the fierce wrath of God."*

51. White, "Reexamining," 321n.5.

when *"the dead will be raised imperishable, and we will be changed"* (v. 52). Verse 54 goes on to say that *"when this mortal will have put on immortality, then will come about the saying that is written, 'death is swallowed up in victory.'"* Andrew Lincoln points out, "The clear temporal reference [to the events of v. 54] is to the *parousia* (cf. verse 52)."[52] Thus, "the end" (15:24) is coterminous with the abolition of death (15:26), which is when our mortal bodies are changed and *"put on immortality"* (15:52–54). Those events all occur at Christ's "coming," i.e., the *parousia* (15:23).[53] That means that Revelation 20 has to recapitulate Revelation 19 and the *parousia* must occur after, not before, the "thousand years."

The premillennialist sequential reading of Revelation 19 and 20, which includes an intermediate millennial kingdom, and *then* the abolition of death, would turn the theme and climax of Paul's argument into a penultimate anti-climax. It would also mean that there would be *two* victories over death—one at the resurrection of Christ's people at the *parousia* and another at the end of the millennium.[54] That, of course, is contrary to the two-age eschatological structure, the significance of the second coming, and the nature of existence in the "age to come" after the *parousia*, discussed previously.

Venema concludes, "The parallels between these visions [Rev 19:11–21 and Rev 20:1–11]—in language, symbolism, use of Old Testament prophecy, and content—is so pervasive and compelling as to yield but one likely explanation: they are describing the same period of history, the same episodes and the same conclusion at the end of the age."[55] Additionally, since at his coming Jesus will raise to glory *all* those who believe in him (e.g., Matt 24:31; John 6:39–40), and according to Rev 19:18, 21 *everyone* else is slain, no one would be left to enter a post-*parousia* "millennium" and repopulate the earth in any event.

The "thousand years"

The broad context of Revelation as a whole, beginning with Rev 1:1's use of *sēmainō* ("communicate by symbols") and *deichnumi* ("show"), together with the repeated introductory formula "I saw" (or similar expressions) throughout the book, *including Rev 20:1*,[56] denote "the general symbolic nature of the communication," as opposed to the merely general conveyance of information.[57] The meaning of visionary terms is not self-evident. Poythress has described that in such cases—*including Rev 20:1–6*—one needs to consider and distinguish four levels of communication: (1) *the linguistic level* (i.e., the textual record itself); (2) *the visionary level* (i.e., what John actually saw; his "visual experience"); (3) *the referential level* (i.e., the historical reference of the various particulars in the description); and (4) *the symbolic level* (i.e., the interpretation of what the symbolic

---

52. Lincoln, *Paradise Now,* 66; see also Appendix 7: 1 Cor 15:20–57: The Resurrection, the *Parousia*, and the Millennium for a detailed discussion of this passage.

53. This is confirmed by Rev 20:14 which says, "Then death and Hades were thrown into the lake of fire. This is the second death, the lake of fire." in other words, death is abolished at the last judgment which takes place at the *parousia*.

54. Strimple, "Amillennialism," 111.

55. Venema, *Promise*, 314–15.

56. See also Rev 4:1; 12:1–3; 13:1–3; 14:1; 17:1–3.

57. Beale, *Revelation*, 973.

imagery actually connotes about its historical referent).[58] The idea that one should interpret "literally" except where one is forced to interpret symbolically by clear contextual
indications "should be turned on its head" in connection with the interpretation of Revelation since "the essence of the book is figurative."[59] That is particularly true of Revelation
20 because in Rev 20:1–6 John:

> employs the words "one thousand years," "resurrection," and "life" because he
> saw, at the visionary level, people who were resurrected and given life for one
> thousand years. Because the objects he sees and what he hears and seen and
> heard in a vision, they are not *first* to be understood literally but viewed as sym-
> bolically portrayed and communicated, which is the *symbolic* level of the vision.
> That this vision is shot through with symbols is apparent merely from the obvious
> symbolic nature of such words as "chain," "abyss," "dragon," "serpent," "locked,"
> "sealed," and "beast." Therefore, the words "resurrection" and "life," for example,
> do not by themselves give a clue about whether the visionary, symbolic portrayal
> has a one-to-one (literal) correspondence to its historical referent together with
> a figurative meaning or only an indirect figurative relation. Thorough exegesis
> must decide in each case.[60]

Insofar as the "thousand years" of Rev 20:2–7 is concerned, Summers points out,
"Numbers are used in apocalyptic literature as symbols of ideas. This has been clearly
demonstrated by comparative studies within the literature."[61] Further, the Bible frequently
uses the number 1000 in a symbolic way. Non-temporal figurative uses of "thousand"
include Deut 1:10–11; 32:30; Josh 23:10; Job 9:3; 33:23; Ps 50:10; 68:17; Song 4:4; Isa 7:23;
30:17; 60:22; Dan 7:10; Amos 5:3. Temporal figurative uses of "thousand" include Deut
7:9; 1 Chron 16:15–17; Ps 84:10; 105:8–10; Eccl 6:6; 7:28.[62] Given the symbolic nature and
symbolic use of numbers in Revelation, and the symbolic use of "thousand" throughout
the Bible, there can be no objection *in principle* to the amillennial view that the "thousand
years" is a symbolic term which stands for a particular or prolonged period of time, as
opposed to a literal thousand years.[63]

The specific context of Revelation 20 itself indicates that the term "thousand years"
is, in fact, a symbolic or figurative term, not a literal thousand-year period of time. Premillennialists Ladd, Osborne, and most other commentators agree.[64] In Rev 20:1–3, "the
multiplication of visual features—key, chain, hand, dragon, throwing, locking, and sealing—underscores the symbolic genre of the entire vision, since John's audience knows
well that Satan is not a literal dragon who can be bound with a physical chain or locked
away in a physical pit."[65] To hold to a "literal" thousand years requires, to be consistent,

---

58. Poythress, "Genre and Hermeneutics," 41–42.

59. Beale, *Revelation*, 52.

60. Ibid., 973–74.

61. Summers, "Revelation 20," 180.

62. Beale and McDonough, "Revelation," 1148; see also Warren, *Revelation Chapter 20*, n.p. (symbolic use of "thousand" discussed relative to Deut 7:9; Ps 50:10–11; 105:8; Isa 7:23; 2 Pet 3:8; Rev 11:3;
12:6; and 14:9).

63. Riddlebarger, *Amillennialism*, 209–10; Venema, *Promise*, 324–27; Beale, *Revelation*, 1017–21.

64. Ladd, *Commentary*, 262; Osborne, *Revelation*, 701.

65. Johnson, *Triumph*, 283.

that the "key" and "chain" held by the angel in Rev 20:1 are a physical key and chain and that the "abyss" of Rev 20:3 is an actual pit in the earth which has a physical lock and physical "seal."[66]

Contrary to such absurdity, Beale reminds us that the abyss is not spatial but "represents a spiritual dimension existing alongside and in the midst of the earthly, not above or below it . . . The abyss is one of the various metaphors representing the spiritual sphere in which the devil and his accomplices operate."[67] Premillennialists, of course, do not contend that the key and chain are "literal." However, it is only their pre-existing theological presuppositions that cause them to interpret some of the words or phrases *in the same passage* "literally" or physically but others figuratively or spiritually.

The "two resurrections"

Erickson says, "The major exegetical problem for amillennialism, however, is not the one thousand years, but the two resurrections."[68] Rev 20:4 talks about those who "come to life" (Greek = *ezēsan*), which is called "the first resurrection" in Rev 20:5b.[69] Amillennialists view the "first resurrection" as our new life in and union with Christ,[70] or as Christ's resurrection in which believers spiritually participate,[71] or as the Christians' translation to heaven upon their physical death.[72]

Premillennialist George E. Ladd says he did not find a sufficient "contextual clue" to justify interpreting the first *ezēsan* spiritually and the second *ezēsan* "literally" or physically.[73] Sydney Page responds:

> Ladd's point that the verb [*ezēsan*] should be interpreted in the same way in both verses unless there is a contextual clue indicating otherwise is well taken, but the reference to the millennium may be the very clue he seeks. If the thousand-year reign in vv 4–6 is coterminous with the thousand-year imprisonment of Satan in vv 1–3, and if the original readers of Revelation believed that the binding of Satan referred to the age in which they lived, they would have understood the coming to life and reigning with Christ as a present reality as well.[74]

It is likely that the original readers *did* interpret Rev 20:1–6 in the manner Page suggests:

> The relevance of this scene of the glory of martyred souls for the early church under persecution from Rome is obvious and commands this interpretation.

66. Waltke, "Kingdom Promises," 273; Jackson, "Examining Premillennialism," n.p.

67. Beale, *Revelation*, 987.

68. Erickson, *Christian Theology*, 1220.

69. *Ezēsan* (Rev 20:4–5) is the aorist tense of the verb *zaō* ("to live"). The word used for "resurrection" in Rev 20:5–6 is the common noun for resurrection, namely, *anastasis*.

70. Augustine, *Civ.*, 20.6–10; White, "Death and the First Resurrection," 22; Shepherd, "Resurrections," 36–38; Venema, *Promise*, 331–36.

71. Hughes, "First Resurrection," 315–18.

72. Kline, "First Resurrection," 366–75.

73. Ladd, "Historic Premillennialism," 37; see also Mounce, *Revelation*, 366.

74. Page, "Revelation 20," 37–38.

What could be more relevant for the persecuted believers of the early church than to be told that the apparent victory of Rome over them in bringing about their deaths was only apparent? What could be more encouraging than to be told that their death was really a promotion to true life, to a participation in the resurrection glory of Christ? Their deaths were really their sharing in the *first resurrection,* while the continued earthly life of those who capitulated to the beast only promised them a part in the *second death.*[75]

Additionally, the wording and the context of Rev 20:4–6 offer compelling reasons why the two uses of *ezēsan* do *not* both represent bodily resurrections separated by thousand literal years.

Parallels of other NT and OT passages with Rev 20:4–6 indicate that the "first resurrection" is spiritual and takes place before the final, general, physical resurrection at the parousia

"Most striking is the observation that elsewhere in the NT *anastasis* [resurrection] and *zaō* ['to live'] (or the cognate noun *zōē,* 'life') and synonyms are used interchangeably of both spiritual and physical resurrection *within the same immediate contexts.*"[76] Further, the verb *zaō* ("to live") also is used for the soul living on after the death of the body in Luke 20:38 and 1 Pet 4:6. *Ezēsan* (Rev 20:4–5) is the aorist tense of *zaō.* Since the words *life* and *resurrection* can be used together to *contrast* a spiritual with a physical state of affairs, the primary hermeneutical objection to the amillennial view—that *ezēsan* in Rev 20:4–5 can only be referring to physical resurrection—is undercut. The amillennial view, which sees the verb *ezēsan* in Rev 20:4 as the spiritual life of Christians that occurs before the general bodily resurrection of all people on the last day and the *ezēsan* of 20:5 as the general resurrection of all people that occurs at the *parousia* is perfectly consistent with the use of that word and with the use of the words "life" and "resurrection" or words that substantively denote these concepts elsewhere in the NT.

The descriptions of the resurrections in John 5 and Revelation 20 are perfectly parallel. In John 5:25 "the coming hour already is: the resurrection life for the physically dead in the end time is already being manifest as life for the spiritually dead," whereas in John 5:28 "the future, final apocalyptic resurrection is in view. The voice of the Son is powerful enough to generate spiritual life now; it will be powerful enough to call forth the dead then."[77] John 5:24 likewise says that the person who believes in Christ *"has passed out of death into life"* (see also 1 John 3:14 [*"We know that we have passed out of death into life"*]). The word for "passed out" is *metabainō* which means "to change from one state or

---

75. Waldron, "Eschatological Kingdom," n.p.

76. Beale, *Revelation,* 1004 (citing Rom 6:4–13 and John 5:24–29; cf. Rom 8:10–11), emphasis in original.

77. Carson, *John,* 257–58; see also Jordan, *The Law,* 57 ("In John 5:21–29, Jesus distinguishes a first resurrection, when those dead in sin will hear the voice of Christ and live (v. 25); and a second resurrection, when those dead in the grave will come forth to a physical resurrection (v. 29). The first resurrection comes in the middle of history to enable men to fulfill the duties of the old creation. The second resurrection comes at the end of history to usher men into the new creation.").

condition to another state."[78] Changing one's state or condition by passing from death into life is the essence of what "resurrection" is. Hence, it appropriate to call such a profound change in one's spiritual condition the "first resurrection." The similarities between the two passages are obvious when seen graphically:[79]

Resurrections	John 5:24–25	Rev 20:4–6	John 5:27–29	Rev 20:12–15
Distinguishing trait	Spiritual resurrection	First resurrection	Physical resurrection	(Second) resurrection
Time of occurrence	Now, before the day of judgment (5:25)	Now, before the day of judgment (20:4)	The day of judgment (5:28; cf. 12:48)	The day of judgment (20:11–15)
Participants	The elect/hearers (5:25)	Believers (20:4)	All/doers of good & evil (5:28–29)	Believers & unbelievers (20:12–13, 15)
Scenario	Elect raised; non-elect dead (5:24–25)	Believers raised; unbelievers dead (20:4–5)	Doers of good raised to life; doers of evil raised to condemnation (5:29)	Believers & unbelievers raised and judged (20:12–15)
Participants' pre-resurrection state	Death; subject to condemnation (5:24)	Subject to second death (20:6)	Death & burial (5:28)	Death & burial (20:13)
Participants' post-resurrection state	Life; free from condemnation (5:24)	Life; free from second death (20:4, 6)	Life for doers of good; condemnation for evildoers (5:29)	Life; free from second death (20:15)

There also is a clear parallel between Eph 2:5–7 and Rev 20:4–6. Eph 2:5–6 uses the phrases "made us alive," "raised us up," and "seated us with him in the heavenly places" to refer to spiritual resurrection with Christ in this age, the present. As N. T. Wright says, "Without downplaying the future hope of actual resurrection itself, the fact that the church lives in the interval between the Messiah's resurrection and its own ultimate new life means that the metaphorical use of 'resurrection' language can be adapted to denote the concrete Christian living described in [Eph] 2:10."[80] That corresponds with Rev 20:4–6 in that, in both cases, the words pertaining to life and resurrection are used spiritually or metaphorically, the participants are sitting in the heavenly realm, and the time period is the present.[81]

78. BDAG, "metabainō," 638.

79. The following comparison is adapted from White, "Death and the First Resurrection," Appendix (tables I–III); see also Shepherd, "Resurrections," 35–36.

80. Wright, Resurrection, 237.

81. In Eph 2:5, the word for "made us alive" is suzōopoieō which is part of the same cognate word group as zaō, from which ezēsan is derived (Trenchard, Complete Vocabulary Guide, 43). In Eph 2:6, the word for "raised us up" is sunegeirō, which is derived from egeirō, an important NT word for "resurrection." Consistent with the use of ezēsan for the "first resurrection" in Rev 20:4, both words in Eph 2:5–6 are being used spiritually or metaphorically.

Similar parallel language is found in Col 2:12–13 (2:12, *"You were also raised up with Him through faith in the working of God, who raised him from the dead"*; 2:13, *"He made you alive together with Him"*) and 3:1–4 (*"Therefore if you have been raised up with Christ, . . . when Christ, who is our life, is revealed, then you also will be revealed with Him in glory"*).[82] Col 2:12 makes a direct comparison between the believers' spiritual resurrection and Christ's physical resurrection. Wright comments:

> The present status of Christians, on the basis of baptism, is that they have already died with the Messiah and been raised with him, as 2.13 makes clear. . . . In the Jewish thought where 'resurrection' was used metaphorically for 'return from exile', one central part of that hope was that Israel's sins would finally be forgiven. Throughout this sequence of thought, the present metaphorical 'resurrection' of Christians, replacing the metaphorical usage in some Jewish texts, denotes their status 'in the Messiah' who has himself been concretely raised from the dead; and it takes its meaning from the fact that it anticipates their future literal 'resurrection', their eventual sharing of the Messiah's glory.[83]

To the same effect is Rom 6:4–5 (*"Therefore we have been buried with Him through baptism into death, so that as Christ was raised from the dead through the glory of the Father, so we too might walk in newness of life. For if we have become united with Him in the likeness of His death, certainly we shall also be in the likeness of His resurrection"*). Wright notes, "Granted, Paul does not use exactly the same terminology here as we find there [in Ephesians and Colossians]; but that is true of almost all parallels and near-parallels between any passages in his various letters. But the questions he asks, and the answers he gives, only make sense if he is affirming a present 'resurrection' life for the Christian as well as a future one."[84] That spiritual rebirth or "resurrection" is as transformative as physical resurrection is similarly expressed in 2 Cor 5:17 and Gal 6:15 where believers are called a "new creature" (or "new creation").

Additional parallels are found within Revelation itself. Rev 20:6 says, *"Blessed and holy is the one who has a part in the first resurrection; over these the second death has no power, but they will be priests of God and of Christ and will reign with Him for a thousand years."* That verse parallels the promises made to the "overcomers" in Revelation 2–3. In Rev 2:10, Jesus says, *"Be faithful until death, and I will give you the crown of life."* Further:

> Revelation 2:11 says, "He who overcomes will not be hurt by the second death." This matches with the statement "over these the second death has no power." Revelation 2:26 reads, "He who overcomes . . . to him I will give authority over the nations." This fits with their reigning with Christ (over the nations) for a thousand years. Revelation 3:12 says, "He who overcomes, I will make him a pillar in the temple of my God. . . ." This fits with the fact that the souls of Revelation 20:4–6 are priests of God in the heavenly temple. Revelation 3:21 reads, "He who overcomes, I will grant to him to sit down with me on my throne. . . ."

---

82. In Col 2:12 and 3:1, the word for the believers' being "raised" is *sunegeirō*, the same word used in Eph 2:6; the word in Col 2:12 for Christ's being raised is *egeirō*, from which sunegeirō is derived. In Col 2:13, the word for *"made you alive"* is *suzōpoieō*, the same word used in Eph 2:5.

83. Wright, *Resurrection*, 238–39.

84. Ibid., 251.

> This matches perfectly with the language of sitting on thrones and reigning with Christ in Revelation 20:4–6.[85]

While the thrust of all of these promises relates to life in the eternal state that commences at the *parousia*, they all find their initial fulfillment in the spiritual transformation that begins in this life and continues in the intermediate state before finding ultimate consummation in the eternal state.

In Rev 20:4, those sitting on the thrones are referred to as *"the souls of those who had been beheaded because of their testimony of Jesus and because of the word of God."* The picture there probably is of souls in the intermediate state because, as Beale points out, "The closest parallel to this is 6.9, where John sees 'the souls of the ones slain on account of the word of God and on account of the witness'. These were believers who had died while holding to their faith despite persecution and whose souls had been translated to heaven in order to receive rest from the Lord."[86]

In addition to the parallels with various NT passages and within Revelation itself, Rev 20:4–6 has parallels with Ezekiel which is similar in structure, language, and imagery. For example, many commentators have observed both the structural and linguistic influence of Ezekiel on Revelation.[87] Beale and McDonough note, "In light of the structural parallelism, the word *ezēsan* ('they came to life') in Rev. 20:4 is to be seen as an echo of Ezek. 37:10, where the identical word is used (so also Ezek. 37:6, 14, though using a future-tense form). If the parallelism is intentional, then it would support a spiritual resurrection in Rev. 20:4–6, since the resurrection in Ezek. 36–37 is also spiritual, or at least metaphorical."[88]

This pattern of spiritual resurrection preceding physical resurrection goes all the way back to Gen 3:15, the *protoevangelium*. R. Fowler White describes this:

> The blessing of redemption from the power of the second death is a reflex of the redemptive victory over eternal death implicitly promised in Gen 3:15. According to that oracle of destiny, the redemptive re-creation of Adam's fallen house was to be fulfilled through the victory of the promised Seed over the serpent. . . . First, lest this re-creation be frustrated by temporal or eternal death, the Seed's victory over the serpent must also entail victories over both temporal death and eternal death. Second, lest these victories be in vain, they must be applied in a particular sequence. That is, the Victor must redeem his house from eternal death before he redeems them from temporal death; otherwise, eternal death will still threaten them after their redemption from temporal death. Likewise, the Victor must redeem his house from eternal death before their temporal death occurs; otherwise, their temporal death will prevent their redemption from eternal death. Therefore, the first victory in which the Victor's house will have a part must answer to the threat of eternal death and must precede their temporal death; in other words, the spiritual resurrection of the Victor's house must have temporal

---

85. Waldron, "Eschatological Kingdom," n.p.; see also Beale, *Revelation*, 996–97; Hoekema, *Bible and Future*, 234–35.

86. Beale, *John's Use*, 375.

87. Beale, *Revelation*, 99, 976–80, 1012–13 and authorities cited therein; Beale and McDonough, "Revelation," 1082 and authorities cited therein.

88. Beale and McDonough, "Revelation," 1148; see also White, "The Millennial Kingdom-City," 17–18.

priority over both their physical deal and their physical resurrection. . . . In all of this, the first resurrection in Rev 20 exhibits all the defining traits of the redemptive victory over eternal death expected in Gen 3. And, remarkably, all of this, including the temporal priority of spiritual resurrection over physical death and resurrection, is thoroughly consistent.[89]

The above passages all have the same structures and concepts and, except for Gen 3:15, use language similar to Rev 20:4–6. More importantly, those passages are consistent with the amillennial view of Rev 20:4–6 but are inconsistent with the premillennial view. Amillennialism is therefore able to demonstrate the overall eschatological unity of the Bible in a way that premillennialism cannot.

The wording of Rev 20:4

Rev 20:4 says, "*I saw the souls of those who had been beheaded . . . and they came to life and reigned with Christ for a thousand years.*" The claim that this (the "first resurrection," Rev 20:5) refers to a bodily resurrection is not justified by the language John uses in Rev 20:4. Waldron points out, "The resurrection is never referred to in the New Testament as 'souls coming to life' and that this is surely a strange way to refer to the resurrection of the body."[90] Hoeksema similarly observes that it is:

> a strange way of referring to persons in the body, whether corruptible or resurrected, . . . to speak of the 'souls of them that were beheaded'! . . . And surely the statement in verse 5, that 'this is the first resurrection,' does not change matters at all. The Chiliast, indeed, adduces this clause in support of his contention that verse 5 refers to risen saints, but he is mistaken. The text plainly says: *this* is the first resurrection. And the pronoun *this* refers back to the statement in verse 4 concerning the souls that reign with Christ. Therefore, in answer to the question, what is the first resurrection, we cannot introduce our own preconceived notion, but we are bound to the text and, therefore, constrained to say: *the reign of the souls of them that were beheaded for the witness of Jesus is the first resurrection!*[91]

Waldron adds, "Though 'souls' may occasionally refer to whole persons, there is good reason to see a reference here to disembodied souls. The context demands the meaning of a disembodied soul. The Greek verb translated, beheaded, is in the perfect tense. This demands a translation like, 'souls in a condition of having been beheaded.' The perfect tense plainly means that the effects of their being beheaded continue into the present. Furthermore, the meaning of 'disembodied soul' is not foreign to the Apocalypse. Rev. 6:9 uses the term, soul, of disembodied souls."[92]

N. T. Wright suggests that the wording of Rev 20:4 (souls "came to life") and 5 ("first resurrection") presents an analogy with the "resurrection" language seen earlier in Romans, Ephesians, and Colossians:

---

89. White, "The Millennial Kingdom-City," 19–20.
90. Waldron, "Eschatological Kingdom," n.p.
91. Hoeksema, "Millennium Period," n.p., emphasis in original.
92. Waldron, "Eschatological Kingdom," n.p.

There, as we saw, the baptized believer, whose current life is based on the past event of Jesus' death and resurrection, and whose body will be raised in the future, is in a sense already 'raised with the Messiah' [Col 3:1]. This metaphorical use of 'resurrection' language to denote the believer's present status seems to me a partial parallel at least to the use in Revelation 20.4 of 'the first resurrection' to denote a new life that these particular 'souls' are given, based on Jesus' resurrection and anticipating the full bodily resurrection still to come. Thus, though the usage is very strange, it can be understood as a bold extension of categories already being tried out within early Christianity, rather than an abandonment of normal Jewish and Christian language.[93]

This also is in accord with what Jesus said in Luke 20:37–38 (see also Matt 22:31–32; Mark 12:26–27), *"But that the dead are raised, even Moses showed, in the passage about the burning bush, where he calls the Lord THE GOD OF ABRAHAM, AND THE GOD OF ISAAC, AND THE GOD OF JACOB. Now He is not the God of the dead but of the living; for all live to Him."* The word used by Jesus for "raised" in v. 37 is *egeirō*, one of the primary words used in the NT for "resurrection." The important point here is that Jesus was using clear "resurrection" language to describe Abraham, Isaac, and Jacob in the intermediate state, not their final bodily resurrected state. In other words, Jesus uses *egeirō* in Luke 20:37 the way amillennialists use the similar word, *anastasis*, in Rev 20:5–6.

The contrasting "first-second" schema of Rev 20:4–6

Additionally, specific "contextual clues" exist in Rev 20:4–6 to justify interpreting the first *ezēsan* (Rev 20:4) ("they lived" or "they came to life") spiritually and the second *ezēsan* (Rev 20:5) physically. In Rev 20:5–6 the "first resurrection" and the "second death" are explicitly mentioned; the "second resurrection" and "first death" are not, but are implied. Although the word *anastasis* ("resurrection") appears 41 times in the New Testament and usually refers to a physical resurrection, in Revelation *anastasis* is only found in Rev 20:5–6. Moreover, "the ordinal 'first' (*prōtos*) with 'resurrection' occurs nowhere else in the OT or the NT. This is a hint that lexical study of words expressing the ideas of 'first' and 'second' needs to be conducted in order to comprehend the full meaning of 'resurrection' in the present context."[94]

That contextual clue—the use of "first" along with "resurrection"—provides the key which demonstrates that the so-called "two resurrections" of Rev 20:4–6 are, in fact, of qualitatively different orders. Over 200 years ago, Alexander Fraser pointed out, "The terms, first and second, are used in Scripture to distinguish subjects which are in some respects similar, but in others are very different, lest we should mistake the one for the other."[95] In Revelation and elsewhere the use of "first" and "second," "old" and "new," "first" and "last," are markers of *qualitative difference*, not temporal sequence of things that are alike.[96] Thus, in Rev 20:5–6 the "first resurrection" is not simply the first of two resur-

93. Wright, *Climax of the Covenant*, 475.

94. Beale, *Revelation*, 1004.

95. Fraser, *Key to the Prophecies*, 418.

96. It is true, of course, that sometimes "first" and "second" are used as ordinal numerals of similar entities (e.g., Rev 4:7–8 [the four living creatures]; Rev 6:1 [seven seals]; Rev 8:6–12 [the seven angels

rections which are alike but is *antithetically contrasted with* the "second death" and with the (implied) "second resurrection." Indeed, the fact that a "second resurrection" is not explicitly mentioned is itself evidence that the "second" resurrection is of a qualitatively different kind than the "first" resurrection: "John refuses to mention the 'second resurrection' by name in 20.13 [or in 20:5–6], not because resurrection is not in view, but because he wishes to discourage the very idea . . . that the 'rest of the dead' will experience 'life' in the deepest sense when they finally 'stand again' in their bodies. . . . The second 'resurrection', that of the unrepentant, can hardly be called such because it issues not in everlasting life, but in the second death."[97]

The use of "first" and "second," "old" and "new," "first" and "last," as terms of *contrast*, not *sequence*, is found throughout the NT. Fraser states, "The Scriptures frequently mention the second or new birth. The first birth is that of the body. Is it necessary that the second should be so too? Will any man, acquainted with the Scriptures, put the question now which Nicodemus formerly proposed to our Lord, 'How can a man be born when he is old? How can he enter the second time into his mother's womb, and be born?' (John iii. 4). The second birth is doubtless an allegory. But does it follow that the first birth is an allegory too?"[98]

In 1 Cor 15:22, 42–46, the "first Adam" had a perishable, natural body and brought death; the "last Adam" has an imperishable, spiritual body and brought life. In 1 Cor 15:47–49, the "first man" is from the earth and is earthy; the "second man" is from heaven and is heavenly. Paul's discussion of the "first and last Adam" and "first and second man" is part of a broader discussion of contrasts, including the "first" or "natural" ("earthly") body and then the "spiritual" ("heavenly") body (1 Cor 15:42–44, 46–49). William Dennison concludes:

> It becomes obvious in the writings of Paul that the two Adams are not only individuals but they are also the representatives of two antithetical orders of life, two aeons and two historical world periods (cf. also Rom. 5:12–21). . . . Adam is first because no aeon comes before him; Christ is "second" or "last" because no aeon comes between Adam and Christ and because no aeon follows Christ. Christ is the eschatological man: He brings the antithetical eschatological aeon. Christ brings, therefore, a mode of existence, a world order, an aeon of history which is absolutely victorious. Although the first Adam inaugurated an aeon of death, the second Adam inaugurated the aeon of resurrection life. Thus, the believer in Christ lives in the blessings of the "eschatological Adam;" the believer is "alive" as opposed to being "dead" (Rom. 5:16–19; I Cor. 15:21, 22).[99]

---

with seven trumpets]; Rev 16:1 [seven angels with seven bowls]; Rev 21:19–20 [twelve foundation stones]). In each of those cases, the function of the numbers as ordinals is obvious, and the ordinals appear before entities of like nature which are immediately referred to (living creatures, seals, angels, trumpets, bowls, foundation stones). Those factors are not present in Rev 20:4–6. The use of "first" and "second" in that context and in the other passages discussed above is distinctive and has a clear theological, not ordinal, significance, indicating contrast, not sequence.

97. Mealy, *After the Thousand Years*, 230n.5; see also Kline, "First Resurrection," 371; Storms, *Kingdom Come*, 465.

98. Fraser, *Key to the Prophecies*, 418.

99. Dennison, *Paul's Two-Age Construction*, 43–44.

In Matt 20:16 Jesus says *"The last shall be first, and the first last"* (see also Matt 19:30; Mark 9:35; 10:31, 44; Luke 13:30). Jesus is not talking about sequence of similar people or events but is speaking about the contrast between the saved and the lost and the radically counter-cultural lifestyle that should characterize the saved. More broadly, in Jesus' parable of the two sons (Matt 21:28–32), the "first" son is the one who did the father's will after saying he would not, but the "second" son did not do the father's will although he said he would. The use of "first" and "second" were not used as markers of birth order, but were used to show the contrast between the responses of the sons to the father, which Jesus then used to compare the contrasting responses of tax collectors and prostitutes, versus the chief priests and elders, to himself.

In Mark 2:21–22 Jesus uses "old" and "new" (cloth and garments; wine and wineskins) to contrast the "newness" of life that Jesus and the gospel bring, as opposed to the "oldness" of Jewish religious rituals (see also Luke 5:36–39). In 2 Cor 5:17 Paul states, *"If anyone is in Christ, he is a new creature; the old things have passed away; behold, new things have come."* Paul's use of "old" and "new" clearly is showing the radical difference of life in Christ as opposed to life without Christ. Similarly, in Eph 4:22–24 and Col 3:9–10 Paul contrasts the "old man" (the unregenerate person) with the "new man" (the regenerate person) (see also Rom 6:4–6).

Meredith Kline points out how Hebrews uses the exact terminology used in Revelation in order to distinguish the "first" or "old," temporary, non-salvific Mosaic Covenant from the "second" or "new," everlasting, salvific New Covenant: "In the Book of Hebrews the terms 'first' and 'new' are used to distinguish the Mosaic and the Messianic administrations of God's redemptive covenant *(cf.* 8:7, 8, 13; 9:1, 15, 18; 10:9). The new covenant is also called 'the second': 'He taketh away the first, that he may establish the second' (10:9). Here then in this terminology for the two-covenant pattern is the identical pairing of terms, including the same alternate for 'new,' that we find in Revelation 20 and 21."[100]

Hebrews does more to establish this pattern. Heb 9:2–12 contrasts the "first tabernacle" (the earthly cultic rituals) with the "second" (the "greater and more perfect tabernacle," i.e., heaven and the eternal redemption brought about by Christ). William Lane summarizes this portion of the argument of Hebrews:

> The writer's distinctive use of *prōtē,* "first," and *deutera,* "second," to describe spatially the two compartments of the tabernacle recalls his use of these numerical terms to designate the old and new covenants (8:7, 13). The "front compartment" (*hē prōtē skēnē*) becomes a spatial metaphor for the time when the "first covenant" (*hē prōtē diathēkē*) was in force. As an illustration for the old age, which is now in the process of dissolution (8:13), it symbolizes the total first covenant order with its daily and annual cultic ritual (9:6, 7). Once the first has been invalidated, the second becomes operative (see 10:9). In the figurative language of the writer, the front compartment of the tabernacle was symbolic of the present age (*ton kairon enestēkota*), which through the intrusion of the *kairos diorthōseōs,* "the time of correction" (v 10), has been superseded.[101]

100. Kline, "First Resurrection," 367–68.

101. Lane, *Hebrews 9–13,* 224

Heb 9:28 continues the pattern by contrasting Christ's first and second comings: *"So Christ also, having been offered once to bear the sins of many, will appear a second time for salvation without reference to sin, to those who eagerly await him."* The first coming was in lowliness to bear the sins of rebellious humanity on the cross; the second coming will be in great glory to vindicate those who are his, bring resurrection, judgment, renewal of the earth, and usher in the fullness of the age to come.

That same pattern is found in Revelation itself. In Revelation 21, which is thematically and proximately related to Revelation 20, *prōtos* ("first") is repeatedly used, *not* as the first in a series of things that are alike but as something that stands *in contrast to* what is described as "new" or "second."[102] "The contextual force of *prōtos* [is] descriptive of the pre-consummate stage of things."[103] Thus, in Rev 21:1 there is antithesis between the "first" (old) creation and the second ("new") creation: "the former was preconsummate or incomplete and the latter consummate or complete."[104] Further, "Rev. 21.1, 4 are a clear allusion to Isa. 65.16–17, where the same qualitative contrasts occur between the 'first affliction' or 'former' earth and 'a new heaven and a new earth.'"[105]

The use of "second death" is another verbal, contextual clue that the "two resurrections" contrast and are of different orders. The phrase "second death" occurs only in the book of Revelation (2:11; 20:6, 14; 21:8). Fraser rhetorically asks, "The Scriptures mention the second death: now, the first death is that of the body. But is it necessary that we understand the second death of the body only? Does it affect the body in the same manner, by putting it in a state of insensibility and putrefacation [sic]?"[106] Just as "first" coupled with "resurrection" provides the contextual clue that the "first resurrection" is not physical, so "second" coupled with "death" indicates that the "second death" likewise is not physical. "The first death is that of the *body,* the second that of the body and soul; the first death is common to the righteous and the wicked, the second is the everlasting portion of the wicked alone."[107] Kline summarizes that the particular nature of the first-second pair in Revelation 20 and 21 is the "contrast between old, pre-consummative and new, consummative."[108]

These many passages confirm the contrasting "first-second" schema. "The first resurrection is distinguished as first because it brings victory, not over physical death (as in a bodily resurrection), but over spiritual death. The second death is second because it means liability to punishment, not in a physical separation of body and soul, but in a spiritual separation or excommunication from God's presence. The term 'second death' seems to confirm, therefore, that the first resurrection is not a physical resurrection."[109]

R. Fowler White describes how Rev 20:5 serves to distinguish the "first resurrection" (which pertains only to Christians) from "the rest of the dead" (i.e., the non-Christians who do not participate in the first resurrection):

102. Kline, "First Resurrection," 366–67, citing Rev 21:1–8.

103. Ibid., 371.

104. Beale, *Revelation,* 1006.

105. Beale, *John's Use,* 381.

106. Fraser, *Key to the Prophecies,* 418.

107. Brown, *Christ's Second Coming,* 217.

108. Kline, "Reaffirmation," 112.

109. Venema, *Promise,* 337–38.

The distinction is achieved by identifying the non-Christian dead as participants only in the (second) resurrection, and the Christian dead as the only participants in the first resurrection. In other words, verse 5 is a profoundly important statement to the effect that the first resurrection is not to be confused with the resurrection in which the Christian dead and the non-Christian dead are both participants—it is not to be confused with the (second [general]) resurrection, which answers to the death of both Christians and non-Christians and has as its ironic consequence the second death of non-Christians. . . . Those who claim that Christians have no part in the resurrection of the dead in v 13 must explain the function of v 5 in its context. To say that only Christians take part in the first resurrection is not to [say] that they have no part in the second.[110]

Rev 20:6 further reinforces the significance of the "first resurrection." It reminds us that those who have taken part in the first resurrection are free from the second death which has power only over those who die in bondage to their sins. The point of 20:6 is that the dead in Rev 20:4 are the ones who, by their participation in the first resurrection, have passed from death to life before they die physically; therefore, they are free from the second death's power when they die physically. They have this freedom because, before they died physically, Christ freed them from the bondage of their sins by his blood made them his kingdom of priests. Only the Christian dead are so blessed. In other words, the Rev 20:6 is a beatitude for the Christian dead.[111]

In sum, the "first resurrection" occurs in this age, is spiritual (i.e., union with God through union with Christ), and applies only to believers; the (implied) "second resurrection" is the general resurrection at the end of the age, is physical, and applies to all people. The (implied) "first death" is a part of this life, is physical, is temporary, and applies to all people; the "second death" occurs after this life is over, is spiritual (i.e., separation from God because of separation from Christ), lasts forever, and applies only to nonbelievers. This contrasting schema "suits the thought of 20:6, since a first, eternal, spiritual resurrection is the minimal condition to prevent one from suffering a second, eternal, spiritual death."[112]

Rev 20:4–6 reflects the following chiasm:[113]

first *physical death* of saints	first *spiritual resurrection* of saints
second *physical resurrection* of wicked	second *spiritual death* of wicked

Summers earlier arrived at a similar chiastic relationship between resurrection and death in the passage:[114]

"First resurrection" [spiritual]	"Second resurrection" (implied)
"First death" (implied) [physical]	"Second death" [spiritual]

110. White, "Death and the First Resurrection," 10–11, 11n.22.

111. I owe this succinct summary of the import of Rev 20:6 to R. Fowler White.

112. Beale, *Revelation*, 1005.

113. Ibid.

114. Summers, "Revelation 20," 182.

There is yet another way of conceptualizing the interrelationship between resurrection and death. This is based on J. Marcellus Kik's insight that:

> the logical way to determine the meaning of the first resurrection is to discover what is the first death. When Adam and Eve sinned their first experience of death was the death of the soul. The apostle Paul describes the state of the Ephesian Christians before conversion as those "who were dead in trespasses and sins." And in I Timothy 5:6 it is stated: "But she that liveth in pleasure is dead while she liveth." That can only refer to the soul. The primary death is that of the soul.[115] . . . Since the first death is primarily the death of the human soul, it is the soul that must be resurrected first.[116]

Hence, the relationship between resurrection and death may be seen this way:

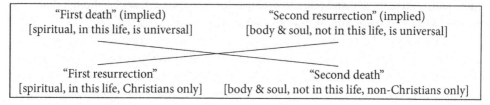

"First death" (implied)	"Second resurrection" (implied)
[spiritual, in this life, is universal]	[body & soul, not in this life, is universal]
"First resurrection"	"Second death"
[spiritual, in this life, Christians only]	[body & soul, not in this life, non-Christians only]

Regardless of how one schematizes it, Kline summarizes the contrasting pattern and antithetical usage of *prōtos* (first) in connection with Revelation 20's discussion of resurrection, life, and death:

> The antithetical usage of *protos* in this context requires a conclusion diametrically opposite to the customary premillennial assumption. If the second resurrection is a bodily resurrection, the first resurrection must be a non-bodily resurrection. . . . [T]he meaning of *protos* in this context is, as we have seen, antithetical to consummation and permanence. That which is "first" belongs to the order of the present passing world. "The first resurrection" must then be something this side of bodily resurrection, some experience that does not bring the subject of it into his consummated condition and final state. . . . Within this schematic pattern, where we would expect to find mention of the second resurrection we find instead "the second death." When describing the event of bodily resurrection that at least includes if it is not exclusively concerned with the unjust (v. 13), the author deliberately does not refer to it as a "resurrection." For the true significance of the event is to be found in the destiny in which it issues and in the case of the unjust the grave delivers them up (v. 13) only to deliver them over to the lake of fire (v. 15). Hence, the real meaning of the resurrection of the unjust to physical life is conveyed by the paradoxical metaphor of death, "the second death" (v. 14).[117]

As Venema puts it, "Only one resurrection is specifically mentioned, and it is particularly defined as the first resurrection because it brings the benefits of the believer's reign with Christ and immunity from the power of the second death."[118] Or, as Beale puts it, "Ironically, the first

---

115. Kik, Eschatology, 230–31; see Gen 2:17; Eph 2:1
116. Ibid., 181; see also Matt 8:22; Luke 9:60; Rom 6:23; Eph 2:5; Col 2:13; Jas 1:15.
117. Kline, "First Resurrection," 370–71.
118. Venema, *Promise*, 334.

physical death of saints translates them into the first spiritual resurrection in heaven, whereas the second physical resurrection translates the ungodly into the second spiritual death."[119]

The nature of the "first resurrection" in light of the contrasting "first-second" schema of Rev 20:4–6

There are three primary ways in which commentators have viewed the "first resurrection" in light of the contrasting "first-second" schema of Rev 20:4–6. In logical order, they are: (1) the first resurrection refers to the *resurrection of Christ* in which believers are participants; (2) the first resurrection refers to the *believers' regeneration*; and (3) the first resurrection refers to the *death of the believer* which (paradoxically) translates him to the intermediate state to "live and reign with Christ for a thousand years." Although different, they are related and overlapping concepts which may be harmonized.

Philip Edgcumbe Hughes is a proponent of the "resurrection of Christ" view. He notes that the resurrection of Christ is central to the gospel and "must be first both in time and significance."[120] Thus, Christ's resurrection is described as the *first fruits* of the resurrection of believers (1 Cor 15:20, 23). More than that, believers are united with Christ in his resurrection. William Dykstra discusses this in the context of 1 Cor 15:20–28, which is consistent with and bears many similarities to Rev 20:4–6:

> The recognition that Christ is not a unique case as the Corinthians supposed, but that he is head of the body, that his relation to his own is one of corporate solidarity—this recognition is indispensable for an understanding of Paul's argument. . . . For in Christ's resurrection the dead in fact rise. Christ is risen as the *aparchē* ["first fruits"]; in his resurrection lies the guarantee that those in Christ shall rise (vv. 20ff.). Calvin had an eye for this element in Paul's argument. Commenting on vv. 13–14, he says, "Christ did not die or rise again for Himself, but for us, therefore His resurrection is the substance (*hypostasis*) of ours."[121]

The Bible says that we are "in Christ" and that God has *"raised us up with Him, and seated us with Him in the heavenly places in Christ Jesus."*[122] As observed earlier, there is a clear parallel between Eph 2:5–7 and Rev 20:4–6. In Eph 2:5–6, being *"made alive"* and *"raised up"* are based on "union with Christ" and "participating in the resurrection of Jesus."[123] Further, Rev 20:6 says, *"Blessed and holy is the one who has a part in [or 'shares in'] the first resurrection."*[124] Hughes comments, "One does not share in one's own but in another's resurrection; and it is precisely the resurrection of Jesus in which believers share in this final age, and even after the experience of physical death during that interval

---

119. Beale, *Revelation*, 1005.

120. Hughes, "First Resurrection," 317.

121. Dykstra, "I Corinthians 15:20–28," 207; see also Wellum, "Christ's Resurrection," 82–83; Holleman, *Resurrection and Parousia*, 44, 55–57.

122. Eph 2:6; see also Col 2:12–13; 3:1–4; Rom 6:4–5; Eph 5:14.

123. BDAG, *"suzōpoieō,"* 954–55; *"sunegeirō,"* 967.

124. The Greek word is *meros*, which can mean "part" or "share." BDAG, *"meros,"* 633–34. In Rev 20:6 *meros* is part of the phrase *echōn meros en,"* which BDAG specifically cites as meaning "having a share in." Ibid., 634.

between death and (the second) resurrection 'as we wait for . . . the redemption of our bodies' (Rom. 8:23)."[125]

The "regeneration" view is closely akin to the "resurrection of Christ" view. It goes back at least as far as Augustine.[126] R. Fowler White summarizes, "In keeping with the doctrine of spiritual resurrection taught in Ezekiel 36–37 and John 5:24–25 (cf. 1 John 3:14), the first resurrection is the spiritual resurrection of those in bondage to their sins, their spiritual redemption from the second death, their spiritual reconstitution as God's kingdom of priests."[127] Norman Shepherd links this to the conversion, transformation, and in-grafting into Christ wrought in baptism.[128]

For Rev 20:6 to affirm that those who take part in the first resurrection will be priests and reign with Christ "is to say that they will do so first on earth before they die and then in heaven after they die" because both propositions "are applicable to Christians as the kingdom of priests ([Rev] 1:6; 5:10)."[129] White adds, "The saints in [Rev 20:]9 are the living constituents of the kingdom of priests on earth, whereas the martyrs in v 4 are its dead constituents in heaven," and "'kingdom of priests' (1:6) is the nominal equivalent of 'they will be priests of God and Christ and will reign with him' (20:6)."[130] He observes, "To say that the second death has no power over those who take part in the first resurrection is simply to say that Christ has freed them from their sins by his blood—a redemptive benefit indisputably applied to believers before they die."[131] White concludes, "In keeping with the doctrine of spiritual resurrection taught in Ezekiel 36–37 and John 5:24–25 (cf. 1 John 3:14), the first resurrection is the spiritual resurrection of those in bondage to their sins, their spiritual redemption from the second death, their spiritual reconstitution as God's kingdom of priests."[132] This is confirmed by Rev 2:11 where:

> we have the same identical promise, that certain persons "shall not be hurt by the second death," the promise relates not to risen and glorified men, but to "him who overcometh" in the struggle for "the crown of life" (Rev. ii. 10, 11). And as exemption from the power of the second death is here made to rest upon a certain character, namely, fidelity to Christ even to death, and in [Rev 20:6] exemption from the power of the same second death is made to rest upon participation in the first resurrection, is it not reasonable to conclude that this "first resurrection" is meant to signify a certain character in the present life, and not the possession of bodily resurrection and glory?[133]

Meredith Kline articulates the third, "death of the believer," view:

---

125. Hughes, "First Resurrection," 317.

126. Augustine, *Civ.,* 20.6–10.

127. White, "Death and the First Resurrection," 22.

128. Shepherd, "Resurrections," 36–38; see also Venema, *Promise,* 331–37; Ulfgard, *Feast and Future,* 62–65.

129. White, "Death and the First Resurrection," 13.

130. Ibid., 14n.28, 15n.32.

131. Ibid., 20.

132. Ibid., 22; see also White, "The Millennial Kingdom-City," 5–6, 17–18.

133. Brown, *Christ's Second Coming,* 219, emphasis in original.

The proper decipherment of "the first resurrection" in the interlocking schema of first-(second) resurrection and (first)-second death is now obvious enough. Just as the resurrection of the unjust is paradoxically identified as "the second death" so the death of the Christian is paradoxically identified as "the first resurrection." . . . The real meaning of their passage from earthly life is to be found in the state to which it leads them. And John sees the Christian dead living and reigning with Christ (vv. 4, 6). . . . Hence the use of the paradoxical metaphor of "the first resurrection" (vv. 5f) for the death of the faithful believer. What for others is the first death is for the Christian a veritable resurrection![134]

Although some may object that the translation of the soul of the believer to heaven in the intermediate state is not elsewhere referred to as a "resurrection,"[135] Beale points out that "the use of 'life' for the intermediate heavenly state prior to physical resurrection can be found elsewhere in the NT and Jewish literature."[136] He adds:

The use of *zaō* ["came to life"] and *anastasis* ["resurrection"] to indicate translation of the soul to a higher state of life in heaven through physical death appears to fall within a legitimate range of use, especially to connote the figurative picture of ironic victory in a context of persecution and earthly defeat. . . . Though the Christian's body appears defeated by the curse of death, at that moment the soul is blessed by rising into God's immediate presence. The ascent of the soul can be conceived of as a "resurrection" because it is an escalated stage of the spiritual resurrection, as well as of kingship and priesthood, that has already taken place in human life.[137]

In harmonizing these three views, it is important to note that all agree on the essentials of the contrasting "first-second" schema of Rev 20:4–6. All are grounded on the believer's regenerated and transformed life, union with Christ, and participation in Christ's resurrection, all of which begin in this life and carry-over into the intermediate state after death. The "resurrection of Christ" and "regeneration" views amount to different ways of articulating the same transformation of believers, the first focusing on the source of the "first resurrection," the second on its subjects. The "death of the believer" view focuses on the contextual specificity of the phrases "came to life" and "first resurrection" in Rev 20:4–5, i.e., the dead believers in heaven.[138]

Beale discusses the compatibility of the different views as follows: "translation from physical death to spiritual life in heaven should not be seen as a spiritual resurrection distinct from regeneration on earth but as a continuation and escalation of regenerate existence in heaven, since regeneration elsewhere is viewed as spiritual resurrection. . . . This understanding of the Augustinian view may be compatible with Kline's position, since regeneration could be seen as the preconsummate phase pointing to the consummate literal resurrection."[139]

---

134. Kline, "First Resurrection," 371; see also Storms, *Kingdom Come,* 451–65.

135. Page, "Revelation 20," 37.

136. Beale, *Revelation,* 1008. See Luke 20:37–38; 1 Pet 4:6; Rev 2:10–11.

137. Ibid., 1010–11.

138. Johnson, *Triumph,* 293.

139. Beale, *Revelation,* 1012; see also Garlington, "Reigning," n.p.n.74.

In fact, each view entails the others. The Christian dead John saw in Rev 20:4 manifest their status as priests and rulers which the "first resurrection" entails but which may not be visible during life on the earth. However, to be manifested, such status first had to be *possessed* by them before their physical deaths.[140] Thus, the three views might better be seen as three different perspectives of the same phenomenon. Regardless of the perspective one uses, the relationship of the "first resurrection" to the "thousand years" rules out premillennialism, as Kline explains: "The way 'the first resurrection' is identified with living and reigning with Christ a thousand years in Revelation 20:4-6 has the effect of connecting the qualifying force of *protos* quite directly to 'the thousand years.' The millennium as such is virtually called a 'first' age. It falls within the days of this present passing world characterized by 'the first things.' The *Parousia* with its concomitant consummative events of resurrection and judgment must then follow these 'thousand years.' The premillennial view of the Second Advent is excluded."[141]

Premillennialist failure to appreciate the contrasting "first-second" schema of Rev 20:4-6

It is the premillennialists' failure to see that the terms "first" and "second" in Rev 20:4-5 indicate *contrast*, not *sequence,* that leads them to insist that both uses of *ezēsan* in Rev 20:4-5 must mean the same thing. Thus, premillennialist Jack S. Deere argues that when *anastasis* ("resurrection") is used in the NT in all cases but one it refers to bodily resurrection, and "the decisive term is not the adjective 'first' but the noun 'resurrection' which it modifies."[142] R. Fowler White responds:

> Deere's statistical argument overlooks two key points. First, of the occurrences of the noun in the NT, the two in Revelation 20 are the only instances modified by an ordinal. The other NT instances of the noun do not form a proper analogy to the occurrences in Rev 20:5-6. Second, the best analogy to "the first resurrection" is "the second death" in Rev 2:11; 20:6, 14; 21:8. In this latter phrase, the noun cannot be the decisive term, else it would not be different in meaning from "death," when in fact we know it is (N.B. 2:10-11): among other things, "death" is death of the preconsummate kind; "the second death," death of the consummate kind. The presence of the ordinal *prōtos* with *anastasis* is therefore decisive, indicating the resurrection of the preconsummate kind, the resurrection that belongs to the preconsummate phase of Christ's kingdom, the resurrection that occurs as long as the first heaven and earth (21:1) remain.[143]

Further, the premillennialist approach to the language of "resurrection" used by the apostle John "neglect[s] the possibility of the presence of a visionary and symbolic

---

140. White, "Death and the First Resurrection," 12-13.

141. Kline, "First Resurrection," 374.

142. Deere, "Premillennialism," 71, 72n.55.

143. White, "Death and the First Resurrection," 2n.4; see also Storms, *Kingdom Come*, 464-65 ("That which is 'first' belongs to the order of this present passing world. 'The first resurrection' must then be something this side of bodily resurrection, some experience that does not bring the subject of it into his consummated condition and final state.").

level . . . [instead moving] almost immediately from the linguistic level to the referential level."[144] Poythress elaborates this important exegetical point:

> The intended historical referent may be either a bodily resurrection, or new birth, or an enthronement of the disembodied souls of martyrs to reign with Christ in heaven. If any of these were the intended referents, the visionary framework would lead us to expect that on the visionary level the events would be vividly visible in concrete bodily form. The imagery of resurrection and life is appropriate. Naturally the linguistic level, as a terse transcription of the visionary level, uses the usual words *anastasis* and *zaō* to describe the vision.
>
> To put it another way, the words for resurrection and life in 20:1–6 are no less and no more "literal" than are the words for beast and wound in 13:1–8. John used the words "beast" and "wound" because on the visionary level he saw a beast and a (healed) wound. In 20:1–6 he used the words for resurrection and life because on the visionary level he saw resurrection and life. In neither case do the words, by themselves, provide any clue as to whether the symbolic, visionary depiction enjoys a direct or indirect relation to its historical referent. The nature of the referent remains unsettled. The vocabulary is what it is because it describes a vision, not because it literally describes the referent of the vision.[145]

Premillennialists are, in fact, arbitrary in insisting that both resurrections be *physical* resurrections since the *nature* and *ends* of the "two resurrections" are opposite: one is to blessing and eternal life, and one is to condemnation and death. Certainly the ends or destinies of the "resurrections" are more important than their mode.[146]

Finally, premillennialists are inconsistent in that they do *not* similarly insist that the "two deaths" be treated exactly alike. As Kline states, "The arbitrariness of the customary premillennial insistence that 'the first resurrection' must be a bodily rising from the grave if the second resurrection is such is exposed by the inconsistent recognition by premillennial exegesis that, although the first death is the loss of physical life, 'the second death' is death of a different kind, death in a metaphorical rather than literal, physical sense."[147]

By not taking into account the significance of "first" coupled with "resurrection," "second" coupled with "death," and the contrasting, as opposed to sequential, "first-second" schema of Rev 20:4–6, the premillennial insistence on "consistency" and "literalism" in fact leads to serious inconsistency, arbitrariness, and to the disregarding of vital aspects of the *parousia* that are clearly and repeatedly established throughout the NT.

Conclusion

The New Testament sets forth a comprehensive two-age scheme in which "this age" of sin and things temporal is succeeded by the "age to come" that will be eternal and without sin. Although it has been inaugurated by Christ's first coming, the "age to come" will be consummated at his second coming which will entail resurrection and judgment for all persons, living and dead, and the restoration of all of creation. Revelation 20 is consistent

---

144. Poythress, "Genre and Hermeneutics," 46.

145. Ibid., 47.

146. See Kline, "First Resurrection," 371.

147. Ibid., 367; see also Venema, *Promise*, 337–38.

with that New Testament pattern. Both Revelation 20 and the rest of Scripture leave no room, either temporally or exegetically, for a provisional "millennial reign" of Christ and his saints following the *parousia*.

Appendix 3

Ezekiel 40–48 (Ezekiel's vision of a new temple)[1]

WHILE ISRAEL WAS IN exile in Babylon, Ezekiel had a vision of a new temple and a New Jerusalem.

The temple Ezekiel saw in his vision was unlike any other physical temple

Ezekiel's temple was square, 500 reeds (about one mile) in size[2]

The size of Ezekiel's temple is approximately the same size as the boundaries of ancient Jerusalem itself during the second temple era.[3] The description by Ezekiel generally lists only lengths and widths, not heights, except for side pillars of 60 cubits (Ezek 40:14).

Ezekiel's temple lacks essential elements from the tabernacle and Solomon's temple

There is no reference to the bronze basin, golden lampstand, table of showbread, altar of incense, veil separating the holy of holies, ark of the covenant, cherubim, anointing oil, or high priest.

As part of the vision, God told Ezekiel that the land of Israel would be divided among the tribes in a completely new way

There were to be thirteen parallel strips of land, apparently of equal widths, running east to west between the Mediterranean Sea and the Jordan River, twelve for the tribes and one for the Lord (Ezek 45:1–8; 47:13–48:29).

---

1. This appendix is part of a larger section entitled "The Temple and the Earth: God's Dwelling Place with Mankind," in Menn, *Biblical Theology*.

2. Ezek 42:15–20; see Ezek 40:5; see also Ezek 48:30–35 which speaks of 4500 cubits per side.

3. Beale, *Temple*, 341.

The temple and city Ezekiel saw in the vision were not intended as plans for construction of a literal temple and city

Several factors indicate that what Ezekiel envisioned was not a "construction plan"

"There is no indication in Ezekiel that the construction of such a city and such a Temple was authorized by God. . . . The new Temple is God's doing. The prophet's only task is to describe it in as full detail as he can."[4] Indeed, "the sheer impracticability of much of the vision leads one to the view that its message is in the symbolism, not in its architecture or in the literal partitioning of the land."[5] Those "impracticabilities" include:

- The reference to the *"very high mountain"* on which the city was located (Ezek 40:2).[6]

- The measurements generally include only lengths and widths but omit heights.

- The absence of any reference to the bronze basin, golden lampstand, table of showbread, altar of incense, veil separating the holy of holies, ark of the covenant, temple furniture, or any "wall around the inner court, to which its three massive gates might stand in relation."[7]

- "The massive size of the gatehouses verges on caricature: their dimensions (25x50 cubits) exceed those of the main hall of the Temple (20x40 cubits); their length is half that of the inner court (100 cubits)!"[8]

To the extent that Ezekiel's temple and God's presence were intended to replace Solomon's temple, they were conditional on Israel's repenting and obeying God completely, which Israel did not do

God's conditions included repentance and obedience (Ezek 43:6–12; 45:9–12) and land redistribution for the Lord, the priests, Levites, tribes, and Gentiles (Ezek 45:1–8; 47:13–48:29). The people did not repent and obey the Lord (see Ezra 10; Hag 1:1–11). The temple they finally built under the leadership of Zerubbabel was not built according to Ezekiel's vision and did not compare in glory even to Solomon's temple (Ezra 3:8–13; Hag 2:1–3). Even after the temple was completed, Israel and its priesthood did not repent of their sinful and disobedient ways (Malachi 1–4). Land redistribution never was done.

---

4. Taylor, "The Temple," 68.

5. Ibid.

6. The fact that Ezekiel did not see an actual city, but only *"a structure like a city"* (Ezek 40:2) indicates that this is not to be taken literally. Dennis Johnson states, "Prophets describe their visions in such cautious and ambiguous similes in order to keep readers from a wooden literalism, lest we forget the limited capacity of human experience and language to convey heavenly reality." Johnson, *Triumph*, 216n.24.

7. Greenberg, "Design and Themes," 193.

8. Ibid.

Certain features of Ezekiel's vision show that it always was intended to be symbolic and heavenly, not physical, in nature

The introductory formula (Ezek 40:1–2)

The introduction in Ezek 40:1–2 contains three elements: (1) reference to a specific date when the experience occurred; (2) a statement that *"the hand of the Lord was upon me"*; and (3) a statement that he saw "visions." The only other places in Ezekiel where that three-fold introductory formula occurs are in Ezek 1:1–3 and 8:1–3. In both of those other cases, the vision which Ezekiel saw was of a *heavenly* temple (i.e., God's dwelling place in heaven), not an earthly one. The heavenly temple is explicitly clear in Ezek 1:1–28 where the focus is exclusively in heaven.

In Ezek 8:1—11:23 the vision is of the heavenly presence that is linked to God's earthly presence with his people. Ezekiel saw the glory of God (8:4), which in the days of Solomon's Temple dwelt in the Temple. However, Ezekiel then saw the abominations which were being done in the physical temple (8:5–17). Therefore, the glory of God began to leave the physical temple (9:3). The scene then shifts to the heavenly temple (10:1–22), and the glory of God completes his departure from the physical temple (10:4; 11:22–23). God's presence is still with the faithful exiles in Babylon (11:16), who are the true earthly temple, even though the physical temple building had been destroyed by the Babylonians.

The river (Ezek 47:2–12)

In Ezekiel's vision, the river must be symbolic and supernatural because even though no tributaries are mentioned, the water gets progressively deeper, from a trickle to a river that could not be forded (47:2–5). Unlike a natural, earthly river, it makes salt water fresh rather than *vice verse* (47:6–12).

The significance of the first coming of Christ

Although Ezekiel wrote using language and imagery that his immediate audience could understand, in light of the coming of Christ Ezekiel's temple could not possibly represent a literal, physical building to be constructed in the future.

- Throughout his vision Ezekiel describes animal sacrifices which are said to have an "atoning" purpose and effect (Ezek 43:13–27; 45:15–25). Such sacrifices could not possibly truly be atoning sacrifices, since that would reverse redemptive history and deny the efficacy and sufficiency of Christ's once-and-for-all sacrifice of himself, contrary to Heb 9:11—10:22. That also would return to the "shadows" in place of the substance and reality (see Col 2:16–17; Heb 8:1–10:22).

- To take "literally" (i.e., physically) Ezekiel's portrait of Jerusalem as the center of the world's worship (Ezekiel 47–48), where non-Israelites are excluded from the temple (Ezek 44:6–9), likewise completely reverses what Christ has done. Jesus eliminated the requirement that worship be conducted at some special place (John 4:21, 23) and eliminated the distinction between Jews and Gentiles among God's people.[9]

- To say that the sacrifices are simply "memorials" of Christ's sacrifice means that there is likewise no reason to take the temple itself "literally" (i.e., as a physical structure). To view the sacrifices referred to by Ezekiel as "memorials" also would dishonor Christ since the only memorial that Christ himself gave to "memorialize" his redemptive work was the Lord's Supper, not a return to OT sacrifices (Luke 22:14–20; 1 Cor 11:23–26).[10]

David Holwerda concludes:

> The essential truth of Ezekiel's temple has become reality apart from a building of stone. That may seem like a surprising twist in the fulfillment of prophecy, but with Stephen and the prophet Isaiah we should know that "the Most High does not dwell in houses made with human hands" (Acts 7:48). God dwells in Jesus and in us (John 14:23), and the reality of Ezekiel's temple exists throughout the world. . . . When fulfillment happens, the institutions that were types or symbols of that reality are no longer necessary. They are displaced by the reality they symbolize. Jesus' body is the new temple because Jesus is both the place of atonement and the place of God's presence. . . . Jesus did not come to turn Ezekiel's architectural blueprints into the most magnificent temple ever constructed by human hands. That the Messiah was supposed to do this was the misunderstanding of Jesus' opponents, a misunderstanding shared by his own disciples until the resurrection opened their minds. Ezekiel's temple of glory is Jesus, a truth revealed in the incarnation, proclaimed in Jesus' teaching, and made understandable by his resurrection [John 2:21–22].[11]

Jesus inaugurated the fulfillment of Ezekiel's vision of a new temple in himself and in his people (the church)

Ezekiel's vision showed the "glory of the Lord" filling the temple, and would dwell among his people forever[12]

John uses language about Jesus reminiscent of Ezekiel: *"And the Word became flesh, and dwelt among us, and we saw his glory, glory as of the only begotten from the Father, full of grace and truth."*[13] Jesus said that, through the Holy Spirit, he would dwell in his people and would always be with us.[14] Fulfillment of that promise began on the Day of Pentecost when the disciples were filled with the Holy Spirit (Acts 2:1–21).

---

9. 1 Cor 12:13; Gal 3:28; Eph 2:11–22; Col 3:11; Rev 5:9; 7:9.

10. See Venema, *Promise*, 285–86. See also Sizer, "The Temple," 254; Sizer, *Zion's Christian Soldiers*, 119.

11. Holwerda, *Jesus and Israel*, 74–75.

12. Ezek 43:1–9; see also Ezek 37:26.

13. John 1:14; see also Luke 9:32; John 2:11; 2 Pet 1:16–18.

14. Matt 28:20; John 14:16–17; Heb 13:5.

Ezekiel's vision showed a river of life-giving water flowing out from under the temple (Ezek 47:1–12)

Since Jesus is God's true temple, he is the true source of life-giving water. In John 4:10–14, he told the Samaritan woman that he is the source of eternal, *"living water."* In John 7:37–39, Jesus said, referring to his giving the Holy Spirit, *"If anyone is thirsty, let him come to me and drink. He who believes in me, as the Scripture said, 'From his innermost being will flow rivers of living water.'"* Since no OT text explicitly says *"from His innermost being will flow rivers of living water,"* it is likely that "a multiple allusion to pertinent scriptures is in mind. Those would be passages that were of prime significance for the meaning of the festival and were read at it: chief among them were the record of the gift of water from the rock in the desert, Exod 17:1–6 (cf. also Pss 78:15–16; 105:40–41), the flowing of the river of living water from the temple in the kingdom of God, Ezek 47:1–11, and the waters that flow in the new age from Jerusalem to the eastern and western seas, Zech 14:8."[15] In other words, Jesus connects the eschatological temple of Ezekiel with himself as the new temple. Hence, the waters flow not from a physical temple in Jerusalem but from Jesus himself. The church is the channel of the life-giving water whose source is Jesus.

Ezekiel's final vision builds upon and consummates what he earlier had said in Ezek 37:26–28

Just as that passage twice said that God would *"set up a sanctuary in their midst forever,"* so Ezek 43:7–9 twice says *"I will dwell among them forever."* In 2 Cor 6:16—7:1 Paul linked the promises of Lev 26:11–12, 2 Sam 7:14, and Ezek 37:27 and showed how fulfillment of those promises was inaugurated in the church.

The New Jerusalem (Rev 21:1—22:5), not a physical building to be constructed on the earth in the future, is the consummation of Ezekiel's temple (Ezekiel 40–48) and is the true reality to which Ezekiel's vision pointed[16]

In Ezek 40:2, Ezekiel was taken to a "very high mountain" where he saw a "structure like a city"

There are no "very high mountains" in or around physical Jerusalem. Further, the fact that he saw a structure "like" a city suggests that Ezekiel is entering into "the realm of symbolic

---

15. Beasley-Murray, *John,* 116.

16. The symbolic nature of Ezekiel's vision is indicated in an intriguing article by Bob Pickle, "Ezekiel's City: Calculating the Circumference of the Earth" (2004). Pickle views the city and land allotment given to Ezekiel as a model of the new earth. He says, "If we enlarge Ezekiel's map [i.e., the 13 strips of land allotted to the tribes and the Lord] till Ezekiel's city is the size of Revelation's New Jerusalem, then Ezekiel's map encircles the globe. The proportion of Ezekiel's city to Revelation's New Jerusalem is the same as that of Ezekiel's map to the earth's circumference." His calculations are based on a number of assumptions: (1) He uses 4500 cubits for each side of Ezekiel's city (Ezek 48:30–35); (2) All 13 strips of land (Ezek 45:1–8; 47:13—48:29) have equal widths of 25,000 cubits (for a total of 325,000 cubits); (3)

geography of heaven and earth that pertains to eschatological conditions."[17] That is confirmed by Rev 21:10 which parallels Ezekiel's language in describing the New Jerusalem. That passage says an angel *"carried me away in the Spirit to a great and high mountain, and showed me the holy city, Jerusalem, coming down out of heaven from God."*

In Ezekiel's vision both the temple and the city are described as square[18]

The identification of Ezekiel's city with the New Jerusalem is confirmed by Rev 21:16 which describes New Jerusalem as "laid out as a square." The Greek word literally is "four-square" (*tetragōnos*). "The Greek OT of Ezek. 45:1–5 and 41:21 uses the same word for the entire temple complex."[19]

The essential element of Ezekiel's vision is that God is present and will dwell among his people forever

The book of Ezekiel ends with the statement, *"the name of the city from that day shall be, 'The Lord is there'"* (Ezek 48:35). That is fulfilled in the New Jerusalem of Revelation 21–22.

- Ezek 43:7–9 twice says *"I will dwell among them forever."* In the Greek OT, the root for "dwell" in Ezek 43:7 is "tabernacle." Rev 21:3 indicates that the New Jerusalem is the consummation of all prophecy, including Ezekiel's vision, by echoing Ezek 43:7, 9 and twice saying *"the tabernacle of God is among men"* and *"He will dwell among them."* Also, three times Rev 21:3 says that God will be *"among"* his people.

- Ezek 43:7 says, *"This is the place of my throne."* Rev 22:1, 3 both state that *"the throne of God and of the Lamb"* will be in New Jerusalem.

- The apostles and the tribes of Israel are described as part of the very structure of New Jerusalem itself: the apostles are the foundation (Rev 21:14); the twelve tribes are the gates (Rev 21:12–13). Not only are Ezekiel's temple and the New Jerusalem the same shape, they both have twelve gates in the same configuration: three on the north; three on the east; three on the south; three on the west.[20] "The integration of the apostles together with the tribes of Israel as part of the city-temple's structure prophesied in Ezekiel 40–48 confirms further our assessment . . . that the multiracial Christian church will be the redeemed group who, together with Christ, will fulfill Ezekiel's prophecy of the future temple and city. This is in line with other NT pas-

---

The size of New Jerusalem (Rev 21:16) is 3000 stadia *per side,* for a *total* of 12,000 stadia, not 12,000 stadia per side (the Greek says only that the measurement was "12,000 stadia" and that *"its length is as great as its width"*); (4) Each Roman stadium is between 606–607 feet in length. Although Pickle's idea is not what is being contended for here, it is intriguing and recognizes that what Ezekiel saw was, at root, to be taken symbolically, rather than as an actual physical building and city to be constructed in the future.

17. Beale, *Temple,* 336.

18. Ezek 42:15–20; 48:15–20.

19. Ibid., 348n.37.

20. Compare Ezek 48:31–34 and Rev 21:12–13.

sages in which the whole covenant community forms a spiritual temple where God's presence dwells (1 Cor. 3:16–17; 6:19; 2 Cor. 6:16; Eph. 2:21–22; 1 Pet. 2:5)."[21]

- Ezekiel's temple is at the center of everything. In New Jerusalem, there is no physical temple building *"for the Lord God the Almighty and the Lamb are its temple"* (Rev 21:22). Thus, the true temple—God and the Lamb—is now central. "The equation of God and the Lamb with the temple approaches closely the essence of the Ezekiel vision, which is God's glorious presence itself (e.g., 48:35, 'the name of the city' is 'the Lord is there'). All that Israel's old temple pointed to, the expanding presence of God, has been fulfilled in Revelation 21:1—22:5, and such a fulfillment has been anticipated within Ezekiel 40–48 itself."[22]

Ezek 47:1–12 describes a river flowing from out of the temple which is healing and life-giving

Rev 22:1–2 uses the same imagery and applies it to the New Jerusalem. The identification of the river in Ezekiel's vision with the river in the New Jerusalem is corroborated by Ezek 47:7, 12 which says that there were trees on both banks of the river. That parallels Rev 22:2 which similarly says that the tree of life was *"on either side of the river."* In both cases the trees are said to bear fruit (Ezek 47:12; Rev 22:2). Further, in both cases the leaves of the trees are "for healing" (Ezek 47:12; Rev 22:2).

Ezekiel's temple would only be a reality for those who had put away their abominations and sins (Ezek 43:6–9)

Echoing Ezek 43:6–9, Rev 21:8, 27 say that *"nothing unclean, and no one who practices abomination"* will be in the New Jerusalem. That shows that Ezekiel's temple could only be referring to people who are "in Christ." Just as Christ inaugurated his kingdom and forever forgave sins at his first coming, so the New Jerusalem forms the consummation of Christ's kingdom, in which sins are forever eliminated.

Ezekiel's Temple: conclusion

Many would see Ezekiel's expansive vision of the Temple (chs. 40–48) as encouraging a belief that there will be an end-time Temple matching Ezekiel's prophetic description. Yet a biblical theologian cannot approach this prophecy without noting the way in which this prophecy is understood by the New Testament writers. Ezekiel's imagery of the river flowing from the Temple (Ezek. 47:1ff) reappears twice in the New Testament. In John 7:37–9 the 'rivers of living water' flow from Jesus himself; meanwhile in Revelation the 'river of the water of life' flows through the middle of the New Jerusalem (Rev. 22:1ff). These two writers have consciously drawn upon Ezekiel's prophecy and applied it to Jesus and the heavenly Jerusalem. As a result, they were presumably not expecting Ezekiel's

21. Beale, *Revelation*, 1070.

22. Beale, *Temple*, 348.

prophecy to be fulfilled literally at some future point in a physical Temple. Instead this prophecy became a brilliant way of speaking pictorially of what God had now achieved in and through Jesus. Paradoxically, therefore, although Ezekiel's vision had focused so much upon the Temple, it found its ultimate fulfillment in that city where there was 'no Temple', because 'its Temple is the Lord God Almighty and the Lamb' (Rev. 21:22).[23]

23. Walker, *Jesus*, 313.

APPENDIX 4

Dan 9:24–27 (the "seventy weeks")

DAN 9:24–27 "PRESENT THE most difficult text in the book, as commentators agree, but they most certainly do not agree as to the right way to understand the figures given. . . . All one can do is to continue to apply agreed criteria as consistently as possible, weigh carefully the conclusions of others, and make suggestions as to the most likely solution to a difficult problem."[1]

Interpretive Issues and Problems with the Passage

There are several issues and problems that make Dan 9:24–27 difficult to interpret. Each one of them requires the interpreter to make a choice. The number and importance of these issues means that there will always be disagreement over the correct interpretation of the passage. To a large degree, these problems stem from the difficulty of the text itself: "The density of the passage, the extreme singularity of its words and expressions, and the complexity of its syntax constitute rather serious obstacles. Moreover, the important divergences between the two basic [Greek] versions . . . do not permit us to draw any definitive conclusions regarding the text."[2]

Almost every phrase in the passage is ambiguous. The following are some, but not all, of the issues and questions the passage raises.

---

1. Baldwin, *Daniel,* 163.
2. Doukhan, "Seventy Weeks," 1.

9:24—"Seventy weeks have been decreed for your people and your holy city, to finish the transgression, to make an end of sin, to make atonement for iniquity, to bring in everlasting righteousness, to seal up vision and prophecy and to anoint the most holy place."

Seventy "weeks"? "sevens"? "periods of time"?

"The basic sense of the word is a 'period of seven'; thus the normal sense is 'week' or 'seven days.' This common usage of the word can be seen in Daniel 10:2, 3. The word can also mean 'a period of seven years'; if taken in this sense, it would be best to translate it as 'sevens' and 70 'sevens' would be 490 years. But the word is definitely ambiguous and it is wise to recognize the ambiguity before positing too rigid an interpretation."[3] "In the preceding context, the original seventy years of Jeremiah's prophecy is in Daniel's mind (Dan. 9:2). Thus years rather than literal weeks is suggested by the prior reference."[4]

On the other hand, Leupold observes a grammatical peculiarity that needs to be taken into account:

> *Shabhu'a*, "week," regularly has as a plural the *feminine* form *shabhu'oth*, "weeks." In this chapter (v. 24, 25, 26, 27) Daniel uses a different form, viz., *shahu'im, masculine* plural. True, in 10:2, 3 this form recurs, seemingly in reminiscence of our chapter, but with the word "days" appended, *shabhu'im yamim*. Now the singular means "a period of seven," "a heptad." . . . Since there is nothing in our chapter that indicates a "heptad of days" as a meaning for *shabhu'im* or a "heptad of years," the only safe translation . . . is seventy "heptads"—seventy "sevens." . . . "Seventy" contains seven multiplied by ten, which, being a round number, signifies perfection, completion. Therefore, "seventy heptads"—7x7x10—is the period in which the divine work of greatest moment is brought to perfection.[5]

Chronology or chronography?

If it is assumed that the "seventy weeks" refers to 70 periods of 7 years, or a total of 490 years, then the question is: Are these periods meant to be taken as a strict *chronology* (i.e., the sequential order in which the events of history occur) or as a *chronography* (i.e., "a stylized scheme of history used to interpret historical data rather than arising from them"[6])?

"Both the numbers 7 and 70 indicate a certain roundness or completeness in Hebrew thought. Seven is not only the number of days in a week, but also the number of years in a sabbatical cycle. And 70 is used, in both OT and NT, of groups of people; it is, for example, the number of disciples sent out by Jesus during his earthly ministry (Lk. 10:1). These and

---

3. Elwell, *Baker Encyclopedia,* 2:1930.

4. Gentry, "Daniel's Seventy Weeks," n.p.

5. Leupold, *Exposition,* 409. "What led Dan. to employ the m. instead of the f. however, is not clear unless it was for the deliberate purpose of calling attention to the fact that the word *sevens* is employed in an unusual sense." Young, *Prophecy of Daniel,* 195.

6. Goldingay, *Daniel,* 257.

other factors indicate that the numbers 7 and 70 may have symbolic significance."[7] Thus, in Matt 18:22 Jesus told Peter to forgive his brother 70 x 7 times. That number clearly is not to be interpreted "literally," as if Peter was supposed to keep a record and was not required to forgive his brother on the 491st occasion.

Even the text is unclear: "The MT [Masoretic Text, the authoritative Hebrew version of the OT, completed about AD 130] places an *atnah* [division] between the seven weeks and the sixty-two weeks [of 9:25]. The RSV and ESV follow the MT and read, "from the going forth of the word to restore and build Jerusalem to the coming of an anointed one, a prince, there shall be seven weeks. Then for sixty-two weeks it shall be built again." Theodotion,[8] however, reads "seven weeks and sixty-two weeks." The NASB, NKJV, and NIV follow Theodotion. If that is the correct version, "sixty-nine weeks must expire before the appearance of the *mashiach,* not seven."[9] If chronography is intended, then the starting points of the different periods of "weeks" may overlap, or the different periods may not follow immediately after each other, or they may not be tied to fixed dates or starting points at all.

What do "finish," "make an end of," "make atonement for," "bring in everlasting righteousness," and "seal up" mean in this context?

"Three times over it is stated that God will cancel ('finish', 'put an end to', 'atone for') the evil done ('the transgression', 'sin', 'iniquity'). The text for this particular verse is not at all certain and several shades of meaning can be read into the various expressions."[10] "The word for 'transgression' is definite and . . . previously 'the transgression' was associated with the attack on Jerusalem and destruction of the temple by Antiochus IV in 167 BC. Others equate 'the transgression' with Israel's rebellion against God and subsequent exile in Babylon, finally ending with the overthrow of Antiochus. Futurist interpreters understand the reference to 'transgression' as a term for 'sin in general' that will not end until the second coming and eternal reign of Jesus Christ."[11]

"The interpretation to *finish* or *complete* does not seem justifiable. The original is difficult, but a good case can be made in defence of the present translation [i.e., 'for restraining the transgression']. . . . [Regarding '*make an end of sin*':] The word may be read *to seal up sin,* and then it is taken in the sense of *taking away,* or *removed out of sight.* However, . . . to seal up sin elsewhere signifies 'to reserve it for punishment' (Job 14:17, cf. Deut. 32:34). The word is difficult."[12] Regarding "*seal up vision and prophecy*": "Sealing elsewhere suggests authenticating (1 Kgs 21:8), and that fits the present context well: the promise is that Jeremiah's prophecy will be fulfilled and thus confirmed."[13] "Alternatively

---

7. Elwell, *Baker Encyclopedia,* 2:1930

8. Hebrew scholar who translated the OT into Greek approximately AD 150.

9. McComiskey, "The Seventy," 19.

10. Russell, *Daniel,* 184.

11. Hill, "Daniel," 169.

12. Young, *Prophecy of Daniel,* 198–99, citations omitted.

13. Goldingay, *Daniel,* 260.

it may mean that the 'vision and prophet' are 'sealed up' in the sense that they have now come to an end, for with the coming of the promised time they are no longer needed."[14]

Who or what is the "most holy" (place? person? or people?) that is to be "anointed"?

"*To anoint a most holy place* (lit. 'a most holy'; the object is not specified; *cf.* RSV mg.). The ambiguity may best be explained by the context."[15] The Hebrew expression translated "most holy" does not have a definite article ("the") in front of it and literally means "a holy of holies." The phrase "occurs at 22 other places in the OT and may refer to equipment in the tabernacle (5 times), sacred areas of land, particularly as dedicated to priests (3), sacrifices (2), the priests' portions of the sacrifices (10), and persons (2). . . . A similar phrase employing the definite article, 'the holy of holies,' occurs 16 additional times, often denoting the most holy place within a sanctuary. But in all these 38 instances outside of Dan 9:24 there is not a single undisputed reference to a temple building."[16]

Different suggestions have been made, including: a rededicated temple building; the Messiah (Christ's baptism); the church as God's "spiritual temple"; the heavenly New Jerusalem; a millennial temple or Christ's enthronement as king in the millennium (dispensationalism); or "in accordance with the usage of the Dead Sea Scrolls, [it may] refer to a community."[17]

For all six of the purposes of the seventy weeks, are they intended in an absolute, perfect, and final sense, or are they intended in the sense of being inaugurated or achieved in principle within the seventy weeks?

9:25—"So you are to know and discern that from the issuing of a decree to restore and rebuild Jerusalem until Messiah the Prince there will be seven weeks and sixty-two weeks; it will be built again, with plaza and moat, even in times of distress."

Which decree (word)?

Some Bibles translate 9:25 as "decree" (NASB; NIV) or "command" (NKJV). The Hebrew uses "the term 'a word' (*dabar*) rather than one of the more specific terms for a royal decree."[18] "The word *dabar* is quite general in its semantic range. It frequently denotes prophetic word, but almost never means 'decree.'"[19]

There have been many suggestions regarding the meaning of the "word to restore and rebuild Jerusalem." Lucas lists seven: "The possibilities are (with dates in brackets): 1. Jeremiah's prophecy about seventy years in Jer. 25:12 (605) or Jer. 29:10 (597). 2. Jeremiah's

---

14. Russell, *Daniel,* 185.
15. Baldwin, *Daniel,* 169.
16. Payne, "Goal," 104–05.
17. Gaston, *No Stone,* 118.
18. Lucas, *Daniel,* 242.
19. McComiskey, "The Seventy," 26.

prophecies of restoration in Jer. 30:18–22; 31:38–40 (587). 3. Gabriel's own words to Daniel (539?). 4. Cyrus's decree recorded in Ezra 1:1–4 (539). 5. Darius's decree recorded in Ezra 6:1–12 (521). 6. Artaxerxes's decree recorded in Ezra 7:12–26 (458). 7. Artaxerxes's warrant given to Nehemiah in Neh. 2:7–8 (445)."[20]

Who is "the anointed one, the prince"?

The NASB and NKJV translate the Hebrew as *"until Messiah the Prince."* The NIV reads *"until the Anointed One, the ruler."* The ESV and RSV read *"to the coming of an anointed one, a prince."* The Hebrew word *mashiach* "has no definite article and should be rendered, 'an anointed one,' a term that could even be applied to a pagan king such as Cyrus, the Persian (Is 45:1). The next word, *nagid,* can refer to a prince (e.g., 1 Sam 2:10, 35; 9:16; 10:1) or a (high) priest (e.g., Lev 4:3; Jer 20:1; Neh 11:11)."[21] "A non-Israelite ruler would more naturally be referred to here as *melek* [as opposed to *nagid*], as commonly in Daniel. In the absence of indication to the contrary, then, 'an anointed, a leader,' is more likely an Israelite figure."[22]

Possible candidates include Cyrus, Nehemiah, the high priest Joshua or Zerubbabel the governor who came to Jerusalem in 538 BC to re-establish the temple, or Jesus Christ.

9:26—"Then after the sixty-two weeks the Messiah will be cut off and have nothing, and the people of the prince who is to come will destroy the city and the sanctuary. And its end will come with a flood; even to the end there will be war; desolations are determined."

Is the "anointed one" of v. 26 the same as the "anointed one" of v. 25?

In neither case is there a definite article ("the") before "anointed one," so both verses read *"an anointed one."* "The description of him as *an* anointed cannot be argued to indicate that he must be the same *mashiach* as the one in v 25 . . . or that he *must* be a different one."[23] On the other hand, "Without any grammatical or literary signals to indicate otherwise, the simplest solution is that the same two terms ['anointed' and 'prince'] in v. 26 also refer to one and the same person—the same individual referred to in v. 25."[24]

The major candidates are Onias III (high priest, murdered in 171 BC) or Jesus Christ. Some hold that he is Antichrist.

20. Lucas, *Daniel,* 242.

21. Pate and Haines, *Doomsday Delusions,* 73.

22. Goldingay, *Daniel,* 261.

23. Ibid., 262.

24. Gentry, "New Exodus," 32.

What does "cut off and have nothing" mean?

"Cut off" is used of "the death penalty, Lev. 7:20; and refers to a violent death, unless some further explanation is given."[25] "The meaning of the words translated 'and shall have nothing' is not certain. They have been rendered variously to mean 'there was nothing against him' or 'he shall have no one [to succeed him]' or 'he shall cease to be' or 'without trial' or 'without a helper.'"[26] Leupold states that, literally, the text reads, "'And there shall not be for Him.' That implies that He shall not have that which normally might be expected to fall to his lot such as followers, influence, and the like."[27] The NKJV reads *"but not for Himself."* Many assert that that translation "is not justified by the original."[28]

Who are "the people of the prince who is to come"?

"If v. 26a refers to Onias' murder, the traditional reading of what follows, 'and the people of the prince who is to come shall destroy the city and the sanctuary', is problematic because Antiochus IV did not destroy Jerusalem and the temple. . . . Goldingay (1989: 262), who adopts the same reading, takes the 'leader who comes' to be one of Onias' successors, probably Jason. However, while his actions are denounced in 2 Macc. 4, the strong language here seems to be more appropriate for the actions of Antiochus IV against the faithful Jews."[29] Others see "a vague reference to enemies who are to destroy Jerusalem and the Temple for a second time, as happened in AD 70 under the Roman general Titus."[30]

On the other hand:

> There is no grammatical issue in identifying the object and subject in this sentence. The meaning of the sentence is also straightforward. The coming ruler must be the Messiah of v. 25 according to the context and the normal rules of literature. Therefore "the people of the coming ruler" are the Jewish people. The statement is telling us that it is the Jewish people who will ruin/spoil the restored city and temple at the arrival of their coming King. Historical records [i.e., Josephus, *J.W.*] confirm that this is precisely right. . . . Although the Roman army actually put the torch to Jerusalem, the destruction of the city was blamed squarely on the Jewish people themselves.[31]

Payne adds this wrinkle:

> The same subject [*mashiach* or *mashiach nagid*] seems to be repeated yet again in 26b, for although "anoint" does not occur the identical qualifying noun, "prince" (cf. v 25), and the same sort of verbal action, "destroying" (cf. the "cutting off" in v 26a), do occur, which seem to identify the same anointed one. The parallelism that this produces suggests that the consonants just before "prince" should

25. Young, *Prophecy of Daniel,* 206.

26. Russell, *Daniel,* 189.

27. Leupold, *Exposition,* 427.

28. Jackson, "Daniel's Prophecy," 10.

29. Lucas, *Daniel,* 244.

30. Baldwin, *Daniel,* 171.

31. Gentry, "New Exodus," 38–39.

be pointed *'im* ("with," according to one Hebrew MS and the ancient versions), rather than *'am,* "people." The text then reads literally, "The city and the sanctuary will be destroyed with the coming prince."[32]

Various candidates have been proposed for the coming prince and his people, including Antiochus Epiphanes and Syrian soldiers or Jewish Hellenizers; Titus and the Romans; Antichrist and his followers; or Jesus Christ and either the Jews who rejected him or the Romans.

What do "the end" and "a flood" refer to?

"The phrase 'its end' is ambiguous. It could refer to the end of the leader, or to that of the people, or to the 'end' that the leader's coming will bring about, the events of v. 27."[33] The "end" may refer to "the city and the Temple or it may refer to 'the end' as such. In either case devastation will come like a flood. Right up to the end there shall be war and desolation."[34] "War *to the end* implies continuing conflict between a powerful enemy and God's cause till the end of the seventy weeks."[35]

No one seems to take "flood" as a literal flood of water (especially since Jerusalem has an elevated geographical location). "Of the 'flood' which comes at the end of the city and the sanctuary we can say nothing, unless a flood of Syrian troops is meant."[36] "The word *overflow* ['flood'] suggests an overwhelming flood. Cf. Nah. 1:8 where it is used of the outpouring of God's wrath. What is the antecedent of *its*? Some refer it to the anointed one, others to the prince. Probably it is best taken as referring to the end of the destruction as such."[37]

9:27—"And he will make a firm covenant with the many for one week, but in the middle of the week he will put a stop to sacrifice and grain offering; and on the wing of abominations will come one who makes desolate, even until a complete destruction, one that is decreed, is poured out on the one who makes desolate."

Who is "he"?

"If *he* refers to the last-named person, 'the prince who is to come', the subject is the enemy of God's cause [if one assumes the 'prince' of 26b is evil]."[38] On the other hand, "As for the prince of verse 26b, whose army is said to advance against the temple-city, he is in any case thematically subordinated to the fate of the temple. Therefore, even if he were to be

---

32. Payne, "Goal," 106.

33. Lucas, *Daniel,* 244.

34. Russell, *Daniel,* 190.

35. Baldwin, *Daniel,* 171.

36. Towner, *Daniel,* 144. Similar "flood" imagery as referring to invasion by military troops is found in Isa 8:5–8 where it refers to an Assyrian invasion of Judah.

37. Young, *Prophecy of Daniel,* 207.

38. Baldwin, *Daniel,* 171.

identified as the head of some foreign nation, he ought not to be preferred over Messiah as the subject of *higbir* [i.e., the 'he' who confirms the covenant in 27a]."[39]

"The indefinite pronoun 'he' does not refer back to 'the prince who is to come' of verse 26. That 'prince' is a subordinate noun; 'the people' is the dominant noun. Thus, the 'he' refers back to the last dominant individual mentioned: 'Messiah' (v. 26a). The Messiah is the leading figure in the whole prophecy, so even the destruction of the Temple is related to his death. In fact, the people who destroy the Temple are providentially 'His armies' (Matt. 22:2–7)."[40]

"He" has been interpreted as Antiochus Epiphanes, Jesus Christ, or an end-time Antichrist.

What is the "covenant"?

"The usual verb for the making of a covenant, karat, was found in verse 26 ['cut']. But in verse 27, the verb higbir was used instead, which means to 'make strong, cause to prevail.'... The use of higbir illustrated that the covenant being 'made strong' or 'prevailing' in verse 27 meant that the covenant in verse 27 was not being made de novo but was a covenant being confirmed or enforced. In other words, the covenant being confirmed in the middle of the seventieth week . . . was a covenant which already existed."[41] The only other use of this form of higbir in the OT is Ps 12:4, which does not involve making or confirming a covenant, "where the sense is simply 'prevail' or 'establish strength.'"[42]

This has been interpreted as the alliance between Antiochus Epiphanes and the Hellenizing Jews; the Abrahamic covenant; the New Covenant that Christ inaugurated; or a political agreement that an end-time Antichrist is said to make with some of the Jews to allow a new Jewish temple and renewed animal sacrifices.

What does "put a stop to sacrifice" refer to?

This has been interpreted as Antiochus' stopping of the Jewish sacrifices; Christ's sacrifice of himself which rendered obsolete the Jewish sacrifices and sacrificial system; the destruction of the temple in AD 70; or an end-time Antichrist's breaking his treaty with the Jews.

What is the "wing of abominations"?

"The language of this passage is extremely difficult."[43] "What the 'wing' refers to is problematic. The Greek and Latin vss took it to refer to some architectural feature of the temple."[44] On the other hand, Hebrew does not appear to use the word *kanaph* ("wing")

---

39. Kline, "Covenant," 463n.31.

40. Gentry, "Daniel's Seventy Weeks," n.p.

41. Riddlebarger, *Amillennialism*, 155.

42. Williamson, *Sealed with an Oath*, 175n.98.

43. Young, *Prophecy of Daniel*, 218.

44. Lucas, *Daniel*, 244–45.

for part of a building.[45] "The term 'wing' can mean 'edge' or 'extremity.' The phrase refers to one causing desolation in association with extreme abominations."[46]

"Desolate" or "desolator"?

Most translations say that destruction will be poured out on the one who *"makes desolate"* (i.e., the "desolator," NASB, RSV, NIV, ESV). Thus, "as in the case of the cruel Assyrian invader (Is. 10:23), an end has been decreed for him, and will be *poured out,* as God's wrath had been on His people (verse 11)."[47]

On the other hand, some translations (NKJV) say that destruction is poured out on the "desolate." Since "the standard transitive form for 'desolator' (cf. 11:31) occurs just six words earlier, it would appear that the normal intransitive meaning ['desolate'] should be retained here at the close of the verse (cf. 9:18, 26). Moreover the party that is foreseen as being desolate and appalled by divine judgment can be none other than Daniel's people and city, which are the subject of his entire revelation of the seventy weeks."[48]

Major Interpretive Approaches to Dan 9:24–27

In the first century AD, Jewish Zealots interpreted Dan 9:24–27 as indicating that Messiah would appear in AD 70 and rescue the Jews from the Romans.[49] On the other hand, first-century Jewish historian Josephus held that the Zealots' themselves, who had killed the high priest, constituted the "abomination of desolation." He concluded that the prophecy had been fulfilled both by Antiochus and by Titus and the Romans.[50]

The apostolic and post-apostolic fathers introduced ideas that have been re-mixed and refined by contemporary interpreters. The *Epistle of Barnabas* 16:6 (c. AD 70–130) is "a Messianic interpretation of *Daniel* ix, with a strong likelihood that it viewed the entire seventy weeks as being fulfilled in the manifestation of Christ, and his work in the church."[51] Several decades later, Irenaeus indicated that 9:27 referred to a future end-time Antichrist.[52] His pupil, Hippolytus, writing about AD 202, held that the starting point for the seventy weeks was the first year of Darius when Daniel received his vision; the return to Jerusalem from Babylon marked the end of the first seven weeks; the high priest Joshua who returned with the people was the anointed one of 9:25; the 62 weeks ended with the birth of Christ; Christ is the "Most Holy" of 9:24; the 70th week takes place at the end of the gospel age before Christ's return; and the "abomination

---

45. See *HALOT,* "kanaph," 1:486; Leupold, *Exposition,* 435.

46. Gentry, "New Exodus," 39.

47. Baldwin, *Daniel,* 172.

48. Payne, "Goal," 112.

49. Gaston, *No Stone,* 462–63.

50. Josephus, *Ant.* 10.11.7; *J.W.* 4.6.3.

51. Knowles, "Interpretation," 138.

52. Irenaeus, *Haer.* 5.25.4. See Knowles, "Interpretation," 138–39.

of desolation" refers to Antichrist who stops the "sacrifice and oblation" being offered around the world by the church.[53]

Most other patristic fathers held that the seventy weeks were fully completed with the first advent of Christ and/or the destruction of Jerusalem in AD 70. Clement of Alexandria, writing about AD 200, held that the beginning of the seventy weeks was the beginning of the exile to Babylon; the completion of all seventy weeks ended with the destruction of Jerusalem by Titus in AD 70; the "Most Holy" of 9:24 refers to Christ; and the "anointed one" of 9:25 refers to the high priest who assumed office at the completion of the rebuilt temple.[54] Tertullian, writing about AD 203, held that the first 62½ weeks covered the period from Darius to the birth of Christ, and the last 7½ weeks defines the period from the birth of Christ to the fall of Jerusalem in AD 70. He finds the fulfillment of the six goals of the prophecy (9:24) in the person and work of Christ at his first advent.[55] "It may very well be Tertullian's thought that the events which took place in principle at the moment of Christ's death found their completion in the final destruction of the holy city of the Jews."[56]

"Up to this point, all who commented on the problem had agreed in assuming that the prophecy referred to weeks of years. Origen [c. 185–254], however, takes them as weeks of decades."[57] He began the "seventy weeks" with the creation of Adam and held that there were 4900 years from Adam to the end of the last week. He held that the "anointed" of 9:25 was Christ, but the "anointed" of 9:26 was the post-exilic high priesthood. He placed the beginning of the 70th week at Pentecost, the destruction of Jerusalem in AD 70 in the middle of the 70th week, and had little to say about the end of the 70th week.[58] J. Paul Tanner summarizes:

> Of the eleven early church fathers surveyed in this study all but one of them held to some form of messianic interpretation of Daniel's prophecy (the lone exception being Hilarianus who held to a fulfillment in the time of Antiochus IV Epiphanes in the second century B.C.). Virtually all these saw the first sixty-nine weeks, if not the entire seventy weeks, as fulfilled at Christ's first advent (the exceptions being Hilarianus and Apollinarus, the latter viewing the seventy weeks as the time between the two advents of Christ). One of the other common points of agreement is that the 'most holy' in Daniel 9:24 refers to Jesus Christ. . . . Despite their agreement about the messianic interpretation in general, they differed greatly in their interpretations of the details.[59]

Contemporary interpretations fall into three main groups: (1) Those that see the passage as primarily concerning historical Jerusalem, culminating in Antiochus Epiphanes and the Maccabean Revolt which ended in 164 BC (Antiochene views); (2) Those that see it as a messianic passage, primarily fulfilled in the first coming of Christ (messianic

---

53. See Knowles, "Interpretation," 139–42, citing Hippolytus, *Comm. Dan.* 2.11–22 (from *ANF*).

54. Clement of Alexandria, *Stromata* 1.21. See Knowles, "Interpretation," 142–45.

55. Tertullian, *An Answer to the Jews* 8. See Knowles, "Interpretation," 145–49.

56. Knowles, "Interpretation," 148.

57. Ibid., 149.

58. Ibid., 152–54.

59. Tanner, "Part 1," 198–99.

views); and (3) Those that see it as culminating with Antichrist and a future Israel and Jerusalem (dispensational views). Each of these major viewpoints is further subdivided into more chronological versus chronographic and literalistic versus idealistic positions (similar to different interpretations of the book of Revelation).

Antiochene views

Classic Antiochene interpretation[60]

The 490 years begin with Jeremiah's prophecy (Jer 25:12) in 605 BC or his prophecies of restoration (Jer 30:18–22; 31:38–40) in 587 BC, include the rebuilding of the temple and Jerusalem, and end with the rededication of the temple and death of Antiochus Epiphanes in 164 BC. This interpretation views at least the first two sets of "sevens" as figurative or schematic, since 605 BC–164 BC is only about 440 years. The "anointed one" of 9:25 is seen as the high priest Joshua and/or governor Zerubbabel. The "cutting off" of the anointed one in 9:26 is taken as referring to the murder of the high priest Onias III in 171 BC. The "covenant" of 9:27 is taken as Antiochus' agreement with Hellenizing Jews. The stopping of sacrifices is Antiochus' stopping of Jewish sacrifices in 167 BC.

Modified Antiochene interpretation[61]

Pate and Haines view the time periods both chronographically and literally. They begin the first seven weeks with Jeremiah's prophecies of restoration (Jer 30:18–22; 31:38–40) in 587 BC, which terminate in 538 BC with Zerubbabel and the high priest Joshua. They date the 62 sevens from Jeremiah's prophecy (Jer 25:12) in 605 BC, which terminates in 171 BC with the death of Onias III. The rest of their interpretation follows classic lines. It thereby accounts for the full 490 years but has the 62 weeks beginning before the seven weeks.

Critique of Antiochene interpretations

"The historical interpretation is surely correct in seeing a primary fulfillment of Daniel's prophecy in the second century BC, but to confine its meaning to that period is to close one's eyes to the witness of Jesus and of the New Testament writers in general that it also had a future significance."[62]

THE SIX-FOLD PURPOSES OF THE "SEVENTY WEEKS" (9:24)

"It is the seventy weeks that are to achieve the six-fold goal; that is, each of the listed purposes should be accomplished within the years designated. This factor is what invalidates

---

60. See Baldwin, *Daniel*, 172–73; Hill, "Daniel," 174–75; Collins, *Daniel*, 352–58; Hartman and Dilella, *Book of Daniel*, 249–53; Russell, *Daniel*, 183–92; Towner, *Daniel*, 140–44; Lucas, *Daniel*, 241–54.

61. Pate and Haines, *Doomsday Delusions*, 69–75.

62. Baldwin, *Daniel*, 173.

the theory of negative Biblical criticism, which puts the 70th week in the Maccabean age, up to 165 B.C.: that era is too soon for the length of time given (490 years from the decree to start Jerusalem's rebuilding, probably in 458 B.C.; compare Ezr 7:6–8 with 4:7–23 and Neh 1:3). It is inadequate as well, because atonement and eternal righteousness were not made available then."[63]

ANTIOCHUS EPIPHANES (9:26)

"Commentators who argue that Antiochus Epiphanes fulfilled this prophecy are at a loss to account for the fact that he destroyed neither the Temple nor the city of Jerusalem, though undoubtedly much damage was done (1 Macc. 1:31, 38)."[64] Towner responds, "Although it seems excessive to say that he 'destroyed the city and the sanctuary,' he at least rendered the latter unusable to observant Jews."[65]

THE "COVENANT" (9:27)

First Macc 1:11–14 says that at the time of Antiochus, unbelieving Jews came to him and received his permission to adopt Gentile ways. Edward Young comments:

> Antiochus gave his royal permission for the Jews to do this, for without such permission they could not have introduced these heathen innovations. Antiochus, therefore, does not make any covenant, nor does he cause any covenant to prevail, unless his granting permission to the Jews to Hellenize be considered as causing a covenant to prevail. However, since the covenant of Dan. 9:27 is to be regarded as already in existence, how can it possibly apply to Antiochus? . . . Those who caused the covenant (if it was a real covenant and not a mere intention to imitate the Greeks) with the nations to prevail were certain transgressors and not Antiochus.[66]

Messianic views

Classic messianic interpretation[67]

The promises of 9:24 are all seen as messianic. Artaxerxes's decree recorded in Ezra 7:12–26 (458 or 457 BC) is taken as the starting point for a literal chronology. The first set of sevens covers the actual rebuilding of Jerusalem (9:25a). The 62 weeks immediately follows and terminates with Jesus' baptism in AD 26 or 27. Jesus is the "anointed one" of 9:25b. The *"prince who is to come"* of 9:26b is often seen as Titus since Jesus cited 9:26–27 in the Olivet Discourse. Others see the "prince" as Christ and his "people" as

63. Payne, "Interpretation," 37.

64. Baldwin, *Daniel*, 171.

65. Towner, *Daniel*, 143.

66. Young, *Prophecy of Daniel*, 210.

67. See Baldwin, *Daniel*, 174–75; Hill, "Daniel," 173–74; Gentry, "Daniel's Seventy Weeks," n.p.; Gentry, "New Exodus," 26–44; Jackson, "Daniel's Prophecy," 1–14; Payne, "Goal," 97–115.

the Jews who rejected him and thereby brought about the destruction of the city by the Romans. In other words, Daniel's prophecy is saying essentially what Christ said in the Olivet Discourse.[68]

Most view the "covenant" of 9:27 as Jesus' finalizing or ratifying the Abrahamic or New Covenant. The "stopping of the sacrifices" is generally seen as Jesus' death on the cross which legally terminated the efficacy of the Jewish sacrificial system, although some see it as Christ's sending "forces of destruction against the Jerusalem temple [in AD 70], so making the old ritual system cease," since "Jesus himself depicted the destruction of Jerusalem as the work of a divine army in the parable of Matthew 22:2ff. (see especially vs. 7)."[69] After the second set of sevens (i.e., half way through the 70th week, in approximately AD 30), Jesus is "cut off" (crucified).

There is no specific termination of the 70th week listed. Some view the 70th week as ending with the death of Stephen; the conversion of Paul or Cornelius and the taking of the Gospel to the Gentiles; or as symbolic of the entire time until Jesus returns. The destruction of Jerusalem was not listed in 9:24 as one of the six predicted goals of the prophecy. "Daniel did not affirm that the actual desolation of the city would occur within the 70 weeks. Rather, the text suggests that Jerusalem's fate would be determined within that span (26b; 27b)."[70] Peter Gentry states:

> The situation is similar to God telling Adam that in the day he ate of the forbidden fruit, he would die. In one sense this did happen on the very day, but took time to be worked out. Just so, when the Jewish people rejected the Messiah and the High Priest blasphemed Jesus, the true Temple, the Herodian temple had to fall and the city had to be destroyed. The coming destruction, symbolized by the curtain protecting the Holy of Holies torn in two at the crucifixion, finally came to pass in A.D. 70, i.e., within the time of that generation which committed this sacrilege.[71]

Therefore, the destruction of Jerusalem by Titus in AD 70 "must be regarded, not as necessarily falling within the 70th seven, but as *consequent* upon the action of the Messiah in causing the sacrifice and oblation to cease."[72] On the other hand, "If making the sacrifice cease in the midst of the seventieth week (Dan. 9:27) refers to Christ's perfecting of Old Testament sacrifice by the sacrifice of himself, rather than his judgment on the Jerusalem temple in AD 70, it would then be possible to regard the latter event as marking the end of the seventy weeks [when viewed chronographically]."[73]

---

68. See Duguid, *Daniel*, 172–73.

69. Kline, "Covenant," 468, 464n.31.

70. Jackson, "Daniel's Prophecy," 12.

71. Gentry, "New Exodus," 40.

72. Young, *Prophecy of Daniel*, 218–19.

73. Kline, "Covenant," 468n.44.

Idealist messianic interpretation[74]

These interpreters view the seventy "weeks" as symbolic periods of time. These interpreters tend to begin the first set of sevens with the decree of Cyrus in 538 BC because of its theological significance: it represented the end of Israel's exile. Meredith Kline says:

> If attention is paid to the unity of this chapter, particularly, if there is due regard for the appropriateness of the response to the urgency of the plea that the divine word through Jeremiah be speedily fulfilled as the passage of the years now demanded (i.e., the seventy years spanned by the date formulae in Dan. 1:1 and 9:1), one can only conclude that the beginning of the seventy weeks coincided with the ending of the seventy years at the time of Daniel's prayer [which] all points to the first year of Cyrus as the start of the seventy weeks. It is then quite impossible to work out the fulfillment in a literal 490-year period. The seventy weeks must be understood symbolically, and it is their sabbatical structure that indicates their specific symbolic significance.[75]

The seventy weeks are generally taken as extending to the *parousia*. Often, "the first period of seven weeks specifies the period of time from Cyrus to the coming of the Messiah (Christ). The second period, 62 weeks, refers to the time since that advent of the Messiah (the present age). The final week, or period, lies still in the future."[76] Most hold the final week or final three and one half years of the seventieth week are symbolic of the entire church age.[77] The references to the "holy city" also are taken spiritually as referring to the church (i.e., spiritual Jerusalem).

The seventy weeks and the New Jerusalem coalesce around the fact that the prophecy is based on ten jubilee periods:

> Before the Jerusalem temple was leveled, the foundations of the everlasting temple of the Spirit, which is Christ and His church, would be laid. This new, antitypical restoration of God's temple would be the achievement of what is portrayed as ten jubilee periods. . . . Since the seventy weeks are ten jubilee eras that issue in the last jubilee, the seventieth week closes with the angelic trumpeting of the earth's redemption and the glorious liberty of the children of God. The acceptable year of the Lord which came with Christ will then have fully come. Then the new Jerusalem whose temple is the Lord and the Lamb will descend from heaven (Rev. 21:10, 22) and the ark of the covenant will be seen (Rev. 11:19), the covenant the Lamb has made to prevail.[78]

74. See Leupold, *Exposition*, 403–40; Young, *Prophecy of Daniel*, 191–221; Kline, "Covenant," 452–69; Duguid, *Daniel*, 162–75.

75. Kline, "Covenant," 459n.19.

76. Elwell, *Baker Encyclopedia*, 1931.

77. Riddlebarger, *Amillennialism*, 156.

78. Kline, "Covenant," 468–69. See also below, the section "The covenantal structure and theological background of Dan 9:24–27 point to Christ."

Appendix 4

Critique of messianic interpretations

The "most holy" (9:24)

"This phrase has been given a messianic interpretation, and has been taken to refer to the anointing of 'a most holy one'. There is no basis for this in the text itself, nor in the book of Daniel as a whole, which has no explicit reference to a 'messiah.'"[79]

On the other hand, Dan 7:13–14 talks about the *"Son of Man"* who was given everlasting and universal *"dominion, glory and a kingdom."* That is clearly messianic, and the NT applies it to Jesus.[80] Baldwin notes, "In 539 BC concern was centered on the holy place in Jerusalem, and the rededication of the Temple was not excluded, but the Lord's anointed was ultimately to be a man (Mt. 12:6, 'a greater thing than the temple is here', RV mg.)."[81]

"The anointed" of 9:25 as Messiah

> The 'messianic' interpretation faces three objections. 1. There is the lack of clear interest in a 'messiah' figure elsewhere in Daniel. 2. It is tied to taking the 'word' of this verse as one of the decrees of Artaxerxes in order to get the chronology even approximately right, and we have seen that this is the least likely referent of the 'word'. 3. It ignores the MT [Masoretic Text] punctuation and follows [Theodotion] in reading 'seven weeks and sixty-two weeks' as the period prior to the anointed leader's appearing. . . . Moreover, there seems no point in saying 'seven and sixty-two' unless something is going to happen after the seven. The most obvious happening is the appearing of 'an anointed leader'.[82]

Titus as the "prince who is to come" (9:26)

Some who have the 70th week ending with Christ see the *"people of the prince"* (v. 26) as the Romans and the "prince" as Titus. However, according to that interpretation, if the "prince to come" (9:26) is Titus, then "he" (9:27) cannot be the same as the "prince to come" because "Titus did not make any covenant with the Jews."[83] Further, according to that interpretation, v. 26 suddenly jumps ahead from the time of Christ to the destruction of Jerusalem and then in v. 27 jumps back to the time of Christ again.

On the other hand, it is not necessary to read verses 26 and 27 as historically sequential. "There is no hint in the text that the events of vs. 27 are to take place after those of vs. 26. To the contrary, vs. 27 is so linked to vs. 26 that it is a further explanation and amplification of what is summarized in the previous verse."[84] In that case, "he" (v. 27) would be the same as Messiah who is *"cut off"* (9:26), and both are referring to Christ. "He

79. Lucas, *Daniel*, 242.

80. Matt 24:30; Mark 13:26; Luke 21:27; Rev 5:5b–7, 9a, 12–13.

81. Baldwin, *Daniel*, 169.

82. Lucas, *Daniel*, 243.

83. Mauro, *Seventy Weeks*, 80.

84. Hasel, "Crossroads," 14.

must cause the covenant to prevail *before* he dies or at least at the same time that He dies. The action of causing the covenant to prevail, therefore, belongs to the 70th seven and is contemporaneous with the death of the Messiah."[85]

The end of the 70th week

Some interpretations end the 69th week with the death of Christ or with the baptism of Christ (his death would then be in the middle of the 70th week). In that case, all that remains for the climactic seventieth week is an unimportant date seven (or 3½) years after Christ's death. That seems to be an incongruous way to end a prophecy based around seventy weeks.

Young responds, "The *terminus ad quem* [ending point] of the 69 weeks is clearly stated, namely, an anointed one, a prince. No such *terminus ad quem,* however, is given for the 70 weeks themselves. It would seem, therefore, that the *terminus ad quem* was not regarded as possessing particular importance or significance. No important event is singled out as marking the termination. All schools of interpretation, therefore, are faced with the difficulty of determining what marked the close of the 70 weeks. And all schools discover this event upon the basis of considerations other than those presented in the text."[86] Again, that objection assumes the seventy weeks are a strictly 490 year chronology, but it is not a valid objection if the seventy weeks are to be seen chronographically.

Dispensational views

Classic dispensational interpretation[87]

According to this view, the prophecy anticipates "the establishment of Israel's covenanted millennial kingdom under the authority of her promised king."[88] This interpretation views the seventy weeks as 490 literal years. The starting point dispensationalists choose is Artaxerxes's warrant given to Nehemiah in Neh 2:7–8 (445 or 444 BC). However, 490 years from that would terminate in about AD 46 or 47 (dates of no significance). The end of the 69th week (483 years) would be in about AD 39 or 40 (dates of no significance). Therefore, to try to get the first 69 weeks to end on some date having something to do with Christ, dispensationalists do not use regular years, but use years consisting of 360 days, which they call "prophetic years." They then turn the "years" into "days" by adding extra days to account for "leap years" and thereby arrive at a total of 173,880 days (which amounts to only 476 "real" years instead of 483). That puts the end of their recalculated 69th week sometime in AD 32 or 33 at what they believe was the date of Christ's triumphal entry into Jerusalem.[89]

85. Young, *Prophecy of Daniel,* 215.

86. Ibid., 220–21.

87. See Baldwin, *Daniel,* 176–77; Hoehner, "Chronological Aspects," 47–65; McClain, *Daniel's Prophecy,* 5–62; Scofield, *New Scofield,* 913n.1; Wood, *Commentary,* 243–63.

88. Pentecost, *Things to Come,* 1362.

89. Hoehner, "Chronological Aspects," 47–65.

The "anointed one" of 9:25 is Jesus. The "cutting off" (9:26) is his death on the cross. Even though his death was *"after the sixty two weeks,"* dispensationalists do not think it occurred *in* the 70th week, but *before* the 70th week. They claim that after 9:25 "the Seventieth Week does not immediately follow the Sixty-ninth Week, but there is a great parenthesis of time between these two which has already lasted for over nineteen hundred years, and therefore the Seventieth Week still lies in the future."[90] They hold that the 70th week relates solely to events that occur just before Christ comes again. Further, "this Seventieth Week is a period of seven years which lies prophetically between the translation [i.e., the 'pretribulational rapture'] of the church and the return of Christ in glory."[91] According to dispensationalists, this seven-year period is the future "tribulation." Indeed, dispensationalist Thomas Ice states, "The seventieth week of Daniel is the basis for our understanding that the future Tribulation will be seven years in length."[92]

Regarding the *"people of the prince who is to come"* (9:26), the *people* are "the Roman people," but the *prince* is not Christ or Titus, but Antichrist, who is the "king of a restored Roman confederacy."[93] The covenant of 9:27 is an agreement Antichrist makes with Israel to "guarantee Israel's safety in the land"[94] or to restore "the Jewish Temple sacrificial system."[95] The stopping of sacrifices is Antichrist's disallowing the sacrifices half way through the 70th week; he then persecutes the Jews but is destroyed at the *parousia*.

Modified dispensational interpretation[96]

Fred Zaspel uses normal years rather than the so-called "prophetic years." Similar to Pate and Haines' modification of the Antiochene interpretation, Zaspel views the sets of sevens as representing 490 total years but separates the first set of sevens from the second set. He dates the first set from 587 BC (God's word to Jeremiah) then inserts a gap. He dates the 62 weeks from 440 BC which is when he believes the rebuilding of Jerusalem under Nehemiah began. With respect to the final seven years and the rest of the interpretation, Zaspel follows classic dispensational lines.

Critique of dispensational interpretations

Although Dan 9:24–27 is one of the most difficult and ambiguous passages in the entire Bible, with multiple textual and historical issues and problems from beginning to end, "The chronology provided in Daniel's prophecy of the Seventy Weeks is a veritable linchpin in the dispensational argument, although it is not crucial to any of the other millennial systems."[97] As such, the entire basis of dispensationalism collapses if their in-

90. McClain, *Daniel's Prophecy*, 25.

91. Ibid., 45.

92. Ice, "Old Testament," 86.

93. Wood, *Commentary*, 255–59.

94. Pentecost, *Things to Come*, 1364

95. McClain, *Daniel's Prophecy*, 51.

96. Zaspel, "Historical and Exegetical," n.p.

97. Gentry, "Daniel's Seventy Weeks," n.p., quoting Walvoord, *Rapture Question*, 24 and Walvoord,

terpretation of this passage is not correct.[98] The fact that dispensationalism is essentially built around its own interpretation of this one highly ambiguous and disputed passage should itself cause one to have reservations about dispensationalism, particularly since the dispensationalist interpretation was not even invented until the 1830s. Dispensationalism also entails a major hermeneutical problem: "The dispensational interpretation of Daniel 9 illustrates the fact that dispensationalists read the New Testament in light of the Old Testament, instead of vice versa."[99]

Specific problems with the dispensationalist interpretation of the passage include the following.

THE 360-DAY "PROPHETIC YEAR"

The 360-day "prophetic year" is only used because 483 years from Artaxerxes's decree of 445/444 BC, which dispensationalists use as their starting point, would place the end of 69 weeks at about 40 AD, a date of no historical or theological significance.[100] "The use of 'prophetic years' is unconvincing special pleading. Although, at various times and places in the ANE [Ancient Near East], calendars with twelve months of thirty days were used, it was always recognized that these ran out of step with the 'real world', and various schemes of intercalary days or months were used to correct for this. It is very unlikely that anyone would have used a 360-day year in chronological calculations."[101]

Indeed, the very context of Daniel 9 itself indicates that a normal 365-day calendar was used and was understood by Daniel: "The Jews knew very well how many days should be in a year; and so as necessary they added an 'intercalary month' to 'correct' their calendar. Moreover, it seems that Daniel himself understood the 'years' of Jeremiah in the usual sense (9:1–2). The prophecy should be understood by counting the years specified, not by adding and/or deleting days which are not specified. That is how Daniel calculated the end of the seventy years' captivity, and this is most naturally how we should understand the years he prophesied also."[102]

TURNING THE "PROPHET YEAR" INTO DAYS DOES NOT ARRIVE AT AN ACCURATE END-POINT

Turning "prophetic years" into 173,880 days amounts to only 476 "real" years, which is seven years too short for 69 weeks of years. However, even using 173,880 days does not end at the date dispensationalists want.

Daniel, 201, 216. See also MacDonald, *Believer's*, 1085 (Dan 9:24–27 is "crucial to understanding God's program").

98. See Riddlebarger, *Amillennialism*, 150.

99. Ibid.

100. This shows that the dispensational interpretation is driven by its own pre-existing theological presuppositions rather than by exegesis of the text. That alone renders the interpretation suspect.

101. Lucas, *Daniel*, 246.

102. Zaspel, "Historical and Exegetical," n.p.

In his classic dispensationalist book *The Coming Prince,* Sir Robert Anderson arrived at the date of April 6, AD 32 as the end of the 69 weeks (which he regarded as the date of Christ's triumphal entry into Jerusalem).[103] He based his calculations on the assumption that Artaxerxes's decree (Neh 2:1–8) was issued on Nisan 1, 445 BC and treated each of the sixty-nine weeks as a 360-day year. He also guessed that Nisan 1 was March 14.[104]

However, even dispensationalists have recognized that Anderson's dates are untenable.[105] Nisan 1 445 BC actually was April 13, not March 14.[106] Indeed, "in the light of new evidence since Anderson's day, the 445 B.C. date is not acceptable for Artaxerxes's twentieth year; instead the decree was given in Nisan, 444 B.C."[107] Further, Anderson's date of Nisan 15 AD 32 for the crucifixion is without basis. "It would mean that Christ was crucified on either a Sunday or Monday. In fact, Anderson realizes the dilemma and he has to do mathematical gymnastics to arrive at a Friday crucifixion. This makes one immediately suspect. Actually there is no good evidence for an A.D. 32 crucifixion date."[108]

Harold Hoehner has tried to preserve Anderson's methodology while, at the same time, correcting his errors.[109] Hoehner proposes Nisan 1 444 BC (which he believes to be March 4 or, more likely, March 5) for Artaxerxes's decree, and March 30, AD 33 for Christ's triumphal entry.[110] Despite those corrections, Hoehner's methodology and conclusions are invalid for several reasons.

Hoehner has an incorrect starting date

"Relying on a source dated 1954, Hoehner sets Xerxes' death and Artaxerxes's succession in December 465 . . . whereas evidence published later sets the date in the preceding August. This error leads Hoehner to misplace the Nisan of Artaxerxes's twentieth year in 444 rather than 445."[111]

Nisan 1, 444 was not March 4 or 5 as assumed by Hoehner, but was April 2 or 3

"If we project today's rabbinical calendar back to the fifth century BC, we find that Nisan 1 began on the Julian date of April 2, which corresponds to a Gregorian date of March 28. Thus, . . . we end up with a date for Nisan 1 a whole month later than the date postulated by Hoehner."[112] Additionally:

103. Anderson, *Coming Prince,* 127–28.

104. Ibid., 122–23.

105. See Pickle, "Chronological Errors," n.p.

106. Rickard, "Sixty-Nine Weeks," n.p.n.1.

107. Hoehner, "Chronological Aspects," 64.

108. Ibid.

109. Hoehner, "Chronological Aspects," 47–65; *Chronological Aspects,* 115–139.

110. Hoehner, "Chronological Aspects," 64; *Chronological Aspects,* 127–128, 138.

111. Rickard, "Sixty-Nine Weeks," n.p.n.1.

112. Pickle, "Chronological Errors," n.p.; see also Rickard, "Sixty-Nine Weeks," n.p.n.1.

analysis of fourteen double-dated Jewish papyri from Elephantine, Egypt, which attempts to ascertain the nature of the Jewish calendar in the fifth century BC . . . give us Julian dates for Nisan 1 ranging from March 26 through April 24. Hoehner's proposed date of March 5 for Nisan 1 in 444 BC is therefore as much as three weeks earlier than the earliest Nisan 1 in the Jewish colony at Elephantine, Egypt. We can therefore confidently conclude, based on the very sources that Hoehner cites, that March 5 in 444 BC was roughly the first of either Adar or Adar II.[113]

Hoehner assumes that the interval from March 5, 444 BC to March 30, AD 33 (both dates Julian) is exactly 483 solar years, or 173,880 days (i.e., sixty-nine weeks of 360-day "prophetic years")

"In order to determine how many days there were between March 5, 444 BC and March 30, 33 AD, Hoehner multiplied 476 by 365.24219879, the number of days he thought there were in a year. The difficulty is that, as he himself acknowledges, he is using Julian dates. That being so, he should have used the figure 365.25, the number of days in a Julian year. By using 365.24219879 instead of 365.25, he introduced an error of four days into his calculation. Instead of there being 173,880 days between the dates in question, there are really 173,884 days.[114]

Like Anderson, Hoehner ignores Jewish sabbatical-year cycles

Jewish years always stay aligned with the seasons, for the Passover has always occurred in the spring. It never has occurred in the fall. Thus, there is no possible way to make Hoehner's calculations align with actual sabbatical cycles. Because he is using a 360-day year instead of a true Jewish year, the Passover falls back 5¼ [days] a year and an entire month every six years. Every 70 years, the Passover would have circled all the way through the seasons back to where it started. The only possible way to make Daniel's 70 weeks line up with actual sabbatical cycles is to use real Jewish years that stay aligned with the seasons. Such years must on average be 365.2425 days in length, not 360.[115]

THE 2000+ YEAR GAP BETWEEN THE 69TH AND 70TH WEEKS

"The insertion of a gap of at least two thousand years between the sixty-ninth and seventieth week is a self-contradictory violation of the dispensationalist's professed literal

---

113. Pickle, "Chronological Difficulties," n.p.

114. Pickle, "Chronological Errors," n.p.; see also Rickard, "Sixty-Nine Weeks," n.p.n.1; Pickle, "Chronological Difficulties," n.p.

115. Pickle, "Chronological Difficulties," n.p.

hermeneutic."[116] Besides that self-contradictory hermeneutical problem within dispensationalism itself, the "gap theory" faces a number of formidable problems.

Dan 9:24–27 is a unity

"It is one period of seventy weeks that must transpire in order to experience the events mentioned; the parts make up a unified whole. . . . The plural 'seventy weeks' is followed by a singular verb 'is decreed,' which indicates the unity of the time period. Dispensationalists even argue vigorously against allowing a gap in the midst of the seventieth week, in that 'the week is one.'"[117] As Apollinarius said of Hippolytus's similarly introducing a lengthy gap between the 69th and 70th weeks, "it is impossible that periods so linked together be wrenched apart, but rather the time-segments must all be joined together in conformity with Daniel's prophecy."[118] Needless to say, the text of Dan 9:24–27 does not mention any "gap" between any of the "weeks."

The literary structure of 9:25–27 is one of "repetition with elaboration" which does not permit a gap

"Dan 9:25–26 cannot be taken as subsequent to 9:24; instead vv 25–26 pick up (repeat and elaborate) the summary of the entire seventy weeks given in v 24. Even so v 27, on the 70th week, would appear to pick up (in the sense of repeating and elaborating) not simply the summary fact of this week's existence as stated in v 24 but also the summary identification of its chief event as stated in v 26—i.e., the cutting off of Messiah."[119] "Verses 26 and 27 related to each other according to the structure: Messiah versus Destroyer (verse 26), Messiah versus Desolator (verse 27). The simple poetic style of Hebrew parallelism in verses 26 and 27 (which is also the poetic arrangement in verse 25) is the most thorough reply of grammatical exegesis to the imposition of a dissecting gap."[120]

9:26a ("Messiah will be cut off") is typically interpreted as referring to the crucifixion of Jesus

"The second half of the verse is then usually taken to be about the coming of the Antichrist at some indefinite time in the future. . . . A time chasm is imported into the text without there being any warrant for it in the text itself."[121]

---

116. Riddlebarger, *Amillennialism*, 153.

117. Gentry, "Daniel's Seventy Weeks," n.p.; see Pentecost, *Things to Come*, 198–99; see also DeMar, *Last Days*, 322–33.

118. Quoted by Jerome, *Commentary on Daniel*, 105.

119. Payne, "Goal," 109.

120. LaRondelle, *Israel of God*, 174.

121. Lucas, *Daniel*, 245.

The "gap" theory of dispensationalism is the problem of dispensationalism itself

Dispensationalism sees the church as a "parenthesis" when, in fact, the church is the culmination of God's purpose in Christ. "As the Epistle to the Hebrews so clearly demonstrates, Christ's death accomplished all that the old sacrifices had foreshadowed, and there can be no way of salvation apart from the way in which He opened for Jew and Gentile. The growth of the kingdom in every part of the world is part and parcel of the purpose of God as seen in Daniel 2:44 and in the teaching of Jesus, and therefore cannot be relegated to a 'parenthesis.'"[122] Even though dispensationalists admit that the death of Christ is referred to in the middle of Daniel's prophecy of the seventy weeks (9:26a), the dispensationalist interpretation places it into an unmentioned "gap" between the 69th and 70th weeks!

THE FULFILLMENT OF THE SIX-FOLD PURPOSES OF THE "70 WEEKS" (9:24)

Dispensationalist J. Dwight Pentecost says that *"everlasting righteousness"* in 9:24 can refer "only to the millennial kingdom promised Israel."[123] Dispensationalist Alva McClain adds that *"to anoint the most holy"* (9:24) refers "to the great millennial Temple which will be consecrated as a place of worship and prayer for all nations at the beginning of Messiah's kingdom."[124]

This dispensationalist insistence that Dan 9:24–27 is fulfilled in a future "millennium" is contrary to the entire purpose of Dan 9:24–27. As Kenneth Gentry points out, the "six results [of 9:24] are the main point of the prophecy, serving as the heading to the explication to follow. . . . There should be, then, correspondences between the events of verse 24 and the prophecy of verses 25–27."[125] However, the dispensationalist view of the fulfillment of the six purposes of Dan 9:24 "means that vs. 24 is describing things beyond the 70th week, events to take place in the millennium. . . . They go against the plain meaning of the Dan 9:24 where the six events described belong to the 70 weeks and not to a period beyond."[126] Further, J. Barton Payne notes, "It is the seventy weeks that are to achieve the six-fold goal; that is, each of the listed purposes should be accomplished within the years designated. This factor also renders suspect the dispensational theory of a 70th week that is still postponed until the future great tribulation, because under this approach neither Christ's atonement (in the gap, which has to be presupposed for verse 26) nor the anointing of the millennial temple (*after* the tribulation) really belong in the seventy weeks."[127]

Dispensationalist John Walvoord, who recognizes the problem, says, "'To make reconciliation for iniquity,' seems to be a rather clear picture of the cross of Christ. . . . While the basic provision for reconciliation was made at the cross, the actual application

122. Baldwin, *Daniel,* 177.

123. Pentecost, *Things to Come,* 241; see also MacDonald, *Believer's,* 1085.

124. McClain, *Daniel's Prophecy,* 59; see also MacDonald, *Believer's,* 1085.

125. Gentry, "Daniel's Seventy Weeks," n.p.

126. Hasel, "Crossroads," 12.

127. Payne, "Interpretation," 37.

of it is again associated with the second advent of Christ as far as Israel is concerned."[128] However, as Philip Mauro states, that is an attempt:

> to escape the force of the evidence of verse 24 by saying that it refers to the time when Israel *as a nation* will *enter into the benefits of* the death and resurrection of Christ. But the words of verse 24 will not bear such an interpretation. They plainly declare that, within the measure of 70 weeks of the history of Daniel's people and city, certain things would take place. The verse says not a word about the time when the Jewish nation should enter into the benefit of the atonement. It speaks definitely of the *happening* of the specified events, quite regardless of whether the Israelites as a nation should ever enter into the benefits thereof. . . . To deny that reconciliation (or atonement) was fully and finally completed when Christ died and rose again would be to deny the very foundation of Christianity. Moreover, the true Israel—the believing part of Daniel's people—*did* enter immediately into the benefits of the atonement. Beyond all question, then, the 70th week of the prophecy was that in which Christ died and rose and ascended into heaven.[129]

In fact, according to dispensationalism, the "everlasting righteousness" promised in 9:24 doesn't even occur in the millennium since the millennium includes sin and ends in a massive rebellion. Thus, Dan 9:24–27 not only is *not* fulfilled within the "seventy weeks," it is not fulfilled for at least a thousand years after the end of dispensationalism's future 70th week. Dispensationalism therefore destroys the very point of the seventy weeks.

THE "PRINCE WHO IS TO COME" AND "HE" (9:26–27)

Dispensationalists agree that the events of 9:26 "were fulfilled in the death of Christ . . . and the destruction of Jerusalem by Rome in A.D. 70."[130] Nevertheless, the dispensationalist interpretation is that *"the prince who is to come"* (9:26) and "he" (9:27) do not refer to Christ, or even to Titus, but to "another 'prince' who is yet to come," a "future Roman prince."[131] Thus, dispensationalism has the prophecy launching thousands of years into the future and dealing with *another* Roman prince, *another* Roman people, *another* rebuilt Jerusalem, *another* rebuilt temple, and *another* sacrificial system. Such an interpretation does great violence to the text, as Young points out:

> vs. 26 states that the city and sanctuary will be destroyed by the people of a prince that will come. All of the above [dispensationalist] writers believe that the allusion is to the destruction of Jerusalem by the Romans. The destroying people are the Romans, but the prince is not Titus, not a prince of the historical Roman empire, but of a future, revived Roman empire. It therefore follows, upon this view, that the people belong to a prince who will not appear for years (nearly 2000 have already elapsed) after they themselves have perished. But how can this be? How can the Roman armies of Titus possibly be regarded as belonging to a prince who has not even yet appeared? . . . But the emphasis in vs. 26 is *not* upon

128. Walvoord, *Daniel*, 221–22; see also MacDonald, *Believer's*, 1085.

129. Mauro, *Seventy Weeks*, 99, emphasis in the original.

130. Scofield, *New Scofield*, 913n.1.

131. Ibid.

a prince from the people, but upon the people who belong to the prince. This prince, therefore, must be one who rules over these people, who can truly say that they are his. In other words, he must be their contemporary, alive when they are alive. We cannot, by any stretch of the imagination, legitimately call the army of George Washington [1776–83] the army of a general, and by that general have reference to Eisenhower [1941–45].[132]

The word for "prince" in 9:26–27 is also against the dispensational view. Daniel uses the term "prince" (Hebrew = *nagid*) for a leader of God's people the only other times he uses the term (Dan 9:25; 11:22). Elsewhere in the OT, *nagid* is regularly used of Israelite leaders, but only once is it used of a foreigner (the "prince of Tyre," Ezek 28:2), and there it is used ironically.

Further, the grammar of 9:26–27 indicates that the reference in those verses is Christ, not Antichrist:

> The indefinite pronoun "he" does not refer back to "the prince who is to come" of verse 26. That "prince" is a subordinate noun; "the people" is the dominant noun. Thus, the "he" refers back to the last dominant individual mentioned: "Messiah" (v. 26a). The Messiah is the leading figure in the whole prophecy, so that even the destruction of the Temple is related to His death. In fact, the people who destroy the Temple are providentially "His armies" (Matt. 22:2–7). It was with the death of Christ that Judaism was legally (covenantally) disestablished, bringing "an end to sacrifice and offering" (Heb. 7:12, 18).[133]

Finally, contrary to the dispensationalist interpretation of 9:26–27, "It is significant that there is in Daniel no mention of a hoped-for rebuilding or rededication of the temple [after AD 70]. In Daniel 2 a great stone 'not made with hands' shatters the fourth kingdom and becomes a 'kingdom which shall never be destroyed' (2:44)."[134] In other words, Daniel himself prophesies that God's kingdom would be inaugurated at the time of the fourth kingdom (Rome, when Jesus appeared); he did not look for a "revival" of the Roman Empire and a new Jewish temple-system thousands of years after that.

THE "COVENANT" (9:27)

The dispensational idea that the "covenant" of 9:27 is a treaty made by Antichrist is contrary to the wording of the verse. "The covenant here is not made, it is confirmed. The usual word for the initial establishment of a covenant is *karat*. This is actually the confirmation of a covenant already extant, i.e., the covenant of God's redemptive grace confirmed by Christ (Rom. 15:8). The word 'confirmed' (Heb.: *higbir*) is the very emphatic form of *gabar*. Not only does the term itself indicate a confirming of covenant, but in its present form it is too strong an expression to apply to a covenant made, then broken by the Antichrist."[135]

---

132. Young, *Prophecy of Daniel,* 211–12.
133. Gentry, "Daniel's Seventy Weeks," n.p.
134. Gaston, *No Stone,* 118.
135. Ibid.

Meredith Kline discusses the background of Isaiah 10 for the Hebrew used in Daniel regarding the covenant and how that affects the interpretation of 9:27:

> According to these futurist reconstructions, antichrist enters into some pact at the beginning of the seventieth week and then what he succeeds in doing during the course of that week is to break his covenant. Such a situation, it must be insisted, would be the diametrical opposite of what verse 27 describes. The evidence on the usage of *higbir* indicates that verse 27 has in view the enforcing of the terms of a covenant previously granted. If so, it can only refer to God's faithful fulfillment of the covenant He has given to His people. . . . Particularly significant for the meaning of *higbir* in Daniel 9:27 is the use of *gibbor* in Isaiah 9 and 10. Isaiah identified the Messiah, the Son of David, as "the mighty God" of the covenant formula by declaring His name to be *el gibbor* (Isa. 9:5, [6]). Then in Isaiah 10 this messianic *el gibbor* is mentioned again in the very passage from which Daniel 9:27 derives its thought and wording alike (see verses 21–23). Isaiah spoke there of God's mighty messianic fulfillment of covenant blessing and curse. . . . Daniel 9:26b, 27 echoes Isaiah's prophecy. . . . The unmistakable dependence of Daniel 9:27 on Isaiah 10:21ff. points directly to the *el gibbor* of Isaiah 10:21 as the inspiration for the *higbir* of Daniel 9:27. This confirms the conclusions that the subject of *higbir* is not antichrist or any other than the anointed one whose name is *el gibbor* and that the object of *higbir*, the covenant made to prevail, is the redemptive covenant sealed by the reconciling blood of Christ.[136]

Further, "Neither history nor Scripture can document a covenant made (not to mention 'confirmed') by a leader of Israel's enemies, whether by Antiochus the Greek, Titus the Roman, or the Antichrist of the future."[137] Finally, although most translations say that the covenant is made "*for one week*," the word "for" is not in the original but has been added by the translators. "The words 'one week' do not refer to the duration of the covenant, but to the time when it was confirmed."[138]

ACCORDING TO CHRIST'S STATEMENTS IN MATT 24:36; MARK 13:31; ACTS 1:7 AND ELSEWHERE, IT IS IMPOSSIBLE TO PREDICT HIS SECOND COMING

"Like other Scriptures, Jesus' words 'No one knows the time' will not pass away until heaven and earth pass away (Mk 13:31). So there can be no future time when someone will know the date of the end—until the end actually comes."[139] The dispensationalist interpretation of Dan 9:24–27 would allow a precise calculation of the date of the *parousia*.[140] Since that is contrary to what Christ said, the dispensationalist interpretation of Dan 9:24–27 cannot be true.

136. Kline, "Covenant," 465, 467.

137. Payne, "Interpretation," 36.

138. Mauro, *Seventy Weeks*, 80.

139. Oropeza, *99 Reasons*, 31. See the main text, chapter 8, the section "The second coming of Christ is totally unpredictable."

140. See Lindsey, *Late Great*, 152; Ice, "Rebuttal," 135–38.

Issues that involve the chronographical versus chronological nature of the "seventy weeks"

The exile itself was not exactly seventy years (see Dan 9:2)

"There are various ways of reckoning the years of exile, none of which comes exactly to seventy years: e.g., 605 BC, the date of Je. 25:11, to 539, the restoration under Cyrus; or 587, the destruction of Jerusalem, to 516, when the Temple restoration was completed. The period of Jerusalem's abandonment, when no worship was offered there, was much less than 70 years (587–538)."[141] "In 2 Chron. 36:17–23 the period of time from the Babylonian conquest of Jerusalem to the establishment of the Persian empire—a period of approximately fifty years—is described in this way, 'All the days that it lay desolate it kept Sabbath to fulfill seventy years.' Thus, even the seventy years of Jeremiah's prophecy were not understood in a strictly literal fashion."[142] Similarly, Zech 1:12 says, *"Then the angel of the LORD said, 'O LORD of hosts, how long will You have no compassion for Jerusalem and the cities of Judah, with which You have been indignant these seventy years?'"* However, Zechariah was written in 520 BC after Israel had been back in the land for approximately 18 years.[143] Therefore, the "70 years" cannot have been viewed as a precisely literal number. Daniel knew of the general time-frame (9:2), but there is no indication that the "seventy years" was intended to be "to-the-day."

Dan 9:24–27 was not viewed as a strict chronology in the NT

"If Daniel's numbers really had been intended, as many interpreters have supposed, to give a precise prediction of the date of Jesus' life and death, then it is surely remarkable that neither Jesus nor New Testament writers appeal to this to support their messianic claims."[144]

The apocalyptic genre of Daniel

Although the years of Jeremiah's prophecy which formed the basis for Daniel's prayer in 9:2 appear to have been normal solar years, "When we move from Jeremiah to Daniel we are not moving only from one historical period to another. We are moving from one literary *genre* to another. We are moving from a book composed primarily of historical and prophetic narrative to one composed primarily of apocalyptic symbolism. The two types of literature have different concerns and different modes of urging their messages. The fact that we have before us apocalyptic imagery in Daniel increases the possibility that we are dealing not with exact chronology, but with a time-scheme, the form of which is, in part, the message."[145]

---

141. Baldwin, *Daniel*, 164n.2.
142. McComiskey, "The Seventy," 40.
143. VanGemeren, *Interpreting*, 193.
144. Travis, *I Believe*, 121–22.
145. McComiskey, "The Seventy," 36–37.

Appendix 4

The symbolic use of "seventy"

"Seventy years was the fixed term of divine indignation (Zc. 1:12). . . . This ritual understanding of the term takes it beyond the merely numerical into the theological and ethical realm. . . . Seventy years had a symbolic significance and so the new term ['seventy weeks'] may be expected to have an element of symbolism, to be taken into account in any attempt at interpretation."[146]

Additionally, the "weeks" appear to be based on the Jewish sabbatical cycle. Collins states:

> The influence of the sabbatical theology of Leviticus 25–26 has been widely noted. According to Lev 25:1–55, a jubilee, or seven weeks of years (forty-nine years), was the maximum period that land could be alienated from its ancestral heirs or that a person could be kept in indentured slavery. Already in 2 Chron 36:18–21, Jeremiah's prophecy is interpreted in the light of Leviticus 'to fulfill the word of the Lord by the mouth of Jeremiah, *until the land had enjoyed its Sabbaths. All the days that it lay desolate it kept Sabbath,* to fulfill seventy years' (cf. Lev 26:34–35). Daniel 9 extends the duration of the desolation to seventy weeks of years, or ten jubilees.[147]

In light of this, the seventy weeks are undoubtedly symbolic:

> Against this background it seems very likely that Daniel's seventy weeks uses number symbolically. . . . The first seven weeks (forty-nine years) may correspond quite well to one way of measuring the exile chronologically, but the figure is probably chosen because it represents the forty-nine years that lead up to a year of jubilee, a year of release for slaves and captives. The antithesis of perfection is sometimes represented by one less than the perfect number (e.g., 666 as the number of the beast in Rev. 13:18). Therefore it is appropriate that the climax of devastation comes at the end of the sixty-ninth week. . . . One week (seven years) provides a suitable symbolic period for sin to reach its completion and be brought to a total end.[148]

Issues involving the chronological use of the "seventy weeks"

Every proposed "starting decree" and "ending date" for the "seventy weeks" is based on certain assumptions and raises various issues.[149] One fundamental issue is: *How precise a chronology is intended by the prophecy?* The literature indicates different dates (usually off by a year) for the dates of the supposed "decrees" that begin the seventy weeks. Without a precisely known starting date one can never have a precise chronology. Similarly, the precise dates of Christ's birth, baptism, and death are not known (both AD 30 and 33 have support as the year of Christ's crucifixion). Without precisely known ending dates one also cannot have a precise chronology. Further, the decrees of 605, 597, 587, 539/538, 521, and 445/444 BC are not 483 or 490 years before a theologically and historically sig-

146. Baldwin, *Daniel,* 164, 168.
147. Collins, *Daniel,* 352, emphasis in original.
148. Lucas, *Daniel,* 248.
149. See Germano, "Decree of Artaxerxes," n.p.

nificant event. On the other hand, if not intended as a "to-the-day" calculation, the decree of 458/457 BC is 483 years (i.e., 69 complete weeks of 7 years) before AD 26/27, the supposed time of Jesus' baptism, a remarkable "coincidence" that appears too close to be accidental. Each decree also entails other issues.

Jeremiah's prophecies (Jer 25:12; 29:10), 605, 597 BC

The first prophecy concerned the seventy years of captivity and God's punishing the Babylonians; the second concerned God's bringing his people back to the land after the seventy years' exile. Neither says anything about *"restoring and rebuilding Jerusalem."* Also, the prophecies were given at the beginning of the exile before Daniel even wrote, so they are unlikely to be what Daniel referred to in Dan 9:25.

Jeremiah's prophecies of restoration (Jer 30:18–22; 31:38–40), 587 BC

Those prophecies do state that the city would be rebuilt. However, they were not themselves *"a decree to restore and rebuild Jerusalem."* Those prophecies also were given before Daniel even wrote, so they are unlikely to be what Daniel referred to in Dan 9:25.

Gabriel's own words to Daniel, or Cyrus's decree (Ezra 1:1–4), 539/538 [or 537] BC

"Daniel had computed the first year of Cyrus (537) as the end of the Exile according to 9:1–2. Ezra 1:1–4 acknowledges Cyrus as the fulfillment of Jeremiah's prophecy."[150] Kline adds:

> If attention is paid to the unity of this chapter, particularly, if there is due regard for the appropriateness of the response to the urgency of the plea that the divine word through Jeremiah be speedily fulfilled as the passage of the years now demanded (i.e., the seventy years spanned by the date formulae in Dan. 1:1 and 9:1), one can only conclude that the beginning of the seventy weeks coincided with the ending of the seventy years at the time of Daniel's prayer [which] all points to the first year of Cyrus as the start of the seventy weeks. It is then quite impossible to work out the fulfillment in a literal 490-year period.[151]

Nevertheless, despite the theological significance of Cyrus's decree, it only speaks specifically of rebuilding the temple, not the city. On the other hand, rebuilding the temple may imply rebuilding the city, since rebuilding the city by Cyrus's decree is referred to in the prophecies of Isa 44:28; 45:13, and "rebuilding the city and rebuilding the temple were one and the same thing to the Jewish people"[152]

---

150. Gentry, "New Exodus," 36.

151. Kline, "Covenant," 459n.19.

152. Gentry, "New Exodus," 35.

Appendix 4

Artaxerxes's decree (Ezra 6:1–12), 521 BC

This decree simply permitted the work on the temple to continue but does not speak about the city itself.

Artaxerxes's decree (Ezra 7:12–26), 458/457 BC

This is the decree typically cited by chronological messianic interpreters since the end of the 69th week yields a date in AD 26/27, the presumed date of Jesus' baptism. The decree permitted Jews to go to Jerusalem, beautify the temple, and worship in it. Ezra 7:18 is a broad warrant to use extra silver and gold as Ezra wishes, but restoring and rebuilding the city are not specifically authorized. Dan 9:25 says, *"You are to know and discern that from the issuing of a decree to restore and rebuild Jerusalem . . ."* Since Daniel himself was an old man by the time of Cyrus in 538 BC, he would have been dead by 457 BC and therefore could not himself have known of or discerned from Artaxerxes's decree. It may be, however, that *"know and discern"* speaks generically and is not limited to Daniel personally.[153]

Artaxerxes's decree (Neh 2:7–8), 445/444 BC

This decree authorized Nehemiah to obtain *"timber to make beams for the gates of the fortress which is by the temple, for the wall of the city and for the house to which I will go."* It did not commission the restoring and rebuilding of Jerusalem itself but simply authorized materials for the construction of walls, gates, and the governor's residence as part of an already ongoing rebuilding project. In fact, Hag 1:2–4, written about seventy years before the decree given to Nehemiah, speaks of people already living in paneled houses in Jerusalem. As with Artaxerxes's earlier decree, Daniel would have been dead by the time of the decree issued in 445/444 BC.

The Christological Nature of Dan 9:24–27

"Critical scholarship, setting the writing of Daniel in the context of the second century BC, sees the period in view as intended to stretch from the sixth century to the time of Antiochus Epiphanes. . . . But from the perspective of the NT, it is hard to avoid the conclusion that the *Anointed One* (25) is fulfilled in Jesus Christ whose coming brings atonement and the end of guilt (24)."[154] Even commentators who have an Antiochene interpretation of the passage agree:

- *Russell*: "He has in mind, no doubt, the deliverance of his people ('you people and your holy city') from the foreign oppression of Antiochus and the Seleucids, but the promised end is much more than this—it is the consummation of God's purpose for his people Israel and the beginning of a new era under his saving rule."[155]

153. This decree is discussed in more detail below in the section "The covenantal structure of Dan 9:24–27 points to Christ."

154. Ferguson, "Daniel," 759.

155. Russell, *Daniel,* 184.

- *Goldingay*: The focus of Daniel 8, 10–12 is on the crisis of Antiochus Epiphanes. The inference is that Dan 9:24–27 has that same focus.

> Yet its allusiveness justifies reapplication of the passage, as is the case with previous chapters, in the following sense. It does not refer specifically to concrete persons and events in the way of historical narrative such as 1 Maccabees, but refers in terms of symbols to what those persons and events embodied, symbols such as sin, justice, an anointed prince, a flood, an abomination. Concrete events and persons are understood in the light of such symbols, but the symbols transcend them. They are not limited in their reference to these particular concrete realities. . . . But if I am justified in believing that Jesus is God's anointed, and that his birth, ministry, death, resurrection, and appearing are God's ultimate means of revealing himself and achieving his purpose in the world, they are also his means of ultimately achieving what the symbols in vv 24–27 speak of.[156]

Goldingay's conclusion is biblically sound because, "to read the Bible contextually *as the Word of God* must include the completed canon as the ultimate context of any particular passage."[157] Both Jesus and the NT writers emphasize that the entire OT, including the OT prophets, ultimately were writing about and find their fulfillment in Jesus Christ.[158] Several factors point to Christ as the true, intended fulfillment of Dan 9:24–27.

The covenantal structure and theological background of Dan 9:24–27 point to Christ

Behind the prophecy is God's covenant relationship with Israel, which included a pattern of Sabbaths, Sabbath years, and the Sabbath Jubilee. Both Daniel's prayer and the answer to that prayer show that. Daniel refers to God *"who keeps His covenant"* (9:4), although Israel has violated the covenant (9:5) and has not listened to God's prophets (9:6, 10). As a result, the curses prescribed by God's covenant have fallen on Israel (9:11–14).

That is the background, and Dan 9:24–27 is God's unique answer to Israel's predicament. "Daniel 9 is the only chapter in Daniel to use God's special covenant name, YHWH ('Lord,' vv. 2, 4, 10, 13, 14, 20; cf. Exo. 6:2–4). This prayer regarding covenant loyalty (Heb.: *hesed*, 9:4) is answered in terms of the covenantal Sabbath pattern of the seventy weeks (9:24–27), which results in the confirmation of covenant (9:27). The recognition of the covenantal framework of the Seventy Weeks is important to its proper interpretation. It virtually demands the focus be on the fulfillment of redemption in the ministry of Christ."[159]

---

156. Goldingay, *Daniel,* 266–68.

157. Johnson, *Him We Proclaim,* 156.

158. Luke 24:25–27; John 5:39–40, 46; Acts 3:18, 24; 10:43; 26:22–23; 1 Pet 1:10–12.

159. Gentry, "Daniel's Seventy Weeks," n.p.

Appendix 4

The seventy weeks, the sabbatical pattern, and the year of Jubilee

"The 'seventy sevens' chronography is probably best understood against the background of Jewish sabbatical years, and the Jubilee year in particular."[160] Additionally, "The goal of the seventy weeks as described in Daniel 9:24 is an ultimate age of fulfillment and completion. Its accomplishments are those found elsewhere in prophecies of God's new and everlasting covenant and of the eschatological jubilee."[161] Kline describes this:

> The covenantal theme emerges in the very structure of Gabriel's revelation—the structure of the seventy weeks (or sevens). This chronological mold in which the prophecy is cast is obviously sabbatical. The basic unit, the *sabua'*, "heptad, period of seven," refers to the seven-years period the seventh year of which was a sabbatical year of rest for the land (Lev. 25:2ff.). The first of the major sections into which the seventy weeks are subdivided comprises seven of these sabbatical years (Dan. 9:25), and so constitutes the forty-nine-year period that issued in the heightened Sabbath of the jubilee (Lev. 25:8ff.), the year of redemption, release, and restoration. The total period of seventy sevens of years thus constituted ten of these jubilee eras, an intensification of the jubilee concept pointing to the ultimate, antitypical jubilee. . . . Therefore, the placing of Gabriel's response to Daniel's prayer in a sabbatical-jubilee framework tells us at once that this prophecy is fundamentally concerned with God's covenant with Israel, and especially with the consummation of that covenant. . . . [In 2 Chron 36:21] each of the seventy years [of Israel's exile] are the equivalent of seventy weeks of years. Under the exile's condition of continuing desolation, 490 years were telescoped into 70 because the desolate land leaped without the normal six-year intervals of labor from one seventh year to the rest immediately to the next sabbatical year. Thus, Gabriel's seventy weeks prophecy actually made use of the very same symbol as the seventy years prophecy of Jeremiah—and that symbol is explained in II Chronicles 36:21 as sabbatical.[162]

God's two-fold plan of the return from exile

According to Dan 9:2, Daniel was concerned about the end of the exile. Yet even before Israel had entered the land under Joshua, God had a plan for his people to return from the exile into which he would send them (Deut 30:1–10). According to Isaiah, God's plan for Israel's return from exile involved two separate stages, as Peter Gentry explains:

> The first stage is the physical return from exile [Isa 42:18—43:21]. . . . The second stage is the spiritual return from exile: it deals with the problem of sin and brings about forgiveness and reconciliation in a renewed covenant between Yahweh and His people [Isa 32:22—44:23]. According to the structure of Isaiah's message, Cyrus is the agent for the return from Babylon, and the Servant of the Lord is the agent for the return from sin. . . . Daniel's prayer is focused upon the physical return from Babylon—the first stage in redemption,

160. Williamson, *Sealed with an Oath*, 174. See Lev 24:8; 25:1–4; 26:43; 2 Chron 36:21.

161. Kline, "Covenant," 462n.25. See Isa 60:21; 61:1–3; Jer 31:34; 32:40; Ezek 16:60–63; 20:37–38; 37:26.

162. Kline, "Covenant," 459–60.

430

but the angelic message and vision of the Seventy Weeks is focused upon the forgiveness of sins and renewal of the covenant and righteousness—the second stage in return from exile.[163]

Kline elaborates the "Servant of the Lord," prophesied by Isaiah, who is to fulfill the prophecy and inaugurate the final, covenantal Jubilee:

> Isaiah had prophesied of this anointed one too, the one anointed with the Spirit to proclaim the jubilee release and renewal (Isa. 61:1ff.), the prince whom God would give when He made the everlasting covenant (Isa. 55:3f.), the servant of the Lord who was a covenant mediator like unto Moses and would himself be the covenant (Isa. 42:6; 49:8), the servant who must be cut off out of the land of the living in order to provide justification for "the many" (Isa. 53:10–12). If the Mosaic treaties provided the framework of administrative rubrics [rules of conduct or procedure] for the covenantal theme in Daniel 9, the Isaianic servant figure was the source for the personal mediator of the covenant of the seventieth week.[164]

The return from exile and the New Covenant

THE UNIVERSAL IMPLICATIONS OF THE RETURN FROM EXILE

The focus of Daniel's prophecy is on the city and the people (Jerusalem and Israel), but there are broader implications for the nations. The Abrahamic Covenant had promised that the nations would be blessed through the seed of Abraham (Gen 12:1–3). The Mosaic Covenant instructed Abraham's physical seed how to live in a right relationship with God, in order to be a blessing to the nations (Exodus 19–24). Gentry describes the situation:

> With the Mosaic Covenant broken, Israel now needs the forgiveness of sins so that the covenant is renewed and the blessings can flow to the nations. Thus, the final and real return from exile is achieved by dealing effectively with Israel's rebellion: the first objective in the list of six [9:24] is to end "the rebellion," i.e., of Israel. Then the blessing can flow to the nations, and this blessing finds fulfillment in the apostolic preaching of the cross and resurrection of Jesus Christ when each one turns from their wicked ways (Acts 3:26). In this way, the second stage of return from exile has implications specifically for Israel, but also universally for the nations.[165]

THE NEW COVENANT

The way in which the Abrahamic Covenant is fulfilled and the nations are blessed, and the way in which Israel receives forgiveness of her sins and rebellion, is through the New Covenant. The New Covenant had been prophesied through Jeremiah (Jer 31:31–34).

---

163. Gentry, "New Exodus," 31.

164. Kline, "Covenant," 462.

165. Gentry, "New Exodus," 32.

It is the only one of God's covenants that promised the forgiveness of sin.[166] Unlike the old Mosaic Covenant, the New Covenant is called an "everlasting covenant."[167] Paul Williamson observes, "Given the Jeremianic context that prompted this revelation (Dan. 9:2; cf. Jer. 25:11–12; 29:10), some explicit association between this climactic Jubilee and the anticipated new covenant is not unexpected."[168] Meredith Kline adds that the form and content of Daniel 9 have prepared the way for a decisive final word about the messianic consummation of God's covenant with Israel in the last of the seventy weeks. "When, therefore, we find a covenant mentioned in verse 27, there should be no doubt as to its identity. The whole context speaks against the supposition that an altogether different covenant from the divine covenant which is the central theme throughout Daniel 9 is abruptly introduced here at the climax of it all."[169] The covenantal structure discussed above indicates that the "covenant" of 9:27 is the New Covenant prophesied by Jeremiah, not an agreement made between Antichrist and Jews.[170]

The literary structure points to Christ

The literary structure of the passage corroborates the theological background of the passage. It shows that the primary focus of the prophecy is the "second (spiritual) stage" of the return from exile—the stage that was, and could only be, effected by Jesus Christ, not by any OT figure. The theological background and literary structure, particularly of Dan 9:25–27, further show that the passage has nothing to do with an end-time Antichrist. Peter Gentry discusses the importance of the literary structure:

> Verses 25–27 are not to be read in a linear manner according to the logic of prose in the western world based upon a Greek and Roman heritage. Instead, the approach in ancient Hebrew literature is to take up a topic and develop it from a particular perspective and then to stop and start anew, taking up the same theme again from another point of view. . . . First, v. 25 introduces the first period of seven weeks and the gap of sixty-two weeks to the climactic seventieth week. This last week is described twice in verses 26 and 27. Verse 26a and 27a describe the work of Messiah in dying vicariously to uphold a covenant with many and deal decisively with sin, thus ending the sacrificial system. Verses 26b and 27b show that ironically, supreme sacrilege against the temple at this time will result in the destruction of the city of Jerusalem. Thus verses 26–27 have an A-B-A'-B' structure. This fits the normal patterns in Hebrew literature to deal with a topic recursively. The literary structure can be diagrammed as follows:
>
> A 26a the beneficial work of the Messiah
>
> B 26b ruin/spoliation of the city by his people and its desolation by war

166. Jer 31:34; see also Jer 32:38–40; 50:4–5; Ezek 11:16–20; 36:24–32; 37:15–28.

167. Gentry, "New Exodus," 38; 43n.33; see Isa 55:3; 61:8; Jer 32:40; 50:5; Ezek 16:60; 37:26.

168. Williamson, *Sealed with an Oath*, 174.

169. Kline, "Covenant," 462–63.

170. Some see the covenant as the Abrahamic Covenant, not the New Covenant. Riddlebarger, *Amillennialism*, 155. The two are related. In fact, the New Covenant is the final realization of the Abrahamic Covenant. For a detailed explanation of how Christ fulfilled the covenants and all of Israel's institutions, see Menn, *Biblical Theology*, 26–93.

A' 27a the beneficial work of the Messiah

B' 27b abominations resulting in destruction of the city by one causing desolation

Observing this literary structure is crucial because one can explain difficulties in one section using the parallel section. For example, "the people of the coming leader" in v. 26b bring ruin to the reconstructed Jerusalem. Verse 27b provides further details showing that the 'one causing desolation' does so in association with abominations. . . . The literary structure also clarifies how the terms *mashiach* and *nagid* in 25 and 26 refer to one and the same individual and moreover make perfect sense of the "strengthening of a covenant" in v. 27a.[171]

Jesus Christ, Daniel 9, and the fulfillment of the New Covenant by the Servant of the Lord

God's plan, as set forth in Daniel's prophecy, was far more than simply getting Israel back into its land from exile in Babylon. That was merely an outward, physical sign of God's overall plan. His overall plan involved ushering in the final Jubilee and inaugurating the everlasting New Covenant. That plan could only be effected by the anointed priest and king, prince and Messiah, also known as the "Servant of the Lord." The agent through whom that plan is brought to completion is none other than Jesus Christ.

Christ is the mashiach ("anointed") nagid ("prince; ruler") of 9:26-27

"Although *nagid*, 'leader, ruler,' is used elsewhere of cultic officials, *nagid* and *mashiach* are conjoined elsewhere only with reference to an anointed king (1 Sam 9:16; 10:1; 1 Chron 29:22)."[172] In the OT, the promised Messiah combined the offices of priest and king (see Ps 110:1-6; Zech 6:13). Historically, the Davidic king ruling in Jerusalem was removed from the throne by the exile in 586 BC. However, the prophets spoke of a coming king from David's line. Gentry states that "the vision given to Daniel associates the king's return with the end of exile and the climactic purposes for Israel and Jerusalem, but with great personal tragedy: he will be cut off, *but not for himself*. The coming king will give his life to deliver his people."[173] Only Jesus Christ met the requirements of being both a priest and a king and fulfilled the prophecies of giving his life to deliver his people.

The death of Christ and the ratification of the New Covenant (Dan 9:26-27)

Dan 9:26-27 links the Messiah and the covenant together. Dan 9:26 speaks of the Messiah being "cut off." The Hebrew for "cut off" is the verb *karat* which is:

regularly employed for the act of ratifying a covenant by a cutting ritual which portrayed the curse of the covenant oath. The statement about the covenant

171. Gentry, "New Exodus," 36.

172. Ibid., 33.

173. Ibid., emphasis in original.

in verse 27 is then in clear continuity with the covenantal allusion in verse 26. Gabriel here assures Daniel that the cutting off of the anointed one (vs. 26) would not mean the failure of His mission but, on the contrary, its accomplishment. . . . It was by His death for the iniquity of His people that the Lord's anointed servant ratified the new covenant in which God's old covenant with Israel is confirmed and finds its consummation.[174]

Dan 9:27 speaks of the "covenant" that will be confirmed in the final, climactic "seven" or "week." As we have seen, that covenant is the New Covenant, prophesied by Jeremiah. Only Jesus Christ has met all the requirements of Daniel 9 and thereby has inaugurated the New Covenant. That is what his life and ministry largely were all about, and he knew it. At the Last Supper, Jesus explicitly stated that he was inaugurating the New Covenant in his blood (Luke 22:20; see 1 Cor 11:25). "The allusions to both the forgiveness anticipated by Jeremiah (Matt. 26:28; Jer. 31:34) and the blood associated with the establishment of the original Mosaic covenant (Luke 22:20; Exod. 24:7) further underline that Jesus understood his death as the inauguration of the new covenant."[175] The New Covenant was confirmed by Jesus in his blood.

As the final covenant, which both takes away sin and is everlasting, the New Covenant also typifies or ushers in the final Jubilee. In Luke 4:14–21 Jesus quoted Isa 61:1–2 and said, *"Today this Scripture has been fulfilled in your hearing."* In substance he was saying, "I am the fulfillment of what that always pointed to; in me the ultimate Jubilee is now here." Iain Duguid summarizes:

> The seventieth week is a kind of "jubilee" week, in which God restores all things to their proper state. . . . With the coming of Jesus into the world, and especially with his death and resurrection, the seventieth week has dawned. In Christ, our jubilee trumpet has sounded, and the victory over sin and transgression has been won. What is more, with the death of Jesus on the cross, the sacrifices of the Old Testament became redundant and worthless. The Son of Man gave his life as a ransom for the many, bringing those whom God had chosen into the new covenant relationship with the Lord (Mark 10:45).[176]

Jesus Christ, the "Servant of the Lord," and "the many" of Dan 9:27

Dan 9:27 refers to the covenant being confirmed with *"the many,"* which almost certainly is a reference to *"the many"* referred to in Isa 53:10–12. Gentry states:

> Without a doubt, Isaiah 53, describing a future Davidic Servant of the Lord, who is also both priest and sacrifice, laying down his life for the many, is the background to the brief comment in Daniel's vision. His death brings an end to the sacrificial system because it is a final solution to the problem of sin. . . . In Dan 9:27a the statement "he will uphold a covenant with the many" refers to the work of the Anointed King in effecting the new covenant described by the prophets at different times and in a variety of ways. . . . The expression "uphold a covenant"

174. Kline, "Covenant," 463–64.

175. Williamson, *Sealed with an Oath,* 184.

176. Duguid, *Daniel,* 171–72.

is chosen and used here because the context entails the return from exile and the 'renewing' of the covenant relationship between Yahweh and Israel.[177]

The anointed "Servant of the Lord" had been prophesied in Isaiah.[178] Isaiah 53, with its reference to *"the many,"* is part of the fourth "Servant Song" (Isa 52:13—53:12). The NT writers describe Jesus as the "Servant,"[179] and they specifically quote and apply the Servant passages to Jesus as the fulfillment of prophecy.[180] Jesus both lived like a Servant and described himself as a Servant.[181] In Rom 5:18–19, Paul alludes to Isa 53:10–12 when he says that Jesus, through his death, will justify *"the many."* Thus, Jesus is the one whom the prophecies were pointing to as the fulfiller of God's plan because he is the anointed "Servant of the Lord."

Artaxerxes's decree of 457 BC, the sabbatical cycle, and Christ

Given the significance of Cyrus's decree of 539–37 BC as being the fulfillment of the prophecies of Jeremiah and Isaiah regarding the return from exile and the rebuilding of the city, it is significant that "Ezra 6:14 speaks of Cyrus, Darius, and Artaxerxes as though they issued a single decree. Darius's decree (Ezra 6) was based upon the fact that Cyrus had *already* issued the decree to permit the return and rebuilding of Jerusalem (see Ezra 5:17—6:7). Ezra 6:14 shows that Artaxerxes's decree (in Ezra 7) is also an extension of Cyrus's original decree. So the decree which Cyrus drafted in 537 to restore the temple is not completed until 457 B.C. under Artaxerxes, which is therefore the date of the 'word to rebuild Jerusalem' starting with its sanctuary."[182]

Dating the decree and its fulfillment

Research indicates that the correct date for this decree was 457 BC, not 458 BC, which would bring the 69th week of Daniel to completion in AD 27.[183] Assuming a 457 BC decree date, both the beginning and ending of Daniel's 69 weeks are consistent with the Jewish sabbatical cycle.[184] "The sabbatical year ended and a new week of years began at Tishri 457 BC. . . . 69 weeks or 483 years later takes us to the fall of 27 AD, which is when the Messiah should have appeared. If Luke used a fall-to-fall calendar with non-accession-year reckoning for Tiberius Caesar, then this would be about the time of Christ's baptism, for Tiberius's fifteenth year by such a reckoning would have commenced in the

---

177. Gentry, "New Exodus," 37–38.

178. Isa 42:1–9; 49:1–6 (or 13); 50:4–9; 52:13–53:12.

179. Acts 3:13, 26; 4:27, 30; Phil 2:7.

180. See, e.g., Matt 8:14–17; 12:17–21; Luke 4:18, 21; 22:37; Acts 8:26–35; 1 Peter 2:21–24.

181. Matt 20:28; Mark 10:45; Luke 22:27; John 13:5–16.

182. Gentry, "New Exodus," 35

183. See Gentry, "New Exodus," 35; Rodriguez, "Seventy Weeks," 1–9; Pickle, "Chronological Difficulties," n.p

184. Gentry, "New Exodus," 36; Pickle, "Sabbatical Cycle," n.p. This also assumes the use of the Zuckermann, rather than the Wacholder, calculation of the sabbatical cycles. Those different calculations of the sabbatical cycles are described by both Pickle and Gentry.

fall of 27 AD (Luke 3:1). Thus His baptism fell at the beginning of the first year of a new sabbatical cycle."[185]

Christ and the fulfillment of Artaxerxes's decree

Assuming the above scenario, the precise *"middle of the [70th] week"* (Dan 9:27) would be AD 31, a date of questionable historical significance. However, both AD 30 and AD 33, the dates in which the crucifixion most likely occurred, fall within that 70th sabbatical cycle. Despite the assumptions and unknowns, and if not presumed to be a "to-the-day" prediction, by using the 457 BC decree date "the prophecy remains an astounding prediction finding fulfillment in Jesus of Nazareth and yet allows for differences as well in calculating the crucifixion [which] is almost always dated between A.D. 27 and 34 [i.e., the 70th sabbatical cycle/seventieth week from 457 BC]."[186] This corroborates that the seventy weeks is based on the sabbatical cycle, the seventy weeks are being used symbolically, and the seventy weeks legitimately can be used chronologically—and all culminate in Christ.

Christ is the ultimate fulfillment of the six purposes of the prophecy stated in Dan 9:24

> All those words [e.g., "sin," "iniquity," "righteousness," "vision," "prophet"] which are used in the prayer [9:1–23] in a definite sense expressing a particularist view ("our," "my," "of the people," "of God," etc.) are suddenly, as soon as they appear in the context of the 70 weeks, used in an indefinite sense expressing a universalistic point of view. We may now understand why *mashiach*, "Messiah," is indefinite—an absolutely exceptional case in OT usage—: In the light of what precedes and on account of its particularity, the term *mashiach* does not mean a particular Messiah among others holding a certain mission, but he is indeed *the* Messiah *par excellence*. . . . He is the Messiah of all the peoples."[187]

As Edward Young puts it, "the primary reference is to Israel after the flesh, and the historical Jerusalem, but since this very vs. [9:24] describes the Messianic work, it also refers to the true people of God, those who will benefit because of the things herein described."[188] Thus, in 9:24, terms like *"your people"* and *"your holy city"* assume the meaning that they have in the NT, when they are used to signify the church, the new, true "Israel of God."[189] In an ultimate sense, therefore, Jesus alone fulfills the six purposes of the seventy weeks described in 9:24:

185. Pickle, "Sabbatical Cycle," n.p.

186. Gentry, "New Exodus," 37.

187. Doukhan, "Seventy Weeks," 21.

188. Young, *Prophecy of Daniel,* 197.

189. Gal 6:16; see also, e.g., Luke 12:32; John 10:15–16; Rom 2:28–29; 4:13–16; 8:14, 16; 9:22–26; 2 Cor 6:16; Gal 3:26, 29; Eph 1:4–5; 2:19; 5:25–32; Phil 3:3; Col 2:11; 3:12; 1 Tim 3:15; Titus 2:14; Heb 8:10; 1 Pet 2:5, 9–10; 5:2–3; 1 John 3:1–2; Rev 1:6; 5:10; 11:2; 21:2–3, 9–14.

"To finish the transgression"

The word "transgression" indicates apostasy and rebellion (see Dan 9:5–11, 15). Young states:

> The work of shutting up sin can only be the work of God, which is to be performed with the introduction of the other blessings herein mentioned. This was done by Christ, the Great Deliverer. He shut up transgression by the act which He performed, namely, His atoning death. . . . And the transgression which He sealed up is . . . not merely the transgression of Israel, but transgression generally. The definite article *the* means that we are to take the reference not to one particular transgression, but to transgression as such. The phrase "upon thy people" etc., does not mean that the blessings described are for the benefit *only* of the literal nation Israel. Such a thought is utterly foreign to the universalistic nature of OT prophecy generally. Rather, the phrase "upon thy people" serves to indicate that as far as Israel is concerned, a period of 70 sevens has been decreed in order to bring about blessing which, while having primary reference to Israel, do as a matter of fact, characterize the New Dispensation.[190]

"To make an end of sin"

Jesus Christ is the Lamb of God who took away the sin of the world by the sacrifice of himself.[191] He "brought about an end to sin and sin offering in that he sealed and overcame in his death once-and-for-all what sin means."[192]

"To make atonement for iniquity"

"The thought seems to be either that the necessary propitiatory sacrifice will be offered and therefore sin expiated, or that the necessary propitiatory sacrifice will be offered and therefore sin is pardoned or forgiven. . . . The text does not say, but who, in the light of the NT revelation, can read these words without coming face to face with that one perfect Sacrifice which was offered by Him?"[193] Wayne Jackson shows the relationship of Dan 9:24 with Isaiah 53:

> It is interesting to note that Daniel emphasized that the Anointed One would address the problems of "transgression," "sin," and "iniquity"—as if to suggest that the Lord is capable of dealing with evil in all of its hideous forms. Similarly, the prophet Isaiah, in the 53rd chapter of his narrative, revealed that the Messiah

---

190. Young, *Prophecy of Daniel*, 198; see John 19:30; Rom 5:17–21; Heb 9:15. Even focusing on Israel's transgression leads us to Jesus: "This finishing (Heb. *kala*) the transgression has to do with Israel's finishing, i.e., completing, her transgression against God. The finishing of that transgression occurs in the ministry of Christ, when Israel culminates her resistance to God by rejecting His Son and having Him crucified." Gentry, "Daniel's Seventy Weeks," n.p.; see Matt 21:33–45; 23:29–39; 27:20–25; Acts 7:51–52.

191. John 1:29; Rom 7:1—8:4; Heb 9:26; 10:11–14; 1 John 3:5.

192. Hasel, "Crossroads," n.p.

193. Young, *Prophecy of Daniel*, 199; see Rom 3:25; Eph 2:16; Col 1:20; Heb 2:17; 1 John 2:2; 4:10.

would sacrifice Himself for "transgression" (5, 8, 12), "sin" (10, 12), and "iniquity" (5, 6, 11). . . . Isaiah 53 frequently is quoted in the New Testament in conjunction with the Lord's atoning work at the time of His first coming. Since Daniel 9:24ff. quite obviously has an identical thrust, it, too, must focus upon the Savior's work at the cross.[194]

"To bring in everlasting righteousness"

The words "everlasting righteousness" do not occur elsewhere in the Old Testament. Of course the noun ["righteousness"] and its cognate forms occur scores of times. . . . This word is used numerous times in Isaiah. Many verses state that the Messiah will transform the nation in righteousness.[195] . . . When Daniel wrote that one of the purposes for the seventy weeks is "to bring in everlasting righteousness" (Dan. 9:24), this would have been freighted with meaning for the Jews, for they were looking forward to what the Messiah, Son of David, would accomplish for Israel as a nation and for the world.[196]

"Because of this atonement to cover sin, the fourth result is that everlasting righteousness is effected. That is, the final, complete atonement establishes righteousness. This was effected by Christ within the seventy week period as well: 'But now the righteousness of God apart from the law is revealed, being witnessed by the Law and the Prophets, even the righteousness of God' (Rom. 3:21–22a)."[197] H. C. Leupold comments on the nature of righteousness: "This is without a doubt the imputed righteousness which is not naturally to be found among men, and so God must 'bring in,' *habhi'*, this much sought treasure. It is not a thing of a moment only but lasts forever as all God's treasures do."[198]

"To seal up the vision and prophecy"

"Vision was a technical name for revelation given to the OT prophets (cf. Isa. 1:1, Amos 1:1, etc.). The *prophet* was the one through whom this vision was revealed to the people. The two words, vision and prophet, therefore, serve to designate the prophetic revelation of the OT period. This revelation was of a temporary, preparatory, typical nature. It pointed forward to the coming of Him who was the great Prophet (Deut. 18:15). When Christ came, there was no further need of prophetic revelation in the OT sense."[199] That is confirmed by Heb 1:1–2 (*"God, after He spoke long ago to the fathers in the prophets in many portions and in many ways, in these last days has spoken to us in His Son"*). Gentry adds, "By this is meant that Christ fulfills (and thereby confirms) the prophecy. . . . Actually, the sealing of prophecy regards the subject of Daniel 9: the accomplishment of

---

194. Jackson, "Daniel's Prophecy," 4.

195. E.g., Isa 1:26; 2:1–4; 11:4–5; 16:5; 32:1; 62:11–12.

196. Tanner, "Part 2," 330.

197. Gentry, "Daniel's Seventy Weeks," n.p.

198. Leupold, *Exposition*, 414; see Matt 3:13–15; Rom 3:21–22; 5:18; 1 Cor 1:30; 2 Cor 5:21.

199. Young, *Prophecy of Daniel*, 200.

redemption from sin, i.e., atonement. This Christ accomplished: 'Behold, we are going up to Jerusalem, and all (!) things that are written by the prophets concerning the Son of Man will be accomplished' (Luke 18:31; cp. Luke 24:44; Acts 3:18)."[200]

"To anoint the Most Holy"

The "most holy" phraseology well speaks of the Messiah, who was "that Holy One who is to be born."[201] It is of Christ that the ultimate redemptive Jubilee is prophesied by Isaiah in these words: "The Spirit of the Lord God is upon Me, because the Lord has anointed Me to preach good tidings to the poor; He has sent Me to heal the brokenhearted, to proclaim liberty to the captives, and the opening of the prison to those who are bound; to proclaim the acceptable year of the Lord" (Isa. 61:1–2a; cp. Luke 4:17–21). It was at His baptismal anointing that the Spirit came upon Him (Mark 1:9–11).[202]

Peter Gentry concludes:

The verb "to anoint" is normally used of consecrating persons for offices. . . . It can also refer to the consecration of the Mosaic Tabernacle and its holy objects. . . . Only in Dan 9:24 do we have the "Holy of Holies" being anointed. This phrase could be construed as "the most holy place" or "the most holy person." The latter meaning would be most unusual. Thus we have a verb that is normally used of a person and an object normally used of a temple. It may suggest that both the future king and temple are one and the same. It finds fulfillment in Jesus of Nazareth as both Messiah and true Temple.[203]

Thus, the NT portrays Christ as the true and greater king (John 18:37; Rev 19:16), the true and greater high priest (Heb 4:14–5:10), and the true and greater temple (John 2:18–22).

---

200. Gentry, "Daniel's Seventy Weeks," n.p.; see also Acts 3:22.

201. Luke 1:35; see also Mark 1:24; Luke 4:34, 41; Acts 2:27; 3:14; 4:27, 30; 10:38; 1 John 2:20; Rev 3:7.

202. Gentry, "Daniel's Seventy Weeks," n.p. Gerhard Hasel adds, "Jesus Christ also anointed the heavenly Most Holy as he himself was also anointed as the heavenly High Priest." Hasel, "Crossroads," n.p.; see Heb 5:1–10; 7:15–8:6; 9:6–26; 10:1–18.

203. Gentry, "New Exodus," 40.

Zechariah 14 (its relation to Christ's two advents)

The Background, Structure, and Themes of Zechariah

The background of Zechariah

The historical situation

"THE HISTORICAL SITUATION IS the same as that of Haggai. The people of Judah had returned from exile in 536 B.C., but the joy and enthusiasm (see Ps. 126) that had characterized their return were gone. Almost twenty years had elapsed, and the temple had not yet been rebuilt. . . . [The people] responded positively to the ministry of Haggai and Zechariah; the temple was dedicated on March 12, 515 B.C. (Ezra 6:15–18)."[1]

Date of Zechariah

"Several months after Haggai had begun preaching (August 29, 520 B.C.; Hag. 1:1), the Lord spoke to Zechariah (1:1). From October to November 520 to December 518 B.C. he proclaimed God's word. The oracles and visions in chapters 1 to 8 are dated by year, month, and day (1:1, 7; 7:1), but chapters 9 to14 contain no such dating formula."[2]

The structure and themes of Zechariah

Basic structure of the book

"Accepting the division between chapters 1 to 8 and 9 to 14, [Brevard] Childs argues in favor of a relationship between the two sections. According to him the second section expands, develops, and sharpens the theological pattern of the 'end time,' which emerges

1. VanGemeren, *Interpreting,* 193.
2. Ibid.

from chapters 1 to 8. The book thus seeks to explain that notwithstanding the return from exile, the full experience of redemption still lies in the future."[3]

Structure of chapters 9–14

Within the basic two-part structure of the book, chapters 9–14 divide into two parts: chapters 9–11 and 12–14. The basic themes of chapters 9 to 14 involve Israel and the nations and the establishment of God's kingdom on earth. Chapters 12 to 14 bring these themes to a climax. VanGemeren outlines them as follows:[4]

The establishment of God's kingdom on earth, 12:1—14:21

   A. Jerusalem and the nations, 12:1–9

      B. Mourning for the pierced one, 12:10–14

         C. Promise of cleansing and forgiveness, 13:1–5

      B'. The shepherd struck, 13:6–9

   A'. Jerusalem and the nations, 14:1–21

      1. Troubles of Jerusalem, 14:1–2

         2. The coming of the King, 14:3–9

            3. Exaltation of Jerusalem, 14:10–11

            3'. Desolation of the nations, 14:12–15

         2'. Universal worship of the King, 14:16–19

      1'. Holiness and peace of Jerusalem, 14:20–21

The function and themes of Zechariah 14

Zechariah 14 serves as the climax to the entire book by drawing together themes woven throughout the previous 13 chapters. These motifs include the return of fertility like that in paradise (cf. 8:12 with 14:6–8); the prosperous city of Jerusalem living securely without walls (cf. 2:9; 9:8 with 14:11); the curse going out all over the land and the ban removed (cf. 5:3 with 14:11); God's judgment on the nations (cf. 2:1–4, 12–13; 9:1–8; 10:11; 12:4 with 14:12–15); the alteration of worship practices (cf. 8:18–23 with 14:20); and the nations coming to Jerusalem to worship (cf. 2:11; 8:20–23 with 14:16).[5]

Interpreting Zechariah

Genre: prophetic-apocalyptic

"The presence of visions, symbolism, and eschatological imagery classify Zechariah [particularly ch. 14] as a prophetic-apocalyptic writing."[6] As such, the guidelines for inter-

---

3. Ibid., 194.

4. Ibid., 195.

5. Klein, *Zechariah*, 395.

6. VanGemeren, *Interpreting*, 194.

preting prophecy and apocalyptic given in the main text, both generally and with respect to Revelation, apply to Zechariah 14.

The use of "prophetic idiom"

In interpreting Zechariah 14, it is important to bear in mind that, in both his descriptions of blessings and plagues that will occur after the Lord's eschatological return to earth, Zechariah uses the language of "prophetic idiom," i.e., the OT prophets speak of Messiah's eternal kingdom *using the language and limited frame of reference of their own physical, Israelite context.*[7] In light of the coming of Christ and the NT, to the extent that Zechariah prophesies about eschatological events, the prophecies cannot be taken "literally."[8] Even Zechariah himself indicates that since he "described it [Jerusalem] as a 'city without walls' (2:4) and composed of 'many nations . . . joined with the Lord' (2:11). He is using Jerusalem as a symbol of the truth about God's kingdom which, Jesus says, is 'not of this world' (John 18:36)."[9]

Historical interpretations of Zechariah 14

As with the book of Revelation and Dan 9:24–27, historically there have been several different interpretations of Zechariah 14. Wolters lists seven: (1) Except for the last 2 verses (which pertain to end-times) the rest of the chapter was fulfilled in connection with the Maccabean Revolt of the 160s BC; (2) It covers the period from Christ's first coming to the second coming; (3) It covers Israel's return from exile to the coming of Christ; (4) It is a non-literal description of the end-times; (5) It is a literal description of the end-times; (6) It concerns the fall of Jerusalem in 586 BC; (7) It is apocalyptic language not specifically tied to any historical or future event.[10]

Eschatological and messianic emphases

Eschatological and messianic emphases in Zechariah 9–14

This section of the book in particular has messianic implications. According to some commentators, "The messianic implications of Zechariah 9–11 focus on events surrounding Christ's first advent. Zechariah 9:9 epitomizes this emphasis: 'See, your king comes to you, righteous and having salvation, gentle and riding on a donkey.' Chapters 12 to 14 encompass Christ's second advent when he establishes the eternal kingdom of God. The theological climax of the Messiah's arrival appears in 14:9: 'The Lord will be king over the

---

7. See the main text, chapter 2, the section "Prophetic idiom."

8. See main text, chapter 3–Old Testament Eschatological Expectations and the Significance of Christ's First Coming.

9. Yilpet, "Zechariah," 1092.

10. Wolters, "Zechariah 14," 39–56.

whole earth. On that day there will be one Lord, and his name the only name.'"[11] That is somewhat of an overstatement. Several passages in chapters 12 to 14 are quoted from or alluded to in the NT as applying to Christ's first advent as well as his second. However, because chapter 14 in particular is clearly eschatological, those passages from chapter 14 that apply to Christ's first advent probably are best seen as doing so because the two advents are connected: the first inaugurated the kingdom; the second consummates the kingdom.

Eschatological and messianic emphases in Zechariah 14

> The only satisfactory interpretation views chap. 14 as a series of momentous prophecies focusing on the future, the eschatological day that Zechariah regularly referred to with the words "on that day." . . . The apocalyptic language, coupled with the universal scope of the prophecies in chap. 14, render any attempt to find a past historical fulfillment to the chapter impossible. Numerous statements in chap. 14 have no equivalent in history. For instance, the following prophecies from chap. 14 demand an eschatological fulfillment: God will "gather all the nations to Jerusalem to fight against it" (v. 2); "it will be a unique day . . . known to the Lord" (v. 7); "the Lord will be king over the whole earth" (v. 9); "never again will it [Jerusalem] be destroyed" (v. 11); and "the survivors from all the nations that have attacked Jerusalem will go up year after year to worship the King, the Lord Almighty" (v. 16). The sevenfold reverberation of the eschatological formula "on that day" (vv. 4, 6, 8, 9, 13, 20, 21) also makes the futuristic outlook of chap. 14 certain.[12]

Zechariah 9–14 applies to Christ's First Advent, and the Kingdom He inaugurated at His First Coming

Zechariah 9–14 is quoted or alluded to as applying to Christ's first advent

Event	Zechariah	Gospels
Entry into Jerusalem on a donkey	9:9	Matt 21:1–9; Mark 11:1–10; Luke 19:29–38; John 12:12–16
Covenant established by blood	9:11	Matt 26:27–28; Mark 14:23–24; Luke 22:20; 1 Cor 11:25
Sheep without a shepherd	10:2	Matt 9:36; Mark 6:34
The flock	11:11	Luke 12:32
30 pieces of silver	11:12	Matt 26:15
Money thrown to the potter	11:13	Matt 27:3–10
Jerusalem is a heavy stone/ trampled	12:3	Luke 21:24; Rev 11:2

11. Klein, *Zechariah*, 398

12. Ibid., 397, 398.

Event	Zechariah	Gospels
They will look on Me whom they have pierced	12:10	John 19:34, 37
Mourning (especially by the women)	12:10–14	Luke 23:27
Forgiveness of sin	13:1	Matt 1:21; Mark 2:10; John 1:29
Shepherd struck; sheep scattered	13:7	Matt 26:31, 56; Mark 14:27, 50; John 16:32
They are my people; I am their God	13:9	Luke 22:20; 2 Cor 6:16; Heb 8:10
The Lord on the Mount of Olives	14:4	Matt 24:3; Mark 13:3; Acts 1:12
Earthquake; appearance of holy ones	14:4–5	Matt 27:51–53
Continual light	14:7	John 1:4, 9; 3:19–21; 8:12; 12:46
Living water at the feast of Tabernacles	14:8, 16–19	John 7:37–38
Cleansing the temple	14:20–21	Matt 21:12–13; Mark 11:15–17; Luke 19:45–46; John 2:13–16

Zech 9:9 (the king enters on a donkey)

Matt 21:1–9; Mark 11:1–10; Luke 19:29–38; and John 12:12–16 all use Zech 9:9 to show that Jesus' symbolic action of riding into Jerusalem on a donkey implies that he fulfills the prophecy and is the messiah, king, savior, and restorer of Israel.[13]

Zech 11:12b (thirty pieces of silver)

"Matthew is the only one to specify the sum of money which Judas was promised by the chief priests for his undertaking to betray Jesus to them. . . . Matthew says that 'they weighed out for him thirty pieces of silver' [Matt 26:15]. This is practically a quotation from [Zech 11:12b], where the prophet tells us that when he asked to be paid for the services he had rendered as 'shepherd of the flock doomed to slaughter', his employers 'weighed out' as his wages 'thirty pieces of silver.'"[14]

Zech 11:13 (throwing down the silver; the potter)

Matthew's dependence on Zechariah's narrative is obvious in the account of Judas's repentance and suicide (an account unique to Matthew). F. F. Bruce notes that the chief priests

13. Carson, "Matthew," 8:437; Blomberg, "Matthew," 63–65; Kostenberger, "John," 472–74; Pao and Schnabel, "Luke," 355; Yilpet, "Zechariah," 1085.

14. Bruce, "Book of Zechariah," 340.

"took the thirty pieces of silver which Judas had thrown down before them in the temple [Matt 27:5], and said: 'It is not lawful to put them into the treasury, since they are blood money.' So they bought the potter's field with them [Matt 27:6–10]. . . . The quotation is readily recognizable as coming from [Zech 11:13], where the prophet tells what he did with the thirty shekels which his employers paid him for looking after their sheep."[15] "Why does Matthew ascribe the prophecy to Jeremiah? Probably because it had already been closely associated, if not conflated, in an earlier set of *testimonia* with two passages from Jeremiah—[Jer 18:2–6] where Jeremiah visits the potter's house, and [Jer 32:6–15] where he buys the family field of Anathoth."[16]

Zech 13:7 (the shepherd is struck; the sheep scatter)

At the Last Supper, in Matt 26:31; Mark 14:27, Jesus quotes this verse of Zechariah and applies it to himself. "When we see the quotation of [Zech 13:7] not as something isolated, but as part of Jesus' presentation of Himself as the good shepherd, we begin to see other things. In particular, we begin to see the germ of the use of Zechariah [9–14] in the Gospels, and especially in the passion narrative. For the figure of the shepherd recurs throughout these six chapters."[17]

Sometimes a prophecy of Zechariah 9–14 is linked in the NT both to Jesus' first advent and his second

The following double references are consistent with the "already, but not yet" nature of the kingdom of God. In no case is Zechariah 9–14 intended to be fulfilled in the present or future literal nation of Israel. Instead, "Christ indeed came to fulfill the expectations of Zechariah 9–14, but in doing so . . . expands the fulfillment to include not only Israel but also the nations"[18]

Zech 12:10 (looking at the one pierced, and mourning)

The "piercing" is explicitly applied to Jesus' first coming in John 19:37 and to his second coming in Rev 1:7. In fact, Rev 1:7 "refers to peoples throughout the earth, although in Zech. 12:10 it is limited to Israelite tribes. The same widening application of Zech. 12:10 is also seen in John 19:37, where the action of a Roman soldier is viewed as a beginning fulfillment of this prophecy."[19]

The "mourning" is explicitly applied to Jesus' second coming in Matt 24:30; Rev 1:7 but implicitly in Luke 23:27 to his first coming (crucifixion).

15. Ibid., 340–41.
16. Ibid., 341.
17. Ibid., 345.
18. Boda, *Haggai, Zechariah*, 63.
19. Beale, *Revelation*, 91.

Appendix 5

Zech 13:9 (they are my people and I am their God)

The essential desire of God that "I will be their God and they will by my people" is fulfilled in Christ's inauguration of the New Covenant (Luke 22:20; 2 Cor 6:16; Heb 8:10) and consummately in the New Jerusalem (Rev 21:3, 7).

Zech 14:8 (living water)

"Living water" is alluded to by Jesus in John 7:37–38 as being inaugurated in his first coming and in Rev 22:1–2 as being consummated in the New Jerusalem.

The Olivet Discourse is a "retelling" of Zechariah 14

The setting of Jesus' Olivet Discourse is the Mount of Olives. "This can hardly be accidental. . . . Jesus seems to intend an allusion to Zechariah 14.4–5. The context is the coming of the divine kingdom (Zechariah 14.9) and the coming great battle of the nations against Jerusalem (14.1–3). . . . The force of the setting then seems to be that this was Jesus' paradoxical retelling of the great story found in Zechariah 14: in predicting Jerusalem's last great struggle, the 'coming' of YHWH, and the final arrival of the divine kingdom, he was acting to fulfil, in his own reinterpreted fashion, the prophecy of Zechariah."[20]

The idea that Jesus was alluding to or "retelling" Zechariah 14 is reinforced by his references to "fleeing,"[21] the sun and the moon being darkened,[22] and his coming with *"all the angels with Him."*[23]

Several aspects of Zechariah 14 relate to Christ's inauguration of the kingdom

Zech 14:4 (Matt 24:3; Mark 13:3; Acts 1:12)

> He will stand *upon the mount of Olives;* this was literally fulfilled when our Lord Jesus was often upon this mountain, especially when thence *he ascended up into heaven,* Acts 1:12. It was the last place on which his feet stood on this earth, the place from which he took rise. The partition-wall between Jews and Gentiles shall be taken away. The *mountains about Jerusalem,* and particularly this, signified it to be an enclosure, and that it stood in the way of those who would approach to it. Between the Gentiles and Jerusalem this *mountain of Bether,* of *division,* stood, Cant. 2:17. But by the destruction of Jerusalem this mountain shall be made to *cleave in the midst,* and so the Jewish pale shall be taken down, and the church laid in common with the Gentiles, who were made one with the Jews by the breaking down of this *middle wall of partition,* Eph. 2:14. . . . The

20. Wright, *Victory,* 344–45. See also Barker, "Zechariah," 824–25 regarding how Zech 14:2 bears on the meaning of Jesus' statement in Luke 21:24 that Jerusalem will be trampled on until the *"times of the Gentiles"* are fulfilled.

21. Matt 24:16; Mark 13:14; Luke 21:21; compare Zech 14:5.

22. Matt 24:29; Mark 13:24; Luke 21:25; compare Zech 14:6.

23. Matt 25:31; compare Zech 14:5b.

mountain being divided, one-half *towards the north* and the other half *towards the south,* there shall be *a very great valley,* that is, a broad way of communication opened between Jerusalem and the Gentile world, by which the Gentiles shall have free admission into the gospel-Jerusalem, and the word of the Lord, that *goes forth from Jerusalem,* shall have a *free course* into the Gentile world.[24]

Zech 14:7 (John 1:4, 9; 3:19–21; 8:12; 12:46)

In the gospel of John, "the dawning of the light [promised in Zech 14:7 to occur *'in that day'*] in the coming of Jesus has been a significant theme. In this age of an inaugurated but not yet consummated kingdom, however, the light is still in mortal combat with darkness."[25]

Zech 14:8 (John 7:37–38)

"In fulfillment of the OT prophetic vision (Zech. 14:8; Ezek. 47:9), Jesus inaugurated the age of God's abundance. Jesus' offer of living water signals the reversal of the curse and the barrenness that are characteristic of the old fallen world."[26] Jesus' statement in John 7:37–38 concerning the *"living water"* likely alludes to a number of OT texts. Those include the water from the rock in the desert, Exod 17:1–6; the river of living water from Ezekiel's temple, Ezek 47:1–11; and the waters that flow in the new age from Jerusalem to the eastern and western seas, Zech 14:8 (see also Pss 78:15–16; 105:40–41).[27] By identifying himself as the rock, the new temple, the New Jerusalem, and the living waters, Jesus was indicating that the OT scriptures are being fulfilled *now:* the eschatological new age has dawned.

Zech 14:16–19 (feast of tabernacles)

The feast of tabernacles was the last of Israel's fall feasts. It commemorated the wandering in the wilderness and celebrated the completion of the fall harvest. Spiritually, in light of its connection with the harvest, tabernacles took on eschatological meaning. It "looked forward to the final joyful harvest, when Israel's mission on earth should be completed by gathering all the nations of the world to the Lord, as prophesied by Zechariah (14:16)."[28] The feast of tabernacles finds its fulfillment in Jesus. Jesus *is* the new, true Israel. John 11:52 makes clear that Jesus is gathering his people.[29] However, his gathering does not involve geographical relocation to Israel or Jerusalem. Jesus said that his being lifted up

---

24. Henry, *Commentary,* 1593.
25. Carson, *John,* 338.
26. Kostenberger, "John," 438.
27. Balfour, "Jewishness of John's Use," 368–78.
28. Hillyer, "First Peter," 40.
29. See also John 4:35; 10:16; Rev 5:9; 7:9.

by his death on the cross is what *"will draw all men to Myself"* (John 12:32). "Jesus, not the 'promised land', is now the focus of this long-awaited 'ingathering'"[30]

Thus, the true fulfillment of Zech 14:16–19 does not involve going to an earthly city to worship the Lord.[31] Zechariah's prophecy (like other OT prophecies) uses the language and symbols of OT physical Israel (which the people at that time could relate to), but in reality it points to Christ himself, the heavenly Jerusalem, a city made without hands, *"whose architect and builder is God"* (Heb 11:8–10; 12:18–24). Pao and Schnabel note the significance of Christ's reorientation of Zechariah, "The notion that the beginning of the messianic age will be noticeable first in Jerusalem, where the good news of repentance and the forgiveness of sins is first proclaimed [Luke 24:47; see also Acts 1:8], also indicates a reversal of the direction assumed by the OT promises concerning the conversion of the Gentiles in the last days. . . . Whereas the Jews expected the nations to come from 'outside' to Jerusalem as the center of the world, Jesus tells his disciples that they will begin in Jerusalem and then move out to the nations."[32]

Zech 14:20–21 (Matt 21:12–13; Mark 11:15–17; Luke 19:45–46; John 2:12–16)

When Jesus drove the money changers and sellers out of the temple, he quoted from Isa 56:7; Jer 7:11 but may also have been alluding to Zech 14:20–21. In effect, he was proclaiming the holiness and the beginning of the messianic transformation of the meaning of the temple. Additionally, Zech 14:20–21 indicates that ordinary cooking pots or utensils in Jerusalem were to be holy vessels. In Mark 11:16, after he "cleansed the temple," Jesus did not permit anyone to carry any merchandise through the temple.[33] Some commentators have suggested, "In this context, it may be that the action reported by Mark 11.16, where Jesus refused to allow anyone to carry vessels through the Temple (something also forbidden in rabbinic literature), was both part of the 'cleansing' side of the story and, more importantly, another symbol, indicating, by veiled allusion to Zechariah 14.20f., that 'the day' had at last arrived."[34]

Regarding Zech 14:21b (*"There will no longer be a Canaanite in the house of the Lord or hosts in that day"*), Canaanites were the historical inhabitants of Israel before they were displaced (Gen 12:6; Josh 3:10). The word for "Canaanite" can also mean "merchant" who bought and sold goods in the temple and elsewhere. That latter sense is how Jesus applied it when he cast out the money changers from the temple. Eschatologically, Canaanites may be referred to "not as a historical entity, but as a powerful literary symbol of illicit

30. Walker, *Jesus*, 189.

31. See John 4:21–24.

32. Pao and Schnabel, "Luke," 401. With respect to OT prophecies (now reversed by Jesus) indicating that Gentiles would come to Jerusalem, see Isa 2:2–5, 14:2; 45:14; 49:22–23; 55:5; 66:20; Jer 16:19–21; Mic 4:1–4; Zeph 3:9–10; Zech 8:20–23; 14:16–19. Those (such as dispensationalists) who take Zech 14:16–21 as indicating that the feast of tabernacles and the associated OT requirements for worship will literally be restored in a future millennium in effect reverse the realities found in Christ and return to the "shadows" and "types" of the OT (see Matt 5:17; 1 Cor 10:1–6; 2 Cor 3:12–16; Gal 3:23—4:7, 21–31; Col 2:16–17; Heb 1:1–2; 8:1—10:22).

33. The word for "merchandise" literally is "a vessel," which includes any kind of receptacle or implement. NASB, Mark 11:16, marginal note; see BDAG, *"skeous,"* 927.

34. Wright, *Victory*, 422.

worship. . . . The complete spiritual restoration will forever remove every vestige of sin from creation, allowing all to worship God righteously."[35]

Zechariah 14 applies to Christ's Second Advent, and the Eternal State He will Inaugurate when He Returns

Zechariah 14 is quoted or alluded to, or is otherwise fulfilled, in connection with Christ's second advent

Event	*Zechariah 14*	*NT Eschatological Fulfillment*
A day for the Lord; that day	14:1, 4, 6–8, 13, 20, 21	Matt 24:36; Mark 13:32; Luke 17:24, 31; 21:34; Acts 2:20; 17:31; Rom 2:5; 13:12; 1 Cor 1:7–8; 3:13; 5:5; 2 Cor 1:14; Eph 4:30; Phil 1:6, 10; 2:16; 1 Thess 5:2, 4; 2 Thess 1:10; 2:1–2; 2 Tim 1:12, 18; 4:8; Heb 10:25; 1 Pet 2:12; 2 Pet 3:10; Rev 6:17; 16:14
All nations gathered by God for war	14:1–2, 14	Rev 16:14–16; 19:19–21; 20:7–9a
The Lord will fight/plague the nations	14:3, 12–15	Rev 8:7–9:20; 16:1–19; 18:8–20; 19:11, 15, 20–21; 20:9b–10
The Lord will return to earth	14:4a	Matt 24:30; Mark 13:26; Luke 21:27; Acts 1:11; 1 Thess 4:16
Mt. of Olives will split like earthquake	14:4–5	Rev 6:14; 8:5; 11:13, 19; 16:18–21; 20:11
The Lord will come with His holy ones	14:5b	Matt 25:31; Mark 8:38; 1 Thess 3:13; 2 Thess 1:7; Rev 19:14
No light on that day	14:6	Matt 24:29; Mark 13:24; Acts 2:20; Rev 6:12
A unique day known to the Lord	14:7a	Matt 24:36; Mark 13:32; Acts 1:7
No day nor night, but there will be light	14:7b	Rev 21:23–25; 22:5
Living waters flow from Jerusalem	14:8	Rev 22:1–2
The Lord will be king of all the earth	14:9	Rev 11:15; 19:6; 21:3, 6–7, 22; 22:5
The land will be changed	14:10	Rom 8:17–25; 2 Pet 3:3–15; Rev 21:10–21
No more curse	14:11	Rev 22:3
Panic; civil war among the ungodly	14:13	Rev 6:15–17; 11:13; 17:16
The nations will worship the Lord	14:16–19	Rev 21:24–26

35. Klein, *Zechariah*, 428–29.

All will be holy to the Lord	14:20–21a	Rev 21:3, 7; 22:3–4
No Canaanite/merchant will be there	14:21b	Rev 21:8, 27; 22:15

The connections between Zechariah 14 and Revelation show how Revelation reinterprets Zechariah 14 Revelation takes every OT image and each limited frame of reference in Zechariah and expands or transforms it.

Zech 14:1–2 (Jerusalem)

"Connections between Zechariah 14 and Isaiah 13 suggest that the prophet is identifying Jerusalem with its former enemy Babylon."[36] Rev 11:8 does the same thing: the phrase *"where also their Lord was crucified"* suggests Jerusalem, but because of its rejection of Christ and persecution of the church physical Jerusalem's true character is described as *"Sodom and Egypt."* Further, it is called *"the great city"* which is consistently used throughout Revelation to describe Babylon the great.[37]

On the other hand, Rev 21:2, 10; 22:19 describe the *New* Jerusalem as the "holy city" (see Rev 11:2). Rev 20:9 specifies that "this is 'the camp of the saints and the beloved city' (20:9) which Jesus calls 'the city of my God' (3:12). The holy city is the spiritual Jerusalem of the saints."[38] Zech 14:2 quotes God as saying, *"I will gather all the nations against Jerusalem to battle."* That indicates that the literal, physical city of Jerusalem is not in view since "it would impossible for everyone from all the nations to come physically to do battle against Jerusalem."[39] Rev 16:14–16; 19:19–21; 20:7–9a make clear that the eschatological "battle" is worldwide and involves God's defeat of all who oppose Christ and the church.

Zech 14:3, 12–15 (eschatological conflict)

In the OT, "it is usually Jahweh himself who marches forth to a victorious warfare to establish his reign over his enemies (Isa. 13:4; 31:4; Ezek. 38–39; Joel 3; Zech. 14:3)."[40] Second Thess 2:8; Rev 2:16; 19:11, 15; 20:9b specify that it is Christ who will slay his enemies at the *parousia* simply by the sword of the word of his mouth. Zech 14:13 reflects an "eschatological state of chaos" like that described in Ezek 38:21; Hag 2:22 and is indicated in Rev 6:15–17; 11:13; 17:16.[41]

36. Boda, *Haggai, Zechariah*, 523; compare Isa 13:3–4 with Zech 14:2; Isa 13:6, 9 with Zech 14:1; Isa 13:10 with Zech 14:6; Isa 13:13–14 with Zech 14:4–5; Isa 13:15–16 with Zech 14:2.

37. Rev 14:8; 17:18; 18:2, 10, 16, 18–19, 21.

38. Kistemaker, "Temple," 437.

39. Klein, *Zechariah*, 400.

40. Ladd, *Commentary*, 252; see also Klein, *Zechariah*, 418.

41. Ladd, *Commentary*, 233; see also Klein, *Zechariah*, 418.

Zech 14:4–5a (His feet will stand on the Mount of Olives)

Zech 14:4 is a depiction of the *parousia*. Although some take this as a literal description of Jesus returning to earth and "touching down" on the Mount of Olives, the combined pictures of Zech 14:4–5 as a whole cannot be taken as literal, physical descriptions, for the following reasons:

- Zech 14:4 "portrays God anthropomorphically, describing his feet standing on Jerusalem's soil. The Lord appears as a colossus astride the mounts surrounding Jerusalem."[42] "*His feet shall stand* (v. 4) [is] a symbol of domination over every foe."[43]

- The OT frequently speaks figuratively of mountains or valleys splitting or quaking when the Lord comes to earth.[44] When Christ returns, according to Rev 6:14; 8:5; 11:13, 19; 16:18–21; 20:11, the earthquake that accompanies the *parousia,* if taken literally, has a much more cosmic scope than does the splitting of the Mount of Olives or earthquake described in Zech 14:4–5.

- Rev 8:7—9:20; 16:1–19; 18:8–20; 19:11, 15, 20–21; 20:9b–10 describe the "plagues" that the Lord will bring on the earth in connection with the *parousia* and also describe how at his coming there will, in fact, be no survivors among the wicked (Rev 19:20–21). Thus, the references to "fleeing" in Zech 14:5 cannot be literal: "Exactly who is it that will make that escape flight when the mountains cleft? It cannot be the wicked, for the Bible teaches that they will be destroyed when the Lord returns (Mt. 25:31–46; 2 Thes. 1:7–9). Moreover, it cannot be the righteous, for they will be 'caught up in the clouds, to meet the Lord in the air' (1 Thes. 4:17). Who, pray tell, is left?"[45] "The ancient imagery should not obscure the theological theme of the verse. The Lord will protect his people and save them from annihilation."[46] That is what Matt 24:31; Mark 13:27; Luke 21:28; 1 Thess 4:16–17; Rev 20:9 assure us.

Zech 14:5b (the Lord will come with the holy ones)

With respect to his coming *"and all the holy ones with Him [Hebrew reads 'with you'],"* many think the "holy ones" are angels, although the term can refer to humans.[47] One commentator argues against that, stating, "The final phrase of verse 5 in the Hebrew text is 'with you' . . . [which] cannot be God since it is a feminine singular pronoun. This is the same form already encountered in 14:1 ('your plunder'; 'among you'), a reference probably to the city of Jerusalem. Thus, the 'holy ones' here are the remnant that has fled from danger and now return under the protection of their Almighty God."[48]

---

42. Klein, *Zechariah,* 403.

43. Higginson, "Zechariah," 801.

44. Isa 64:1, 3; Ezek 38:19–20; Joel 3:16; Mic 1:3–4; Nah 1:5; Hab 3:6, 10.

45. Jackson, "Dispensationalism," n.p.

46. Klein, *Zechariah,* 405.

47. See Lev 21:7; Num 16:5; 2 Chron 35:3; Job 5:1; Ps 89:5, 7.

48. Boda, *Haggai, Zechariah,* 524–25.

The NT indicates that *"all the holy ones"* refers to Christians who accompany Christ at the *parousia* (or Christians along with angels). First Thess 3:13 speaks of *"at the coming of our Lord Jesus with all his saints ['holy ones']."* Jeffrey Weima states that, for the quotation in 1 Thess 3:13, there is good evidence that Paul depends on Zech. 14:5 LXX in which "holy ones" refers to angels, but Paul appears to have reinterpreted "holy ones" to mean believers because every other time he uses the plural *haigoi* ("saints" or "holy ones") he refers to believers.[49] His statement in 1 Thess 3:13 that "all" the saints will be with the Lord Jesus at his coming is consistent with or anticipates his argument in 1 Thess 4:14–15 that God "will bring with him" all believers, both those who are alive and those who have "fallen asleep."[50] The *Didache* 16:6–7 cited the reference to the saints or holy ones in Zech 14:5 as evidence for the resurrection of believers.

Zech 14:6 (there will be no light)

In Zech 14:6 *"there will be no light; the luminaries will dwindle"*; that is paralleled by Rev 6:12; 8:12; 16:10 (and by Christ's statements in Matt 24:29; Mark 13:24–25; Luke 21:25).[51]

Zech 14:7 (a unique day; light at night)

Zech 14:7 says there will be neither day nor night, yet there will be light, but it does not indicate the eschatological source of light. Rev 22:5 specifies that the source of light for the new heavens and new earth will be the Lord himself. "Since this day is unique, never having occurred before, it is beyond human experience or comprehension. . . . There is a finality about this day that signals the beginning of the eternal state when 'there will be no more night' (Rev. 22:5). This congealing of the astral bodies resonates with Revelation's affirmation that there will be no need of 'the light of the sun' (22:5)."[52] "The unique character of the day reflects a completely new order on earth. Like the statement in v. 6a, this prophecy continues the reversal of God's first action in creation, the distinction between day and night (Gen 1:3–5)."[53]

---

49. Weima, "1–2 Thessalonians," 875. See Rom 1:7; 8:27; 12:13; 15:25; 1 Cor. 1:2; 6:1–2; 2 Cor. 1:1; Eph. 2:19; 3:8; Phil. 1:1; 4:22; Col. 1:4, 26; 3:12; 1 Tim. 5:10; see also Rev 17:14; 19:14.

50. See Weima, "1–2 Thessalonians," 875.

51. As was discussed in the main text regarding the Olivet Discourse and the book of Revelation, the cosmic changes such as are described by Zechariah may or may not be literal. With respect to Zechariah specifically, Thomas McComiskey states, "Such cosmic changes characterize other prophetic descriptions of divine intervention. . . . To take them always as literal depictions of actual physical phenomena is to miss the nature of prophetic language in general and of apocalyptic symbolism in particular." McComiskey, "Zechariah," 1233.

52. Ibid.

53. Klein, *Zechariah*, 409.

Zech 14:8 (living water)

Zech 14:8 "depicts the life-giving water flowing eastward and westward, never ceasing to provide for the people because it flows continually, both 'summer and winter.'"[54] "Zechariah sets this hope in symbols relating to the land, for the waters flow to the Mediterranean as well as to the Dead Sea. These seas functioned as boundaries of the promised land (Num. 34:12; Deut 11:24; 34:2)."[55] The reference to *"in that day"* indicates eschatological finality. Rev 22:1 parallels Zechariah's vision by describing the *"the river of the water of life . . . coming from the throne of God and of the Lamb."* Further, Revelation expands Zechariah's vision by applying it to the entire new earth.

Zech 14:9 (the Lord will be king over all)

Zech 14:9 says, *"The Lord will be king over all the earth; in that day the Lord will be the only one, and His name the only one."* Rev 1:8; 3:12; 4:8; 5:5–14; 7:9–12; 11:15–17; 14:1; 21:3–7, 22–23; 22:1–5 have a much more Christocentric focus and equate "God and the Lamb." Unlike Zech 14:9, the closeness of the Lord and his people in the new earth is indicated by Rev 22:5 which says the *saints "will reign forever and ever."* The corporate reign of God, the Lamb, and the saints is something that never could have been imagined in the OT.

Zech 14:10 (the [New] Jerusalem)

In Zech 14:10, "The dimensions of the city are those of the eighth-century capital in its prime, with mention of the Benjamin (e.g., Jer. 20:2), First and Corner (e.g., 31:38) Gates, the Tower of Hananel (e.g., 31:38), and the royal winepresses (39:4)."[56] Rev 21:10–21 changes that picture, and turns the New Jerusalem into a Holy of Holies that is equivalent to the entire new earth.[57]

Zech 14:11 (no more curse)

Zech 14:11 anticipates Rev 21:1 in which all is new and *"the first earth passed away."* When 14:11 says there is no more "curse" it uses the Hebrew term *herem* which refers to "putting under the ban" or destroying idolaters and enemies such as the Canaanites when Israel entered the land.[58] It also speaks of Jerusalem dwelling in security. Rev 21:1, 25, which speak of no more sea and gates never being shut, likewise imply perfect security. Rev 21:4 goes well beyond that by speaking of no more tears, death, mourning, crying, or pain.

Rev 22:3 says *"there will no longer be any curse."* The phrase is taken from Zech 14:11, but the "curse" goes beyond the *herem*. The new heavens and new earth are the restoration

---

54. McComiskey, "Zechariah," 1233.

55. Ibid., 1234.

56. Boda, *Haggai, Zechariah*, 527.

57. See main text, chapter 11, the section "Overview of major ideas and sections," regarding Rev 21:1—22:5.

58. See, e.g., Deut 7:1–2; Josh 6:17–18; 11:1–15.

or new creation of the entire world. Thus, reference to the curse goes back to Gen 3:13–19: "physical and spiritual death set on the human race by Adam in the first garden is permanently removed by the Lamb in the last garden at the time of the new creation."[59]

Zech 14:16–19 *(feast of tabernacles)*

The feast of tabernacles was required by the OT law of Moses.[60] God's withholding rain was an Old Covenant curse for covenantal disobedience.[61] Zechariah expresses the eschatological future in OT terms: the nations come to Jerusalem; they celebrate the feast of tabernacles; God withholds rain for failure to celebrate the feast. As with Zechariah's other images, these cannot be taken literally because the entire Old Covenant and all its feasts have been superseded in Christ.[62] Therefore, when Christ comes again he will not re-establish the Jewish sacrificial system and festivals, including the Feast of Tabernacles, in the physical city of Jerusalem. Further, there cannot be covenant curses in the New Jerusalem since, according to Rev 20:15; 21:27, no one whose name is not written in the book of life is able to enter the New Jerusalem but has been cast into the lake of fire. Indeed, the fact that Zechariah indicates that *"any who are left of all the nations"* will celebrate the feast of tabernacles shows that Zechariah is "anticipating the inclusion of the Gentiles in the covenant community—precisely what John [in Revelation] is depicting in his portrayal of the church as the New Israel."[63]

Zech 14:20–21 *(the house of the Lord and perfect holiness)*

Zech 14:20–21 indicates that there still will be a *"house of the Lord"* in the restored Jerusalem. Revelation 21–22 goes well beyond that. Revelation specifies that in the New Jerusalem there is no temple *"for the Lord God the Almighty and the Lamb are its temple"* (Rev 21:22). Also, it so closely identifies the New Jerusalem with the people of God that it may be a metaphor for God's people and his relationship with them. "The dwelling of God with man *in the form of a city* may . . . suggest the perfect social union of the redeemed with one another as God's final and eternal answer to the successive societal failures littering the course of human history."[64]

Zech 14:20–21 does point to a change in OT law, however. "The reference to 'bells of the horses' is interesting, especially considering that the horse is a ritually unclean animal (Lev. 11:1–8). . . . Furthermore, the cooking pots in the temple will share the status of the sacred bowls at the altar, and common pots throughout Jerusalem and Judah will share the

---

59. Beale, *Revelation*, 1112.

60. Exod 23:16–17; 34:22–23; Lev 23:33–43; Num 29:12–38; Deut 16:13–15.

61. Deut 11:17; 28:22–24; 1 Kgs 8:35.

62. John 7:2, 37–38; 8:12; Gal 3:10—5:4; Col 2:16–17; Heb 8:6–13; 10:9. See Menn, *Biblical Theology*, 26–93.

63. Smith, "Portrayal of the Church," 116.

64. Ortlund, *God's Unfaithful Wife*, 166n.73; see Rev 21:2, 9–10; cf. Rev 19:7–8.

status of the cooking pots. These verses transform the ritual categories of Torah."[65] All of those changes and more were enacted by Christ, who freed us from the entire OT law.[66]

"The final scene of Zechariah anticipates Revelation 11:15, toward which all history is steadily moving—'the kingdom of the world has become the kingdom of our Lord and of his Christ, and he will reign for ever and ever'—and Revelation 19:16—'On his robe and on his thigh he has this name written: KING OF KINGS AND LORD OF LORDS.'"[67] It also anticipates the absolute holiness of the new heaven and new earth, which symbolically is a new Holy of Holies.[68] "When every vessel in Jerusalem is as holy as the temple vessels, the whole city will have become the Holy of Holies, filled with God's presence."[69]

65. Boda, *Haggai, Zechariah,* 528.

66. E.g., Matt 11:13; Mark 7:19; Luke 16:16; Acts 10:15; Gal 3:10—5:4; Eph 2:14–15; Col 2:13–14; Heb 8:6–13; 10:9.

67. Barker, "Zechariah," 833

68. Compare 1 Kgs 6:16–20; 2 Chron 3:8 and Rev 21:16.

69. Johnson, *Triumph,* 309–10n.12.

Rom 11:25–26 ("and so all Israel will be saved")

25For I do not want you, brethren, to be uninformed of this mystery—so that you will not be wise in your own estimation—that a partial hardening has happened to Israel until the fullness of the Gentiles has come in; 26and so all Israel will be saved; just as it is written, "The Deliverer will come from Zion, He will remove ungodliness from Jacob."

Context of Romans 11:25-26

"All acknowledge that Romans 9–11 forms a unit in Paul's thought. Therefore, any interpretation of Romans 11 must also be consistent with Romans 9 and 10."[1]

The issue of Romans 9–11

The nation of Israel in large part rejected Christ as the Messiah, despite having had covenants, promises, and many other benefits (Rom 9:1–5). The issue was whether God's OT word had failed (Rom 9:6). Paul's answer is that, in God's sovereign plan, not all ethnic Israel is true Israel (Rom 9:6–7). In Romans 9, Paul explains God's sovereign plan and ability to choose whom he wants to for salvation—including Gentiles, not just Israelites (Rom 9:8–33). In Romans 10, he explains that the Jews had been ignorant of God's righteousness, and had sought to establish their own righteousness (Rom 10:3); the Gentiles had discovered that the good news of salvation is found through faith in Christ (Rom 10:6–21).

That leads to Romans 11, in which Paul raises the issue that follows from his discussion in Romans 9–10: "Has God completely cast off or rejected the Jews?" (Rom 11:1). Paul begins his answer by denying that God has completely rejected the Jews. He cites as proof the fact that he himself is *"an Israelite, a descendant of Abraham, of he tribe of Benjamin"* (Rom 11:1). Greg Bahnsen summarizes the rest of Paul's answer, "God has not totally rejected the Jews (vv. 2–4). His love and election necessitates a remnant among Israel (vv.

---

1. Merkle, "Romans 11," 711.

5–6), even though many were hardened by their self-righteousness (vv. 7–10). We could say, then that Israel has stumbled. Was it God's purpose to have Israel stumble so that she might utterly fall? Paul denies it (v. 11). Rather, Israel has rejected the Messiah as her savior, with the result that salvation would come to the Gentiles (cf. Acts 13:46, 18:6, 28:28)."[2]

The olive tree (Rom 11:17–24)

The image of the olive tree is taken from Jer 11:16 and Hos 14:5–6. Rom 11:1–6 begins by pointing out that God has kept his promises to Israel through the faithful remnant (of which Paul, a member of the church, is a member). Paul then likens Israel to a good olive tree:

> God has removed some of the branches of this Olive Tree because of their un-belief in His Son, their Messiah. At the same time, He has taken some branches from a wild olive, and has grafted them in among the branches of the good Olive Tree. But these newly engrafted branches should not boast because of their position, glorying over the Jews who were cut off. The Jewish branches were cut off because of their *unbelief.* The Gentile branches were grafted in because of their *belief.* If these Gentiles fall into *unbelief,* they too will be cut off. Position in the good Olive Tree is due to *faith alone.*[3]

Bell adds this important point regarding the grafting in of the Gentiles:

> It should be noted that the believing Jews, represented by the good natural branches, did not move. They were not transferred to a new tree, etc. It was the Gentile Christians who became a part of the already-existing good olive tree (Israel) and who share with the already-present natural branches (Jews). . . . Romans 11, in perfect harmony with other Pauline passages such as Ephesians 2 and with the New Testament generally, teaches that God's promises to Israel were never intended for the physical descendants as a whole, but for believing Israelites only, the remnant of Israel, represented in Paul's day by himself and other believing Jews, and that these promises have now been extended to believing Gentiles as well who, by admission to ancient Israel (the grafting into the good olive tree), share with the believing Jews; they together comprising spiritual Israel and/or the Christian church.[4]

Interpretive Issues Regarding Rom 11:25–26

11:25—What does "until" mean?

The Greek for "until" is *achris hou.* O. Palmer Robertson states, "The phrase brings matters 'up to' a certain point or 'until' a certain goal is reached. It does not itself determine the state of affairs after the termination."[5] What happens after the "until" point is reached can only be determined from the context.

2. Bahnsen, "Gospel Prosperity," 6.
3. Bear, "People of God," 152.
4. Bell, "Critical Evaluation," 116, 118.
5. Robertson, *Israel of God,* 179.

There are two main views of the partial hardening of Israel *until* the fullness of the Gentiles comes in: (1) Those who view "until" as implying a change in condition *after* some future point when *"the fullness of the Gentiles"* has *"come in"* (i.e., at that point the "hardening of Israel" will be *removed*); and (2) Those who do not see a "removal" of the hardening (i.e., the Gentiles will continue to *"come in"* until the *parousia;* Jews will continue to be saved throughout the age, but there will be no specific point in the future when God works with Israel in a new or distinctive way).

The meaning of Rom 11:25 obviously is key to this debate. Robertson points out that many interpreters appear to instinctively leap to the conclusion that "until" implies a change after the "until point" is reached, although the text does not say that: "Too often 'until' has been understood as marking the beginning of a new state of things with regard to Israel. It has hardly been considered that 'until' more naturally should be interpreted as reaching an eschatological termination point. The phrase implies not a new beginning after a termination, but the continuation of a circumstance until the end of time."[6] As Woudstra puts it, "The apostle's emphasis is not upon some later point in time when there will be a reversal in the hardening in part of the Jews. Rather, the emphasis is upon the word 'so' or 'thus,' 'in this way' [11:26a]. All Israel will be saved in the way of the bringing in of the fullness of the Gentiles."[7]

11:25—What is "the fullness of the Gentiles"?

The same word, *plērōma* ("fullness"), is used in both v. 25 and in v. 12, although it is sometimes translated differently, even within the same translation of the Bible.[8] Leon Morris states, "NIV may well be right in seeing a reference to number. In that case a certain number of Gentiles are to be saved, and God is waiting until that number has been reached before taking action for Israel."[9] However, there is another possible meaning. "It is also possible to understand the expression as the fullness of the blessing of the Gentiles or the full contribution of the Gentiles, or the Gentiles as a whole. Whichever way we take it, the fullness is regarded as active and as entering the scene (it 'comes in'). . . . We should probably see a reference to the fulfillment of God's purpose in bringing Gentiles into his kingdom, however we understand the individual words."[10] Douglas Moo adds that *plērōma* "consistently has a qualitative meaning in the Bible—'fulfillment,' 'completion,' 'fullness.' Some scholars therefore think that 'fullness of the Gentiles' means simply the 'full blessing' that God intends to bestow on the Gentiles, or perhaps the 'completion' of the Gentile mission."[11]

---

6. Ibid., 180.

7. Woudstra, "Israel and the Church," 236.

8. v. 12: "fulfillment" (NASB); "full inclusion" (RSV; ESV); "fullness" (NKJV; NIV). v. 25: "fullness" (NASB; ESV; NKJV); "full number" (RSV; NIV).

9. Morris, *Romans,* 420.

10. Ibid.

11. Moo, *Romans,* 718. P. H. R. van Houwelingen comments that "fullness" does not have an eschatological meaning here (i.e., the full number of the elect), but the "fullness" in v. 12 "stands in contrast to 'loss' [or 'failure']. In other words, the fullness of Israel will be achieved when lost ground has been made up. So it will be with the nations." van Houwelingen, "Redemptive-Historical Dynamics," 304.

Those who adopt an "end-time" interpretation[12] typically regard *the fullness of the Gentiles*" as "a fixed number of people whom God has destined for salvation . . . a numerical completion: God has determined to save a certain number of Gentiles, and only when that number has been reached will Israel's hardness be removed."[13] That is also compatible with the non-end-time "all Israel" as the elect of ethnic Israel throughout history interpretation: "This gathering of the fulness of the Gentiles does not take place just at the end-time, but goes on throughout the history of the church."[14] Ben Merkle observes, "Since virtually every scholar interprets 'the fullness of the Gentiles' as referring to the full number of elect Gentiles throughout history, is it not also likely that the 'fullness' of Israel [11:12] refers to the full number of elect Jews throughout history? Since verses 12 and 15 are parallel, the 'acceptance' of verse 15 also refers to the consummation of all elect Jews. . . . Therefore, the 'fullness' refers to the full number of elect Israelites, not just the salvation of the remnant at any one time."[15]

11:26—What does "and so" (Greek = kai houtōs) mean?

There are four basic options in interpreting the word *houtōs*.

(1) *Houtōs* might have a temporal meaning, i.e., "And then [after the events depicted in v. 25b] all Israel will be saved." However, Moo notes that "a temporal meaning of *houtōs* is not otherwise found in Greek."[16]

(2) *Houtōs* could introduce a consequence or conclusion, i.e., "And in consequence of this process [v. 25b] all Israel will be saved." Moo comments, "This use of *houtōs* is attested in Greek and in Paul, but is rare, and there seems no good reason to abandon the usual meaning of the word, which is to denote the manner in which an action takes place [i.e., 'in this manner' all Israel will be saved]."[17]

(3) *Houtōs* could have its usual meaning of denoting the manner in which an action takes place [i.e., 'in this manner' all Israel will be saved]" and be connected with the "just as it is written" formula that follows, i.e., "It is in this way that Israel will be saved: namely, just as it is written. . . ." However, Moo again notes, "Paul never elsewhere pairs *houtōs* and 'just as it is written.'"[18]

(4) In light of the problems with the first three options, Moo concludes, "Taking *houtōs* to indicate manner and linking it with what comes before—is to be preferred: 'And

12. Both "end-time" and "non-end-time" interpretations of the passage are discussed in detail below.

13. Moo, *Romans*, 719.

14. Hoekema, *Bible and Future*, 144.

15. Merkle, "Romans 11," 718.

16. Moo, *Romans*, 719–20; but see van Houwelingen, "Redemptive-Historical Dynamics," 305, who cites sources arguing that Paul does use *kai houtōs* with a temporal meaning in other contexts, and is thinking temporally here because "until" in 11:25 indicates the passage of time as does the "then-now" scheme in vv. 30–31.

17. Moo, *Romans*, 720.

18. Ibid.

in this manner all Israel will be saved.' The 'manner' of Israel's salvation is the process that Paul has outlined in vv. 11–24 and summarized in v. 25b: God imposes a hardening on most of Israel while Gentiles come into the messianic salvation, with the Gentiles' salvation leading in turn to Israel's jealousy and her own salvation."[19]

11:26—What does "all Israel will be saved" mean?

There are three main interpretations of the phrase "all Israel will be saved." "All Israel" is seen either as: (1) all the elect, both Jew and Gentile; (2) the ethnic nation of Israel as a whole; or (3) all the elect of ethnic Israel throughout history. Merkel explains the three positions:

(1) *All the elect, both Jew and Gentile.* Scholars such as Calvin, Jeremías, Barth, and Wright have held this interpretation. In his commentary on Romans Calvin states, "I extend the word 'Israel' to all the people of God, according to this meaning: when the Gentiles shall come in, the Jews also shall return from their defection to the obedience of faith, and thus shall be completed the salvation of the whole Israel of God, which must be gathered from both." . . .

(2) *The ethnic nation of Israel as a whole.* This second interpretation is by far the majority view.[20] Although there are some who maintain that every individual Jew will be saved, most simply interpret "all" as referring to ethnic Israel as a whole. That is, "all Israel" refers to the mass of Jews living on the earth at the end of time, who, after the full number of elect Gentiles are gathered in, will be a part of a large-scale mass conversion. This event will take place just previous to (or at the moment of) Christ's return.[21] . . .

(3) *The elect of ethnic Israel throughout history.* The third interpretation is often included in surveys but is usually simply dismissed rather than refuted.[22] . . . This interpretation maintains that God will always save a remnant of Jews throughout history. Israel will experience only a partial hardening until the end of time (i.e., until the fullness of the Gentiles come in).[23]

19. Ibid., 719–20.

20. Although the second view is the majority today, that has not always been the case. The first view was held by a number of the church fathers (e.g., Irenaeus, Clement of Alexandria), and "became especially widespread among Protestant Continental theologians in the late sixteenth and seventeenth centuries." Moo, "Romans 11," 720–21n.45.

21. If the second of the three main views is what is meant, then it is significant that "Paul writes 'all Israel,' not 'every Israelite'—and the difference is an important one. 'All Israel,' as the OT and Jewish sources demonstrate, has a corporate significance, referring to the nation as a whole and not to every single individual who is a part of that nation. The phrase is similar, then, to those that we sometimes use to denote a large and representative number from a group; that is, 'the whole school turned out to see the football game.'" Moo, *Romans*, 722–23; see also van Houwelingen, "Redemptive-Historical Dynamics," 306–7.

22. Well-regarded scholars who hold this view include Herman Bavinck, Louis Berkhof, William Hendriksen, Anthony Hoekema, Herman Hoeksema, Richard Lenski, Herman Ridderbos, and O. Palmer Robertson. See Merkle, "Romans 11," 711n.11.

23. Merkle, "Romans 11," 709–11.

11:26—What does "the Deliverer will come from Zion" mean and when does that occur?

Paul is quoting from Isa 59:20, but is not quoting verbatim, and has made significant changes to that verse. With respect to the meaning of "Zion," P. W. L. Walker asks, "Is this a reference to physical Jerusalem, or does it now refer to the 'heavenly Zion/Jerusalem? Is the event predicted in the Old Testament still future to Paul, or has it already begun to take place? Thirdly, why has Paul not retained the original wording of Isaiah 59:20 (which in the Masoretic text had read, 'the Deliverer will come *to* Zion')?"[24]

Moo discusses other aspects of this difficult and ambiguous quotation:

> He quotes Isa. 59:20–21a in vv. 26b–27a and a clause from Isa. 27:9 in v. 27b.[25] Both parts of the quotation follow the LXX closely, with one notable exception: where the LXX of Isa. 59:20 says that "the redeemer will come *for the sake of* [*heneken*] Zion," Paul says "the redeemer will come *out of* [*ek*] Zion." And not only does Paul's reading differ from the LXX, it differs also from the Hebrew text and from every known pre-Pauline text and version. How are we to account for this variation? Paul may have inadvertently assimilated this text to others in the OT that speak of Israel's deliverance as coming "from Zion" (cf. Ps. 13:7; 53:7; 110:2). He may have deliberately changed the wording to make a point: to show that Christ, "the redeemer," originates from the Jewish people (cf. 9:5); to show that the final "missionary" to the Gentiles, Christ, comes, like the present missionaries to the Gentiles, from Jerusalem (cf. 15:19); or to show that Christ will save Israel by coming from the "heavenly" Zion at his *parousia*. Or Paul may, in fact, be faithfully quoting from a form of the LXX text that we no longer have.[26]

Interpretive Approaches to Rom 11:25–26

As with Dan 9:24–27, there are many different interpretations of Rom 11:25–26. The interpretations tend to fall into two main groups: (1) Those that see the passage as indicating a future, end-time mass conversion of ethnic Jews to Christ just before or at the time of the *parousia* (end-time interpretations); and (2) Those that do not see the passage as indicating an end-time mass conversion of Jews to Christ (non-end-time interpretations).[27] In some cases, however, even the difference between some "end-time" and "non-end-time" views can be very small.[28]

---

24. Walker, *Jesus*, 137–38; see also Holwerda, *Jesus and Israel*, 172; Morris, *Romans*, 421.

25. Murray holds that in 11:26–27 "the first part of the quotation is from Isaiah 59:20, 21 and the last part derived from Jeremiah 31:34." Murray, *Romans*, 98–99.

26. Moo, *Romans*, 727.

27. Sam Storms calls the two major camps the *Future Restoration* and the *Historical Remnant* views. Storms, *Kingdom Come*, 303–34. There are also preterist interpretations of the passage which view it as having been fulfilled with the destruction of Jerusalem in AD 70. King, "And So All Israel," n.p.; Thompson, "Romans 11:11–32," n.p. Those interpretations are mentioned here but will not be discussed since they are held only be very few and have little influence outside of preterist circles.

28. Compare Holwerda, *Jesus and Israel*, 163–75 and Hoekema, *Bible and Future*, 139–47.

Appendix 6

End-time interpretations

Non-dispensationalist interpretation[29]

"Until" (11:25) implies a change after some future point toward the end of this age

This interpretation holds that the word "until" suggests a reversal of the present condition. Moo explains, "Israel's partial hardening will last only *until* the fullness of the Gentiles comes in—and then it will be removed. But decisive for this interpretation is the context, for Paul has throughout vv. 11–24 implied that Israel would one day experience a spiritual rejuvenation that would extend far beyond the present bounds of the remnant ('their fullness' contrasted with 'their defeat' in v. 12; 'their acceptance' contrasted with 'their rejection' in v. 15; the 'holiness' of even the broken-off branches in v. 16; the hope that these branches might be grafted in again in v. 24)."[30]

"All Israel" (11:26) refers to the nation of ethnic Israel as a whole

According to this interpretation, "Paul has used the term 'Israel' ten times so far in Rom. 9–11, and each refers to ethnic Israel. This clearly is the meaning of the term in v. 25b, and a shift from this ethnic denotation to a purely religious one in v. 26a—despite the 'all'—is unlikely. . . . Paul is probably using the phrase 'all Israel' to denote the corporate entity of the nation of Israel as it exists at a particular point in time [i.e., the end-time]."[31]

There will be a mass conversion of ethnic Israelites in connection with the second coming of Christ

Moo lists three reasons for his view that there will be a mass, end-time conversion of ethnic Jews to Christ:

(1) The prediction of v. 26a seems to match the third step in the salvation-historical process that Paul describes throughout these verses ('their fullness' [v. 12]; 'their acceptance' [v. 15]; the grafting in again of natural branches [v. 24]; cf. also vv. 30–31). Since Paul makes clear that this reintegration of Israel is in contrast to the situation as it exists in his own time—when Israel is 'rejected'—it must be a future event.

---

29. E.g., Bahnsen, "Gospel Prosperity," 4–7; Holwerda, *Jesus and Israel,* 163–75; Moo, *Romans,* 715–28; Murray, *Romans,* 91–103; Riddlebarger, *Amillennialism,* 180–94.

30. Moo, *Romans,* 717–18.

31. Ibid., 721, 723. Merkle counters this by noting, "If 'all' meant a great number of Jews at the end of time, does that interpretation do justice to the meaning of all? It would in fact only include a small fraction of Jews which is not as climactic as it might first appear." Merkle, "Romans 11," 717. Although Moo is a proponent of end-time interpretation, he acknowledges that "the interpretation that takes the phrase to refer to the elect among Israel throughout time deserves consideration as a serious alternative." Moo, *Romans,* 723.

(2) The specific point in the future when this will occur is indicated by Paul's probable connection between Israel's 'acceptance' and the eschatological resurrection of the dead (v. 15).

(3) The implication of v. 25b is that the current partial hardening of Israel will be reversed when all the elect Gentiles have been saved; and it is unlikely that Paul would think that salvation would be closed to Gentiles before the end.[32]

Because the phrase *"all Israel"* has a corporate meaning and does not mean "every Israelite," it is impossible to predict the actual percentage of Jews living at the time who will convert to Christ. However, "the contrast between the remnant and 'all Israel' would suggest a significantly larger percentage than was the case in Paul's day."[33] It is also not possible to predict the exact timing of any such conversion, although, as Moo states, "the fact that it will take place only after the salvation of all elect Gentiles suggests that it will be closely associated with the return of Christ in glory."[34] Finally, as to the manner of any such end-time conversion, "Jews, like Gentiles, can be saved only by responding to the gospel and being grafted into the one people of God. . . . The end-time conversion of a large number of Jews will therefore come about only through their faith in the gospel of Jesus the Messiah."[35] In other words, "as Israel's 'trespass' (vv. 11, 12) and 'rejection' (v. 15) trigger the stage of salvation history in which Paul (and we) are located, a stage in which God is specially blessing Gentiles, so Israel's 'fullness' (v. 12) and 'acceptance' (v. 15) will trigger the climactic end of salvation history."[36]

Dispensationalist interpretation

The dispensationalist interpretation follows the basic outline of the non-dispensationalist end-time interpretation but adds its own distinctive doctrines:

---

32. Moo, *Romans*, 723–24. Contrary to the idea that it is the appearance of Christ that causes the conversion of Israel, van Houwelingen points out, "This position, however, raises serious questions. Why would Paul have had such deep and unceasing anguish in his heart (Rom. 9:3) if, at the same time, he nurtured the hope that in the end all would be well with Israel? Furthermore, would this not lead, for the unbelieving part of Israel, to a reluctant election? Finally, the prophetic expectation usually mentions the restoration of Israel first and, after that, a consequent coming in of the Gentiles. Paul's order is exactly the reverse. For these reasons, this is not a credible position." van Houwelingen, "Redemptive-Historical Dynamics," 311.

33. Moo, *Romans*, 724.

34. Ibid., 725.

35. Ibid., 726.

36. Ibid., 696. Even the position that an end-time conversion of Israel will occur after the mission to the Gentiles has reached its completion and there is an opening to Israel for the gospel, raises serious questions: "To what extent can the generation of the end-time still be considered as all Israel? This possibility does not fit any eschatological scheme, and it has not, according to Ridderbos, been argued cogently by even one single exegete." van Houwelingen, "Redemptive-Historical Dynamics," 311.

Appendix 6

"*The fulness of the Gentiles* began with the calling out of the Church. . . . It will continue until the Rapture of the Church. Blindness and hardening of Israel will continue as long as the Church is present in the world."[37]

NATIONAL SALVATION FROM TRIBULATION, NOT FROM SIN

The salvation or deliverance is a *national* one: "It is perhaps better to refer to the time when God shall close this Gentile dispensation, and when Israel's national salvation shall take place. Liddon refers it to the time when 'the full number of the heathen shall have been converted' (*cf.* Luke xxi. 24)."[38] "*And so all Israel will be saved*" means that the nation of Israel will be "delivered . . . from the terrible Tribulation by the Messiah, the Deliverer."[39] Walvoord first said that "their restoration as a nation [is] indicated in Romans 11:26–32," and "*all Israel shall be saved*" is "a national promise, namely, that at the time of the end when her period of suffering has been fulfilled, Israel as a nation or Israel as a whole shall be delivered from her enemies. The salvation in view is not that of freedom from the guilt of sin, but deliverance from persecution and trial."[40] However, he later wrote that "*all Israel will be saved*" means "a remnant of Israel will be delivered from end-time judgment."[41] J. Dwight Pentecost claimed, "The nation Israel is to experience a conversion, which will prepare them to meet the Messiah and to be in His millennial kingdom. Paul establishes the fact that this conversion is effected at the second advent."[42] At that time, the "New Covenant" (Jer 31:31–34) will be made with the nation of Israel.[43]

ISRAEL'S DOMINANCE DURING THE MILLENNIUM

The millennium will reflect the nation of Israel's dominance in which "the Gentiles will be Israel's servants."[44] "Although in the present Christian dispensation, individual Jews and individual Gentiles combine to form one Church, the Body of Christ, yet in the great future to which the Apostle looks, national distinctions will remain, and the Jew, the Gentile, and the Church of God will be kept separate until that day when 'God shall be all in all.'"[45]

---

37. McGee, *Reasoning Through Romans*, 27; see also MacDonald, *Believer's*, 1727.
38. Thomas, "St. Paul's Epistle," 303.
39. Witmer, "Romans," 486.
40. Walvoord, *Israel in Prophecy*, 58, 112.
41. Walvoord, *New Millennium*, 108.
42. Pentecost, *Things to Come*, 505–06.
43. Barnhouse, *Romans*, 4:152–54; Pentecost, *Things to Come*, 119–21; Witmer, "Romans," 486.
44. Pentecost, *Things to Come*, 508.
45. Thomas, "St. Paul's Epistle," 313.

CRITIQUE

None of dispensationalism's unique doctrines (the pretribulational rapture, the restoration of Israel as a nation, the millennium) is found in Romans at all. Paul's concern in Romans 9–11 is with Israel's *spiritual* condition; nothing is stated or implied about any national, political, or physical restoration. The following commentators state much more biblically the real issues that Paul is addressing in Romans 11, in contrast to the dispensationalist view.

- *Kim Riddlebarger*:

  Paul made no mention of Jews returning to the promised land, nor do we find any reference to a millennial kingdom in which Jesus rules the earth as a Davidic king during an earthly millennium. Nor do we find any reference made by Paul to a postmillennial golden age in which the world will be largely Christianized. One would certainly think that since Paul is addressing the subject of Israel's future and if Israel's future entailed the things dispensationalists and postmillenarians claim that it does, this would be the ideal time for Paul to mention them. But he does not. . . . Paul limits his discussion to Israel's future, and that future is in no way tied to an earthly millennium.[46]

- *R. T. France*: "In fact, the New Testament writers never suggest that Old Testament prophecy is to be fulfilled in a political restoration of the Jewish nation. When Paul asserts that the 'hardened' part of Israel will one day be reintegrated into the true people of God, and so 'all Israel will be saved', he gives no hint that he is thinking of anything other than their spiritual conversion."[47]

- *John Murray*: Paul's quotations in 11:26–27 "specify for us what is involved in the salvation of Israel. These are redemption, the turning away from ungodliness, the sealing of the covenant of grace, and the taking away of sins, the kernel blessings of the gospel, and they are an index of what the salvation of Israel means. There is no suggestion of any privilege or status but that which is common to Jew and Gentile in the faith of Christ."[48]

Finally, Jesus said that he was inaugurating the New Covenant in his blood (Luke 22:20). Second Cor 3:2–18; 4:3–6 and Hebrews 8–10 apply the New Covenant to the church now, not to national Israel in the "millennium."

Non-End-time interpretations

"All Israel" is the elect of ethnic Israel throughout history" interpretation[49]

In Rom 10:12 Paul says that *"there is no distinction between Jew and Gentile"* concerning the plan of salvation. "If God has a separate plan for saving Israel in the future, this view

---

46. Riddlebarger, *Amillennialism*, 183.
47. France, "Old Testament Prophecy," 77–78; see also Schnabel, *40 Questions*, 126.
48. Murray, *Romans*, 99.
49. E.g., Hoekema, *Bible and Future*, 139–47; Lehrer, *New Covenant Theology*, 93–105; Merkle,

would seem to go contrary to Paul's statement in verse 12. Nowhere in chapters 9 or 10 do we anticipate Paul speaking of a mass end-time conversion of Jews."[50] In other words, "Israel will continue to turn to the Lord until the *Parousia*, while at the same time the fullness of the Gentiles is being gathered in. And in this way all Israel will be saved: not just the last generation of Israelites, but all true Israelites. . . . Another way of putting this would be: *all Israel* in Romans 11:26 means the totality of the elect among Israel. The salvation of Israel, therefore, does not take place exclusively at the end-time, but takes place throughout the era between Christ's first and second coming."[51]

The issue of Romans 11 does not deal with a supposed mass end-time conversion of Jews, but with the manner by which God still saves Israel despite its rejection of its Messiah

The issue of 11:1 "is *not*, 'Has God cast off ethnic Israel with respect to his special plan for their future?' . . . The question Paul asks is, 'Has God cut off ethnic Israel *altogether*?' . . . The same could be said of the question in verse 11 where Paul asks, 'have they stumbled that they should fall?' Again, Paul is not asking if there is going to be a future mass conversion of Israel. Rather, he is asking if Israel has completely forfeited their past privilege."[52]

Paul's primary concern is not the future, but the *present*. Steve Lehrer points out:

> In Romans 11:1, Paul's answer to the question about whether God had rejected his people deals with Paul's first century salvation, not something in the distant future. In verse 5, Paul answers the question about God's rejection of Israel with a reference to his contemporary situation. . . . In verses 13 and 14 Paul refers to his hope that his own evangelistic work with the Gentiles in the first century will arouse Israelites in that general time period. . . . In verses 30 and 31 Paul tells us that the salvation of the Gentiles—which leads to the jealousy of the Jews, which leads to the salvation of the Jews—was all taking place "now" in Paul's day.[53]

With respect to the partial "hardening" of Israel (11:7, 25), in both vv. 7 and 25 Paul is speaking quantitatively, not temporally. In other words, the verses do not mean "for a while hardening has happened to Israel" but "a partial hardening (or 'a hardening in part') has happened to Israel."[54] Further, when Paul says that a *partial hardening has happened to Israel*" he "does not mean that all of Israel is only partially hardened, but that some are fully hardened while the elect remnant is being saved. In no way does the phrase suggest that God intends to initiate a special salvation era for Israel in the future."[55]

"Romans 11," 709–21.

50. Merkle, "Romans 11," 712.

51. Hoekema, *Bible and Future*, 145.

52. Merkle, "Romans 11," 713.

53. Lehrer, *New Covenant Theology*, 96.

54. Merkle, "Romans 11," 715.

55. Ibid.

"UNTIL" (11:25) DOES NOT IMPLY A CHANGE AFTER SOME FUTURE POINT TOWARD THE END OF THIS AGE

Merkle puts it this way: "A hardening will occur throughout the whole of the present age until the return of Christ. Paul is not suggesting a time when the hardening will be reversed but a time when the hardening is eschatologically fulfilled."[56] Hoekema lists three factors that bear on the meaning of "until":

> (1) The main point of Paul's previous discussion in Romans 11 has been to indicate that God, who in times past dealt almost exclusively with Israel as far as the bringing of salvation to his people was concerned, is now dealing with Jews and Gentiles together. . . . To make verse 26 refer to a time of salvation for Jews which will be separate from (because subsequent to) the time when Gentiles are saved is to go contrary to the main thrust of the chapter.
>
> (2) The gathering of the fullness, or full number, of the Gentiles takes place throughout history, not just at the end-time. Why should the gathering of the fullness of the Jews be different?
>
> (3) . . . In verses 30–31, where Paul is summing up the argument of the chapter, he speaks not in terms of what will happen in the future but in terms of what is happening *now*.[57]

"AND SO" ALL ISRAEL WILL BE SAVED (11:26) REFERS TO THE MANNER IN WHICH ISRAEL IS SAVED, NOT THE TIME WHEN IT IS SAVED

By saying that a partial hardening has occurred *until* the full number of the Gentiles has come in, *and so* all Israel will be saved, Paul is not saying that *then* (i.e., *after* the full number of the Gentiles has come in) all Israel will be saved, but *in this manner* all Israel will be saved. The manner in which "all Israel will be saved" is what Paul has been describing in the earlier part of the chapter: "(a) through the unbelief of many Israelites salvation is coming to the Gentiles, and (b) by the salvation of the Gentiles Israelites are being moved to jealousy. This has been happening in the past, it is happening now, and will continue to happen."[58] Robertson summarizes that, when Paul says *kai houtōs* ("and so"), he is not looking into the future (i.e., beyond the point where "the fullness of the Gentiles" comes in); rather, he is considering God's past dealings with Jews and Gentiles as the template for the future:

> First the promises and the Messiah were given to Israel. Then in God's mysterious plan, Israel rejected its Messiah and was cut off from its position of distinctive privilege. . . . The nations then obtained by faith what Israel could not find by seeking in the strength of their own flesh. Frustrated over seeing the blessings of their messianic kingdom heaped on the Gentiles, individual Jews are moved to jealousy. Consequently, they too repent, believe, and share in the promises originally made to them. "And in this manner" *(kai houtos)*, by such a fantastic

---

56. Ibid., 715, 716.

57. Hoekema, *Bible and Future,* 146.

58. Ibid., 145.

process which shall continue throughout he present age "up to" *(achris hou)* the point where the full number of the Gentiles is brought in, all Israel is saved.[59]

Paul distinguishes between the elect and the non-elect within ethnic Israel itself

In Rom 9:6 Paul draws an important distinction *within the nation of Israel itself*: "God's promises to Abraham never included the promise that his descendants would be saved based on their ethnic identity. True Israel consists of those who are the children of promise, rather than children of the flesh. . . . Therefore, Paul refutes the notion that God's Word has failed by pointing out that God's promises apply to the spiritual offspring within ethnic Israel."[60]

"All Israel" (11:26) does refer to ethnic Israel but not to ethnic Israel as a whole; rather, "all Israel" refers to the elect remnant within ethnic Israel

It is clear that the reference to "Israel" in verse 25 must refer to ethnic Israel and not a spiritual Israel consisting of both Jews and Gentiles since that is contrary to Paul's usage of the term in Romans 9–11. We see no reason, however, why Paul could not shift the meaning of Israel within two verses—the first reference to the nation of Israel as a whole [v. 25] and the second to the elect within the nation of Israel [v. 26]. For example, in Rom 9:6 Paul states [that] not all who are from the nation of Israel are part of the elect remnant of Israel. In the same sentence Paul uses Israel to refer to both the nation and then the elect within the nation. We submit that this is precisely the pattern that Paul uses in 11:25–26. Furthermore, there is a similar pattern in chapter 11 itself. In verse 7 Paul declares, "What then? Israel has not obtained what it seeks; but the elect have obtained it, and the rest were hardened." Within Israel Paul describes two groups: the "elect" and the "rest."[61]

In other words, "'The fullness of the Gentiles' = the full number of the saved Gentiles, *all* of them; 'all Israel' = the fullness of Jews, the full number of non-petrified, i.e., of saved Jews."[62]

Charles Horne adds:

If Paul is speaking in 11:26 of a future mass conversion of the nation of Israel, then he is destroying the entire development of his argument in chaps. 9–11. For the one important point he is trying to establish constantly is exactly this: that God's promises attain fulfillment not in the nation as such (that is, all of ethnic Israel) but rather in the remnant according to the election of grace. It would

---

59. Robertson, *Israel of God,* 182.

60. Merkle, "Romans 11," 711–12.

61. Ibid., 720; see also Storms, *Kingdom Come,* 326–33.

62. Lenski, *Interpretation,* 727.

seem from this fact therefore that the widely-held theory that the term 'all Israel' refers to the nation as a whole is incorrect—though the correct element in this view is that Israel refers to Jews.[63]

Finally, a mass conversion of Israel at the end of history appears to be inconsistent with 1 Thess 2:14b–16 where "Paul states that the wrath of God will come upon the Jews until the end *(eis telos)*. It seems clear from this text that Paul does not imagine a time when this judgment will be reversed with a special dispensation for the nation of Israel."[64]

"'All Israel' is the church (all the elect, both Jew and Gentile)" interpretation[65]

This interpretation adopts the same basic perspective on the passage as the "all Israel is the elect of ethnic Israel throughout history" interpretation but defines "all Israel" as the church (i.e., elect Jews and Gentiles), rather than "all Israel" as only elect Jews.

"Until" (11:25) does not imply a change after some future point toward the end of this age

The mention of "the fullness of the Gentiles" indicates that it is relevant to the manner in which "all Israel will be saved." Likewise, the "partial hardening" of Israel is integrally related to the coming in of the full number of the Gentiles. Lee Irons explains, "God has sovereignly caused many (though not all) Israelites to be hardened and thus cut off expressly so that many Gentiles could be saved, and this hardening and cutting off will continue for as long as is necessary for the fulness of the Gentiles to be grafted in. . . . It is precisely by means of Israel's own partial hardening that Israel is saved. The intermediate link is that by means of Israel's partial hardening, the Gentiles are grafted into the covenant tree in the place of those branches which were cut off."[66]

The key point is that the covenantal "olive tree" of Rom 11:17–24 is what is meant by the phrase *"all Israel."* In other words, *"all Israel"* does not refer only to one part of the olive tree (elect Jews) but to the *entire tree* which includes all the elect, both Jews and Gentiles. That is confirmed by the reference to the Gentiles "coming in" (11:25). They manifestly are "coming in" to the one olive tree of God. Indeed, "coming in" is equivalent to the "grafting in" of 11:17–24. Paul uses different imagery to make the same point in Eph 2:12–22, where he states that Gentiles had been excluded from the *"commonwealth of Israel"* but now are *"fellow citizens with the saints."*

God could have chosen to save the Gentiles in a way that did not involve the hardening of the Jews, but in his mysterious wisdom he opened salvation for the Gentiles in a way that "involves them in the very mechanism of God's faithfulness to his covenantal olive tree."[67] When Paul says that he does not want us to be uninformed of this "mystery,"

---

63. Horne, "Meaning of the Phrase," 333; see also Hoekema, *Bible and Future,* 145.

64. Merkle, "Romans 11," 718.

65. E.g., Irons, "Paul's Theology," 101–24; Robertson, *Israel of God,* 167–92.

66. Irons, "Paul's Theology," 111–12.

67. Ibid., 112.

he means that the salvation of the Gentiles "is not a new election in place of the election of the Jews but rather a subordinate (though necessary) element in the grand redemption of 'all Israel.'... The revelation that 'all Israel' is to be saved by means of the salvation of the Gentiles, is definitely a revelation fittingly denominated a mystery."[68]

The "all" in "all Israel" (11:26) suggests that "Israel" (11:25) and "all Israel" (11:26) mean different things

Rom 11:25 refers simply to "Israel," whereas Rom 11:26 refers to "all Israel." The use of "all" indicates that there is a difference in the meaning of "Israel" in the two verses: v. 25 refers to the ethnic Israel; v. 26 refers to spiritual Israel, which consists of all saved Jews and Gentiles. Irons notes that similar uses of the word "all" are found elsewhere in Romans:

> A similar use of "all" to expand the referent of a term originally limited to ethnic Israel may be found in Romans 4:13 and 16. . . . [There] Paul is arguing that the promise originally made to Abraham and his genetic seed was based on the principle of justification by faith so that the Gentiles could be included as well. When he wants to refer to the genetic seed of Abraham, he uses the simple "his seed," but when he wants to expand the reference to include the true spiritual offspring of Abraham, he uses "all the seed." . . . In [11:32] "all" is employed again with an ethnically universal connotation, as occurs so often in Paul's epistles. . . . Not only v. 32 but an earlier reference to the ethnically universal sin of man and the equally universal scope of the gospel [Rom 3:9, 21–23] adds credibility to taking "all Israel" as inclusive of Jews and Gentiles.[69]

An important theme throughout Romans is the redefinition of "Israel" to include both Jews and Gentiles

One of the things Paul has been doing throughout Romans essentially is to redefine "true Israel." For example, in Rom 2:25–29 he redefined the value of circumcision.[70] In Rom 9:6–8, 24–26, 30–33 Paul made clear that there is an Israel within Israel, and that membership among God's people is not related to circumcision or ethnic relation to Abraham. In other words, "If being an Israelite doesn't necessarily make one a *true* Israelite, then one need not be an *Israelite* to be a true Israelite. The door has now been opened to allow for Gentiles to be reckoned as true Israelites."[71] Indeed, in Rom 10:4–12 Paul proclaims that the only criterion to define "Israel" is faith in Christ. Irons concludes:

> Paul intentionally established the radical distinction between two Israels, two elections, and two circumcisions for the very purpose of preparing the way for

---

68. Ibid., 114.

69. Ibid., 108–10.

70. Paul reaffirms and elaborates this at 1 Cor 7:18–19; Gal 2:11–12; 5:2–12; 6:14–15; Eph 2:11–22; Phil 3:2–3; Col 2:10–12; Titus 1:10–11.

71. Irons, "Paul's Theology," 119.

this climactic conclusion (11:26). . . . Therefore, to take "all Israel" as a reference to the church is not only natural (since the reader has been primed for it ever since chapter two) but *necessary* in order to achieve a satisfying resolution to the issues that have been raised throughout the course of Paul's extended argument. This interpretation has the great advantage of unifying the first eleven chapters of Romans and bringing the whole to a climactic crescendo of redemptive-historical insight.[72]

ONLY THROUGH THE CHURCH (I.E., "ALL ISRAEL") DOES GOD DEMONSTRATE HIS FAITHFULNESS TO HIS PROMISES

Taking *"all Israel"* as Paul's redefined Israel-of-faith, consisting of believing Jews and Gentiles together, provides a satisfying answer to the question: "Has God rejected his people?" (Rom 11:1). Irons concludes his discussion by focusing on the question that Paul addresses in Romans 11: "How is it that the vast majority of post-pentecost Jews have rejected Jesus as the Messiah and are therefore lost?" He answers:

> Given this undeniable datum, how are we going to justify theologically the non-negotiable truth that God's promises to Israel as a *people,* a *corporate* identity, cannot be broken? I posit that . . . the church is the continuation, in fact, the consummation of God's promises to Israel. Individual branches may be removed from the covenant olive tree, but the faithfulness of God guarantees that the olive tree itself will endure, even if that means that new branches must be found to replace the old. God's faithfulness to the promises made to the patriarchs finds expression, not in the salvation of the remnant of elect Jews merely, much less in a future national conversion, but in the entrance of Gentiles into the covenant fold, along with the concomitant jealousy which provokes elect Jews to faith in Christ throughout the church age. It is in this manner that 'all Israel' will be saved. What, then, is Paul's theology of Israel's future? In a word, the church.[73]

Additional Comments Regarding Rom 11:25–26

Non-end-time interpretations of Rom 11:25–26 are not inconsistent with large-scale conversions of Jews[74]

"Even if we adopt the viable alternative interpretation of 'all Israel will be saved' as a reference to the ultimate salvation of all the elect from the people of Israel throughout history

---

72. Ibid., 119–20.

73. Ibid., 122.

74. "Although the redemptive-historical approach [i.e., the preaching of Paul and other evangelists once their mission to the Gentiles has been completed] provides the best perspective, it needs to be augmented with a future-directed dynamic. . . . It is possible that Paul saw the history of redemption and the end-time as existing on the same line [cf. Matt. 24:14; Mark 13:10]. For the apostle Paul, this was entirely consistent with his missionary strategy: first the Jews and then the Gentiles. Then why not, by extension, make another move toward the Jews, either by himself or by his successors?" van Houwelingen, "Redemptive-Historical Dynamics," 312.

[or that 'all Israel' means 'the church'], a great end-time conversion of Jews is not excluded. Verse 26a would then simply summarize the process by which Jews are saved that Paul has described throughout this chapter."[75] There could, in fact, be more than one such large-scale turning of Jews to Christ in the future. Hoekema points out, "There is nothing in the passage which would rule out such a future conversion or future conversions, as long as one does not insist that the passage points *only* to the future, or that it describes a conversion of Israel which occurs *after* the full number of Gentiles has been gathered in."[76] There have been large-scale conversions of Jews in the past. After all, the church began largely through mass conversions of Jews (Acts 2:37–41). Since large numbers of Jews have converted to Christ in the past, there is no reason why that might not happen again in the future.

The "fullness" (11:12), "acceptance" (11:15), and "grafting in" (11:23–24), including any mass conversions of Jews that may occur, should not be divorced from the process of gospel-proclamation inaugurated at Christ's first advent

Several factors, including contextual indicators within Romans 9–11, suggest that if large-scale conversions of ethnic Israel are to occur, they cannot be limited to a mass conversion of Jews immediately before or in connection with the *parousia*.

To view Romans 11 as teaching a mass conversion of Jews only at the end of history in connection with the parousia is inconsistent with the NT's and Paul's emphasis on mission

Christ made clear that the gospel must be preached to the whole world *"even to the end of the age."*[77] In Rom 10:8–17 Paul argued that Jews and Gentiles are in the same position and will be converted by the same means: the preaching of the gospel. "Paul's point here is that *as far as the obtaining of salvation is concerned,* there is no distinction between Jew and Greek. If this is so, a future period of time in which only Jews will be saved, or in which Jews will be saved in a way different from the way in which Greeks or Gentiles are saved, would seem to be ruled out."[78]

The "end-time mass conversion of ethnic Israel" view has important implications regarding the efficacy of the gospel and of missions. First, "it suggests that the gospel is not effective in the end, which would have been cause for Paul to abandon his continuing concern with a Jewish mission, or to be ashamed of the power of the gospel, positions he certainly denied (1:16)."[79] Second, that view makes the salvation of the fullness of Israel,

---

75. Moo, *Romans,* 724n.59.

76. Hoekema, *Bible and Future,* 147.

77. Matt 28:18–20; see also Matt 24:14; Acts 1:8.

78. Hoekema, *Bible and Future,* 142, emphasis in original..

79. Nanos, *The Mystery,* 257. To view Romans 11 as teaching a mass conversion of Jews only at the *parousia* (i.e., "an apocalyptic miracle of conversion," Ridderbos, *Paul: An Outline,* 358–59n.70) turns the *parousia* into a *deus ex machina* ("a god out of a machine," i.e., a literary device whereby a seemingly hopeless problem is abruptly solved by the contrived and unexpected intervention of some new event

different or distinct from the salvation of the fullness of the Gentiles, both in manner and in time. In other words, the end-time mass conversion of Israel:

> does not result directly or at least not primarily from the gospel and the preaching mission of the Church in the world. Instead the salvation of the fullness of Israel, in distinction from the remnant, will be accomplished only when the One who is himself the content of the gospel reappears. . . . While indeed the Deliverer himself will remove blindness from Israel, Paul does seem to teach that the removal of hardness from Jewish Israel will be associated with the active power of the gospel. Speaking of hardened Israel, the apostle writes that when a person turns to the Lord in response to the gospel, it is through Christ that the hardness is removed (II Corinthians 3:14–16). One need not assume that Christ removes blindness or hardness only by coming in person.[80]

Romans 11 indicates that the process for converting mass numbers of ethnic Israel was inaugurated at Christ's first advent

"Paul's conviction that 'jealousy' will provoke Israel's response [Rom 11:11] sits uneasily with the notion of an end-time event."[81] In 11:17–24 Paul uses the metaphor of the olive tree, and the "grafting in" of both Gentiles and Jews who come to faith in Christ. That is a metaphor of the *present* conversion of Jews: "This participation by being 'grafted in' cannot be postponed to some future time, while Gentile believers immediately experience the blessing of the covenant. Just like every present Gentile believer, every present Jewish believer will be grafted in. Like the previous sections of Romans 11, this paragraph emphasizes the present significance of the Jews in fulfilling God's purposes of salvation."[82]

Similarly, 11:25–27 *is* related to what Paul has said in vv. 17–24 and involves action in the present, not simply the end-time future. That is indicated by the fact that 11:25 begins with the word "for." Additionally, the reference in 11:27 to the *"covenant . . . when I take away their sins"* confirms that Paul was referring to Christ's first advent, not his second. That is a reference to the "New Covenant" (Jer 31:31–34), which is the only covenant that promised the forgiveness of sins. Christ inaugurated the New Covenant in his blood on the cross.[83] Further, in the Greek, 11:27 is phrased *hotan aphelōmai* ("when I take away"). *Hotan* is indefinite, and often is translated "whenever." Thus, "11:27b enables Paul to include the idea of recurring action. 'Whenever' God takes away their sins, i.e., whenever Jews come to believe in Christ and so enter the family of God, in that moment the promises God made long ago to the patriarchs are being reaffirmed."[84]

---

or character). "This is the stuff that bad fiction or drama is made of, so it is no surprise that *deus ex machina* is usually applied to narrative works, especially to the work of playwrights and novelists who find themselves . . . incapable of bringing their plots to a close without relying on improbable coincidence." Ehrlich, *Amo, Amas, Amat,* 104.

80. Holwerda, *Jesus and Israel,* 172–73.

81. Walker, *Jesus,* 141n.103.

82. Robertson, *Israel of God,* 170.

83. Luke 22:20; 1 Cor 11:25; Hebrews 8–10.

84. Wright, *Climax of the Covenant,* 251.

> The same thing is found in Rom 11:30–32. That part of Paul's argument indicates that salvation is always given to those in disobedience. Holwerda explains Paul's point: Gentiles in their disobedience received God's mercy because of the disobedience of unbelieving Jewish Israel. Now disobedient Jewish Israel may receive mercy by the mercy shown to the Gentiles. This reciprocal and interrelated process clearly seems to establish the view that salvation is received in the same manner by Jews and Gentiles alike through the efficacy of the Word working in history. . . . This process, which *now* (Romans 11:30) brought God's mercy to the Gentile world, would have its effect that unbelieving Jewish Israel would receive that same mercy. If the "now" found in some manuscripts in Romans 11:31 is included, then Paul is clearly relating the conversion of Israel to the process inaugurated by the first coming of Christ and the subsequent preaching of the gospel.[85]

It is not the removal of the church from the earth (dispensationalism) or the end of Gentile conversions that leads to the conversion of the Jews but *"the mercy shown to you"* (11:31): "It was through the Jews' disobedience that the Gentiles came to experience God's mercy but it will be through the mercy God has shown to the Gentiles that he will bring mercy to the Jews."[86] That implies the presence and winsome witness of Gentile believers to the Jews. Ridderbos summarizes, "Jealousy of the gentiles must come to fill Israel (v. 11), and the preaching of the gospel to and by the gentiles must save Israel (v. 14) and move them not to persevere in their unbelief (v. 22), and by the mercy shown to the gentiles it will make them, too, in their turn, obtain mercy with God (v. 31)."[87]

Even though he holds an "end-time" interpretation, Moo similarly sees that the "now" of 11:31 "reveals that typical NT perspective which views the new era of fulfillment as already having dawned and all the events belonging to that era as therefore near in time. The salvation experienced by the Gentiles means that Israel is 'now' in the position to experience again God's mercy."[88] Ridderbos concludes, "The entire wrestling of the apostle for Israel's conversion, his pain, his effort to be permitted to save a few of his hardened brethren, his declaration that he is himself willing to be cut off from Christ, loses its tension when the real decision loses its present, historical character and is shifted to 'post-history.'"[89]

Paul's other uses of "Zion" indicate that "the Deliverer will come from Zion" (Rom 11:26) refers to Christ's first advent

The quotation in 11:26 is taken from Isa 59:20. Paul's frequent quotations from Isaiah suggest the meaning of his use of Isaiah here. For example, in 2 Cor 6:2 he quotes from Isa 49:8 and in 2 Cor 6:17 he quotes from Isa 52:11. Both passages relate to the meaning of "Zion" in Rom 11:26. Isa 49:8 had defined *"the day of salvation"* as the time when God would *"restore the land,"* Zion would no longer be "forsaken" (see Isa 49:14–21), and the

85. Holwerda, *Jesus and Israel*, 173–74.

86. Morris, *Romans*, 425.

87. Ridderbos, *Paul: An Outline*, 358.

88. Moo, *Romans*, 735.

89. Ridderbos, *Paul: An Outline*, 359n.70.

Gentiles would help bring God's people to the land (Isa 49:22–23). In Isa 52:11 God had told his people to "depart" from Babylon because the Lord *"has redeemed Jerusalem"* (Isa 52:9). P. W. L. Walker comments on the significance of these other "Zion" prophecies:

> Paul applied these prophecies without explanation to the Corinthians! He could only do so with integrity if he believed these prophecies *had now been fulfilled.* . . . 'Jerusalem' therefore had been 'redeemed'—in the sense that the exile which had *partly* ended in the time of Isaiah had now been *fully* brought to an end in the work of Jesus. In keeping with this is the section in Romans 10 where he again quoted from Isaiah 52 (v. 7 in Rom. 10:15), thereby identifying the Christian 'good news' (*evaggelion*) with the 'good news' proclaimed by Isaiah of the exile's end. . . . In all these instances Paul was taking verses which originally had spoken of a specific work of God in and for Jerusalem and was applying them to God's work in the gospel. He believed God's act in Christ was a fulfill-ment of these Zion-prophecies.[90]

Paul treats "Zion" similarly in Rom 9:32–33. There, he conflates quotes from Isa 8:14 and 28:6. "From the context it is clear that Paul is seeking to explain the 'stumbling' that had occurred in his own generation in the response of his fellow-Jews to the gospel: the 'stone' is Jesus, whilst God's act of 'laying in Zion' refers to his sending Jesus to Israel, but especially to Zion/Jerusalem, the very heart of Israel's life."[91]

Paul's understanding of "Zion," as indicated by these other uses of Isaiah, helps us to understand his reference to "Zion" in Rom 11:26. Although Isaiah's prophecy, as quoted by Paul, is in the future tense ("the Deliverer *will come* from Zion"), the issue is: Future to whom? What was future to Isaiah might not be for Paul. Walker discusses this:

> In keeping with the earlier usage of 'Zion' (Rom. 9:33), there is an increased likelihood that 'Zion' is associated in Paul's mind, not with some future event, but chiefly with Jesus' recent work accomplished in Zion/Jerusalem. . . . Paul retains the prophet's syntax, in order to show that this had now been fulfilled. . . . Because he believes that Jesus was truly the Deliverer sent by God (v. 26b) he has faith that the divinely intended consequences will follow: 'he *will* banish ungodliness from Jacob' (v. 26c). . . . Paul is not predicting a 'large-scale, last-minute salvation of Jews' but speaking of an ongoing process which has now begun through the gospel.[92]

That also makes sense of Paul's replacing "*to* Zion" (the way Isaiah originally phrased the prophecy) with "*from* Zion." If "Zion" refers to Jerusalem, then Paul certainly would not have denied that Christ had come "to Zion." Indeed, as indicated in Rom 9:33, Paul already had spoken of Jesus' coming to Zion. Now, however, Paul is focusing on the consequences of that coming for those far removed *from* Zion. Walker concludes that Paul's substitution of "from" in place of "to" reveals his conviction that "Zion's principle role in God's economy was that of being the divine channel of divine blessing to the nations. . . . Although in the gospel God had acted specifically in Zion and for Zion, through the resurrection and the gift

---

90. Walker, *Jesus*, 139.

91. Ibid., 140.

92. Ibid., 140–41.

of the Spirit he had now unleashed Zion's potential to be the place from which the 'word of the Lord' could 'go forth.'"[93]

If the "fullness of Israel" is limited to a mass end-time conversion, it is contrary to the purpose of the "fullness of Israel," which is to bless the Gentiles and the world (Rom 11:12, 15)

Paul argues that the *effect* of the conversion of Jews is the blessing of the Gentiles and the world. Rom 11:12 says, *"If their [Israel's] transgression is riches for the world and their failure is riches for the Gentiles, how much more will their fulfillment be!"* The Greek for "riches" in this context indicates "the richness of spiritual blessing. Paul frequently uses the word to refer to the riches of God's grace and mercy (cf. Rom. 2:4; 9:23; 11:33; Eph. 1:7, 18; 2:7; 3:8, 16; Phil. 4:17; Col. 1:27). . . . The logic of Paul's sentence implies that the blessing that will come to the Gentiles at the time of Israel's 'fullness' will be much greater."[94]

Given his "end-time" perspective, Moo believes that the great blessing referred to in 11:12, 15 is the "new life that comes after resurrection," although he acknowledges that "Paul is silent about the timing of these events."[95] Resurrection and the new heavens and new earth are indeed the ultimate and final blessing for the world. However, Paul does not use the word for "resurrection" here, and "the words Paul uses here are not used elsewhere for the general resurrection."[96]

Just as the Gentiles and the world have experienced their spiritual "riches" during this age, Paul's argument suggests that Israel's "fullness" will lead to great spiritual blessings yet to be experienced during this age, similar to the prodigal son's return in Luke 15:24 (*"This son of mine was dead and has come to life again"*). John Murray states:

> In verse 12 the fullness of Israel is said to bring much greater blessing to the Gentiles. . . . But if "the fulness of the Gentiles" means the full [number] of the elect of the Gentiles, then the fulness of Israel would terminate any further expansion among the Gentiles of the kind of blessing which verse 12 suggests. The contextual data, therefore, point to the conclusion that "the fulness of the Gentiles" refers to blessing for the Gentiles that is parallel and similar to the expansion of blessing for Israel denoted by "their fulness" (vs. 12) and the "receiving" (vs. 15). . . . "The fulness of the Gentiles" denotes unprecedented blessing for them but does not exclude even greater blessing to follow. It is to this subsequent blessing that the restoration of Israel contributes.[97]

93. Ibid., 138–42; see Isa 2:3; Mic 4:2; Rom 15:19; 1 Thess 1:8.

94. Moo, *Romans*, 688n.28, 689.

95. Ibid., 695, 696.

96. Morris, *Romans*, 411.

97. Murray, *Romans*, 95–96. The above argument is premised on the idea that "Israel" refers to ethnic Jews, not the church. On the other hand, Irons sets forth cogent reasons why 11:12, 15 are not talking about blessings that will accrue for the Gentiles or the world *after* the conversion of Jews. Rather, since Irons's position is that "Israel" is the church, "the nature of this great wealth" *is* "the glory of Christ's church composed of both Jews and Gentiles." Irons, "Paul's Theology," 122–24.

A mass conversion of Jews limited to the end of history is inconsistent with the unpredictability of the second coming

The timing of the *parousia* is completely unpredictable.[98] If the "fullness of Israel" is limited only to an end-time occurrence, that would suggest the predictability of the *parousia*. On the other hand:

> The sign of the salvation of the fullness of Israel [that is not limited to the end-time] does not enable us to date the second coming of Christ with exactness. It tells us that Jews will continue to be converted to Christianity throughout the entire era between the first and second comings of Christ, as the full number of the Gentiles is being gathered in. In such Jewish conversions, therefore, we are to see a sign of the certainty of Christ's return [but not its timing]. In the meantime, this sign should bind on our hearts the urgency of the church's mission to the Jews.[99]

98. See main text, chapter 8, the section "The second coming of Christ is totally unpredictable."
99. Hoekema, *Bible and Future,* 147.

1 Cor 15:20–57: The Resurrection, the *Parousia*, and the Millennium

> [20] *But now Christ has been raised from the dead, the first fruits of those who are asleep.* [21] *For since by a man came death, by a man also came the resurrection of the dead.* [22] *For as in Adam all die, so also in Christ all will be made alive.* [23] *But each in his own order: Christ the first fruits, after that those who are Christ's at His coming,* [24] *then comes the end, when He hands over the kingdom to the God and Father, when He has abolished all rule and all authority and power.* [25] *For He must reign until He has put all His enemies under His feet.* [26] *The last enemy that will be abolished is death.* [27] *For HE HAS PUT ALL THINGS IN SUBJECTION UNDER HIS FEET. But when He says, "All things are put in subjection," it is evident that He is excepted who put all things in subjection to Him.* [28] *When all things are subjected to Him, then the Son Himself also will be subjected to the One who subjected all things to Him, so that God may be all in all.*

Introduction

FIRST CORINTHIANS 15 IS Paul's most detailed discussion of the resurrection and has been described as "the *locus classicus* in the writings of Paul . . . of the concluding events of this eon, that is, of present history."[1] Paul sets forth the essence of the gospel and Christ's resurrection in vv. 1–11. He then expresses his surprise that some people in the church (v. 12) did believe in the resurrection of Christ (vv. 1–4) but did not believe that they or other believers would have a bodily resurrection. In vv. 12–19 he explains how deadly that idea is to the faith. Verses 20–28 then state the heart of his argument that believers are united with Christ and will be bodily raised at his coming. Verses 29–34 continue the argument by emphasizing that our fullness will come in the future but is not realized in the present (in contrast with the "over-realized eschatology" of those resurrection-deniers in Corinth who were preoccupied with spiritual gifts and the present). He then concludes his argument in vv. 35–57 by discussing how the resurrection will occur and why transformation is necessary to enter into the fullness of the kingdom. Verse 58 ends the chapter with a

---

1. Boers, "Apocalyptic Eschatology," 52.

word of encouragement for believers to persevere in faithfulness, knowing that their work is not in vain.

One issue this passage raises is whether or not it is consistent with the existence of a temporary, post-*parousia*, "millennial kingdom." In fact, other than Rev 20:1–7, the consensus among premillennialists of all stripes is that "there is only one other passage in the New Testament which may envisage a temporal reign of Christ between his *parousia* and the *telos* [the "end"]: 1 Cor 15:23–24."[2] If such a millennium (i.e., the "thousand years" of Rev 20:1–7) is to be found in 1 Corinthians 15, it is seen as occurring between vv. 23–24. D. Edmund Hiebert says, "the crux of the millennial issue" is "the indefinite phrase, *eita to telos* ['then (comes) the end'], which begins verse 24."[3] Necessary to premillennial exegesis of 1 Corinthians 15 are the following: (1) In vv. 23–24 *epeita* ("after that") and *eita to telos* ("then the end") form a temporal sequence following the *parousia* into which fits the millennium.[4] (2) In vv. 23–24 the phrase *"but each in his own order"* refers to three, not two, *tagma* ("order, rank, class") of persons to be resurrected: (A) Christ; (B) believers; and (C) "the end" (i.e., unbelievers; or all those who live during the "millennium," including unbelievers).[5] In fact, however, the grammar and context of vv. 23–24, and the grammar, context, and theology of vv. 20–28 and 1 Corinthians 15 as a whole do not support a premillennial interpretation of the passage. Instead, they are consistent with the amillennial position.

Analysis of the Passage

Epeita ("after that") and *eita to telos* ("then the end"): grammatical considerations

Epeita ("after that," v. 23) and *eita* ("then," v. 24) often denote temporal sequencing. On the other hand, a sequence denoted either by *epeita* or *eita* "is often without a chronological reference at all. And when a lapse of time is supposed it can be of the shortest possible duration, as is the case with the 'span' between the resurrection of the dead in Christ and the transformation of the living faithful at the *parousia* as portrayed in I Thess. 4:17, where *epeita* is used to link these two events."[6] Ralph Smith adds:

> There is no example in the New Testament of *eita* being used of a long interval. But in the premillennial scheme, the interval from the *parousia* to the end is at least 1000 years—and it may be longer, for some premillennialists understand the 1000 years of Revelation figuratively. Neither in the LXX, nor in the Apocrypha, nor in the New Testament is there any example of *eita* being used to imply such an extended period of time. It seems all the more unlikely, then, that Paul would take a word which regularly connotes a relatively short interval

2. Ladd, *Commentary*, 267; see also Blaising and Bock, *Progressive Dispensationalism*, 273; Culver, "A Neglected Millennial Passage," 150.

3. Hiebert, "Evidence," 229–30.

4. Wallis, "The Problem," 230–33; Culver, "A Neglected Millennial Passage," 148–49.

5. Blaising and Bock, *Progressive Dispensationalism*, 273; Ladd, *Gospel of the Kingdom*, 43–44; Zaspel, "The Kingdom," 7–8.

6. Hill, "Paul's Understanding," 308; see also BDAG, "*eita*," 295.

and include within it not only the time, but also all the glory of the millennial kingdom.[7]

Paul uses the same words, *epeita* and *eita*, to show the temporal sequencing of Christ's post-resurrection appearances in 1 Cor 15:5–7: "[5] *and that He appeared to Cephas, then [eita] to the twelve.* [6] *After that [epeita] He appeared to more than five hundred brethren at one time, most of whom remain until now, but some have fallen asleep;* [7] *then [epeita] He appeared to James, then [eita] to all the apostles.*" Significantly, in that passage: (1) those adverbs are used to describe a series of related events connected closely in time (unlike a third supposed *tagma* at "the end" of a millennium); and (2) syntactically, in 1 Cor 15:5–7 *eita* and *epeita* are used to show structural contrast, with *eita* being the adverb which shows a close linkage of events and *epeita* showing events lacking a close linkage (exactly opposite of how premillennialists use the terms in their construal of 1 Cor 15:23–24). Gerald Borchert explains, "The Greek [in 1 Cor 15:5–7] suggests an order to the appearances: (a) the appearance to Cephas is listed first and linked closely (*eita*) with the appearance to the Twelve; (b) thereafter (*epeita*) comes the appearance to the five hundred; (c) thereafter (*epeita*) is the appearance to James, and this appearance is linked closely (*eita*) with the appearance to all the apostles; and (d) finally (*eschaton*) the appearance to Paul is noted."[8]

Further, Joseph Plevnik notes the different function that *eita* serves in 1 Cor 15:5–7 compared with 1 Cor 15:23–24:

> In [1 Cor 15:5–7] *eita* is employed in the enumeration of the resurrection appearances and brings out the repetition of the appearances of the risen Jesus. Every item enumerated here is an event of the same kind. In vv. 23–24, however, the enumeration occurs only in the first two instances—the resurrection of Christ, presented as the *aparche* ["first fruits"] and the resurrection of the faithful—which are clearly separated by *epeita*; the "order" (*tagma*) of the resurrection thus extends only to these two events. The *eita* that links *to telos* to the second event does not add another, third instance of the same—it does not imply that after those who belong to Christ have been raised, the "rest" would be raised—but, rather, terminates the sequence. This *eita* introduces a comment on the second phase of the resurrection: it emphasizes that the completion will not come until the resurrection of the faithful.[9]

Hence, Barrett states that "then (*eita*) may well mean thereupon."[10] Strimple correctly concludes that since "either of these 'adverbs of sequence' can also be used in the sense of *immediate* sequence . . . [n]ot the adverb itself . . . but only the context can determine for us the length of the interval marked by the adverb."[11]

7. Smith, "A Neglected," n.p., citing Mark 4:17, 28; 8:25; Luke 8:12; John 13:5; 19:27; 20:27; 1 Cor 15:5, 7, 24; 1 Tim 2:13; 3:10; Heb 12:9; James 1:15; see also Venema, *The Promise*, 248–50; Kennedy, *St. Paul's Conceptions*, 323.

8. Borchert, "The Resurrection," 404.

9. Plevnik, *Paul and the Parousia*, 126.

10. Barrett, *First Epistle to the Corinthians*, 356.

11. Strimple, "Amillennialism," 109–10.

Epeita and *eita to telos*: contextual considerations

Contextual clues indicate that *eita to telos* in 1 Cor 15:24 cannot imply the existence of a millennial period. Christ's own words in the Olivet Discourse (Matthew 24) equate "the end" (*to telos*) with the *parousia* (Matt 24:14—*tote heksei to telos*, "then comes the end").

Within the general context of 1 Corinthians itself, the "eschatological emphasis of 1:7, 8 is the underlying motif of the entire letter."[12] That passage (1 Cor 1:7-8) "brings together the revelation (*apokalypsis*) of our Lord Jesus Christ, the end [*to telos*], and the day of our Lord Jesus Christ."[13] Thus, in this very epistle:

> Paul clearly understands the "end" to be coterminous with the second coming: "as you wait for the revealing of our Lord Jesus Christ; who will sustain you to the end (*telos*), guiltless in the day of our Lord Jesus Christ" (1 Cor. 1:7-8, italics added). The "day of the Lord" is clearly the day of the second coming, as may be seen from 1 Thessalonians 5:2, "the day of the Lord will come like a thief in the night." The point is that the "end" does not come, say, a thousand years after the second coming; for Paul, the second coming is the end.[14]

It is therefore unreasonable to say that Paul meant something entirely different by *to telos* ("the end") when he used that same term just a few chapters later in 1 Cor 15:24.

The same thing is seen in the specific context of 1 Cor 15:23-24. The grammar of those verses reinforces the thrust of Paul's emphasis on the *parousia* as "the end." R. C. H. Lenski discusses this:

> "Then" in v. 23 is not the word that tells us about the interval between Christ's resurrection and that of the Christians. "Then," *epeita*, may mean immediately after or at any time after. It is the final phrase "at his Parousia" which informs us about the interval that will occur in this case. Paul adds no corresponding phrase or corresponding expression when he writes "Then the end." What right have we to insert or to assume such a phrase: "Then the end—after a thousand years"; or: "Then the end—after an indefinitely long interval"? . . . In v. 23 "then" or "thereupon," *epeita* = "at his *Parousia*." Paul himself defines the adverb by means of the phrase. He does the same in v. 24 with regard to "then," *eita*; this he defines by two "when" clauses: "Then . . . when (*hotan*)." And "then . . . when" go together even more closely than "then . . . at" (*ev*) in v. 23. . . . "Then the end," with neither a verb nor tense of any kind, means: then at the *Parousia*. No known rule of language allows us to supply a future tense, to say nothing about a long interval.[15]

Simon Kistemaker rightly concludes, "With the word then Paul introduces not the resurrection of a third group but simply the end. In other words, this adverb does not necessarily suggest an interlude between the resurrection of believers and the end of time. Because of its brevity, the clause then comes the end does not appear to support the teaching of an intermediate kingdom before the consummation of the age. Rather,

---

12. Arrington, *Paul's Aeon Theology*, 13.
13. Strimple, "Amillennialism," 110.
14. Davis, *Christ's Victorious Kingdom*, 57.
15. Lenski, *The Interpretation*, 672–73.

it signifies that 'after all this has happened, will the end or the consummation of Christ's Messianic work come.'"[16]

*Tagma*ta and *to telos*: grammatical considerations

Essential to the premillennial position is the necessity to find three *tagmata* ("orders, ranks, classes"), or stages of resurrection, in vv. 23–24: (1) Christ, the first fruits; (2) those who are Christ's at his coming; and (3) "the end" (which necessarily includes the rest of humanity, the unbelievers).[17] However, in v. 24 *to telos* cannot support the concept of a third resurrection *tagma*.

Verse 23 describes the resurrection as occurring *"each in his own order."* The word translated "order" is *tagma*. Some premillennialists have based their exegesis largely on the meaning that *tagma* had in classical Greek, where it meant a military detachment or division of troops.[18] However, as Barrett points out, "In later Greek (including the LXX) its use widened, so that it could be applied to any sort of group, military or civilian, and could mean place or position, or even ordinance."[19] Jean Héring observes, "The fact is that the first group is constituted by Christ alone and we must therefore translate '*tagma*' by 'rank.'"[20]

Grammatically, according to v. 23, there are only two *tagmata*, not three. Lenski makes this clear: "The fact remains that 'as first fruits' is a predicate noun that is attached to 'Christ': 'as first fruits Christ,' and it is thus different from the two adverbs that follow. Again, the fact is that 'first fruits' has and can have only one correlative, namely the general harvest which consists of 'those that are Christ's.' Thus 'Christ' and 'those of Christ' constitute a complete whole."[21] In other words, v. 23 itself describes and defines the "orders" (*tagmata*) of the resurrection: *"Christ the first fruits, after that those who are Christ's at His coming."* *To telos* ("the end") could not be a *tagma* because *to telos* is a temporal event signifying the completion of Christ's reign from heaven, when he finally defeats all enemies and "hands over the kingdom to the God and Father"; it is not a category, or "rank," or "order" of groups being resurrected at all.[22]

Finally, if *eita to telos* ("then the end") is read as a continuation of the series of resurrection *tagmata* ("orders"), then, of necessity, *to telos* ("the end") would have to mean

---

16. Kistemaker, *Exposition*, 552, quoting Hoekema, *Bible and Future*, 184; see also, Ridderbos, *Paul: An Outline*, 558 ("The words 'thereafter the end' are intended to say that 'then and not before' will the end, the consummation, have come"); Plevnik, *Paul and the Parousia*, 126–27.

17. See Blaising and Bock, *Progressive Dispensationalism*, 273; Ladd, *Gospel of the Kingdom*, 43–44; Zaspel, "The Resurrection," 7–8.

18. See Culver, "A Neglected Millennial Passage," 147; Zaspel, "The Resurrection," 8.

19. Barrett, *First Epistle to the Corinthians*, 354.

20. Héring, *First Epistle of St. Paul*, 165.

21. Lenski, *The Interpretation*, 671; see also Héring, *First Epistle of St. Paul*, 165–66; Kistemaker, *Exposition*, 551.

22. See Lambrecht, "Paul's Christological Use," 505, 509n.16; Héring, *First Epistle of St. Paul*, 165–66; Hill, "Paul's Understanding," 309; Fee, *First Epistle to the Corinthians*, 753–54; Lenski, *The Interpretation*, 672–74; Schmithals, "The Pre-Pauline Tradition," 362.

"the rest," i.e., all the rest of the dead.[23] However, to interpret *to telos* as referring to the resurrection of unbelievers would be a "revisionist reading," since "no known Greek usage allows 'the end' (*to telos*) to be construed as the rest (of those to be raised)."[24] Grammatically, therefore, *to telos* does not bear the interpretation that it must have in order to be consistent with the premillennialist view of this passage. Hill notes that "some recent efforts to explain Paul's eschatology as found in this passage along chiliastic [i.e., premillennial] lines abandon the attempt to see in *to telos* a third *tagma* of the resurrected. But it should be recognized that if *to telos* will not bear this interpretation there is no call for a third *tagma* anywhere in the passage and hence no hint that Paul might be thinking of two mass resurrections of humanity separated by an earthly reign of Christ."[25]

*Tagma*ta and *to telos*: contextual considerations

To telos means "the end." Significantly, in 1 Cor 1:8 Paul correlates *telos* (*eōs telous* ["until the end"]) with the *parousia*.[26] Since Paul used the word *telos* earlier in this very epistle to signify the *parousia*, it would be inconsistent to take that same term as meaning something considerably different in 1 Cor 15:24. In fact, the context of its use in 1 Cor 15:24 indicates that *to telos* is the end of Christ's reign from heaven—the end of "this age" when all opposition and enemies are defeated. *To telos* is "a technical phrase denoting the final consummation."[27] Or, as Holleman puts it, *to telos* is "the absolute end of human history, the very last day on which the old aeon will be finished completely and the new aeon will start."[28] The end of "this age" and the beginning of the "age to come" occurs at the *parousia*.[29]

Contextually, *to telos* cannot support the concept of a third resurrection *tagma* which is resurrected 1000 years after Christ's *parousia* because such an idea is completely contrary to Paul's argument and line of thought in 1 Corinthians 15, as Ridderbos reminds us:

> One must surely keep the purport of the whole argument in view here. Paul polemicizes against those who as members of the church (cf. 1 Cor. 15:12) apparently did believe in the resurrection of Christ but no longer expected a resurrection of the dead. Over against this error Paul sets the divine order: Christ as the firstfruits; thereafter, at the *parousia*, those who are Christ's. In this train of thought not only

---

23. Conzelmann, *1 Corinthians*, 270.

24. Collins, *First Corinthians*, 552; see also Garland, *1 Corinthians*, 709; Conzelmann, *1 Corinthians*, 27–71; Héring, *First Epistle of St. Paul*, 166 ("this translation seems impossible, because we have been unable to find a single text, sacred or secular, in which '*telos*' has this sense"); Lenski, *The Interpretation*, 673 (the meaning of *telos* as "the rest" is "unknown even to the dictionaries"); Schmittals, "The Pre-Pauline Tradition," 362 ("*telos* does not have the meaning of 'remnant'"); Thistleton, *First Epistle to the Corinthians*, 1231 (to construe *to telos* as a resurrection *tagma* "does not reflect the lexicographical scope of *to telos*") Fee, *First Epistle to the Corinthians*, 754n.39 ("not only is there no evidence for such a meaning for this word . . . but Paul is perfectly capable of saying *hoi loipoi* ('the rest,' 'the others') when that is what he intends").

25. Hill, "Paul's Understanding," 309.

26. See BDAG, "*telos*," 998 ("it means to the end=until the *parousia*").

27. Davies, *Paul and Rabbinic Judaism*, 295.

28. Holleman, *Resurrection and Parousia*, 60.

29. See main text, chapter 4–Interpreting Biblical Eschatology in Light of its Overall Structure.

is there no occasion for a third category following that, but it also falls entirely outside the sphere of thought.[30]

Other Considerations Rule Out a Premillennial Interpretation of the Passage

Other aspects of 1 Corinthians 15 rule out a premillennial interpretation of the passage. The first is abolition of death (v. 26), particularly as demonstrated by the parallel between vv. 23–26 and vv. 50–57, which occurs at the *parousia*, not 1000 years thereafter. Second, the nature of the supposed "millennial kingdom" is contrary to the nature of Christ's "reign" as described in 1 Cor 15:20–28.

Eita, tote, and the abolition of death

First Cor 15:23–26 states that believers shall be made alive at Christ's *parousia* (v. 23). Verse 24 begins *eita to telos* ("then the end")—at that time he will "deliver up the kingdom to God the Father" (v. 24), and *"then the son himself"* (*tote kai autos ho huios*) will be subjected to the Father (v. 28). That will occur when Christ *"abolishes death"* (vv. 25–26). The question is: When is death abolished—at Christ's *parousia* or 1000 years

---

30. Ridderbos, *Paul: An Outline*, 558. Much has been written on whether the two *pantes* ("all") in v. 22 are perfectly parallel and include all people without exception. Some take the view that just as Adam brought death to every person, so in Christ every person (believer and unbeliever alike) will be resurrected. See Culver, "A Neglected Millennial Passage," 144–45; Wallis, "The Problem," 234–37; Dahl, *The Resurrection*, 34n.2. Others emphasize the *en tō Christō* ("in Christ") and *zōopoiēthēsontai* ("will be made alive") as qualifying the second *pantes* and limiting it only to believers. See Héring, *First Epistle of St. Paul*, 165; Kennedy, St. *Paul's Conceptions*, 310–11; Borchert, "The Resurrection," 407; Crockett, "The Ultimate Restoration," 83–85; Vos, *Pauline Eschatology*, 238; Hill, "Paul's Understanding," 305–07; Kistemaker, *Exposition*, 550; Holleman, *Resurrection and Parousia*, 52–55 ("The parallelism between the two clauses of verse 22 does not lie in the fact that both groups are identical, but in the fact that for both groups the representative determines the fate of the group. The unity with Adam leads to death, the unity with Christ leads to resurrection.").

Elsewhere in the NT it is clear that Paul did teach that, at Christ's Second Coming, unbelievers will also be raised for the purpose of eternal judgment. See Acts 24:15; 2 Thess 1:6–10. The issue here, however, is the reading into 1 Cor 15:20–28 what it does not say, based upon one's presuppositions gained elsewhere. Regardless of how one construes *pantes*, the issue of the fate of unbelievers simply is not relevant to, or even within the scope of, this passage. See Crockett, "The Ultimate Restoration," 86 ("The fact that Paul's present concern is with those who are 'in Christ' does not mean that the rest of mankind will not one day themselves be found 'in Christ'. This, in fact, may be the case, but such a conclusion cannot be derived from the above text."); Wellum, "Christ's Resurrection," 91n.27 ("In terms of the fate of unbelievers, Paul is not addressing that issue in this text"); Beckwith, *The Apocalypse*, 99 ("an argument upon the resurrection of all men would be foreign to the Apostle's purpose in this paragraph, which is solely designed to show the doubting Christians at Corinth that their resurrection is assured through their union with Christ"); Blomberg, *1 Corinthians*, 304 ("Paul simply does not address the question of the fate of unbelievers in this passage"). Even premillennialist Wallis acknowledges that Paul's "main purpose in the entire argument is to assure his readers that believers will enjoy the ultimate eschatological victory through Christ (verse 57)." Wallis, "The Problem," 234. Since Paul's purpose and argument in 1 Corinthians 15 were not designed to deal with the fate of unbelievers, it is improvident to read into his use of the word *pantes* more than he intended, and then to read into other verses in this passage answers to questions that Paul had not asked and did not specifically address.

thereafter, following the "millennium"? Vos states that, grammatically, "*eita* can be used just as well as *tote* ["then," "at that time"] to express momentary sequence of events."[31] Zaspel (a premillennialist) disagrees. He distinguishes Paul's use of *eita* in v. 24 from *tote* in v. 28 ("which does indicate concurrent events") to argue that "the eternal state follows immediately not when Christ returns but when after His return He has brought His kingdom to its consummation."[32]

Paul answers the question of when Christ abolishes death in the context of this very passage when he describes the consummation in vv. 50–57. He begins in v. 50 by saying that "*flesh and blood cannot inherit the kingdom of God; nor does the perishable inherit the imperishable.*" He goes on to state when the perishable will "*put on the imperishable, and this mortal must put on immortality*" (v. 53; cf. v. 51). That occurs at "*the last trumpet*" when "*the dead will be raised imperishable, and we will be changed*" (v. 52). Verse 54 goes on to say that, "*when this mortal will have put on immortality, then [tote] will come about the saying that is written, 'death is swallowed up in victory.*'" Lincoln points out, "the clear temporal reference [to the events of v. 54] is to the *parousia* (cf. verse 52)."[33] Thus, "*the end*" (v. 24) is coterminous with the abolition of death (v. 26); both occur at Christ's "coming" (i.e., the *parousia*, v. 23). Venema states, "The believer's victory over death is said in 1 Corinthians 15:54–55 to occur when believers receive resurrection bodies. This coincides with what is said in 1 Corinthians 15:23–26 to occur in conjunction with both the 'coming' of Christ and the 'end', when the believer's last enemy, death, will be overcome."[34] This corresponds with Rev 20:14 which says that at the eschatological judgment which is part of what Christ's *parousia* entails, "*death and Hades were thrown into the lake of fire.*" Sydney Pages observes, "For both John and Paul the last scene in the drama of redemption before the inauguration of the eternal state is the elimination of death."[35] Kennedy summarizes: "When [the last enemy, death] has been vanquished, Christ's dominion is complete. Obviously, this final abolition of death *is revealed by* the event of the Resurrection, when the redeemed of the Lord prove by their rising that they are also stronger than death—that the indwelling might of the *pneuma* ["spirit"] of Christ has vanquished the darkness of the grave."[36]

The argument throughout 1 Corinthians 15 is focused on the resurrection of the dead and the abolition of death which occur at Christ's *parousia*. The premillennial conception of an intermediate millennial kingdom, the resurrection of third *tagma* 1000 years after the *parousia*, and *then* the abolition of death would turn the theme and climax of Paul's argument into a penultimate anti-climax.[37] According to premillennialism, there would be two victories over death—one at the resurrection of Christ's people at the *parousia*, and another at the end of the millennium.[38] That duplication of events is

---

31. Vos, *Pauline Eschatology*, 243.

32. Zaspel, "The Resurrection," 8.

33. Lincoln, *Paradise Now*, 66.

34. Venema, *Promise*, 250; see also Vos, *Pauline Eschatology*, 245–46; Plevnik, *Paul and the Parousia*, 128–29; Holleman, *Resurrection and Parousia*, 65.

35. Page, "Revelation 20," 42.

36. Kennedy, St. *Paul's Conceptions*, 329–30, emphasis added.

37. See Plevnik, *Paul and the Parousia*, 129; Vos, *Pauline Eschatology*, 76.

38. See Strimple, "Amillennialism," 111.

not hinted at in the text, which clearly indicates a single vanquishing of death. Thus, the premillennial view of this passage is actually contrary to Paul's line of thought and reason for writing this chapter.

Christ's "Reign" Versus the "Millennium"

Christ *"must reign until He has put all His enemies under His feet"* (v. 25). Does this "reign" refer to a current reign of Christ from heaven or to a future reign of Christ on earth during the "millennium"? Further, is the nature of Christ's "reign" consistent or inconsistent with the nature of a temporary "millennium"? To those questions we now turn.

The timing of Christ's "reign"

Verse 26 tells us that *"the last enemy that will be abolished is death."* As we have seen, death will be abolished at the *parousia*. Consequently, Christ must have begun his reign before, not after, the *parousia*.[39] In fact, Christ's "reign" began with his resurrection and ascension; he is now at the right hand of God reigning in power.[40] This is seen by Paul's quoting or alluding to Ps 110:1 (*"The LORD said to my Lord, 'Sit at my right hand until I make your enemies your footstool'"*) in v. 25[41] and Ps 8:6 (*"You made him ruler over the works of your hands and placed all things under his feet"*) in v. 27.

Keener discusses the significance of Ps 110:1 in this context: "Paul's eschatological scheme here depends on his interpretation of Ps 110:1, which becomes clear in 15:25. Because 'the Lord' will reign at God's right hand until all enemies are subdued beneath his feet (Ps 110:1), Christ must reign at God's right hand in the present until his enemies are subdued (15:25)."[42] Christ has been exalted and is ruling from heaven now in the "already" phase of his kingdom. That is clear from other passages which discuss Christ's present reign: "In Col. ii. 15 [Paul] speaks of the conquest of the *archai* ["rulers"] and *exousiai* ["authorities"] [both of which are referred to in 1 Cor 15:24] as having in principle been accomplished in the cross of Christ. In Rom. viii. 38, 39 he assumes that even

39. The Greek wording in v. 26 indicates this. The word translated "abolished" (*katargeitai*) is in the present passive tense. Grosheide comments, "The present tense in vs. 26 implies that death is being abolished. The action has begun already because Christ has been raised up as firstfruits." Grosheide, *Commentary*, 368; see also Fee, *First Epistle to the Corinthians*, 757; Thistleton, *First Epistle to the Corinthians*, 1234–35.

40. See Mark 16:19; Luke 22:69; Acts 2:22–36; 7:55–56; Rom 1:4; 8:34; Eph 1:20–22; Phil 2:9–10; 3:20–21; Col 1:13; 3:1; Heb 1:3; 8:1; 10:12; 12:2; 1 Pet 3:22; Rev 1:5; see also Fee, *First Epistle to the Corinthians*, 747. Even most premillennialists concede that Christ's resurrection, not the *parousia*, commenced his reign, although they contend that the "reign" referred to in v. 25 continues after the *parousia*, through the millennium, to "the end." See Ladd, *Theology*, 407, 450; Ladd, "Historic Premillennialism," 29–32; Blaising and Bock, *Progressive Dispensationalism*, 273.

41. See also Matt 22:44 where Jesus quotes Ps 110:1 in relation to himself, and uses language derived from the LXX translation which does not refer to "footstool" but, similar to Paul's reference in 1 Cor 15:25, speaks of placing his enemies "beneath" or "under" his feet. Because of the context, Paul uses the third person singular, rather than the first person singular, in his reference to Ps 110:1.

42. Keener, *1–2 Corinthians*, 127; see also Bauckham, *God Crucified*, 29–30; Hill, "Paul's Understanding," 312–14; Smith, "A Neglected," n.p.

now Christ so reigns over and controls death and life and principalities and powers as to preclude every separation of the Christian from the love of God in Him."[43] According to Ps 110:1, Christ will continue to rule from heaven until all foes are subdued. It is the *parousia* itself which manifests the completion of Christ's final victory (i.e., ushers in the consummation—the "not yet," eternal phase of the kingdom).

The premillennial view is completely contradictory to Ps 110:1 as referred to in 1 Cor 15:25. According to Ps 110:1, Christ sits at the Father's right hand in heaven "until" all enemies have been *"put under his feet"* (i.e., made his footstool). Premillennialism would have Christ leaving heaven 1000 years *before* he has put *"all enemies under his feet."* It would then have Christ reign on earth for 1000 years but then face a massive Satanic uprising against Christ and his people at the end of the thousand years. Christ's enemies, including death, would only be overcome (i.e., *"put under his feet"*) at the end of the "millennium."

The quotation of Ps 8:6 (*"He has put all things in subjection under His feet"*) in 1 Cor 15:27 similarly shows that Christ's "reign" is a present phenomenon. The verb "has put" (*hupotasso*) in that sentence is in the past (aorist) tense (*hupetaksen*). Waldron comments, "The unavoidable impression with which one is left is that Paul felt that the beginning of Christ's reign of conquest was a matter of past history. Certainly the manner in which Paul brings in this quotation is misleading if this is not the implication."[44] The only other occasion in the NT in which that sentence from Ps 8:6 is quoted in the third person (as in 1 Cor 15:27) as applying to Christ—Eph 1:22—likewise clearly speaks of Christ's reign as having begun at his resurrection. Frank Thielman points out that, in Eph 1:22, "the thought is close to Paul's argument in 1 Cor. 15, where he claims that at Christ's resurrection 'the last Adam' and 'the second man' reversed the curse of death that came to all people through Adam (15:22, 45, 47) and set in motion the events that eventually would lead to the demise of 'every rule and every authority and power' (15:24), including death itself (15:26, 54)."[45]

Ladd summarizes:

> The New Testament does not make the reign of Christ one that is limited to Israel in the millennium [quoting 1 Cor 15:24–26]. It is a spiritual reign in heaven which has already been inaugurated, and its primary purpose is to destroy Christ's spiritual enemies, the last of which is death. . . . Lordship and kingship are interchangeable terms. This is seen in 1 Timothy 6:15. God is our "blessed and only Sovereign, the King of kings and Lord of lords." While this verse speaks of the Father, it is by the mediatorial work of the Lord Jesus that every enemy shall be put beneath his feet. When this has been accomplished and he has destroyed "every rule and every

---

43. Vos, *Pauline Eschatology*, 245.

44. Waldron, "The Eschatological Kingdom," sec. II.B.2; see also Borchert, "The Resurrection," 408 ("The use of the past tense [v. 27] probably indicates that Paul considers that the reign of Christ has already begun in the resurrection/exaltation event").

45. Thielman, "Ephesians," 816. The three other quotations or allusions to this sentence from Ps 8:6 in the NT, Phil 3:21, Heb 2:8, and 1 Pet 3:22, all in context similarly see Christ's reign as already having been commenced. See Guthrie, "Hebrews," 946–47; see also Matt 28:18; Acts 2:29–36; Rom 1:4; Eph 1:20–22; Phil 2:9; Col 2:10.

authority and power," Jesus the Lord will deliver the kingdom to God the Father (1 Cor. 15:24).[46]

The nature of Christ's "reign"

Having been *"declared the Son of God with power by the resurrection from the dead"* (Rom 1:4), Christ is now actively reigning as Lord and even now is defeating all his enemies (Matt 12:22–29; Luke 10:18; 11:20). With respect to 1 Cor 15:26 (*"the last enemy that will be abolished is death"*), B. B. Warfield states, "The essence of Paul's representation is not that Christ is striving against evil, but progressively (*eschatos* ["last"], verse 26) overcoming evil, throughout this period."[47] Indeed, in this very epistle Paul speaks of *"the rulers of this age, who are passing away"* (1 Cor 2:6).[48] In a sense, the invisible powers have become the unwilling servants of Christ.[49] Dykstra points out, "It is clear from Ephesians 1:20f. that Christ has already been exalted to lordship, and that the powers are included under his sway. The same thing is evident from such passages as Colossians 1:15ff. and Philippians 2:4–10."[50]

Christ's victory over the powers was achieved at the cross. "By taking on the body of our flesh, and becoming subject to the law—the very instruments whereby the powers operate against us—Christ was able to free us from the powers. This comes out most clearly in Colossians 2:14–15. Christ has taken our body of flesh which was against us because of the law . . . and nailed it to the cross. That is how Christ's cross constitutes the defeat of the powers."[51] Paul confirms this in 1 Cor 2:8 which says that if the rulers of this age had understood the significance of the cross, *"they would not have crucified the Lord of glory."* Through his death, resurrection, and ascension, Christ set in motion a process which will end in the total defeat of all hostile powers, including death.

Further, Paul contrasted Adam and Christ in 1 Cor 15:21–22 in that, just as Adam brought death, so Christ brings life. Christ's reign is about bringing the dead to life (Eph 2:1–5; Col 2:13). Thomas Schreiner explains, "Sin manifests its reign (*ebasileusen*) in the dominion of death (Rom 5:21). Apart from Christ people are 'slaves' to sin (*douleuein*, Rom 6:6), whereas believers have been freed from the sin that enslaved them and are

---

46. Ladd, "Historic Premillennialism," 30; see also Warfield, *Biblical and Theological*, 487 ("The period between the two advents is the period of Christ's kingdom, and when He comes again it is not to institute His kingdom, but to lay it down").

47. Warfield, *Biblical and Theological*, 485.

48. The connection of 1 Cor 2:6 and 1 Cor 15:24, 26 is clear. In 2:6 "rulers" is *archontōn*, the genitive plural masculine of *archōn*; in 15:24, when he speaks of Christ's having abolished all "rule," Paul uses the related, feminine form *archēn*. In 2:6 "passing away" is a participle form of the verb *katargeō*; in 15:24 and 15:26 for "abolished" Paul uses the aorist active subjunctive and present passive indicative forms of that same Greek verb.

49. Dykstra, "The Reign of Christ," 65–66, citing Cullmann, *Christ and Time*, 196–98.

50. Dykstra, "The Reign of Christ," 63; see also Vos, *Pauline Eschatology*, 246 ("This conclusion also follows from the equivalence of the *kuriotēs* [lordship] of Christ and the *Basileia* [kingship] of Christ. The *kuriotēs* begins with the resurrection of the Saviour, therefore his *Basileia* cannot begin at a later point. Phil. ii. 9–11 connects with Christ's exaltation to the *kuriotēs* the same things that 1 Cor. xv. 24–28 connects with his reign as King.").

51. Dykstra, "The Reign of Christ," 64.

now enslaved to righteousness (Rom 6:16–18, 20, 22)."[52] Thus, Christ is defeating his enemies, even death, *now* by *"saving his people from their sins"* (Matt 1:21; see also Luke 24:44–49; Acts 2:38; 10:43; 13:38–39; 26:18) and giving new life to people (John 10:10, *"I came that they may have life, and have it abundantly"*).[53] The manner in which Christ defeats death and gives life (giving the Spirit as a pledge) is by grace through faith and then by transforming his people at the resurrection (which occurs at the *parousia*).

Some premillennialists contend that Christ's current reign is "seen only by the eye of faith [but is] unseen and unrecognized by the world"; therefore, an earthly "reign of power" during the millennium is necessary to manifest in history the lordship that is Christ's already.[54] Although one might posit any number of reasons why a "millennium" or other event might be useful, human reasoning cannot stand if it is contrary to Scripture. Regardless of that, the contention that Christ's current reign is "unseen and unrecognized by the world" is not entirely true. Christ's reign is visible in the world through *the church*. Eph 3:9–10 says that the preaching of the gospel brings to light *"what is the administration of the mystery which for ages has been hidden in God who created all things; so that the manifold wisdom of God might now be made known through the church to the rulers and the authorities in the heavenly places."* Further, Christ even now is appearing to thousands of people, particularly in areas closed to overt Christian witness, through visions, dreams, miraculous signs, and answers to prayer.[55] He is saving millions of people *"from every tribe and tongue and people and nation"* (Rev 5:9); their love and changed lifestyles are visible manifestations of Christ's power and the presence of his kingdom.[56]

In addition to the church's manifesting the reign of Christ on the earth, there is a sense in which the "world" demonstrates the present reign of Christ. Although nonbelievers do not consciously admit Christ's sovereignty and reign, "human culture, advance in medicine, war on crime and poverty, and the healing of racial antagonisms can be at least signs of this fact. . . . Human culture to that extent is not continuous with the kingdom. It remains a sign, a pointer to what is not yet; it is always 'in part.'"[57] The good produced by human culture is the outward and visible manifestation of the "common grace" Christ bestows on the world.

From the foregoing we see that the kingdom has an "already/not yet" nature, consistent with the "two ages" and the two-stage nature of salvation described throughout the NT. Paul clearly describes the two-stage nature of the kingdom in 1 Cor 15:22–28: Christ is reigning now, but faces opposition (the "already" of the kingdom); however,

52. Schreiner, *Paul: Apostle*, 128.

53. See also Mark 10:29–30; John 3:16, 36; 4:13–14; 5:24–25, 40; 6:33, 35, 40, 47–54; 10:27–28; 11:25–26; 14:6; 20:31; Rom 5:12–21; 6:22–23; 2 Cor 5:1–5; Eph 2:1–6; Col 2:13–15; 2 Tim 1:8–10; 1 John 5:11–12).

54. Ladd, "Historic Premillennialism," 32; Ladd, "The Revelation," 14.

55. See Woodberry, Shubin, and Marks, "Why Muslims Follow," 80–85; Woodberry and Shubin, "Muslims tell," n.p.; see also Greeson, *The Camel*, 50, 79–91; Greenham, "A Study," 166–67; Dunning, "Palestinian Muslims," 285–86; Abdulahugli, "Factors Leading," 162.

56. See Houssney, *Engaging Islam*, 186–87; Woodberry and Shubin, 2001: "Muslims tell," n.p.; Singer, "A Survey," 1–16; Greenham, "A Study," 162; Abdulahugli, "Factors Leading," 162; see also Kik, *Eschatology*, 209–28.

57. Dykstra, "The Reign of Christ," 75–77.

when the last enemy (death) is abolished, then all things will be subjected to him and the kingdom will exist in all its glory (the "not yet" of the kingdom). Christ will then *"hand over the kingdom to the Father"* (v. 25).

The "reign" of Christ as described in 1 Corinthians 15 is inconsistent with premillennialism

The characteristics of the reign of Christ are inconsistent with the "millennium" as conceived by premillennialists in at least three ways. First, the "millennium" is supposed to be a 1000 year period of time before the abolition of death in which Christ possesses absolute control, all opposition to him is eliminated, and there is worldwide peace and harmony.[58] However, the language Paul uses in 1 Cor 15:24–26 is completely contrary to a "millennium" in which all submit to the Messiah and there is worldwide peace. R. H. Charles notes that the character of Christ's kingdom as portrayed in 1 Cor 15:22–26 "is wholly at variance with that of the temporary Messianic Kingdom of Apocalyptic and the Millennium of the Apocalypse; for the Messianic reign is here one of unintermitting strife, whereas in the [premillennial] literature . . . it is always one of peaceful dominion and blessedness."[59] Further, "The language employed here is therefore about the reign of Christ, the powers, the conflict, the subjugation, and the annihilation. It contains war imagery, probably in association with Ps 110:1, alluded to in v. 25. . . . It interprets the reign of Christ (*basileuein*), mentioned in v. 24 (*basileian*), as an active enforcement of Christ's rule over the powers in the cosmos, as an ongoing conflict in which Christ is subjugating and annihilating these powers."[60] As discussed above, Christ defeated the hostile powers through the cross, his resurrection, and ascension and is now subduing those powers, including the power of death, by saving his people from their sins and giving them new life. A "millennium" cannot contribute anything to the defeat of death. There could be nothing different about how Christ might give new life in a "millennium" compared to what he does now. Consequently, not only is the language that Paul uses in 1 Corinthians 15 concerning Christ's reign contrary to the nature of the premillennialists' "millennium," but the millennium itself is unnecessary to bring about the primary purpose of that reign.

Second, a primary purpose of the entire chapter is to give Christians hope—the hope of the resurrection which, at the *parousia*, demonstrably removes the "sting of death" (1 Cor 15:54–57).[61] Premillennialism negates that hope:

> The chief thing to note in connection with the millennium is that it occurs prior to the final destruction of the enemies. Revelations [sic] 20:7ff. indicates that Satan and the enemies of the saints shall engage in one last offensive "when the thousand

---

58. See Erickson, *A Basic Guide*, 101–02; Osborne, *Revelation*, 703.

59. Charles, *Critical and Exegetical*, 448.

60. Plevnik, *Paul and the Parousia*, 127.

61. See, Boers, "Apocalyptic Eschatology," 62 ("Christian existence is characterized by faith in the resurrection of Christ and hope in a personal resurrection effected by his *parousia*. This is the substance of I Corinthians 15."); Borchert, "The Resurrection," 409 ("His goal is to provide those 'in Christ' with a sense of hope and security in their salvation").

years are finished" (vs. 7). Accordingly, these events as well as the millennium itself would have to be prior to the destruction of the last foe (I Cor. 15:26). . . . The final hostilities of Satan and his allies are clearly directed against the saints (Rev. 20:7). To maintain that Christians would again be exposed to the raging of the powers subsequent to their resurrection would destroy the essence of the hope of the resurrection as preached by Paul. For Paul, as we have seen, the glory of the resurrection is precisely the definitive exchange of the body of the flesh with the body energized by the Spirit of the age to come (I Cor. 15:44, 49, 50–54), whereby the powers have lost their only instrument against us.[62]

Third, the *parousia* is the *terminal point*, not a *midpoint*, of the kingdom or reign of Christ. The reference to Christ's handing over "the kingdom" to God (v. 24) and Christ's "reigning" (v. 25) demonstrates the present, active (as opposed to future, post-*parousia*) reign of Christ. This is seen in the distinction between the phrases: the "reign" of Christ (v. 25) or "kingdom of Christ" (see Col 1:13) versus the "kingdom of God." "Whenever Paul speaks of a kingdom that is to come he thinks of a *basileia tou theo* ('kingdom of God')."[63] On the other hand, Col 1:13 states, "*He rescued us from the domain of darkness and transferred us to the kingdom of His beloved Son.*" That verse is consistent with 1 Cor 15:25 in regarding Christ's "reign" and "kingdom" as present, not future, realities. "The Resurrection had designated Christ the Son of God, and from that moment the Kingdom of the Son was 'actualized'; the victory of the Cross was the beginning of that triumph of Christ over the evil powers mentioned in I Cor. 15.24. It is not after but before the *Parousia* that the Messianic Kingdom lies in the mind of Paul."[64]

The final portion of Paul's argument in 1 Corinthians 15 continues the distinction between the "reign" (or, kingdom) of Christ (v. 25) and the "kingdom of God" (see vv. 24, 28) and demonstrates why Christ's "reign" terminates with the *parousia* instead of continuing for 1000 years thereafter through a supposed millennium. Verse 50 introduces the final section of the chapter. That verse refers to the "kingdom of God," which indicates that the *final* state (not a temporary millennium) begins at the *parousia* because, as Vos notes, "the Apostle does not say 'the kingdom of Christ,' as he ought to have said according to the chiliastic [i.e., premillienial] exegesis of vss. 24–28."[65] In other words, "God has delegated his *basileia*, 'kingship,' to Christ for a definite period, from the raising of Christ (which of course is his exaltation) to his *parousia*, and for a definite end, the annihilation of the hostile powers."[66] Dykstra summarizes:

> Christ is in the process of dethroning every rule and authority and power (vs. 24). The end of this process is marked by the abolition of death (vs. 26). . . . Death draws up the end of the line as the last vestige of the curse brought upon all things

---

62. Dykstra, "The Reign of Christ," 86–87; see also Riddlebarger, *Amillennialism*, 85–87; Kennedy, *St. Paul's Conceptions*, 330 (the idea of a "further process of conflict" after the Lord's return "would be utterly alien to the apostle's standpoint").

63. Davies, *Paul and Rabbinic Judaism*, 295, citing 1 Cor 6:9–10; 15:50; Gal 5:21; Col 4:11; 1 Thess 2:12; 2 Thess 1:4–5.

64. Ibid., 296.

65. Vos, *Pauline Eschatology*, 246; see also Davies, *Paul and Rabbinic Judaism*, 295–96.

66. Conzelmann, *1 Corinthians*, 271; see also Kistemaker, *Exposition*, 552 ("God entrusted the kingdom to Christ for the period lasting from his first coming to his second coming. . . . At the end of time, Christ will deliver the kingdom to God the Father when he has destroyed all the hostile spiritual forces.").

by Adam (Rom. 8:20). Now the connection between Christ's reign and the resurrection becomes clear. The crowning act of Christ's reign is the final *katargesis* ("destruction") of death, and this is but the obverse of the final resurrection. What marks the *katargesis* of death is the resurrection of the dead and the change of the mortal to immortality at Christ's *parousia* (vv. 51–54; cf. vs. 23b.).[67]

One question remains: What of the duration of events associated with the *parousia* itself? The reason for this question is that the *parousia* involves judgment and the restoration of creation as well as resurrection.[68] As Page puts it, "In Paul's eschatology the return of Christ, the physical resurrection of believers, and final judgment appear as a single complex of events, and it is hard to imagine that he would have found congenial the notion of a provisional kingdom following the *parousia*."[69] It might be maintained that those events of necessity would have to occur after the *parousia*/resurrection *per se*. Consequently, the *eita* ("then") in the phrase *eita to telos* ("then the end"; v. 24) would allow for an interval of time between the *parousia* and "the end." Héring, for example, speaks of "the end" as "the events between the *Parousia* and the final establishment of the Kingdom of God."[70] Assuming that there is some period of time between the *parousia* and "the end" (when Christ hands over the kingdom to the Father) does not contradict the above analysis. The reason is that any events—i.e., judgment and re-creation—which take place between the *parousia* and "the end" not only are immediately associated in time with the *parousia* but are the very things which describe what the *parousia* entails and demonstrate the epoch-changing significance of the *parousia* itself. They are the very things that "usher in" the final consummation, i.e., "the end."[71] Even Daniel Wallace, a premillennialist, acknowledges:

> The most we can get out of 1 Cor 15:21–28 is that there may be some time for Christ to do his "clean-up operation"—that is, to bring everything, including death, under submission to his sovereignty. But to read into this text a one thousand year period is unwarranted. Indeed, it seems equally plausible to extract from this text the notion that Christ is now reigning and is bringing everything under his submission (v 25). "Then comes the end" (v 24), in this scenario, would support a postmillennial/amillennial position. Suffice it to say that the millennium is anything but clear in this text.[72]

Conclusion

The concept of a temporary "millennial kingdom" between the *parousia* and the institution of the eternal state is not found in—indeed, is inconsistent with—Paul's most

67. Dykstra, "The Reign of Christ," 46–47.

68. See discussion in main text, chapter 5–The Eschatological Significance of Christ's Second Coming.

69. Page, "Revelation 20," 40.

70. Héring, *First Epistle of St. Paul*, 166.

71. See Davies, *Paul and Rabbinic Judaism*, 295; Lenski, *Interpretation*, 674; Hill, "Paul's Understanding," 319; Smith, "A Neglected," n.p.

72. Wallace, "New Testament Eschatology," n.p.

extensive discussion of the events surrounding the eschatological resurrection. The crucial pericope, 1 Cor 15:20–57, does not support premillennialism but rather is consistent with amillennial eschatology. It is noteworthy that for premillennialists, "the value of this text can ever only lie in what it leaves unsaid, certainly not in what it does say."[73] Thus, although premillennialist D. Edmund Hiebert calls the phrase *eita to telos* ("then the end") in v. 24 the "crux of the millennial issue," the most he can say about it is that if it establishes an interval between the *parousia* and the consummation, then Paul "at the very least, leaves room for an end-time millennial kingdom."[74] However, neither that phrase nor anything else in the entire passage actually mentions Christ's reigning on the earth, a millennial kingdom, a revolt at the end of 1000 years, a third resurrection *tagma* involving unbelievers, or any aspect of the so-called "millennium." Those concepts all have to be read into the text, not gleaned from it.[75] Given the reason why he was writing and the specific subjects he was discussing in this passage, "it seems unthinkable that Paul, if he believed in such a [millennial] kingdom, should pass over it without a word."[76] In light of the above, even some premillennialists acknowledge that, "the attempt to attribute to Paul a belief in the millennium on the basis of 1 Cor 15:20–28 is unconvincing."[77]

Contrary to such premillennial eisegesis, both the grammar and the context of the passage explicitly teach what is taught elsewhere by Paul and the other NT writers, namely, Christ is reigning from heaven now, and this phase of his reign is marked by conflict. However, there is coming a day, the *parousia*, when he will return to earth. In connection with that event (not 1000 years thereafter) the dead shall be resurrected, conflict will be ended, the new heavens and new earth which will last forever will be ushered in, and death will be swallowed up in victory.

73. Hill, "Paul's Understanding," 308n.31.

74. Hiebert, "Evidence," 229–30; see also Blaising, "Premillennialism," 204; Blomberg, *1 Corinthians*, 304; Wellum, "Christ's Resurrection," 91n.31.

75. Ridderbos, *Paul: An Outline*, 557–58.

76. Barrett, *First Epistle to the Corinthians*, 356; see also Fee, *First Epistle to the Corinthians*, 753n.38 (Paul "neither explicitly nor allusively speaks of such [a millennial kingdom], which he was fully capable of doing, had it been of any interest to him").

77. Mounce, *Revelation*, 367n.12; see also Caird, *St. John the Divine*, 251; Beckwith, *The Apocalypse*, 99, 735; Wallace, "New Testament Eschatology," n.p.

Bibliography

Pseudepigrapha

1 Enoch [*The Book of Enoch*]. Translated by Andy McCraken. Online: http://www.scriptural-truth.com/stuff/BookOfEnoch.pdf.
2 Baruch [*Apocalypse of Baruch*]. Online: http://www.pseudepigrapha.com/pseudepigrapha/2Baruch.html.

Greco-Roman Writings

Herodotus. *The History of Herodotus*. 2 volumes. Translated by G. C. Macaulay. London: MacMillan, 1890. Online: http://wps.pearsoncustom.com/wps/media/objects/2426/2484749/chap_assets/bookshelf/herodotus.pdf.
Josephus. *Antiquities of the Jews*. In *The Works of Josephus*, new updated ed., translated by William Whiston, 27–542. Peabody, MA: Hendrickson, 1987. Online (another edition): http://www.ccel.org/ccel/josephus/works/files/works.html.
———. *Wars of the Jews*. In *The Works of Josephus*, new updated ed., translated by William Whiston, 543–772. Peabody, MA: Hendrickson, 1987. Online (another edition): http://www.ccel.org/ccel/josephus/works/files/works.html.

Early Christian Writings

Apostles' Creed. Online: http://www.ccel.org/ccel/schaff/creeds1.iv.ii.html.
Athanasian Creed. Online: http://www.ccel.org/ccel/schaff/creeds1.iv.v.html.
Augustine. *The City of God*. Translated by Marcus Dods. New York: Random House, 1950. Online: http://www.ccel.org/ccel/schaff/npnf102.toc.html.
———. *Quaestiones in Heptateuchum*. Online (another edition): http://www.augustinus.it/latino/questioni_ettateuco/index2.htm.
1 Clement. In *The Apostolic Fathers*, 2nd ed., edited and revised by Michael Holmes, translated by J. B. Lightfoot and J. R. Harmer, 28–64. Grand Rapids: Baker, 1989. Online (another edition): http://www.ccel.org/ccel/lightfoot/fathers.ii.i.html.
2 Clement. In *The Apostolic Fathers*, 2nd ed., edited and revised by Michael Holmes, translated by J. B. Lightfoot and J. R. Harmer, 68–78. Grand Rapids: Baker, 1989. Online (another edition): http://www.ccel.org/ccel/lightfoot/fathers.ii.ii.html.
Clement of Alexandria, *Stromata*. In *ANF*, vol. 2, edited by Alexander Roberts and James Donaldson, revised by A. Cleveland Coxe, 299–567. New York: Christian Literature Publishing Company, 1885. Reprint, Peabody, MA: Hendrickson, 1994. Online (another edition): http://www.ccel.org/ccel/schaff/anf02.vi.iv.html.

Cyprian, *Treatise on Jealousy and Envy*. In *ANF*, vol. 5, edited by Alexander Roberts and James Donaldson, revised by A. Cleveland Coxe, 4–91. New York: Christian Literature Publishing Company, 1886. Reprint, Peabody, MA: Hendrickson, 1994. Online (another edition): http://www.ccel.org/ccel/schaff/anf05.iv.v.x.html.

The Didache. In *The Apostolic Fathers*, 2nd ed., edited and revised by Michael Holmes, translated by J. B. Lightfoot and J. R. Harmer, 145–58. Grand Rapids: Baker, 1989. Online (another edition): http: // www.ccel.org/ccel/lightfoot/fathers.ii.xii.html.

Dionysius Syrus. "Rev 20:2, 3" (extracts). Online: http://www.tertullian.org/fathers/dionysius_syrus_revelation_01.htm#C5.

The Epistle of Barnabas. In *The Apostolic Fathers*, 2nd ed., edited and revised by Michael Holmes, translated by J. B. Lightfoot and J. R. Harmer, 162–88. Grand Rapids: Baker, 1989. Online (another edition): http://www.ccel.org/ccel/lightfoot/fathers.ii.xiii.html.

Eusebius. *Ecclesiastical History*. In *Nicene and Post-Nicene Fathers*, first series, vol. 1, edited by Philip Schaff, 73–403. New York: Christian Literature Publishing Company, 1890. Reprint, Peabody, MA: Hendrickson, 1994. Online (another edition): http://www.ccel.org/ccel/schaff/npnf201.iii.html.

Hippolytus. *Commentary on Daniel* (fragments). In *ANF*, vol. 5, edited by Alexander Roberts and James Donaldson, revised by A. Cleveland Coxe, 177–91. New York: Christian Literature Publishing Company, 1886. Reprint, Peabody, MA: Hendrickson, 1994. Online (another edition): http://www.ccel.org/ccel/schaff/anf05.iii.iv.i.x.i.html.

————. *Expository Treatise Against the Jews*. In *ANF*, vol. 5, edited by Alexander Roberts and James Donaldson, revised by A. Cleveland Coxe, 219–21. New York: Christian Literature Publishing Company, 1886. Reprint, Peabody, MA: Hendrickson, 1994. Online (another edition): http://www.ccel.org/ccel/schaff/anf05.iii.iv.ii.ii.html.

————. *Hippolyte Commentaire sur Daniel* (SC 14) (complete text). Text established and translated by Maurice Lefèvre. Paris: Éditions du Cerf, 1947.

————. *Treatise on Christ and Antichrist*. In *ANF*, vol. 5, edited by Alexander Roberts and James Donaldson, revised by A. Cleveland Coxe, 204–19. New York: Christian Literature Publishing Company, 1886. Reprint, Peabody, MA: Hendrickson, 1994. Online (another edition): http://www.ccel.org/ccel/schaff/anf05.iii.iv.ii.i.html.

Ignatius. "To the Ephesians." In *The Apostolic Fathers*, 2nd ed., edited and revised by Michael Holmes, translated by J. B. Lightfoot and J. R. Harmer, 86–93. Grand Rapids: Baker, 1989. Online (another edition): http://www.ccel.org/ccel/lightfoot/fathers.ii.iii.html.

————. "To the Magnesians." In *The Apostolic Fathers*, 2nd ed., edited and revised by Michael Holmes, translated by J. B. Lightfoot and J. R. Harmer, 93–97. Grand Rapids: Baker, 1989. Online (another edition): http://www.ccel.org/ccel/lightfoot/fathers.ii.iv.html.

————. "To Polycarp." In *The Apostolic Fathers*, 2nd ed., edited and revised by Michael Holmes, translated by J. B. Lightfoot and J. R. Harmer, 115–18. Grand Rapids: Baker, 1989. Online (another edition): http://www.ccel.org/ccel/lightfoot/fathers.ii.ix.html.

Irenaeus. *Against Heresies*. In *ANF*, vol. 1, edited by Alexander Roberts and James Donaldson, revised by A. Cleveland Coxe, 315–567. New York: Christian Literature Publishing Company, 1885. Reprint, Peabody, MA: Hendrickson, 1994. Online (another edition): http://www.ccel.org/ccel/schaff/anf01.ix.i.html.

Jerome. *Commentary on Daniel*. Translated by Gleason Archer. Grand Rapids: Baker, 1958. Online: http://www.tertullian.org/fathers/jerome_daniel_02_text.htm.

Justin Martyr. *Dialogue with Trypho*. In *ANF*, vol. 1, edited by Alexander Roberts and James Donaldson, revised by A. Cleveland Coxe, 194–270. New York: Christian Literature Publishing Company, 1885. Reprint, Peabody, MA: Hendrickson, 1994. Online (another edition): http://www.ccel.org/ccel/schaff/anf01.viii.iv.html.

————. *First Apology*. In *ANF*, vol. 1, edited by Alexander Roberts and James Donaldson, revised by A. Cleveland Coxe, 159–87. New York: Christian Literature Publishing Company, 1885. Reprint, Peabody, MA: Hendrickson, 1994. Online (another edition): http://www.ccel.org/ccel/schaff/anf01.viii.ii.html.

Lactantius. *Divine Institutes*. In *ANF*, vol. 7, edited by Alexander Roberts and James Donaldson, revised by A. Cleveland Coxe, 9–223. New York: Christian Literature Publishing Company, 1886. Reprint,

Peabody, MA: Hendrickson, 1994. Online (another edition): http://www.ccel.org/ccel/schaff/anf07.iii.ii.html.

Nicene-Constantinople Creed. Online: http://www.ccel.org/ccel/schaff/creeds1.iv.iii.html.

Origen. *Against Celsus*. In *ANF*, vol. 4, edited by Alexander Roberts and James Donaldson, revised by A. Cleveland Coxe, 395–670. New York: Christian Literature Publishing Company, 1885. Reprint, Peabody, MA: Hendrickson, 1994. Online (another edition): http://www.ccel.org/ccel/schaff/anf04.vi.ix.i.i.html.

Papias. "Fragments." In *The Apostolic Fathers*, 2nd ed., edited and revised by Michael Holmes, translated by J. B. Lightfoot and J. R. Harmer, 311–29. Grand Rapids: Baker, 1989. Online (another edition): http://www.ccel.org/ccel/schaff/anf01.vii.ii.html.

Polycarp. "To the Philippians." In *The Apostolic Fathers*, 2nd ed., edited and revised by Michael Holmes, translated by J. B. Lightfoot and J. R. Harmer, 123–30. Grand Rapids: Baker, 1989. Online (another edition): http://www.ccel.org/ccel/lightfoot/fathers.ii.x.html.

The Shepherd of Hermas. In *The Apostolic Fathers*, 2nd ed., edited and revised by Michael Holmes, translated by J. B. Lightfoot and J. R. Harmer, 194–290. Grand Rapids: Baker, 1989. Online (another edition): http://www.ccel.org/ccel/lightfoot/fathers.ii.xiv.html.

Tertullian. *Against Marcion*. In *ANF*, vol. 3, edited by Alexander Roberts and James Donaldson, revised by A. Cleveland Coxe, 269–423. New York: Christian Literature Publishing Company, 1885. Reprint, Peabody, MA: Hendrickson, 1994. Online (another edition): http://www.ccel.org/ccel/schaff/anf03.v.iv.i.html.

———. *An Answer to the Jews*. In *ANF*, vol. 3, edited by Alexander Roberts and James Donaldson, revised by A. Cleveland Coxe, 151–73. New York: Christian Literature Publishing Company, 1885. Reprint, Peabody, MA: Hendrickson, 1994. Online (another edition): http://www.ccel.org/ccel/schaff/anf03.iv.ix.i.html.

———. *Apology*. In *ANF*, vol. 3, edited by Alexander Roberts and James Donaldson, revised by A. Cleveland Coxe, 17–55. New York: Christian Literature Publishing Company, 1885. Reprint, Peabody, MA: Hendrickson, 1994. Online (another edition): http://www.ccel.org/ccel/schaff/anf03.iv.iii.i.html.

———. *On the Resurrection of the Flesh*. In *ANF*, vol. 3, edited by Alexander Roberts and James Donaldson, revised by A. Cleveland Coxe, 545–94. New York: Christian Literature Publishing Company, 1885. Reprint, Peabody, MA: Hendrickson, 1994. Online (another edition): http://www.ccel.org/ccel/schaff/anf03.v.viii.i.html.

———. *Prescription Against Heretics*. In *ANF*, vol. 3, edited by Alexander Roberts and James Donaldson, revised by A. Cleveland Coxe, 243–65. Peabody, MA: Hendrickson, 1994. Online (another edition): http://www.ccel.org/ccel/schaff/anf03.v.iii.i.html.

———. *The Shows*. In *ANF*, vol. 3, edited by Alexander Roberts and James Donaldson, revised by A. Cleveland Coxe, 79–91. New York: Christian Literature Publishing Company, 1885. Reprint, Peabody, MA: Hendrickson, 1994. Online (another edition): http://www.ccel.org/ccel/schaff/anf03.iv.v.i.html.

Victorinus of Pettau. *Commentary on the Apocalypse*. In *Ancient Christian Texts: Latin Commentaries on Revelation*, translated and edited by William Weinrich, 1–22. Downers Grove, IL: IVP Academic, 2012. Online (another edition): http://www.bombaxo.com/victapoc.html.

Contemporary Works

Abdulahugli, Hasan. "Factors Leading to Conversion among Central Asian Muslims." In *From the Straight Path to the Narrow Way*, ed. David Greenlee, 157–66. Waynesboro, GA: Authentic, 2005.

Adeyemo, Tokunboh. "Daniel." In *Africa Bible Commentary*, edited by Tokunboh Adeyemo, 989–1012. Nairobi: WordAlive, 2006.

Alexander, T. Desmond. *From Eden to the New Jerusalem*. Nottingham, England: Inter-Varsity, 2008.

Alford, Henry. *The Greek Testament*, new ed. 4 vols. Boston: Lee and Shepard, 1878. Online: http://archive.org/stream/GreekTestamentCriticalExegeticalCommentaryByHenry/04.GreekTestament.CritExegComm.v4.Heb.toRevel.Alford.1878.#page/n9/mode/2up.

Allen, David. *Hebrews* (NAC 35). Nashville: B&H, 2010.

Allison, Dale. *The End of the Ages Has Come: An Early Interpretation of the Passion and Resurrection of Jesus.* Philadelphia: Fortress, 1985.

Anderson, Gary. "Sacrifice and Sacrificial Offerings (OT)." In *The Anchor Bible Dictionary,* vol. 5, edited by David Freedman, 870–86. New York: Doubleday, 1992.

Anderson, Robert. *The Coming Prince,* 16th ed. Grand Rapids: Kregel, 1967.

Archer, Gleason, et al. *The Rapture: Pre-, Mid-, or Post-Tribulational?* Grand Rapids: Academie, 1984.

Arrington, French L. *Paul's Aeon Theology in 1 Corinthians.* Washington, D.C.: University Press of America, 1978.

Arthur, Kay. *How to Study Your Bible.* Eugene, OR: Harvest House, 1994.

Aune, David. *Prophecy in Early Christianity and the Ancient Mediterranean World.* Grand Rapids: Eerdmans, 1983.

———. *Revelation 1–5* (WBC 52A). Dallas: Word, 1997.

———. *Revelation 6–16* (WBC 52B). Nashville: Thomas Nelson, 1998.

———. *Revelation 17–22* (WBC 52C). Nashville: Thomas Nelson, 1998.

Azurdia, Arturo. *Sermon Series on the Book of Revelation.* Audio mp3. Online: http://www.monergism. com/thethreshold/articles/onsite/azurdia_revelation.html.

Bahnsen, Greg. "Gospel Prosperity and the Future of Israel." *Calvinism Today* 3 (1993) 4–7. Online: http: //www.cmfnow.com/articles/pt158.htm.

———. *Victory in Jesus,* 2nd ed. Nacogdoches, TX: Covenant Media Press, 2015.

Baldwin, Joyce. *Daniel: An Introductory Commentary* (TOTC). Leicester, England: Inter-Varsity, 1978.

Balfour, Glenn. "The Jewishness of John's Use of the Scriptures in John 6:31 and 7:37–38." *TynBul* 46 (1995) 368–79. Online: http://www.tyndalehouse.com/tynbul/library/TynBull_1995_46_2_08_ Balfour_John6_7.pdf.

Bandstra, Andrew. "'Kingship and Priests': Inaugurated Eschatology in the Apocalypse," *CTJ* 27 (1992) 10–25.

Barker, Kenneth. "Zechariah." In *The Expositor's Bible Commentary,* vol. 8, rev. ed., edited by Tremper Longman III and David Garland, 721–833. Grand Rapids: Zondervan, 2008.

Barnhouse, Donald. *Romans.* 4 vols. Grand Rapids: Eerdmans, 1952–1964. Reprint, Grand Rapids: Eerdmans, 1973.

Barrett, C. K. *The First Epistle to the Corinthians* (HNTC). New York: Harper & Row, 1968.

———. *The New Testament Background Selected Documents,* rev. ed. San Francisco: Harper & Row, 1989.

Bartlett, John. "Maccabees, The Books of the." In *The Oxford Companion to the Bible,* edited by Bruce Metzger and Michael Coogan, 475–82. New York: Oxford, 1993.

Bauckham, Richard. *The Bible in Politics: How to Read the Bible Politically.* London: SPCK, 1989.

———. *The Climax of Prophecy: Studies on the Book of Revelation.* Edinburgh: T&T Clark, 1993.

———. "The Delay of the Parousia." *TynBul* 31 (1980) 3–36. Online: http://www.tyndalehouse.com/ tynbul/library/TynBull_1980_31_01_Bauckham_DelayOfParousia.pdf.

———. "The Economic Critique of Rome in Revelation 18." In *Images of Empire* (JSOTSup 122), edited by Loveday Alexander, 47–90. Sheffield, England: Sheffield Academic Press, 1991.

———. *God Crucified: Monotheism and Christology in the New Testament.* Grand Rapids: Eerdmans, 1998.

———. "The Great Tribulation in the Shepherd of Hermas." *JTS* 25 (1974) 27–40.

———. "The List of Tribes in Revelation 7 Again." *JSNT* 42 (1991) 99–115.

———. *The Theology of the Book of Revelation.* Cambridge, England: Cambridge University Press, 1993.

Beal, Jr, R. S. "Can A Premillennialist Consistently Entertain A Concern for the Environment? A Rejoinder to Al Truesdale." *Perspectives on Science and Christian Faith* 46 (1994) 172–77. Online: http:// resources.asa3.org/FMPro?-db=asadb49.fm4&-format=%2fasadb%2fdetail3.html&-lay=layout1&- sortfield=first%20author&-op=cn&combo%5ftag=beal&-lop=or&-max=2147483647&- recid=34359&-find=.

Beale, G. K. *The Book of Revelation: A Commentary on the Greek Text* (NIGTC). Grand Rapids: Eerdmans, 1999.

———. *John's Use of the Old Testament in Revelation* (JSNTSup 166). Sheffield, England: Sheffield Academic Press, 1998.

———. *A New Testament Biblical Theology: The Unfolding of the Old Testament in the New.* Grand Rapids: Baker Academic, 2011.

———."The Purpose of Symbolism in the Book of Revelation." *CTJ* 41 (2006) 53–66. Online: http://www .calvin.edu/library/database/crcpi/fulltext/ctj/CTJ06Ap/124804.pdf.

———. "Review Article: J. W. Mealy *After the Thousand Years*." *EvQ* 66 (1994) 229–49. Online: https:// biblicalstudies.org.uk/pdf/eq/1994-3_229.pdf.

———. *Sermon Series on the Book of Revelation*. Audio mp3. 2008. Online: http://resources. thegospelcoalition.org/library?f%5Bbook%5D%5B%5D=Revelation&f%5Bcontributors%5D%5B% 5D=Beale%2C+G.K.&page=2&sort=contributors.

———. *The Temple and the Church's Mission: A Biblical Theology of the Dwelling Place of God* (NSBT 17). Downers Grove, IL: InterVarsity, 2004.

Beale, G. K., and Sean McDonough. "Revelation." In *Commentary on the New Testament Use of the Old Testament*, edited by G. K. Beale and D. A. Carson, 1081–1161. Grand Rapids: Baker Academic, 2007.

Bear, James. "The People of God in the Light of the Teaching of the New Testament." *USR* 52 (1940–41) 129–58.

Beasley-Murray, George. *The Book of Revelation*. Grand Rapids: Eerdmans, 1974.

———. *A Commentary on Mark Thirteen*. London: Macmillan, 1957.

———. "Ezekiel." In *The New Bible Commentary*, 3rd ed., edited by D. Guthrie et al., 664–87. Carmel, NY: Guideposts, 1970.

———. "The Interpretation of Daniel 7." *CBQ* 45 (1983) 44–58.

———. *Jesus and the Last Days: The Interpretation of the Olivet Discourse*. Peabody, MA: Hendrickson, 1993.

———. *John*, 2nd ed. (WBC 36). Nashville: Thomas Nelson, 1999.

———. "The Revelation." In *The New Bible Commentary*, 3rd ed., edited by D. Guthrie et al., 1279–1310. Carmel, NY: Guideposts, 1970.

Beckwith, Isbon. *The Apocalypse of John*. New York: Macmillan, 1919. Reprint, Grand Rapids: Baker, 1967. Online: https://archive.org/details/apocalypseofjohnoobeck.

Bell, William Everett, Jr. "A Critical Evaluation of the Pretribulation Rapture Doctrine in Christian Eschatology." PhD diss., New York University, 1967.

Belleville, Linda. "'Under Law': Structural Analysis and the Pauline Concept of Law in Galatians 3:21– 4:11." *JSNT* 26 (1986) 53–78.

Berkhof, Louis. *The History of Christian Doctrines*. Grand Rapids: Baker, 1937. Reprint, Carlisle, PA: Banner of Truth, 2002.

Berkouwer, G. C. *The Return of Christ*. Translated by James Van Oosterom. Grand Rapids: Eerdmans, 1972.

Blaising, Craig A. "Premillennialism." In *Three Views on the Millennium and Beyond*. edited by Darrell L. Bock, 157–227. Grand Rapids: Zondervan, 1999.

Blaising, Craig A., and Darrell L. Bock. *Progressive Dispensationalism*. Grand Rapids: Baker, 1993.

Blaising, Craig, et al. *Three Views on the Rapture: Pretribulation, Prewrath, or Posttribulation*, 2nd ed. Grand Rapids: Zondervan, 2010.

Bloch, Ruth. *Visionary Republic: Millennial Themes in American Thought, 1756–1800*. Cambridge: Cambridge University Press, 1985.

Blomberg, Craig. *1 Corinthians* (NIVAC). Grand Rapids: Baker, 1994.

———. *Matthew* (NAC 22). Nashville: Broadman, 1992.

———. "Matthew." In *Commentary on the New Testament Use of the Old Testament*, edited by G. K. Beale and D. A. Carson, 1–109. Grand Rapids: Baker Academic, 2007.

Bock, Darrell. "The Reign of the Lord Jesus Christ." In *Dispensationalism, Israel and the Church*, edited by Craig Blaising and Darrell Bock, 37–67. Grand Rapids: Zondervan, 1992.

Bock, Darrell, et al. *Three Views on the Millennium and Beyond*. Grand Rapids: Zondervan, 1999.

Boda, Mark. *Haggai, Zechariah* (NIVAC). Grand Rapids: Zondervan, 2004.

Boers, H. W. "Apocalyptic Eschatology in I Corinthians 15." *Int* 21 (1967) 50–65.

Boettner, Loraine. "Postmillennialism." In *The Meaning of the Millennium: Four Views*, edited by Robert Clouse, 117–41. Downers Grove, IL: InterVarsity, 1977.

———. "A Postmillennial Response." In *The Meaning of the Millennium: Four Views*, edited by Robert Clouse, 199–208. Downers Grove, IL: InterVarsity, 1977.

Boff, Leonardo, and Clodovis Boff. *Introducing Liberation Theology.* Translated by Paul Burns. Maryknoll, NY: Orbis, 1987.

Boice, James. *Foundations of the Christian Faith,* rev. ed. Downers Grove, IL: InterVarsity, 1986.

Bolt, Peter. "Mark 13: An Apocalyptic Precursor to the Passion Narrative." *RTR* 54 (1995) 10–32.

Bonhoeffer, Dietrich. *Letters and Papers from Prison,* enlarged edition. Edited by Eberhard Bethge. New York: Touchstone, 1997.

Borchert, Gerald L. "The Resurrection: 1 Corinthians 15." *RevExp* 80 (1983) 401–15.

Boxall, Ian. *The Revelation of St. John* (BNTC). Grand Rapids: Baker Academic, 2009.

Boyd, Alan Patrick. "A Dispensational Premillennial Analysis of the Eschatology of the Post-Apostolic Fathers (Until the Death of Justin Martyr)." Master's thesis, Dallas Theological Seminary, 1977. Theological Research Exchange Network No. 001–0593 (www.tren.com).

Boyer, Paul. *When Time Shall Be No More.* Cambridge, MA: Belknap, 1992.

Brown, David. *Christ's Second Coming: Will it be Premillennial?* 7th ed. Edinburgh: T&T Clark, 1882. Online: https://books.google.com/books?id=RaRTHQNejWQC.

Brown, Schuyler. "The Hour of Trial (Rev 3:10)." *JBL* 85 (1966) 308–14.

Bruce, F. F. "The Book of Zechariah and the Passion Narrative." *BJRL* 43 (1961) 336–53. Online: http://www.biblicalstudies.org.uk/pdf/bjrl/zechariah_bruce.pdf.

———. "The Earliest Latin Commentary on the Apocalypse." *EvQ* 10 (1938) 352–66. Online: https://biblicalstudies.org.uk/pdf/eq/1938-4_352.pdf

———. "1 and 2 Thessalonians." In *The New Bible Commentary,* 3rd ed., edited by D. Guthrie et al., 1154–65. Carmel, NY: Guideposts, 1970.

———. *1 and 2 Thessalonians* (WBC 45). Waco, TX: Word, 1982.

Burke, Trevor. *Adopted into God's Family: Exploring a Pauline Metaphor* (NSBT 22). Nottingham, England: Apollos, 2006.

Caird, G. B. *The Apostolic Age,* rev. ed. London: Duckworth, 1975.

———. *A Commentary on the Revelation of St. John the Divine* (HNTC). New York: Harper & Row, 1966.

Calvin, John. "Commentary on the Second Epistle to the Thessalonians." In *Commentaries on the Epistles of Paul the Apostle to the Philippians, Colossians, and Thessalonians,* translated and edited by John Pringle, 307–62. Edinburgh: Calvin Translation Society, 1851. Online: http://www.ccel.org/ccel/calvin/calcom42.toc.html.

Campbell, Gordon. "Antithetical Feminine-Urban Imagery and a Tale of Two Women-Cities in the Book of Revelation." *TynBul* 55 (2004) 81–108. Online: http://www.tyndalehouse.com/TynBul/Library/TynBull_2004_55_1_05_Campbell_UrbanImageryinRevelation.pdf.

Carson, D. A. *Christ and Culture Revisited.* Grand Rapids: Eerdmans, 2008.

———. *The Gospel According to John* (PNTC). Grand Rapids: Eerdmans, 1991.

———. "Matthew." In *The Expositor's Bible Commentary,* vol. 8, edited by Frank Gaebelein, 3–599. Grand Rapids: Zondervan, 1984.

———. "Matthew." In *The Expositor's Bible Commentary,* rev. ed., vol. 9, edited by Tremper Longman III and David Garland, 23–670. Grand Rapids: Zondervan, 2010.

———. *Preaching Apocalyptic.* 2009. Audio mp3. Online: http://thegospelcoalition.org/index.php?/resources/name-index/a/DA_Carson/topic/End+Times.

———. *Sermons and Lectures on the Book of Revelation.* 1994–2010. Audio mp3. Online: http://resources.thegospelcoalition.org/library?f%5Bbook%5D%5B%5D=Revelation&f%5Bcontributors%5D%5B%5D=Carson%2C+D.+A.&sort=contributors., 2005.

———. "This Present Evil Age." In *These Last Days: A Christian View of History,* edited by Richard Phillips and Gabriel Fluhrer, 17–37. Phillipsburg, NJ: P&R. Online: https://thelogcollege.files.wordpress.com/2013/09/2011_present_evil_age.pdf.

Charles, R. H. *A Critical and Exegetical Commentary on the Revelation of St. John* (ICC). 2 vols. Edinburgh: T&T Clark, 1920. Online: https://books.google.com/books?id=LW83AQAAMAAJ.

———. *Eschatology.* New York: Schocken, 1963.

Chesebrough, David, ed. *God Ordained This War: Sermons on the Sectional Crisis, 1830–1865.* Columbia, SC: University of South Carolina Press, 1991.

Chilton, David. *Days of Vengeance: An Exposition of the Book of Revelation.* Ft. Worth, TX: Dominion, 1987. Online: http://www.garynorth.com/freebooks/docs/pdf/days_of_vengeance.pdf.

————. *Paradise Restored.* Tyler, TX: Dominion, 1985. Online: http://www.garynorth.com/freebooks/docs/pdf/paradise_restored.pdf.

Chisholm, Robert. "When Prophecy Appears to Fail, Check Your Hermeneutic." *JETS* 53 (2010) 561–77. Online: http://www.etsjets.org/files/JETS-PDFs/53/53-3/Chisholm_JETS_53_3_pp_561-577.pdf.

Clouse, Robert, ed. *The Meaning of the Millennium: Four Views.* Downers Grove, IL: InterVarsity, 1977.

Clowney, Edmund. "The Final Temple." *WTJ* 35 (1972–73) 156–89. Online: http://beginningwithmoses.org/bt-articles/230/the-final-temple.

Code of Canon Law of the Roman Catholic Church. 1983. Online: http://www.vatican.va/archive/ENG1104/_INDEX.HTM.

Cole, Victor Babajide. "Mark." In *Africa Bible Commentary,* edited by Tokunboh Adeyemo, 1171–1202. Nairobi: WordAlive, 2006.

Collins, John. *Daniel* (Hermeneia). Minneapolis: Fortress, 1993.

Collins, Raymond F. *First Corinthians* (SP 7). Collegeville, MN: The Liturgical Press, 1999.

Conzelmann, Hans. *1 Corinthians* (Hermeneia). Translated by James W. Leitch. Philadelphia: Fortress, 1975.

Cooper, Charles. "The Prophetic Pillars of the Prewrath Position, Part 4: God Almighty Takes Back His Rule of the Earth After the Seventieth Week of Daniel, But Before Armageddon." *Parousia* 15 (2000)2–10. Online: http://www.solagroup.org/products/pdf_files/parousia15.pdf.

Court, John. *Myth and History in the Book of Revelation.* Atlanta: John Knox, 1979.

Crampton, W. Gary. *What Calvin Says.* Jefferson, MD: The Trinity Foundation, 1992.

Crockett, William. "The Ultimate Restoration of all Mankind: 1 Corinthians 15:22." In *Studia Biblica 1978: II, Papers on Paul and Other New Testament Authors,* edited by E. A. Livingstone, 83–86. Sheffield, England: JSOT, 1980.

Crockett, William, ed. *Four Views on Hell.* Grand Rapids: Zondervan, 1992.

Crutchfield, Larry. 1988. "The Apostle John and Asia Minor as a Source of Premillennialism in the Early Church Fathers." *JETS* 31 (1988) 411–27. Online: http://www.etsjets.org/files/JETS-PDFs/31/31-4/31-4-pp411-427_JETS.pdf.

Cullmann, Oscar. *Christ and Time,* rev. ed. Translated by Floyd Filson. Philadelphia: Westminster, 1964.

Culver, Robert. "A Neglected Millennial Passage from Saint Paul." *BSac* 113 (1956) 141–52.

Curry-Roper, Janel. "Contemporary Christian Eschatologies and Their Relation to Environmental Stewardship." *Professional Geographer* 42 (1990) 157–69.

Dahl, M. E. *The Resurrection of the Body.* London: SCM, 1962.

Davies, J. G. *The Early Christian Church.* Grand Rapids: Baker, 1965.

Davies, W. D. *Paul and Rabbinic Judaism,* 4th ed. Philadelphia: Fortress, 1980.

Davies, W. D., and Dale Allison. *The Gospel According to St. Matthew* (ICC). 3 vols. Edinburgh: T&T Clark, 1991.

Davis, John Jefferson. *Christ's Victorious Kingdom.* Grand Rapids, Mich.: Baker, 1986.

Dayton, Donald. *Discovering an Evangelical Heritage.* New York: Harper & Row, 1976.

de Boer, M. C. "Paul and Apocalyptic Eschatology." In *The Encyclopedia of Apocalypticism,* vol. 1, edited by John Collins, 345–83. New York: Continuum, 1998.

Deere, Jack S. "Premillennialism in Revelation 20:4–6." *BSac* 35 (1978) 58–73.

DeMar, Gary. *Last Days Madness,* 4th ed. Powder Springs, GA, 1999: American Vision. Preview online: https://books.google.com/books?isbn=0915815354.

Dennison, William. *Paul's Two-Age Construction and Apologetics.* Lanham, MD: University Press of America, 1985.

Deutsch, Celia. "Transformation of Symbols: The New Jerusalem in Rv 21:1–22:5." *ZNW* 78 (1987) 106–26.

Di Sabatino, David. "The Jesus People Movement: Countercultural Revival and Evangelical Renewal." Master's thesis, McMaster University, 1994.

Dobson, Ed, and Ed Hindson. "Apocalypse Now? What Fundamentalists Believe About the End of the World." *Policy Review* 38 (1986) 16–22. Online: http://www.unz.org/Pub/PolicyRev-1986q4-00016.

Dodd, C. H. *More New Testament Studies.* Grand Rapids: Eerdmans, 1968.

Doukhan, Jacques. "The Seventy Weeks of Dan 9: An Exegetical Study." *AUSS* 17 (1979) 1–22. Online: https://digitalcommons.andrews.edu/cgi/viewcontent.cgi?article=1078&context=old-testament-pubs.

Duguid, Iain. *Daniel* (REC). Phillipsburg, NJ: P&R, 2008.

Dunning, Craig. 2013. "Palestinian Muslims Converting to Christianity: Effective Evangelistic Methods in the West Bank." Ph.D. diss. University of Pretoria. 2013. Online: https://www.academia.edu/5769303/Palestinian_Muslims_converting_to_Christianity_effective_evangelistic_methods_in_the_West_Bank.

Dykstra, William. "I Corinthians 15:20–28, An Essential Part of Paul's Argument Against Those Who Deny the Resurrection." *CTJ* 4 (1969) 195–211.

———. "The Reign of Christ and Salvation History in I Corinthians 15:20–28." Master's thesis, Calvin Theological Seminary, 1969.

Edwards, James. *The Gospel According to Mark* (PNTC). Grand Rapids: Eerdmans, 2002.

Ehrlich, Eugene. *Amo, Amas, Amat and More.* New York: Harper & Row, 1985.

Elwell, Walter. "Revelation." In *Evangelical Commentary on the Bible,* edited by Walter Elwell, 1195–1229. Grand Rapids: Baker, 1989.

Elwell, Walter, ed. *Baker Encyclopedia of the Bible.* 2 vols. Grand Rapids: Baker, 1988.

Erickson, Millard. *A Basic Guide to Eschatology: Making Sense of the Millennium.* Grand Rapids Baker, 1998.

———. *Christian Theology,* 2nd ed. Grand Rapids: Baker, 1998.

———. *Contemporary Options in Eschatology: A Study of the Millennium.* Grand Rapids: Baker, 1977.

Evans, Craig. *Mark 8:27–16:20* (WBC 34B). Nashville: Thomas Nelson, 2001.

Ewert, David. "1–2 Thessalonians." In *Evangelical Commentary on the Bible,* edited by Walter Elwell, 1064–97. Grand Rapids: Baker, 1989.

Fee, Gordon. *The First Epistle to the Corinthians* (NICNT). Grand Rapids: Eerdmans, 1987.

———. *1 and 2 Timothy, Titus* (NIBC). Peabody, MA: Hendrickson, 1988.

Fee, Gordon, and Douglas Stuart. *How to Read the Bible for All Its Worth.* Grand Rapids: Academie, 1982.

Feinberg, Charles. *Millennialism: The Two Major Views,* 3rd ed. Chicago: Moody, 1980.

Ferguson, Sinclair. "Daniel." In *New Bible Commentary,* 4th ed., edited by D. A. Carson et al., 745–63. Leicester, England: Inter-Varsity, 1994.

Fesko, John. *Lecture Series on the Book of Revelation.* 2010. Audio mp3. Online: http://www.genevaopc.org/audio/fesko-lectures/72-revelation-lecture-series.html.

Fison, J. E. *The Christian Hope: The Presence and the Parousia.* London: Longmans, Green and Co, 1954.

Fletcher-Louis, Crispin. "The Destruction of the Temple and the Relativization of the Old Covenant: Mark 13:31 and Matthew 5:18." In *Eschatology in Bible and Theology: Evangelical Essays at the Dawn of a New Millennium,* edited by Kent Brower and Mark Elliott, 145–69. Downers Grove, IL: InterVarsity, 1997. Online: http://independent.academia.edu/CrispinFletcherLouis/Papers/963053/The_Destruction_of_the_Temple_and_the_Relativization_of_the_Old_Covenant_Mark_13_31_and_Matthew_5_18.

Ford, Desmond. *The Abomination of Desolation in Biblical Eschatology.* Washington, DC: University Press of America, 1979.

France, R. T. *The Gospel of Matthew* (NICNT). Grand Rapids: Eerdmans, 2007.

———. "Old Testament Prophecy and the Future of Israel: A Study of the Teaching of Jesus." *TynBul* 26 (1975) 53–78. Online: http://www.tyndalehouse.com/TynBul/Library/TynBull_1975_26_03_France_OTProphecyIsrael.pdf.

Fraser, Alexander. *A Key to the Prophecies of the Old and New Testaments which are Not Yet Accomplished.* Philadelphia: John Bioren, 1802. Online: https://books.google.com/books?id=6700AAAAMAAJ.

Froom, LeRoy. *The Prophetic Faith of Our Fathers.* 4 vols. Washington, DC: Review and Herald, 1948.

Gaebelein, Frank. "The Unity of the Bible." In *Revelation and the Bible: Contemporary Evangelical Thought,* edited by Carl F. H. Henry, 389–401. Grand Rapids: Baker, 1958. Online: http://www.biblicalstudies.org.uk/pdf/rev-henry/24_unity_gaebelein.pdf.

Garland, David E. *1 Corinthians* (BECNT). Grand Rapids: Baker Academic, 2003.

Garlington, Don. "Reigning With Christ (Revelation 20:1–6 In Its Salvation-Historical Setting)." Not dated. No pages. Online: http://www.mountainretreatorg.net/eschatology/reigning.html.

Gaston, Lloyd. *No Stone On Another.* Leiden: Brill, 1970.

Gay, John. "Remnant Theology: Different Perspectives on the Church and Israel." 2002. No pages. Online: http://www.leaderu.com/theology/remnanttheo.html.

Gentry, Kenneth. *Before Jerusalem Fell: Dating the Book of Revelation.* Powder Springs, GA: American Vision, 1989. Online: http://www.garynorth.com/freebooks/docs/pdf/before_jerusalem_fell.pdf.

———. "A Brief Theological Analysis of Hyper-Preterism." 2010. No pages. Online: https://chalcedon.edu/magazine/a-brief-theological-analysis-of-hyper-preterism.

———. "Daniel's Seventy Weeks." Not dated. No pages. Online: http://www.cmfnow.com/articles/pt551.htm.

———. *The Greatness of the Great Commission.* Tyler, TX: Institute for Christian Economics, 1990. Online: http://www.garynorth.com/freebooks/docs/pdf/the_great_commission.pdf.

———. "The Great Tribulation is Future: Rebuttal." In *The Great Tribulation: Past or Future? Two Evangelicals Debate the Question,* 165–99. Grand Rapids: Kregel, 1999.

———. "The Great Tribulation is Past: Exposition." In *The Great Tribulation: Past or Future? Two Evangelicals Debate the Question,* 33–66. Grand Rapids: Kregel, 1999.

———. "The Great Tribulation is Past: Foundation." In *The Great Tribulation: Past or Future? Two Evangelicals Debate the Question,* 11–32. Grand Rapids: Kregel, 1999

———. *He Shall Have Dominion.* Tyler, TX: Institute for Christian Economics, 1992. Online: http://www.garynorth.com/freebooks/docs/pdf/he_shall_have_dominion.pdf.

———. "A Preterist View of Revelation." In *Four Views on the Book of Revelation,* 37–92. Grand Rapids, MI: Zondervan, 1998. Online: https://books.google.com/books?isbn=0310872391.

———. "The Transition Text in Matthew 24: An Answer to Full Preterism." 2000. No pages. Online: http://www.preteristarchive.com/Modern/2000_gentry_transitional-verses.html.

Gentry, Peter. "Daniel's Seventy Weeks and the New Exodus." *SBJT* 14 (2010) 26–44. Online: http://equip.sbts.edu/wp-content/uploads/2010/05/sbjt_v14_n1_gentry.pdf.

Germano, Michael. "The Decree of Artaxerxes: Is It the Key to the Date of the Crucifixion?" *Perspectives* 5 (2002) no pages. Online: http://web.archive.org/web/20050919085931/www.bibarch.com/Perspectives/5.1.htm.

Glasson, T. Francis. "The Ensign of the Son of Man (Matt. XXIV. 30)." *JTS* 15 (1964) 299–300.

———. "Theophany and Parousia." *NTS* 34 (1988) 259–70.

Goldingay, John. *Daniel* (WBC 30). Dallas: Word, 1989.

Goldsworthy, Graeme. *According to Plan: The Unfolding Revelation of God in the Bible.* Downers Grove, IL: InterVarsity, 1991.

———. *Preaching the Whole Bible as Christian Scripture.* Grand Rapids: Eerdmans, 2000.

Goppelt, Leonhard. *Typos: The Typological Interpretation of the Old Testament in the New.* Translated by Donald Madvig. Grand Rapids: Eerdmans, 1982.

Gourgues, Michel. "The Thousand-Year Reign (Rev 20:1–6): Terrestrial or Celestial?" *CBQ* 47 (1985)676–81.

Graham, Billy. *Approaching Hoofbeats: The Four Horsemen of the Apocalypse.* Waco, TX: Word, 1983.

Gray, John. *The Biblical Doctrine of the Reign of God.* Edinburgh: T. & T. Clark, 1979.

Green, Joel. *How to Read Prophecy.* Downers Grove, IL: InterVarsity, 1984.

Greenberg, Moshe. "The Design and Themes of Ezekiel's Program of Restoration." *Int* 38 (1984) 181–208.

Greenham, Ant(hony). "A Study of Palestinian Muslim Conversions to Christ." *St. Francis Magazine* 6 (2010) 116–75.

Greeson, Kevin. *The Camel.* Arkadelphia, AR: WIGTake Resources, 2007.

Gregg, Steve, ed. *Revelation: Four Views: A Parallel Commentary.* Nashville, TN: Thomas Nelson, 1997.

Grenz, Stanley. *The Millennial Maze.* Downers Grove, IL: InterVarsity, 1992.

Grosheide, F. W. *Commentary on the First Epistle to the Corinthians* (NICNT). Grand Rapids: Eerdmans, 1953.

Grudem, Wayne. *Systematic Theology.* Leicester, England: Inter-Varsity, 1994.

Gundry, Robert. *Matthew,* 2nd ed. Grand Rapids: Eerdmans, 1994.

———. "The New Jerusalem: People as Place, Not Place for People." *NovT* 29 (1987) 254–64.

Guth, James, et al. "Faith and the Environment: Religious Belief and Attitudes on Environmental Policy." *American Journal of Political Science* 39 (1995) 364–82. Online: http://spot.colorado.edu/~bairdv/Green_Guth.pdf.

Guthrie, George. "Hebrews." In *Commentary on the New Testament Use of the Old Testament,* edited by G. K. Beale and D. A. Carson, 919–95. Grand Rapids: Baker Academic, 2007.

Hagner, Donald. *Matthew 14–28* (WBC 33B). Dallas, TX: Word, 1995.

Hamstra, Sam. "An Idealist View of Revelation." In *Four Views on the Book of Revelation,* 95–131. Grand Rapids: Zondervan, 1998. Online: https://books.google.com/books?isbn=0310872391.

Harink, Douglas. *1 & 2 Peter.* Grand Rapids: Brazos, 2009.

Harper, Larry. *The AntiChrist,* 2nd ed. Mesquite, TX: The Elijah Project, 2003.

Hartman, Louis, and Alexander Dilella. *The Book of Daniel* (AB). New York: Doubleday, 1977.

Harvey, Paul. "'Yankee Faith' and Southern Redemption: White Southern Baptist Ministers, 1850–1890." In *Religion and the American Civil War,* edited by Randall Miller et al., 167–86. New York: Oxford University Press, 1998.

Harvey, Robert, and Philip Towner. *2 Peter & Jude* (IVPNTC). Downers Grove, IL: InterVarsity, 2009.

Hasel, Gerhard. "Crossroads in Prophetic Interpretation: Historicism versus Futurism." Paper presented at the 1990 World Ministers Council, Indianapolis, Indiana on July 3, 1990. Online: http://www.scribd.com/doc/59053975/Crossroads-in-Prophetic-Interpretation.

Haydock, George. *Catholic Bible Commentary.* 1859. Online: http://haydock1859.tripod.com/.

Heil, John. "The Fifth Seal (Rev 6.9–11) as a Key to the Book of Revelation." *Biblica* 74 (1993) 220–43.

Hendriksen, William. *Exposition of the Gospel According to Matthew* (NTC). Grand Rapids: Baker, 1973.

———. *More Than Conquerors.* Grand Rapids, Baker, 1962. Reprint, Grand Rapids: Baker, 1982.

Henry, Matthew. *Matthew Henry's Commentary on the Whole Bible.* Peabody, Mass.: Hendrickson, 1991. Online: http://www.biblestudytools.com/commentaries/matthew-henry-complete/.

Héring, Jean. *The First Epistle of St. Paul to the Corinthians.* Translated by A. W. Heathcote and P. J. Allcock. London: Epworth, 1962.

Herrmann, John, and Annewies van den Hoek. "Apocalyptic Themes in the Monumental and Minor Art of Early Christianity." In *Apocalyptic Thought in Early Christianity,* edited by Robert Daly, 33–80. Grand Rapids: Baker Academic, 2009.

Hiebert, D. Edmund. "Evidence from 1 Corinthians 15." In *A Case for Premillennialism,* edited by Donald K. Campbell and Jeffrey L. Townsend, 225–34. Chicago: Moody, 1992.

———. *The Thessalonian Epistles: A Call to Readiness.* Chicago: Moody, 1971.

Higgins, A. J. B. "The Sign of the Son of Man (Matt. XXIV. 30)." *NTS* 9 (1962–63) 380–82.

Higgins, John. *The Manasseh Effect: Your Appointment With Destiny.* Phoenix, AZ: Josiah Publications, 1995.

Higginson, R. E. "Zechariah." In *The New Bible Commentary,* 3rd ed., edited by D. Guthrie et al., 786–803. Carmel, NY: Guideposts, 1970.

Hill, Andrew. "Daniel." In *The Expositor's Bible Commentary,* vol. 8, rev. ed., edited by Tremper Longman III and David Garland, 19–212. Grand Rapids: Zondervan, 2008.

Hill, C. E. "Paul's Understanding of Christ's Kingdom in I Corinthians 15:20–28." *NovT* 30 (1988) 297–320.

Hill, Charles. *Regnum Caelorum: Patterns of Millennial Thought in Early Christianity,* 2nd ed. Grand Rapids: Eerdmans, 2001.

Hillyer, Norman. "First Peter and the Feast of Tabernacles," *TynBul* 21 (1970) 39–70. Online: http://www.tyndalehouse.com/tynbul/library/TynBull_1970_21_02_Hillyer_1PeterFeastTabernacles.pdf.

Hodge, Charles. *Systematic Theology.* 3 vols. New York: Charles Scribner & Co., 1871–1872. Reprint, Grand Rapids: Eerdmans, 1986. Online: http://www.ccel.org/ccel/hodge?show=worksBy.

Hoehner, Harold. "Chronological Aspects of the Life of Christ—Part IV: Daniel's Seventy Weeks and New Testament Chronology." *BSac* 132 (1975) 47–65.

———. *Chronological Aspects of the Life of Christ.* Grand Rapids: Zondervan, 1977.

Hoekema, Anthony. "Amillennialism." In *The Meaning of the Millennium: Four Views,* ed. Robert Clouse, 155–87. Downers Grove, IL: InterVarsity, 1977.

———. *The Bible and the Future.* Grand Rapids: Eerdmans, 1979.

Hoeksema, Herman. "The Millennium Period." 2000. No pages. Online: http://www.prca.org/pamphlets/pamphlet_5.html.

Holleman, Joost. *Resurrection and Parousia: A Traditio-Historical Study of Paul's Eschatology in 1 Corinthians 15.* Leiden: Brill, 1996.

Holmes, Michael. *1 and 2 Thessalonians* (NIVAC). Grand Rapids: Zondervan, 1998.

Holmes, Michael, ed. *The Apostolic Fathers,* 2nd ed. Translated by J. B. Lightfoot and J. R. Harmer. Grand Rapids: Baker, 1989.

Holwerda, David. "Eschatology and History: A Look at Calvin's Eschatological Vision." In *Readings in Calvin's Theology,* edited by Donald Kim, 311–42. Grand Rapids: Baker, 1984.

———. *Jesus and Israel: One Covenant or Two?* Grand Rapids: Eerdmans, 1995.

Hooker, Morna. *The Son of Man in Mark.* Montreal: McGill University Press, 1967.

Horne, Charles. "The Meaning of the Phrase 'And Thus All Israel Will Be Saved' (Romans 11:26)." *JETS* 21 (1978) 329–34. Online: http://www.etsjets.org/files/JETS-PDFs/21/21-4/21-4-pp329-334_JETS.pdf.

House, H. Wayne. *Charts of Christian Theology & Doctrine.* Grand Rapids: Zondervan, 1992.

Houssney, Georges. *Engaging Islam.* Boulder, CO: Treeline, 2010.

Hoyt, Herman. "Dispensational Premillennialism." In *The Meaning of the Millennium: Four Views,* ed. Robert Clouse, 63–92. Downers Grove, IL: InterVarsity, 1977.

Hughes, Philip Edgcumbe. *A Commentary on the Epistle to the Hebrews.* Grand Rapids: Eerdmans, 1977.

———. "The First Resurrection: Another Interpretation." *WTJ* 39 (1977) 315–18.

Hunt, Dave. *A Woman Rides the Beast.* Eugene, OR: Harvest House, 1994.

Ice, Thomas. "The Great Tribulation is Future: The New Testament." In *The Great Tribulation: Past or Future? Two Evangelicals Debate the Question,* 93–119. Grand Rapids: Kregel, 1999.

———. "The Great Tribulation is Future: The Old Testament." In *The Great Tribulation: Past or Future? Two Evangelicals Debate the Question,* 69–92. Grand Rapids: Kregel, 1999.

———. "The Great Tribulation is Past: Rebuttal." In *The Great Tribulation: Past or Future? Two Evangelicals Debate the Question,* 123–63. Grand Rapids: Kregel, 1999.

———. "Why the Rapture and Second Coming are Distinct Events," 1–4. Washington, DC: Pre-Trib Research Center, 1994.

Ice, Thomas, and Kenneth Gentry. *The Great Tribulation: Past or Future? Two Evangelicals Debate the Question.* Grand Rapids: Kregel, 1999.

Irons, Lee. "Paul's Theology of Israel's Future: A Non-Millennial Interpretation of Romans 11." *Reformation & Revival* 6 (1997) 101–26. Online: https://biblicalstudies.org.uk/pdf/ref-rev/06-2/6-2_irons.pdf.

———. "Prophetic Idiom." Audio mp3. Not dated. Online: http://www.upper-register.com/mp3/TUM/55_TUM_Prophets.mp3.

Ironside, Harry. *The Great Parenthesis.* Grand Rapids: Zondervan, 1943. Online: http://bartimaeus.us/pub_dom/the_great_parenthesis.html.

Jackson, Wayne. "Daniel's Prophecy of the 'Seventy Weeks.'" 1–14. Montgomery, AL: Apologetics Press, Not dated. Online: http://espanol.apologeticspress.org/rr/reprints/Daniels-70-Weeks.pdf.

———. "Dispensationalism and Zechariah 14." 1999. No pages. Online: http://www.christiancourier.com/articles/120-dispensationalism-and-zechariah-14.

———. "Examining Premillennialism." 2001. No pages. Online: http://www.christiancourier.com/articles/322-examining-premillennialism.

———. "The Menace of Radical Preterism." 1999. No pages. Online: http://www.christiancourier.com/articles/91-the-menace-of-radical-preterism.

———. "A Study of Matthew Twenty-Four." 1998. No pages. Online: http://www.christiancourier.com/articles/19-a-study-of-matthew-24.

Jenkins, Philip. "Chilembwe's rising." *Christian Century* (February 18, 2015) 45.

Jeremias, Joachim. "'Flesh and Blood Cannot Inherit the Kingdom of God' (1 Cor. XV. 50)." *NTS* 2 (1956)151–59.

Johnson, Alan. "Revelation." In *The Expositor's Bible Commentary,* vol. 12, edited by Frank Gaebelein, 399–603. Grand Rapids: Zondervan, 1981.

Johnson, Dennis. *Him We Proclaim: Preaching Christ from All the Scriptures.* Phillipsburg, NJ: P&R, 2007.

———. *Triumph of the Lamb: A Commentary on Revelation.* Phillipsburg, NJ: P&R, 2001.

Jordan, James. *The Law of the Covenant.* Tyler, TX: Institute for Christian Economics, 1984. Online: http://www.garynorth.com/freebooks/docs/pdf/the_law_of_the_covenant.pdf.

Keener, Craig. *1–2 Corinthians* (NCBC). Cambridge: Cambridge University Press, 2005.

Keller, Timothy. *The Reason for God.* New York: Dutton, 2008.

Kennedy, H. A. A. *St. Paul's Conceptions of the Last Things.* London: Hodder and Stoughton, 1904.

Kerkeslager, Allen. "The Day of the Lord, the 'Hour' in the Book of Revelation, and Rev 3:10." Unpublished paper presented at the annual national meeting for the Society of Biblical Literature, Kansas City, Missouri, November 23–26, 1991.

Kevan, E. F. "The Covenants and the Interpretation of the Old Testament." *EvQ* 26 (1954) 19–28. Online: https://biblicalstudies.org.uk/pdf/eq/1954-1_kevan.pdf.

Kiddle, Martin. *The Revelation of St. John* (MNTC). London: Harper and Bros., 1940.

Kik, J. Marcellus. *An Eschatology of Victory.* Phillipsburg, NJ: Presbyterian and Reformed, 1971.

King, Max. "And So All Israel Will Be Saved." 2005. No pages. Online: http://livingthequestion.org/did-paul -mean-all-israel-will-be-saved-rom/.

———. *The Cross and the Parousia of Christ.* Warren, OH: M. R. King, 1987. Online: https://www. preteristarchive.com/Hyper/1987_king_cross-parousia.html.

Kistemaker, Simon. *Exposition of the First Epistle to the Corinthians* (NTC). Grand Rapids: Baker, 1993.

———. "The Temple in the Apocalypse." *JETS* 43 (2000) 433–41. Online: http://www.etsjets.org/files/ JETS-PDFs/43/43-3/43-3-pp433-441_JETS.pdf.

Klassen, Ken. "A Reexamination of the Nature of the First Resurrection of Revelation 20:4–6 in Light of the Eschatology of the Ante-Nicene Fathers." Master's thesis, Briercrest Biblical Seminary, 1995. Theological Research Exchange Network No. 047–0009 (www.tren.com).

Klein, George. *Zechariah* (NAC 21B). Nashville: B&H, 2008.

Kline, Meredith. "The Covenant of the Seventieth Week." In *The Law and the Prophets,* ed. John Skilton, 452–69. Nutley, NJ: Presbyterian and Reformed, 1974. Online: http://www.meredithkline.com/ klines-works/articles-and-essays/the-covenant-of-the-seventieth-week/.

———. "Double Trouble." *JETS* 32 (1989) 171–79. Online: http://www.etsjets.org/files/JETS-PDFs/32/32- 2/32-2-pp171-179_JETS.pdf.

———. "The First Resurrection." *WTJ* 37 (1975) 366–75. Online: http://www.meredithkline.com/klines- works/articles-and-essays/the-first-resurrection/.

———. "The First Resurrection: A Reaffirmation." *WTJ* 39 (1976) 110–19. Online: http://www. meredithkline.com/klines-works/articles-and-essays/the-first-resurrection-a-reaffirmation/.

———. "Har Magedon: The End of the Millenium." *JETS* 39 (1996) 207–22. Online: http://www.etsjets. org/files/JETS-PDFs/39/39-2/39-2-pp207-222_JETS.pdf.

Knowles, Louis. "The Interpretation of the Seventy Weeks of Daniel in the Early Fathers." *WTJ* 7 (1945) 136–60.

Koopmans, William. "*Brq.*" In *NIDOTTE,* vol. 1, edited by Willem VanGemeren, 769–70. Grand Rapids: Zondervan, 1997.

Korner, Ralph. "'And I Saw . . .' An Apocalyptic Literary Convention for Structural Identification in the Apocalypse." *NovT* 42 (2000) 160–83.

Kostenberger, Andreas. "John." In *Commentary on the New Testament Use of the Old Testament,* edited by G. K. Beale and D. A. Carson, 415–512. Grand Rapids: Baker Academic, 2007.

Kraftchick, Steven. *Jude, 2 Peter* (ANTC). Nashville: Abingdon, 2002.

Kromminga, D. H. *The Millennium in the Church: Studies in the History of Christian Chiliasm.* Grand Rapids: Eerdmans, 1945.

Ladd, George Eldon. "Apocalyptic and New Testament Theology." In *Reconciliation and Hope. New Testament Essays on Atonement and Eschatology Presented to L.L. Morris on his 60th Birthday,* edited by Robert Banks, 285–96. Carlisle, PA: Paternoster, 1974. Online: http://www.biblicalstudies.org.uk/ pdf/rh/apocalyptic_ladd.pdf.

———. *The Blessed Hope.* Grand Rapids: Eerdmans, 1956.

———. *A Commentary on the Revelation of John.* Grand Rapids: Eerdmans, 1972.

———. *The Gospel of the Kingdom.* Grand Rapids: Eerdmans, 1959.

———. "Historic Premillennialism." In *The Meaning of the Millennium: Four Views,* edited by Robert Clouse, 17–40. Downers Grove, IL: InterVarsity, 1977.

———. *The Last Things.* Grand Rapids: Eerdmans, 1978.

———. "Revelation 20 and the Millennium." *RevExp* 57 (1960) 167–75.

———. "The Revelation of Christ's Glory." *Christianity Today* (September 1958) 13–14.

———. A Theology of the New Testament, rev. ed. Grand Rapids: Eerdmans, 1974.

Lambrecht, Jan. "Paul's Christological Use of Scripture in 1 Cor. 15.20–28." *NTS* 28 (1981) 502–27.

Lane, William. *The Gospel According to Mark* (NICNT). Grand Rapids: Eerdmans, 1974.

———. *Hebrews 9–13* (WBC 47B). Nashville: Thomas Nelson, 1991.

LaRondelle, Hans. *The Israel of God in Prophecy: Principles of Prophetic Interpretation.* Berrien Springs, MI: Andrews University Press, 1983.

Lausanne Covenant. 1974. No pages. Online: http://www.lausanne.org/covenant.

Lehrer, Steve. *New Covenant Theology: Questions Answered*. Steve Lehrer, 2006. Online: http://www. redmoonrising.com/newexodus/nctbook.pdf.

Leinenweber, John. *Love One Another, My Friends: St. Augustine's Homilies on the First Letter of John*. San Francisco: Harper & Row, 1989.

Lenski, R. C. H. *The Interpretation of St. Paul's Epistle to the Romans*. Columbus, OH: Wartburg, 1945. Reprint, Minneapolis: Augsburg, 1963.

———. *The Interpretation of St. Paul's First and Second Epistles to the Corinthians*. Minneapolis: Augsburg, 1937. Reprint 1963.

Leupold, H. C. *Exposition of Daniel*. Columbus, OH: Wartburg, 1949. Reprint, Grand Rapids, MI: Baker, 1969.

Levenson, Jon. *Creation and the Persistence of Evil*. San Francisco: Harper & Row, 1988.

Lewis, Arthur. *The Dark Side of the Millennium: The Problem of Evil in Rev. 20:1–10*. Grand Rapids: Baker, 1980.

Lewis, C. S. "Introduction." In *On the Incarnation*, rev. ed., by St. Athanasius, 3–10. Translated by Penelope Lawson. Crestwood, NY: St. Vladimir's Seminary Press, 1996. Online: http://www.romans45.org/history/ath-inc.htm.

———. *The Weight of Glory*, rev. ed. New York: Macmillan, 1949. Reprint, New York: Macmillan, 1980.

Lewis, Charlton, and Charles Short. *Harpers' Latin Dictionary*, rev. ed. New York: American Book Company, 1907.

Lincoln, Abraham. *Speeches and Writings, 1832–1858*. New York: The Library of America, 1989.

Lincoln, Andrew. *Paradise Now and Not Yet*. Grand Rapids: Baker, 1981.

———. "Sabbath, Rest, and Eschatology in the New Testament." In *From Sabbath to Lord's Day: A Biblical, Historical and Theological Investigation*, edited by D. A. Carson, 197–220. Grand Rapids: Zondervan, 1982.

Lindsey, Hal. *The Late Great Planet Earth*. Grand Rapids: Zondervan, 1970.

Longenecker, Richard. *Galatians* (WBC 41). Nashville, TN: Thomas Nelson, 1990.

Longman III, Tremper, and Daniel Reid. *God is a Warrior*. Grand Rapids: Zondervan, 1995.

Lovelace, Richard. *Dynamics of Spiritual Life*. Downers Grove, IL: InterVarsity, 1980.

Lucas, Ernest. *Daniel* (AOTC 20). Leicester, England: Apollos, 2002.

Luter, A. Boyd, and Emily Hunter. "The 'Earth Dwellers' and the 'Heaven Dwellers': An Overlooked Interpretive Key to the Apocalypse." *Faith & Mission* 20 (2003) 3–18. Online: http: //digitalcommons.liberty.edu/cgi/viewcontent.cgi?article=1285&context=lts_fac_pubs&sei -redir=1&referer=http%3A%2F%2Fwww.google.com%2Furl%3Fsa%3Dt%26rct%3Dj%26q%3Dlu ter%2520%2522earth%2520dwellers%2522%26source%3Dweb%26cd%3D1%26ved%3D0CB8QF jAA%26url%3Dhttp%253A%252F%252Fdigitalcommons.liberty.edu%252Fcgi%252Fviewcontent .cgi%253Farticle%253D1285%2526context%253Dlts_fac_pubs%26ei%3DAwlnUJGlIqmaoQG3r4 HICg%26usg%3DAFQjCNEsbnwnxuloaM41yu7cOJTqZY7HYg#search=%22luter%20earth%20 dwellers%22.

Luther, Martin. *Three Treatises*, rev. ed. Philadelphia: Muhlenberg, 1947. Reprint, Philadelphia: Fortress, 1970.

MacDonald, William. *Believer's Bible Commentary*, edited by Art Farstad. Nashville: Thomas Nelson, 1995.

Marshall, I. Howard. "Acts." In *Commentary on the New Testament Use of the Old Testament*, edited by G. K. Beale and D. A. Carson, 513–606. Grand Rapids, MI: Baker Academic, 2007.

Mathison, Keith. *Postmillennialism: An Eschatology of Hope*. Phillipsburg, NJ: P&R, 1999.

Mattill, A. J. "The Way of Tribulation." *JBL* 98 (1979): 531–46.

Mauro, Philip. *The Seventy Weeks and the Great Tribulation*, rev. ed. Swengel, PA: I. C. Herendeen, 1944. Abridgment online: http://www.bullartistry.com.au/pdf_lastdays/CompleteBooks/SeventyWeeks-Mauro.pdf.

Mayer, Jeremy. "Christian Fundamentalists and Public Opinion Toward the Middle East: Israel's New Best Friends?" *Social Science Quarterly* 85 (2004) 695–712.

McCartney, Dan. "*Ecce Homo*: The Coming of the Kingdom as the Restoration of Human Vicegerency." *WTJ* 56 (1994) 1–21. Online: http://files.wts.edu/uploads/pdf/articles/mccartney-vicegerency.pdf.

McClain, Alva. *Daniel's Prophecy of the Seventy Weeks*. Grand Rapids: Zondervan, 1969.

McComiskey, Thomas. "The Seventy 'Weeks' of Daniel Against the Background of Ancient Near Eastern Literature." *WTJ* 47 (1985) 18–45.

———. "Zechariah." In *The Minor Prophets: An Exegetical and Expository Commentary,* vol. 3, edited by Thomas McComiskey, 1003–1244. Grand Rapids: Baker, 1998.

McDurmon, Joel. *Jesus v. Jerusalem.* Powder Springs, GA: American Vision, 2011.

McGee, J. Vernon. *Reasoning Through Romans—Part II (Chapters 9–16).* Pasadena, CA: Thru the Bible Books, 1981.

McGinn, Bernard. *Anti-Christ: Two Thousand Years of the Human Fascination with Evil.* New York: HarperSanFrancisco, 1994.

———. *Visions of the End: Apocalyptic Traditions in the Middle Ages.* New York: Columbia University Press, 1979.

McKnight, Scot. *Galatians* (NIVAC). Grand Rapids: Zondervan, 1995.

Mealy, J. Webb. *After the Thousand Years: Resurrection and Judgment in Revelation 20.* Sheffield: Sheffield Academic Press, 1992.

———. *The End of the Unrepentant.* Eugene, OR: Wipf & Stock, 2013.

———. *New Creation Millennialism.* 2017. [unpublished draft].

———. "Revelation is One: Revelation 20 and the Quest to Make the Scriptures Agree." In *Reconsidering the Relationship between Systematic and Biblical Theology in the New Testament,* edited by Benjamin Reynolds, Brian Lugioyo, and Kevin Vanhoozer, 131–53. Tübingen: Mohr Siebeck, 2014. Online: http://www.academia.edu/21465652/Revelation_is_One_Revelation_20_and_the_Quest_to_Make_the_Scriptures_Agree.

Menn, Jonathan. *Biblical Interpretation.* 2017. Online: http://www.eclea.net/courses.html#interpretation.

———. *Biblical Theology.* 2016. Online: http://www.eclea.net/courses.html#theology.

———. *Sermon Series: Revelation.* Not dated. Online: http://www.eclea.net/sermons.html#revelation.

Merkle, Ben. "Romans 11 and the Future of Ethnic Israel." *JETS* 43 (2000) 701–21. Online: http://www.etsjets.org/files/JETS-PDFs/43/43-4/43-4-pp709-721_JETS.pdf.

Metzger, Bruce. *An Introduction to the Apocrypha.* New York: Oxford, 1957.

Michaels, J. Ramsay. *1 Peter* (WBC 49). Nashville: Thomas Nelson, 1988.

Milligan, William. *The Book of Revelation.* New York: Armstrong, 1896. Online: https://books.google.com/books?id=98DYAAAAMAAJ.

———. *Discussions on the Apocalypse.* London: Macmillan, 1893. Preview online: https://books.google.com/books?isbn=155635763X.

Moo, Douglas. "The Case for the Posttribulation Rapture Position." In *The Rapture: Pre-, Mid-, or Post-Tribulational?* 171–211. Grand Rapids: Academie, 1984.

———. *The Epistle to the Romans* (NICNT). Grand Rapids: Eerdmans, 1996.

Moo, Jonathan. "The Sea that is No More: Rev 21:1 and the Function of Sea Imagery in the Apocalypse of John." *NovT* 51 (2009) 148–67.

Moore, A. L. *The Parousia in the New Testament* (NTSup 13). Leiden: Brill, 1966.

Morris, Leon. *The Epistle to the Romans.* Grand Rapids: Eerdmans, 1988.

———. *Revelation* (TNTC), 2nd ed. Grand Rapids: Eerdmans, 1987.

Mounce, Robert. *The Book of Revelation* (NICNT), rev. ed. Grand Rapids: Eerdmans, 1998.

———. *Matthew* (NIBC). Peabody, MA: Hendrickson, 1985.

Mueller, Ekkehardt. "Recapitulation in Revelation 4–11." Not dated. No pages. Online: http://adventistbiblicalresearch.org/sites/default/files/pdf/rev4-11.pdf.

Murray, John. *The Epistle to the Romans* (NICNT). Grand Rapids: Eerdmans, 1968.

———. "The Interadventual Period and the Advent: Matthew 24 and 25." In *Collected Works,* vol. 2, 387–400. Edinburgh: Banner of Truth, 1977.

Nanos, Mark. *The Mystery of Romans.* Minneapolis: Fortress, 1996.

Nelson, Neil. "'This Generation in Matt 24:34: A Literary Critical Perspective." *JETS* 38 (1996) 369–85. Online: http://www.etsjets.org/files/JETS-PDFs/38/38-3/JETS_38-3_Nelson_369-386.pdf.

Ngundu, Onesimus. "Revelation." In *Africa Bible Commentary,* edited by Tokunboh Adeyemo, 2006, 1543–79. Nairobi: WordAlive.

Nigro, H. L. *Before God's Wrath,* rev. ed. Bellefonte, PA: Strong Tower, 2004.

Nixon, R. E. "Matthew." In *The New Bible Commentary,* 3rd ed., edited by D. Guthrie et al., 813–50. Carmel, NY: Guideposts, 1970.

Noe, John. "An Exegetical Basis for a Preterist-Idealist Understanding of the Book of Revelation." *JETS* 49 (2006) 767–96. Online: http://www.etsjets.org/files/JETS-PDFs/49/49-4/JETS_49-4_767-796_Noe.pdf.

Nolland, John. *The Gospel of Matthew* (NIGTC). Grand Rapids: Eerdmans, 2005.

———. *Luke 18:35–24:53* (WBC 35C). Dallas, TX: Word, 1993.

O'Brien, Peter. *The Letter to the Ephesians* (PNTC). Grand Rapids: Eerdmans, 1999.

———. *The Letter to the Hebrews* (PNTC). Grand Rapids: Eerdmans, 2010.

Oepke, Albrecht. "*Parousia, Pareimi.*" In *TDNT* 5:858–71.

Olshausen, Hermann. *Commentary on the Gospels and Acts.* 4 volumes. Edinburgh: T. & T. Clark, 1850. Online: https://catalog.hathitrust.org/Record/008925520.

Oropeza, B. J. *99 Reasons Why No One Knows When Christ Will Return.* Downers Grove, IL: InterVarsity, 1994.

Ortlund, Raymond. *God's Unfaithful Wife: A Biblical Theology of Spiritual Adultery* (NSBT 2). Downers Grove, IL: InterVarsity, 1996.

Osborne, Grant. *The Hermeneutical Spiral.* Downers Grove, IL: InterVarsity, 1991.

———. *Revelation* (BECNT). Grand Rapids: Baker Academic, 2002.

Otto, Randall. "Jesus the Preterist: a review of R. C. Sproul's The Last Days According to Jesus." *Quodlibet Journal* 1 (1999) no pages. Online: https://www.preteristarchive.com/1999_otto_jesus-the-preterist-a-review-of-r-c-sprouls-the-last-days-according-to-jesus/.

Owen, John. *Indwelling Sin in Believers.* Philadelphia: Presbyterian Board of Publication, 1842. Reprint, Grand Rapids: Baker, 1979.

Ozment, Steven. *Protestants: The Birth of a Revolution.* New York: Doubleday, 1992.

Pache, Rene. *The Return of Jesus Christ.* Translated by William Sanford LaSor. Chicago: Moody, 1955.

Page, Sydney. "Revelation 20 and Pauline Eschatology." *JETS* 23 (1980) 31–43. Online http://www.etsjets.org/files/JETS-PDFs/23/23-1/23-1-pp031-043_JETS.pdf.

Pao, David, and Eckhard Schnabel. "Luke." In *Commentary on the New Testament Use of the Old Testament,* edited by G. K. Beale and D. A. Carson, 251–414. Grand Rapids: Baker Academic, 2007.

Pate, C. Marvin. *The End of the Ages Has Come.* Grand Rapids: Zondervan, 1995.

———. "Introduction to Revelation." In *Four Views on the Book of Revelation,* 9–34. Grand Rapids: Zondervan, 1998. Online: https://books.google.com/books?isbn=0310872391.

———. "A Progressive Dispensationalist View of Revelation." In *Four Views on the Book of Revelation,* 135–75. Grand Rapids: Zondervan, 1998. Online: https://books.google.com/books?isbn=0310872391.

———. *Reading Revelation: A Comparison of Four Interpretive Translations of the Apocalypse.* Grand Rapids: Kregel, 2009.

———. "Revelation 6: An Early Interpretation of the Olivet Discourse." *CTR* 8 (2011) 45–55.

Pate, C. Marvin, and Calvin Haines. *Doomsday Delusions: What's Wrong with Predictions About the End of the World.* Downers Grove, IL: InterVarsity, 1995.

Pate, C. Marvin, et al. *Four Views on the Book of Revelation.* Grand Rapids: Zondervan, 1998. Online: https://books.google.com/books?isbn=0310872391.

Paulien, Jon. "The Role of the Hebrew Cultus, Sanctuary, and Temple in the Plot and Structure of the Book of Revelation." *AUSS* 33 (1995) 245–64. Online: http://www.bibelschule.info/streaming/Jon-Paulien—-The-Role-of-the-Hebrew-Cultus,-Sanctuary,-and-Temple-in-the-Plot-and-Structure-of-the-Book-of-Revelation_24036.pdf.

Payne, J. Barton. *Encyclopedia of Biblical Prophecy.* New York: Harper & Row, 1973. Reprint, Grand Rapids: Baker, 1980.

———. The Goal of Daniel's Seventy Weeks." *JETS* 21 (1978) 97–115. Online: http://www.etsjets.org/files/JETS-PDFs/21/21-2/21-2-pp097-115_JETS.pdf.

———. "The Goal of Daniel's Seventy Weeks: Interpretation By Context." *Covenant Seminary Review* 4 (1978) 33–38.

Pentecost, J. Dwight. "Daniel." In *Bible Knowledge Commentary: Old Testament,* edited by John Walvoord and Roy Zuck, 1323–75. Wheaton, IL: Victor, 1985.

———. *Things to Come: A Study in Biblical Eschatology.* Grand Rapids: Academie, 1958.

Peterson, David. *The Acts of the Apostles* (PNTC). Grand Rapids: Eerdmans, 2009.

———. "The Prophecy of the New Covenant in the Argument of Hebrews." *RTR* 38 (1979) 74–81.

Peterson, Robert. *Hell on Trial: The Case for Eternal Punishment.* Phillipsburg, NJ: P&R, 1995.

Phillips, John. *Exploring Revelation,* rev. ed. Chicago: Moody, 1987.

Pickle, Bob. "Daniel 9's Seventy Weeks and the Sabbatical Cycle: When Were the Sabbatical Years?" 2006. No pages. Online: http://www.pickle-publishing.com/papers/sabbatical-years.htm.

———. "An Examination of Anderson's Chronological Errors: Regarding Daniel 9's First 69 Weeks." 2006. No pages. Online: http://www.pickle-publishing.com/papers/sir-robert-anderson.htm.

———. "An Examination of the Chronological Difficulties of Hoehner and Ice's Calculations of Daniel 9's First 69 Weeks." 2006. No pages. Online: http://www.pickle-publishing.com/papers/harold-hoehner-70-weeks.htm.

———. "Ezekiel's City: Calculating the Circumference of the Earth." 2004. Online: http://www.pickle-publishing.com/papers/ezekiels-city-circumference-of-the-earth.htm.

Plevnik, Joseph. *Paul and the Parousia: An Exegetical and Theological Investigation.* Peabody, MA: Hendrickson, 1997.

Plummer, Alfred. *A Critical and Exegetical Commentary on the Gospel According to St. Luke* (ICC), 5th ed. Edinburgh: T&T Clark, 1922. Reprint, Edinburgh: T&T Clark, 1942.

Porter, Stanley. *Idioms of the Greek New Testament,* 2nd ed. Sheffield, England: Sheffield Academic Press, 1999.

Poythress, Vern. "Genre and Hermeneutics in Rev 20:1–6," *JETS* 36 (1993) 41–54. Online: http://www.etsjets.org/files/JETS-PDFs/36/36-1/JETS_36-1_041-054_Poythress.pdf.

———. *The Shadow of Christ in the Law of Moses.* Brentwood, TN: Wolgemuth & Hyatt, 1991.

Preston, Don. *AD 70: A Shadow of the "Real" End?* Ardmore, OK: JaDon Management, 2013.

———. *Like Father, Like Son, On Clouds of Glory,* 2nd ed. Ardmore, OK: JaDon Management, 2010.

Ramm, Bernard. *Protestant Biblical Interpretation,* 3rd rev. ed. Grand Rapids: Baker, 1970. Online: http://www.glasovipisma.pbf.rs/phocadownload/knjige/bernard%20ramm%20protestant%20biblical%20interpretation.pdf.

Ramsay, William. "Triumphus." In *A Dictionary of Greek and Roman Antiquities,* edited by William Smith, 1163–67. London: John Murray, 1875. Online: http://penelope.uchicago.edu/Thayer/E/Roma/Texts/secondary/SMIGRA*/Triumphus.html.

Reader, W. "The Riddle of the Identification of the Polis in Rev. 11:1–13." In *Studia Evangelica,* vol. VII, edited by Elizabeth Livingstone, 407–14. Berlin: Akademie-Verlag, 1982.

Resseguie, James. *The Revelation of John: A Narrative Commentary.* Grand Rapids: Baker Academic, 2009.

Rickard, Ed. "The Sixty-Nine Weeks of Daniel, Lesson 1: Event Starting the Clock." 2007. No pages. Online: http://archive.is/5FHm.

Ridderbos, Herman. *Paul: An Outline of His Theology.* Translated by John DeWitt. Grand Rapids: Eerdmans, 1975.

Riddlebarger, Kim. "The Antichrist." *Modern Reformation* 3, no. 3 (1994): 4–6. Online: https://www.whitehorseinn.org/article/the-antichrist/.

———. *A Case for Amillennialism.* Grand Rapids: Baker, 2003.

———. *Sermon Series on the Book of Revelation.* 2001–2002. Online: http://www.christreformed.org/kim-riddlebarger/#Revelation (audio mp3); http://kimriddlebarger.squarespace.com/downloadable-sermons-on-the-bo/ (written transcripts).

Rissi, Mathias. *Time and History: A Study of Revelation.* Translated by Gordon Winsor. Richmond, VA: John Knox, 1966.

Rist, Martin, and Lynn Harold Hough. "The Revelation of St. John the Divine." In *The Interpreter's Bible,* vol. 12, edited by George Buttrick, 345–613. New York: Abingdon, 1957.

Robertson, O. Palmer. *The Israel of God.* Phillipsburg, NJ: P&R, 2000.

"Rome." *Wikipedia.* 2012. No pages. Online: http://en.wikipedia.org/wiki/Rome.

Rosenthal, Marvin. *The Pre-Wrath Rapture of the Church.* Nashville, TN: Thomas Nelson, 1990.

Rowden, Harold. "The Brethren." In *Introduction to the History of Christianity,* edited by Tim Dowley, 526–27. Minneapolis: Fortress, 2002.

Rushdoony, R. J. *Thy Kingdom Come.* Vallecito, CA: Ross House, 1970.

Russell, J. Stewart. *The Parousia: The New Testament Doctrine of Our Lord's Second Coming.* London: London: Daldy, Isbister & Co., 1878. Online: https://books.google.com/books?id=oPgUAAAAYAAJ.

Russell, John. *Daniel.* Edinburgh: Saint Andrew, 1981.

Ryle, J. C. *Expository Thoughts on Matthew.* London: Hodder and Stoughton, 1900. Reprint, Edinburgh: Banner of Truth, 1995. Online (another edition): https://www.ccel.org/ccel/ryle/matthew.i.html.

Ryrie, Charles. *Dispensationalism Today.* Chicago: Moody, 1965.

———. *The Holy Spirit.* Chicago: Moody, 1965.

———. *The Holy Spirit,* rev. ed. Chicago: Moody, 1997.

Sasse, Hermann. "*Aiōn, Aiōnios.*" In *TDNT* 1:197–209.

Savoy Declaration of Faith and Order. 1658. No pages. Online: http://www.reformed.org/master/index
.html?mainframe=/documents/Savoy_Declaration/index.html.

Schaeffer, Francis. *Escape From Reason.* In *The Complete Works of Francis Schaeffer,* vol. 1, 205–70.
Westchester, IL: Crossway, 1982.

———. *How Then Shall We Live?* In *The Complete Works of Francis Schaeffer,* vol. 5, 79–277. Westchester,
IL: Crossway, 1982.

———. *Pollution and the Death of Man.* In *The Complete Works of Francis Schaeffer,* vol. 5, 1–76.
Westchester, IL: Crossway, 1982.

Schaff, Philip. *The Creeds of Christendom, With a History and Critical Notes,* 6th ed. 3 vols. New York:
Harper & Row, 1931. Reprint, Grand Rapids: Baker, 1990. Online: http://www.ccel.org/ccel/schaff/
creeds1.html.

———. *History of the Christian Church.* 10 vols. Grand Rapids: Eerdmans, 1910. Online: http://www.ccel
.org/ccel/schaff/hcc1.

Schaff, Philip, ed., *Nicene and Post-Nicene Fathers,* first series. 14 vols. New York: Christian Literature
Publishing Company, 1890–1889. Reprint, Peabody, MA: Hendrickson, 1994. Online: http://www.
ccel.org/ccel/schaff/npnf101.i.html.

Schaff, Philip, and Henry Wace, ed. *Nicene and Post-Nicene Fathers,* second series, 14 vols. New York:
Christian Literature Publishing Company, 1890–1900. Reprint, Peabody, MA: Hendrikson, 1994.
Online: http://www.ccel.org/ccel/schaff/npnf201.i.html.

Schlier, Heinrich. "*Thlibō, Thlipsis.*" In *TDNT* 3:139–48.

Schillebeeckx, Edward. *God the Future of Man.* New York: Sheed and Ward, 1968.

Schmithals, Walter. "The Pre-Pauline Tradition in 1 Corinthians 15:20–28." *Perspectives in Religious
Studies* 20 (1993) 357–80.

Schnabel, Eckhard. *40 Questions About the End Times.* Grand Rapids: Kregel, 2011.

———. "Israel, the People of God, and the Nation." *JETS* 45 (2002) 35–57. Online: http://www.etsjets.
org/files/JETS-PDFs/45/45-1/45-1-PP035-057_JETS.pdf.

Schneider, Johannes. "*Homoios, Homoiotēs, Homoioō, Homoiōsis, Homoiōma, Aphomoioō, Paromoios,
Paromoiazō.*" In *TDNT* 5:186–99.

Schreiner, Thomas. *1, 2 Peter, Jude* (NAC 37). Nashville, TN: Broadman & Holman, 2003.

———. *Paul: Apostle of God's Glory in Christ.* Downers Grove, Ill.: IVP Academic, 2001.

Schüssler Fiorenza, Elisabeth. "Apokalypsis and Propheteia: The Book of Revelation in the Context of
Early Christian Prophecy." In *L'Apocalypse Johannique et l'Apocalyptique dans le Nouveau Testament,*
edited by J. Lambrecht, 105–28. Leuven: University Press, 1980.

———. *Revelation: Vision of a Just World* (PC). Minneapolis: Fortress, 1991.

Scofield, C. I., ed. *The New Scofield Reference Bible.* New York: Oxford, 1967.

Scott, Jr., Jack. "But What Will They Do With Luke 17?" Not dated. No pages. Online: https://www.
preteristarchive.com/0000_scott_what-will-do-luke/.

"Second Helvetic Confession, The." In *The Creeds of Christendom, With a History and Critical Notes,* 6th
ed. 3 vols. Edited by Philip Schaff. 1:390–420. Grand Rapids: Baker, 1990. Online: http://www.ccel.
org/creeds/helvetic.htm.

Shakespeare, William. "The Merchant of Venice." In *The Comedies of William Shakespeare,* edited by W.
G. Clark and W. Aldis Wright, 93–117. Garden City, NY: International Collectors Library, not dated.
Online: http://shakespeare.mit.edu/merchant/full.html.

Shea, William. "The Parallel Literary Structure of Revelation 12 and 20." *AUSS* 23 (1985) 37–54. Online:
https://www.andrews.edu/library/car/cardigital/Periodicals/AUSS/1985-1/1985-1-04.pdf.

Shepherd, Norman. "The Resurrections of Revelation 20." *WTJ* 37 (1974) 34–43.

Showers, Renald. *The Pre-Wrath Rapture View: An Examination and Critique.* Grand Rapids: Kregel, 2001.

Silva, Moisés, ed. *NIDNTTE.* 5 volumes. Grand Rapids: Zondervan, 2014.

Singer, Dwight. 1980. "A Survey of Muslim Converts in Iran." Online: https://drive.google.com/file/
d/0BwJ7iUsxP3zkRDZKRnJRRTNHVkk/view?pli=1.

Sittema, John. *Meeting Jesus at the Feast: Israel's Festivals and the Gospel.* Grandville, MI: Reformed Fellowship, 2013.

Sizer, Stephen. "The Temple in Contemporary Christian Zionism." In *Heaven on Earth: The Temple in Biblical Theology,* edited by T. Desmond Alexander and Simon Gathercole, 231–66. Carlisle, Cumbria, UK: Paternoster, 2004.

———. *Zion's Christian Soldiers?* Nottingham, England: Inter-Varsity, 2007.

Smalley, Stephen. *The Revelation to John.* Downers Grove, IL: InterVarsity, 2005.

Smith, Christopher. "The Portrayal of the Church as the New Israel in the Names and Order of the Tribes in Revelation 7.5–8." *JSNT* 39 (1990) 111–18.

———. "The Tribes of Revelation 7 and the Literary Competence of John the Seer." *JETS* 38 (1995)213–18. Online: http://www.etsjets.org/files/JETS-PDFs/38/38-2/38-2-pp213-218_JETS.pdf.

Smith, Chuck. *The Tribulation and the Church.* Costa Mesa, CA: The Word for Today, 1980.

———. *What The World Is Coming To.* Costa Mesa, CA: The Word for Today, 1980.

Smith, Ralph Allan. "A Neglected Millennial Passage from Saint Paul." 1999. No pages. Online: http://www.berith.org/essays/cor/.

Smith, Wilber. "Revelation." In *The Wycliffe Bible Commentary,* edited by Charles Pfeiffer and Everett Harrison, 1491–1525. Chicago: Moody, 1962.

Solzhenitsyn, Aleksandr. *The Gulag Archipelago 1918–1956: An Experiment in Literary Investigation.* Translated by Thomas Whitney and Harry Willetts. Abridged by Edward Ericson. New York: Harper & Row, 1985.

Sproul, R. C. *The Last Days According To Jesus.* Grand Rapids: Baker, 1998.

Stefanovic, Ranko. "Finding Meaning in the Literary Patterns of Revelation." *JATS* 13 (2002) 27–43. Online: http://www.atsjats.org/publication_file.php?pub_id=60&journal=1&type=pdf.

Steinmann, Andrew. "The Tripartite Structure of the Sixth Seal, the Sixth Trumpet, and the Sixth Bowl of John's Apocalypse (Rev 6:12–7:17; 9:13–11:14; 16:12–16)." *JETS* 35 (1992) 69–79. Online: http://www.etsjets.org/files/JETS-PDFs/35/35-1/JETS_35-1_069-079_Steinmann.pdf.

Stephens, Mark. *Annihilation or Renewal?* Tübingen, Germany: Mohr Siebeck, 2011.

Storms, Sam. *Kingdom Come: The Amillennial Alternative.* Tain, Scotland: Mentor, 2013.

Stott, John. *What Christ Thinks of the Church.* Wheaton, IL: Harold Shaw, 1990.

Stout, Harry. *The New England Soul.* New York: Oxford University Press, 1986.

Strand, Kenneth. "The Two Witnesses of Rev 11:3–12." *AUSS* 19 (1981) 127–35. Online: http://digitalcommons.andrews.edu/cgi/viewcontent.cgi?article=1526&context=auss.

Strimple, Robert B. "Amillennialism." In *Three Views on the Millennium and Beyond,* edited by Darrell L. Bock, 83–129. Grand Rapids: Zondervan, 1999.

Stylianopoulos, Theodore. "'I Know Your Works': Grace and Judgment in the Apocalypse." In *Apocalyptic Thought in Early Christianity,* edited by Robert Daly, 17–32. Grand Rapids: Baker Academic, 2009.

Such, W. A. *The Abomination of Desolation in the Gospel of Mark.* Lanham, MD: University Press of America, 1999.

Summers, Ray. "Revelation 20: An Interpretation." *RevExp* 57 (1960) 176–83.

Sweeney, James. "Jesus, Paul, and the Temple: An Exploration of Some Patterns of Continuity." *JETS* 46 (2003) 605–31. Online: http://www.etsjets.org/files/JETS-PDFs/46/46-4/46-4-pp605-631_JETS.pdf.

Sykes, Stephen. *The Story of Atonement.* London: Darton, Longman & Todd, Ltd., 1997.

Tanner, J. Paul. "Is Daniel's Seventy-Weeks Prophecy Messianic? Part 1." *BSac* 166 (2009) 181–200.

———. "Is Daniel's Seventy-Weeks Prophecy Messianic? Part 2." *BSac* 166 (2009) 319–35. Online: http://paultanner.org/English%20HTML/Publ%20Articles/Daniel%27s%2070th%20Wk%20-%20BibSac%20Article%202%20-%20Dr%20Tanner.pdf.

Taylor, John. "The Temple in Ezekiel." In *Heaven on Earth: The Temple in Biblical Theology,* edited by T. Desmond Alexander and Simon Gathercole, 59–70. Carlisle, Cumbria, UK: Paternoster, 2004.

Thielman, Frank. 2007. "Ephesians." In *Commentary on the New Testament Use of the Old Testament,* edited by G. K. Beale and D. A. Carson, 813–33. Grand Rapids: Baker Academic.

Thistleton, Anthony C. *The First Epistle to the Corinthians* (NIGTC). Grand Rapids: Eerdmans, 2000.

Thomas, Robert. "An Analysis of the Seventh Bowl of the Apocalypse." *MSJ* 5 (1994)73–95. Online: https://www.tms.edu/m/tmsj5d.pdf.

———. "The Chronological Interpretation of Revelation 2–3." *BSac* 124 (1967) 321–31.

————. "A Classical Dispensationalist View of Revelation." In *Four Views on the Book of Revelation*, 179–229. Grand Rapids, MI: Zondervan, 1998. Online: https://books.google.com/books?isbn=0310872391.

————. *Revelation 1–7: An Exegetical Commentary*. Chicago: Moody, 1992.

————. *Revelation 8–22: An Exegetical Commentary*. Chicago: Moody, 1995.

————. "The Structure of the Apocalypse: Recapitulation or Progression?" *MSJ* 4 (1993) 45–66. Online: https://www.tms.edu/m/tmsj4c.pdf.

Thomas, W. H. Griffith. *St. Paul's Epistle to the Romans*. Grand Rapids: Eerdmans, 1974.

Thompson, Daniel. "Romans 11:11–32: A Commentary." Not dated. No pages. Online: http://www.solidrock.net/library/thompson/romans_11_11-32.php.

Torrance, Thomas. *The Apocalypse Today*. Grand Rapids: Eerdmans, 1959.

Toussaint, Stanley. "A Critique of the Preterist View of the Olivet Discourse." *BSac* 161 (2004)469–90. Online: http://www.dts.edu/download/publications/bibliotheca/BibSac-Toussaint-CritiqueOfThePreterestView.pdf.

Towner, W. Sibley. *Daniel* (Int). Louisville, KY: John Knox, 1984.

————. "Lightning." In *Harper's Bible Dictionary*, edited by Paul Achtemeier, 561. San Francisco: Harper & Row, 1985.

Travis, Stephen. *I Believe in the Second Coming of Jesus*. Grand Rapids: Eerdmans, 1982.

Trench, Richard. *Synonyms of the New Testament*. Grand Rapids: Baker, 1989. Online (another edition): http://archive.org/details/synonymsofnewtesootreniala.

Trenchard, Warren. *Complete Vocabulary Guide to the Greek New Testament*, rev. ed. Grand Rapids, Zondervan, 1998.

Truesdale, Al. "Last Things First: The Impact of Eschatology on Ecology." *Perspectives on Science and Christian Faith* 46 (1994) 116–22. Online: http://www.asa3.org/ASA/PSCF/1994/PSCF6-94Truesdale.html.

Turner, David. "The Structure and Sequence of Matthew 24:1–41: Interaction with Evangelical Treatments." *Grace Theological Journal* 10 (1989) 3–27. Online: https://faculty.gordon.edu/hu/bi/ted_hildebrandt/ntesources/ntarticles/gtj-nt/turner-mat24-gtj-88.htm.

Turner, James. *Without God, Without Creed: The Origins of Unbelief in America*. Baltimore, MD: The Johns Hopkins University Press, 1985.

Tyndale, William. *Doctrinal Treatises*, edited by Henry Walter. Cambridge: The University Press, 1848. Online: https://books.google.com/books?id=JV0JAAAAQAAJ.

Ulfgard, Håkan. *Feast and Future: Revelation 7:9–17 and the Feast of Tabernacles*. Stockholm: Almqvist & Wiksell, 1989.

Van Deventer, Jack. "Comparison of the Four Millennial Views." *Credenda Agenda* 10, no. 3 (2012)38–39.

VanGemeren, Willem. "Daniel." In *Evangelical Commentary on the Bible*, edited by Walter Elwell, 589–601. Grand Rapids: Baker, 1989.

————. *Interpreting the Prophetic Word*. Grand Rapids: Zondervan, 1990.

van Houwelingen, P. H. R. "The Redemptive-Historical Dynamics of the Salvation of 'All Israel' (Ro. 11:26a)." *CTJ* 46 (2011) 301–14. Online: http://www.biblicalstudies.org.uk/pdf/ctj/46_301.pdf.

Van Kampen, Robert. *The Sign*, 3rd ed. Wheaton, IL: Crossway, 2000.

Venema, Cornelis. *The Promise of the Future*. Carlisle, PA: Banner of Truth, 2000.

Vos, Geerhardus. *The Pauline Eschatology*. Princeton: Princeton University Press, 1930. Reprint, Grand Rapids: Baker, 1979.

Waldron, Samuel. *The End Times Made Simple: How Could Everybody Be So Wrong about Biblical Prophecy*. Amityville, NY: Calvary, 2007.

————. "The Eschatological Kingdom." In *Lecture Notes on Eschatology*, 2000. No pages. Online: http://www.vor.org/truth/rbst/escatology00.html.

————. "The General Judgment," In *Lecture Notes on Eschatology*, 2000. No pages. Online: http://www.vor.org/truth/rbst/escatology00.html.

————. "Preterism." In *Lecture Notes on Eschatology*, 2000. No pages. Online: http://www.vor.org/truth/rbst/escatology00.html.

————. "Structural Considerations." In *Lecture Notes on Eschatology*, 2000. No pages. Online: http://www.vor.org/truth/rbst/escatology00.html.

Walker, P. W. L. *Jesus and the Holy City: New Testament Perspectives on Jerusalem*. Grand Rapids: Eerdmans, 1996.

Wallace, Daniel B. "New Testament Eschatology in the Light of Progressive Revelation." 2004. No pages. Online: https://bible.org/article/new-testament-eschatology-light-progressive-revelation.

Wallis, Wilber. "The Problem of an Intermediate Kingdom in I Corinthians 15:20–28." *JETS* 18 (1975)229–42. Online: http://www.etsjets.org/files/JETS-PDFs/18/18-4/18-4-pp229-242_JETS.pdf

Waltke, Bruce. "Kingdom Promises as Spiritual." In *Continuity and Discontinuity: Perspectives on the Relationship Between the Old and New Testaments,* edited by John Feinberg, 263–87. Westchester, IL: Crossway, 1988.

Walvoord, John. *Daniel: The Key to Prophetic Revelation.* Chicago: Moody, 1971.

———. *The Holy Spirit.* Wheaton, IL: Van Kampen, 1954.

———. *Israel in Prophecy.* Grand Rapids: Zondervan, 1962.

———. "The Literal View." In *Four Views on Hell,* edited by William Crockett, 11–28. Grand Rapids: Zondervan, 1992.

———. *The Millennial Kingdom,* rev. ed. Finlay, OH: Dunham, 1963.

———. *Prophecy in the New Millennium.* Grand Rapids: Kregel, 2001.

———. *The Rapture Question.* Grand Rapids: Zondervan, 1957.

———. *The Rapture Question,* rev. ed. Grand Rapids: Zondervan, 1979.

———. *The Revelation of Jesus Christ.* Chicago: Moody, 1966.

Warfield, B. B. *Biblical and Theological Studies.* Edited by Samuel Craig. Philadelphia: Presbyterian and Reformed, 1952.

Warner, Tim. "The Rapture & Second Coming: An Important Distinction–Rebuttal." 2003. No pages. Online: http://starbacks.ca/~lasttrumpet/debate2_2b.html (this link appears to no longer be operative).

Warren, Tony. *An Exposition of Revelation Chapter 20.* 2000. No pages. Online: http://www.mountainretreatorg.net/eschatology/rev20.html.

Waterman, G. Henry. "The Sources of Paul's Teaching on the 2nd Coming of Christ in 1 and 2 Thessalonians." *JETS* 18 (1975) 105–13. Online: http://www.etsjets.org/files/JETS-PDFs/18/18-2/18-2-pp105-113_JETS.pdf.

Watts, Rikk. "Mark." In *Commentary on the New Testament Use of the Old Testament,* edited by G. K. Beale and D. A. Carson, 111–249. Grand Rapids: Baker Academic, 2007.

Webb, William. *Slaves, Women & Homosexuals: Exploring the Hermeneutics of Cultural Analysis.* Downers Grove, IL: IVP Academic, 2001.

Weber, Timothy. *Living in the Shadow of the Second Coming: American Premillennialism 1875–1982,* enlarged ed. Grand Rapids: Zondervan, 1983.

———. *On the Road to Armageddon: How Evangelicals Became Israel's Best Friend.* Grand Rapids: Baker Academic, 2004.

Weima, Jeffrey. "1–2 Thessalonians." In *Commentary on the New Testament Use of the Old Testament,* edited by G. K. Beale and D. A. Carson, 871–89. Grand Rapids: Baker Academic, 2007.

Wellum, Stephen. "Christ's Resurrection and Ours (1 Corinthians 15)." *SBJT* 6 (2002) 76–93. Online: http://www.sbts.edu/media/publications/sbjt/sbjt_2002fall6.pdf.

Wendland, Paul. "[B-Greek] Another Latin LXX quote." (2003). Online: http://lists.ibiblio.org/pipermail/b-greek/2003-May/025469.html.

Whisenant, Edgar. *88 Reasons Why The Rapture Will Be In 1988.* Nashville, TN: World Bible Society, 1988. Online: https://archive.org/details/ReasonsWhyTheRaptureWillBeIn1988PDF.

White, R. Fowler. "Agony, Irony, and Victory in Inaugurated Eschatology: Reflections on the Current Amillennial-Postmillennial Debate." *WTJ* 62 (2000) 161–76.

———. "Death and the First Resurrection in Revelation 20: A Response to Meredith G. Kline." Unpublished paper presented at the Eastern Regional meeting for the Evangelical Theological Society, Lanham, Maryland, April 3, 1992. Theological Research Exchange Network No. ETS-0524 (www.tren.com).

———. "Making Sense of Rev 20:1–10? Harold Hoehner Versus Recapitulation." *JETS* 37 (1994) 539–51. Online: http://www.etsjets.org/files/JETS-PDFs/37/37-4/JETS_37-4_539-551_White.pdf.

———. "The Millennial Kingdom-City: Epic Themes, Ezek 36–39, and the Interpretation of Rev 20:4–10." Unpublished paper presented at the annual meeting of the Evangelical Theological Society held 21 November1991. Theological Research Exchange Network No. ETS-4318 (www.tren.com).

———. "On the Hermeneutics and Interpretation of Rev 20:1–3: A Preconsummationist Perspective." *JETS* 42 (1999) 53–68. Online: http://www.etsjets.org/files/JETS-PDFs/42/42-1/42-1-pp053-068_JETS.pdf.

———. "Reexamining the Evidence for Recapitulation in Rev 20:1–10." *WTJ* 51 (1989) 319–44. Online: http://www.apuritansmind.com/the-christian-walk/recapitulation-in-revelation-201-10-by-dr-r-fowler-white/.

Williamson, Paul. *Sealed with an Oath: Covenant in God's Unfolding Purpose* (NSBT 23). Nottingham, England: Apollos, 2007.

Wilson, Charles Reagan. "Religion and the American Civil War in Comparative Perspective." In *Religion and the American Civil War*, edited by Randall Miller, Harry Stout, and Charles Reagan Wilson, 385–407. New York: Oxford University Press, 1998.

Wilson, Dwight. *Armageddon Now!* Grand Rapids: Baker, 1977. Online: http://www.garynorth.com/freebooks/docs/pdf/armageddon_now.pdf.

Witherington, Ben. *Revelation* (NCBC). Cambridge, England: Cambridge University Press, 2003.

Witmer, John. "Romans." In *Bible Knowledge Commentary: New Testament*, edited by John Walvoord and Roy Zuck, 435–503. Wheaton, IL: Victor, 1983.

Wolters, Al. "Zechariah 14: A Dialogue with the History of Interpretation." *Mid-America Journal of Theology* 13 (2002) 39–56. Online: http://www.midamerica.edu/uploads/files/pdf/journal/13-wolters.pdf.

Wolvaardt, Bennie. *How to Interpret the Bible: A Do-It-Yourself Manual.* London: Veritas College, 2005.

Wood, Leon. *A Commentary on Daniel.* Grand Rapids: Regency Reference Library, 1973.

Woodberry, J. Dudley, and Russell Shubin. "Muslims tell . . . 'Why I Chose Jesus.'" *Mission Frontiers* (March 2001). Online: https://www.missionfrontiers.org/issue/article/muslims-tell. . .-why-i-chose-jesus.

Woodberry, J. Dudley, Russell Shubin, and G. Marks. "Why Muslims Follow Jesus." *Christianity Today* (October 2007) 80–85. Online: http://www.christianitytoday.com/ct/2007/october/42.80.html.

Woudstra, Marten. "Israel and the Church: A Case for Continuity." In *Continuity and Discontinuity: Perspectives on the Relationship Between the Old and New Testaments,* edited by John Feinberg, 221–38. Westchester, Ill.: Crossway, 1988.

Wright, N. T. *The Climax of the Covenant: Christ and the Law in Pauline Theology.* Minneapolis: Fortress, 1992.

———. *Jesus and the Victory of God.* Minneapolis: Fortress, 1996.

———. *The Resurrection of the Son of God.* Minneapolis, MN: Fortress, 2003.

Yarbro Collins, Adela. "The Book of Revelation." In *The Encyclopedia of Apocalypticism,* vol. 1, edited by John Collins, 384–414. New York: Continuum, 1998.

———. "The Political Perspective of the Revelation to John." *JBL* 96 (1977) 241–56.

Yarbrough, Robert. "Biblical Theology." In *Evangelical Dictionary of Biblical Theology,* edited by Walter Elwell, 61–66. Grand Rapids: Baker, 1996. Online: http://www.biblestudytools.com/dictionaries/bakers-evangelical-dictionary/biblical-theology.html.

Yilpet, Yoilah. "Zechariah." In *Africa Bible Commentary,* edited by Tokunboh Adeyemo, 1077–92. Nairobi: WordAlive, 2006.

Young, Edward. *My Servants the Prophets.* Grand Rapids: Eerdmans, 1952.

———. *The Prophecy of Daniel: A Commentary.* Grand Rapids: Eerdmans, 1949.

Zakai, Avihu. "Theocracy in Massachusetts: The Puritan Universe of Sacred Imagination." *Studies in the Literary Imagination* 27 (1994) 23–31. Online: http://pluto.mscc.huji.ac.il/~msavihu/AvihuZakai/SacredImagination.pdf.

Zaspel, Fred. "Daniel's 'Seventy Weeks': An Historical and Exegetical Analysis. 1991. No pages. Online: http://www.biblicalstudies.com/bstudy/eschatology/daniel.htm (this link appears to be no longer operative).

———. "The Kingdom, The Millennium, & The Eschaton." 1995. No pages. Online: https://theologue.files.wordpress.com/2014/06/thekingdom-themillennium-theeschaton-fredzaspel.pdf.

Zodhiates, Spiros. *The Complete Word Study Dictionary: New Testament,* rev. ed. Chattanooga, TN: AMG, 1993.

Index of Ancient Documents

Old Testament

Genesis

Exodus

Proverbs

Ecclesiastes

Song of Solomon

Isaiah

Ephesians

Philippians

Revelation (*continued*)

Index of Subjects

Numbers

Other significant numbers are listed in this index in the order in which they are spelled.

A

N

O

S

Made in the USA
Coppell, TX
05 August 2020